# INTERNATIONAL
# POLITICS

# INTERNATIONAL POLITICS

## Enduring Concepts and Contemporary Issues

EIGHTH EDITION

### ROBERT J. ART
*Brandeis University*

### ROBERT JERVIS
*Columbia University*

PEARSON
Longman

New York • San Francisco • Boston
London • Toronto • Sydney • Tokyo • Singapore • Madrid
Mexico City • Munich • Paris • Cape Town • Hong Kong • Montreal

Editor-in-Chief: Eric Stano
Senior Marketing Manager: Elizabeth Fogarty
Production Manager: Denise Phillip
Project Coordination, Text Design, and Electronic Page Makeup: Stratford Publishing
    Services
Cover Designer/Manager: John Callahan
Cover Images: Left image courtesy of Planet Art. Right image courtesy of PhotoDisc
Senior Manufacturing Buyer: Dennis J. Para
Printer and Binder: R. R. Donnelley & Sons
Cover Printer: Phoenix Color Graphics

Please visit us at www.ablongman.com

ISBN 0-321-45291-7

1 2 3 4 5 6 7 8 9 10—DOC—09   08   07   06

# BRIEF CONTENTS

Detailed Contents    vii

Preface    xiii

## PART 1   ANARCHY AND ITS CONSEQUENCES   1

Power and Principle in Statecraft    7
The Consequences of Anarchy    29
The Mitigation of Anarchy    69

## PART 2   THE USES OF FORCE   137

The Political Uses of Force    141
The Political Utility of Force Today    205
The Spread of Nuclear Weapons    239

## PART 3   THE INTERNATIONAL POLITICAL ECONOMY   261

Perspectives on Political Economy    267
The Meaning of Globalization    309
The Pros and Cons of Globalization    347

## PART 4   CONTEMPORARY WORLD POLITICS   369

Conflict, War, and Terrorism    375
The Uses of, and Reactions to, American Power    417
Failed States, Civil Wars, and Nation-Building    451
The Environment and Climate Change    495
New Actors and New Forces    517

# DETAILED CONTENTS

PREFACE                                                                xiii

PART 1    Anarchy and Its Consequences                                    1

POWER AND PRINCIPLE IN STATECRAFT                                         7

    HANS J. MORGENTHAU
      *Six Principles of Political Realism    7*

    J. ANN TICKNER
      *A Critique of Morgenthau's*
      *Principles of Political Realism    15*

THE CONSEQUENCES OF ANARCHY                                              29

    KENNETH N. WALTZ
      *The Anarchic Structure of World Politics    29*

    JOHN J. MEARSHEIMER
      *Anarchy and the Struggle for Power    50*

    ALEXANDER WENDT
      *Anarchy Is What States Make of It    61*

THE MITIGATION OF ANARCHY                                                69

    KENNETH A. OYE
      *The Conditions for Cooperation*
      *in World Politics    69*

    MICHAEL W. DOYLE
      *Kant, Liberal Legacies, and Foreign Affairs    83*

    STEPHEN M. WALT
      *Alliances: Balancing and Bandwagoning    96*

    HANS J. MORGENTHAU
      *The Future of Diplomacy    104*

STANLEY HOFFMANN
*The Uses and Limits of International Law*  114

ROBERT O. KEOHANE
*International Institutions:
   Can Interdependence Work?*  119

ADAM ROBERTS
*The United Nations and International Security*  127


PART **2**    **The Uses of Force**                          **137**

**THE POLITICAL USES OF FORCE**                               **141**

ROBERT J. ART
*The Four Functions of Force*  141

THOMAS C. SCHELLING
*The Diplomacy of Violence*  149

ROBERT J. ART
*Coercive Diplomacy*  163

ROBERT JERVIS
*Offense, Defense, and the Security Dilemma*  177

BRUCE HOFFMAN
*What Is Terrorism?*  198

**THE POLITICAL UTILITY OF FORCE TODAY**                     **205**

ROBERT J. ART
*The Fungibility of Force*  205

ROBERT A. PAPE
*The Strategic Logic of Suicide Terrorism*  221

**THE SPREAD OF NUCLEAR WEAPONS**                            **239**

SCOTT D. SAGAN
*Nuclear Instability in South Asia*  239

KENNETH N. WALTZ
*Nuclear Stability in South Asia*  250

PART **3**   The International Political Economy        **261**

PERSPECTIVES ON POLITICAL ECONOMY                    267

ROBERT GILPIN
*The Nature of Political Economy*   267

ROBERT O. KEOHANE
*Hegemony in the World Political Economy*   283

BRUCE R. SCOTT
*The Great Divide in the Global Village*   296

THE MEANING OF GLOBALIZATION                         309

JEFFREY FRANKEL
*Globalization of the Economy*   309

MARTIN WOLF
*Will Globalization Survive?*   325

KENNETH N. WALTZ
*Globalization and Governance*   335

THE PROS AND CONS OF GLOBALIZATION                   347

DANI RODRIK
*Trading in Illusions*   347

GEOFFREY GARRETT
*Globalization's Missing Middle*   355

JOHN MICKLETHWAIT AND ADRIAN WOOLDRIDGE
*Why the Globalization Backlash is Stupid*   361

PART **4**   Contemporary World Politics              **369**

CONFLICT, WAR, AND TERRORISM                         375

ROBERT JERVIS
*The Era of Leading Power Peace*   375

SAMUEL P. HUNTINGTON
*The Clash of Civilizations?*   391

FAREED ZAKARIA
*Why Do They Hate Us?* 406

## THE USES OF, AND REACTIONS TO, AMERICAN POWER     417

ROBERT JERVIS
*Explaining the Bush Doctrine* 417

F. GREGORY GAUSE III
*Can Democracy Stop Terrorism?* 432

STEPHEN M. WALT
*Taming American Power* 441

## FAILED STATES, CIVIL WARS, AND NATION-BUILDING     451

ROBERT I. ROTBERG
*Failed States, Collapsed States,
Weak States: Causes and Indicators* 451

CHAIM KAUFMANN
*Possible and Impossible Solutions
to Ethnic Civil Wars* 459

JAMES DOBBINS
*Nation-Building: UN Surpasses
U.S. on Learning Curve* 481

JAMES L. PAYNE
*Deconstructing Nation Building* 490

## THE ENVIRONMENT AND CLIMATE CHANGE     495

GARRETT HARDIN
*The Tragedy of the Commons* 495

THOMAS HOMER-DIXON
*Environmental Changes as Causes
of Acute Conflict* 501

JOHN BROWNE
*Beyond Kyoto* 508

## NEW ACTORS AND NEW FORCES                                    517

RICHARD K. BETTS AND THOMAS J. CHRISTENSEN
*The Rise of China: Getting the Questions Right*    517

ANDREW MORAVCSIK
*Europe Without Illusions*    526

MARGARET E. KECK AND KATHRYN SIKKINK
*Transnational Activist Networks*    532

SEBASTIAN MALLABY
*NGOs: Fighting Poverty, Hurting the Poor*    539

RHODA E. HOWARD AND JACK DONNELLY
*Human Rights in World Politics*    546

MOISÉS NAÍM
*The Five Wars of Globalization*    558

DANIEL W. DREZNER
*The Global Governance of the Internet:*
    *Bringing the State Back In*    567

STEVEN R. RATNER
*International Law: The Trials of Global Norms*    581

# PREFACE

The first edition of *International Politics* appeared in 1973. Since then, the field of international relations has experienced a dramatic enrichment in the subjects studied and the quality of works published. Political economy came into its own as an important subfield in the 1970s. New and important works in the field of security studies appeared. The literature on cooperation among states flourished in the early 1980s, and important studies about the environment began to appear in the mid-1980s. Feminist, post-modernist, and constructivist critiques of the mainstream made their appearance also. With the end of the Cold War, these new issues came to the fore: human rights, the tension between state sovereignty and the obligations of the international community, the global environment, civil wars, failed states, and nation-building. The growing diversity of the field has closely mirrored the actual developments in international relations.

As for the previous editions, in fashioning the eighth, we have kept in mind both the new developments in world politics and the literature that has accompanied them. Central to this edition, though, as for the other seven, is our belief that the realm of international politics differs fundamentally from that of domestic politics. Therefore, we have continued to put both the developments and the literature in the context of the patterns that still remain valid for understanding the differences between politics in an anarchic environment and politics that takes place under a government. As in the previous seven, the theme for this edition continues to revolve around enduring concepts and contemporary issues in world politics.

The eighth edition retains the four major subdivisions of the seventh edition. We have left Part One as it appears in the seventh edition. Part Two retains the three subsections of the seventh edition, but has a new selection by Bruce Hoffman on terrorism. Part Three has two new selections on globalization – one by Martin Wolf and another by Geoffrey Garrett. Most of the changes in the eighth edition come in Part Four. We have retained the four subdivisions of the seventh edition, but have added eleven new selections: articles by Fareed Zakaria, Gregory Gause, Stephen Walt, James Dobbins, James Payne, Thomas Homer-Dixon, John Browne, Richard Betts and Thomas Christensen, Andrew Moravcsik, Sebastian Mallaby, and Daniel Drezner.

The eighth edition of *International Politics* has fourteen new selections and is a little over 25 percent new, but it continues to follow the four principles that have guided us throughout all previous editions:

1. A selection of subjects that, while not exhaustively covering the field of international politics, nevertheless encompasses most of the essential topics that we teach in our introductory courses.

**2.** Individual readings that are mainly analytical in content, that take issue with one another, and that thereby introduce the student to the fundamental debates and points of view in the field.

**3.** Editors' introductions to each part that summarize the central concepts the student must master, that organize the central themes of each part, and that relate the readings to one another.

**4.** A reader that can be used either as the core around which to design an introductory course or as the primary supplement to enrich an assigned text.

Finally, in putting together this and previous editions, we received excellent advice from the following colleagues, whom we would like to thank for the time and care they took: Andrew Bennett, Georgetown University; Timothy McKeown, University of North Carolina at Chapel Hill; Roslin Simowitz, University of Texas at Arlington; Robert J. Griffiths, University of North Carolina at Greensboro; Linda S. Adams, Baylor University; Timothy M. Cole, University of Maine; Robert C. Gray, Franklin & Marshall College; James A. Mitchell, California State University, Northridge; Margaret E. Scranton, University of Arkansas at Little Rock; David G. Becker, Dartmouth College; James A. Caporaso, University of Washington; Ken Wise, Creighton University; Sonia Gardenas, Trinity College; Philip Schrodt, University of Kansas; and Jane Cramer, University of Oregon.

ROBERT J. ART

ROBERT JERVIS

# INTERNATIONAL
# POLITICS

PART
1

# Anarchy and Its Consequences

Unlike domestic politics, international politics takes place in an arena that has no central governing body. From this central fact flow important consequences for the behavior of states. In Part One, we explore three of them: the role that principles and morality can and should play in statecraft; the effects that anarchy has on how states view and relate to one another; and the ways that the harsher edges of anarchy can be mitigated, even if not wholly removed.

## POWER AND PRINCIPLE IN STATECRAFT

Citizens, students, and scholars alike often take up the study of international politics because they want their country to behave in as principled a way as possible. But they soon discover that principle and power, morality and statecraft do not easily mix. Why should this be? Is it inevitable? Can and should states seek to do good in the world? Will they endanger themselves and harm others if they try?

These are timeless questions, having been asked by observers of international politics in nearly every previous era. They therefore make a good starting point for thinking about the nature of international politics and the choices states face in our era. Hans J. Morgenthau, one of the leading proponents of the approach known as Realism (also known as Power Politics), takes the classic Realist position: universal standards of morality cannot be an invariable guide to statecraft because there is an "ineluctable tension between the moral command and the requirements of successful political action." Rather than base statecraft on morality, Morgenthau argues that state actors must think and act in terms of power and must do whatever it takes to defend the national interests of their state. J. Ann Tickner, commenting on the primacy of power in Morgenthau's writings, explains that what he considers to be a realistic description of international politics is only a picture of the past and therefore not a prediction about the future, and proposes what she considers to be a feminist alternative. A world in which state actors think of power in terms of collective empowerment, not in terms of leverage over one another, could produce more cooperative outcomes and pose fewer conflicts between the dictates of morality and the power of self-interest.

## THE CONSEQUENCES OF ANARCHY

Even those who argue that morality should play a large role in statecraft acknowledge that international politics is not like domestic politics. In the latter, there is government; in the former, there is none. As a consequence, no agency exists above the individual states with authority and power to make laws and settle disputes. States can make commitments and treaties, but no sovereign power ensures compliance and punishes deviations. This—the absence of a supreme power—is what is meant by the anarchic environment of international politics. Anarchy is therefore said to constitute a *state of war:* when all else fails, force is the *ultima ratio*—the final and legitimate arbiter of disputes among states.

The state of war does not mean that every nation is constantly at the brink of war or actually at war with other nations. Most countries, though, do feel threatened by some states at some time, and every state has experienced periods of intense insecurity. No two contiguous states, moreover, have had a history of close, friendly relations uninterrupted by severe tension if not outright war. Because a nation cannot look to a supreme body to enforce laws, nor count on other nations for constant aid and support, it must rely on its own efforts, particularly for defense against attack. Coexistence in an anarchic environment thus requires *self-help.* The psychological outlook that self-help breeds is best described by a saying common among British statesmen since Palmerston: "Great Britain has no permanent enemies or permanent friends, she has only permanent interests."

Although states must provide the wherewithal to achieve their own ends, they do not always reach their foreign policy goals. The goals may be grandiose; the means available, meager. The goals may be attainable; the means selected, inappropriate. But even if the goals are realistic and the means both available and appropriate, a state can be frustrated in pursuit of its ends. The reason is simple but fundamental to an understanding of international politics: what one state does will inevitably impinge on some other states—on some beneficially, but on others adversely. What one state desires, another may covet. What one thinks its just due, another may find threatening. Steps that a state takes to achieve its goals may be rendered useless by the countersteps others take. No state, therefore, can afford to disregard the effects its actions will have on other nations' behavior. In this sense state behavior is contingent: what one state does is dependent in part upon what others do. Mutual dependence means that each must take the others into account.

Mutual dependence affects nothing more powerfully than it does security—the measures states take to protect their territory. Like other foreign-policy goals, the security of one state is contingent upon the behavior of other states. Herein lies the *security dilemma* to which each state is subject: in its efforts to preserve or enhance its own security, one state can take measures that decrease the security of other states and cause them to take countermeasures that neutralize the actions of the first state and that may even menace it. The first state may feel impelled to take further actions, provoking additional countermeasures . . . and so forth. The security dilemma means that an action-reaction spiral can occur between two states or among several of them, forcing each to spend ever larger sums on arms to be no more secure than before. All will run faster merely to stay where they are.

At the heart of the security dilemma are these two constraints: the inherent difficulty in distinguishing between offensive and defensive postures, and the inability of one state to believe or trust that another state's present pacific intentions will remain so. The capability to defend can also provide the capability to attack. In adding to its arms, state A may know that its aim is defensive, that its intentions are peaceful, and therefore that it has no aggressive designs on state B. In a world where states must look to themselves for protection, however, B will examine A's actions carefully and suspiciously. B may think that A will attack him when A's arms become powerful enough and that A's protestations of friendship are designed to lull him into lowering his guard. But even if B believes A's actions are not directed against him, B cannot assume that A's intentions will remain peaceful. Anarchy makes it impossible for A to bind itself to continuing to respect B's interests in the future. B must allow for the possibility that what A can do to him, A sometime might do. The need to assess capabilities along with intentions, or, the equivalent, to allow for a change in intentions, makes state actors profoundly conservative. They prefer to err on the side of safety, to have too much rather than too little. Because security is the basis of existence and the prerequisite for the achievement of all other goals, state actors must be acutely sensitive to the security actions of others. The security dilemma thus means that state actors cannot risk *not* reacting to the security actions of other states, but that in so reacting they can produce circumstances that leave them worse off than before.

The anarchic environment of international politics, then, allows every state to be the final judge of its own interests, but requires that each provide the means to attain them. Because the absence of a central authority permits wars to occur, security considerations become paramount. Because of the effects of the security dilemma, efforts of state leaders to protect their peoples can lead to severe tension and war even when all parties sincerely desire peace. Two states, or two groups of states, each satisfied with the status quo and seeking only security, may not be able to achieve it. Conflicts and wars with no economic or ideological basis can occur. The outbreak of war, therefore, does not necessarily mean that some or all states seek expansion, or that humans have an innate drive for power. That states go to war when none of them wants to, however, does not imply that they never seek war. The security dilemma may explain some wars; it does not explain all wars. States often do experience conflicts of interest over trade, real estate, ideology, and prestige. For example, when someone asked Francis I what differences led to his constant wars with Charles V, he replied: "None whatever. We agree perfectly. We both want control of Italy!" (Cited in Frederick L. Schuman, *International Politics,* 7th ed., New York, 1953, p. 283.) If states cannot obtain what they want by blackmail, bribery, or threats, they may resort to war. Wars can occur when no one wants them; wars usually do occur when someone wants them.

Realists argue that even under propitious circumstances, international cooperation is difficult to achieve because in anarchy, states are often more concerned with relative advantages than with absolute gains. That is, because international politics is a self-help system in which each state must be prepared to rely on its own resources and strength to further its interests, national leaders often seek to become more powerful than their potential adversaries. Cooperation is then made difficult not only by the fear that others will cheat and fail to live up to their agreements, but also by the perceived need to gain a superior position. The reason is not that state actors are concerned with status, but that they fear that arrangements which benefit all, but provide greater benefits to others than to them, will render their country vulnerable to pressure and coercion in the future.

Kenneth N. Waltz develops the above points more fully by analyzing the differences between hierarchic (domestic) and anarchic (international) political systems. He shows why the distribution of capabilities (the relative power positions of states) in anarchic systems is so important and lays out the ways in which political behavior differs in hierarchic and anarchic systems.

There is broad agreement among Realists on the consequences of anarchy for states behavior, but not total agreement. One brand of Realists, who are called the "offensive Realists," argue that the consequences of anarchy go far beyond producing security dilemmas and making cooperation hard to come by. They assert that anarchy forces states, and especially the great powers, to become "power maximizers" because the only way to assure the state's security is to be the most powerful state in the system. Offensive realism envisions a "dog-eat-dog" world of international politics in which power and fear dominate great power interactions and in which war, or the threat of war, among the great powers or among their proxies is a constant feature of international relations. John J. Mearsheimer lays out the tenets of this brand of Realism.

In an anarchic condition, however, the question to ask may not be, "Why does war occur?" but rather "Why does war not occur more frequently than it does?" Instead of asking "Why do states not cooperate more to achieve common interests?" we should ask "Given anarchy and the security dilemma, how is it that states are able to cooperate at all?" Anarchy and the security dilemma do not produce their effects automatically, and it is not self evident that states are power maximizers. Thus Alexander Wendt argues that Waltz and other Realists have missed the extent to which the unpleasant patterns they describe are "socially constructed"— i.e., stem from the actors' beliefs, perceptions, and interpretations of others' behavior. If national leaders believe that anarchy requires an assertive stance that endangers others, conflict will be generated. But if they think they have more freedom of action and do not take the hostility of others for granted, they may be able to create more peaceful relationships. In this view, structure (anarchy) does not determine state action; agency (human decision) does.

## THE MITIGATION OF ANARCHY

Even Realists note that conflict and warfare is not a constant characteristic of international politics. Most states remain at peace with most others most of the time. State actors have developed a number of ways of coping with anarchy, of gaining more than a modicum of security, of regulating their competition with other states, and of developing patterns that contain, but do not eliminate, the dangers of aggression.

Kenneth A. Oye shows that even if anarchy and the security dilemma inhibit cooperation, they do not prevent it. A number of conditions and national strategies can make it easier for states to achieve common ends. Cooperation is usually easier if there are a small number of actors. Not only can each more carefully observe the others, but all actors know that their impact on the system is great enough so that if they fail to cooperate with others, joint enterprises are likely to fail. Furthermore, when the number of actors is large, there may be mechanisms and institutions that group them together, thereby reproducing some of the advantages of small numbers.

The conditions actors face also influence their fates. The barriers of anarchy are more likely to be overcome when actors have long time horizons, when even successfully exploiting others produces an outcome that is only a little better than mutual cooperation, when being exploited by others is only slightly worse than mutual noncooperation, and when mutual cooperation is much better than unrestricted competition. Under such circumstances, states are particularly likely to undertake contingent strategies such as tit-for-tat. That is, they will cooperate with others if others do likewise and refuse to cooperate if others have refused to cooperate with them.

Most strikingly, it appears that democracies may never have gone to war against each other. This is not to say, as Woodrow Wilson did, that democracies are inherently peaceful. They seem to fight as many wars as do dictatorships. But, as Michael W. Doyle shows, they do not fight each other. If this is correct—and, of course, both the evidence and the reasons are open to dispute—it implies that anarchy and the security dilemma do not prevent peaceful and even harmonious relations among states that share certain common values and beliefs.

Democracies are relatively recent developments. For a longer period of time, two specific devices—international law and diplomacy—have proven useful in resolving conflicts among states. Although not enforced by a world government, international law can provide norms for behavior and mechanisms for settling disputes. The effectiveness of international law derives from the willingness of states to observe it. Its power extends no further than the disposition of states "to agree to agree." Where less than vital interests are at stake, state actors may accept settlements that are not entirely satisfactory because they think the precedents or principles justify the compromises made. Much of international law reflects a consensus among states on what is of equal benefit to all, as, for example, the rules regulating international communications. Diplomacy, too, can facilitate cooperation and resolve disputes. If diplomacy is skillful, and the legitimate interests of the parties in dispute are taken into account, understandings can often be reached on issues that might otherwise lead to war. These points and others are explored more fully by Stanley Hoffmann and Hans J. Morgenthau.

National leaders use these two traditional tools within a balance-of-power system. Much maligned by President Wilson and his followers and misunderstood by many others, balance of power refers to the way in which stability is achieved through the conflicting efforts of individual states, whether or not any or all of them deliberately pursue that goal. Just as Adam Smith argued that if every individual pursued his or her own self-interest, the interaction of individual egoisms would enhance national wealth, so international relations theorists have argued that even if every state seeks power at the expense of the others, no one state will likely dominate. In both cases a general good can be the unintended product of selfish individual actions. Moreover, even if most states desire only to keep what they have, their own interests dictate that they band together in order to resist any state or coalition of states that threatens to dominate them.

The balance-of-power system is likely to prevent any one state's acquiring hegemony. It will not, however, benefit all states equally nor maintain the peace permanently. Rewards will be unequal because of inequalities in power and expertise. Wars will occur because they are one of the means by which states can preserve what they have or acquire what they covet. Small states may even be eliminated by their more powerful neighbors. The international system will be unstable, however, only if states flock to what they think is the strongest side. What is called *bandwagoning* or the *domino theory* argues that the international system is precarious because successful aggression will attract many followers, either out of fear or out of a desire to share the spoils of victory. Stephen M. Walt disagrees, drawing on balance-of-power theory and historical evidence to argue that, rather than bandwagoning, under most conditions states balance against emerging threats. They do not throw in their lot with the stronger side. Instead, they join with others to prevent any state from becoming so strong that it could dominate the system.

Power balancing is a strategy followed by individual states acting on their own. Other ways of coping with anarchy, which may supplement or exist alongside this impulse, are more explicitly collective. Regimes and institutions can help overcome anarchy and facilitate cooperation. When states agree on the principles, rules, and norms that should govern behavior, they can often ameliorate the security dilemma and increase the scope for cooperation. Institutions may not only embody common understandings but, as Robert O. Keohane argues, they can also help states work toward mutually desired outcomes by providing a framework for long-run agreements, making it easier for each state to see whether others are living up to their promises, and increasing the costs the state will pay if it cheats.

In the security area, the United Nations has the potential to be an especially important institution. Adam Roberts assesses the United Nations' role in coping with conflict within states through the mechanism of peacekeeping missions. He finds that the demand for such missions since the end of the Cold War has expanded dramatically, but notes the formidable obstacles that must be overcome if the UN is to fulfill the hopes that so many state leaders and citizens have for it in this area.

# POWER AND PRINCIPLE IN STATECRAFT

## Six Principles of Political Realism

### HANS J. MORGENTHAU

1. Political realism believes that politics, like society in general, is governed by objective laws that have their roots in human nature. In order to improve society it is first necessary to understand the laws by which society lives. The operation of these laws being impervious to our preferences, men will challenge them only at the risk of failure.

Realism, believing as it does in the objectivity of the laws of politics, must also believe in the possibility of developing a rational theory that reflects, however imperfectly and one-sidedly, these objective laws. It believes also, then, in the possibility of distinguishing in politics between truth and opinion—between what is true objectively and rationally, supported by evidence and illuminated by reason, and what is only a subjective judgment, divorced from the facts as they are and informed by prejudice and wishful thinking.

Human nature, in which the laws of politics have their roots, has not changed since the classical philosophies of China, India, and Greece endeavored to discover these laws. Hence, novelty is not necessarily a virtue in political theory, nor is old age a defect. The fact that a theory of politics, if there be such a theory, has never been heard of before tends to create a presumption against, rather than in favor of, its soundness. Conversely, the fact that a theory of politics was developed hundreds or even thousands of years ago—as was the theory of the balance of power—does not create a presumption that it must be outmoded and obsolete. . . .

For realism, theory consists in ascertaining facts and giving them meaning through reason. It assumes that the character of a foreign policy can be ascertained

From *Politics Among Nations,* 5th edition by Hans J. Morgenthau. Copyright © 1972 by Alfred A. Knopf, a division of Random House, Inc. Reprinted by permission of Alfred A. Knopf, a division of Random House, Inc. Portions of the text and some footnotes have been omitted.

only through the examination of the political acts performed and of the foreseeable consequences of these acts. Thus we can find out what statesmen have actually done, and from the foreseeable consequences of their acts we can surmise what their objectives might have been.

Yet examination of the facts is not enough. To give meaning to the factual raw material of foreign policy, we must approach political reality with a kind of rational outline, a map that suggests to us the possible meanings of foreign policy. In other words, we put ourselves in the position of a statesman who must meet a certain problem of foreign policy under certain circumstances, and we ask ourselves what the rational alternatives are from which a statesman may choose who must meet this problem under these circumstances (presuming always that he acts in a rational manner), and which of these rational alternatives this particular statesman, acting under these circumstances, is likely to choose. It is the testing of this rational hypothesis against the actual facts and their consequences that gives theoretical meaning to the facts of international politics.

2. The main signpost that helps political realism to find its way through the landscape of international politics is the concept of interest defined in terms of power. This concept provides the link between reason trying to understand international politics and the facts to be understood. It sets politics as an autonomous sphere of action and understanding apart from other spheres, such as economics (understood in terms of interest defined as wealth), ethics, aesthetics, or religion. Without such a concept a theory of politics, international or domestic, would be altogether impossible, for without it we could not distinguish between political and nonpolitical facts, nor could we bring at least a measure of systematic order to the political sphere.

We assume that statesmen think and act in terms of interest defined as power, and the evidence of history bears that assumption out. That assumption allows us to retrace and anticipate, as it were, the steps a statesman—past, present, or future—has taken or will take on the political scene. We look over his shoulder when he writes his dispatches; we listen in on his conversation with other statesmen; we read and anticipate his very thoughts. Thinking in terms of interest defined as power, we think as he does, and as disinterested observers we understand his thoughts and actions perhaps better than he, the actor on the political scene, does himself.

The concept of interest defined as power imposes intellectual discipline upon the observer, infuses rational order into the subject matter of politics, and thus makes the theoretical understanding of politics possible. On the side of the actor, it provides for rational discipline in action and creates that astounding continuity in foreign policy which makes American, British, or Russian foreign policy appear as an intelligible, rational continuum, by and large consistent within itself, regardless of the different motives, preferences, and intellectual and moral qualities of successive statesmen. A realist theory of international politics, then, will guard against two popular fallacies: the concern with motives and the concern with ideological preferences.

To search for the clue to foreign policy exclusively in the motives of statesmen is both futile and deceptive. It is futile because motives are the most illusive of psychological data, distorted as they are, frequently beyond recognition, by the interests and emotions of actor and observer alike. Do we really know what our own motives are? And what do we know of the motives of others?

Yet even if we had access to the real motives of statesmen, that knowledge would help us little in understanding foreign policies, and might well lead us astray. It is true that the knowledge of the statesman's motives may give us one among many clues as to what the direction of his foreign policy might be. It cannot give us, however, the one clue by which to predict his foreign policies. History shows no exact and necessary correlation between the quality of motives and the quality of foreign policy. This is true in both moral and political terms.

We cannot conclude from the good intentions of a statesman that his foreign policies will be either morally praiseworthy or politically successful. Judging his motives, we can say that he will not intentionally pursue policies that are morally wrong, but we can say nothing about the probability of their success. If we want to know the moral and political qualities of his actions, we must know them, not his motives. How often have statesmen been motivated by the desire to improve the world, and ended by making it worse? And how often have they sought one goal, and ended by achieving something they neither expected nor desired? . . .

A realist theory of international politics will also avoid the other popular fallacy of equating the foreign policies of a statesman with his philosophic or political sympathies, and of deducing the former from the latter. Statesmen, especially under contemporary conditions, may well make a habit of presenting their foreign policies in terms of their philosophic and political sympathies in order to gain popular support for them. Yet they will distinguish with Lincoln between their "*official duty*," which is to think and act in terms of the national interest, and their "*personal wish*," which is to see their own moral values and political principles realized throughout the world. Political realism does not require, nor does it condone, indifference to political ideals and moral principles, but it requires indeed a sharp distinction between the desirable and the possible—between what is desirable everywhere and at all times and what is possible under the concrete circumstances of time and place.

It stands to reason that not all foreign policies have always followed so rational, objective, and unemotional a course. The contingent elements of personality, prejudice, and subjective preference, and of all the weaknesses of intellect and will which flesh is heir to, are bound to deflect foreign policies from their rational course. Especially where foreign policy is conducted under the conditions of democratic control, the need to marshal popular emotions to the support of foreign policy cannot fail to impair the rationality of foreign policy itself. Yet a theory of foreign policy which aims at rationality must for the time being, as it were, abstract from these irrational elements and seek to paint a picture of foreign policy which presents the rational essence to be found in experience, without the contingent deviations from rationality which are also found in experience. . . .

The difference between international politics as it actually is and a rational theory derived from it is like the difference between a photograph and a painted portrait. The photograph shows everything that can be seen by the naked eye; the painted portrait does not show everything that can be seen by the naked eye, but it shows, or at least seeks to show, one thing that the naked eye cannot see: the human essence of the person portrayed.

Political realism contains not only a theoretical but also a normative element. It knows that political reality is replete with contingencies and systemic irrationalities and points to the typical influences they exert upon foreign policy. Yet it shares with all social theory the need, for the sake of theoretical understanding, to stress the rational elements of political reality; for it is these rational elements that make reality intelligible for theory. Political realism presents the theoretical construct of a rational foreign policy which experience can never completely achieve.

At the same time political realism considers a rational foreign policy to be good foreign policy; for only a rational foreign policy minimizes risks and maximizes benefits and, hence, complies both with the moral precept of prudence and the political requirement of success. Political realism wants the photographic picture of the political world to resemble as much as possible its painted portrait. Aware of the inevitable gap between good—that is, rational—foreign policy and foreign policy as it actually is, political realism maintains not only that theory must focus upon the rational elements of political reality, but also that foreign policy ought to be rational in view of its own moral and practical purposes.

Hence, it is no argument against the theory here presented that actual foreign policy does not or cannot live up to it. That argument misunderstands the intention of this book, which is to present not an indiscriminate description of political reality, but a rational theory of international politics. Far from being invalidated by the fact that, for instance, a perfect balance of power policy will scarcely be found in reality, it assumes that reality, being deficient in this respect, must be understood and evaluated as an approximation to an ideal system of balance of power.

3. Realism assumes that its key concept of interest defined as power is an objective category which is universally valid, but it does not endow that concept with a meaning that is fixed once and for all. The idea of interest is indeed of the essence of politics and is unaffected by the circumstances of time and place. Thucydides' statement, born of the experiences of ancient Greece, that "identity of interests is the surest of bonds whether between states or individuals" was taken up in the nineteenth century by Lord Salisbury's remark that "the only bond of union that endures" among nations is "the absence of all clashing interests." It was erected into a general principle of government by George Washington:

> A small knowledge of human nature will convince us, that, with far the greatest part of mankind, interest is the governing principle; and that almost every man is more or less, under its influence. Motives of public virtue may for a time, or in particular instances, actuate men to the observance of a conduct purely disinterested; but they are not of themselves sufficient to produce persevering conformity to the refined dictates and obligations of social duty. Few men are capable of making a continual sacrifice of all views of private interest, or advantage, to the common good. It is vain to exclaim against the depravity of human nature on this account; the fact is so, the experience of every age and nation has proved it and we must in a great measure, change the constitution of man, before we can make it otherwise. No institution, not built on the presumptive truth of these maxims can succeed.[1]

It was echoed and enlarged upon in our century by Max Weber's observation:

> Interests (material and ideal), not ideas, dominate directly the actions of men. Yet the "images of the world" created by these ideas have very often served as switches determining the tracks on which the dynamism of interests kept actions moving.[2]

Yet the kind of interest determining political action in a particular period of history depends upon the political and cultural context within which foreign policy is formulated. The goals that might be pursued by nations in their foreign policy can run the whole gamut of objectives any nation has ever pursued or might possibly pursue.

The same observations apply to the concept of power. Its content and the manner of its use are determined by the political and cultural environment. Power may comprise anything that establishes and maintains the control of man over man. Thus power covers all social relationships which serve that end, from physical violence to the most subtle psychological ties by which one mind controls another. Power covers the domination of man by man, both when it is disciplined by moral ends and controlled by constitutional safeguards, as in Western democracies, and when it is that untamed and barbaric force which finds its laws in nothing but its own strength and its sole justification in its aggrandizement.

Political realism does not assume that the contemporary conditions under which foreign policy operates, with their extreme instability and the ever present threat of large-scale violence, cannot be changed. The balance of power, for instance, is indeed a perennial element of all pluralistic societies, as the authors of *The Federalist* papers well knew; yet it is capable of operating, as it does in the United States, under the conditions of relative stability and peaceful conflict. If the factors that have given rise to these conditions can be duplicated on the international scene, similar conditions of stability and peace will then prevail there, as they have over long stretches of history among certain nations.

What is true of the general character of international relations is also true of the nation state as the ultimate point of reference of contemporary foreign policy. While the realist indeed believes that interest is the perennial standard by which political action must be judged and directed, the contemporary connection between interest and the nation state is a product of history, and is therefore bound to disappear in the course of history. Nothing in the realist position militates against the assumption that the present division of the political world into nation states will be replaced by larger units of a quite different character, more in keeping with the technical potentialities and the moral requirements of the contemporary world.

The realist parts company with other schools of thought before the all-important question of how the contemporary world is to be transformed. The realist is persuaded that this transformation can be achieved only through the workmanlike manipulation of the perennial forces that have shaped the past as they will the future. The realist cannot be persuaded that we can bring about that transformation by confronting a political reality that has its own laws with an abstract ideal that refuses to take those laws into account.

4. Political realism is aware of the moral significance of political action. It is also aware of the ineluctable tension between the moral command and the requirements of successful political action. And it is unwilling to gloss over and obliterate that tension and thus to obfuscate both the moral and the political issue by making it appear as though the stark facts of politics were morally more satisfying than they actually are, and the moral law less exacting than it actually is.

Realism maintains that universal moral principles cannot be applied to the actions of states in their abstract universal formulation, but that they must be filtered through the concrete circumstances of time and place. The individual may say for himself: "*Fiat justitia, pereat mundus* (Let justice be done, even if the world perish)," but the state has no right to say so in the name of those who are in its care. Both individual and state must judge political action by universal moral principles, such as that of liberty. Yet while the individual has a moral right to sacrifice himself in defense of such a moral principle, the state has no right to let its moral disapprobation of the infringement of liberty get in the way of successful political action, itself inspired by the moral principle of national survival. There can be no political morality without prudence; that is, without consideration of the political consequences of seemingly moral action. Realism, then, considers prudence—the weighing of the consequences of alternative political actions—to be the supreme virtue in politics. Ethics in the abstract judges action by its conformity with the moral law; political ethics judges action by its political consequences. Classical and medieval philosophy knew this, and so did Lincoln when he said:

> I do the very best I know how, the very best I can, and I mean to keep doing so until the end. If the end brings me out all right, what is said against me won't amount to anything. If the end brings me out wrong, ten angels swearing I was right would make no difference.

5. Political realism refuses to identify the moral aspirations of a particular nation with the moral laws that govern the universe. As it distinguishes between truth and opinion, so it distinguishes between truth and idolatry. All nations are tempted—and few have been able to resist the temptation for long—to clothe their own particular aspirations and actions in the moral purposes of the universe. To know that nations are subject to the moral law is one thing, while to pretend to know with certainty what is good and evil in the relations among nations is quite another. There is a world of difference between the belief that all nations stand under the judgment of God, inscrutable to the human mind, and the blasphemous conviction that God is always on one's side and that what one wills oneself cannot fail to be willed by God also.

The lighthearted equation between a particular nationalism and the counsels of Providence is morally indefensible, for it is that very sin of pride against which the Greek tragedians and the Biblical prophets have warned rulers and ruled. That equation is also politically pernicious, for it is liable to engender the distortion in judgement which, in the blindness of crusading frenzy, destroys nations and civilizations—in the name of moral principle, ideal, or God himself.

On the other hand, it is exactly the concept of interest defined in terms of power that saves us from both that moral excess and that political folly. For if we look at all nations, our own included, as political entities pursuing their respective interests defined in terms of power, we are able to do justice to all of them. And we are able to do justice to all of them in a dual sense: We are able to judge other nations as we judge our own and, having judged them in this fashion, we are then capable of pursuing policies that respect the interests of other nations, while protecting and promoting those of our own. Moderation in policy cannot fail to reflect the moderation of moral judgment.

6. The difference, then, between political realism and other schools of thought is real, and it is profound. However much the theory of political realism may have been misunderstood and misinterpreted, there is no gainsaying its distinctive intellectual and moral attitude to matters political.

Intellectually, the political realist maintains the autonomy of the political sphere, as the economist, the lawyer, the moralist maintain theirs. He thinks in terms of interest defined as power, as the economist thinks in terms of interest defined as wealth; the lawyer, of the conformity of action with legal rules; the moralist, of the conformity of action with moral principles. The economist asks: "How does this policy affect the wealth of society, or a segment of it?" The lawyer asks: "Is this policy in accord with the rules of law?" The moralist asks: "Is this policy in accord with moral principles?" And the political realist asks: "How does this policy affect the power of the nation?" (Or of the federal government, of Congress, of the party, of agriculture, as the case may be.)

The political realist is not unaware of the existence and relevance of standards of thought other than political ones. As political realist, he cannot but subordinate these other standards to those of politics. And he parts company with other schools when they impose standards of thought appropriate to other spheres upon the political sphere. . . .

This realist defense of the autonomy of the political sphere against its subversion by other modes of thought does not imply disregard for the existence and importance of these other modes of thought. It rather implies that each should be assigned its proper sphere and function. Political realism is based upon a pluralistic conception of human nature. Real man is a composite of "economic man," "political man," "moral man," "religious man," etc. A man who was nothing but "political man" would be a beast, for he would be completely lacking in moral restraints. A man who was nothing but "moral man" would be a fool, for he would be completely lacking in prudence. A man who was nothing but "religious man" would be a saint, for he would be completely lacking in worldly desires.

Recognizing that these different facets of human nature exist, political realism also recognizes that in order to understand one of them one has to deal with it on its own terms. That is to say, if I want to understand "religious man," I must for the time being abstract from the other aspects of human nature and deal with its religious aspect as if it were the only one. Furthermore, I must apply to the religious sphere the standards of thought appropriate to it, always remaining aware of the existence of other standards and their actual influence upon the religious qualities of man. What is true of this facet of human nature is true of all the others. No modern economist, for instance, would conceive of his science and its relations to other sciences of man in any other way. It is exactly through such a process of emancipation from other standards of thought, and the development of one appropriate to its subject matter, that economics has developed as an autonomous theory of the economic activities of man. To contribute to a similar development in the field of politics is indeed the purpose of political realism.

It is in the nature of things that a theory of politics which is based upon such principles will not meet with unanimous approval—nor does, for that matter, such a foreign policy. For theory and policy alike run counter to two trends in our culture which are not able to reconcile themselves to the assumptions and results of a rational, objective theory of politics. One of these trends disparages the role of power in society on grounds that stem from the experience and philosophy of the nineteenth century; we shall address ourselves to this tendency later in greater detail. The other trend, opposed to the realist theory and practice of politics, stems from the very relationship that exists, and must exist, between the human mind and the political sphere. . . . The human mind in its day-by-day operations cannot bear to look the truth of politics straight in the face. It must disguise, distort, belittle, and embellish the truth—the more so, the more the individual is actively involved in the processes of politics, and particularly in those of international politics. For only by deceiving himself about the nature of politics and the role he plays on the political scene is man able to live contentedly as a political animal with himself and his fellow men.

Thus it is inevitable that a theory which tries to understand international politics as it actually is and as it ought to be in view of its intrinsic nature, rather than as people would like to see it, must overcome a psychological resistance that most other branches of learning need not face.

## NOTES

1. *The Writings of George Washington*, edited by John C. Fitzpatrick (Washington: United States Printing Office, 1931–44), Vol. X, p. 363.
2. Marianne Weber, *Max Weber* (Tuebingen: J. C. B. Mohr, 1926), pp. 347–8. See also Max Weber, *Gesammelte Aufsätze zur Religionssociology* (Tuebingen: J. C. B. Mohr, 1920), p. 252.

# A Critique of Morgenthau's Principles of Political Realism

## J. ANN TICKNER

*It is not in giving life but in risking life that man is raised above the animal: that is why superiority has been accorded in humanity not to the sex that brings forth but to that which kills.*

SIMONE DE BEAUVOIR[1]

International politics is a man's world, a world of power and conflict in which warfare is a privileged activity. Traditionally, diplomacy, military service and the science of international politics have been largely male domains. In the past women have rarely been included in the ranks of professional diplomats or the military; of the relatively few women who specialize in the academic discipline of international relations, few are security specialists. Women political scientists who do study international relations tend to focus on areas such as international political economy, North–South relations and matters of distributive justice.

Today, in the United States, where women are entering the military and the foreign service in greater numbers than ever before, they are rarely to be found in positions of military leadership or at the top of the foreign policy establishment.[2] One notable exception, Jeane Kirkpatrick, who was U.S. ambassador to the United Nations in the early 1980s, has described herself as "a mouse in a man's world"; for, in spite of her authoritative and forceful public style and strong conservative credentials, Kirkpatrick maintains that she failed to win the respect or attention of her male colleagues on matters of foreign policy.[3]

Kirkpatrick's story could serve to illustrate the discrimination that women often encounter when they rise to high political office. However, the doubts as to whether a woman would be strong enough to press the nuclear button (an issue raised when a tearful Patricia Schroeder was pictured sobbing on her husband's shoulder as she bowed out of the 1988 U.S. presidential race), suggest that there may be an even more fundamental barrier to women's entry into the highest ranks of the military or of foreign policy making. Nuclear strategy, with its vocabulary of power, threat, force and deterrence, has a distinctly masculine ring;[4] moreover,

From J. Ann Tickner, "A Critique of Morgenthau's Principles of Political Realism" in *Gender and International Relations*, eds. Rebecca Grant and Kathleen Newland. Published by Indiana University Press. Reprinted by permission of Kathleen Newland. Portions of the text and some footnotes have been omitted.

women are stereotypically judged to be lacking in qualities which these terms evoke. It has also been suggested that, although more women are entering the world of public policy, they are more comfortable dealing with domestic issues such as social welfare that are more compatible with their nurturing skills. Yet the large number of women in the ranks of the peace movement suggests that women are not uninterested in issues of war and peace, although their frequent dissent from national security policy has often branded them as naive, uninformed or even unpatriotic.

In this chapter I propose to explore the question of why international politics is perceived as a man's world and why women remain so underrepresented in the higher echelons of the foreign policy establishment, the military and the academic discipline of international relations. Since I believe that there is something about this field that renders it particularly inhospitable and unattractive to women, I intend to focus on the nature of the discipline itself rather than on possible strategies to remove barriers to women's access to high policy positions. As I have already suggested, the issues that are given priority in foreign policy are issues with which men have had a special affinity. Moreover, if it is primarily men who are describing these issues and constructing theories to explain the workings of the international system, might we not expect to find a masculine perspective in the academic discipline also? If this were so then it could be argued that the exclusion of women has operated not only at the level of discrimination but also through a process of self-selection which begins with the way in which we are taught about international relations.

In order to investigate this claim that the discipline of international relations, as it has traditionally been defined by realism, is based on a masculine world view, I propose to examine the six principles of political realism formulated by Hans J. Morgenthau in his classic work *Politics Among Nations*. I shall use some ideas from feminist theory to show that the way in which Morgenthau describes and explains international politics, and the prescriptions that ensue are embedded in a masculine perspective. Then I shall suggest some ways in which feminist theory might help us begin to conceptualize a world view from a feminine perspective and to formulate a feminist epistemology of international relations. Drawing on these observations I shall conclude with a reformulation of Morgenthau's six principles. Male critics of contemporary realism have already raised many of the same questions about realism that I shall address. However, in undertaking this exercise, I hope to make a link between a growing critical perspective on international relations theory and feminist writers interested in global issues. Adding a feminist perspective to its discourse could also help to make the field of international relations more accessible to women scholars and practitioners.

## HANS J. MORGENTHAU'S PRINCIPLES OF POLITICAL REALISM: A MASCULINE PERSPECTIVE?

I have chosen to focus on Hans J. Morgenthau's six principles of political realism because they represent one of the most important statements of contemporary realism from which several generations of scholars and practitioners of international relations in the United States have been nourished. Although Morgenthau has frequently been criticized for his lack of scientific rigour and ambiguous use of language, these six principles have significantly framed the way in which the majority of international relations scholars and practitioners in the West have thought about international politics since 1945.[5]

Morgenthau's principles of political realism can be summarized as follows:

1. Politics, like society in general, is governed by objective laws that have their roots in human nature, which is unchanging: therefore it is possible to develop a rational theory that reflects these objective laws.
2. The main signpost of political realism is the concept of interest defined in terms of power which infuses rational order into the subject matter of politics, and thus makes the theoretical understanding of politics possible. Political realism stresses the rational, objective and unemotional.
3. Realism assumes that interest defined as power is an objective category which is universally valid but not with a meaning that is fixed once and for all. Power is the control of man over man.
4. Political realism is aware of the moral significance of political action. It is also aware of the tension between the moral command and the requirements of successful political action.
5. Political realism refuses to identify the moral aspirations of a particular nation with the moral laws that govern the universe. It is the concept of interest defined in terms of power that saves us from moral excess and political folly.
6. The political realist maintains the autonomy of the political sphere; he asks "How does this policy affect the power of the nation?" Political realism is based on a pluralistic conception of human nature. A man who was nothing but "political man" would be a beast, for he would be completely lacking in moral restraints. But, in order to develop an autonomous theory of political behaviour, "political man" must be abstracted from other aspects of human nature.[6]

I am not going to argue that Morgenthau is incorrect in his portrayal of the international system. I do believe, however, that it is a partial description of international politics because it is based on assumptions about human nature that are partial and that privilege masculinity. First, it is necessary to define masculinity and femininity. According to almost all feminist theorists, masculinity and femininity refer to a set of socially constructed categories, which vary in time and place, rather than to biological determinants. In the West, conceptual dichotomies such as objectivity vs. subjectivity, reason vs. emotion, mind vs. body, culture vs. nature, self vs. other or autonomy vs. relatedness, knowing vs. being and public vs. private have typically been used to describe male/female differences by feminists and non-feminists alike.[7] In the United States, psychological tests conducted across different socioeconomic groups confirm that individuals perceive these dichotomies as masculine and feminine and also that the characteristics associated with masculinity are more highly valued by men and women alike.[8] It is important to stress, however, that these characteristics are stereotypical; they do not necessarily describe individual men or women, who can exhibit characteristics and modes of thought associated with the opposite sex.

Using a vocabulary that contains many of the words associated with masculinity as I have identified it, Morgenthau asserts that it is possible to develop a rational (and unemotional) theory of international politics based on objective laws that have their roots in human nature. Since Morgenthau wrote the first edition of *Politics Among Nations* in 1948, this search for an objective science of international politics based on the model of the natural sciences has been an important part of the realist and neorealist agenda. In her feminist critique of the natural sciences, Evelyn Fox Keller points out that most scientific communities share the "assumption that the universe they study is directly accessible, represented by concepts and shaped not by language but only by the demands of logic and experiment."[9] The laws of nature, according to this view of science, are "beyond the relativity of language." Like most feminists, Keller rejects this view of science which, she asserts, imposes a coercive, hierarchical and conformist pattern on scientific inquiry. Feminists in general are sceptical about the possibility of finding a universal and objective foundation for knowledge, which Morgenthau claims is possible. Most share the belief that knowledge is socially constructed: since it is language that transmits knowledge, the use of language and its claims to objectivity must continually be questioned.

Keller argues that objectivity, as it is usually defined in our culture, is associated with masculinity. She identifies it as "a network of interactions between gender development, a belief system that equates objectivity with masculinity, and a set of cultural values that simultaneously (and cojointly) elevates what is defined as scientific and what is defined as masculine."[10] Keller links the separation of self from other, an important stage of masculine gender development, with this notion of objectivity. Translated into scientific inquiry this becomes the striving for the separation of subject and object, an important goal of modern science and one which, Keller asserts, is based on the need for control; hence objectivity becomes associated with power and domination.

The need for control has been an important motivating force for modern realism. To begin his search for an objective, rational theory of international politics, which could impose order on a chaotic and conflictual world, Morgenthau constructs an abstraction which he calls political man, a beast completely lacking in moral restraints. Morgenthau is deeply aware that real men, like real states, are both moral and bestial but, because states do not live up to the universal moral laws that govern the universe, those who behave morally in international politics are doomed to failure because of the immoral actions of others. To solve this tension Morgenthau postulates a realm of international politics in which the amoral behaviour of political man is not only permissible but prudent. It is a Hobbesian world, separate and distinct from the world of domestic order. In it, states may act like beasts, for survival depends on a maximization of power and a willingness to fight.

Having long argued that the personal is political, most feminist theory would reject the validity of constructing an autonomous political sphere around which boundaries of permissible modes of conduct have been drawn. As Keller maintains, "the demarcation between public and private not only defines and defends the boundaries of the political but also helps form its content and style."[11] Morgenthau's political man is a social construct based on a partial representation of human nature. One might well ask where the women were in Hobbes's state of nature; presumably they must have been involved in reproduction and childrearing, rather than warfare, if life was to go on for more than one generation.[12] Morgenthau's emphasis on the conflictual aspects of the international system contributes to a tendency, shared by other realists, to de-emphasize elements of cooperation and regeneration which are also aspects of international relations.[13]

Morgenthau's construction of an amoral realm of international power politics is an attempt to resolve what he sees as a fundamental tension between the moral laws that govern the universe and the requirements of successful political action in a world where states use morality as a cloak to justify the pursuit of their own national interests. Morgenthau's universalistic morality postulates the highest form of morality as an abstract ideal, similar to the Golden Rule, to which states seldom adhere: the morality of states, by contrast, is an instrumental morality guided by self-interest.

Morgenthau's hierarchical ordering of morality contains parallels with the work of psychologist Lawrence Kohlberg. Based on a study of the moral development of 84 American boys, Kohlberg concludes that the highest stage of human moral development (which he calls stage 6) is the ability to recognize abstract universal principles of justice; lower on the scale (stage 2) is an instrumental morality concerned with serving one's own interests while recognizing that others have interests too. Between these two is an interpersonal morality which is contextual and characterized by sensitivity to the needs of others (stage 3).[14]

In her critique of Kohlberg's stages of moral development, Carol Gilligan argues that they are based on a masculine conception of morality. On Kohlberg's scale women rarely rise above the third or contextual stage. Gilligan claims that this is not a sign of inferiority but of difference. Since women are socialized into a mode of thinking which is contextual and narrative, rather than formal and abstract, they tend to see issues in contextual rather than in abstract terms.[15] In international relations the tendency to think about morality either in terms of abstract, universal and unattainable standards or as purely instrumental, as Morgenthau does, detracts from our ability to tolerate cultural differences and to seek potential for building community in spite of these differences.

Using examples from feminist literature I have suggested that Morgenthau's attempt to construct an objective, universal theory of international politics is rooted in assumptions about human nature and morality that, in modern Western culture, are associated with masculinity. Further evidence that Morgenthau's principles are not the basis for a universalistic and objective theory is contained in his frequent references to the failure of what he calls the "legalistic–moralistic" or idealist approach to world politics which he claims was largely responsible for both the world wars. Having laid the blame for the Second World War on the misguided morality of appeasement, Morgenthau's *realpolitik* prescriptions for successful political action appear as prescriptions for avoiding the mistakes of the 1930s rather than as prescriptions with timeless applicability.

If Morgenthau's world view is embedded in the traumas of the Second World War, are his prescriptions still valid as we move further away from this event? I share with other critics of realism the view that, in a rapidly changing world, we must begin to search for modes of behaviour different from those prescribed by Morgenthau. Given that any war between the major powers is likely to be nuclear, increasing security by increasing power could be suicidal.[16] Moreover, the nation state, the primary constitutive element of the international system for Morgenthau and other realists, is no longer able to deal with an increasingly pluralistic array of problems ranging from economic interdependence to environmental degradation. Could feminist theory make a contribution to international relations theory by constructing an alternative, feminist perspective on international politics that might help us to search for more appropriate solutions?

## A FEMINIST PERSPECTIVE ON INTERNATIONAL RELATIONS?

If the way in which we describe reality has an effect on the ways we perceive and act upon our environment, new perspectives might lead us to consider alternative courses of action. With this in mind I shall first examine two important concepts in international relations, power and security, from a feminist perspective and then discuss some feminist approaches to conflict resolution.

Morgenthau's definition of power, the control of man over man, is typical of the way power is usually defined in international relations. Nancy Hartsock argues that this type of power-as-domination has always been associated with masculinity, since the exercise of power has generally been a masculine activity: rarely have women exercised legitimized power in the public domain. When women write about power they stress energy, capacity and potential, says Hartsock. She notes that women theorists, even when they have little else in common, offer similar definitions of power which differ substantially from the understanding of power as domination.[17]

Hannah Arendt, frequently cited by feminists writing about power, defines power as the human ability to act in concert, or to take action in connection with others who share similar concerns.[18] This definition of power is similar to that of psychologist David McClelland's portrayal of female power, which he describes as shared rather than assertive.[19] Jane Jaquette argues that, since women have had less access to the instruments of coercion, they have been more apt to rely on power as persuasion; she compares women's domestic activities to coalition building.[20]

All of these writers are portraying power as a relationship of mutual enablement. Tying her definition of female power to international relations, Jaquette sees similarities between female strategies of persuasion and strategies of small states operating from a position of weakness in the international system. There are also examples of states' behaviour that contain elements of the female strategy of coalition building. One such example is the Southern African Development Coordination Conference (SADCC), which is designed to build regional infrastructure based on mutual cooperation and collective self-reliance in order to decrease dependence on the South African economy. Another is the European Community, which has had considerable success in building mutual cooperation in an area of the world whose history would not predict such a course of events.[21] It is rare, however, that cooperative outcomes in international relations are described in these terms, although Karl Deutsch's notion of pluralistic security communities might be one such example where power is associated with building community.[22] I am not denying that power as domination is a pervasive reality in international relations. However, there are also instances of cooperation in interstate relations, which tend to be obscured when power is seen solely as domination. Thinking about power in this multidimensional sense may help us to think constructively about the potential for cooperation as well as conflict, an aspect of international relations generally played down by realism.

Redefining national security is another way in which feminist theory could contribute to new thinking about international relations.[23] Traditionally in the West, the concept of national security has been tied to military strength and its role in the physical protection of the nation state from external threats. Morgenthau's notion of defending the national interest in terms of power is consistent with this definition. But this traditional definition of national security is partial at best in today's world.[24] The technologically advanced states are highly interdependent, and rely on weapons whose effects would be equally devastating to winners and losers alike. For them to defend national security by relying on war as the last resort no longer appears very useful. Moreover, if one thinks of security in North–South rather than East–West terms, for a large portion of the world's population security has as much to do with the satisfaction of basic material needs as with military threats. According to Johan Galtung's notion of structural violence, to suffer a lower life expectancy by virtue of one's place of birth is a form of violence whose effects can be as devastating as war.[25]

Basic needs satisfaction has a great deal to do with women, but only recently have women's roles as providers of basic needs, and in development more generally, become visible as important components in development strategies.[26] Traditionally the development literature has focused on aspects of the development process that are in the public sphere, are technologically complex and are usually undertaken by men. Thinking about the role of women in development and the way in which we can define development and basic needs satisfaction to be inclusive of women's roles and needs are topics that deserve higher priority on the international agenda. Typically, however, this is an area about which traditional international relations theory, with the priority it gives to order over justice, has had very little to say.

A further threat to national security, more broadly defined, which has also been missing from the agenda of traditional international relations, concerns the environment. Carolyn Merchant argues that a mechanistic view of nature, contained in modern science, has helped to guide an industrial and technological development which has resulted in environmental damage that has now become a matter of global concern. In the introduction to her book *The Death of Nature*, Merchant suggests that, "Women and nature have an age-old association—an affiliation that has persisted throughout culture, language, and history."[27] Hence she maintains that the ecology movement, which is growing up in response to environmental threats, and the women's movement are deeply interconnected. Both stress living in equilibrium with nature rather than dominating it, both see nature as a living non-hierarchical entity in which each part is mutually dependent on the whole. Ecologists, as well as many feminists, are now suggesting that only such a fundamental change of world view will allow the human species to survive the damage it is inflicting on the environment.

Thinking about military, economic and environmental security in interdependent terms suggests the need for new methods of conflict resolution that seek to achieve mutually beneficial, rather than zero sum, outcomes. One such method comes from Sara Ruddick's work on "maternal thinking."[28] Ruddick describes maternal thinking as focused on the preservation of life and the growth of children. To foster a domestic environment conducive to these goals, tranquility must be preserved by avoiding conflict where possible, engaging in it non-violently and restoring community when it is over. In such an environment the ends for which disputes are fought are subordinate to the means by which they are resolved. This method of conflict resolution involves making contextual judgements rather than appealing to absolute standards and thus has much in common with Gilligan's definition of female morality.

While non-violent resolution of conflict in the domestic sphere is a widely accepted norm, passive resistance in the public realm is regarded as deviant. But, as Ruddick argues, the peaceful resolution of conflict by mothers does not usually extend to the children of one's enemies, an important reason why women have been ready to support men's wars.[29] The question for Ruddick then becomes how to get maternal thinking, a mode of thinking which she believes can be found in men as well as women, out into the public realm. Ruddick believes that finding a common humanity among one's opponents has become a condition of survival in the nuclear age when the notion of winners and losers has become questionable.[30] Portraying the adversary as less than human has all too often been a technique of the nation state to command loyalty and to increase its legitimacy in the eyes of its citizens. Such behaviour in an age of weapons of mass destruction may be self-defeating.

We might also look to Gilligan's work for a feminist perspective on conflict resolution. Reporting on a study of playground behaviour of American boys and girls, Gilligan argues that girls are less able to tolerate high levels of conflict, and more likely than boys to play games that involve taking turns and in which the success of one does not depend on the failure of another.[31] While Gilligan's study does not take into account attitudes toward other groups (racial, ethnic, economic or national), it does suggest the validity of investigating whether girls are socialized to use different modes of problem solving when dealing with conflict, and whether such behaviour might be useful in thinking about international conflict resolution.

## TOWARD A FEMINIST EPISTEMOLOGY OF INTERNATIONAL RELATIONS

I am deeply aware that there is no *one* feminist approach but many, which come out of various disciplines and intellectual traditions. Yet there are common themes in the different feminist literatures that I have reviewed which could help us to begin to formulate a feminist epistemology of international relations. Morgenthau encourages us to try to stand back from the world and to think about theory building in terms of constructing a rational outline or map that has universal applications. In contrast, the feminist literature reviewed here emphasizes connection and contingency. Keller argues for a form of knowledge, which she calls "dynamic objectivity," "that grants to the world around us its independent integrity, but does so in a way that remains cognizant of, indeed relies on, our connectivity with that world."[32] Keller illustrates this mode of thinking in her study of Barbara McClintock, whose work on genetic transposition won her a Nobel prize after many years of marginalization by the scientific community.[33] McClintock, Keller argues, was a scientist with a respect for complexity, diversity and individual difference whose methodology allowed her data to speak rather than imposing explanations on it.

Keller's portrayal of McClintock's science contains parallels with what Sandra Harding calls an African world view.[34] Harding tells us that the Western liberal notion of rational economic man, an individualist and a welfare maximizer, similar to the image of rational political man on which realism has based its theoretical investigations, does not make any sense in the African world view where the individual is seen as part of the social order acting within that order rather than upon it. Harding believes that this view of human behaviour has much in common with a feminist perspective. If we combine this view of human behaviour with Merchant's holistic perspective which stresses the interconnectedness of all things, including nature, it may help us to begin to think from a more global perspective. Such a perspective appreciates cultural diversity but at the same time recognizes a growing interdependence, which makes anachronistic the exclusionary thinking fostered by the nation state system.

Keller's dynamic objectivity, Harding's African world view and Merchant's ecological thinking all point us in the direction of an appreciation of the "other" as a subject whose views are as legitimate as our own, a way of thinking that has been sadly lacking in the history of international relations. Just as Keller cautions us against the construction of a feminist science which could perpetuate similar exclusionary attitudes, Harding warns us against schema that contrast people by race, gender or class and that originate within projects of social domination. Feminist thinkers generally dislike dichotomization and the distancing of subject from object that goes with abstract thinking, both of which, they believe, encourage a we/they attitude characteristic of international relations. Instead, feminist literature urges us to construct epistemologies that value ambiguity and difference. These qualities could stand us in good stead as we begin to build a human or ungendered theory of international relations which contains elements of both masculine and feminine modes of thought.

## MORGENTHAU'S PRINCIPLES OF POLITICAL REALISM: A FEMINIST REFORMULATION

The first part of this paper used feminist theory to develop a critique of Morgenthau's principles of political realism in order to demonstrate how the theory and practice of international relations may exhibit a masculine bias. The second part suggested some contributions that feminist theory might make to reconceptualizing some important elements in international relations and to thinking about a feminist epistemology. Drawing on these observations, this conclusion will present a feminist reformulation of Morgenthau's six principles of political realism, outlined earlier in this paper, which might help us to begin to think differently about international relations. I shall not use the term realism since feminists believe that there are multiple real ities: a truly realistic picture of international politics must recognize elements of cooperation as well as conflict, morality as well as *realpolitik,* and the strivings for justice as well as order.[35] This reformulation may help us to think in these multidimensional terms.

1. A feminist perspective believes that objectivity, as it is culturally defined, is associated with masculinity. Therefore, supposedly "objective" laws of human nature are based on a partial, masculine view of human nature. Human nature is both masculine and feminine; it contains elements of social reproduction and development as well as political domination. Dynamic objectivity offers us a more connected view of objectivity with less potential for domination.

2. A feminist perspective believes that the national interest is multidimensional and contextually contingent. Therefore, it cannot be defined solely in terms of power. In the contemporary world the national interest demands cooperative rather than zero sum solutions to a set of interdependent global problems which include nuclear war, economic well-being and environmental degradation.

3. Power cannot be infused with meaning that is universally valid. Power as domination and control privileges masculinity and ignores the possibility of collective empowerment, another aspect of power often associated with femininity.

4. A feminist perspective rejects the possibility of separating moral command from political action. All political action has moral significance. The realist agenda for maximizing order through power and control gives priority to the moral command of order over those of justice and the satisfaction of basic needs necessary to ensure social reproduction.

5. While recognizing that the moral aspirations of particular nations cannot be equated with universal moral principles, a feminist perspective seeks to find common moral elements in human aspirations which could become the basis for de-escalating international conflict and building international community.

6. A feminist perspective denies the autonomy of the political. Since autonomy is associated with masculinity in Western culture, disciplinary efforts to construct a world view which does not rest on a pluralistic conception of human nature are partial and masculine. Building boundaries around a narrowly defined political realm defines political in a way that excludes the concerns and contributions of women.

To construct this feminist alternative is not to deny the validity of Morgenthau's work. But adding a feminist perspective to the epistemology of international relations is a stage through which we must pass if we are to think about constructing an ungendered or human science of international politics which is sensitive to, but goes beyond, both masculine and feminine perspectives. Such inclusionary thinking, as Simone de Beauvoir tells us, values the bringing forth of life as much as the risking of life; it is becoming imperative in a world in which the technology of war and a fragile natural environment threaten human existence. An ungendered, or human, discourse becomes possible only when women are adequately represented in the discipline and when there is equal respect for the contributions of women and men alike.

## NOTES

An earlier version of this paper was presented at a symposium on Gender and International Relations at the London School of Economics in June 1988. I would like to thank the editors of *Millennium,* who organized this symposium, for encouraging me to undertake this rewriting. I am also grateful to Hayward Alker Jr. and Susan Okin for their careful reading of the manuscript and helpful suggestions.

1. Quoted in Sandra Harding, *The Science Question in Feminism* (Ithaca, N.Y.: Cornell University Press, 1986), p. 148.
2. In 1987 only 4.8 per cent of the top career Foreign Service employees were women. Statement of Patricia Schroeder before the Committee on Foreign Affairs, U.S. House of Representatives, p. 4; *Women's Perspectives on U.S. Foreign Policy: A Compilation of Views* (Washington, D.C.: U.S. Government Printing Office, 1988). For an analysis of women's roles in the American military, see Cynthia Enloe, *Does Khaki Become You? The Militarisation of Women's Lives* (London: Pluto Press, 1983).
3. Edward P. Crapol (ed.), *Women and American Foreign Policy* (Westport, Conn.: Greenwood Press, 1987), p. 167.
4. For an analysis of the role of masculine language in shaping strategic thinking see Carol Cohn, "Sex and Death in the Rational World of Defense Intellectuals," *Signs: Journal of Women in Culture and Society* (Vol. 12, No. 4, Summer 1987).
5. The claim for the dominance of the realist paradigm is supported by John A. Vasquez, "Colouring It Morgenthau: New Evidence for an Old Thesis on Quantitative International Studies," *British Journal of International Studies* (Vol. 3, No. 5, October 1979), pp. 210–28. For a critique of Morgenthau's ambiguous use of language see Inis L. Claude Jr., *Power and International Relations* (New York: Random House, 1962), especially pp. 25–37.
6. These are drawn from Hans Morgenthau, *Politics Among Nations: The Struggle for Power and Peace,* 5th revised edition (New York: Alfred Knopf, 1973), pp. 4–15. I am aware that these principles embody only a partial statement of Morgenthau's very rich study of international politics, a study which deserves a much more detailed analysis than I can give here.
7. This list is a composite of the male/female dichotomies which appear in Evelyn Fox Keller's *Reflections on Gender and Science* (New Haven, Conn.: Yale University Press, 1985) and Harding, *op. cit.*

8. Inge K. Broverman, Susan R. Vogel, Donald M. Broverman, Frank E. Clarkson and Paul S. Rosenkranz, "Sex-role Stereotypes: A Current Appraisal," *Journal of Social Issues* (Vol. 28, No. 2, 1972), pp. 59–78. Replication of this research in the 1980s confirms that these perceptions still hold.

9. Keller, *op. cit.,* p. 130.

10. *Ibid.,* p. 89.

11. *Ibid.,* p. 9.

12. Sara Ann Ketchum, "Female Culture, Woman Culture and Conceptual Change: Toward a Philosophy of Women's Studies," *Social Theory and Practice* (Vol. 6, No. 2, Summer 1980).

13. Others have questioned whether Hobbes's state of nature provides an accurate description of the international system. See for example Charles Beitz, *Political Theory and International Relations* (Princeton, N.J.: Princeton University Press, 1979), pp. 35–50 and Stanley Hoffmann, *Duties Beyond Borders* (Syracuse, N.Y.: Syracuse University Press, 1981), chap. 1.

14. Kohlberg's stages of moral development are described and discussed in Robert Kegan, *The Evolving Self: Problem and Process in Human Development* (Cambridge, Mass.: Harvard University Press, 1982), chap. 2.

15. Carol Gilligan, *In a Different Voice: Psychological Theory and Women's Development* (Cambridge, Mass.: Harvard University Press, 1982). See chap. 1 for Gilligan's critique of Kohlberg.

16. There is evidence that, toward the end of his life, Morgenthau himself was aware that his own prescriptions were becoming anachronistic. In a seminar presentation in 1978 he suggested that power politics as the guiding principle for the conduct of international relations had become fatally defective. For a description of this seminar presentation see Francis Anthony Boyle, *World Politics and International Law* (Durham, N.C.: Duke University Press, 1985), pp. 70–4.

17. Nancy C. M. Hartsock, *Money, Sex and Power: Toward a Feminist Historical Materialism* (Boston: Northeastern University Press, 1983), p. 210.

18. Hannah Arendt, *On Violence* (New York: Harcourt, Brace and World, 1969), p. 44. Arendt's definition of power, as it relates to international relations, is discussed more extensively in Jean Bethke Elshtain's "Reflections on War and Political Discourse: Realism, Just War, and Feminism in a Nuclear Age," *Political Theory* (Vol. 13, No. 1, February 1985), pp. 39–57.

19. David McClelland, "Power and the Feminine Role," in David McClelland, *Power: The Inner Experience* (New York: Wiley, 1975).

20. Jane S. Jaquette, "Power as Ideology: A Feminist Analysis," in Judith H. Stiehm (ed.), *Women's Views of the Political World of Men* (Dobbs Ferry, N.Y.: Transnational Publishers, 1984).

21. These examples are cited by Christine Sylvester, "The Emperor's Theories and Transformations: Looking at the Field through Feminist Lenses," in Dennis Pirages and Christine Sylvester (eds.), *Transformations in the Global Political Economy* (Basingstoke: Macmillan, 1989).

22. Karl W. Deutsch et al., *Political Community and the North Atlantic Area* (Princeton, N.J.: Princeton University Press, 1957).

23. New thinking is a term that is also being used in the Soviet Union to describe foreign policy reformulations under Gorbachev. There are indications that the Soviets are beginning to conceptualize security in the multidimensional terms described here. See Margot Light, *The Soviet Theory of International Relations* (New York: St. Martin's Press, 1988), chap. 10.

24. This is the argument made by Edward Azar and Chung-in Moon, "Third World National Security: Toward a New Conceptual Framework," *International Interactions* (Vol. 11, No. 2, 1984), pp. 103–35.

25. Johan Galtung, "Violence, Peace, and Peace Research," in Galtung, *Essays in Peace Research*, Vol. I (Copenhagen: Christian Ejlers, 1975).

26. See, for example, Gita Sen and Caren Grown, *Development, Crises and Alternative Visions: Third World Women's Perspectives* (New York: Monthly Review Press, 1987). This is an example of a growing literature on women and development which deserves more attention from the international relations community.

27. Carolyn Merchant, *The Death of Nature: Women, Ecology and the Scientific Revolution* (New York: Harper and Row, 1982), p. xv.

28. Sara Ruddick, "Maternal Thinking" and "Preservative Love and Military Destruction: Some Reflections on Mothering and Peace," in Joyce Treblicot, *Mothering: Essays in Feminist Theory* (Totowa, N.J.: Rowman and Allenhead, 1984).

29. For a more extensive analysis of this issue see Jean Bethke Elshtain, *Women and War* (New York: Basic Books, 1987).

30. This type of conflict resolution contains similarities with the problem solving approach of Edward Azar, John Burton and Herbert Kelman. See, for example, Edward E. Azar and John W. Burton, *International Conflict Resolution: Theory and Practice* (Brighton: Wheatsheaf, 1986) and Herbert C. Kelman, "Interactive Problem Solving: A Social-Psychological Approach to Conflict Resolution," in W. Klassen (ed.), *Dialogue Toward Inter-Faith Understanding* (Tantur/Jerusalem: Ecumenical Institute for Theoretical Research, 1986), pp. 293–314.

31. Gilligan, *op. cit.,* pp. 9–10.

32. Keller, *op. cit.,* p. 117.

33. Evelyn Fox Keller, *A Feeling for the Organism: The Life and Work of Barbara McClintock* (New York: Freeman, 1983).

34. Harding, *op. cit.,* chap. 7.

35. "Utopia and reality are . . . the two facets of political science. Sound political thought and sound political life will be found only where both have their place": E. H. Carr, *The Twenty Years Crisis: 1919–1939* (New York: Harper and Row, 1964), p. 10.

# THE CONSEQUENCES OF ANARCHY

## The Anarchic Structure of World Politics

### KENNETH N. WALTZ

## POLITICAL STRUCTURES

Only through some sort of systems theory can international politics be understood. To be a success, such a theory has to show how international politics can be conceived of as a domain distinct from the economic, social, and other international domains that one may conceive of. To mark international-political systems off from other international systems, and to distinguish systems-level from unit-level forces, requires showing how political structures are generated and how they affect, and are affected by, the units of the system. How can we conceive of international politics as a distinct system? What is it that intervenes between interacting units and the results that their acts and interactions produce? To answer these questions, this chapter first examines the concept of social structure and then defines structure as a concept appropriate for national and for international politics.

A system is composed of a structure and of interacting units. The structure is the system-wide component that makes it possible to think of the system as a whole. The problem is . . . to contrive a definition of structure free of the attributes and the interactions of units. Definitions of structure must leave aside, or abstract from, the characteristics of units, their behavior, and their interactions. Why must those obviously important matters be omitted? They must be omitted so that we can distinguish between variables at the level of the units and variables at the level of the system. The problem is to develop theoretically useful concepts to replace the vague and varying systemic notions that are customarily employed—notions such as environment, situation, context, and milieu. Structure is a useful concept if it gives clear and fixed meaning to such vague and varying terms.

We know what we have to omit from any definition of structure if the definition is to be useful theoretically. Abstracting from the attributes of units means leaving aside questions about the kinds of political leaders, social and economic institutions, and ideological commitments states may have. Abstracting from relations means leaving aside questions about the cultural, economic, political, and military interactions of states. To say what is to be left out does not indicate what is to be put in. The negative point is important nevertheless because the instruction to omit attributes is often violated and the instruction to omit interactions almost always goes unobserved. But if attributes and interactions are omitted, what is left? The question is answered by considering the double meaning of the term "relation." As S. F. Nadel points out, ordinary language obscures a distinction that is important in theory. "Relation" is used to mean both the interaction of units and the positions they occupy vis-à-vis each other.[1] To define a structure requires ignoring how units relate with one another (how they interact) and concentrating on how they stand in relation to one another (how they are arranged or positioned). Interactions, as I have insisted, take place at the level of the units. How units stand in relation to one another, the way they are arranged or positioned, is not a property of the units. The arrangement of units is a property of the system.

By leaving aside the personality of actors, their behavior, and their interactions, one arrives at a purely positional picture of society. Three propositions follow from this. First, structures may endure while personality, behavior, and interactions vary widely. Structure is sharply distinguished from actions and interactions. Second, a structural definition applies to realms of widely different substance so long as the arrangement of parts is similar.[2] Third, because this is so, theories developed for one realm may with some modification be applicable to other realms as well. . . .

The concept of structure is based on the fact that units differently juxtaposed and combined behave differently and in interacting produce different outcomes. I first want to show how internal political structure can be defined. In a book on international-political theory, domestic political structure has to be examined in order to draw a distinction between expectations about behavior and outcomes in the internal and external realms. Moreover, considering domestic political structure now will make the elusive international-political structure easier to catch later on.

Structure defines the arrangement, or the ordering, of the parts of a system. Structure is not a collection of political institutions but rather the arrangement of them. How is the arrangement defined? The constitution of a state describes some parts of the arrangement, but political structures as they develop are not identical with formal constitutions. In defining structures, the first question to answer is this: What is the principle by which the parts are arranged?

Domestic politics is hierarchically ordered. The units—institutions and agencies—stand vis-à-vis each other in relations of super- and subordination. The ordering principle of a system gives the first, and basic, bit of information about how the parts of a realm are related to each other. In a polity the hierarchy of offices is by no means completely articulated, nor are all ambiguities about relations of super- and subordination removed. Nevertheless, political actors are formally differentiated according to the degrees of their authority, and their distinct functions are specified. By "specified" I do not mean that the law of the land fully describes the duties that different agencies perform, but only that broad agreement prevails on the tasks that various parts of a government are to undertake and on the extent of the power they legitimately wield. Thus Congress supplies the military forces; the President commands them. Congress makes the laws; the executive branch enforces them; agencies administer laws; judges interpret them. Such specification of roles and differentiation of functions is found in any state, the more fully so as the state is more highly developed. The specification of functions of formally differentiated parts gives the second bit of structural information. This second part of the definition adds some content to the structure, but only enough to say more fully how the units stand in relation to one another. The roles and the functions of the British Prime Minister and Parliament, for example, differ from those of the American President and Congress. When offices are juxtaposed and functions are combined in different ways, different behaviors and outcomes result, as I shall shortly show.

The placement of units in relation to one another is not fully defined by a system's ordering principle and by the formal differentiation of its parts. The standing of the units also changes with changes in their relative capabilities. In the performance of their functions, agencies may gain capabilities or lose them. The relation of Prime Minister to Parliament and of President to Congress depends on, and varies with, their relative capabilities. The third part of the definition of structure acknowledges that even while specified functions remain unchanged, units come to stand in different relation to each other through changes in relative capability.

A domestic political structure is thus defined: first, according to the principle by which it is ordered; second, by specification of the functions of formally differentiated units; and third, by the distribution of capabilities across those units. Structure is a highly abstract notion, but the definition of structure does not abstract from everything. To do so would be to leave everything aside and to include nothing at all. The three-part definition of structure includes only what is required to show how the units of the system are positioned or arranged. Everything else is omitted. Concern for tradition and culture, analysis of the character and personality of political actors, consideration of the conflictive and accommodative processes of politics, description of the making and execution of policy—all such matters are left aside. Their omission does not imply their unimportance. They are omitted because we want to figure out the expected effects of structure on process and of process on structure. That can be done only if structure and process are distinctly defined.

I defined domestic political structures first by the principle according to which they are organized or ordered, second by the differentiation of units and the specification of their functions, and third by the distribution of capabilities across units. Let us see how the three terms of the definition apply to international politics.

## 1. Ordering Principles

Structural questions are questions about the arrangement of the parts of a system. The parts of domestic political systems stand in relations of super- and subordinaion. Some are entitled to command; others are required to obey. Domestic systems are centralized and hierarchic. The parts of international-political systems stand in relations of coordination. Formally, each is the equal of all the others. None is entitled to command; none is required to obey. International systems are decentralized and anarchic. The ordering principles of the two structures are distinctly different, indeed, contrary to each other. Domestic political structures have governmental institutions and offices as their concrete counterparts. International politics, in contrast, has been called "politics in the absence of government."[3] International organizations do exist, and in ever-growing numbers. Supranational agents able to act effectively, however, either themselves acquire some of the attributes and capabilities of states, as did the medieval papacy in the era of Innocent III, or they soon reveal their inability to act in important ways except with the support, or at least the acquiescence, of the principal states concerned with the matters at hand. Whatever elements of authority emerge internationally are barely once removed from the capability that provides the foundation for the appearance of those elements. Authority quickly reduces to a particular expression of capability. In the absence of agents with system-wide authority, formal relations of super and subordination fail to develop.

The first term of a structural definition states the principle by which the system is ordered. Structure is an organizational concept. The prominent characteristic of international politics, however, seems to be the lack of order and of organization. How can one think of international politics as being any kind of an order at all? The anarchy of politics internationally is often referred to. If structure is an organizational concept, the terms "structure" and "anarchy" seem to be in contradiction. If international politics is "politics in the absence of government," what are we in the presence of? In looking for international structure, one is brought face to face with the invisible, an uncomfortable position to be in.

The problem is this: how to conceive of an order without an orderer and of organizational effects where formal organization is lacking. Because these are difficult questions, I shall answer them through analogy with microeconomic theory. Reasoning by analogy is helpful where one can move from a domain for which theory is well developed to one where it is not. Reasoning by analogy is permissible where different domains are structurally similar.

Classical economic theory, developed by Adam Smith and his followers, is microtheory. Political scientists tend to think that microtheory is theory about small-scale matters, a usage that ill accords with its established meaning. The term "micro" in economic theory indicates the way in which the theory is constructed rather than the scope of the matters it pertains to. Microeconomic theory describes how an order is spontaneously formed from the self-interested acts and interactions of individual units—in this case, persons and firms. The theory then turns upon the two central concepts of the economic units and of the market. Economic units and economic markets are concepts, not descriptive realities or concrete entities. This must be emphasized since from the early eighteenth century to the present, from the sociologist Auguste Comte to the psychologist George Katona, economic theory has been faulted because its assumptions fail to correspond with realities.[4] Unrealistically, economic theorists conceive of an economy operating in isolation from its society and polity. Unrealistically, economists assume that the economic world is the world of the world. Unrealistically, economists think of the acting unit, the famous "economic man," as a single-minded profit maximizer. They single out one aspect of man and leave aside the wondrous variety of human life. As any moderately sensible economist knows, "economic man" does not exist. Anyone who asks businessmen how they make their decisions will find that the assumption that men are economic maximizers grossly distorts their characters. The assumption that men behave as economic men, which is known to be false as a descriptive statement, turns out to be useful in the construction of theory.

Markets are the second major concept invented by microeconomic theorists. Two general questions must be asked about markets: How are they formed? How do they work? The answer to the first question is this: The market of a decentralized economy is individualist in origin, spontaneously generated, and unintended. The market arises out of the activities of separate units—persons and firms—whose aims and efforts are directed not toward creating an order but rather toward fulfilling their own internally defined interests by whatever means they can muster. The individual unit acts for itself. From the coaction of like units emerges a structure that affects and constrains all of them. Once formed, a market becomes a force in itself, and a force that the constitutive units acting singly or in small numbers cannot control. Instead, in lesser or greater degree as market conditions vary, the creators become the creatures of the market that their activity gave rise to. Adam Smith's great achievement was to show how self-interested, greed-driven actions may produce good social outcomes if only political and social conditions permit free competition. If a laissez-faire economy is harmonious, it is so because the intentions of actors do not correspond with the outcomes their actions produce. What intervenes between the actors and the objects of their action in order to thwart their purposes? To account for the unexpectedly favorable outcomes of selfish acts, the concept of a market is brought into play. Each unit seeks its own good; the result of a number of units simultaneously doing so transcends the motives and the aims of the separate units. Each would like to work less hard and price his product higher. Taken together, all have to work harder and price their products lower. Each firm seeks to increase its profit; the result of many firms doing so drives the profit rate downward. Each man seeks his own end, and, in doing so, produces a result that was no part of his intention. Out of the mean ambition of its members, the greater good of society is produced.

The market is a cause interposed between the economic actors and the results they produce. It conditions their calculations, their behaviors, and their interactions. It is not an agent in the sense of A being the agent that produces outcome X. Rather it is a structural cause. A market constrains the units that comprise it from taking certain actions and disposes them toward taking others. The market, created by self-directed interacting economic units, selects behaviors according to their consequences. The market rewards some with high profits and assigns others to bankruptcy. Since a market is not an institution or an agent in any concrete or palpable sense, such statements become impressive only if they can be reliably inferred from a theory as part of a set of more elaborate expectations. They can be. Microeconomic theory explains how an economy operates and why certain effects are to be expected. . . .

International-political systems, like economic markets, are formed by the co-action of self-regarding units. International structures are defined in terms of the primary political units of an era, be they city states, empires, or nations. Structures emerge from the coexistence of states. No state intends to participate in the formation of a structure by which it and others will be constrained. International-political systems, like economic markets, are individualist in origin, spontaneously generated, and unintended. In both systems, structures are formed by the coaction of their units. Whether those units live, prosper, or die depends on their own efforts. Both systems are formed and maintained on a principle of self-help that applies to the units. . . .

In a microtheory, whether of international politics or of economics, the motivation of the actors is assumed rather than realistically described. I assume that states seek to ensure their survival. The assumption is a radical simplification made for the sake of constructing theory. The question to ask of the assumption, as ever, is not whether it is true but whether it is the most sensible and useful one that can be made. Whether it is a useful assumption depends on whether a theory based on the assumption can be contrived, a theory from which important consequences not otherwise obvious can be inferred. Whether it is a sensible assumption can be directly discussed.

Beyond the survival motive, the aims of states may be endlessly varied; they may range from the ambition to conquer the world to the desire merely to be left alone. Survival is a prerequisite to achieving any goals that states may have, other than the goal of promoting their own disappearance as political entities. The survival motive is taken as the ground of action in a world where the security of states is not assured, rather than as a realistic description of the impulse that lies behind every act of state. The assumption allows for the fact that no state always acts exclusively to ensure its survival. It allows for the fact that some states may persistently seek goals that they value more highly than survival; they may, for example, prefer amalgamation with other states to their own survival in form. It allows for the fact that in pursuit of its security no state will act with perfect knowledge and wisdom—if indeed we could know what those terms might mean. . . .

Actors may perceive the structure that constrains them and understand how it serves to reward some kinds of behavior and to penalize others. But then again they either may not see it or, seeing it, may for any of many reasons fail to conform their actions to the patterns that are most often rewarded and least often punished. To say that "the structure selects" means simply that those who conform to accepted and successful practices more often rise to the top and are likelier to stay there. The game one has to win is defined by the structure that determines the kind of player who is likely to prosper. . . .

## 2. The Character of the Units

The second term in the definition of domestic political structure specifies the functions performed by differentiated units. Hierarchy entails relations of super- and subordination among a system's parts, and that implies their differentiation. In defining domestic political structure the second term, like the first and third, is needed because each term points to a possible source of structural variation. The states that are the units of international-political systems are not formally differentiated by the functions they perform. Anarchy entails relations of coordination among a system's units, and that implies their sameness. The second term is not needed in defining international-political structure, because, so long as anarchy endures, states remain like units. International structures vary only through a change of organizing principle or, failing that, through variations in the capabilities of units. Nevertheless I shall discuss these like units here, because it is by their interactions that international-politics structures are generated.

Two questions arise: Why should states be taken as the units of the system? Given a wide variety of states, how can one call them "like units"? Questioning the choice of states as the primary units of international-political systems became popular in the 1960s and 1970s as it was at the turn of the century. Once one understands what is logically involved, the issue is easily resolved. Those who question the state-centric view do so for two main reasons. First, states are not the only actors of importance on the international scene. Second, states are declining in importance, and other actors are gaining, or so it is said. Neither reason is cogent, as the following discussion shows.

States are not and never have been the only international actors. But then structures are defined not by all of the actors that flourish within them but by the major ones. In defining a system's structure one chooses one or some of the infinitely many objects comprising the system and defines its structure in terms of them. For international-political systems, as for any system, one must first decide which units to take as being the parts of the system. Here the economic analogy will help again. The structure of a market is defined by the number of firms zcompeting. If many roughly equal firms contend, a condition of perfect competition is approximated. If a few firms dominate the market, competition is said to be oligopolistic even though many smaller firms may also be in the field. But we are told that definitions of this sort cannot be applied to international politics because of the interpenetration of states, because of their inability to control the environment of their action, and because rising multinational corporations and other nonstate actors are difficult to regulate and may rival some states in influence. The importance of nonstate actors and the extent of transnational activities are obvious. The conclusion that the state-centric conception of international politics is made obsolete by them does not follow. That economists and economically minded politics scientists have thought that it does is ironic. The irony lies in the fact that all of the reasons given for scrapping the state-centric concept can be related more strongly and applied to firms. Firms competing with numerous others have no hope of controlling their market, and oligopolistic firms constantly struggle with imperfect success to do so. Firms interpenetrate, merge, and buy each up at a merry pace. Moreover, firms are constantly threatened and regulated by, shall we say, "nonfirm" actors. Some governments encourage concentration; others work to prevent it. The market structure of parts of an economy may move from a wider to a narrower competition or may move in the opposite direction, but whatever the extent and the frequency of change, market structures, generated by the interaction of firms, are defined in terms of them.

Just as economists define markets in terms of firms, so I define international-political structures in terms of states. If Charles P. Kindleberger were right in saying that "the nation-state is just about through as an economic unit,"[5] then the structure of international politics would have to be redefined. That would be necessary because economic capabilities cannot be separated from the other capabilities of states. The distinction frequently drawn between matters of high and low politics is misplaced. States use economic means for military and political ends; and military and political means for the achievement of economic interests.

An amended version of Kindleberger's statement may hold: Some states may be nearly washed up as economic entities, and others not. That poses no problem for international-political theory since international politics is mostly about inequalities anyway. So long as the major states are the major actors, the structure of international politics is defined in terms of them. That theoretical statement is of course borne out in practice. States set the scene in which they, along with nonstate actors, state their dramas or carry on their humdrum affairs. Though they may choose to interfere little in the affairs of nonstate actors for long periods of time, states nevertheless set the terms of intercourse, whether by passively permitting informal rules to develop or by actively intervening to change rules that no longer suit them. When the crunch comes, states remake the rules by which other actors operate. Indeed, one may be struck by the ability of weak states to impede the operation of strong international corporations and by the attention the latter pay to the wishes of the former. . . .

States are the units whose interactions form the structure of international-political systems. They will long remain so. The death rate among states is remarkably low. Few states die; many firms do. . . . To call states "like units" is to say that each state is like all other states in being an autonomous political unit. It is another way of saying that states are sovereign. But sovereignty is also a bothersome concept. Many believe, as the anthropologist M. G. Smith has said, that "in a system of sovereign states no state is sovereign."[6] The error lies in identifying the sovereignty of states with their ability to do as they wish. To say that states are sovereign is not to say that they can do as they please, that they are free of others' influence, that they are able to get what they want. Sovereign states may be hardpressed all around, constrained to act in ways they would like to avoid, and able to do hardly anything just as they would like to. The sovereignty of states has never entailed their insulation from the effects of other states' actions. To be sovereign and to be dependent are not contradictory conditions. Sovereign states have seldom led free and easy lives. What then is sovereignty? To say that a state is sovereign means that it decides for itself how it will cope with its internal and external problems, including whether or not to seek assistance from others and in doing so to limit its freedom by making commitments to them. States develop their own strategies, chart their own courses, make their own decisions about how to meet whatever needs they experience and whatever desires they develop. It is no more contradictory to say that sovereign states are always constrained and often tightly so than it is to say that free individuals often make decisions under the heavy pressure of events.

Each state, like every other state, is a sovereign political entity. And yet the differences across states, from Costa Rica to the Soviet Union, from Gambia to the

United States, are immense. States are alike, and they are also different. So are corporations, apples, universities, and people. Whenever we put two or more objects in the same category, we are saying that they are alike not in all respects but in some. No two objects in this world are identical, yet they can often be usefully compared and combined. "You can't add apples and oranges" is an old saying that seems to be especially popular among salesmen who do not want you to compare their wares with others. But we all know that the trick of adding dissimilar objects is to express the result in terms of a category that comprises them. Three apples plus four oranges equals seven pieces of fruit. The only interesting question is whether the category that classifies objects according to their common qualities is useful. One can add up a large number of widely varied objects and say that one has eight million things, but seldom need one do that.

States vary widely in size, wealth, power, and form. And yet variations in these and in other respects are variations among like units. In what way are they like units? How can they be placed in a single category? States are alike in the tasks that they face, though not in their abilities to perform them. The differences are of capability, not of function. States perform or try to perform tasks, most of which are common to all of them; the ends they aspire to are similar. Each state duplicates the activities of other states at least to a considerable extent. Each state has its agencies for making, executing, and interpreting laws and regulations, for raising revenues, and for defending itself. Each state supplies out of its own resources and by its own means most of the food, clothing, housing, transportation, and amenities consumed and used by its citizens. All states, except the smallest ones, do much more of their business at home than abroad. One has to be impressed with the functional similarity of states and, now more than ever before, with the similar lines their development follows. From the rich to the poor states, from the old to the new ones, nearly all of them take a larger hand in matters of economic regulation, of education, health, and housing, of culture and the arts, and so on almost endlessly. The increase of the activities of states is a strong and strikingly uniform international trend. The functions of states are similar, and distinctions among them arise principally from their varied capabilities. International politics consists of like units duplicating one another's activities.

## 3. The Distribution of Capabilities

The parts of a hierarchic system are related to one another in ways that are determined both by their functional differentiation and by the extent of their capabilities. The units of an anarchic system are functionally undifferentiated. The units of such an order are then distinguished primarily by their greater or lesser capabilities for performing similar tasks. This states formally what students of international politics have long noticed. The great powers of an era have always been marked off from others by practitioners and theorists alike. Students of national government make such distinctions as that between parliamentary and presidential systems; governmental systems differ in form. Students of international politics make distinctions between international-political systems only according to the number of their great powers. The structure of a system changes with changes in the distribution of capabilities across the system's units. And changes in structure change expectations about how the units of the system will behave and about the outcomes their interactions will produce. Domestically, the differentiated parts of a system may perform similar tasks. We know from observing the American government that executives sometimes legislate and legislatures sometimes execute. Internationally, like units sometimes perform different tasks . . . but two problems should be considered.

The first problem is this: Capability tells us something about units. Defining structure partly in terms of the distribution of capabilities seems to violate my instruction to keep unit attributes out of structural definitions. As I remarked earlier, structure is a highly but not entirely abstract concept. The maximum of abstraction allows a minimum of content, and that minimum is what is needed to enable one to say how the units stand in relation to one another. States are differently placed by their power. And yet one may wonder why only *capability* is included in the third part of the definition, and not such characteristics as ideology, form of government, peacefulness, bellicosity, or whatever. The answer is this: Power is estimated by comparing the capabilities of a number of units. Although capabilities are attributes of units, the distribution of capabilities across units is not. The distribution of capabilities is not a unit attribute, but rather a system-wide concept. . . .

The second problem is this: Though relations defined in terms of interactions must be excluded from structural definitions, relations defined in terms of grouping of states do seem to tell us something about how states are placed in the system. Why not specify how states stand in relation to one another by considering the alliances they form? Would doing so not be comparable to defining national political structures partly in terms of how presidents and prime ministers are related to other political agents? It would not be. Nationally as internationally, structural definitions deal with the relation of agents and agencies in terms of the organization of realms and not in terms of the accommodations and conflicts that may occur within them or the groupings that may now and then form. Parts of a government may draw together or pull apart, may oppose each other or cooperate in greater or lesser degree. These are the relations that form and dissolve within a system rather than structural alterations that mark a change from one system to another. This is made clear by the example that runs nicely parallel to the case of alliances. Distinguishing systems of political parties according to their number is common. A multiparty system changes if, say, eight parties become two, but not if two groupings of the eight form merely for the occasion of fighting an election. By the same logic, an international-political system in which three or more great powers have split into two alliances remains a multipolar system—structurally distinct from a bipolar system, a system in which no third power is able to challenge the top two. . . .

In defining international-political structures we take states with whatever traditions, habits, objectives, desires, and forms of government they may have. We do not ask whether states are revolutionary or legitimate, authoritarian or democratic, ideological or pragmatic. We abstract from every attribute of states except their capabilities. Nor in thinking about structure do we ask about the relations of states—their feelings of friendship and hostility, their diplomatic exchanges, the alliances they form, and the extent of the contacts and exchanges among them. We ask what range of expectations arises merely from looking at the type of order that prevails among them and at the distribution of capabilities within that order. We abstract from any particular qualities of states and from all of their concrete connections. What emerges is a positional picture, a general description of the ordered overall arrangement of a society written in terms of the placement of units rather than in terms of their qualities. . . .

## ANARCHIC STRUCTURES AND BALANCES OF POWER

[We must now] examine the characteristics of anarchy and the expectations about outcomes associated with anarchic realms. . . . [This] is best accomplished by drawing some comparisons between behavior and outcomes in anarchic and hierarchic realms.

### 4. Violence at Home and Abroad

The state among states, it is often said, conducts its affairs in the brooding shadow of violence. Because some states may at any time use force, all states must be prepared to do so—or live at the mercy of their militarily more vigorous neighbors. Among states, the state of nature is a state of war. This is meant not in the sense that war constantly occurs but in the sense that, with each state deciding for itself whether or not to use force, war may at any time break out. Whether in the family, the community, or the world at large, contact without at least occasional conflict is inconceivable; and the hope that in the absence of an agent to manage or to manipulate conflicting parties the use of force will always be avoided cannot be realistically entertained. Among men as among states, anarchy, or the absence of government, is associated with the occurrence of violence.

The threat of violence and the recurrent use of force are said to distinguish international from national affairs. But in the history of the world surely most rulers have had to bear in mind that their subjects might use force to resist or overthrow them. If the absence of government is associated with the threat of violence, so also is its presence. A haphazard list of national tragedies illustrates the point all too well. The most destructive wars of the hundred years following the defeat of Napoleon took place not among states but *within* them. Estimates of deaths in China's Taiping Rebellion, which began in 1851 and lasted 13 years, range as high as 20 million. In the American Civil War some 600 thousand people lost their lives. In more recent history, forced collectivation and Stalin's purges eliminated 5 million Russians, and Hitler exterminated 6 million Jews. In some Latin American countries, coups d'états and rebellions have been normal features of national life. Between 1948 and 1957, for example, 200 thousand Colombians were killed in civil strife. In the middle 1970s most inhabitants of Idi Amin's Uganda must have felt their lives becoming nasty, brutish, and short, quite as in Thomas Hobbes's state of nature. If such cases constitute aberrations, they are uncomfortably common ones. We easily lose sight of the fact that struggles to achieve and maintain power, to establish order, and to contrive a kind of justice within states may be bloodier than wars among them.

If anarchy is identified with chaos, destruction, and death, then the distinction between anarchy and government does not tell us much. Which is more precarious: the life of a state among states, or of a government in relation to its subjects? The answer varies with time and place. Among some states at some times, the actual or expected occurrence of violence is low. Within some states at some times, the actual or expected occurrence of violence is high. The use of force, or the constant fear of its use, are not sufficient grounds for distinguishing international from domestic affairs. If the possible and the actual use of force mark both national and international orders, then no durable distinction between the two realms can be drawn in terms of the use or the nonuse of force. No human order is proof against violence.

To discover qualitative differences between internal and external affairs one must look for a criterion other than the occurrence of violence. The distinction between international and national realms of politics is not found in the use or the nonuse of force but in their different structures. But if the dangers of being violently attacked are greater, say, in taking an evening stroll through downtown Detroit than they are in picnicking along the French and German border, what practical difference does the difference of structure make? Nationally as internationally, contact generates conflict and at times issues in violence. The difference between national and international politics lies not in the use of force but in the different modes of organization for doing something about it. A government, ruling by some standard of legitimacy, arrogates to itself the right to use force—that is, to apply a variety of sanctions to control the use of force by its subjects. If some use private force, others may appeal to the government. A government has no monopoly on the use of force, as is all too evident. An effective government, however, has a monopoly on the *legitimate* use of force, and legitimate here means that public agents are organized to prevent and to counter the private use of force. Citizens need not prepare to defend themselves. Public agencies do that. A national system is not one of self-help. The international system is.

## 5. Interdependence and Integration

The political significance of interdependence varies depending on whether a realm is organized, with relations of authority specified and established, or remains formally unorganized. Insofar as a realm is formally organized, its units are free to specialize, to pursue their own interests without concern for developing the means of maintaining their identity and preserving their security in the presence of others. They are free to specialize because they have no reason to fear the increased interdependence that goes with specialization. If those who specialize most benefit most, then competition in specialization ensues. Goods are manufactured, grain is produced, law and order are maintained, commerce is conducted, and financial services are provided by people who ever more narrowly specialize. In simple economic terms, the cobbler depends on the tailor for his pants and the tailor on the cobbler for his shoes, and each would be ill-clad without the services of the other. In simple political terms, Kansas depends on Washington for protection and regulation and Washington depends on Kansas for beef and wheat. In saying that in such situations interdependence is close, one need not maintain that the one part could not learn to live without the other. One need only say that the cost of breaking the interdependent relation would be high. Persons and institutions depend heavily on one another because of the different tasks they perform and the different goods they produce and exchange. The parts of a polity bind themselves together by their differences.[7]

Differences between national and international structures are reflected in the ways the units of each system define their ends and develop the means for reaching them. In anarchic realms, like units coact. In hierarchic realms, unlike units interact. In an anarchic realm, the units are functionally similar and tend to remain so. Like units work to maintain a measure of independence and may even strive for autarchy. In a hierarchic realm, the units are differentiated, and they tend to increase the extent of their specialization. Differentiated units become closely interdependent, the more closely so as their specialization proceeds. Because of the difference of structure, interdependence within and interdependence among nations are two distinct concepts. So as to follow the logicians' admonition to keep a single meaning for a given term throughout one's discourse, I shall use "integration" to describe the condition within nations and "interdependence" to describe the condition among them.

Although states are like units functionally, they differ vastly in their capabilities. Out of such differences something of a division of labor develops. The division of labor across nations, however, is slight in comparison with the highly articulated division of labor within them. Integration draws the parts of a nation closely together. Interdependence among nations leaves them loosely connected. Although the integration of nations is often talked about, it seldom takes place. Nations could mutually enrich themselves by further dividing not just the labor that goes into the production of goods but also some of the other tasks they perform, such as political management and military defense. Why does their integration not take place? The structure of international politics limits the cooperation of states in two ways.

In a self-help system each of the units spends a portion of its effort, not in forwarding its own good, but in providing the means of protecting itself against others. Specialization in a system of divided labor works to everyone's advantage, though not equally so. Inequality in the expected distribution of the increased product works strongly against extension of the division of labor internationally. When faced with the possibility of cooperating for mutual gain, states that feel insecure must ask how the gain will be divided. They are compelled to ask not "Will both of us gain?" but "Who will gain more?" If an expected gain is to be divided, say, in the ratio of two to one, one state may use its disproportionate gain to implement a policy intended to damage or destroy the other. Even the prospect of large absolute gains for both parties does not elicit their cooperation so long as each fears how the other will use its increased capabilities. Notice that the impediments to collaboration may not lie in the character and the immediate intention of either party. Instead, the condition of insecurity—at the least, the uncertainty of each about the other's future intentions and actions—works against their cooperation. . . .

A state worries about a division of possible gains that may favor others more than itself. That is the first way in which the structure of international politics limits the cooperation of states. A state also worries lest it become dependent on others through cooperative endeavors and exchanges of goods and services. That is the second way in which the structure of international politics limits the cooperation of states. The more a state specializes, the more it relies on others to supply the materials and goods that it is not producing. The larger a state's imports and exports, the more it depends on others. The world's well-being would be increased if an ever more elaborate division of labor were developed, but states would thereby place themselves in situations of ever closer interdependence. Some states may not resist that. For small and ill-endowed states the costs of doing so are excessively high. But states that can resist becoming ever more enmeshed with others ordinarily do so in either or both of two ways. States that are heavily dependent, or closely interdependent, worry about securing that which they depend on. The high interdependence of states means that the states in question experience, or are subject to, the common vulnerability that high interdependence entails. Like other organizations, states seek to control what they depend on or to lessen the extent of their dependency. This simple thought explains quite a bit of the behavior of states: their imperial thrusts to widen the scope of their control and their autarchic strivings toward greater self-sufficiency.

Structures encourage certain behaviors and penalize those who do not respond to the encouragement. Nationally, many lament the extreme development of the division of labor, a development that results in the allocation of ever narrower tasks to individuals. And yet specialization proceeds, and its extent is a measure of the development of societies. In a formally organized realm a premium is put on each unit's being able to specialize in order to increase its value to others in a system of divided labor. The domestic imperative is "specialize"! Internationally, many lament the resources states spend unproductively for their own defense and the opportunities they miss to enhance the welfare of their people through cooperation with other states. And yet the ways of states change little. In an unorganized realm each unit's incentive is to put itself in a position to be able to take care of itself since no one else can be counted on to do so. The international imperative is "take care of yourself"! Some leaders of nations may understand that the well-being of all of them would increase through their participation in a fuller division of labor. But to act on the idea would be to act on a domestic imperative, an imperative that does not run internationally. What one might want to do in the absence of structural constraints is different from what one is encouraged to do in their presence. States do not willingly place themselves in situations of increased dependence. In a self-help system, considerations of security subordinate economic gain to political interest. . . .

## 6. Structures and Strategies

That motives and outcomes may well be disjoined should now be easily seen. Structures cause nations to have consequences they were not intended to have. Surely most of the actors will notice that, and at least some of them will be able to figure out why. They may develop a pretty good sense of just how structures work their effects. Will they not then be able to achieve their original ends by appropriately adjusting their strategies? Unfortunately, they often cannot. To show why this is so I shall give only a few examples; once the point is made, the reader will easily think of others.

If shortage of a commodity is expected, all are collectively better off if they buy less of it in order to moderate price increases and to distribute shortages equitably. But because some will be better off if they lay in extra supplies quickly, all have a strong incentive to do so. If one expects others to make a run on a bank, one's prudent course is to run faster then they do even while knowing that if few others run, the bank will remain solvent, and if many run, it will fail. In such cases, pursuit of individual interest produces collective results that nobody wants, yet individuals by behaving differently will hurt themselves without altering outcomes. These two much used examples establish the main point. Some courses of action I cannot sensibly follow unless we are pretty sure that many others will as well. . . .

We may well notice that our behavior produces unwanted outcomes, but we are also likely to see that such instances as these are examples of what Alfred E. Kahn describes as "large" changes that are brought about by the accumulation of "small" decisions. In such situations people are victims of the "tyranny of small decisions," a phrase suggesting that "if one hundred consumers choose option $x$, and this causes the market to make decision $X$ (where $X$ equals $100x$), it is not necessarily true that those same consumers would have voted for that outcome if that large decision had ever been presented for their explicit consideration."[8] If the market does not present the large question for decision, then individuals are doomed to making decisions that are sensible within their narrow contexts even though they know all the while that in making such decisions they are bringing about a result that most of them do not want. Either that or they organize to overcome some of the effects of the market by changing its structure—for example, by bringing consumer units roughly up to the size of the units that are making producers' decisions. This nicely makes the point: So long as one leaves the structure unaffected it is not possible for changes in the intentions and the actions of particular actors to produce desirable outcomes or to avoid undesirable ones. . . . The only remedies for strong structural effects are structural changes.

Structural constraints cannot be wished away, although many fail to understand this. In every age and place, the units of self-help systems—nations, corporations, or whatever—are told that the greater good, along with their own, requires them to act for the sake of the system and not for their own narrowly defined advantage. In the 1950s, as fear of the world's destruction in nuclear war grew, some concluded that the alternative to world destruction was world disarmament. In the 1970s, with the rapid growth of population, poverty, and pollution, some concluded, as one political scientist put it, that "states must meet the needs of the political ecosystem in its global dimensions or court annihilation."[9] The international interest must be served; and if that means anything at all, it means that national interests are subordinate to it. The problems are found at the global level. Solutions to the problems continue to depend on national policies. What are the conditions that would make nations more or less willing to obey the injunctions that are so often laid on them?

How can they resolve the tension between pursuing their own interests and acting for the sake of the system? No one has shown how that can be done, although many wring their hands and plead for rational behavior. The very problem, however, is that rational behavior, given structural constraints, does not lead to the wanted results. With each country constrained to take care of itself, no one can take care of the system.[10]

A strong sense of peril and doom may lead to a clear definition of ends that must be achieved. Their achievement is not thereby made possible. The possibility of effective action depends on the ability to provide necessary means. It depends even more so on the existence of conditions that permit nations and other organizations to follow appropriate policies and strategies. World-shaking problems cry for global solutions, but there is no global agency to provide them. Necessities do not create possibilities. Wishing that final causes were efficient ones does not make them so.

Great tasks can be accomplished only by agents of great capability. That is why states, and especially the major ones, are called on to do what is necessary for the world's survival. But states have to do whatever they think necessary for their own preservation, since no one can be relied on to do it for them. Why the advice to place the international interest above national interests is meaningless can be explained precisely in terms of the distinction between micro- and macrotheories. . . .

Some have hoped that changes in the awareness and purpose, in the organization and ideology of states would change the quality of international life. Over the centuries states have changed in many ways, but the quality of international life has remained much the same. States may seek reasonable and worthy ends, but they cannot figure out how to reach them. The problem is not in their stupidity or ill will, although one does not want to claim that those qualities are lacking. The depth of the difficulty is not understood until one realizes that intelligence and goodwill cannot discover and act on adequate programs. Early in this century Winston Churchill observed that the British-German naval race promised disaster *and* that Britain had no realistic choice other than to run it. States facing global problems are like individual consumers trapped by the "tyranny of small decisions." States, like consumers, can get out of the trap only by changing the structure of their field of activity. The message bears repeating: The only remedy for a strong structural effect is a structural change.

## 7. The Virtues of Anarchy

To achieve their objectives and maintain their security, units in a condition of anarchy—be they people, corporations, states, or whatever—must rely on the means they can generate and the arrangements they can make for themselves. Self-help is necessarily the principle of action in an anarchic order. A self-help situation is one of high risk—of bankruptcy in the economic realm and of war in a world of free states. It is also one in which organizational costs are low. Within an economy or within an international order, risks may be avoided or lessened by moving from a situation of coordinate action to one of super- and subordination, that is, by erecting agencies with effective authority and extending a system of rules. Government emerges where the functions of regulation and management themselves become distinct and specialized tasks. The costs of maintaining a hierarchic order are frequently ignored by those who deplore its absence. Organizations have at least two aims: to get something done and to maintain themselves as organizations. Many of their activities are directed toward the second purpose. The leaders of organizations, and political leaders preeminently, are not masters of the matters their organizations deal with. They have become leaders not by being experts on one thing or another but by excelling in the organizational arts—in maintaining control of a group's members, in eliciting predictable and satisfactory efforts from them, in holding a group together. In making political decisions, the first and most important concern is not to achieve the aims the members of an organization may have but to secure the continuity and health of the organization itself.[11]

Along with the advantages of hierarchic orders go the costs. In hierarchic orders, moreover, the means of control become an object of struggle. Substantive issues become entwined with efforts to influence or control the controllers. The hierarchic ordering of politics adds one to the already numerous objects of struggle, and the object added is at a new order of magnitude.

If the risks of war are unbearably high, can they be reduced by organizing to manage the affairs of nations? At a minimum, management requires controlling the military forces that are at the disposal of states. Within nations, organizations have to work to maintain themselves. As organizations, nations, in working to maintain themselves, sometimes have to use force against dissident elements and areas. As hierarchical systems, governments nationally or globally are disrupted by the defection of major parts. In a society of states with little coherence, attempts at world government would founder on the inability of an emerging central authority to mobilize the resources needed to create and maintain the unity of the system by regulating and managing its parts. The prospect of world government would be an invitation to prepare for world civil war. . . . States cannot entrust managerial powers to a central agency unless that agency is able to protect its client states. The more powerful the clients and the more the power of each of them appears as a threat to the others, the greater the power lodged in the center must be. The greater the power of the center, the stronger the incentive for states to engage in a struggle to control it.

States, like people, are insecure in proportion to the extent of their freedom. If freedom is wanted, insecurity must be accepted. Organizations that establish relations of authority and control may increase insecurity as they decrease freedom. If might does not make right, whether among people or states, then some institution or agency has intervened to lift them out of nature's realm. The more influential the agency, the stronger the desire to control it becomes. In contrast, units in an anarchic order act for their own sakes and not for the sake of preserving an organization and furthering their fortunes within it. Force is used for one's own interest. In the absence of organization, people or states are free to leave one another alone. Even when they do not do so, they are better able, in the absence of the politics of the organization, to concentrate on the politics of the problem and to aim for a minimum agreement that will permit their separate existence rather than a maximum agreement for the sake of maintaining unity. If might decides, then bloody struggles over right can more easily be avoided.

Nationally, the force of a government is exercised in the name of right and justice. Internationally, the force of a state is employed for the sake of its own protection and advantage. Rebels challenge a government's claim to authority; they question the rightfulness of its rule. Wars among states cannot settle questions of authority and right; they can only determine the allocation of gains and losses among contenders and settle for a time the question of who is the stronger. Nationally, relations of authority are established. Internationally, only relations of strength result. Nationally, private force used against a government threatens the political system. Force used by a state—a public body—is, from the international perspective, the private use of force; but there is no government to overthrow and no governmental apparatus to capture. Short of a drive toward world hegemony, the private use of force does not threaten the system of international politics, only some of its members. War pits some states against others in a struggle among similarly constituted entities. The power of the strong may deter the weak from asserting their claims, not because the weak recognize a kind of rightfulness of rule on the part of the strong, but simply because it is not sensible to tangle with them. Conversely, the weak may enjoy considerable freedom of action if they are so far removed in their capabilities from the strong that the latter are not much bothered by their actions or much concerned by marginal increases in their capabilities.

National politics is the realm of authority, of administration, and of law. International politics is the realm of power, of struggle, and of accommodation. The international realm is preeminently a political one. The national realm is variously described as being hierarchic, vertical, centralized, heterogeneous, directed, and contrived; the international realm, as being anarchic, horizontal, decentralized, homogeneous, undirected, and mutually adaptive. The more centralized the order, the nearer to the top the locus of decisions ascends. Internationally, decisions are made at the bottom level, there being scarcely any other. In the vertical–horizontal dichotomy, international structures assume the prone position. Adjustments are made internationally, but they are made without a formal or authoritative adjuster. Adjustment and accommodation proceed by mutual adaptation.[12] Action and reaction, and reaction to the reaction, proceed by a piecemeal process. The parties feel each other out, so to speak, and define a situation simultaneously with its development. Among coordinate units, adjustment is achieved and accommodations arrived at by the exchange of "considerations," in a condition, as Chester Barnard put it, "in which the duty of command and the desire to obey are essentially absent."[13] Where the contest is over considerations, the parties seek to maintain or improve their positions by maneuvering, by bargaining, or by fighting. The manner and intensity of the competition is determined by the desires and the abilities of parties that are at once separate and interacting.

Whether or not by force, each state plots the course it thinks will best serve its interests. If force is used by one state or its use is expected, the recourse of other states is to use force or be prepared to use it singly or in combination. No appeal can be made to a higher entity clothed with the authority and equipped with the ability to act on its own initiative. Under such conditions the possibility that force will be used by one or another of the parties looms always as a threat in the background. In politics force is said to be the *ultima ratio*. In international politics force serves, not only as the *ultima ratio,* but indeed as the first and constant one. To limit force to being the *ultima ratio* of politics implies, in the words of Ortega y Gasset, "the previous submission of force to methods of reason."[14] The constant possibility that force will be used limits manipulations, moderates demands, and serves as an incentive for the settlement of disputes. One who knows that pressing too hard may lead to war has strong reason to consider whether possible gains are worth the risks entailed. The threat of force internationally is comparable to the role of the strike in labor and management bargaining. "The few strikes that take place are in a sense," as Livernash has said, "the cost of the strike option which produces settlements in the large mass of negotiations."[15] Even if workers seldom strike, their doing so is always a possibility. The possibility of industrial disputes leading to long and costly strikes encourages labor and management to face difficult issues, to try to understand each other's problems, and to work hard to find accommodations. The possibility that conflicts among nations may lead to long and costly wars has similarly sobering effects.

## 8. Anarchy and Hierarchy

I have described anarchies and hierarchies as though every political order were of one type or the other. Many, and I suppose most, political scientists who write of structures allow for a greater, and sometimes for a bewildering, variety of types. Anarchy is seen as one end of a continuum whose other end is marked by the presence of a legitimate and competent government. International politics is then described as being flecked with particles of government and alloyed with elements of community—supranational organizations whether universal or regional, alliances, multinational corporations, networks of trade, and whatnot. International-political systems are thought of as being more or less anarchic.

Those who view the world as a modified anarchy do so, it seems, for two reasons. First, anarchy is taken to mean not just the absence of government but also the presence of disorder and chaos. Since world politics, although not reliably peaceful, falls short of unrelieved chaos, students are inclined to see a lessening of anarchy in each outbreak of peace. Since world politics, although not formally organized, is not entirely without institutions and orderly procedures, students are inclined to see a lessening of anarchy when alliances form, when transactions across national borders increase, and when international agencies multiply. Such views confuse structure with process, and I have drawn attention to that error often enough.

Second, the two simple categories of anarchy and hierarchy do not seem to accommodate the infinite social variety our senses record. Why insist on reducing the types of structure to two instead of allowing for a greater variety? Anarchies are ordered by the juxtaposition of similar units, but those similar units are not identical. Some specialization by function develops among them. Hierarchies are ordered by the social division of labor among units specializing in different tasks, but the resemblance of units does not vanish. Much duplication of effort continues. All societies are organized segmentally or hierarchically in greater or lesser degree. Why not, then, define additional social types according to the mixture of organizing principles they embody? One might conceive of some societies approaching the purely anarchic, of others approaching the purely hierarchic, and of still others reflecting specified mixes of the two organizational types. In anarchies the exact likeness of units and the determination of relations by capability alone would describe a realm wholly of politics and power with none of the interaction of units guided by adminis-tration and conditioned by authority. In hierarchies the complete differentiation of parts and the full specification of their functions would produce a realm wholly of authority and administration with none of the interaction of parts affected by politics and power. Although such pure orders do not exist, to distinguish realms by their organizing principles is nevertheless proper and important.

Increasing the number of categories would bring the classification of societies closer to reality. But that would be to move away from a theory claiming explanatory power to a less theoretical system promising greater descriptive accuracy. One who wishes to explain rather than to describe should resist moving in that direction if resistance is reasonable. Is it? What does one gain by insisting on two types when admitting three or four would still be to simplify boldly? One gains clarity and econ-omy of concepts. A new concept should be introduced only to cover matters that existing concepts do not reach. If some societies are neither anarchic or hierarchic, if their structures are defined by some third ordering principle, then we would have to define a third system.[16] All societies are mixed. Elements in them represent both of the ordering principles. That does not mean that some societies are ordered according to a third principle. Usually one can easily identify the principle by which a society is ordered. The appearance of anarchic sectors within hierarchies does not alter and should not obscure the ordering principle of the larger system, for those sectors are anarchic only within limits. The attributes and behavior of the units populating those sectors within the larger system differ, moreover, from what they should be and how they would behave outside of it. Firms in oligopolistic markets again are perfect examples of this. They struggle against one another, but because they need not prepare to defend themselves physically, they can afford to specialize and to participate more fully in the division of economic labor than states can. Nor do the states that populate an anarchic world find it impossible to work with one another, to make agreements limiting their arms, and to cooperate in establishing organizations. Hierarchic elements within international structures limit and restrain the exercise of sovereignty but only in ways strongly conditioned by the anarchy of the larger system. The anarchy of that order strongly affects the likelihood of cooperation, the extent of arms agreements, and the jurisdiction of international organizations. . . .

## NOTES

1. S. F. Nadel, *The Theory of Social Structure* (Glencoe, Ill.: Free Press, 1957), pp. 8–11.
2. Ibid., pp. 104–9.
3. William T. R. Fox, "The Uses of International Relations Theory," in William T. R. Fox, ed., *Theoretical Aspects of International Relations* (Notre Dame, Ind.: University of Notre Dame Press, 1959), p. 35.

4.  Marriet Martineau, *The Positive Philosophy of Auguste Comte: Freely Translated and Condensed,* 3rd ed. (London: Kegan Paul, Trench, Trubner, 1983), Vol. 2, pp. 51–53; George Katona, "Rational Behavior and Economic Behavior," *Psychological Review* 60 (September 1953).

5.  Charles P. Kindleberger, *American Business Abroad* (New Haven, Ct.: Yale University Press, 1969), p. 207.

6.  Smith should know better. Translated into terms that he has himself so effectively used, to say that states are sovereign is to say that they are segments of a plural society. See his "A Structural Approach to Comparative Politics" in David Easton, ed., *Varieties of Politics Theories* (Englewood Cliffs, N.J.: Prentice Hall, 1966), p. 122; cf. his "On Segmentary Lineage Systems," *Journal of the Royal Anthropological Society of Great Britain and Ireland* 86 (July–December 1956).

7.  Émile Durkheim, *The Division of Labor in Society,* trans. George Simpson (New York: Free Press, 1964), p. 212.

8.  Alfred E. Kahn, "The Tyranny of Small Decision: Market Failure, Imperfections and Limits of Econometrics," in Bruce M. Russett, ed., *Economic Theories of International Relations* (Chicago, Ill.: Markham, 1966), p. 23.

9.  Richard W. Sterling, *Macropolitics: International Relations in a Global Society* (New York: Knopf, 1974), p. 336.

10. Put differently, states face a "prisoners' dilemma." If each of two parties follows his own interest, both end up worse off than if each acted to achieve joint interests. For thorough examination of the logic of such situations, see Glenn H. Snyder and Paul Diesing, *Conflict among Nations* (Princeton, N.J.: Princeton University Press, 1977); for brief and suggestive international applications, see Robert Jervis, "Cooperation under the Security Dilemma," *World Politics* 30 (January 1978).

11. Cf. Paul Diesing, *Reason in Society* (Urbana, Ill.: University of Illinois Press, 1962), pp. 198–204; Anthony Downs, *Inside Bureaucracy* (Boston: Little, Brown, 1967), pp. 262–70.

12. Cf. Chester I. Barnard, "On Planning for World Government," in Chester I. Barnard, ed., *Organization and Management* (Cambridge, Mass.: Harvard University Press, 1948), pp. 148–52; Michael Polanyi, "The Growth of Thought in Society," *Economica* 8 (November 1941), pp. 428–56.

13. Barnard, "On Planning," pp. 150–51.

14. Quoted in Chalmers A. Johnson, *Revolutionary Change* (Boston: Little, Brown, 1966), p. 13.

15. E. R. Livernash, "The Relation of Power to the Structure and Process of Collective Bargaining," in Bruce M. Russett, ed., *Economic Theories of International Politics* (Chicago, Ill.: Markham, 1963), p. 430.

16. Émile Durkheim's depiction of solidary and mechanical societies still provides the best explication of the two ordering principles, and his logic in limiting the types of society to two continues to be compelling despite the efforts of his many critics to overthrow it (see esp. *The Division of Labor in Society*).

# Anarchy and the Struggle for Power

## JOHN J. MEARSHEIMER

Great powers, I argue, are always searching for opportunities to gain power over their rivals, with hegemony as their final goal. This perspective does not allow for status quo powers, except for the unusual state that achieves preponderance. Instead, the system is populated with great powers that have revisionist intentions at their core. This chapter presents a theory that explains this competition for power. Specifically, I attempt to show that there is a compelling logic behind my claim that great powers seek to maximize their share of world power. . . .

## WHY STATES PURSUE POWER

My explanation for why great powers vie with each other for power and strive for hegemony is derived from five assumptions about the international system. None of these assumptions alone mandates that states behave competitively. Taken together, however, they depict a world in which states have considerable reason to think and sometimes behave aggressively. In particular, the system encourages states to look for opportunities to maximize their power vis-à-vis other states. . . .

The first assumption is that the international system is anarchic, which does not mean that it is chaotic or riven by disorder. It is easy to draw that conclusion, since realism depicts a world characterized by security competition and war. By itself, however, the realist notion of anarchy has nothing to do with conflict; it is an ordering principle, which says that the system comprises independent states that have no central authority above them. Sovereignty, in other words, inheres in states because there is no higher ruling body in the international system. There is no "government over governments."

The second assumption is that great powers inherently possess some offensive military capability, which gives them the wherewithal to hurt and possibly destroy each other. States are potentially dangerous to each other, although some states have more military might than others and are therefore more dangerous. A state's military power is usually identified with the particular weaponry at its disposal, although even if there were no weapons, the individuals in those states could still use their feet and hands to attack the population of another state. After all, for every neck, there are two hands to choke it.

The third assumption is that states can never be certain about other states' intentions. Specifically, no state can be sure that another state will not use its offensive

Excerpts from *Tragedy of Great Power Politics* by John Mearsheimer, pp. 29–40, 46–53. Copyright © 2001 by John J. Mearsheimer. Used by permission of W. W. Norton & Company, Inc.

military capability to attack the first state. This is not to say that states necessarily have hostile intentions. Indeed, all of the states in the system may be reliably benign, but it is impossible to be sure of that judgment because intentions are impossible to divine with 100 percent certainty. There are many possible causes of aggression, and no state can be sure that another state is not motivated by one of them. Furthermore, intentions can change quickly, so a state's intentions can be benign one day and hostile the next. Uncertainty about intentions is unavoidable, which means that states can never be sure that other states do not have offensive intentions to go along with their offensive capabilities.

The fourth assumption is that survival is the primary goal of great powers. Specifically, states seek to maintain their territorial integrity and the autonomy of their domestic political order. Survival dominates other motives because, once a state is conquered, it is unlikely to be in a position to pursue other aims. . . . States can and do pursue other goals, of course, but security is their most important objective.

The fifth assumption is that great powers are rational actors. They are aware of their external environment and they think strategically about how to survive in it. In particular, they consider the preferences of other states and how their own behavior is likely to affect the behavior of those other states, and how the behavior of those other states is likely to affect their own strategy for survival. Moreover, states pay attention to the long term as well as the immediate consequences of their actions.

As emphasized, none of these assumptions alone dictates that great powers as a general rule *should* behave aggressively toward each other. There is surely the possibility that some state might have hostile intentions, but the only assumption dealing with a specific motive that is common to all states says that their principal objective is to survive, which by itself is a rather harmless goal. Nevertheless, when the five assumptions are married together, they create powerful incentives for great powers to think and act offensively with regard to each other. In particular, three general patterns of behavior result: fear, self-help, and power maximization.

## STATE BEHAVIOR

Great powers fear each other. They regard each other with suspicion, and they worry that war might be in the offing. They anticipate danger. There is little room for trust among states. For sure, the level of fear varies across time and space, but it cannot be reduced to a trivial level. From the perspective of any one great power, all other great powers are potential enemies. This point is illustrated by the reaction of the United Kingdom and France to German reunification at the end of the Cold War. Despite the fact that these three states had been close allies for almost forty-five years, both the United Kingdom and France immediately began worrying about the potential dangers of a united Germany.

The basis of this fear is that in a world where great powers have the capability to attack each other and might have the motive to do so, any state bent on survival must be at least suspicious of other states and reluctant to trust them. Add to this the "911" problem—the absence of a central authority to which a threatened state can turn for help—and states have even greater incentive to fear each other. Moreover, there is no mechanism, other than the possible self-interest of third parties, for punishing an aggressor. Because it is sometimes difficult to deter potential aggressors, states have ample reason not to trust other states and to be prepared for war with them.

The possible consequences of falling victim to aggression further amplify the importance of fear as a motivating force in world politics. Great powers do not compete with each other as if international politics were merely an economic marketplace. Political competition among states is a much more dangerous business than mere economic intercourse; the former can lead to war, and war often means mass killing on the battlefield as well as mass murder of civilians. In extreme cases, war can even lead to the destruction of states. The horrible consequences of war sometimes cause states to view each other not just as competitors, but as potentially deadly enemies. Political antagonism, in short, tends to be intense, because the stakes are great.

States in the international system also aim to guarantee their own survival. Because other states are potential threats, and because there is no higher authority to come to their rescue when they dial 911, states cannot depend on others for their own security. Each state tends to see itself as vulnerable and alone, and therefore it aims to provide for its own survival. In international politics, God helps those who help themselves. This emphasis on self-help does not preclude states from forming alliances. But alliances are only temporary marriages of convenience: today's alliance partner might be tomorrow's enemy, and today's enemy might be tomorrow's alliance partner. For example, the United States fought with China and the Soviet Union against Germany and Japan in World War II, but soon thereafter flip-flopped enemies and partners and allied with West Germany and Japan against China and the Soviet Union during the Cold War.

States operating in a self-help world almost always act according to their own self-interest and do not subordinate their interests to the interests of other states, or to the interests of the so-called international community. The reason is simple: it pays to be selfish in a self-help world. This is true in the short term as well as in the long term, because if a state loses in the short run, it might not be around for the long haul.

Apprehensive about the ultimate intentions of other states, and aware that they operate in a self-help system, states quickly understand that the best way to ensure their survival is to be the most powerful state in the system. The stronger a state is relative to its potential rivals, the less likely it is that any of those rivals will attack it and threaten its survival. Weaker states will be reluctant to pick fights with more powerful states because the weaker states are likely to suffer military defeat. Indeed, the bigger the gap in power between any two states, the less likely it is that the weaker will attack the stronger. Neither Canada nor Mexico, for example, would countenance attacking the United States, which is far more powerful than its neighbors. The ideal situation is to be the hegemon in the system. . . . Survival would then be almost guaranteed.

Consequently, states pay close attention to how power is distributed among them, and they make a special effort to maximize their share of world power.

Specifically, they look for opportunities to alter the balance of power by acquiring additional increments of power at the expense of potential rivals. States employ a variety of means—economic, diplomatic, and military—to shift the balance of power in their favor, even if doing so makes other states suspicious or even hostile. Because one state's gain in power is another state's loss, great powers tend to have a zero-sum mentality when dealing with each other. The trick, of course, is to be the winner in this competition and to dominate the other states in the system. Thus, the claim that states maximize relative power is tantamount to arguing that states are disposed to think offensively toward other states, even though their ultimate motive is simply to survive. In short, great powers have aggressive intentions.

Even when a great power achieves a distinct military advantage over its rivals, it continues looking for chances to gain more power. The pursuit of power stops only when hegemony is achieved. The idea that a great power might feel secure without dominating the system, provided it has an "appropriate amount" of power, is not persuasive, for two reasons. First, it is difficult to assess how much relative power one state must have over its rivals before it is secure. Is twice as much power an appropriate threshold? Or is three times as much power the magic number? The root of the problem is that power calculations alone do not determine which side wins a war. Clever strategies, for example, sometimes allow less powerful states to defeat more powerful foes.

Second, determining how much power is enough becomes even more complicated when great powers contemplate how power will be distributed among them ten or twenty years down the road. The capabilities of individual states vary over time, sometimes markedly, and it is often difficult to predict the direction and scope of change in the balance of power. Remember, few in the West anticipated the collapse of the Soviet Union before it happened. In fact, during the first half of the Cold War, many in the West feared that the Soviet economy would eventually generate greater wealth than the American economy, which would cause a marked power shift against the United States and its allies. What the future holds for China and Russia and what the balance of power will look like in 2020 is difficult to foresee.

Given the difficulty of determining how much power is enough for today and tomorrow, great powers recognize that the best way to ensure their security is to achieve hegemony now, thus eliminating any possibility of a challenge by another great power. Only a misguided state would pass up an opportunity to be the hegemon in the system because it thought it already had sufficient power to survive. But even if a great power does not have the wherewithal to achieve hegemony (and that is usually the case), it will still act offensively to amass as much power as it can, because states are almost always better off with more rather than less power. In short, states do not become status quo powers until they completely dominate the system.

All states are influenced by this logic, which means that not only do they look for opportunities to take advantage of one another, they also work to ensure that other states do not take advantage of them. After all, rival states are driven by the same logic, and most states are likely to recognize their own motives at play in the actions of other states. In short, states ultimately pay attention to defense as well as offense. They think about conquest themselves, and they work to check aggressor states from gaining power at their expense. This inexorably leads to a world of constant security competition, where states are willing to lie, cheat, and use brute force if it helps them gain advantage over their rivals. Peace, if one defines that concept as a state of tranquility or mutual concord, is not likely to break out in this world. . . .

It should be apparent from this discussion that saying that states are power maximizers is tantamount to saying that they care about relative power, not absolute power. There is an important distinction here, because states concerned about relative power behave differently than do states interested in absolute power. States that maximize relative power are concerned primarily with the distribution of material capabilities. In particular, they try to gain as large a power advantage as possible over potential rivals, because power is the best means to survival in a dangerous world. Thus, states motivated by relative power concerns are likely to forgo large gains in their own power, if such gains give rival states even greater power, for smaller national gains that nevertheless provide them with a power advantage over their rivals. States that maximize absolute power, on the other hand, care only about the size of their own gains, not those of other states. They are not motivated by balance-of-power logic but instead are concerned with amassing power without regard to how much power other states control. They would jump at the opportunity for large gains, even if a rival gained more in the deal. Power, according to this logic, is not a means to an end (survival), but an end in itself.

## CALCULATED AGGRESSION

There is obviously little room for status quo powers in a world where states are inclined to look for opportunities to gain more power. Nevertheless, great powers cannot always act on their offensive intentions, because behavior is influenced not only by what states want, but also by their capacity to realize these desires. Every state might want to be king of the hill, but not every state has the wherewithal to compete for that lofty position, much less achieve it. Much depends on how military might is distributed among the great powers. A great power that has a marked power advantage over its rivals is likely to behave more aggressively, because it has the capability as well as the incentive to do so.

By contrast, great powers facing powerful opponents will be less inclined to consider offensive action and more concerned with defending the existing balance of power from threats by their more powerful opponents. Let there be an opportunity for those weaker states to revise the balance in their own favor, however, and they will take advantage of it.

In short, great powers are not mindless aggressors so bent on gaining power that they charge headlong into losing wars or pursue Pyrrhic victories. On the contrary, before great powers take offensive actions, they think carefully about the balance of power and about how other states will react to their moves. They weigh the costs and risks of offense against the likely benefits. If the benefits do not outweigh the risks, they sit tight and wait for a more propitious moment. Nor do states start arms races that are unlikely to improve their overall position. . . . States sometimes limit defense spending either because spending more would bring no strategic advantage or because spending more would weaken the economy and undermine the state's power in the long run. To paraphrase Clint Eastwood, a state has to know its limitations to survive in the international system.

Nevertheless, great powers miscalculate from time to time because they invariably make important decisions on the basis of imperfect information. States hardly ever have complete information about any situation they confront. There are two dimensions to this problem. Potential adversaries have incentives to misrepresent their own strength or weakness, and to conceal their true aims. For example, a weaker state trying to deter a stronger state is likely to exaggerate its own power to discourage the potential aggressor from attacking. On the other hand, a state bent on aggression is likely to emphasize its peaceful goals while exaggerating its military weakness, so that the potential victim does not build up its own arms and thus leaves itself vulnerable to attack. Probably no national leader was better at practicing this kind of deception than Adolf Hitler.

But even if disinformation was not a problem, great powers are often unsure about how their own military forces, as well as the adversary's, will perform on the battlefield. For example, it is sometimes difficult to determine in advance how new weapons and untested combat units will perform in the face of enemy fire. Peacetime maneuvers and war games are helpful but imperfect indicators of what is likely to happen in actual combat. Fighting wars is a complicated business in which it is often difficult to predict outcomes. . . .

Great powers are also sometimes unsure about the resolve of opposing states as well as allies. For example, Germany believed that if it went to war against France and Russia in the summer of 1914, the United Kingdom would probably stay out of the fight. Saddam Hussein expected the United States to stand aside when he invaded Kuwait in August 1990. Both aggressors guessed wrong, but each had good reason to think that its initial judgment was correct. In the 1930s, Adolf Hitler believed that his great-power rivals would be easy to exploit and isolate because each had little interest in fighting Germany and instead was determined to get someone else to assume that burden. He guessed right. In short, great powers constantly find themselves confronting situations in which they have to make important decisions with incomplete information. Not surprisingly, they sometimes make faulty judgments and end up doing themselves serious harm.

Some defensive realists go so far as to suggest that the constraints of the international system are so powerful that offense rarely succeeds, and that aggressive great powers invariably end up being punished. . . . They emphasize that 1) threatened states balance against aggressors and ultimately crush them, and 2) there is an offense-defense balance that is usually heavily tilted toward the defense, thus making conquest especially difficult. Great powers, therefore, should be content with the existing balance of power and not try to change it by force. . . .

There is no question that systemic factors constrain aggression, especially balancing by threatened states. But defensive realists exaggerate those restraining forces. Indeed, the historical record provides little support for their claim that offense rarely succeeds. One study estimates that there were 63 wars between 1815 and 1980, and the initiator won 39 times, which translates into about a 60 percent success rate.... In short, the historical record shows that offense sometimes succeeds and sometimes does not. The trick for a sophisticated power maximizer is to figure out when to raise and when to fold.

## HEGEMONY'S LIMITS

Great powers, as I have emphasized, strive to gain power over their rivals and hopefully become hegemons. Once a state achieves that exalted position, it becomes a status quo power. More needs to be said, however, about the meaning of hegemony.

A hegemon is a state that is so powerful that it dominates all the other states in the system. No other state has the military wherewithal to put up a serious fight against it. In essence, a hegemon is the only great power in the system. A state that is substantially more powerful than the other great powers in the system is not a hegemon, because it faces, by definition, other great powers. The United Kingdom in the mid-nineteenth century, for example, is sometimes called a hegemon. But it was not a hegemon, because there were four other great powers in Europe at the time—Austria, France, Prussia, and Russia—and the United Kingdom did not dominate them in any meaningful way. In fact, during that period, the United Kingdom considered France to be a serious threat to the balance of power. Europe in the nineteenth century was multipolar, not unipolar.

Hegemony means domination of the system, which is usually interpreted to mean the entire world. It is possible, however, to apply the concept of a system more narrowly and use it to describe particular regions, such as Europe, Northeast Asia, and the Western Hemisphere. Thus, one can distinguish between *global hegemons*, which dominate the world, and *regional hegemons*, which dominate distinct geographical areas. The United States has been a regional hegemon in the Western Hemisphere for at least the past one hundred years. No other state in the Americas has sufficient military might to challenge it, which is why the United States is widely recognized as the only great power in its region. . . .

## POWER AND FEAR

That great powers fear each other is a central aspect of life in the international system. But as noted, the level of fear varies from case to case. For example, the Soviet Union worried much less about Germany in 1930 than it did in 1939. How much states fear each other matters greatly, because the amount of fear between them largely determines the severity of their security competition, as well as the probability that they will fight a war. The more profound the fear is, the more intense is the security competition, and the more likely is war. The logic is straight-forward: a scared state will look especially hard for ways to enhance its security, and it will be disposed to pursue risky policies to achieve that end. Therefore, it is important to understand what causes states to fear each other more or less intensely.

Fear among great powers derives from the fact that they invariably have some offensive military capability that they can use against each other, and the fact that one can never be certain that other states do not intend to use that power against oneself. Moreover, because states operate in an anarchic system, there is no night watchman to whom they can turn for help if another great power attacks them. Although anarchy and uncertainty about other states' intentions create an irreducible level of fear among states that leads to power-maximizing behavior, they cannot account for why sometimes that level of fear is greater than at other times. The reason is that anarchy and the difficulty of discerning state intentions are constant facts of life, and constants cannot explain variation. The capability that states have to threaten each other, however, varies from case to case, and it is the key factor that drives fear levels up and down. Specifically, the more power a state possesses, the more fear it generates among its rivals. Germany, for example, was much more powerful at the end of the 1930s than it was at the decade's beginning, which is why the Soviets became increasingly fearful of Germany over the course of that decade. . . .

## THE HIERARCHY OF STATE GOALS

Survival is the number one goal of great powers, according to my theory. In practice, however, states pursue non-security goals as well. For example, great powers invariably seek greater economic prosperity to enhance the welfare of their citizenry. They sometimes seek to promote a particular ideology abroad, as happened during the Cold War when the United States tried to spread democracy around the world and the Soviet Union tried to sell communism. National unification is another goal that sometimes motivates states, as it did with Prussia and Italy in the nineteenth century and Germany after the Cold War. Great powers also occasionally try to foster human rights around the globe. States might pursue any of these, as well as a number of other non-security goals.

Offensive realism certainly recognizes that great powers might pursue these non-security goals, but it has little to say about them, save for one important point: states can pursue them as long as the requisite behavior does not conflict with balance-of-power logic, which is often the case. Indeed, the pursuit of these non-security goals sometimes complements the hunt for relative power. For example, Nazi Germany expanded into eastern Europe for both ideological and realist reasons, and the superpowers competed with each other during the Cold War for similar reasons. Furthermore, greater economic prosperity invariably means greater wealth, which has significant implications for security, because wealth is the foundation of military power. Wealthy states can afford powerful military forces, which enhance a state's prospects for survival. . . .

Sometimes the pursuit of non-security goals has hardly any effect on the balance of power, one way or the other. Human rights interventions usually fit this description, because they tend to be small-scale operations that cost little and do not detract from a great power's prospects for survival. For better or for worse, states are rarely willing to expend blood and treasure to protect foreign populations from gross abuses, including genocide. For instance, despite claims that American foreign policy is infused with moralism, Somalia (1992–93) is the only instance during the past one hundred years in which U.S. soldiers were killed in action on a humanitarian mission. And in that case, the loss of a mere eighteen soldiers in an infamous firefight in October 1993 so traumatized American policy-makers that they immediately pulled all U.S. troops out of Somalia and then refused to intervene in Rwanda in the spring of 1994, when ethnic Hutu went on a genocidal rampage against their Tutsi neighbors. Stopping that genocide would have been relatively easy and it would have had virtually no effect on the position of the United States in the balance of power. Yet nothing was done. In short, although realism does not prescribe human rights interventions, it does not necessarily proscribe them.

But sometimes the pursuit of non-security goals conflicts with balance-of-power logic, in which case states usually act according to the dictates of realism. For example, despite the U.S. commitment to spreading democracy across the globe, it helped overthrow democratically elected governments and embraced a number of authoritarian regimes during the Cold War, when American policymakers felt that these actions would help contain the Soviet Union. In World War II, the liberal democracies put aside their antipathy for communism and formed an alliance with the Soviet Union against Nazi Germany. "I can't take communism," Franklin Roosevelt emphasized, but to defeat Hitler "I would hold hands with the Devil." In the same way, Stalin repeatedly demonstrated that when his ideological preferences clashed with power considerations, the latter won out. To take the most blatant example of his realism, the Soviet Union formed a non-aggression pact with Nazi Germany in August 1939—the infamous Molotov-Ribbentrop Pact—in hopes that the agreement would at least temporarily satisfy Hitler's territorial ambitions in eastern Europe and turn the Wehrmacht toward France and the United Kingdom. When great powers confront a serious threat, in short, they pay little attention to ideology as they search for alliance partners.

Security also trumps wealth when those two goals conflict, because "defence," as Adam Smith wrote in *The Wealth of Nations*, "is of much more importance than opulence." Smith provides a good illustration of how states behave when forced to choose between wealth and relative power. In 1651, England put into effect the famous Navigation Act, protectionist legislation designed to damage Holland's commerce and ultimately cripple the Dutch economy. The legislation mandated that all goods imported into England be carried either in English ships or ships owned by the country that originally produced the goods. Since the Dutch produced few goods themselves, this measure would badly damage their shipping, the central ingredient in their economic success. Of course, the Navigation Act would hurt England's economy as well, mainly because it would rob England of the benefits of free trade. "The act of navigation," Smith wrote, "is not favorable to foreign commerce, or to the growth of that opulence that can arise from it." Nevertheless, Smith considered the legislation "the wisest of all the commercial regulations of England" because it did more damage to the Dutch economy than to the English economy, and in the mid-seventeenth century Holland was "the only naval power which could endanger the security of England." . . .

## COOPERATION AMONG STATES

One might conclude from the preceding discussion that my theory does not allow for any cooperation among the great powers. But this conclusion would be wrong. States can cooperate, although cooperation is sometimes difficult to achieve and always difficult to sustain. Two factors inhibit cooperation: considerations about relative gains and concern about cheating. Ultimately, great powers live in a fundamentally competitive world where they view each other as real, or at least potential, enemies, and they therefore look to gain power at each other's expense.

Any two states contemplating cooperation must consider how profits or gains will be distributed between them. They can think about the division in terms of either absolute or relative gains (recall the distinction made earlier between pursuing either absolute power or relative power; the concept here is the same). With absolute gains, each side is concerned with maximizing its own profits and cares little about how much the other side gains or loses in the deal. Each side cares about the other only to the extent that the other side's behavior affects its own prospects for achieving maximum profits. With relative gains, on the other hand, each side considers not only its own individual gain, but also how well it fares compared to the other side.

Because great powers care deeply about the balance of power, their thinking focuses on relative gains when they consider cooperating with other states. For sure, each state tries to maximize its absolute gains; still, it is more important for a state to make sure that it does no worse, and perhaps better, than the other state in any agreement. Cooperation is more difficult to achieve, however, when states are attuned to relative gains rather than absolute gains. This is because states concerned about absolute gains have to make sure that if the pie is expanding, they are getting at least some portion of the increase, whereas states that worry about relative gains must pay careful attention to how the pie is divided, which complicates cooperative efforts.

Concerns about cheating also hinder cooperation. Great powers are often reluctant to enter into cooperative agreements for fear that the other side will cheat on the agreement and gain a significant advantage. This concern is especially acute in the military realm, causing a "special peril of defection," because the nature of military weaponry allows for rapid shifts in the balance of power. Such a development could create a window of opportunity for the state that cheats to inflict a decisive defeat on its victim.

These barriers to cooperation notwithstanding, great powers do cooperate in a realist world. Balance-of-power logic often causes great powers to form alliances and cooperate against common enemies. The United Kingdom, France, and Russia, for example, were allies against Germany before and during World War I. States sometimes cooperate to gang up on a third state, as Germany and the Soviet Union did against Poland in 1939. More recently, Serbia and Croatia agreed to conquer and divide Bosnia between them, although the United States and its European allies prevented them from executing their agreement. Rivals as well as allies cooperate. After all, deals can be struck that roughly reflect the distribution of power and satisfy concerns about cheating. The various arms control agreements signed by the superpowers during the Cold War illustrate this point.

The bottom line, however, is that cooperation takes place in a world that is competitive at its core—one where states have powerful incentives to take advantage of other states. This point is graphically highlighted by the state of European politics in the forty years before World War I. The great powers cooperated frequently during this period, but that did not stop them from going to war on August 1, 1914. The United States and the Soviet Union also cooperated considerably during World War II, but that cooperation did not prevent the outbreak of the Cold War shortly after Germany and Japan were defeated. Perhaps most amazingly, there was significant economic and military cooperation between Nazi Germany and the Soviet Union during the two years before the Wehrmacht attacked the Red Army. No amount of cooperation can eliminate the dominating logic of security competition. Genuine peace, or a world in which states do not compete for power, is not likely as long as the state system remains anarchic.

# Anarchy Is What States Make of It

## ALEXANDER WENDT

Classical realists such as Thomas Hobbes, Reinhold Niebuhr, and Hans J. Morgenthau attributed egoism and power politics primarily to human nature, whereas structural realists or neorealists emphasize anarchy. The difference stems in part from different interpretations of anarchy's causal powers. Kenneth Waltz's work is important for both. In *Man, the State, and War,* he defines anarchy as a condition of possibility for or "permissive" cause of war, arguing that "wars occur because there is nothing to prevent them."[1] It is the human nature or domestic politics of predator states, however, that provide the initial impetus or "efficient" cause of conflict which forces other states to respond in kind. . . . But . . . In Waltz's *Theory of International Politics* . . . the logic of anarchy seems by itself to constitute self-help and power politics as necessary features of world politics.[2] . . .

Waltz defines political structure in three dimensions: ordering principles (in this case, anarchy), principles of differentiation (which here drop out), and the distribution of capabilities.[3] By itself, this definition predicts little about state behavior. It does not predict whether two states will be friends or foes, will recognize each other's sovereignty, will have dynastic ties, will be revisionist or status quo powers, and so on. These factors, which are fundamentally intersubjective, affect states' security interests and thus the character of their interaction under anarchy. . . . Put more generally, without assumptions about the structure of identities and interests in the system, Waltz's definition of structure cannot predict the content or dynamics of anarchy. Self-help is one such intersubjective structure and, as such, does the decisive explanatory work in the theory. The question is whether self-help is a logical or contingent feature of anarchy. In this section, I develop the concept of a "structure of identity and interest" and show that no particular one follows logically from anarchy.

A fundamental principle of constructivist social theory is that people act toward objects, including other actors, on the basis of the meanings that the objects have for them. States act differently toward enemies than they do toward friends because enemies are threatening and friends are not. Anarchy and the distribution of power are insufficient to tell us which is which. U.S. military power has a different significance for Canada than for Cuba, despite their similar "structural" positions, just as British missiles have a different significance for the United States than do Soviet missiles. The distribution of power may always affect states' calculations, but how it does so depends on the intersubjective understandings and expectations, on the "distribution of knowledge," that constitute their conceptions of self and other.[4] If society "forgets" what a university is, the powers and practices of professor and student cease

From Alexander Wendt, "Anarchy Is What States Make of It: The Social Construction of Power Politics," *International Organization,* Vol. 46, No. 2 (Spring 1992), pp. 391–425. © 1992 by the World Peace Foundation and the Massachusetts Institute of Technology. Reprinted by permission of The MIT Press. Portions of the text and some footnotes have been omitted.

to exist; if the United States and Soviet Union decide that they are no longer enemies, "the Cold War is over." It is collective meanings that constitute the structures which organize our actions.

Actors acquire identities—relatively stable, role-specific understandings and expectations about self—by participating in such collective meanings. Identities are inherently relational: "Identity, with its appropriate attachments of psychological reality, is always identity within a specific, socially constructed world," Peter Berger argues.[5] Each person has many identities linked to institutional roles, such as brother, son, teacher, and citizen. Similarly, a state may have multiple identities as "sovereign," "leader of the free world," "imperial power," and so on. The commitment to and the salience of particular identities vary, but each identity is an inherently social definition of the actor grounded in the theories which actors collectively hold about themselves and one another and which constitute the structure of the social world.

Identities are the basis of interests. Actors do not have a "portfolio" of interests that they carry around independent of social context; instead, they define their interests on the process of defining situations. . . . Sometimes situations are unprecedented in our experience, and in these cases we have to construct their meaning, and thus our interests, by analogy or invent them de novo. More often they have routine qualities in which we assign meanings on the basis of institutionally defined roles. When we say that professors have an "interest" in teaching, research, or going on leave, we are saying that to function in the role identity of "professor," they have to define certain situations as calling for certain actions. This does not mean that they will necessarily do so (expectations and competence do not equal performance), but if they do not, they will not get tenure. The absence or failure of roles makes defining situations and interests more difficult, and identity confusion may result. This seems to be happening today in the United States and the former Soviet Union: Without the cold war's mutual attributions of threat and hostility to define their identities, these states seem unsure of what their "interests" should be.

An institution is a relatively stable set or "structure" of identities and interests. Such structures are often codified in formal rules and norms, but these have motivational force only in virtue of actors' socialization to and participation in collective knowledge. Institutions are fundamentally cognitive entities that do not exist apart from actors' ideas about how the world works. This does not mean that institutions are not real or objective, that they are "nothing but" beliefs. As collective knowledge, they are experienced as having an existence "over and above the individuals who happen to embody them at the moment."[6] In this way, institutions come to confront individuals as more or less coercive social facts, but they are still a function of what actors collectively "know." Identities and such collective cognitions do not exist apart from each other; they are "mutually constitutive." On this view, institutionalization is a process of internalizing new identities and interests, not something occurring outside them and affecting only behavior; socialization is a cognitive process, not just a behavioral one. Conceived in this way, institutions may be cooperative or conflictual, a point sometimes lost in scholarship on international regimes, which tends to equate institutions with cooperation. There are important differences between conflictual and cooperative institutions to be sure, but all relatively stable self-other relations—even those of "enemies"—are defined intersubjectively.

Self-help is an institution, one of various structures of identity and interest that may exist under anarchy. Processes of identity formation under anarchy are concerned first and foremost with preservation or "security" of the self. Concepts of security therefore differ in the extent to which and the manner in which the self is identified cognitively with the other, and, I want to suggest, it is upon this cognitive variation that the meaning of anarchy and the distribution of power depends. Let me illustrate with a standard continuum of security systems.

At one end is the "competitive" security system, in which states identify negatively with each other's security so that ego's gain is seen as alter's loss. Negative identification under anarchy constitutes systems of "realist" power politics: risk-averse actors that infer intentions from capabilities and worry about relative gains and losses. At the limit—in the Hobbesian war of all against all—collective action is nearly impossible in such a system because each actor must constantly fear being stabbed in the back.

In the middle is the "individualistic" security system, in which states are indifferent to the relationship between their own and others' security. This constitutes "neoliberal" systems: States are still self-regarding about their security but are concerned primarily with absolute gains rather than relative gains. One's position in the distribution of power is less important, and collective action is more possible (though still subject to free riding because states continue to be "egoists").

Competitive and individualistic systems are both "self-help" forms of anarchy in the sense that states do not positively identify the security of self with that of others but instead treat security as the individual responsibility of each. Given the lack of a positive cognitive identification on the basis of which to build security regimes, power politics within such systems will necessarily consist of efforts to manipulate others to satisfy self-regarding interests.

This contrasts with the "cooperative" security system, in which states identify positively with one another so that the security of each is perceived as the responsibility of all. This is not self-help in any interesting sense, since the "self" in terms of which interests are defined is the community; national interests are international interests. In practice, of course, the extent to which states identify with the community varies from the limited form found in "concerts" to the full-blown form seen in "collective security" arrangements. Depending on how well developed the collective self is, it will produce security practices that are in varying degrees altruistic or prosocial. This makes collective action less dependent on the presence of active threats and less prone to free riding. Moreover, it restructures efforts to advance one's objectives, or "power politics," in terms of shared norms rather than relative power.

On this view, the tendency in international relations scholarship to view power and institutions as two opposing explanations of foreign policy is therefore misleading, since anarchy and the distribution of power only have meaning for state action in virtue of the understandings and expectations that constitute institutional identities and interests. Self-help is one such institution, constituting one kind of anarchy but not the only kind. Waltz's three-part definition of structure therefore seems underspecified. In order to go from structure to action, we need to add a fourth: the intersubjectively constituted structure of identities and interests in the system.

This has an important implication for the way in which we conceive of states in the state of nature before their first encounter with each other. Because states do not have conceptions of self and other, and thus security interests, apart from or prior to interaction, we assume too much about the state of nature if we concur with Waltz that, in virtue of anarchy, "international political systems, like economic markets, are formed by the coaction of self-regarding units."[7] We also assume too much if we argue that, in virtue of anarchy, states in the state of nature necessarily face a "stag hunt" or "security dilemma."[8] These claims presuppose a history of interaction in which actors have acquired "selfish" identities and interests; before interaction (and still in abstraction from first- and second-image factors) they would have no experience upon which to base such definitions of self and other. To assume otherwise is to attribute to states in the state of nature qualities that they can only possess in society. Self-help is an institution, not a constitutive feature of anarchy.

What, then, *is* a constitutive feature of the state of nature before interaction? Two things are left if we strip away those properties of the self which presuppose interaction with others. The first is the material substrate of agency, including its zintrinsic capabilities. For human beings, this is the body; for states, it is an organizational apparatus of governance. In effect, I am suggesting for rhetorical purposes that the raw material out of which members of the state system are constituted is created by domestic society before states enter the constitutive process of international society, although this process implies neither stable territoriality nor sovereignty, which are internationally negotiated terms of individuality (as discussed further below). The second is a desire to preserve this material substrate, to survive. This does not entail "self-regardingness," however, since actors do not have a self prior to interaction with another; how they view the meaning and requirements of this survival therefore depends on the processes by which conceptions of self evolve.

This may all seem very arcane, but there is an important issue at stake: Are the foreign policy identities and interests of states exogenous or endogenous to the state system? The former is the answer of an individualistic or undersocialized systemic theory for which rationalism is appropriate; the latter is the answer of a fully socialized systemic theory. Waltz seems to offer the latter and proposes two mechanisms, competition and socialization, by which structure conditions state action.[9] The content of his argument about this conditioning, however, presupposes a self-help system that is not itself a constitutive feature of anarchy. As James Morrow points out, Waltz's two mechanisms condition behavior, not identity and interest. . . .[10]

If self-help is not a constitutive feature of anarchy, it must emerge causally from processes in which anarchy plays only a permissive role. This reflects a second principle of constructivism: that the meanings in terms of which action is organized arise out of interaction. . . .

Consider two actors—ego and alter—encountering each other for the first time.[11] Each wants to survive and has certain material capabilities, but neither actor has biological or domestic imperatives for power, glory, or conquest . . . and there is no history of security or insecurity between the two. What should they do? Realists would probably argue that each should act on the basis of worst-case assumptions about the other's intentions, justifying such an attitude as prudent in view of the possibility of death from making a mistake. Such a possibility always exists, even in civil society; however, society would be impossible if people made decisions purely on the basis of worst-case possibilities. Instead, most decisions are and should be made on the basis of probabilities, and these are produced by interaction, by what actors *do*.

In the beginning is ego's gesture, which may consist, for example, of an advance, a retreat, a brandishing of arms, a laying down of arms, or an attack. For ego, this gesture represents the basis on which it is prepared to respond to alter. This basis is unknown to alter, however, and so it must make an inference or "attribution" about ego's intentions and, in particular, given that this is anarchy, about whether ego is a threat. The content of this inference will largely depend on two considerations. The first is the gesture's and ego's physical qualities, which are in part contrived by ego and which include the direction of movement, noise, numbers, and immediate consequences of the gesture. The second consideration concerns what alter would intend by such qualities were it to make such a gesture itself. Alter may make an attributional "error" in its inference about ego's intent, but there is also no reason for it to assume a priori—before the gesture—that ego is threatening, since it is only through a process of signaling and interpreting that the costs and probabilities of being wrong can be determined. Social threats are constructed, not natural.

Consider an example. Would we assume, a priori, that we were about to be attacked if we are ever contacted by members of an alien civilization? I think not. We would be highly alert, of course, but whether we placed our military forces on alert or launched an attack would depend on how we interpreted the import of their first gesture for our security—if only to avoid making an immediate enemy out of what may be a dangerous adversary. The possibility of error, in other words, does not force us to act on the assumption that the aliens are threatening: Action depends on the probabilities we assign, and these are in key part a function of what the aliens do; prior to their gesture, we have no systemic basis for assigning probabilities. If their first gesture is to appear with a thousand spaceships and destroy New York, we will define the situation as threatening and respond accordingly. But if they appear with one spaceship, saying what seems to be "we come in peace," we will feel "reassured" and will probably respond with a gesture intended to reassure them, even if this gesture is not necessarily interpreted by them as such.

This process of signaling, interpreting, and responding completes a "social act" and begins the process of creating intersubjective meanings. It advances the same way. The first social act creates expectations on both sides about each other's future behavior: potentially mistaken and certainly tentative, but expectations nonetheless. Based on this tentative knowledge, ego makes a new gesture, again signifying the basis on which it will respond to alter, and again alter responds, adding to the pool of knowledge each has about the other, and so on over time. The mechanism here is reinforcement; interaction rewards actors for holding certain ideas about each other and discourages them from holding others. If repeated long enough, these "reciprocal typifications" will create relatively stable concepts of self and other regarding the issue at stake in the interaction.[12]

Competitive systems of interaction are prone to security "dilemmas," in which the efforts of actors to enhance their security unilaterally threatens the security of the others, perpetuating distrust and alienation. The forms of identity and interest that constitute such dilemmas, however, are themselves ongoing effects of, not exogenous to, the interaction; identities are produced in and through "situated activity."[13] We do not *begin* our relationship with the aliens in a security dilemma; security dilemmas are not given by anarchy or nature. . . .

The mirror theory of identity formation is a crude account of how the process of creating identities and interests might work, but it does not tell us why a system of states—such as, arguably, our own—would have ended up with self-regarding and not collective identities. In this section, I examine an efficient cause, predation, which, in conjunction with anarchy as a permissive cause, may generate a self-help system. In so doing, however, I show the key role that the structure of identities and interests plays in mediating anarchy's explanatory role.

The predator argument is straightforward and compelling. For whatever reasons—biology, domestic politics, or systemic victimization—some states may become predisposed toward aggression. The aggressive behavior of these predators or "bad apples" forces other states to engage in competitive power politics, to meet fire with fire, since failure to do so may degrade or destroy them. One predator will best a hundred pacifists because anarchy provides no guarantees. This argument is powerful in part because it is so weak: Rather than making the strong assumption that all states are inherently power-seeking (a purely reductionist theory of power politics), it assumes that just one is power-seeking and that the others have to follow suit because anarchy permits the one to exploit them.

In making this argument, it is important to reiterate that the possibility of predation does not in itself force states to anticipate it a priori with competitive power politics of their own. The possibility of predation does not mean that "war may at any moment occur"; it may in fact be extremely unlikely. Once a predator emerges, however, it may condition identity and interest formation in the following manner.

In an anarchy of two, if ego is predatory, alter must either define its security in self-help terms or pay the price. . . . The timing of the emergence of predation relative to the history of identity formation in the community is therefore crucial to anarchy's explanatory role as a permissive cause. Predation will always lead victims to defend themselves, but whether defense will be collective or not depends on the history of interaction within the potential collective as much as on the ambitions of the predator. Will the disappearance of the Soviet threat renew old insecurities among the members of the North Atlantic Treaty Organization? Perhaps, but not if they have reasons independent of that threat for identifying their security with one another. Identities and interests are relationship-specific, not intrinsic attributes of a "portfolio"; states may be competitive in some relationships and solidary in others. . . .

The source of predation also matters. If it stems from unit-level causes that are immune to systemic impacts (causes such as human nature or domestic politics taken in isolation), then it functions in a manner analogous to a "genetic trait" in the constructed world of the state system. Even if successful, this trait does not select for other predators in an evolutionary sense so much as it teaches other states to respond in kind, but since traits cannot be unlearned, the other states will continue competitive behavior until the predator is either destroyed or transformed from within. However, in the more likely event that predation stems at least in part from prior systemic interaction—perhaps as a result of being victimized in the past (one thinks here of Nazi Germany or the Soviet Union)—then it is more a response to a learned identity and, as such, might be transformed by future social interaction in the form of appeasement, reassurances that security needs will be met, systemic effects on domestic politics, and so on. In this case, in other words, there is more hope that process can transform a bad apple into a good one. . . .

This raises anew the question of exactly how much and what kind of role human nature and domestic politics play in world politics. The greater and more destructive this role, the more significant predation will be, and the less amenable anarchy will be to formation of collective identities. Classical realists, of course, assumed that human nature was possessed by an inherent lust for power or glory. My argument suggests that assumptions such as this were made for a reason: An unchanging Hobbesian man provides the powerful efficient cause necessary for a relentless pessimism about world politics that anarchic structure alone, or even structure plus intermittent predation, cannot supply. . . .

Assuming for now that systemic theories of identity formation in world politics are worth pursuing, let me conclude by suggesting that the realist-rationalist alliance "reifies" self-help in the sense of treating it as something separate from the practices by which it is produced and sustained. Peter Berger and Thomas Luckmann define reification as follows: "[It] is the apprehension of the products of human activity *as if* they were something else than human products—such as facts of nature, results of cosmic laws, or manifestations of divine will. Reification implies that man is capable of forgetting his own authorship of the human world, and further, that the dialectic between man, the producer, and his products is lost to consciousness. The reified world is . . . experienced by man as a strange facticity, an *opus alienum* over which he has no control rather than as the *opus proprium* of his own productive activity."[14] By denying or bracketing states' collective authorship of their identities and interests, in other words, the realist-rationalist alliance denies or brackets the fact that competitive power politics help create a very "problem of order" they are supposed to solve—that realism is a selffulfilling prophecy. Far from being exogenously given, the intersubjective knowledge that constitutes competitive identities and interests is constructed every day by processes of "social will formation."[15] It is what states have made of themselves.

## NOTES

1. Kenneth Waltz, *Man, the State, and War* (New York: Columbia University Press, 1959), p. 232.
2. Kenneth Waltz, *Theory of International Politics* (Boston: Addison-Wesley, 1979).
3. Waltz, *Theory of International Politics*, pp. 79–101.
4. The phrase "distribution of knowledge" is Barry Barnes's, as discussed in his work *The Nature of Power* (Cambridge: Polity Press, 1988); see also Peter Berger and Thomas Luckmann, *The Social Construction of Reality* (New York: Anchor Books, 1966).

5. Berger, "Identity as a Problem in the Sociology of Knowledge," *European Journal of Sociology*, 7, 1 (1966), 111.

6. Berger and Luckmann, p. 58.

7. Waltz, *Theory of International Politics*, p. 91.

8. See Waltz, *Man, the State, and War;* and Robert Jervis, "Cooperation Under the Security Dilemma," *World Politics* 30 (January 1978), 167–214.

9. Waltz, *Theory of International Politics*, pp. 74–77.

10. See James Morrow, "Social Choice and System Structure in World Politics," *World Politics* 41 (October 1988), 89.

11. This situation is not entirely metaphorical in world politics, since throughout history states have "discovered" each other, generating an instant anarchy as it were. A systematic empirical study of first contacts would be interesting.

12. On "reciprocal typifications," see Berger and Luckmann, pp. 54–58.

13. See C. Norman Alexander and Mary Glenn Wiley, "Situated Activity and Identity Formation," in Morris Rosenberg and Ralph Turner, eds., *Social Psychology: Sociological Perspectives* (New York: Basic Books, 1981), pp. 269–89.

14. See Berger and Luckmann, p. 89.

15. See Richard Ashley, "Social Will and International Anarchy," in Hayward Alker and Richard Ashley, eds., *After Realism,* work in progress, Massachusetts Institute of Technology, Cambridge, and Arizona State University, Tempe, 1992.

# THE MITIGATION
# OF ANARCHY

## The Conditions for Cooperation in World Politics

### KENNETH A. OYE

## I. INTRODUCTION

Nations dwell in perpetual anarchy, for no central authority imposes limits on the pursuit of sovereign interests. This common condition gives rise to diverse outcomes. Relations among states are marked by war and concert, arms races and arms control, trade wars and tariff truces, financial panics and rescues, competitive devaluation and monetary stabilization. At times, the absence of centralized international authority precludes attainment of common goals. Because, as states, they cannot cede ultimate control over their conduct to a supranational sovereign, they cannot guarantee that they will adhere to their promises. The possibility of a breach of promise can impede cooperation even when cooperation would leave all better off. Yet, at other times, states do realize common goals through cooperation under anarchy. Despite the absence of any ultimate international authority, governments often bind themselves to mutually advantageous courses of action. And, though no international sovereign stands ready to enforce the terms of agreement, states can realize common interests through tacit cooperation, formal bilateral and multi-lateral negotiation, and the creation of international regimes. The question is: if international relations can approximate both a Hobbesian state of nature and a Lockean evil society, why does cooperation emerge in some cases and not in others?

From "Explaining Cooperation under Anarchy: Hypothesis and Strategies" by Kenneth A. Oye from *World Politics*, pp. 1–22. Reprinted by permission of Johns Hopkins University Press. Portions of the text and some footnotes have been omitted.

[Scholars] address both explanatory and prescriptive aspects of this perennial question. *First, what circumstances favor the emergence of cooperation under anarchy?* Given the lack of a central authority to guarantee adherence to agreements, what features of situations encourage or permit states to bind themselves to mutually beneficial courses of action? What features of situations preclude cooperation? *Second, what strategies can states adopt to foster the emergence of cooperation by altering the circumstances they confront?* Governments need not necessarily accept circumstances as given. To what extent are situational impediments to cooperation subject to willful modification? Through what higher order strategies can states create the preconditions for cooperation? . . .

I submit that three circumstantial dimensions serve both as proximate explanations of cooperation and as targets of longer-term strategies to promote cooperation. Each of the three major sections of this piece defines a dimension, explains how that dimension accounts for the incidence of cooperation and conflict in the absence of centralized authority, and examines associated strategies for enhancing the prospects for cooperation.

In the section entitled "Payoff Structure: Mutual and Conflicting Preferences," I discuss how payoffs affect the prospects for cooperation and present strategies to improve the prospects for cooperation by altering payoffs. Orthodox game theorists identify optimal strategies *given* ordinally defined classes of games, and their familiar insights provide the starting point for the discussion. Recent works in security studies, institutional microeconomics, and international political economy suggest strategies to *alter* payoff structures and thereby improve the prospects for cooperation.[1]

In the next section, entitled "Shadow of the Future: Single-play and Iterated Games," I discuss how the prospect of continuing interaction affects the likelihood of cooperation; examine how strategies of reciprocity can provide direct paths to cooperative outcomes under iterated conditions; and suggest strategies to lengthen the shadow of the future.[2] In addition, this section shows that recognition and control capabilities—the ability to distinguish between cooperation and defection by others and to respond in kind—can affect the power of reciprocity, and suggests strategies to improve recognition capabilities.

In the third section, "Number of Players: Two-Person and N-Person Games," I explain why cooperation becomes more difficult as the number of actors increases; present strategies for promoting cooperation in N-actor situations; and offer strategies for promoting cooperation by reducing the number of actors necessary to the realization of common interests. Game theorists and oligopoly theorists have long noted that cooperation becomes more difficult as numbers increase, and their insights provide a starting point for discussion. Recent work in political economy focuses on two strategies for promoting cooperation in thorny N-person situations: functionalist analysts of regimes suggest strategies for increasing the likelihood and robustness of cooperation *given* large numbers of actors,[3] analysts of *ad hoc* bargaining in international political economy suggest strategies of bilateral and regional decomposition to *reduce* the number of actors necessary to the realization of some mutual interests, at the expense of the magnitude of gains from cooperation. . . . [4]

# II. PAYOFF STRUCTURE: MUTUAL AND CONFLICTING PREFERENCES

The structure of payoffs in a given round of play—the benefits of mutual cooperation (CC) relative to mutual defection (DD) and the benefits of unilateral defection (DC) relative to unrequited cooperation (CD)—is fundamental to the analysis of cooperation. The argument proceeds in three stages. First, how does payoff structure affect the significance of cooperation? More narrowly, when is cooperation, defined in terms of conscious policy coordination, necessary to the realization of mutual interests? Second, how does payoff structure affect the likelihood and robustness of cooperation? Third, through what strategies can states increase the long-term prospects for cooperation by altering payoff structures?

Before turning to these questions, consider briefly some tangible and intangible determinants of payoff structures. The security and political economy literatures examine the effects of military force structure and doctrine, economic ideology, the size of currency reserves, macroeconomic circumstance, and a host of other factors on national assessments of national interests. In "Cooperation under the Security Dilemma," Robert Jervis has explained how the diffusion of offensive military technology and strategies can increase rewards from defection and thereby reduce the prospects for cooperation. In "International Regimes, Transactions, and Chance: Embedded Liberalism in the Postwar Economic Order," John Ruggie has demonstrated how the diffusion of liberal economic ideas increased the perceived benefits of mutual economic openness over mutual closure (CC-DD), and diminished the perceived rewards from asymmetric defection relative to asymmetric cooperation (DC-CD). In "Firms and Tariff Regime Change," Timothy McKeown has shown how downturns in the business cycle alter national tastes for protection and thereby decrease the perceived benefits of mutual openness relative to mutual closure and increase the perceived rewards of asymmetric defection. . . . [5]

## A. Payoff Structure and Cooperation

How does payoff structure determine the significance of cooperation? More narrowly, when is *cooperation,* defined in terms of conscious policy coordination, *necessary* to the realization of *mutual benefits?* For a *mutual benefit* to exist, actors must prefer mutual cooperation (CC) to mutual defection (DD). For coordination to be *necessary* to the realization of the mutual benefit, actors must prefer unilateral defection (DC) to unrequited cooperation (CD). These preference orderings are consistent with the familiar games of Prisoners' Dilemma, Stag Hunt, and Chicken. Indeed, these games have attracted a disproportionate share of scholarly attention precisely because cooperation is desirable but not automatic. In these cases, the capacity of states to cooperate under anarchy, to bind themselves to mutually beneficial courses of action without resort to any ultimate central authority, is vital to the realization of a common good. . . .

In the class of games—including Prisoners' Dilemma, Stag Hunt, and Chicken—where cooperation is necessary to the realization of mutual benefits, how does payoff structure affect the likelihood and robustness of cooperation in these situations? Cooperation will be less likely in Prisoners' Dilemma than in Stag Hunt or Chicken. To understand why, consider each of these games in conjunction with the illustrative stories from which they derive their names.

*Prisoners' Dilemma:* Two prisoners are suspected of a major crime. The authorities possess evidence to secure conviction on only a minor charge. If neither prisoner squeals, both will draw a light sentence on the minor charge (CC). If one prisoner squeals and the other stonewalls, the rat will go free (DC) and the sucker will draw a very heavy sentence (CD). If both squeal, both will draw a moderate sentence (DD). Each prisoner's preference ordering is: DC > CC > DD > CD. If the prisoners expect to "play" only one time, each prisoner will be better off squealing than stonewalling, no matter what his partner chooses to do (DC > CC and DD > CD). The temptation of the rat payoff and fear of the sucker payoff will drive single-play Prisoners' Dilemmas toward mutual defection. Unfortunately, if both prisoners act on this reasoning, they will draw a moderate sentence on the major charge, while cooperation could have led to a light sentence on the minor charge (CC > DD). In single-play Prisoners' Dilemmas, individually rational actions produce a collectively suboptimal outcome.

*Stag Hunt:* A group of hunters surround a stag. If all cooperate to trap the stag, all will eat well (CC). If one person defects to chase a passing rabbit, the stag will escape. The defector will eat lightly (DC) and none of the others will eat at all (CD). If all chase rabbits, all will have some chance of catching a rabbit and eating lightly (DD). Each hunter's preference ordering is: CC > DC > DD > CD. The mutual interest in plentiful venison (CC) relative to all other outcomes militates strongly against defection. However, because a rabbit in the hand (DC) is better than a stag in the bush (CD), cooperation will be assured only if each hunter believes that all hunters will cooperate. In single-play Stag Hunt, the temptation to defect to protect against the defection of others is balanced by the strong universal preference for stag over rabbit.

*Chicken:* Two drivers race down the center of a road from opposite directions. If one swerves and the other does not, then the first will suffer the stigma of being known as a chicken (CD) while the second will enjoy being known as a hero (DC). If neither swerves, both will suffer grievously in the ensuing collision (DD). If both swerve, damage to the reputation of each will be limited (CC). Each driver's preference ordering is: DC > CC > CD > DD. If each believes that the other will swerve, then each will be tempted to defect by continuing down the center of the road. Better to be a live hero than a live chicken. If both succumb to this temptation, however, defection will result in collision. The fear that the other driver may not swerve decreases the appeal of continuing down the center of the road. In single-play Chicken, the temptations of unilateral defection are balanced by fear of mutual defection.

In games that are not repeated, only ordinally defined preferences matter. Under single-play conditions, interval-level payoffs in ordinally defined categories of games cannot (in theory) affect the likelihood of cooperation. In the illustrations above, discussions of dominant strategies do not hinge on the magnitude of differences among the payoffs. Yet the magnitude of differences between CC and DD and between DC and CD can be large or small, if not precisely measurable, and can increase or decrease. Changes in the magnitude of differences in the value placed on outcomes can influence the prospects for cooperation through two paths.

First, changes in the value attached to outcomes can transform situations from one ordinally defined class of game into another. For example, in "Cooperation under the Security Dilemma," Robert Jervis described how difficult Prisoners' Dilemmas may evolve into less challenging Stag Hunts if the gains from mutual cooperation (CC) increase relative to the gains from exploitation (DC). He related the structure of payoffs to traditional concepts of offensive and defensive dominance, and offensive and defensive dominance to technological and doctrinal shifts. Ernst Haas, Mary Pat Williams, and Don Babai have emphasized the importance of cognitive congruence as a determinant of technological cooperation. The diffusion of common conceptions of the nature and effects of technology enhanced perceived gains from cooperation and diminished perceived gains from defection, and may have transformed some Prisoners' Dilemmas into Harmony.[6]

Second, under iterated conditions, the magnitude of differences among payoffs *within* a given class of games can be an important determinant of cooperation. The more substantial the gains from mutual cooperation (CC-DD) and the less substantial the gains from unilateral defection (DC-CD), the greater the likelihood of cooperation. In iterated situations, the magnitude of the difference between CC and DD and between DC and CD in present and future rounds of play affects the likelihood of cooperation in the present. This point is developed at length in the section on the shadow of the future.

## B. Strategies to Alter Payoff Structure

If payoff structure affects the likelihood of cooperation, to what extent can states alter situations by modifying payoff structures, and thereby increase the long-term likelihood of cooperation? Many of the tangible and intangible determinants of payoff structure, discussed at the outset of this section, are subject to willful modification through unilateral, bilateral, and multilateral strategies. In "Cooperation under the Security Dilemma," Robert Jervis has offered specific suggestions for altering payoff structures through unilateral strategies. Procurement policy can affect the prospects for cooperation. If one superpower favors procurement of defensive over offensive weapons, it can reduce its own gains from exploitation through surprise attack (DC) and reduce its adversary's fear of exploitation (CD). Members of alliances have often resorted to the device of deploying troops on troubled frontiers to increase the likelihood of cooperation. A state's use of troops as hostages is designed to diminish the payoff from its own defection—to reduce its gains from exploitation (DC)—and thereby render defensive defection by its partner less likely. Publicizing an agreement diminishes payoffs associated with defection from the agreement, and thereby lessens gains from exploitation. These observations in international relations are paralleled by recent developments in microeconomics. Oliver Williamson has identified unilateral and bilateral techniques used by firms to facilitate interfirm cooperation by diminishing gains from exploitation. He distinguishes between specific and nonspecific costs associated with adherence to agreements. Specific costs, such as specialized training, machine tools, and construction, cannot be recovered in the event of the breakdown of an agreement. When parties to an agreement incur high specific costs, repudiation of commitments will entail substantial losses. Firms can thus reduce their gains from exploitation through the technique of acquiring dedicated assets that serve as hostages to continuing cooperation. Nonspecific assets, such as general-purpose trucks and airplanes, are salvageable if agreements break down; firms can reduce their fear of being exploited by maximizing the use of nonspecific assets, but such assets cannot diminish gains from exploitation by serving as hostages.[7] Unilateral strategies can improve the prospects of cooperation by reducing both the costs of being exploited (CD) and the gains from exploitation (DC). The new literature on interfirm cooperation indirectly raises an old question on the costs of unilateral strategies to promote cooperation in international relations.

In many instances, unilateral actions that limit one's gains from exploitation may have the effect of increasing one's vulnerability to exploitation by others. For example, a state could limit gains from defection from liberal international economic norms by permitting the expansion of sectors of comparative advantage and by permitting liquidation of inefficient sectors. Because a specialized economy is a hostage to international economic cooperation, this strategy would unquestionably increase the credibility of the nation's commitment to liberalism. It also has the effect, however, of increasing the nation's vulnerability to protection by others. In the troops-as-hostage example, the government that stations troops may promote cooperation by diminishing an ally's fear of abandonment, but in so doing it raises its own fears of exploitation by the ally. . . .

Unilateral strategies do not exhaust the range of options that states may use to alter payoff structures. Bilateral strategies—most significantly strategies of issue linkage—can be used to alter payoff structures by combining dissimilar games. Because resort to issue linkage generally assumes iteration, analysis of how issue linkage can be used to alter payoffs is presented in the section on the shadow of the future. Furthermore, bilateral "instructional" strategies can aim at altering another country's understanding of cause-and-effect relationships, and result in altered perceptions of interest. For example, American negotiators in SALT I sought to instruct their Soviet counterparts on the logic of mutual assured destruction.[8]

Multilateral strategies, centering on the formation of international regimes, can be used to alter payoff structures in two ways. First, norms generated by regimes may be internalized by states, and thereby alter payoff structure. Second, information generated by regimes may alter states' understanding of their interests. As Ernst Haas argues, new regimes may gather and distribute information that can highlight cause-and-effect relationships not previously understood. Changing perceptions of means-ends hierarchies can, in turn, result in changing perceptions of interest.[9]

## III. THE SHADOW OF THE FUTURE: SINGLE-PLAY AND ITERATED GAMES

The distinction between cases in which similar transactions among parties are unlikely to be repeated and cases in which the expectation of future interaction can influence decisions in the present is fundamental to the emergence of cooperation among egotists. As the previous section suggests, states confronting strategic situations that resemble single-play Prisoners' Dilemma and, to a lesser extent, single-play Stag Hunt and Chicken, are constantly tempted by immediate gains from unilateral defection, and fearful of immediate losses from unrequited cooperation. How does continuing interaction affect prospects for cooperation? The argument proceeds in four stages. First, why do iterated conditions improve the prospects for cooperation in Prisoners' Dilemma and Stag Hunt while diminishing the prospects for cooperation in Chicken? Second, how do strategies of reciprocity improve the prospects for cooperation under iterated conditions? Third, why does the effectiveness of reciprocity hinge on conditions of play—the ability of actors to distinguish reliably between cooperation and defection by others and to respond in kind? Fourth, through what strategies can states improve conditions of play and lengthen the shadow of the future?

Before turning to these questions, consider the attributes of iterated situations. First, states must expect to continue dealing with each other. This condition is, in practice, not particularly restrictive. With the possible exception of global thermonuclear war, international politics is characterized by the expectation of future interaction. Second, payoff structures must not change substantially over time. In other words, each round of play should not alter the structure of the game in the future. This condition is, in practice, quite restrictive. For example, states considering surprise attack when offense is dominant are in a situation that has many of the characteristics of a single-play game: Attack alters options and payoffs in future rounds of interaction. Conversely, nations considering increases or decreases in their military budgets are in a situation that has many of the characteristics of an iterated game: Spending options and associated marginal increases or decreases in military strength are likely to remain fairly stable over future rounds of interaction. In international monetary affairs, governments considering or fearing devaluation under a gold-exchange standard are in a situation that has many of the characteristics of a single-play game: Devaluation may diminish the value of another state's foreign currency reserves on a one-time basis, while reductions in holdings of reserves would diminish possible losses on a one-time basis. Conversely, governments considering intervention under a floating system with minimal reserves are in a situation that has many of the characteristics of an iterated game: Depreciation or appreciation of a currency would not produce substantial one-time losses or gains. Third, the size of the discount rate applied to the future affects the iterativeness of games. If a government places little value on future payoffs, its situation has many of the characteristics of a single-play game. If it places a high value on future payoffs, its situation may have many of the characteristics of an iterated game. For example, political leaders in their final term are likely to discount the future more substantially than political leaders running for, or certain of, reelection.

## A. The Shadow of the Future and Cooperation

How does the shadow of the future affect the likelihood of cooperation? Under single-play conditions without a sovereign, adherence to agreements is often irrational. Consider the single-play Prisoners' Dilemma. Each prisoner is better off squealing, whether or not his partner decides to squeal. In the absence of continuing interaction, defection would emerge as the dominant strategy. Because the prisoners can neither turn to a central authority for enforcement of an agreement to cooperate nor rely on the anticipation of retaliation to deter present defection, cooperation will be unlikely under single-play conditions. If the prisoners expect to be placed in similar situations in the future, the prospects for cooperation improve. Experimental evidence suggests that under iterated Prisoners' Dilemma the incidence of cooperation rises substantially.[10] Even in the absence of centralized authority, tacit agreements to cooperate through mutual stonewalling are frequently reached and maintained. Under iterated Prisoners' Dilemma, a potential defector compares the immediate gain from squealing with the possible sacrifice of future gains that may result from squealing. In single-play Stag Hunt, each hunter is tempted to defect in order to defend himself against the possibility of defection by others. A reputation for reliability, for resisting temptation, reduces the likelihood of defection. If the hunters are a permanent group, and expect to hunt together again, the immediate gains from unilateral defection relative to unrequited cooperation must be balanced against the cost of diminished cooperation in the future. In both Prisoners' Dilemma and Stag Hunt, defection in the present *decreases* the likelihood of cooperation in the future. In both, therefore, iteration improves the prospects for cooperation. In Chicken, iteration may decrease the prospects for cooperation. Under single-play conditions, the temptation of unilateral defection is balanced by the fear of the collision that follows from mutual defection. How does iteration affect this balance? If the game is repeated indefinitely, then each driver may refrain from swerving in the present to coerce the other driver into swerving in the future. Each driver may seek to acquire a reputation for not swerving to cause the other driver to swerve. In iterated Chicken, one driver's defection in the present may decrease the likelihood of the other driver's defection in the future.

## B. Strategies of Reciprocity and Conditions of Play

It is at this juncture that strategy enters the explanation. Although the expectation of continuing interaction has varying effects on the likelihood of cooperation in the illustrations above, an iterated environment permits resort to strategies of reciprocity that may improve the prospects of cooperation in Chicken as well as in Prisoners' Dilemma and Stag Hunt. Robert Axelrod argues that strategies of reciprocity have the effect of promoting cooperation by establishing a direct connection between an actor's present behavior and anticipated future benefits. Tit-for-tat, or conditional cooperation, can increase the likelihood of joint cooperation by shaping the future consequences of present cooperation or defection.

In iterated Prisoners' Dilemma and Stag Hunt, reciprocity underscores the future consequences of present cooperation and defection. The argument presented above—that iteration enhances the prospects for cooperation in these games—rests on the assumption that defection in the present will decrease the likelihood of cooperation in the future. Adoption of an implicit or explicit strategy of matching stonewalling with stonewalling, squealing with squealing, rabbit chasing with rabbit chasing, and cooperative hunting with cooperative hunting validates the assumption. In iterated Chicken, a strategy of reciprocity can offset the perverse effects of reputational considerations on the prospects for cooperation. Recall that in iterated Chicken, each driver may refrain from swerving in the present to coerce the other driver into swerving in the future. Adoption of an implicit or explicit strategy of tit-for-tat in iterated games of Chicken alters the failure stream of benefits associated with present defection. If a strategy of reciprocity is credible, then the mutual losses associated with future collisions can encourage present swerving. In all three games, a promise to respond to present cooperation with future cooperation and a threat to respond to present defection with future defection can improve the prospects for cooperation.

The effectiveness of strategies of reciprocity hinges on conditions of play—the ability of actors to distinguish reliably between cooperation and defection by others and to respond in kind. In the illustrations provided above, the meaning of "defect" and "cooperate" is unambiguous. Dichotomous choices—between squeal and stonewall, chase the rabbit or capture the stag, continue down the road or swerve—limit the likelihood of misperception. Further, the actions of all are transparent. Given the definitions of the situations, prisoners, hunters, and drivers can reliably detect defection and cooperation by other actors. Finally, the definition of the actors eliminates the possibility of control problems. Unitary prisoners, hunters, and drivers do not suffer from factional, organizational, or bureaucratic dysfunctions that might hinder implementation of strategies of reciprocity.

In international relations, conditions of play can limit the effectiveness of reciprocity. The definition of cooperation and defection may be ambiguous. For example, the Soviet Union and the United States hold to markedly different definitions of "defection" from the terms of détente as presented in the Basic Principles Agreement;[11] the European Community and the United States differ over whether domestic sectoral policies comprise indirect export subsidies. Further, actions may not be transparent. For example, governments may not be able to detect one another's violations of arms control agreements or indirect export subsidies. If defection cannot be reliably detected, the effect of present cooperation on possible future reprisals will erode. Together, ambiguous definitions and a lack of transparency can limit the ability of states to recognize cooperation and defection by others.

Because reciprocity requires flexibility, control is as important as recognition. Internal factional, organizational, and bureaucratic dysfunctions may limit the ability of nations to implement tit-for-tat strategies. It may be easier to sell one unvarying line of policy than to sell a strategy of shifting between lines of policy in response to the actions of others. For example, arms suppliers and defense planners tend to resist the cancellation of weapons systems even if the cancellation is a response to the actions of a rival. Import-competing industries tend to resist the removal of barriers to imports, even if trade liberalization is in response to liberalization by another state. At times, national decision makers may be unable to implement strategies of reciprocity. On other occasions, they must invest heavily in selling reciprocity. For these reasons, national decision makers may display a bias against conditional strategies: The domestic costs of pursuing such strategies may partially offset the value of the discounted stream of future benefits that conditional policies are expected to yield. . . .

## C. Strategies to Improve Recognition and Lengthen the Shadow of the Future

To what extent can governments promote cooperation by creating favorable conditions of play and by lengthening the shadow of the future? The literature on international regimes offers several techniques for creating favorable conditions of play. Explicit codification of norms can limit definitional ambiguity. The very act of clarifying standards of conduct, of defining cooperative and uncooperative behavior, can permit more effective resort to strategies of reciprocity. Further, provisions for surveillance—for example, mechanisms for verification in arms control agreements or for sharing information on the nature and effects of domestic sectoral policies—can increase transparency. In practice, the goal of enhancing recognition capabilities is often central to negotiations under anarchy.

The game-theoretic and institutional microeconomic literatures offer several approaches to increasing the iterative character of situations. Thomas Schelling and Robert Axelrod suggest tactics of decomposition over time to lengthen the shadow of the future.[12] For example, the temptation to defect in a deal promising thirty billion dollars for a billion barrels of oil may be reduced if the deal is sliced up into a series of payments and deliveries. Cooperation in arms reduction or in territorial disengagement may be difficult if the reduction or disengagement must be achieved in one jump. If a reduction or disengagement can be sliced up into increments, the problem of cooperation may be rendered more tractable. Finally, strategies of issue linkage can be used to alter payoff structures and to interject elements of iterativeness into single-play situations. Relations among states are rarely limited to one single-play issue of overriding importance. When nations confront a single-play game on one issue, present defection may be deterred by threats of retaliation on other iterated issues. In international monetary affairs, for instance, a government fearing one-time reserve losses if another state devalues its currency may link devaluation to an iterated trade game. By establishing a direct connection between present behavior in a single-play game and future benefits in an iterated game, tacit or explicit cross-issue linkage can lengthen the shadow of the future. . . .

## IV. NUMBER OF PLAYERS: TWO-PERSON AND N-PERSON GAMES

Up to now, I have discussed the effects of payoff structure and the shadow of the future on the prospects of cooperation in terms of two-person situations. What happens to the prospects for cooperation as the number of significant actors rises? In this section, I explain why the prospects for cooperation diminish as the number of players increases; examine the function of international regimes as a response to the problems created by large numbers; and offer strategies to improve the prospects for cooperation by altering situations to diminish the number of significant players.

The numbers problem is central to many areas of the social sciences. Mancur Olson's theory of collective action focuses on N-person versions of Prisoners' Dilemma. The optimism of our earlier discussions of cooperation under iterated

Prisoners' Dilemma gives way to the pessimism of analyses of cooperation in the provision of public goods. Applications of Olsonian theory to problems ranging from cartelization to the provision of public goods in alliances underscore the significance of "free-riding" as an impediment to cooperation.[13] In international relations, the numbers problem has been central to two debates. The longstanding controversy over the stability of bipolar versus multipolar systems reduces to a debate over the impact of the number of significant actors on international conflict.[14] A more recent controversy, between proponents of the theory of hegemonic stability and advocates of international regimes, reduces to a debate over the effects of large numbers on the robustness of cooperation.[15]

## A. Number of Players and Cooperation

How do numbers affect the likelihood of cooperation? There are at least three important channels of influence.[16] First, cooperation requires recognition of opportunities for the advancement of mutual interests, as well as policy coordination once these opportunities have been identified. As the number of players increases, transactions and information costs rise. In simple terms, the complexity of N-person situations militates against identification and realization of common interests. Avoiding nuclear war during the Cuban missile crisis called for cooperation by the Soviet Union and the United States. The transaction and information costs in this particularly harrowing crisis, though substantial, did not preclude cooperation. By contrast, the problem of identifying significant actors, defining interests, and negotiating agreements that embodied mutual interests in the N-actor case of 1914 was far more difficult. These secondary costs associated with attaining cooperative outcomes in N-actor cases erode the difference between CC and DD. More significantly, the intrinsic difficulty of anticipating the behavior of other players and of weighing the value of the future goes up with the number of players. The complexity of solving N-person games, even in the purely deductive sense, has stunted the development of formal work on the problem. This complexity is even greater in real situations, and operates against multilateral cooperation.

Second, as the number of players increases, the likelihood of autonomous defection and of recognition and control problems increases. Cooperative behavior rests on calculations of expected utility—merging discount rates, payoff structures, and anticipated behavior of other players. Discount rates and approaches to calculation are likely to vary across actors, and the prospects for mutual cooperation may decline as the number of players and probable heterogeneity of actors increases. The chances of including a state that discounts the future heavily, that is too weak (domestically) to detect, react, or implement a strategy of reciprocity, that cannot distinguish reliably between cooperation and defection by other states, or that departs from even minimal standards of rationality increase with the number of states in a game. For example, many pessimistic analyses of the consequences of nuclear proliferation focus on how breakdowns of deterrence may become more likely as the number of countries with nuclear weapons increases.

Third, as the number of players increases, the feasibility of sanctioning defectors diminishes. Strategies of reciprocity become more difficult to implement without triggering a collapse of cooperation. In two-person games, tit-for-tat works well because the costs of defection are focused on only one other party. If defection imposes costs on all parties in an N-person game, however, the power of strategies of reciprocity is undermined. The infeasibility of sanctioning defectors creates the possibility of free-riding. What happens if we increase the number of actors in the iterated Prisoners' Dilemma from 2 to 20? Confession by any one of them could lead to the conviction of all on the major charge; therefore, the threat to retaliate against defection in the present with defection in the future will impose costs on all prisoners, and could lead to wholesale defection in subsequent rounds. For example, under the 1914 system of alliances, retaliation against one member of the alliance was the equivalent of retaliation against all. In N-person games, a strategy of conditional defection can have the effect of spreading, rather than containing, defection.

## B. Strategies of Institutionalization and Decomposition

Given a large number of players, what strategies can states use to increase the likelihood of cooperation? Regime creation can increase the likelihood of cooperation in N-person games. First, conventions provide rules of thumb that can diminish transaction and information costs. Second, collective enforcement mechanisms both decrease the likelihood of autonomous defection and permit selective punishment of violators of norms. These two functions of international regimes directly address problems created by large numbers of players. For example, Japan and the members of NATO profess a mutual interest in limiting flows of militarily useful goods and technology to the Soviet Union. Obviously, all suppliers of militarily useful goods and technology must cooperate to deny the Soviet Union access to such items. Although governments differ in their assessment of the military value of some goods and technologies, there is consensus on a rather lengthy list of prohibited items. By facilitating agreement of the prohibited list, the Coordinating Committee on the Consultative Group of NATO (CoCom) provides a relatively clear definition of what exports would constitute defection. By defining the scope of defection, the CoCom list forestalls the necessity of retaliation against nations that ship technology or goods that do not fall within the consensual definition of defection. Generally, cooperation is a prerequisite of regime creation. The creation of rules of thumb and mechanisms of collective enforcement and the maintenance and administration of regimes can demand an extraordinary degree of cooperation. This problem may limit the range of situations susceptible to modification through regimist strategies.

What strategies can reduce the number of significant players in a game and thereby render cooperation more likely? When governments are unable to cooperate on a global scale, they often turn to discriminatory strategies to encourage bilateral or regional cooperation. Tactics of decomposition across actors can, at times, improve the prospects for cooperation. Both the possibilities and the limits of strategies to reduce the number of players are evident in the discussions that follow. First, reductions in the number of actors can usually be purchased at the expense of the magnitude of gains from cooperation. The benefits of regional openness are smaller than the gains from global openness. A bilateral clearing arrangement is less economically efficient than a multilateral clearing arrangement. Strategies to reduce the number of players in a game generally diminish the gains from cooperation while they increase the likelihood and robustness of cooperation. Second, strategies to reduce the number of players generally impose substantial costs on third parties. These externalities may motivate third parties to undermine the limited area of cooperation or may serve as an impetus for a third party to enlarge the zone of cooperation. In the 1930s, for example, wholesale resort to discriminatory trading policies facilitated creation of exclusive zones of commercial openness. When confronted by a shrinking market share, Great Britain adopted a less liberal and more discriminatory commercial policy in order to secure preferential access to its empire and to undermine preferential agreements between other countries. As the American market share diminished, the United States adopted a more liberal and more discriminatory commercial policy to increase its access to export markets. It is not possible, however, to reduce the number of players in all situations. For example, compare the example of limited commercial openness with the example of a limited strategic embargo. To reduce the number of actors in a trade war, market access can simply be offered to only one country and withheld from others. By contrast, defection by only one supplier can permit the target of a strategic embargo to obtain a critical technology. These problems may limit the range of situations susceptible to modification through strategies that reduce the number of players in games.

## NOTES

1. For examples, see Robert Jervis, "Cooperation under the Security Dilemma," *World Politics* 30 (January 1978), pp. 167–214; Oliver E. Williamson, "Credible Commitments: Using Hostages to Support Exchange," *American Economic Review* (September 1983), pp. 519–40; John Gerard Ruggie, "International Regimes, Transactions, and Change: Embedded Liberalism in the Postwar Economic Order," in Stephen D. Krasner, ed., *International Regimes* (Ithaca, N.Y.: Cornell University Press, 1983).

2. For orthodox game-theoretic analyses of the importance of iteration, see R. Duncan Luce and Howard Raiffa, *Games and Decisions* (New York: Wiley, 1957), Appendix 8, and David M. Kreps, Paul Milgram, John Roberts, and Robert Wilson, "Rational Cooperation in Finitely-Repeated Prisoner's Dilemma," *Journal of Economic Theory* 27 (August 1982), pp. 245–52. For the results of laboratory experiments, see Robert Radlow, "An Experimental Study of Cooperation in the Prisoners' Dilemma Game," *Journal of Conflict Resolution* 9 (June 1965), pp. 221–27. On the importance of indefinite iteration to the emergence of cooperation in business transactions, see Robert Telsor, "A Theory of Self-Enforcing Agreements," *Journal of Business* 53 (January 1980), pp. 27–44.

3. See Robert O. Keohane, *After Hegemony: Cooperation and Discord in the World Political Economy* (Princeton, N.J.: Princeton University Press, 1984), and Krasner (fn. 1).

4. See John A. C. Conybeare, "International Organization and the Theory of Property Rights," *International Organization* 34 (Summer 1980), pp. 307–34, and Kenneth A. Oye, "Belief Systems, Bargaining, and Breakdown: International Political Economy 1929–1936," Ph.D. diss. (Harvard University, 1983), chap. 3.

5. See Jervis (fn. 1); Ruggie (fn. 1); Timothy J. McKeown, "Firms and Tariff Regime Change: Explaining the Demand for Protection," *World Politics* 36 (January 1984),

pp. 215–33. On the effects of *ambiguity* of preferences on the prospects of cooperation, see the concluding sections of Jervis (fn. 1).

6. Haas, Williams, and Babai, *Scientists and World Order: The Uses of Technical Knowledge in International Organizations* (Berkeley: University of California Press, 1977).
7. Williamson (fn. 1).
8. See John Newhouse, *Cold Dawn: The Story of SALT I* (New York: Holt, Rinehart & Winston, 1973).
9. See Haas, "Words Can Hurt You; Or Who Said What to Whom About Regimes," in Krasner (fn. 1).
10. See Anatol Rapoport and Albert Chammah, *Prisoners' Dilemma* (Ann Arbor: University of Michigan Press, 1965), and subsequent essays in *Journal of Conflict Resolution*.
11. See Alexander L. George, *Managing U.S.–Soviet Rivalry: Problems of Crisis Prevention* (Boulder, Colo.: Westview, 1983).
12. Schelling, *Strategy of Conflict* (Cambridge, Mass.: Harvard University Press, 1960), pp. 43–46.
13. See Mancur Olson, Jr., *The Logic of Collective Action: Public Goods and the Theory of Groups* (Cambridge, Mass.: Harvard University Press, 1965), and Mancur Olson and Richard Zeckhauser, "An Economic Theory of Alliances," *Review of Economics and Statistics* 48 (August 1966), pp. 266–79. For a recent elegant summary and extension of the large literature on dilemmas of collective action, see Russell Hardin, *Collective Action* (Baltimore: Johns Hopkins University Press, 1982).
14. See Kenneth N. Waltz, "The Stability of a Bipolar World," *Daedalus* 93 (Summer 1964), and Richard N. Rosecrance, "Bipolarity, Multipolarity, and the Future," *Journal of Conflict Resolution* (September 1966), pp. 314–27.
15. On hegemony, see Robert Gilpin, *U.S. Power and the Multinational Corporation* (New York: Basic Books, 1975), pp. 258–59. On duopoly, see Timothy McKeown, "Hegemonic Stability Theory and 19th-Century Tariff Levels in Europe," *International Organization* 37 (Winter 1983), pp. 73–91.
16. See Keohane (fn. 3), chap. 6, for extensions of these points.

# Kant, Liberal Legacies, and Foreign Affairs

## MICHAEL W. DOYLE

## I

What difference do liberal principles and institutions make to the conduct of the foreign affairs of liberal states? A thicket of conflicting judgments suggests that the legacies of liberalism have not been clearly appreciated. For many citizens of liberal states, liberal principles and institutions have so fully absorbed domestic politics that their influence on foreign affairs tends to be either overlooked altogether or, when perceived, exaggerated. Liberalism becomes either unselfconsciously patriotic or inherently "peace-loving." For many scholars and diplomats, the relations among independent states appear to differ so significantly from domestic politics that influences of liberal principles and domestic liberal institutions are denied or denigrated. They judge that international relations are governed by perceptions of national security and the balance of power; liberal principles and institutions, when they do intrude, confuse and disrupt the pursuit of balance-of-power politics.

Although liberalism is misinterpreted from both these points of view, a crucial aspect of the liberal legacy is captured by each. Liberalism is a distinct ideology and set of institutions that has shaped the perceptions of and capacities for foreign relations of political societies that range from social welfare or social democratic to laissez faire. It defines much of the content of the liberal patriot's nationalism. Liberalism does appear to disrupt the pursuit of balance-of-power politics. Thus its foreign relations cannot be adequately explained (or prescribed) by a sole reliance on the balance of power. But liberalism is not inherently "peace-loving"; nor is it consistently restrained or peaceful in intent. Furthermore, liberal practice may reduce the probability that states will successfully exercise the consistent restraint and peaceful intentions that a world peace may well require in the nuclear age. Yet the peaceful intent and restraint that liberalism does manifest in limited aspects of its foreign affairs announces the possibility of a world peace this side of the grave or of world conquest. It has strengthened the prospects for a world peace established by the steady expansion of a separate peace among liberal societies. . . .

From Michael W. Doyle, "Kant, Liberal Legacies, and Foreign Affairs, Part 1," *Philosophy & Public Affairs*, Vol. 12, No. 3 (Summer 1983), pp. 205–232. Reprinted by permission of Blackwell Publishing.

# II

Liberalism has been identified with an essential principle—the importance of the freedom of the individual. Above all, this is a belief in the importance of moral freedom, of the right to be treated and a duty to treat others as ethical subjects, and not as objects or means only. This principle has generated rights and institutions.

A commitment to a threefold set of rights forms the foundation of liberalism. Liberalism calls for freedom from arbitrary authority, often called "negative freedom," which includes freedom of conscience, a free press and free speech, equality under the law, and the right to hold, and therefore to exchange, property without fear of arbitrary seizure. Liberalism also calls for those rights necessary to protect and promote the capacity and opportunity for freedom, the "positive freedoms." Such social and economic rights as equality of opportunity in education and rights to health care and employment, necessary for effective self-expression and participation, are thus among liberal rights. A third liberal right, democratic participation or representation, is necessary to guarantee the other two. To ensure that morally autonomous individuals remain free in those areas of social action where public authority is needed, public legislation has to express the will of the citizens making laws for their own community.

These three sets of rights, taken together, seem to meet the challenge that Kant identified:

> To organize a group of rational beings who demand general laws for their survival, but of whom each inclines toward exempting himself, and to establish their constitution in such a way that, in spite of the fact their private attitudes are opposed, these private attitudes mutually impede each other in such a manner that [their] public behavior is the same as if they did not have such evil attitudes.[1]

But the dilemma within liberalism is how to reconcile the three sets of liberal rights. The right to private property, for example, can conflict with equality of opportunity and both rights can be violated by democratic legislation. During the 180 years since Kant wrote, the liberal tradition has evolved two high roads to individual freedom and social order; one is laissez-faire, or "conservative," liberalism and the other is social welfare, or social democratic, or "liberal," liberalism. Both reconcile these conflicting rights (though in differing ways) by successfully organizing free individuals into a political order.

The political order of laissez-faire and social welfare liberals is marked by a shared commitment to four essential institutions. First, citizens possess juridical equality and other fundamental civil rights such as freedom of religion and the press. Second, the effective sovereigns of the state are representative legislatures deriving their authority from the consent of the electorate and exercising their authority free from all restraint apart from the requirement that basic civic rights be preserved. Most pertinently for the impact of liberalism on foreign affairs, the state is subject to neither the external authority of other states nor to the internal authority of special prerogatives held, for example, by monarchs or military castes over foreign policy. Third, the economy rests on a recognition of the rights of private property including the ownership of means of production. Property is justified by individual acquisition (for example, by labor) or by social agreement or social utility. This excludes state socialism or state capitalism, but it need not exclude market socialism or various forms of the mixed economy. Fourth, economic decisions are predominantly shaped by the forces of supply and demand, domestically and internationally, and are free from strict control by bureaucracies. . . .

## III

In foreign affairs liberalism has shown, as it has in the domestic realm, serious weaknesses. But unlike liberalism's domestic realm, its foreign affairs have experienced startling but less than fully appreciated successes. Together they shape an unrecognized dilemma, for both these successes and weaknesses in large part spring from the same cause: the international implications of liberal principles and institutions.

The basic postulate of liberal international theory holds that states have the right to be free from foreign intervention. Since morally autonomous citizens hold rights to liberty, the states that democratically represent them have the right to exercise political independence. Mutual respect for these rights then becomes the touchstone of international liberal theory. When states respect each other's rights, individuals are free to establish private international ties without state interference. Profitable exchange between merchants and educational exchanges among scholars then create a web of mutual advantages and commitments that bolsters sentiments of public respect.

These conventions of mutual respect have formed a cooperative foundation for relations among liberal democracies of a remarkably effective kind. *Even though liberal states have become involved in numerous wars with nonliberal states, constitutionally secure liberal states have yet to engage in war with one another.*[2] No one should argue that such wars are impossible; but preliminary evidence does appear to indicate that there exists a significant predisposition against warfare between liberal states. Indeed, threats of war also have been regarded as illegitimate. A liberal zone of peace, a pacific union, has been maintained and has expanded despite numerous particular conflicts of economic and strategic interest. . . .

Statistically, war between any two states (in any single year or other short period of time) is a low probability event. War between any two adjacent states, considered over a long period of time, may be somewhat more probable. The apparent absence of war among the more clearly liberal states, whether adjacent or not, for almost two hundred years thus has some significance. Politically more significant, perhaps, is that, when states are forced to decide, by the pressure of an impinging world war, on which side of a world contest they will fight, liberal states wind up all on the same side, despite the real complexity of the historical, economic, and political factors that affect their foreign policies. And historically, we should recall that medieval and early modern Europe were the warring cockpits of states, wherein France and England and the Low Countries engaged in near constant strife. Then in the late eighteenth century there began to emerge liberal regimes. At first hesitant and confused, and later clear and confident as liberal regimes gained deeper domestic foundations and longer international experience, a pacific union of these liberal states became established.

The realist model of international relations, which provides a plausible explanation of the general insecurity of states, offers little guidance in explaining the pacification of the liberal world. Realism, in its classical formation, holds that the state is and should be formally sovereign, effectively unbounded by individual rights nationally and thus capable of determining its own scope of authority. (This determination can be made democratically, oligarchically, or autocratically.) Internationally, the sovereign state exists in an anarchical society in which it is radically independent, neither bounded nor protected by international "law" or treaties or duties, and hence, insecure. Hobbes, one of the seventeenth-century founders of the realist approach, drew the international implications of realism when he argued that the existence of international anarchy, the very independence of states, best accounts for the competition, the fear, and the temptation toward preventive war that characterize international relations. Politics among nations is not a continuous combat, but it is in this view a "state of war . . . a tract of time, wherein the will to contend by battle is sufficiently known."[3] . . .

Finding that all states, including liberal states, do engage in war, the realist concludes that the effects of differing domestic regimes (whether liberal or not) are overridden by the international anarchy under which all states live.[4] . . . But the ends that shape the international state of war are decreed for the realist by the anarchy of the international order and the fundamental quest for power that directs the policy of all states, irrespective of differences in their domestic regimes. As Rousseau argued, international peace therefore depends on the abolition of international relations either by the achievement of a world state or by a radical isolationism (Corsica). Realists judge neither to be possible.

Recent additions to game theory specify some of the circumstances under which prudence could lead to peace. Experience; geography; expectations of cooperation and belief patterns; and the differing payoffs to cooperation (peace) or conflict associated with various types of military technology all appear to influence the calculus.[5] But when it comes to acquiring the techniques of peaceable interaction, nations appear to be slow, or at least erratic, learners. The balance of power (more below) is regarded as a primary lesson in the realist primer, but centuries of experience did not prevent either France (Louis XIV, Napoleon I) or Germany (Wilhelm II, Hitler) from attempting to conquer Europe, twice each. Yet some, very new, black African states appear to have achieved a twenty-year-old system of impressively effective standards of mutual toleration. These standards are not completely effective (as in Tanzania's invasion of Uganda); but they have confounded expectations of a scramble to redivide Africa.[6] Geography—"insular security" and "continental insecurity"—may affect foreign policy attitudes; but it does not appear to determine behavior, as the bellicose records of England and Japan suggest. Beliefs, expectations, and attitudes of leaders and masses should influence strategic behavior. . . . Nevertheless, it would be difficult to determine if liberal leaders have had more peaceable attitudes than leaders who lead nonliberal states. But even if one did make that discovery, he also would have to account for why these peaceable attitudes only appear to be effective in relations with other liberals (since wars with nonliberals have not been uniformly defensive). . . .

Second, at the level of social determinants, some might argue that relations among any group of states with similar social structures or with compatible values would be peaceful. But again, the evidence for feudal societies, communist societies, fascist societies, or socialist societies does not support this conclusion. Feudal warfare was frequent and very much a sport of the monarchs and nobility. There have not been enough truly totalitarian, fascist powers (nor have they lasted long enough) to test fairly their pacific compatibility; but fascist powers in the wider sense of nationalist, capitalist, military dictatorships fought each other in the 1930s. Communist powers have engaged in wars more recently in East Asia. And we have not had enough socialist societies to consider the relevance of socialist pacification. The more abstract category of pluralism does not suffice. Certainly Germany was pluralist when it engaged in war with liberal states in 1914; Japan as well in 1941. But they were not liberal.

And third, at the level of interstate relations, neither specific regional attributes nor historic alliances or friendships can account for the wide reach of the liberal peace. The peace extends as far as, and no further than, the relations among liberal states, not including nonliberal states in an otherwise liberal region (such as the north Atlantic in the 1930s) nor excluding liberal states in a nonliberal region (such as Central America or Africa).

At this level, Raymond Aron has identified three types of interstate peace: empire, hegemony, and equilibrium.[7] An empire generally succeeds in creating an internal peace, but this is not an explanation of peace among independent liberal states. Hegemony can create peace by over-awing potential rivals. Although far from perfect and certainly precarious, United States hegemony, as Aron notes, might account for the interstate peace in South America in the postwar period during the height of the Cold War conflict. However, the liberal peace cannot be attributed merely to effective international policing by a predominant hegemon—Britain in the nineteenth century, the United States in the postwar period. Even though a hegemon might well have an interest in enforcing a peace for the sake of commerce or investments or as a means of enhancing its prestige or security, hegemons such as seventeenth-century France were not peace-enforcing police, and the liberal peace persisted in the interwar period when international society lacked a predominant hegemonic power. Moreover, this explanation overestimates hegemonic control in both periods. Neither England nor the United States was able to prevent direct challenges to its interests (colonial competition in the nineteenth century, Middle East diplomacy and conflicts over trading with the enemy in the postwar period). Where then was the capacity to prevent all armed conflicts between liberal regimes, many of which were remote and others strategically or economically insignificant? Liberal hegemony and leadership are important, but they are not sufficient to explain a liberal peace. . . .

Finally, some realists might suggest that the liberal peace simply reflects the absence of deep conflicts of interest among liberal states. Wars occur outside the liberal zone because conflicts of interest are deeper there. But this argument does nothing more than raise the question of why liberal states have fewer or less fundamental conflicts of interest with other liberal states than liberal states have with nonliberal, or nonliberal states have with other nonliberals. We must therefore examine the workings of liberalism among its own kind—a special pacification of the "state of war" resting on liberalism and nothing either more specific or more general.

# IV

Most liberal theorists have offered inadequate guidance in understanding the exceptional nature of liberal pacification. Some have argued that democratic states would be inherently peaceful simply and solely because in these states citizens rule the polity and bear the costs of wars. Unlike monarchs, citizens are not able to indulge their aggressive passions and have the consequences suffered by someone else. Other liberals have argued that laissez-faire capitalism contains an inherent tendency toward rationalism, and that, since war is irrational, liberal capitalisms will be pacifistic. Others still, such as Montesquieu, claim that "commerce is the cure for the most destructive prejudices," and "Peace is the natural effect of trade."[8] While these developments can help account for the liberal peace, they do not explain the fact that liberal states are peaceful only in relations with other liberal states. France and England fought expansionist, colonial wars throughout the nineteenth century (in the 1830s and 1840s against Algeria and China); the United States fought a similar war with Mexico in 1848 and intervened again in 1914 under president Wilson. Liberal states are as aggressive and war prone as any other form of government or society in their relations with nonliberal states.

Immanuel Kant offers the best guidance. "Perpetual Peace," written in 1795, predicts the ever-widening pacification of the liberal pacific union, explains that pacification, and at the same time suggests why liberal states are not pacific in their relations with nonliberal states. . . .

Kant shows how republics, once established, lead to peaceful relations. He argues that once the aggressive interests of absolutist monarchies are tamed and once the habit of respect for individual rights is engrained by republican government, wars would appear as the disaster to the people's welfare that he and the other liberals thought them to be. The fundamental reason is this:

> If the consent of the citizens is required in order to decide that war should be declared (and in this constitution it cannot but be the case), nothing is more natural than that they would be very cautious in commencing such a poor game, decreeing for themselves all the calamities of war. Among the latter would be: having to fight, having to pay the costs of war from their own resources, having painfully to repair the devastation war leaves behind, and, to fill up the measure of evils, load themselves with a heavy national debt that would embitter peace itself and that can never be liquidated on account of constant wars in the future. But, on the other hand, in a constitution which is not republican, and under which the subjects are not citizens, a declaration of war is the easiest thing in the world to decide upon, because war does not require of the ruler, who is the proprietor and not a member of the state, the least sacrifice of the pleasure of his table, the chase, his country houses, his court functions, and the like. He may, therefore, resolve on war as on a pleasure party for the most trivial reasons, and with perfect indifference leave the justification which decency requires to the diplomatic corps who are ever ready to provide it.[9]

One could add to Kant's list another source of pacification specific to liberal constitutions. The regular rotation of office in liberal democratic polities is a nontrivial device that helps ensure that personal animosities among heads of government provide no lasting, escalating source of tension.

These domestic republican restraints do not end war. If they did, liberal states would not be warlike, which is far from the case. They do introduce Kant's "caution" in place of monarchical caprice. Liberal wars are only fought for popular, liberal purposes. To see how this removes the occasion of wars among liberal states and not wars between liberal and nonliberal states, we need to shift our attention from constitutional law to international law, Kant's second source.

Complementing the constitutional guarantee of caution, *international law* adds a second source—a guarantee of respect. The separation of nations that asocial sociability encourages is reinforced by the development of separate languages and religions. These further guarantee a world of separate states—an essential condition needed to avoid a "global, soul-less despotism." Yet, at the same time, they also morally integrate liberal states "as culture progresses and men gradually come closer together toward a greater agreement on principles for peace and understanding."[10] As republics emerge (the first source) and as culture progresses, an understanding of the legitimate rights of all citizens and of all republics comes into play; and this, now that caution characterizes policy, sets up the moral foundations for the liberal peace. Correspondingly, international law highlights the importance of Kantian publicity. Domestically, publicity helps ensure that the officials of republics act according to the principles they profess to hold just and according to the interests of the electors they claim to represent. Internationally, free speech and the effective communication of accurate conceptions of the political life of foreign peoples is essential to establish and preserve the understanding on which the guarantee of respect depends. In short, domestically just republics, which rest on consent, presume foreign republics to be also consensual, just, and therefore deserving of accommodation. The experience of cooperation helps engender further cooperative behavior when the consequences of state policy are unclear but (potentially) mutually beneficial.[11]

Lastly, *cosmopolitan law* adds material incentives to moral commitments. The cosmopolitan right to hospitality permits the "spirit of commerce" sooner or later to take hold of every nation, thus impelling states to promote peace and to try to avert war.

Liberal economic theory holds that these cosmopolitan ties derive from a cooperative international division of labor and free trade according to comparative advantage. Each economy is said to be better off than it would have been under autarky; each thus acquires an incentive to avoid policies that would lead the other to break these economic ties. Since keeping open markets rests upon the assumption that the next set of transactions will also be determined by prices rather than coercion, a sense of mutual security is vital to avoid security-motivated searches for economic autarky. Thus, avoiding a challenge to another liberal state's security or even enhancing each other's security by means of alliance naturally follows economic interdependence.

A further cosmopolitan source of liberal peace is that the international market removes difficult decisions of production and distribution from the direct sphere of state policy. A foreign state thus does not appear directly responsible for these outcomes; states can stand aside from, and to some degree above, these contentious market rivalries and be ready to step in to resolve crises. Furthermore, the interdependence of commerce and the connections of state officials help create crosscutting transnational ties that serve as lobbies for mutual accommodation. According to modern liberal scholars, international financiers and transnational, bureaucratic, and domestic organizations create interests in favor of accommodation and have ensured by their variety that no single conflict sours an entire relationship.[12]

No one of these constitutional, international or cosmopolitan sources is alone sufficient, but together (and only where together) they plausibly connect the characteristics of liberal politics and economies with sustained liberal peace. Liberal states have not escaped from the realists' "security dilemma," the insecurity caused by anarchy in the world political system considered as a whole. But the effects of international anarchy have been tamed in the relations among states of a similarly liberal character. Alliances of purely mutual strategic interest among liberal and nonliberal states have been broken, economic ties between liberal and nonliberal states have proven fragile, but the political bond of liberal rights and interests has proven a remarkably firm foundation for mutual nonaggression. A separate peace exists among liberal states.

## NOTES

1. Immanuel Kant, "Perpetual Peace" (1795), in *The Philosophy of Kant*, ed. Carl J. Friedrich (New York: Modern Library, 1949), p. 453.
2. There appear to be some exceptions to the tendency for liberal states not to engage in a war with each other. Peru and Ecuador, for example, entered into conflict. But for each, the war came within one to three years after the establishment of a liberal regime, that is, before the pacifying effects of liberalism could become deeply ingrained. The Palestinians and the Israelis clashed frequently along the Lebanese border, which Lebanon could not hold secure from either belligerent. But at the beginning of the 1967 War, Lebanon seems to have sent a flight of its own jets into Israel. The jets were repulsed. Alone among Israel's Arab neighbors, Lebanon engaged in no further hostilities with Israel. Israel's recent attack on the territory of Lebanon was an attack on a country that had already been occupied by Syria (and the P.L.O.). Whether Israel actually will withdraw (if Syria withdraws) and restore an independent Lebanon is yet to be determined.
3. Thomas Hobbes, *Leviathan* (New York: Penguin, 1980), I, chap. 13, 62, p. 186.
4. Kenneth N. Waltz, *Man, the State, and War* (New York: Columbia University Press, 1954, 1959), pp. 120–23; and see his *Theory of International Politics* (Reading, Mass.: Addison-Wesley, 1979). The classic sources of this form of Realism are Hobbes and, more particularly, Rousseau's "Essay on St. Pierre's Peace Project" and his "State of War" in *A Lasting Peace* (London: Constable, 1917), E. H. Carr's *The Twenty Year's Crisis: 1919–1939* (London: Macmillan & Co., 1951), and the works of Hans Morgenthau.
5. Jervis, "Cooperation under the Security Dilemma," *World Politics* 30, no. 1 (January 1978), pp. 172–86.
6. Robert H. Jackson and Carl G. Rosberg, "Why West Africa's Weak States Persist," *World Politics* 35, No. 1 (October 1962).
7. Raymond Aron, *Peace and War* (New York: Praeger, 1968), pp. 151–54.
8. The incompatibility of democracy and war is forcefully asserted by Paine in *The Rights of Man*. The connection between liberal capitalism, democracy, and peace is argued by,

among others, Joseph Schumpeter in *Imperialism and Social Classes* (New York: Meridian, 1955); and Montesquieu, *Spirit of the Laws* I, bk. 20, chap. 1. This literature is surveyed and analyzed by Albert Hirschman, "Rival Interpretations of Market Society: Civilizing, Destructive, or Feeble?" *Journal of Economic Literature* 20 (December 1982).

9. Immanuel Kant, "Perpetual Peace," in *The Enlightenment,* ed. Peter Gay (New York: Simon & Schuster, 1974), pp. 790–92.

10. Kant, *The Philosophy of Kant,* p. 454. These factors also have a bearing on Karl Deutsch's "compatibility of values" and "predictability of behavior."

11. A highly stylized version of this effect can be found in the realist's "Prisoners' Dilemma" game. There, a failure of mutual trust and the incentives to enhance one's own position produce a noncooperative solution that makes both parties worse off. Contrarily, cooperation, a commitment to avoid exploiting the other party, produces joint gains. The significance of the game in this context is the character of its participants. The "prisoners" are presumed to be felonious, unrelated apart from their partnership in crime, and lacking in mutual trust—competitive nation-states in an anarchic world. A similar game between fraternal or sororal twins—Kant's republics—would be likely to lead to different results. See Robert Jervis, "Hypotheses on Misperception," *World Politics* 20, No. 3 (April 1968), for an exposition of the role of presumptions; and "Cooperation under the Security Dilemma," *World Politics* 30, No. 2 (January 1978), for the factors realists see as mitigating the security dilemma caused by anarchy.

    Also, expectations (including theory and history) can influence behavior, making liberal states expect (and fulfill) pacific policies toward each other. These effects are explored at a theoretical level in R. Dacey, "Some Implications of 'Theory Absorption' for Economic Theory and the Economics Information," in *Philosophical Dimensions of Economics,* ed. J Pitt (Dordrecht, Holland: D. Reidel, 1980).

12. Karl Polanyi, *The Great Transformation* (Boston: Beacon Press, 1944), chaps. 1–2 and Samuel Huntington and Z. Brzezinski, *Political Power: USA/USSR* (New York: Viking Press, 1963, 1964), chap. 9. And see Richard Neustadt, *Alliance Politics* (New York: Columbia University Press, 1970) for a detailed case study of interliberal politics.

TABLE 1 ■ WARS INVOLVING LIBERAL REGIMES

| Period | Liberal regimes and the pacific union (by date "liberal")[a] | Total number |
|---|---|---|
| 18th century | Swiss Cantons[b]<br>French Republic 1790–1795<br>  the United States[b] 1776– | 3 |
| 1800–1850 | Swiss Confederation, the United States<br>France 1830–1849<br>Belgium 1830–<br>Great Britain 1832–<br>Netherlands 1848–<br>Piedmont 1848–<br>Denmark 1849– | 8 |
| 1850–1900 | Switzerland, the United States, Belgium, Great Britain,<br>  Netherlands<br>Piedmont 1861, Italy 1861–<br>Denmark 1866<br>Sweden 1864–<br>Greece 1864–<br>Canada 1867–<br>France 1871–<br>Argentina 1880–<br>Chile 1891– | 13 |
| 1900–1945 | Switzerland, the United States, Great Britain, Sweden,<br>  Canada<br>Greece 1911, 1928–1936<br>Italy 1922<br>Belgium 1940<br>Netherlands 1940<br>Argentina 1943<br>France 1940<br>Chile 1924, 1932<br>Australia 1901–<br>Norway 1905–1940<br>New Zealand 1907–<br>Colombia 1910–1949<br>Denmark 1914–1940<br>Poland 1917–1935<br>Latvia 1922–1934<br>Germany 1918–1932<br>Austria 1918–1934<br>Estonia 1919–1934<br>Finland 1919–<br>Uruguay 1919–<br>Costa Rica 1919–<br>Czechoslovakia 1920–1939<br>Ireland 1920–<br>Mexico 1928–<br>Lebanon 1944– | 29 |

TABLE 1  ■  (Continued)

| Period | Liberal regimes and the pacific union (by date "liberal")[a] | Total number |
|---|---|---|
| 1945[c] | Switzerland, the United States, Great Britain, Sweden, Canada, Australia, New Zealand, Finland, Ireland, Mexico | 49 |
| | Uruguay 1973 | |
| | Chile 1973 | |
| | Lebanon 1975 | |
| | Costa Rica 1948, 1953– | |
| | Iceland 1944– | |
| | France 1945– | |
| | Denmark 1945– | |
| | Norway 1945– | |
| | Austria 1945– | |
| | Brazil 1945–1954, 1955–1964 | |
| | Belgium 1946– | |
| | Luxemburg 1946– | |
| | Netherlands 1946– | |
| | Italy 1946– | |
| | Philippines 1946–1972 | |
| | India 1947–1975, 1977– | |
| | Sri Lanka 1948–1961, 1963–1977, 1978– | |
| | Ecuador 1948–1963, 1979– | |
| | Israel 1949– | |
| | West Germany 1949– | |
| | Peru 1950–1962, 1963–1968, 1980– | |
| | El Salvador 1950–1961 | |
| | Turkey 1950–1960, 1966–1971 | |
| | Japan 1951– | |
| | Bolivia 1956–1969 | |
| | Colombia 1958– | |
| | Venezuela 1959– | |
| | Nigeria 1961–1964, 1979– | |
| | Jamaica 1962– | |
| | Trinidad 1962– | |
| | Senegal 1963– | |
| | Malaysia 1963– | |
| | South Korea 1963–1972 | |
| | Botswana 1966– | |
| | Singapore 1965– | |
| | Greece 1975– | |
| | Portugal 1976– | |
| | Spain 1978– | |
| | Dominican Republic 1978– | |

[a] I have drawn up this approximate list of "Liberal Regimes" according to the four institutions described as essential: market and private property economies; politics that are extremely sovereign; citizens who possess juridical rights; and "republican" (whether republican or monarchical),

representative, government. This latter includes the requirement that the legislative branch have an effective role in public policy and be formally and competitively, either potentially or actually, elected. Furthermore, I have taken into account whether male suffrage is wide (that is, 30 percent) or open to "achievement" by inhabitants (for example, to poll-tax payers or householders) of the national or metropolitan territory. Female suffrage is granted within a generation of its being demanded; and representative government is internally sovereign (for example, including and especially over military and foreign affairs) as well as stable (in existence for at least three years).

[b] There are domestic variations within these liberal regimes. For example, Switzerland was liberal only in certain cantons; the United States was liberal only north of the Mason-Dixon line until 1865, when it became liberal throughout. These lists also exclude ancient "republics," since none appear to fit Kant's criteria. See Stephen Holmes, "Aristippus in and out of Athens," *American Political Science Review* 73, No. 1 (March 1979).

[c] Selected list, excludes liberal regimes with populations less than one million.

*Sources:* Arthur Banks and W. Overstreet, eds., *The Political Handbook of the World*, 1980 (New York: McGraw-Hill, 1980; Foreign and Commonwealth Office. *A Year Book of the Commonwealth* 1980 (London: HMSO, 1980); *Europa Yearbook* 1981 (London: Europe, 1981); W. L. Langer, *An Encyclopedia of World History* (Boston: Houghton-Mifflin, 1968); Department of State, *Country Reports on Human Rights Practices* (Washington, D.C.: U.S. Government Printing Office, 1981); and *Freedom at Issue*, No. 54 (January–February 1980).

## TABLE 2  ■  INTERNATIONAL WARS LISTED CHRONOLOGICALLY

| | |
|---|---|
| British-Maharattan (1817–1818) | Franco-Mexican (1862–1867) |
| Greek (1821–1828) | Ecuadorian-Colombian (1863) |
| Franco-Spanish (1823) | Second Polish (1863–1864) |
| First Anglo-Burmese (1823–1826) | Spanish-Santo Dominican (1863–1865) |
| Japanese (1825–1830) | Second Schleswig-Holstein (1864) |
| Russo-Persian (1826–1828) | Lopez (1864–1870) |
| Russo-Turkish (1828–1829) | Spanish-Chilean (1865–1866) |
| First Polish (1831) | Seven Weeks (1866) |
| First Syrian (1831–1832) | Ten Years (1868–1878) |
| Texan (1835–1836) | Franco-Prussian (1870–1871) |
| First British-Afghan (1838–1842) | Dutch-Achinese (1873–1878) |
| Second Syrian (1839–1840) | Balkan (1875–1877) |
| Franco-Algerian (1839–1847) | Russo-Turkish (1877–1878) |
| Peruvian-Bolivian (1841) | Bosnian (1878) |
| First British-Sikh (1845–1846) | Second British-Afghan (1878–1880) |
| Mexican-American (1846–1848) | Pacific (1879–1880) |
| Austro-Sardinian (1848–1849) | British-Zulu (1879) |
| First Schleswig-Holstein (1848–1849) | Franco-Indochinese (1882–1884) |
| Hungarian (1848–1849) | Mahdist (1882–1885) |
| Second British-Sikh (1848–1849) | Sino-French (1884–1885) |
| Roman Republic (1849) | Central American (1885) |
| La Plata (1851–1852) | Serbo-Bulgarian (1885) |
| First Turco-Montenegran (1852–1853) | Sino-Japanese (1894–1895) |
| Crimean (1853–1856) | Franco-Madagascan (1894–1895) |
| Sepoy (1857–1859) | Cuban (1895–1896) |
| Second Turco-Montenegran (1858–1859) | Italo-Ethiopian (1895–1896) |
| Italian Unification (1859) | First Philippine (1896–1898) |
| Spanish-Moroccan (1859–1860) | Greco-Turkish (1897) |
| Italo-Roman (1860) | Spanish-American (1898) |
| Italo-Sicilian (1860–1861) | Second Philippine (1899–1902) |

**TABLE 2 ■ (Continued)**

| | |
|---|---|
| Boer (1899–1902) | Palestine (1948–1949) |
| Boxer Rebellion (1900) | Hyderabad (1948) |
| Ilinden (1903) | Madagascan (1947–1948) |
| Russo-Japanese (1904–1905) | First Kashmir (1947–1949) |
| Central American (1906) | Korean (1950–1953) |
| Central American (1907) | Algerian (1954–1962) |
| Spanish-Moroccan (1909–1910) | Russo-Hungarian (1956) |
| Italo-Turkish (1911–1912) | Sinai (1956) |
| First Balkan (1912–1913) | Tibetan (1956–1959) |
| Second Balkan (1913) | Sino-Indian (1962) |
| World War I (1914–1918) | Vietnamese (1965–1975) |
| Russian Nationalities (1917–1921) | Second Kashmir (1965) |
| Russo-Polish (1919–1920) | Six Day (1967) |
| Hungarian-Allies (1919) | Israeli-Egyptian (1969–1970) |
| Greco-Turkish (1919–1922) | Football (1969) |
| Riffian (1921–1926) | Bangladesh (1971) |
| Druze (1925–1927) | Philippine-MNLF (1972–) |
| Sino-Soviet (1929) | Yom Kippur (1973) |
| Manchurian (1931–1933) | Turco-Cypriot (1974) |
| Chaco (1932–1935) | Ethiopian-Eritrean (1974–) |
| Italo-Ethiopian (1935–1936) | Vietnamese-Cambodian (1975–) |
| Sino-Japanese (1937–1941) | Timor (1975–) |
| Changkufeng (1938) | Saharan (1975–) |
| Nomohan (1939) | Ogaden (1976–) |
| World War II (1939–1945) | Ugandan-Tanzanian (1978–1979) |
| Russo-Finnish (1939–1940) | Sino-Vietnamese (1979) |
| Franco-Thai (1940–1941) | Russo-Afghan (1979–1989) |
| Indonesian (1945–1946) | Irani-Iraqi (1980–1988) |
| Indochinese (1945–1954) | |

* Table 2 is from Melvin Small and J. David Singer, *Resort to Arms*, pp. 79–80. Copyright © 1982 by Sage Publications, Inc. Reprinted by permission of Sage Publications, Inc. This is a partial list of international wars fought between 1816 and 1980. In Appendices A and B of *Resort to Arms*, Small and Singer identify a total of 575 wars in this period, but approximately 159 of them appear to be largely domestic or civil wars.

This definition of war excludes covert interventions, some of which have been directed by liberal regimes against other liberal regimes. One example is the United States' effort to destabilize the Chilean election and Allende's government. Nonetheless, it is significant . . . that such interventions are not pursued publicly as acknowledged policy. The covert destabilization campaign against Chile is recounted in U.S. Congress, Senate, Select Committee to Study Governmental Operations with Respect to Intelligence Activities, *Covert Action in Chile*, 1963–73, 94th Congress, 1st Session (Washington, D.C.: U.S. Government Printing Office, 1975).

# Alliances: Balancing and Bandwagoning

## STEPHEN M. WALT

When confronted by a significant external threat, states may either balance or bandwagon. *Balancing* is defined as allying with others against the prevailing threat; *bandwagoning* refers to alignment with the source of danger. Thus two distinct hypotheses about how states will select their alliance partners can be identified on the basis of whether the states ally against or with the principal external threat.[1]

These two hypotheses depict very different worlds. If balancing is more common than bandwagoning, then states are more secure, because aggressors will face combined opposition. But if bandwagoning is the dominant tendency, then security is scarce, because successful aggressors will attract additional allies, enhancing their power while reducing that of their opponents. . . .

## BALANCING BEHAVIOR

The belief that states form alliances in order to prevent stronger powers from dominating them lies at the heart of traditional balance-of-power theory. According to this view, states join alliances to protect themselves from states or coalitions whose superior resources could pose a threat. States choose to balance for two main reasons.

First, they place their survival at risk if they fail to curb a potential hegemon before it becomes too strong. To ally with the dominant power means placing one's trust in its continued benevolence. The safer strategy is to join with those who cannot readily dominate their allies, in order to avoid being dominated by those who can. As Winston Churchill explained Britain's traditional alliance policy: "For four hundred years the foreign policy of England has been to oppose the strongest, most aggressive, most dominating power on the Continent. . . . [I]t would have been easy . . . and tempting to join with the stronger and share the fruits of his conquest. However, we always took the harder course, joined with the less strong powers, . . . and thus defeated the Continental military tyrant whoever he was."[2] More recently, Henry Kissinger advocated a rapprochement with China, because he believed that in a triangular relationship, it was better to align with the weaker side.

Second, joining the weaker side increases the new member's influence within the alliance, because the weaker side has greater need for assistance. Allying with the strong side, by contrast, gives the new member little influence (because it adds relatively less to the coalition) and leaves it vulnerable to the whims of its partners. Joining the weaker side should be the preferred choice.

## BANDWAGONING BEHAVIOR

The belief that states will balance is unsurprising, given the many familiar examples of states joining together to resist a threatening state or coalition. Yet, despite the powerful evidence that history provides in support of the balancing hypothesis, the belief that the opposite response is more likely is widespread. According to one scholar: "In international politics, nothing succeeds like success. Momentum accrues to the gainer and accelerates his movement. The appearance of irreversibility in his gains enfeebles one side and stimulates the other all the more. The bandwagon collects those on the sidelines."[3]

The bandwagoning hypothesis is especially popular with statesmen seeking to justify overseas involvements or increased military budgets. For example, German admiral Alfred von Tirpitz's famous risk theory rested on this type of logic. By building a great battle fleet, Tirpitz argued, Germany could force England into neutrality or alliance with her by posing a threat to England's vital maritime supremacy.

Bandwagoning beliefs have also been a recurring theme throughout the Cold War. Soviet efforts to intimidate both Norway and Turkey into not joining NATO reveal the Soviet conviction that states will accommodate readily to threats, although these moves merely encouraged Norway and Turkey to align more closely with the West.[4] Soviet officials made a similar error in believing that the growth of Soviet military power in the 1960s and 1970s would lead to a permanent shift in the correlation of forces against the West. Instead, it contributed to a Sino-American rapprochement in the 1970s and the largest peacetime increase in U.S. military power in the 1980s.

American officials have been equally fond of bandwagoning notions. According to NSC–68, the classified study that helped justify a major U.S. military buildup in the 1950s: "In the absence of an affirmative decision [to increase U.S. military capabilities] . . . our friends will become more than a liability to us, they will become a positive increment to Soviet power."[5] President John F. Kennedy once claimed that "if the United States were to falter, the whole world . . . would inevitably begin to move toward the Communist bloc."[6] And though Henry Kissinger often argued that the United States should form balancing alliances to contain the Soviet Union, he apparently believed that U.S. allies were likely to bandwagon. As he put it, "If leaders around the world . . . assume that the U.S. lacked either the forces or the will . . . they will accommodate themselves to what they will regard as the dominant trend."[7] Ronald Reagan's claim, "If we cannot defend ourselves [in Central America] . . . then we cannot expect to prevail elsewhere. . . . [O]ur credibility will collapse and our alliances will crumble," reveals the same logic in a familiar role—that of justifying overseas intervention.[8]

Balancing and bandwagoning are usually framed solely in terms of capabilities. Balancing is alignment with the weaker side, bandwagoning with the stronger. This conception should be revised, however, to account for the other factors that statesmen consider when deciding with whom to ally. Although power is an important part of the equation, it is not the only one. It is more accurate to say that states tend to ally with or against the foreign power that poses the greatest threat. For example, states may balance by allying with other strong states if a weaker power is more dangerous for other reasons. Thus the coalitions that defeated Germany in World War I and World War II were vastly superior in total resources, but they came together when it became clear that the aggressive aims of the Wilhelmines and Nazis posed the greater danger. Because balancing and bandwagoning are more accurately viewed as a response to threats, it is important to consider other factors that will affect the level of threat that states may pose: aggregate power, geographic proximity, offensive power, and aggressive intentions. . . .

By defining the basic hypotheses in terms of threats rather than power alone, we gain a more complete picture of the factors that statesmen will consider when making alliance choices. One cannot determine a priori, however, which sources of threat will be most important in any given case; one can say only that all of them are likely to play a role. And the greater the threat, the greater the probability that the vulnerable state will seek an alliance.

## THE IMPLICATIONS OF BALANCING AND BANDWAGONING

The two general hypotheses of balancing and bandwagoning paint starkly contrasting pictures of international politics. Resolving the question of which hypothesis is more accurate is especially important, because each implies very different policy prescriptions. What sort of world does each depict, and what policies are implied?

If balancing is the dominant tendency, then threatening states will provoke others to align against them. Because those who seek to dominate others will attract widespread opposition, status quo states can take a relatively sanguine view of threats. Credibility is less important in a balancing world, because one's allies will resist threatening states out of their own self-interest, not because they expect others to do it for them. Thus the fear of allies defecting will decline. Moreover, if balancing is the norm and if statesmen understand this tendency, aggression will be discouraged because those who contemplate it will anticipate resistance.

In a balancing world, policies that convey restraint and benevolence are best. Strong states may be valued as allies because they have much to offer their partners, but they must take particular care to avoid appearing aggressive. Foreign and defense policies that minimize the threat one poses to others make the most sense in such a world.

A bandwagoning world, by contrast, is much more competitive. If states tend to ally with those who seem most dangerous, then great powers will be rewarded if they appear both strong and potentially aggressive. International rivalries will be more intense, because a single defeat may signal the decline of one side and the ascendancy of the other. This situation is especially alarming in a bandwagoning world, because additional defections and a further decline in position are to be expected. Moreover, if statesmen believe that bandwagoning is widespread, they will be more inclined to use force. This tendency is true for both aggressors and status quo powers. The former will use force because they will assume that others will be unlikely to balance against them and because they can attract more allies through belligerence or brinkmanship. The latter will follow suit because they will fear the gains their opponents will make by appearing powerful and resolute.[9]

Finally, misperceiving the relative propensity to balance or bandwagon is dangerous, because the policies that are appropriate for one situation will backfire in the other. If statesmen follow the balancing prescription in a bandwagoning world, their moderate responses and relaxed view of threats will encourage their allies to defect, leaving them isolated against an overwhelming coalition. Conversely, following the bandwagoning prescription in a world of balancers (employing power and threats frequently) will lead others to oppose you more and more vigorously.[10]

These concerns are not merely theoretical. In the 1930s, France failed to recognize that her allies in the Little Entente were prone to bandwagon, a tendency that French military and diplomatic policies reinforced. As noted earlier, Soviet attempts to intimidate Turkey and Norway after World War II reveal the opposite error; they merely provoked a greater U.S. commitment to these regions and cemented their entry into NATO. Likewise, the self-encircling bellicosity of Wilhelmine Germany and Imperial Japan reflected the assumption, prevalent in both states, that bandwagoning was the dominant tendency in international affairs.

## WHEN DO STATES BALANCE? WHEN DO THEY BANDWAGON?

These examples highlight the importance of identifying whether states are more likely to balance or bandwagon and which sources of threat have the greatest impact on the decision. . . . In general, we should expect balancing behavior to be much more common than bandwagoning, and we should expect bandwagoning to occur only under certain identifiable conditions.

Although many statesmen fear that potential allies will align with the strongest side, this fear receives little support from most of international history. For example, every attempt to achieve hegemony in Europe since the Thirty Years' War has been thwarted by a defensive coalition formed precisely for the purpose of defeating the potential hegemon. Other examples are equally telling. Although isolated cases of bandwagoning do occur, the great powers have shown a remarkable tendency to ignore other temptations and follow the balancing prescription when necessary.

This tendency should not surprise us. Balancing should be preferred for the simple reason that no statesman can be completely sure of what another will do. Bandwagoning is dangerous because it increases the resources available to a threatening power and requires placing trust in its continued forbearance. Because perceptions are unreliable and intentions can change, it is safer to balance against potential threats than to rely on the hope that a state will remain benevolently disposed.

But if balancing is to be expected, bandwagoning remains a possibility. Several factors may affect the relative propensity for states to select this course.

## Strong versus Weak States

In general, the weaker the state, the more likely it is to bandwagon rather than balance. This situation occurs because weak states add little to the strength of a defensive coalition but incur the wrath of the more threatening states nonetheless. Because weak states can do little to affect the outcome (and may suffer grievously in the process), they must choose the winning side. Only when their decision can affect the outcome is it rational for them to join the weaker alliance. By contrast, strong states can turn a losing coalition into a winning one. And because their decision may mean the difference between victory and defeat, they are likely to be amply rewarded for their contribution.

Weak states are also likely to be especially sensitive to proximate power. Where great powers have both global interests and global capabilities, weak states will be concerned primarily with events in their immediate vicinity. Moreover, weak states can be expected to balance when threatened by states with roughly equal capabilities but they will be tempted to bandwagon when threatened by a great power. Obviously, when the great power is capable of rapid and effective action (i.e., when its offensive capabilities are especially strong), this temptation will be even greater.

## The Availability of Allies

States will also be tempted to bandwagon when allies are simply unavailable. This statement is not simply tautological, because states may balance by mobilizing their own resources instead of relying on allied support. They are more likely to do so, however, when they are confident that allied assistance will be available. Thus a further prerequisite for balancing behavior is an effective system of diplomatic communication. The ability to communicate enables potential allies to recognize their shared interests and coordinate their responses. If weak states see no possibility of outside assistance, however, they may be forced to accommodate the most imminent threat. Thus the first Shah of Iran saw the British withdrawal from Kandahar in 1881 as a signal to bandwagon with Russia. As he told the British representative, all he had received from Great Britain was "good advice and honeyed words—nothing else."[11] Finland's policy of partial alignment with the Soviet Union suggests the same lesson. When Finland joined forces with Nazi Germany during World War II, it alienated the potential allies (the United States and Great Britain) that might otherwise have helped protect it from Soviet pressure after the war.

Of course, excessive confidence in allied support will encourage weak states to free-ride, relying on the efforts of others to provide security. Free-riding is the optimal policy for a weak state, because its efforts will contribute little in any case. Among the great powers, the belief that allies are readily available encourages buck-passing; states that are threatened strive to pass to others the burdens of standing up to the aggressor. Neither response is a form of bandwagoning, but both suggest that effective balancing behavior is more likely to occur when members of an alliance are not convinced that their partners are unconditionally loyal.

Taken together, these factors help explain the formation of spheres of influence surrounding the great powers. Although strong neighbors of strong states are likely to balance, small and weak neighbors of the great powers may be more inclined to bandwagon. Because they will be the first victims of expansion, because they lack the capabilities to stand alone, and because a defensive alliance may operate too slowly to do them much good, accommodating a threatening great power may be tempting.

## Peace and War

Finally, the context in which alliance choices are made will affect decisions to balance or bandwagon. States are more likely to balance in peacetime or in the early stages of a war, as they seek to deter or defeat the powers posing the greatest threat. But once the outcome appears certain, some will be tempted to defect from the losing side at an opportune moment. Thus both Rumania and Bulgaria allied with Nazi Germany initially and then abandoned Germany for the Allies, as the tides of war ebbed and flowed across Europe in World War II.

The restoration of peace, however, restores the incentive to balance. As many observers have noted, victorious coalitions are likely to disintegrate with the conclusion of peace. Prominent examples include Austria and Prussia after their war with Denmark in 1864, Britain and France after World War I, the Soviet Union and the United States after World War II, and China and Vietnam after the U.S. withdrawal from Vietnam. This recurring pattern provides further support for the proposition that balancing is the dominant tendency in international politics and that bandwagoning is the opportunistic exception.

## SUMMARY OF HYPOTHESES ON BALANCING AND BANDWAGONING

### Hypotheses on Balancing

1. *General form:* States facing an external threat will align with others to oppose the states posing the threat.
2. The greater the threatening state's aggregate power, the greater the tendency for others to align against it.
3. The nearer a powerful state, the greater the tendency for those nearby to align against it. Therefore, neighboring states are less likely to be allies than are states separated by at least one other power.
4. The greater a state's offensive capabilities, the greater the tendency for others to align against it. Therefore, states with offensively oriented military capabilities are likely to provoke other states to form defensive coalitions.
5. The more aggressive a state's perceived intentions, the more likely others are to align against that state.
6. Alliances formed during wartime will disintegrate when the enemy is defeated.

## Hypotheses on Bandwagoning

The hypotheses on bandwagoning are the opposite of those on balancing.

1. *General form:* States facing an external threat will ally with the most threatening power.
2. The greater a state's aggregate capabilities, the greater the tendency for others to align with it.
3. The nearer a powerful state, the greater the tendency for those nearby to align with it.
4. The greater a state's offensive capabilities, the greater the tendency for others to align with it.
5. The more aggressive a state's perceived intentions, the less likely other states are to align against it.
6. Alliances formed to oppose a threat will disintegrate when the threat becomes serious.

## Hypotheses on the Conditions Favoring Balancing or Bandwagoning

1. Balancing is more common than bandwagoning.
2. The stronger the state, the greater its tendency to balance. Weak states will balance against other weak states but may bandwagon when threatened by great powers.
3. The greater the probability of allied support, the greater the tendency to balance. When adequate allied support is certain, however, the tendency for free-riding or buck-passing increases.
4. The more unalterably aggressive a state is perceived to be, the greater the tendency for others to balance against it.
5. In wartime, the closer one side is to victory, the greater the tendency for others to bandwagon with it.

## NOTES

1. My use of the terms *balancing* and *bandwagoning* follows that of Kenneth Waltz (who credits it to Stephen Van Evera) in his *Theory of International Politics* (Reading, Mass., 1979). Arnold Wolfers uses a similar terminology in his essay "The Balance of Power in Theory and Practice," in *Discord and Collaboration: Essays on International Politics* (Baltimore, Md., 1962), pp. 122–24.
2. Winston S. Churchill, *The Second World War*, vol. 1: *The Gathering Storm* (Boston, 1948), pp. 207–8.
3. W. Scott Thompson, "The Communist International System," *Orbis* 20, no. 4 (1977).
4. For the effects of the Soviet pressure on Turkey, see George Lenczowski, *The Middle East in World Affairs*, 4th ed. (Ithaca, 1980), pp. 134–38; and Bruce R. Kuniholm, *The Origins of the Cold War in the Near East* (Princeton, N.J., 1980), pp. 355–78. For the Norwegian response to Soviet pressure, see Herbert Feis, *From Trust to Terror: The Onset of the*

*Cold War, 1945–50* (New York, 1970), p. 381; and Geir Lundestad, *America, Scandinavia, and the Cold War: 1945–1949* (New York, 1980), pp. 308–9.

5. NSC–68 ("United States Objectives and Programs for National Security"), reprinted in Gaddis and Etzold, *Containment*, p. 404. Similar passages can be found on pp. 389, 414, and 434.

6. Quoted in Seyom Brown, *The Faces of Power: Constancy and Change in United States Foreign Policy from Truman to Johnson* (New York, 1968), p. 217.

7. Quoted in U.S. House Committee on Foreign Affairs, *The Soviet Union and the Third World: Watershed in Great Power Policy?* 97th Cong., 1st sess., 1977, pp. 157–58.

8. *New York Times*, April 28, 1983, p. A12. In the same speech, Reagan also said: "If Central America were to fall, what would the consequences be for our position in Asia and Europe and for alliances such as NATO? . . . Which ally, which friend would trust us then?"

9. It is worth noting that Napoleon and Hitler underestimated the costs of aggression by assuming that their potential enemies would bandwagon. After Munich, for example, Hitler dismissed the possibility of opposition by claiming that British and French statesmen were "little worms." Napoleon apparently believed that England could not "reasonably make war on us unaided" and assumed that the Peace of Amiens guaranteed that England had abandoned its opposition to France. Because Hitler and Napoleon believed in a bandwagoning world, they were excessively eager to go to war.

10. This situation is analogous to Robert Jervis's distinction between the deterrence model and the spiral model. The former calls for opposition to a suspected aggressor, the latter for appeasement. Balancing and bandwagoning are the alliance equivalents of deterring and appeasing. See Robert Jervis, *Perception and Misperception in International Politics* (Princeton, N.J., 1976), chap. 3.

11. Quoted in C. J. Lowe, *The Reluctant Imperialists* (New York, 1967), p. 85.

# The Future of Diplomacy

## HANS J. MORGENTHAU

### FOUR TASKS OF DIPLOMACY

. . . Diplomacy [is] an element of national power. The importance of diplomacy for the preservation of international peace is but a particular aspect of that general function. For a diplomacy that ends in war has failed in its primary objective: the promotion of the national interest by peaceful means. This has always been so and is particularly so in view of the destructive potentialities of total war.

Taken in its widest meaning, comprising the whole range of foreign policy, the task of diplomacy is fourfold: (1) Diplomacy must determine its objectives in the light of the power actually and potentially available for the pursuit of these objectives. (2) Diplomacy must assess the objectives of other nations and the power actually and potentially available for the pursuit of these objectives. (3) Diplomacy must determine to what extent these different objectives are compatible with each other. (4) Diplomacy must employ the means suited to the pursuit of its objectives. Failure in any one of these tasks may jeopardize the success of foreign policy and with it the peace of the world.

A nation that sets itself goals which it has not the power to attain may have to face the risk of war on two counts. Such a nation is likely to dissipate its strength and not to be strong enough at all points of friction to deter a hostile nation from challenging it beyond endurance. The failure of its foreign policy may force the nation to retrace its steps and to redefine its objectives in view of its actual strength. Yet it is more likely that, under the pressure of an inflamed public opinion, such a nation will go forward on the road toward an unattainable goal, strain all its resources to achieve it, and finally, confounding the national interest with that goal, seek in war the solution to a problem that cannot be solved by peaceful means.

A nation will also invite war if its diplomacy wrongly assesses the objectives of other nations and the power at their disposal. . . . A nation that mistakes a policy of imperialism for a policy of the status quo will be unprepared to meet the threat to its own existence which the other nation's policy entails. Its weakness will invite attack and may make war inevitable. A nation that mistakes a policy of the status quo for a policy of imperialism will evoke through its disproportionate reaction the very danger of war which it is trying to avoid. For as A mistakes B's policy for imperialism, so B might mistake A's defensive reaction for imperialism. Thus both nations, each intent upon forestalling imaginary aggression from the other side,

From *Politics Among Nations*, 5th edition by Hans J. Morgenthau, copyright © 1972 by Alfred A. Knopf, a division of Random House, Inc. Used by permission of Alfred A. Knopf, a division of Random House, Inc.

will rush to arms. Similarly, the confusion of one type of imperialism with another may call for disproportionate reaction and thus evoke the risk of war.

As for the assessment of the power of other nations, either to overrate or to underrate it may be equally fatal to the cause of peace. By overrating the power of B, A may prefer to yield to B's demands until, finally, A is forced to fight for its very existence under the most unfavorable conditions. By underrating the power of B, A may become overconfident in its assumed superiority. A may advance demands and impose conditions upon B which the latter is supposedly too weak to resist. Unsuspecting B's actual power of resistance, A may be faced with the alternative of either retreating and conceding defeat or of advancing and risking war.

A nation that seeks to pursue an intelligent and peaceful foreign policy cannot cease comparing its own objectives and the objectives of other nations in the light of their compatibility. If they are compatible, no problem arises. If they are not compatible, nation A must determine whether its objectives are so vital to itself that they must be pursued despite that incompatibility with the objectives of B. If it is found that A's vital interests can be safeguarded without the attainment of these objectives, they ought to be abandoned. On the other hand, if A finds that these objectives are essential for its vital interests, A must then ask itself whether B's objectives, incompatible with its own, are essential for B's vital interests. If the answer seems to be in the negative, A must try to induce B to abandon its objectives, offering B equivalents not vital to A. In other words, through diplomatic bargaining, the give and take of compromise, a way must be sought by which the interests of A and B can be reconciled.

Finally, if the incompatible objectives of A and B should prove to be vital to either side, a way might still be sought in which the vital interests of A and B might be redefined, reconciled, and their objectives thus made compatible with each other. Here, however—even provided that both sides pursue intelligent and peaceful policies—A and B are moving dangerously close to the brink of war.

It is the final task of an intelligent diplomacy, intent upon preserving peace, to choose the appropriate means for pursuing its objectives. The means at the disposal of diplomacy are three: persuasion, compromise, and threat of force. No diplomacy relying only upon the threat of force can claim to be both intelligent and peaceful. No diplomacy that would stake everything on persuasion and compromise deserves to be called intelligent. Rarely, if ever, in the conduct of the foreign policy of a great power is there justification for using only one method to the exclusion of the others. Generally, the diplomatic representative of a great power, in order to be able to serve both the interests of his country and the interests of peace, must at the same time use persuasion, hold out the advantages of a compromise, and impress the other side with the military strength of his country.

The art of diplomacy consists in putting the right emphasis at any particular moment on each of these three means at its disposal. A diplomacy that has been successfully discharged in its other functions may well fail in advancing the national interest and preserving peace if it stresses persuasion when the give and take of compromise is primarily required by the circumstances of the case. A diplomacy that puts most of its eggs in the basket of compromise when the military might of the nation should be predominantly displayed, or stresses military might when the political situation calls for persuasion and compromise, will likewise fail. . . .

## The Promise of Diplomacy: Its Nine Rules[1]

Diplomacy could revive if it would part with [the] vices, which in recent years have well-nigh destroyed its usefulness, and if it would restore the techniques which have controlled the mutual relations of nations since time immemorial. By doing so, however, diplomacy would realize only one of the preconditions for the preservation of peace. The contribution of a revived diplomacy to the cause of peace would depend upon the methods and purposes of its use. . . .

We have already formulated the four main tasks with which a foreign policy must cope successfully in order to be able to promote the national interest and preserve peace. It remains for us now to reformulate those tasks in the light of the special problems with which contemporary world politics confront diplomacy. . . .

The main reason for [the] threatening aspect of contemporary world politics [lies] in the character of modern war, which has changed profoundly under the impact of nationalistic universalism° and modern technology. The effects of modern technology cannot be undone. The only variable that remains subject to deliberate manipulation is the new moral force of nationalistic universalism. The attempt to reverse the trend toward war through the techniques of a revived diplomacy must start with this phenomenon. That means, in negative terms, that a revived diplomacy will have a chance to preserve peace only when it is not used as the instrument of a political religion aiming at universal dominion.

### Four Fundamental Rules

**Diplomacy Must Be Divested of the Crusading Spirit**    This is the first of the rules that diplomacy can neglect only at the risk of war. In the words of William Graham Sumner:

> If you want war, nourish a doctrine. Doctrines are the most frightful tyrants to which men ever are subject, because doctrines get inside of a man's own reason and betray him against himself. Civilised men have done their fiercest fighting for doctrines. The reconquest of the Holy Sepulcher, "the balance of power," "no universal dominion," "trade follows the flag," "he who holds the land will hold the sea," "the throne and the altar," the revolution, the faith—these are the things for which men have given their lives. . . . Now when any doctrine arrives at that degree of authority, the name of it is a club which any demagogue may swing over you at any time and apropos of anything. In order to describe a doctrine, we must have recourse to theological language. A doctrine is an article of faith. It is something which you are bound to believe, not because you have some rational grounds for believing it is true, but because you belong to such and such a church or denomination. . . . A policy in a state we can understand; for instance, it was the policy of the United States at the end of the eighteenth century to get the free navigation of the Mississippi to its mouth, even at the expense of war with Spain. That policy had reason and justice in it; it was founded in our interests; it had positive form and definite scope. A doctrine is an abstract principle; it is necessarily absolute in its

---

° [Editors' Note: By this term Professor Morgenthau refers to the injection of ideology into international politics and to each nation's claim that its own ethical code would serve as the basis of international conduct for all nations.]

scope and abstruse in its terms; it is metaphysical assertion. It is never true, because it is absolute, and the affairs of men are all conditioned and relative. . . . Now to turn back to politics, just think what an abomination in statecraft an abstract doctrine must be. Any politician or editor can, at any moment, put a new extension on it. The people acquiesce in the doctrine and applaud it because they hear the politicians and editors repeat it, and the politicians and editors repeat it because they think it is popular. So it grows. . . . It may mean anything or nothing, at any moment, and no one knows how it will be. You accede to it now, within the vague limits of what you suppose it to be; therefore, you will have to accede to it tomorrow when the same name is made to cover something which you never have heard or thought of. If you allow a political catchword to go on and grow, you will awaken some day to find it standing over you, the arbiter of your destiny, against which you are powerless, as men are powerless against delusions. . . . What can be more contrary to sound statesmanship and common sense than to put forth an abstract assertion which has no definite relation to any interest of ours now at stake, but which has in it any number of possibilities of producing complications which we cannot foresee, but which are sure to be embarrassing when they arise![2]

The Wars of Religion have shown that the attempt to impose one's own religion as the only true one upon the rest of the world is as futile as it is costly. A century of almost unprecedented bloodshed, devastation, and barbarization was needed to convince the contestants that the two religions could live together in mutual toleration. The two political religions of our time have taken the place of the two great Christian denominations of the sixteenth and seventeenth centuries. Will the political religions of our time need the lesson of the Thirty Years' War, or will they rid themselves in time of the universalistic aspirations that inevitably issue in inconclusive war?

Upon the answer to that question depends the cause of peace. For only if it is answered in the affirmative can a moral consensus, emerging from shared convictions and common values, develop—a moral consensus within which a peace-preserving diplomacy will have a chance to grow. Only then will diplomacy have a chance to face the concrete political problems that require peaceful solution. If the objectives of foreign policy are not to be defined in terms of a world-embracing political religion, how are they to be defined? This is a fundamental problem to be solved once the crusading aspirations of nationalistic universalism have been discarded.

### The Objectives of Foreign Policy Must Be Defined in Terms of the National Interest and Must Be Supported with Adequate Power

This is the second rule of a peace-preserving diplomacy. The national interest of a peace-loving nation can only be defined in terms of national security, and national security must be defined as integrity of the national territory and of its institutions. National security, then, is the irreducible minimum that diplomacy must defend with adequate power without compromise. But diplomacy must ever be alive to the radical transformation that national security has undergone under the impact of the nuclear age. Until the advent of that age, a nation could use its diplomacy to purchase its security at the expense of another nation. Today, short of a radical change in the atomic balance of power in favor of a particular nation, diplomacy, in order to make one nation secure from nuclear destruction, must make them all secure. With the national interest defined in such restrictive and transcendent terms, diplomacy must observe the third of its rules.

**Diplomacy Must Look at the Political Scene from the Point of View of Other Nations** "Nothing is so fatal to a nation as an extreme of self-partiality, and the total want of consideration of what others will naturally hope or fear."[3] What are the national interests of other nations in terms of national security and are they compatible with one's own? The definition of the national interest in terms of national security is easier, and the interests of the two opposing nations are more likely to be compatible in a bipolar system than in any other system of the balance of power. The bipolar system, as we have seen, is more unsafe from the point of view of peace than any other, when both blocs are in competitive contact throughout the world and the ambition of both is fired by the crusading zeal of a universal mission. ". . . Vicinity, or nearness of situation, constitutes nations natural enemies."[4]

Yet once they have defined their national interests in terms of national security, they can draw back from their outlying positions, located close to, or within, the sphere of national security of the other side, and retreat into their respective spheres, each self-contained within its orbit. Those outlying positions add nothing to national security; they are but liabilities, positions that cannot be held in case of war. Each bloc will be the more secure the wider it makes the distance that separates both spheres of national security. Each side can draw a line far distant from each other, making it understood that to touch or even to approach it means war. What then about the interjacent spaces, stretching between the two lines of demarcation? Here the fourth rule of diplomacy applies.

**Nations Must Be Willing to Compromise on All Issues that Are Not Vital to Them**

> All government, indeed every human benefit and enjoyment, every virtue and every prudent act, is founded on compromise and barter. We balance inconveniences; we give and take; we remit some rights, that we may enjoy others; and we choose rather to be happy citizens than subtle disputants. As we must give away some natural liberties, for the advantages to be derived from the communion and fellowship of a great empire. But, in all fair dealings, the thing bought must bear some proportion to the purchase paid. None will barter away the immediate jewel of his soul.[5]

Here diplomacy meets its most difficult task. For minds not beclouded by the crusading zeal of a political religion and capable of viewing the national interests of both sides with objectivity, the delimitation of these vital interests should not prove too difficult. Compromise on secondary issues is a different matter. Here the task is not to separate and define interests that by their very nature already tend toward separation and definition, but to keep in balance interests that touch each other at many points and may be intertwined beyond the possibility of separation. It is an immense task to allow the other side a certain influence in those interjacent spaces without allowing them to be absorbed into the orbit of the other side. It is hardly a less immense task to keep the other side's influence as small as possible in the regions close to one's own security zone without absorbing those regions into one's own orbit. For the performance of these tasks, no formula stands ready for automatic application. It is only through a continuous process of adaptation, supported both by firmness and self-restraint, that compromise on secondary issues can be made to work. It is, however, possible to indicate a priori what approaches will facilitate or hamper the success of policies of compromise.

First of all, it is worth noting to what extent the success of compromise—that is, compliance with the fourth rule—depends upon compliance with the other three rules, which in turn are similarly interdependent. As the compliance with the second rule depends upon the realization of the first, so the third rule must await its realization from compliance with the second. A nation can only take a rational view of its national interests after it has parted company with the crusading spirit of a political creed. A nation is able to consider the national interests of the other side with objectivity only after it has become secure in what it considers its own national interests. Compromise on any issue, however minor, is impossible so long as both sides are not secure in their national interests. Thus nations cannot hope to comply with the fourth rule if they are not willing to comply with the other three. Both morality and expediency require compliance with these four fundamental rules.

Compliance makes compromise possible, but it does not assure its success. To give compromise, made possible through compliance with the first three rules, a chance to succeed, five other rules must be observed.

### Five Prerequisites of Compromise

***Give up the Shadow of Worthless Rights for the Substance of Real Advantage***
A diplomacy that thinks in legalistic and propagandistic terms is particularly tempted to insist upon the letter of the law, as it interprets the law, and to lose sight of the consequences such insistence may have for its own nation and for humanity. Since there are rights to be defended, this kind of diplomacy thinks that the issue cannot be compromised. Yet the choice that confronts the diplomat is not between legality and illegality, but between political wisdom and political folly. "The question with me," said Edmund Burke, "is not whether you have a right to render your people miserable, but whether it is not your interest to make them happy. It is not what a lawyer tells me I *may* do, but what humanity, reason and justice tell me I ought to do."[6]

***Never Put Yourself in a Position from Which You Cannot Retreat Without Losing Face and from Which You Cannot Advance Without Grave Risks***    The violation of this rule often results from disregard for the preceding one. A diplomacy that confounds the shadow of legal right with the actuality of political advantage is likely to find itself in a position where it may have a legal right, but no political business, to be. In other words, a nation may identify itself with a position, which it may or may not have a right to hold, regardless of the political consequences. And again compromise becomes a difficult matter. A nation cannot retreat from that position without incurring a serious loss of prestige. It cannot advance from that position without exposing itself to political risks, perhaps even the risk of war. That heedless rush into untenable positions and, more particularly, the stubborn refusal to extricate oneself from them in time is the earmark of incompetent diplomacy. Its classic examples are the policy of Napoleon III on the eve of the Franco-Prussian War of 1870 and the policies of Austria and Germany on the eve of the First World War. These examples also show how closely the risk of war is allied with the violation of this rule.

***Never Allow a Weak Ally to Make Decisions for You***   Strong nations that are oblivious to the preceding rules are particularly susceptible to violating this one. They lose their freedom of action by identifying their own national interests completely with those of the weak ally. Secure in the support of its powerful friend, the weak ally can choose the objectives and methods of its foreign policy to suit itself. The powerful nation then finds that it must support interests not its own and that it is unable to compromise on issues that are vital not to itself, but only to its ally.

The classic example of the violation of this rule is to be found in the way in which Turkey forced the hand of Great Britain and France on the eve of the Crimean War in 1853. The Concert of Europe had virtually agreed upon a compromise settling the conflict between Russia and Turkey, when Turkey, knowing that the Western powers would support it in a war with Russia, did its best to provoke that war and thus involved Great Britain and France in it against their will. Thus Turkey went far in deciding the issue of war and peace for Great Britain and France according to its own national interests. Great Britain and France had to accept that decision even though their national interests did not require war with Russia and they had almost succeeded in preventing its outbreak. They had surrendered their freedom of action to a weak ally, which used its control over their policies for its own purposes.

***The Armed Forces Are the Instrument of Foreign Policy, Not Its Master***
No successful and no peaceful foreign policy is possible without observance of this rule. No nation can pursue a policy of compromise with the military determining the ends and means of foreign policy. The armed forces are instruments of war; foreign policy is an instrument of peace. It is true that the ultimate objectives of the conduct of war and of the conduct of foreign policy are identical: Both serve the national interest. Both, however, differ fundamentally in their immediate objective, in the means they employ, and in the modes of thought they bring to bear upon their respective tasks.

The objective of war is simple and unconditional: to break the will of the enemy. Its methods are equally simple and unconditional: to bring the greatest amount of violence to bear upon the most vulnerable spot in the enemy's armor. Consequently, the military leader must think in absolute terms. He lives in the present and in the immediate future. The sole question before him is how to win victories as cheaply and quickly as possible and how to avoid defeat.

The objective of foreign policy is relative and conditional: to bend, not to break, the will of the other side as far as necessary in order to safeguard one's own vital interests without hurting those of the other side. The methods of foreign policy are relative and conditional: not to advance by destroying the obstacles in one's way, but to retreat before them, to circumvent them, to maneuver around them, to soften and dissolve them slowly by means of persuasion, negotiation, and pressure. In consequence, the mind of the diplomat is complicated and subtle. It sees the issue in hand as a moment in history, and beyond the victory of tomorrow it anticipates the incalculable possibilities of the future. In the words of Bolingbroke:

> Here let me only say, that the glory of taking towns, and winning battles, is to be measured by the utility that results from those victories. Victories that bring honour to the arms, may bring shame to the councils, of a nation. To win a battle, to take a town, is the glory of a general, and of an army. . . . But the glow of a nation is to proportion the ends she proposes, to her interest and her strength; the means she employs to the ends she proposes, and the vigour she exerts to both.[7]

To surrender the conduct of foreign affairs to the military, then, is to destroy the possibility of compromise and thus surrender the cause of peace. The military mind knows how to operate between the absolutes of victory and defeat. It knows nothing of that patient intricate and subtle maneuvering of diplomacy, whose main purpose is to avoid the absolutes of victory and defeat and meet the other side on the middle ground of negotiated compromise. A foreign policy conducted by military men according to the rules of the military art can only end in war, for "what we prepare for is what we shall get."[8]

For nations conscious of the potentialities of modern war, peace must be the goal of their foreign policies. Foreign policy must be conducted in such a way as to make the preservation of peace possible and not make the outbreak of war inevitable. In a society of sovereign nations, military force is a necessary instrument of foreign policy. Yet the instrument of foreign policy should not become the master of foreign policy. As war is fought in order to make peace possible, foreign policy should be conducted in order to make peace permanent. For the performance of both tasks, the subordination of the military under the civilian authorities which are constitutionally responsible for the conduct of foreign affairs is an indispensable prerequisite.

***The Government Is the Leader of Public Opinion, Not Its Slave***    Those responsible for the conduct of foreign policy will not be able to comply with the foregoing principles of diplomacy if they do not keep this principle constantly in mind. As has been pointed out above in greater detail, the rational requirements of good foreign policy cannot from the outset count upon the support of a public opinion whose preferences are emotional rather than rational. This is bound to be particularly true of a foreign policy whose goal is compromise, and which, therefore, must concede some of the objectives of the other side and give up some of its own. Especially when foreign policy is conducted under conditions of democratic control and is inspired by the crusading zeal of a political religion, statesmen are always tempted to sacrifice the requirements of good foreign policy to the applause of the masses. On the other hand, the statesmen who would defend the integrity of these requirements against even the slightest contamination with popular passion would seal his own doom as a political leader and, with it, the doom of his foreign policy, for he would lose the popular support which put and keeps him in power.

The statesman, then, is allowed neither to surrender to popular passions nor disregard them. He must strike a prudent balance between adapting himself to them and marshaling them to the support of his policies. In one word, he must lead. He must perform that highest feat of statesmanship: trimming his sails to the winds of popular passion while using them to carry the ship to the port of good foreign policy, on however roundabout and zigzag a course.

## CONCLUSION

The road to international peace which we have outlined cannot compete in inspirational qualities with the simple and fascinating formulae that for a century and a half have fired the imagination of a war-weary world. There is something spectacular in the radial simplicity of a formula that with one sweep seems to dispose of the problem of war once and for all. This has been the promise of such solutions as free trade, arbitration, disarmament, collective security, universal socialism, international government, and the world state. There is nothing spectacular, fascinating, or inspiring, at least for the people at large, in the business of diplomacy.

We have made the point, however, that these solutions, insofar as they deal with the real problem and not merely with some of its symptoms, presuppose the existence of an integrated international society, which actually does not exist. To bring into existence such an international society and keep it in being, the accommodating techniques of diplomacy are required. As the integration of domestic society and its peace develop from the unspectacular and almost unnoticed day-by-day operations of the techniques of accommodation and change, so the ultimate ideal of international life—that is, to transcend itself in a supranational society—must await its realization from the techniques of persuasion, negotiation, and pressure, which are the traditional instruments of diplomacy.

The reader who has followed us to this point may well ask: But has not diplomacy failed in preventing war in the past? To that legitimate question two answers can be given.

Diplomacy has failed many times, and it has succeeded many times, in its peace-preserving task. It has failed sometimes because nobody wanted it to succeed. We have seen how different in their objectives and methods the limited wars of the past have been from the total war of our time. When war was the normal activity of kings, the task of diplomacy was not to prevent it, but to bring it about at the most propitious moment.

On the other hand, when nations have used diplomacy for the purpose of preventing war, they have often succeeded. The outstanding example of a successful war-preventing diplomacy in modern times is the Congress of Berlin of 1878. By the peaceful means of an accommodating diplomacy, that Congress settled, or at least made susceptible of settlement, the issues that had separated Great Britain and Russia since the end of the Napoleonic Wars. During the better part of the nineteenth century, the conflict between Great Britain and Russia over the Balkans, the Dardanelles, and the Eastern Mediterranean hung like a suspended sword over the peace of the world. Yet, during the fifty years following the Crimean War, though hostilities between Great Britain and Russia threatened to break out time and again, they never actually did break out. The main credit for the preservation of peace must go to the techniques of an accommodating diplomacy which culminated in the Congress of Berlin. When British Prime Minister Disraeli returned from that Congress to London, he declared with pride that he was bringing home "peace . . . with honor." In fact, he had brought peace for later generations, too; for a century there has been no war between Great Britain and Russia.

We have, however, recognized the precariousness of peace in a society of sovereign nations. The continuing success of diplomacy in preserving peace depends, as we have seen, upon extraordinary moral and intellectual qualities that all the leading participants must possess. A mistake in the evaluation of one of the elements of national power, made by one or the other of the leading statesmen, may spell the difference between peace and war. So may an accident spoiling a plan or a power calculation.

Diplomacy is the best means of preserving peace which a society of sovereign nations has to offer, but, especially under the conditions of contemporary world politics and of contemporary war, it is not good enough. It is only when nations have surrendered to a higher authority the means of destruction which modern technology has put in their hands—when they have given up their sovereignty—that international peace can be made as secure as domestic peace. Diplomacy can make peace more secure than it is today, and the world state can make peace more secure than it would be if nations were to abide by the rules of diplomacy. Yet, as there can be no permanent peace without a world state, there can be no world state without the peace-preserving and community-building processes of diplomacy. For the world state to be more than a dim vision, the accommodating processes of diplomacy, mitigating and minimizing conflicts, must be revived. Whatever one's conception of the ultimate state of international affairs may be, in the recognition of that need and in the demand that it be met all men of good will can join.

## NOTES

1. We by no means intend to give here an exhaustive account of rules of diplomacy. We propose to discuss only those which seem to have a special bearing upon the contemporary situation.
2. "War." *Essays of William Graham Sumner* (New Haven, Conn.: Yale University Press, 1934), Vol. I, pp. 169 ff.
3. Edmund Burke, "Remarks on the Policy of the Allies with Respect to France" (1793), *Works*, Vol. IV (Boston: Little, Brown and Company, 1889), p. 447.
4. *The Federalist*, No. 6.
5. Edmund Burke, "Speech on the Conciliation with America," *loc. cit.*, Vol. II, p. 169.
6. "Speech on Conciliation with the Colonies" (1775), *The Works of Edmund Burke*, Vol. II (Boston: Little, Brown and Company, 1865), p. 140.
7. *Bolingbroke's Defense of the Treaty of Utrecht* (Cambridge: Cambridge University Press, 1932), p. 95.
8. William Graham Sumner, *op. cit.*, p. 173.

# The Uses and Limits of International Law

## STANLEY HOFFMANN

The student of international law who examines its functions in the present international system and in the foreign policy of states will, unless he takes refuge in the comforting seclusion from reality that the pure theory of law once provided, be reduced to one of three attitudes. He will become a cynic, if he chooses to stress, like Giraudoux in *Tiger at the Gates*, the way in which legal claims are shaped to support any position a state deems useful or necessary on nonlegal grounds, or if he gets fascinated by the combination of cacophony and silence that characterizes international law as a system of world public order. He will become a hypocrite, if he chooses to rationalize either the conflicting interpretations and uses of law by states as a somehow converging effort destined to lead to some such system endowed with sufficient stability and solidity, or else if he endorses one particular construction (that of his own statesmen) as a privileged and enlightened contribution to the achievement of such a system. He will be overcome by consternation, if he reflects upon the gap between, on the one hand, the ideal of a world in which traditional self-help will be at least moderated by procedures and rules made even more indispensable by the proliferation both of states and of lethal weapons, and, on the other hand, the realities of inexpiable conflicts, sacred egoisms, and mutual recriminations. . . .

1. Some of the functions of international law constitute *assets both for the policy maker and from the viewpoint of world order*, i.e., of providing the international milieu with a framework of predictability and with procedures for the transaction of interstate business.

    (a) International law is an instrument of *communication*. To present one's claims in legal terms means, 1, to signal to one's partner or opponent which "basic conduct norms" (to use Professor Scheinman's expression) one considers relevant or essential, and 2, to indicate which procedures one intends to follow and would like the other side to follow. At a time when both the size of a highly heterogeneous international milieu and the imperatives of prudence in the resort to force make communication essential and often turn international relations into a psychological contest, international law provides a kind of common language that does not amount to a common code of legitimacy yet can serve as a joint frame of reference. (One must however remember, 1, that communication is no guarantee against misperception, and 2, that what is being communicated may well determine the other side's response to the message: If "we" communicate to "them" an understanding of the situation that threatens their basic values or goals—like our interpretation of the war in South Vietnam as a case of aggression—there will be no joint frame of reference at all, and in fact the competition may become fiercer.)

(b) International law affords means of *channeling conflict*—of diverting inevitable tensions and clashes from the resort to force. Whenever there have been strong independent reasons for avoiding armed conflict—in an international system in which the superpowers in particular have excellent reasons for "managing" their confrontations, either by keeping them nonviolent, or by using proxies—international law has provided statesmen both with alibis for shunning force and with alternatives to violence. . . . In Berlin, both the Soviets and the West shaped their moves in such a way as to leave to the other side full responsibility for a first use of force, and to avoid the kind of frontal collision with the other side's legal claim that could have obliged the opponent to resort to force in order not to lose power or face. Thus, today as in earlier periods, law can indeed. . . serve as an alternative to confrontation whenever states are eager or forced to look for an alternative.

2. International law also plays various useful roles in the policy process, which however do not ipso facto contribute to world order. Here, we are concerned with *law as a tool of policy* in the competition of state visions, objectives, and tactics.

(a) The establishment of a network of rights and obligations, or the resort to legal arguments can be useful for the *protection or enhancement of a position*: if one wants to give oneself a full range of means with which to buttress a threatened status quo (cf. the present position of the West in Berlin; this is also what treaties of alliance frequently are for); if one wants to enhance one's power in a way that is demonstrably authorized by principles in international law (cf. Nasser's claim when he nationalized the Suez Canal, and Sukarno's invocation of the principle of self-determination against Malaysia); if one wants to restore a political position badly battered by an adversary's move, so that the resort to legal arguments becomes part of a strategy of restoring the status quo ante (Western position during the Berlin blockade; Kennedy's strategy during the Cuban missile crisis; Western powers' attempts during the first phase of the Suez crisis; Soviet tactics in the U.N. General Assembly debates on the financing of peace-keeping operations).

(b) In all those instances, policy makers use law as a way of putting pressure on an opponent by *mobilizing international support* behind the legal rules invoked: law serves as a focal point, as the tool for "internationalizing" a national interest and as the cement of a political coalition. States that may have political misgivings about pledging direct support to a certain power whose interests only partly coincide with theirs, or because they do not want to antagonize another power thereby, may find it both easier and useful to rally to the defense of a legal principle in whose maintenance or promotion they may have a stake.

(c) A policy maker who ignores international law leaves the field of political-competition-through-legal-manipulation open to his opponents or rivals. International law provides one of the numerous *chessboards* on which state contests occur.

3. Obviously, this indicates not only that to the statesmen international law provides an instrument rather than a guide for action, but also that this tool is often *not used*, when resort to it would hamper the state's interest as defined by the policy maker.

(a) One of the reasons why international law often serves as a technique of political mobilization is the appeal of reciprocity: "You must support my invocation of the rule against him, because if you let the rule be violated at my expense, someday it may be breached at yours; and we both have an interest in its preservation." But *reciprocity cuts both ways*: My using a certain legal argument to buttress my case against him may encourage him, now or later, to resort to the same argument against me; I may therefore be unwise to play on a chessboard in which, given the solemn and abstract nature of legal rights and obligations, I may not be able to make the kind of distinction between my (good) case and your (bad) one that can best be made by resort to ad hoc, political and circumstantial evidence that is irrelevant or ruled out in legal argumentation. Thus . . . during the Cuban crisis, when the United States tried to distinguish between Soviet missiles in Cuba and American ones in Turkey in order to build its case and get support, America's use of the OAS [Organization of American States] Charter as the legal basis for its "quarantine" established a dangerous precedent which the Soviets could use some day, against the U.S. or its allies, on behalf of the Warsaw Pact. And in the tragicomedy of the battle over Article 19 of the U.N. Charter, one reason why the U.S. finally climbed down from its high legal horse and gave up the attempt to deprive the Soviets of their right to vote, unless they paid their share, was the growing awareness of the peril which the principle of the exercise of the U.N. taxing power by the General Assembly could constitute some day for the United States if it lost control of the Assembly.

(b) One of the things that international law "communicates" is the solemnity of a commitment: a treaty, or a provision of the Charter, serves as a kind of tripwire or burglar alarm. When it fails to deter, the victim and third parties have a fateful choice between upholding the legal principle by all means, at the cost of a possible escalation in violence, and choosing to settle the dispute more peacefully, at the cost of *fuzzing the legal issue*. For excellent political reasons, the latter course is frequently adopted . . . in the form of dropping any reference to the legal principle at stake. . . .

(c) The very *ambiguity* of international law, which in many essential areas displays either gaping holes or conflicting principles, allows policy makers in an emergency to act as if international law were irrelevant—as if it were neither a restraint nor a guide. . . .

However, precisely because there is a legal chessboard for state competition, the fact that international law does not, in a crisis, really restrict one's freedom of action, does not mean that one will forgo legal rationalizations of the moves selected. Here we come to the last set of considerations about the role of law:

**4.** The resort to legal arguments by policy makers may be *detrimental to world order and thereby counterproductive for the state* that used such arguments.

(a) In the legal vacuum or confusion which prevails in areas as vital to states as internal war or the use of force, each state tries to justify its conduct with legal rationalizations. The result is a kind of *escalation of claims and counterclaims*, whose consequence, in turn, is both a further devaluation of international law and a "credibility gap" at the expense of those states who have debased·the currency. America's rather indiscriminate resort to highly debatable legal arguments to support its Vietnam policy is a case in point. The unsubtle reduction of international law to a mere storehouse of convenient *ex post* justifications (as in the case of British intervention at Suez, or American interventions in Santo Domingo and Vietnam) undermines the very pretense of contributing to world order with which these states have tried to justify their unilateral acts.

(b) Much of contemporary international law authorizes states to *increase their power*. In this connection, Nasser's nationalization of the Suez Canal Company was probably quite legal, and those who accept the rather tortured argument put forth by the State Department legal advisers to justify the Cuban "quarantine" have concluded that this partial blockade was authorized by the OAS Charter and not in contradiction with the U.N. Charter. Yet it is obvious that a full exploitation by all states of all permissions granted by international law would be a perfect recipe for chaos.

(c) *Attempts to enforce or to strengthen international law*, far from consolidating a system of desirable restraints on state (mis)behavior, may actually *backfire* if the political conditions are not ripe. This is the central lesson of the long story of the financing of U.N. peace-keeping operations. American self-intoxication with the importance of the rule of law, fed by misleading analogies between the U.N. Charter and the U.S. Constitution, resulted ultimately in a weakening of the influence of the World Court (which largely followed America's line of reasoning), and in an overplaying of America's hand during the "non-session" of the General Assembly in the fall of 1964 and winter of 1965.

These are sobering considerations. But what they tell us is not, as so many political scientists seem to believe, that international law is, at best, a farce, and, at worst, even a potential danger; what they tell us is that *the nature of the international system condemns international law to all the weaknesses and perversions that it is so easy to deride*. International law is merely a magnifying mirror that reflects faithfully and cruelly the essence and the logic of international politics. In a fragmented world, there is no "global perspective" from which anyone can authoritatively assess, endorse, or reject the separate national efforts at making international law serve national interests above all. Like the somber universe of Albert Camus' Caligula, this is a judgeless world where no one is innocent. . . .

The permanent plight of international law is that, now as before, it shows on its body of rules all the scars inflicted by the international state of war. The tragedy of contemporary international law is that of a double divorce: first, between the old liberal dream of a world rule of law, and the realities of an international system of multiple minidramas that always threaten to become major catastrophes; second, between the old dream and the new requirements of moderation which in the circumstances of the present system suggest a *down-playing* of formal law in the realm of peace-and-war issues, and an *upgrading* of more flexible techniques, until the system has become less fierce. The interest of international law for the political scientist is that there is no better way of grasping the continuing differences between order within a national society and the fragile order of international affairs than to study how and when states use legal language, symbols, and documents, and with what results. . . .

# International Institutions: Can Interdependence Work?

## ROBERT O. KEOHANE

To analyze world politics in the [current era] is to discuss international institutions: the rules that govern elements of world politics and the organizations that help implement those rules. . . . Under what conditions should China be admitted to the World Trade Organization (WTO)? How many billions of dollars does the International Monetary Fund (IMF) need at its disposal to remain an effective "lender of last resort" for countries such as Indonesia, Korea, and Thailand that were threatened in 1997 with financial collapse? Will the tentative Kyoto Protocol on Climate Change be renegotiated, ratified, and implemented effectively? Can future United Nations peacekeeping practices—in contrast to the UN fiascoes in Bosnia and Somalia—be made more effective?

These questions help illustrate the growing importance of international institutions for maintaining world order. . . . Superpowers need general rules because they seek to influence events around the world. Even an unchallenged superpower such as the United States would be unable to achieve its goals through the bilateral exercise of influence: the costs of such massive "arm-twisting" would be too great.

International institutions are increasingly important, but they are not always successful. Ineffective institutions such as the United Nations Industrial Development Organization or the Organization of African Unity exist alongside effectual ones such as the Montreal Protocol on Substances that Deplete the Ozone Layer and the European Union. In recent years, we have gained insight into what makes some institutions more capable than others—how such institutions best promote cooperation among states and what mechanics of bargaining they use. But our knowledge is incomplete, and as the world moves toward new forms of global regulation and governance, the increasing impact of international institutions has raised new questions about how these institutions themselves are governed.

## THEORY AND REALITY, 1919–89

Academic "scribblers" did not always have to pay much attention to international institutions. The 1919 Versailles Treaty constituted an attempt to construct an institution for multilateral diplomacy—the League of Nations. But the rejection of the

From Robert O. Keohane, "International Institutions: Can Interdependence Work?" *Foreign Policy*, issue #110 (Spring 1998), pp. 82–94. © 1998 by the Carnegie Endowment for International Peace. Reprinted with permission.

League Covenant by the U.S. Senate ensured that until World War II the most important negotiations in world politics—from the secret German-Russian deals of the 1920s to the 1938 Munich conference—took place on an ad hoc basis. Only after the United Nations was founded in 1945, with strong support from the United States and a multiplicity of specialized agencies performing different tasks, did international institutions begin to command substantial international attention. . . .

[After 1945], however, even the most powerful states [came to] rely increasingly on international institutions. . . . From the late 1960s onward, the Treaty on the Non-Proliferation of Nuclear Weapons was the chief vehicle for efforts to prevent the dangerous spread of nuclear weapons. NATO was not only the most successful multilateral alliance in history but also the most highly institutionalized, with a secretary-general, a permanent staff, and elaborate rules governing relations among members. From its founding in 1947 through the Uruguay Round that concluded in 1993, the General Agreement on Tariffs and Trade (GATT) presided over a series of trade rounds that have reduced import tariffs among industrialized countries by up to 90 percent, boosting international trade. After a shaky start in the 1940s, the IMF had—by the 1960s—become the centerpiece of efforts by the major capitalist democracies to regulate their monetary affairs. When that function atrophied with the onset of flexible exchange rates in the 1970s, it became their leading agent for financing and promoting economic development in Africa, Asia, and Latin America. The sheer number of inter-governmental organizations also rose dramatically—from about 30 in 1910 to 70 in 1940 to more than 1,000 by 1981.

The exchange rate and oil crises of the early 1970s helped bring perceptions in line with reality. Suddenly, both top policymakers and academic observers in the United States realized that global issues required systematic policy coordination and that such coordination required institutions. In 1974, then secretary of state Henry Kissinger, who had paid little attention to international institutions, helped establish the International Energy Agency to enable Western countries to deal cooperatively with the threat of future oil embargoes like the 1973 OPEC embargo of the Netherlands and United States. And the Ford administration sought to construct a new international monetary regime based on flexible rather than pegged exchange rates. Confronted with complex interdependence and the efforts of states to manage it, political scientists began to redefine the study of international institutions, broadening it to encompass what they called "international regimes"—structures of rules and norms that could be more or less informal. The international trade regime, for example, did not have strong formal rules or integrated, centralized management; rather, it provided a set of interlocking institutions, including regular meetings of the GATT contracting parties, formal dispute settlement arrangements, and delegation of technical tasks to a secretariat, which gradually developed a body of case law and practice. . . .

In the 1980s, research on international regimes moved from attempts to describe the phenomena of interdependence and international regimes to closer analysis of the conditions under which countries cooperate. How does cooperation occur among sovereign states and how do international institutions affect it? From the standpoint of political realism, both the reliance placed by states on certain international institutions and the explosion in their numbers were puzzling. Why should international institutions exist at all in a world dominated by sovereign states? This question seemed unanswerable if institutions were seen as opposed to, or above, the state but not if they were viewed as devices to help states accomplish their objectives.

The new research on international institutions broke decisively with legalism—the view that law can be effective regardless of political conditions—as well as with the idealism associated with the field's origins. Instead, scholars adopted the assumptions of realism, accepting that relative state power and competing interests were key factors in world politics, but at the same time drawing new conclusions about the influence of institutions on the process. Institutions create the capability for states to cooperate in mutually beneficial ways by reducing the costs of making and enforcing agreements—what economists refer to as "transaction costs." They rarely engage in centralized enforcement of agreements, but they do reinforce practices of reciprocity, which provide incentives for governments to keep their own commitments to ensure that others do so as well. Even powerful states have an interest, most of the time, in following the rules of well-established international institutions, since general conformity to rules makes the behavior of other states more predictable.

This scholarship drew heavily on the twin concepts of uncertainty and credibility. Theorists increasingly recognized that the preferences of states amount to "private information"—that absent full transparency, states are uncertain about what their partners and rivals value at any given time. They naturally respond to uncertainty by being less willing to enter into agreements, since they are unsure how their partners will later interpret the terms of such agreements. International institutions can reduce this uncertainty by promoting negotiations in which transparency is encouraged; by dealing with a series of issues over many years and under similar rules, thus encouraging honesty in order to preserve future reputation; and by systematically monitoring the compliance of governments with their commitments.

Even if a government genuinely desires an international agreement, it may be unable to persuade its partners that it will, in the future, be willing and able to implement it. Successful international negotiations may therefore require changes in domestic institutions. For instance, without "fast-track" authority on trade, the United States' negotiating partners have no assurance that Congress will refrain from adding new provisions to trade agreements as a condition for their ratification. Hence, other states are reluctant to enter into trade negotiations with the United States since they may be confronted, at the end of tortuous negotiations, with a redesigned agreement less favorable to them than the draft they initialed. By the same token, without fast-track authority, no promise by the U.S. government to abide by negotiated terms has much credibility, due to the president's lack of control over Congress.

In short, this new school of thought argued that, rather than imposing themselves on states, international institutions should respond to the demand by states for cooperative ways to fulfill their own purposes. By reducing uncertainty and the costs of making and enforcing agreements, international institutions help states achieve collective gains.

## YESTERDAY'S CONTROVERSIES: 1989–95

This new institutionalism was not without its critics, who focused their attacks on three perceived shortcomings: First, they claimed that international institutions are fundamentally insignificant since states wield the only real power in world politics. They emphasized the weakness of efforts by the UN or League of Nations to achieve collective security against aggression by great powers, and they pointed to the dominant role of major contributors in international economic organizations. Hence, any effects of these international institutions were attributed more to the efforts of their great power backers than to the institutions themselves.

This argument was overstated. Of course, great powers such as the United States exercise enormous influence within international institutions. But the policies that emerge from these institutions are different from those that the United States would have adopted unilaterally. . . . Where agreement by many states is necessary for policy to be effective, even the United States finds it useful to compromise on substance to obtain the institutional seal of approval. Therefore, the decision-making procedures and general rules of international institutions matter. They affect both the substance of policy and the degree to which other states accept it.

The second counterargument focused on "anarchy": the absence of a world government or effective international legal system to which victims of injustice can appeal. As a result of anarchy, critics argued, states prefer relative gains (i.e., doing better than other states) to absolute gains. They seek to protect their power and status and will resist even mutually beneficial cooperation if their partners are likely to benefit more than they are. For instance, throughout the American-Soviet arms race, both sides focused on their relative positions—who was ahead or threatening to gain a decisive advantage—rather than on their own levels of armaments. Similar dynamics appear on certain economic issues, such as the fierce Euro-American competition (i.e., Airbus Industrie versus Boeing) in the production of large passenger jets.

Scholarly disputes about the "relative gains question" were intense but short-lived. It turned out that the question needed to be reframed: not, "do states seek relative or absolute gains?" but "under what conditions do they forego even mutually beneficial cooperation to preserve their relative power and status?" When there are only two major players, and one side's gains may decisively change power relationships, relative gains loom large: in arms races, for example, or monopolistic competition (as between Airbus and Boeing). Most issues of potential cooperation, however, from trade liberalization to climate change, involve multilateral negotiations that make relative gains hard to calculate and entail little risk of decisive power shifts for one side over another. Therefore, states can be expected most of the time to seek to enhance their own welfare without being worried that others will also make advances. So the relative gains argument merely highlights the difficulties of cooperation where there is tough bilateral competition; it does not by any means undermine prospects for cooperation in general.

The third objection to theories of cooperation was less radical but more enduring. Theorists of cooperation had recognized that cooperation is not harmonious: it emerges out of discord and takes place through tough bargaining. Nevertheless, they claimed that the potential joint gains from such cooperation explained the dramatic increases in the number and scope of cooperative multilateral institutions. Critics pointed out, however, that bargaining problems could produce obstacles to achieving joint gains. For instance, whether the Kyoto Protocol will lead to a global agreement is questionable in part because developing countries refused to accept binding limits on their emissions and the U.S. Senate declared its unwillingness to ratify any agreement not containing such commitments by developing countries. Both sides staked out tough bargaining positions, hindering efforts at credible compromise. As a result of these bargaining problems, the fact that possible deals could produce joint gains does not assure that cooperative solutions will be reached. The tactics of political actors and the information they have available about one another are both key aspects of a process that does not necessarily lead to cooperation. Institutions may help provide "focal points," on which competing actors may agree, but new issues often lack such institutions. In this case, both the pace and the extent of cooperation become more problematic.

## TODAY'S DEBATES

The general problem of bargaining raises specific issues about how institutions affect international negotiations, which always involve a mixture of discord and potential cooperation. Thinking about bargaining leads to concerns about subjectivity, since bargaining depends so heavily on the beliefs of the parties involved. And the most fundamental question scholars wish to answer concerns effectiveness: What structures, processes, and practices make international institutions more or less capable of affecting policies—and outcomes—in desired ways?

The impact of institutional arrangements on bargaining remains puzzling. We understand from observation, from game theory, and from explorations of bargaining in a variety of contexts that outcomes depend on more than the resources available to the actors or the pay-offs they receive. Institutions affect bargaining patterns in complex and nuanced ways. Who, for example, has authority over the agenda? In the 1980s, Jacques Delors used his authority as head of the European Commission to structure the agenda of the European Community, thus leading to the Single European Act and the Maastricht Treaty. What voting or consensus arrangements are used and who interprets ambiguities? At the Kyoto Conference, agreement on a rule of "consensus" did not prevent the conference chair from ignoring objections as he gaveled through provision after provision in the final session. Can disgruntled participants block implementation of formally ratified agreements? In the GATT, until 1993, losers could prevent the findings of dispute resolution panels from being implemented; but in the WTO, panel recommendations take effect unless there is a consensus not to implement them. Asking such questions systematically about international institutions may well yield significant new insights in future years.

Institutional maneuvers take place within a larger ideological context that helps define which purposes such institutions pursue and which practices they find acceptable. The Mandates System of the League of Nations depended in part on specific institutional arrangements, but more fundamental was the shared understanding that continued European rule over non-European peoples was acceptable. No system of rule by Europeans over non-Europeans could remain legitimate after the collapse of that consensus during the 15 years following World War II. . . .

The procedures and rules of international institutions create informational structures. They determine what principles are acceptable as the basis for reducing conflicts and whether governmental actions are legitimate or illegitimate. Consequently, they help shape actors' expectations. For instance, trade conflicts are increasingly ritualized in a process of protesting in the WTO—promising tough action on behalf of one's own industries, engaging in quasi-judicial dispute resolution procedures, claiming victory if possible, or complaining about defeat when necessary. There is much sound and fury, but regularly institutionalized processes usually relegate conflict to the realm of dramatic expression. Institutions thereby create differentiated information. "Insiders" can interpret the language directed toward "outsiders" and use their own understandings to interpret, or manipulate, others' beliefs.

Finally, students of international institutions continue to try to understand why some institutions are so much more effective than others. Variation in the coherence of institutional policy or members' conformity with institutional rules is partially accounted for by the degree of common interests and the distribution of power among members. Institutions whose members share social values and have similar political systems—such as NATO or the European Union—are likely to be stronger than those such as the Organization for Security and Cooperation in Europe or the Association of South East Asian Nations, whose more diverse membership does not necessarily have the same kind of deep common interests. Additionally, the character of domestic politics, . . . has a substantial impact on international institutions. The distribution of power is also important. Institutions dominated by a small number of members—for example, the IMF, with its weighted voting system—can typically take more decisive action than those where influence is more widely diffused, such as the UN General Assembly.

## OVERCOMING THE DEMOCRATIC DEFICIT

Even as scholars pursue these areas of inquiry, they are in danger of overlooking a major normative issue: the "democratic deficit" that exists in many of the world's most important international institutions. As illustrated most recently by the far-reaching interventions of the IMF in East Asia, the globalization of the world economy and the expanding role of international institutions are creating a powerful form of global regulation. Major international institutions are increasingly laying down rules and guidelines that governments, if they wish to attract foreign investment and generate growth, must follow. But these international institutions are managed by technocrats and supervised by high governmental officials. That is, they are run by élites. Only in the most attenuated sense is democratic control exercised over major international organizations. Key negotiations in the WTO are made in closed sessions. The IMF negotiates in secret with potential borrowers, and it has only begun in the last few months to provide the conditions it imposes on recipients. . . .

Admittedly, democracy does not always work well. American politicians regularly engage in diatribes against international institutions, playing on the dismay of a vocal segment of their electorates at the excessive number of foreigners in the United Nations. More seriously, an argument can be made that the IMF, like central banks, can only be effective if it is insulated from direct democratic control. Ever since 1787, however, practitioners and theorists have explored how authoritative decision making can be combined with accountability to publics and indirect democratic control. The U.S. Constitution is based on such a theory—the idea that popular sovereignty, though essential, is best exercised indirectly, through rather elaborate institutions. An issue that scholars should now explore is how to devise international institutions that are not only competent and effective but also accountable, at least ultimately, to democratic publics.

One possible response is to say that all is well, since international institutions are responsible to governments—which, in turn, are accountable in democracies to their own people. International regulation simply adds another link to the chain of delegation. But long chains of delegation, in which the public affects action only at several removes, reduce actual public authority. If the terms of multilateral cooperation are to reflect the interests of broader democratic publics rather than just those of narrow élites, traditional patterns of delegation will have to be supplemented by other means of ensuring greater accountability to public opinion.

One promising approach would be to seek to invigorate transnational society in the form of networks among individuals and nongovernmental organizations. The growth of such networks—of scientists, professionals in various fields, and human rights and environmental activists—has been aided greatly by the fax machine and the Internet and by institutional arrangements that incorporate these networks into decision making. For example, natural and social scientists developed the scientific consensus underlying the Kyoto Protocol through the Intergovernmental Panel on Climate Change (IPCC) whose scientific work was organized by scientists who did not have to answer to any governments. The Kyoto Protocol was negotiated, but governments opposed to effective action on climate change could not hope to renegotiate the scientific guidelines set by the IPCC. . . .

Therefore, the future accountability of international institutions to their publics may rest only partly on delegation through formal democratic institutions. Its other pillar may be voluntary pluralism under conditions of maximum transparency. International policies may increasingly be monitored by loose groupings of scientists or other professionals, or by issue advocacy networks such as Amnesty International and Greenpeace, whose members, scattered around the world, will be linked even more closely by modern information technology. Accountability will be enhanced not only by chains of official responsibility, but by the requirement of transparency. Official actions, negotiated among state representatives in international organizations, will be subjected to scrutiny by transnational networks.

Such transparency, however, represents nongovernmental organizations and networks more than ordinary people, who may be as excluded from élite networks as they are from government circles. That is, transnational civil society may be a necessary but insufficient condition for democratic accountability. Democracies should insist that, wherever feasible, international organizations maintain sufficient transparency for transnational networks of advocacy groups, domestic legislators, and democratic publics to evaluate their actions. But proponents of democratic accountability should also seek counterparts to the mechanisms of control embedded in national democratic institutions. Governors of the Federal Reserve Board are, after all, nominated by the president and confirmed by the Senate, even if they exercise great authority during their terms of office. If Madison, Hamilton, and Jay could invent indirect mechanisms of popular control in the *Federalist Papers* two centuries ago, it should not be beyond our competence to devise comparable mechanisms at the global level in the twenty-first century.

# The United Nations and International Security

## ADAM ROBERTS

In recent years, there has been a remarkable growth in demands for the services of the United Nations (UN) in the field of international security. The 1991 authorized action in Iraq was quickly followed in 1992 by a fivefold increase in the numbers of troops deployed in UN peace-keeping activities and by an increase in the types of roles they perform. At long last, the United Nations seemed to offer the prospect of moving decisively away from the anarchic reliance on force, largely on a unilateral basis, by individual sovereign states. The United Nations has, and will probably continue to have, a far more central role in security issues than it did during the Cold War.

However, the United Nations' multifaceted role in the security field faces a huge array of problems. Almost every difficulty connected with the preparation, deployment, and use of force has re-emerged in a UN context and does not appear to be any easier to address. Excessive demands have been placed on the United Nations, which has been asked to pour the oil of peace-keeping on the troubled waters of a huge number of conflicts, to develop its role in preventing breaches of the peace, and to play a central part in defeating aggression and tackling the after-effects of war. Arms control, too, is embroiled in controversy, with various states—Iraq and North Korea being the clearest examples—challenging what they see as a discriminatory non-proliferation regime. Above all, the increasing role of the United Nations in international security raises two central questions: First, is there a real coherence in the vast array of security activities undertaken by the United Nations? Second, is there a danger that the elemental force of ethnic conflict could defeat the United Nations' efforts? . . .

This article advances the following propositions about the United Nations' post–Cold War role in the field of international security:

1. The United Nations has become seriously overloaded with security issues, for good and enduring reasons. The extent to which it can transfer these responsibilities to regional organizations is debatable.
2. Most conflicts in the contemporary world involve an element of civil war or inter-ethnic struggle. They are different in character from those conflicts, essentially interstate, that the United Nations was established to tackle.

Excerpts from Adam Roberts, "The United Nations and International Security," *Survival: The IISS Quarterly,* Vol. 35, No. 2 (Summer 1993), pp. 3–30. Reprinted by permission of the author and Taylor & Francis Ltd. http://www.tandf.co.uk/journals.

3. There is only limited agreement among the major powers about the basis of international security and only a limited shared interest in ensuring that international norms are effectively implemented.

4. The structure of the Security Council, including the system of five veto-wielding permanent members, is in danger of losing its legitimacy. Although a formal change of membership or powers will be very hard to achieve, changes in the Council's procedures and practices may be both desirable and possible.

5. There are some advantages in the practice whereby enforcement has taken the form of authorized military action by groups of states, rather than coming under direct UN command as a literal reading of the UN Charter would suggest. . . .

6. Although the United Nations' role is increasing, basic questions about collective security remain. There is no prospect of a general system of collective security supplanting existing strategic arrangements.

These propositions . . . are in no way intended as criticism of the increased emphasis given to the United Nations and its role in the foreign policies of many states. Rather, they constitute a plea for the sober assessment of both the merits and defects of an increased role, as well as for constructive thinking about some of the difficult issues it poses, and a caution against the hasty abandonment of some still-valuable aspects of traditional approaches to international relations.

## THE OVERLOAD PROBLEM

. . . Reasons for such a heavy demand to deal with wars, civil strife, and other crises are numerous and persuasive. Whatever difficulties the United Nations may face in the coming years, these reasons will not suddenly disappear. Three stand out. First, the impressive record of the United Nations in the years 1987–92 has raised expectations. The United Nations has contributed to the settlement of numerous regional conflicts, including the Iran–Iraq War, the South African presence in Namibia, the Soviet presence in Afghanistan, and the Vietnamese presence in Cambodia. It provided a framework for the expulsion of Iraq from Kuwait. Second, given a choice, states contemplating the use of force beyond their borders often prefer to do it in a multilateral, especially UN, context. A multilateral approach helps neutralize domestic political opposition, increases the opportunity that operations have limited and legitimate goals, and reduces the risk of large-scale force being used by adversaries or rival powers. Third, the United Nations has some notable advantages over regional organizations in tackling security problems: It is universal; it has a reputation, even if it is now under threat, for impartiality; and it has a more clear set of arrangements for making decisions on security issues than do most regional organizations, including even the North Atlantic Treaty Organization (NATO). . . .

Recognizing that the United Nations is seriously overloaded, much thought has been given to the question of cooperation with regional security organizations. . . . The idea that the United Nations and regional institutions could share responsibility for security seems to be emerging, albeit hesitantly, in Europe. The proliferation of

European bodies with responsibilities in the security field is notorious: The Conference on Security and Cooperation in Europe (CSCE), NATO, the European Community (EC), the Western European Union (WEU), and the North Atlantic Cooperation Council (NACC) all play roles of varying importance. . . . Despite such developments, enlarging the international security role of regional organizations is easier said than done. These organizations have a bewildering variety of purposes and memberships, and they often have great difficulty in reaching decisions and in taking action. Many regional bodies are seen as too partial to one side. Moreover, it is often far from self-evident which regional body should have the principal role in addressing a given problem. The United Nations has often encouraged regional bodies to handle crises only to find that important aspects of the problems remained within its own domain.

## THE CHANGING CHARACTER OF CONFLICT

Many of the conflicts in the contemporary world have a very different character from those that the United Nations was designed to address. Above all, those who framed the UN Charter had in mind the problem of international war, waged by well-organized states. This reflected the view, still common today, that aggression and international war constitute the supreme problem of international relations. Although the problem of interstate war has by no means disappeared, for many, civil war—whether internationalized or not—has always represented the deadlier threat. Some of the twentieth century's principal political philosophies have underestimated the significance of ethnicity, however defined, as a powerful political force and source of conflict; this is now changing through the pressure of events. . . .

In the overwhelming majority of UN Security Council operations today, there is a strong element of civil war and communal conflict. For the United Nations, involvement in such a conflict is hardly new, as the long-standing and continuing problems of Palestine/Israel and Cyprus bear witness. The collapse of large multinational states and empires almost always causes severe dislocations, including the emergence or re-emergence of ethnic, religious, regional, and other animosities. The absence of fully legitimate political systems, traditions, regimes, and state frontiers all increase the likelihood that a narrowly ethnic definition of "nations" prevails. These difficulties are compounded by the fact that, for the most part, the geographical distribution of populations is so messy that the harmonious realization of national self-determination is impossible. Conflict-ridden parts of the former Yugoslavia and the former Soviet Union are merely the two most conspicuous contemporary examples of imperial collapse leading to inter-ethnic war. In both cases, the taboo against changing old "colonial" frontiers has been undermined much more quickly and seriously than occurred in post-colonial states in Africa and elsewhere in the decades following European decolonization. . . . It is by no means impossible that internal conflicts could drag the United Nations down; its inability to prevent a resumption of war in Angola following the September 1992 elections is an ominous indicator of this type of hazard.

Internal conflicts, especially those with a communal or ethnic dimension, present special risks for international engagement, whether in the form of mediation, peace-keeping, or forceful military intervention. First, internal conflicts tend to be "nasty, brutish, and long," and they leave communities with deep and enduring mutual suspicions based on traumatic experiences and continuing proximity. Intervention requires a willingness to stay what may be a very long course. Second, internal conflicts are typically conducted under the leadership of non-governmental or semi-governmental entities, which may see great advantages in the degree of recognition involved in negotiating with UN representatives and yet be unwilling or unable to carry out the terms of agreements. Third, internal conflicts typically involve the use of force directed against the civilian populations, thus becoming especially bitter and posing difficult problems related to the protection of dispersed and vulnerable civilians. Fourth, internal conflicts are often conducted with small weapons: rifles, knives and the arsonist's match. It is very difficult to control the use of such weaponry by bombing, arms embargoes, or formal methods of arms control. Finally, in cases such as these, there is frequently no territorial *status quo ante* to which to return. Cease-fires and other agreements are vulnerable to the charge that they legitimize the use of force and that they create impossibly complicated "leopard-spot" territorial arrangements, based on ethnic territorial units that are small and separated and, thus, difficult to defend. . . .

Communal and ethnic conflicts raise awkward issues about the criteria used in recognizing political entities as states and in favoring their admission to the United Nations. When the United Nations admits member-states, it is in fact conferring a particularly important form of recognition, and it is also implicitly underwriting the inviolability of their frontiers. Yet, the United Nations does not appear to be taking sufficient account of traditional criteria for recognition, which include careful consideration of whether a state really exists and coheres as a political and social entity. Many European states also forgot these traditional criteria in some of their recent acts of recognition, many of which did not involve setting up diplomatic missions. If the results of recognition are risky security commitments to purported states that never really attained internal cohesion, public support for UN action may be weakened.

Such conflicts also raise issues about the appropriateness of certain principles derived from interstate relations, including the principle that changing frontiers by force can never be accepted. This principle, which is very important in contemporary international relations, has been frequently reiterated by the international community in connection with the Yugoslav crisis. A successful armed grab for territory on largely ethnic grounds would indeed set a deeply worrying precedent. Yet, it must be asked whether it is wise to express this legal principle so forcefully in circumstances in which existing "frontiers" have no physical existence, in which they lack both logic and legitimacy, in which there are such deep-seated ethnic problems, and in which almost any imaginable outcome will involve recognition of the consequences of frontier violations.

## LIMITED HARMONY AMONG THE MAJOR POWERS

. . . It is undeniable, and very welcome, that there is more agreement among states about international security issues now than there was during the Cold War. However, there remain fundamental differences of both interest and perception. These may not be enough to prevent the Security Council from reaching decisions on key issues, but they can frustrate efforts to turn decisions into actions in fast-changing situations. . . .

Differences of interest amongst states are complemented by differences in perceptions about the fundamental nature of world politics. Depending largely on their different historical experiences, some states view colonial domination and imperialism as the most serious problems in international relations; others see civil war as the most dangerous threat to international security; yet others view aggressive conquest and international war as the central problems.

Such serious differences of perception and interest are, of course, reflected in the proceedings of the UN Security Council. One should not necessarily expect relations among major powers to be good, and there may be perfectly valid reasons why countries perceive major security problems differently. [For example,] China's world-view, although undergoing important changes, retains distinctive elements—including a fear of foreign subversion, a strong belief in state sovereignty, and some identification with developing states—which could set it against other Security Council members.

## THE PROBLEMATIC STRUCTURE OF THE SECURITY COUNCIL

. . . If the United Nations is indeed to have an enlarged role in security affairs, its system of decision-making must be seen to be legitimate.

The powers of the Security Council are, in theory, very extensive: "The Members of the United Nations agree to accept and carry out the decisions of the Security Council in accordance with the present Charter." In practice, the Security Council cannot impose its will on the membership in the way this statement implies and, despite the absence of any system of formal constitutional challenge, there is no sign of the emergence of a doctrine even hinting at the infallibility of UN Security Council pronouncements. However, these limitations on the power of the Security Council do not mean that states, having successfully retained considerable sovereign powers in security matters, see the existing arrangements as satisfactory.

The criticisms of the composition of the Security Council involve several elements: doubt about preserving unaltered, half a century later, the special position of those countries that were allies in the Second World War; concern that three of those powers—France, Britain, and the United States—make most of the agenda-setting decisions in running the Security Council; irritation, especially on the part of Germany and Japan, about "taxation without representation," and frustration that the views of the non-permanent members of the Security Council, and indeed of the great majority of the 181-strong General Assembly, count for little. These criticisms could become much more serious if events take such a turn that they coincide with a perception that the Security Council has made serious misjudgments on central issues. . . .

In the history of the United Nations, much more has been achieved by changes in practice, rather than Charter revision. More thought will have to be given to how the Security Council might develop its procedures and practices: for example, by strengthening the selection of non-permanent members to reflect their contributions to the United Nations' work and developing more regular Security Council consultation with major states and interested parties. Such changes, although difficult to implement, might go at least some way towards meeting the strong concerns of certain states about being left out of decisions that affect them vitally.

## THE PROBLEM OF ORGANIZING ENFORCEMENT ACTIONS

The issue of organizing enforcement actions is central to almost every discussion of the United Nations' future role. It brings out the conflict between "Charter fundamentalists," who would like such actions to be organized precisely in accord with the UN Charter, and those with a "common law" approach, who believe the most important guide is UN practice.

Three times in the UN era, major military action authorized by the United Nations has been under US, not UN, command: in Korea in 1950–53, Iraq in 1990–91, and Somalia in 1992–93. These episodes suggest the emergence of a system in which the United Nations authorizes military actions, which are then placed under the control of a state or group of states. There are important advantages to such an arrangement. First, it reflects the reality that not all states feel equally involved in every enforcement action. Moreover, military actions require extremely close coordination between intelligence-gathering and operations, a smoothly functioning decision-making machine, and forces with some experience of working together to perform dangerous and complex tasks. These things are more likely to be achieved through existing national armed forces, alliances, and military relationships, than they are within the structure of a UN command. As habits of cooperation between armed forces develop, and as the United Nations itself grows, the scope for action under direct UN command may increase, but this will inevitably be a slow process. . . .

Experience seems to show that mobilizing for collective security only works when one power takes the lead. However, as a result of the effort, that same power may be reluctant to continue assuming the entire burden of collective security. After the Korean War, the United States tried to set up regional alliances to reduce its direct military obligation. After the 1991 Gulf War, the United States was manifestly reluctant to get entangled in Iraq and to underwrite all security arrangements in the area. . . . The issue of UN versus authorized national command arises in non-enforcement connections as well. As UN-controlled peace-keeping forces become involved in more complex missions, in which neat distinctions between peace-keeping and enforcement are eroded, the adequacy of the United Nations' existing machinery for controlling complex operations in distant countries is increasingly called into question. . . .

## PROSPECTS FOR COLLECTIVE SECURITY

Is it possible to say that out of the rubble of the Cold War a system of collective security is emerging? . . . The term "collective security" normally refers to a system in which each state in the system accepts that the security of one is the concern of all and agrees to join in a collective response to aggression. In this sense, it is distinct from collective defense or alliance systems, in which groups of states ally with each other, principally against possible external threats.

"Collective security" proposals have been in circulation since the beginning of the modern states system and were indeed aired at the negotiations that led to the 1648 Peace of Westphalia. The attractive theory of collective security, when tested against some basic questions, often reveals some fundamental flaws.

*Whose collective security?* There is always a risk that a collective security system will be seen as protecting only certain countries or interests or as privileging certain principles at the expense of others. Some countries may, for whatever reason, feel excluded from its benefits or threatened by it. The anxieties expressed by some countries in the developing world regarding the concept of the "New World Order," while they have not yet crystallized into definite opposition to any specific UN action, are evidence of concern on this point.

*Can there be consistent responses to security problems?* Although the UN system is the first truly global international system and although it involves the subscription of virtually all countries in the world to a common set of principles, it is not yet evident that the same principles and practices could or should be applied consistently to different problems, countries, and regions. Difficulties can arise both from the consistent application of principles to situations that are fundamentally different and from the inconsistent application of principles. It is also not yet apparent that collective security can operate as effectively for East Timor or Tibet as for Kuwait. The widespread perception that Israel has successfully defied UN Security Council resolutions while other states have not, although arguably facile in certain respects, illustrates the explosiveness of emerging accusations of "double standards" at the United Nations. The political price of apparent inconsistency could be high.

*Against which types of threat is a system of collective security intended to operate?* There is no agreement that collective security should apply equally to the following: massive aggression and annexation; cross-border incursions; environmental despoliation; acts of terrorism; human rights violations within a state; communal and ethnic conflict; and the collapse of state structures under assault from internal opposition. In 1990–91, many people argued that it was the particularly flagrant nature of the Iraqi invasion, occupation, and annexation of Kuwait that justified the coalition's response; even then, the international military response was far from unanimous. The fact that this argument was so widely used underlines the point that in cases in which aggression is not so blatant, it might be much harder to secure an international military response; a state caught up in such a conflict might have to look after its own interests. Since 1991, inspired partly by the establishment of "safe havens" in northern Iraq and partly by a trend of opinion, admittedly far from universal, in favor of democracy, there has been some increased advocacy, not least in France and the United States, of a right of intervention in states even in the absence of a formal invitation. This remains a deeply contentious issue and serves as a useful reminder that the ends towards which collective security efforts might be directed are not fixed.

*How collective does enforcement have to be?* Is complete unanimity impossible to attain, especially in the case of military action? Is there still space for some states to be neutral? In practice, there has never been, on the global level, a truly "collective" case (let alone system) of collective security. In the Gulf crisis of 1990–91, the key UN Security Council resolution avoided the call for all states to take military action. Instead, it merely authorized "member-states co-operating with the Government of Kuwait" to use "all necessary means" to implement relevant UN resolutions. This implied that it was still legitimate for a state to have a status of neutrality or non-belligerency in this conflict. It marked an interesting and realistic interpretation of some optimistic provisions in Chapter VII of the UN Charter.

*How can a system of collective security actively deter a particular threat to a particular country?* In the wake of the 1991 Gulf War, there was much discussion as to possible means by which, in the future, invasions could be deterred before disaster struck. . . . Following a unanimous Security Council decision of 11 December 1992, the idea was implemented by the United Nations for the first time in Macedonia. Ironically, a state that until April 1993 remained a non-member was thus receiving protection from a state, Yugoslavia, that was still, for most practical purposes, a UN member. Despite remarkable progress, the idea of "preventive deployment" is fraught with difficulty. There is the risk that large numbers of states would request it, that it would be insufficient to discourage aggression, and that it might be used by a government as an alternative to providing for its own defense. It should not, however, be taken for granted that military deployments are absolutely essential. There may also be some residual deterrent value in the lessons of Korea (1950–53) and Kuwait (1990–91); twice, under UN auspices, the United States has led coalitions that have gone to the defense of invaded states to which the United States was not bound by formal alliance commitments and in which it had no troops deployed at the time. This curious fact may not be entirely lost on would-be aggressors. Yet, there are bound to be cases in which some kinds of preventive UN deployments, of which Macedonia is a harbinger, are considered necessary.

*Who pays for collective security?* The question of burden-sharing in international security matters is notoriously complex, as shown by the experience of NATO, of UN peace-keeping, and of the US-led operations in the 1990–91 Gulf crisis. In 1992, the annual cost of UN peace-keeping activities was the highest ever—about $2.8 billion. Unpaid contributions towards UN peace-keeping operations in September 1992 stood at $844 million, but by the beginning of 1993, this figure was reduced to about $670 million. States have responded well to the increased costs of peace-keeping. However if more UN peace-keeping (or other) operations go badly, there could be added difficulty in securing payment. Even if they do not, there are problems to be addressed. During the US presidential campaign, Bill Clinton, while indicating that he would act on payment of the US debt to the United Nations, repeatedly called for new agreements for sharing the costs of maintaining peace and suggested that the US apportionment of UN peace-keeping costs be reduced from 30.4% to 25%. The extraordinary paradox of the country most deeply involved in military support for an international organization being simultaneously its major (though steadily repaying) defaulter is yet one more illustration of the gulf between the theory of collective security and its practice.

However, future payment difficulties may come from states not involved in, or critical of, Security Council decisions.

*What is the place of disarmament and arms control in a system of collective security?* Most proposals for collective security call for lower levels of armaments, consistent with the needs of internal security and international obligations. . . . However, the United Nations has yet to work out a coherent philosophy to guide its efforts in the field of disarmament and arms control in the post–Cold War era. "Arms control" is still seen by many as a suspect, meliorist concept. Attempts to develop guidelines for conventional arms transfers have many sharp critics, including China. The rationale for arms reductions, for control of arms transfers, and for nuclear non-proliferation efforts, all still need to be carefully examined and refined. This is especially important in view of the common fears that existing arms control arrangements are discriminatory—fears that could be exacerbated if the Security Council assumes a more central role in non-proliferation matters.

# 2 | The Uses of Force

With the end of both the Cold War and the Soviet Union, the nightmare of an all-out nuclear war between the superpowers that so dominated world politics since 1945 ended. It is not likely that a new danger of the same magnitude will arise, at least for the economically developed democracies of North America, Japan, and Western Europe. Indeed, for the first time since the formation of these nation-states, the citizens of these countries may live out their lives without worrying that they or their children will have to die or kill in a major war.

This fact, however, does not mean that we should no longer be concerned with how states use force. Even if the optimistic prediction is correct, we still need to understand previous eras in which warfare played such a large role. We cannot understand the course of the Cold War without studying the role nuclear weapons played in it. Moreover, an understanding of the role that nuclear weapons played in that era is central for determining the role they will play in this era. This is true for no other reason than that national leaders' views of the present are heavily influenced by their reading of the past. Furthermore, even within the developed rich world, where a great-power war is unlikely, military power still remains useful to the conduct of statecraft. If it were not, these states would have already disarmed. They have not because the use of force must always be available, even if it is not always necessary. For much of the rest of the world, unfortunately, circumstances are different. Threats to the security of states remain real, and war among them has not been abolished. For all states, then—those likely to enjoy peace and those that will have to endure war—what has changed is not so much the utility of military power as how it can be usefully employed.

## THE POLITICAL USES OF FORCE

The use of force almost always represents the partial failure of a policy. The exception, of course, is the case in which fighting is valued for its own sake—when it is believed that war brings out heroic values and purifies individuals and cultures, or when fighting is seen as entertainment. Changes in states' values and the increased destructiveness of war, however, have led state actors to view armed conflicts as the last resort. Threats are a second choice to diplomatic maneuvers; actual use of force follows only if the threats fail.

Because of the high costs of violence, its use is tempered by restraints and bargaining. As bloody as most wars are, they could always be bloodier. Brutalities are limited in part by the combatants' shared interests, if not by their scruples. Even if two states differ enough to go to war, it does not necessarily follow that they have no common interests. Only when everything that is good for one side is bad for the other (a "zero-sum" situation) do the opponents gain nothing by bargaining. In most cases, however, certain outcomes are clearly bad for both sides; therefore, even though they are at war, each side shares an interest in avoiding them.

The shared nature of the interest, as Thomas Schelling points out, stems from the fact that it is easier to destroy than to create. Force can be used to take—or to bargain. If you can take what you want, you do not need your adversary's cooperation and do not have to bargain with him. A country may use force to seize disputed territory just as a robber may kill you to get your wallet. Most of the things people and nations want, however, cannot be taken in this way. A nation not only wants to take territory, it wants to govern and exploit it. A nation may want others to stop menacing it; it may even want others to adopt its values. Brute force alone cannot achieve these goals. A nation that wants to stop others from menacing it may not want to fight them in order to remove the threat. A nation that wants others to adopt its values cannot impose them solely through conquest. Where the cooperation of an adversary is needed, bargaining will ensue. The robber does not need the cooperation of his victim if he kills him to get his wallet. However, the thief who must obtain the combination of a safe from the hostage who carries it only in his head does need such cooperation. The thief may use force to demonstrate that the hostage can lose his life if he does not surrender the combination. But the thief no more wishes to kill the hostage and lose the combination than the hostage wishes to die. The hostage may trade the combination for his life. The bargain may be unequal or unfair, but it is still a bargain.

The mutual avoidance of certain outcomes explains why past wars have not been as bloody as they could have been; but an analysis of why wars were not more destructive should not blind us to the factors that made them as destructive as they were. By 1914, for example, all the statesmen of Europe believed a war inevitable, and all were ready to exploit it. None, however, imagined the staggering losses that their respective nations would inflict and bear in the field, or the extent to which noncombatants would be attacked. Yet by the second year of the war, the same men were accepting the deaths of hundreds or thousands for a few yards' gain in the front lines; and by the end of the war, they were planning large-scale aerial gas attacks on each other's major cities. The German bombing of Guernica in 1937 and Rotterdam in 1940 shocked statesmen and citizens alike, but by the middle of the war both were accepting as routine the total destruction of German and Japanese cities.

Three factors largely account for the increasing destructiveness of the wars of the last two centuries. First was the steady technological improvement in weaponry. Weapons such as machine guns, submarines, poison gas, and aircraft made it feasible to maim or kill large numbers of people quickly. The rapidity of destruction that is possible with nuclear weapons is only the most recent, albeit biggest, advance. Second was the growth in the capacity, and thus the need, of states to field ever larger numbers of forces. As states became more industrialized and centralized, they acquired the wealth and developed the administrative apparatus to move men on a grand scale. Concomitant with the increase in military potential was the necessity to realize this potential. As soon as one state expanded the forces at its disposal, all other states had to follow suit. Thus when Prussia instituted universal conscription and the general-staff system, and then demonstrated their advantages with swift victories over Austria and France, the rest of the continent quickly adopted its methods. An increase in the potential power of states led to an increase in their standing power.

Third was the gradual "democratization" of war: the expansion of the battlefield and hence the indiscriminate mass killing of noncombatants. Everyone, citizens and soldiers alike, began fighting and dying. World War II, with its extensive use of air-power, marked not the debut but the zenith of this mass killing. As war changed from the province of the princes to the burden of the masses, the distinction between combatants and noncombatants increasingly blurred. Most of the wars of the eighteenth century did impinge upon the citizenry, but mainly financially; few civilians died in them. With the widespread use of conscription in the nineteenth and twentieth centuries, however, more citizens became soldiers. With the advent of industrialization and with the increasing division of labor, the citizens who did not fight remained behind to produce weapons. Now a nation not only had to conquer its enemy's armies but also had to destroy the industrial plant that supplied their weapons. Gradually the total energy of a country was diverted into waging wars, and as the costs of wars increased, so did the justifications given for them and the bene-fits claimed to derive from them. The greater the sacrifices asked, the larger the vic-tory spoils demanded. Because wars became literally wars of, by, and for the people, governments depended increasingly upon the support of their citizens. As wars became democratized, so too did they become popularized and propagandized.

The readings in the first section explore how force has been and can be used in a changing world. Robert J. Art notes that the threat and use of force has four dis-tinct functions and shows how their relative importance varies from one situation to another. Thomas Schelling examines the differences between the uses of con-ventional and nuclear weapons and the links between force and foreign policy goals. Robert Art analyzes the concept of coercive diplomacy—the resort to force short of all-out war—and demonstrates why it is difficult to execute. Robert Jervis argues that the extent to which states can make themselves more secure without menacing others depends in large part on whether offensive postures can be dis-tinguished from defensive ones and whether the offense is believed to be more efficacious than the defense. Terrorism has never been absent from world politics, and Bruce Hoffman discusses its changing forms and purposes, and distinguishes terrorism from guerrilla warfare and criminal activity.

## THE POLITICAL UTILITY OF FORCE TODAY

It is a mistake to examine the possible use of force in a vacuum. As Clausewitz stressed, force is an instrument for reaching political goals. Its utility, as well as the likelihood of its use, depends not only on the costs and perceived benefits of fighting but on the general political context, the values statesmen and citizens hold, the alternative policy instruments available, and the objectives sought.

Realism, represented in many of the readings in Part One, stresses the importance of military power. The two readings in this section demonstrate the continuing relevance of force to political outcomes. Robert J. Art argues that military power is fungible—that is, it can be used to reach a number of goals, even for a state like the United States that lacks strong state enemies. Robert A. Pape examines the political logic of suicide terrorism, surveys the universe of cases of this unfortunate phenomenon from 1980–2001, and argues that "it pays" because it has forced liberal democracies to compromise.

## THE SPREAD OF NUCLEAR WEAPONS

During the Cold War, nuclear weapons, it was argued, helped make competition between the two superpowers safer than it would otherwise have been. That is, nuclear weapons made the two superpowers scared, not safe, and this restrained them. Each had to worry that if it pushed the other too far, matters could get out of hand and escalate to nuclear war. Each learned, especially after the Cuban Missile Crisis of 1962, not to push the other to the point where it faced the choice of upping the ante and risking loss of control, or backing down and risking humiliation. Rules of the road between the two superpowers gradually developed, and their subsequent competition proved safer in the last twenty-eight years of the Cold War than it had been in the first fifteen.

How relevant for today is the superpower experience with nuclear weapons? Will states that experience intense political conflicts with one another be deterred from pushing one another too far? Or will they be less restrained than were the superpowers and find themselves in the horror of escalating to the use of nuclear weapons? How valid a model is the US-Soviet experience for dyadic conflicts today?

Scott Sagan and Kenneth Waltz analyze what is today the most dangerous political conflict between two nuclear armed states—the Pakistani-Indian conflict over the state of Kashmir. They look at the 1999 shooting conflict over Kargil and draw opposite conclusions from it. Sagan argues that we should take no comfort from the fact that a large war did not ensue because there were too many near misses and because next time the two states might not be so lucky. Waltz argues that the limited use of force by both sides in 1999 shows clearly how the mutual possession of nuclear weapons causes states to restrain their ambitions and reign in their military. The Kargil case serves as a good exemplar by which to extrapolate the other possible conflicts between nuclear armed adversaries that the world may experience in the future.

# THE POLITICAL USES OF FORCE

## The Four Functions of Force

### ROBERT J. ART

In view of what is likely to be before us, it is vital to think carefully and precisely about the uses and limits of military power. That is the purpose of this essay. It is intended as a backdrop for policy debates, not a prescription of specific policies. It consciously eschews elaborate detail on the requisite military forces for scenarios *a . . . n* and focuses instead on what military power has and has not done, can and cannot do. Every model of how the world works has policy implications. But not every policy is based on a clear view of how the world works. What, then, are the uses to which military power can be put? How have nuclear weapons affected these uses? And what is the future of force in a world of nuclear parity and increasing economic interdependence?

## WHAT ARE THE USES OF FORCE?

The goals that states pursue range widely and vary considerably from case to case. Military power is more useful for realizing some goals than others, though it is generally considered of some use by most states for all of the goals that they hold. If we attempt, however, to be descriptively accurate, to enumerate all of the purposes for which states use force, we shall simply end up with a bewildering list. Descriptive accuracy is not a virtue *per se* for analysis. In fact, descriptive accuracy is generally bought at the cost of analytical utility. (A concept that is descriptively accurate is usually analytically useless.) Therefore, rather than compile an exhaustive list of such purposes, I have selected four categories that themselves analytically exhaust the functions that force can serve: defense, deterrence, compellence, and "swaggering."

From "To What Ends Military Power" by Robert J. Art, in *International Security*, Vol. 4 (Spring 1980), pp. 4–35. Portions of the text and the footnotes have been omitted.

Not all four functions are necessarily well or equally served by a given military posture. In fact, usually only the great powers have the wherewithal to develop military forces that can serve more than two functions at once. Even then, this is achieved only vis-á-vis smaller powers, not vis-á-vis the other great ones. The measure of the capabilities of a state's military forces must be made relative to those of another state, not with reference to some absolute scale. A state that can compel another state can also defend against it and usually deter it. A state that can defend against another state cannot thereby automatically deter or compel it. A state can deter another state without having the ability to either defend against or compel it. A state that can swagger vis-á-vis another may or may not be able to perform any of the other three functions relative to it. Where feasible, defense is the goal that all states aim for first. If defense is not possible, deterrence is generally the next priority. Swaggering is the function most difficult to pin down analytically; deterrence, the one whose achievement is the most difficult to demonstrate; compellence, the easiest to demonstrate but among the hardest to achieve. The following discussion develops these points more fully.

The *defensive* use of force is the deployment of military power so as to be able to do two things—to ward off an attack and to minimize damage to oneself if attacked. For defensive purposes, a state will direct its forces against those of a potential or actual attacker, but not against his unarmed population. For defensive purposes, a state can deploy its forces in place prior to an attack, use them after an attack has occurred to repel it, or strike first if it believes that an attack upon it is imminent or inevitable. The defensive use of force can thus involve both peaceful and physical employment and both repellent (second) strikes and offensive (first) strikes. If a state strikes first when it believes an attack upon it is imminent, it is launching a preemptive blow. If it strikes first when it believes an attack is inevitable but not momentary, it is launching a preventive blow. Preemptive and preventive blows are undertaken when a state calculates, first, that others plan to attack it and, second, that to delay in striking offensively is against its interests. A state preempts in order to wrest the advantage of the first strike from an opponent. A state launches a preventive attack because it believes that others will attack it when the balance of forces turns in their favor and therefore attacks while the balance of forces is in its favor. In both cases it is better to strike first than to be struck first. The major distinction between preemption and prevention is the calculation about when an opponent's attack will occur. For preemption, it is a matter of hours, days, or even a few weeks at the most; for prevention, months or even a few years. In the case of preemption, the state has almost no control over the timing of its attack; in the case of prevention, the state can in a more leisurely way contemplate the timing of its attack. For both cases, it is the belief in the certainty of war that governs the offensive, defensive attack. For both cases, the maxim, "the best defense is a good offense," makes good sense.

The *deterrent* use of force is the deployment of military power so as to be able to prevent an adversary from doing something that one does not want him to do and that he might otherwise be tempted to do by threatening him with unacceptable punishment if he does it. Deterrence is thus the threat of retaliation. Its purpose is to prevent something undesirable from happening. The threat of punishment is directed at the adversary's population and/or industrial infrastructure. The effectiveness of the threat depends upon a state's ability to convince a potential adversary that it has both the will and power to punish him severely if he undertakes the undesirable action in question. Deterrence therefore employs force peacefully. It is the threat to resort to force in order to punish that is the essence of deterrence. If the threat has to be carried out, deterrence by definition has failed. A deterrent threat is made precisely with the intent that it will not have to be carried out. Threats are made to prevent actions from being undertaken. If the threat has to be implemented, the action has already been undertaken. Hence deterrence can be judged successful only if the retaliatory threats have not been implemented.

Deterrence and defense are alike in that both are intended to protect the state or its closest allies from physical attacks. The purpose of both is dissuasion—persuading others *not* to undertake actions harmful to oneself. The defensive use of force dissuades by convincing an adversary that he cannot conquer one's military forces. The deterrent use of force dissuades by convincing the adversary that his population and territory will suffer terrible damage if he initiates the undesirable action. Defense dissuades by presenting an unvanquishable military force. Deterrence dissuades by presenting the certainty of retaliatory devastation.

Defense is possible without deterrence, and deterrence is possible without defense. A state can have the military wherewithal to repel an invasion without also being able to threaten devastation to the invader's population or territory. Similarly, a state can have the wherewithal credibly to threaten an adversary with such devastation and yet be unable to repel his invading force. Defense, therefore, does not necessarily buy deterrence, nor deterrence defense. A state that can defend itself from attack, moreover, will have little need to develop the wherewithal to deter. If physical attacks can be repelled or if the damage from them drastically minimized, the incentive to develop a retaliatory capability is low. A state that cannot defend itself, however, will try to develop an effective deterrent if that be possible. No state will leave its population and territory open to attack if it has the means to redress the situation. Whether a given state can defend or deter or do both vis-á-vis another depends upon two factors: (1) the quantitative balance of forces between it and its adversary; and (2) the qualitative balance of forces, that is, whether the extant military technology favors the offense or the defense. These two factors are situation-specific and therefore require careful analysis of the case at hand.

The *compellent* use of force is the deployment of military power so as to be able either to stop an adversary from doing something that he has already undertaken or to get him to do something that he has not yet undertaken. Compellence, in Schelling's words, "involves initiating an action . . . that can cease, or become harmless, only if the opponent responds." Compellence can employ force either physically or peacefully. A state can start actually harming another with physical destruction until the latter abides by the former's wishes. Or, a state can take actions against another that do not cause physical harm but that require the latter to pay some type of significant price until it changes its behavior. America's bombing of North Vietnam in early 1965 was an example of physical compellence; Tirpitz's building of a German fleet aimed against England's in the two decades before World War I, an example of peaceful compellence. In the first case, the United

States started bombing North Vietnam in order to compel it to stop assisting the Vietcong forces in South Vietnam. In the latter case, Germany built a battlefleet that in an engagement threatened to cripple England's in order to compel her to make a general political settlement advantageous to Germany. In both cases, one state initiated some type of action against another precisely so as to be able to stop it, to bargain it away for the appropriate response from the "put upon" state.

The distinction between compellence and deterrence is one between the active and passive use of force. The success of a deterrent threat is measured by its not having to be used. The success of a compellent action is measured by how closely and quickly the adversary conforms to one's stipulated wishes. In the case of successful deterrence, one is trying to demonstrate a negative, to show why something did not happen. It can never be clear whether one's actions were crucial to, or irrelevant to, why another state chose *not* to do something. In the case of successful compellence, the clear sequence of actions and reactions lends a compelling plausibility to the centrality of one's actions. Figure 1 illustrates the distinction. In successful compellence, state B can claim that its pressure deflected state A from its course of action. In successful deterrence, state B has no change in state A's behavior to point to, but instead must resort to claiming that its threats were responsible for the continuity in A's behavior. State A may have changed its behavior for reasons other than state B's compellent action. State A may have continued with its same behavior for reasons other than state B's deterrent threat. "Proving" the importance of B's influence on A for either case is not easy, but it is more plausible to claim that B influenced A when there is a change in A's behavior than when there is not. Explaining why something did not happen is more difficult than explaining why something did.

Compellence may be easier to demonstrate than deterrence, but it is harder to achieve. Schelling argues that compellent actions tend to be vaguer in their

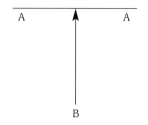

| COMPELLENCE | DETERRENCE |
|---|---|
| (1) A is doing something that B cannot tolerate | (1) A is presently not doing anything that B finds intolerable |
| (2) B initiates action against A in order to get him to stop his intolerable actions | (2) B tells A that if A changes his behavior and does something intolerable, B will punish him |
| (3) A stops his intolerable actions and B stops his (or both cease simultaneously) | (3) A continues not to do anything B finds intolerable |

**FIGURE 1** ■

objectives than deterrent threats and for that reason more difficult to attain. If an adversary has a hard time understanding what it is that one wished him to do, his compliance with one's wishes is made more difficult. There is, however, no inherent reason why a compellent action must be vaguer than a deterrent threat with regard to how clearly the adversary understands what is wanted from him. "Do not attack me" is not any clearer in its ultimate meaning than "stop attacking my friend." A state can be as confused or as clear about what it wishes to prevent as it can be about what it wishes to stop. The clarity, or lack of it, of the objectives of compellent actions and deterrent threats does not vary according to whether the given action is compellent or deterrent in nature, but rather according to a welter of particularities associated with the given action. Some objectives, for example, are inherently clearer and hence easier to perceive than others. Some statesmen communicate more clearly than others. Some states have more power to bring to bear for a given objective than others. It is the specifics of a given situation, not any intrinsic difference between compellence and deterrence, that determines the clarity with which an objective is perceived.

We must, therefore, look elsewhere for the reason as to why compellence is comparatively harder to achieve than deterrence. It lies, not in what one asks another to do, but in *how* one asks. With deterrence, state B asks something of state A in this fashion: "Do not take action X; for if you do, I will bash you over the head with this club." With compellence, state B asks something of state A in this fashion: "I am now going to bash you over the head with this club and will continue to do so until you do what I want." In the former case, state A can easily deny with great plausibility any intention of having planned to take action X. In the latter case, state A cannot deny either that it is engaged in a given course of action or that it is being subjected to pressure by state B. If they are to be successful, compellent actions require a state to alter its behavior in a manner quite visible to all in response to an equally visible forceful initiative taken by another state. In contrast to compellent actions, deterrent threats are both easier to appear to have ignored or easier to acquiesce to without great loss of face. In contrast to deterrent threats, compellent actions more directly engage the prestige and the passions of the put-upon state. Less prestige is lost in not doing something than in clearly altering behavior due to pressure from another. In the case of compellence, a state has publicly committed its prestige and resources to a given line of conduct that it is now asked to give up. This is not so for deterrence. Thus, compellence is intrinsically harder to attain than deterrence, not because its objectives are vaguer, but because it demands mere humiliation from the compelled state.

The fourth purpose to which military power can be put is the most difficult to be precise about. *Swaggering* is in part a residual category, the deployment of military power for purposes other than defense, deterrence, or compellence. Force is not aimed directly at dissuading another state from attacking, at repelling attacks, nor at compelling it to do something specific. The objectives for swaggering are more diffuse, ill-defined, and problematic than that. Swaggering almost always involves only the peaceful use of force and is expressed usually in one of two ways: displaying one's military might at military exercises and national demonstrations and buying or building the era's most prestigious weapons. The swagger use of force is the most egoistic: It aims to enhance the national pride of a people or to satisfy the personal ambitions of its ruler. A state or statesman swaggers in order to look and feel more powerful and important, to be taken seriously by others in the councils of international decision making, to enhance the nation's image in the eyes of others. If its image is enhanced, the nation's defense, deterrent, and compellent capabilities may also be enhanced; but swaggering is not undertaken solely or even primarily for these specific purposes. Swaggering is pursued because it offers to bring prestige "on the cheap." Swaggering is pursued because of the fundamental yearning of states and statesmen for respect and prestige. Swaggering is more something to be enjoyed for itself than to be employed for a specific, consciously thought-out end.

And yet, the instrumental role of swaggering cannot be totally discounted because of the fundamental relation between force and foreign policy that it obtains in an anarchic environment. Because there is a connection between the military might that a nation is thought to possess and the success that it achieves in attaining its objectives, the enhancement of a state's stature in the eyes of others can always be justified on *realpolitik* lines. If swaggering causes other states to take one's interests more seriously into account, then the general interests of the state will benefit. Even in its instrumental role, however, swaggering is undertaken less for any given end than for all ends. The swaggering function of military power is thus at one and the same time the most comprehensive and the most diffuse, the most versatile in its effects and the least focused in its immediate aims, the most instrumental in the long run and the least instrumental in the short run, easy to justify on hardheaded grounds and often undertaken on emotional grounds. Swaggering mixes the rational and irrational more than the other three functions of military power and, for that reason, remains both pervasive in international relations and elusive to describe.

Defense, deterrence, compellence, and swaggering—these are the four general purposes for which force can be employed. Discriminating among them analytically, however, is easier than applying them in practice. This is due to two factors. First, we need to know the motives behind an act in order to judge its purpose; but the problem is that motives cannot be readily inferred from actions because several motives can be served by the same action. But neither can one readily infer the motives of a state from what it publicly or officially proclaims them to be. Such statements should not necessarily be taken at face value because of the role that bluff and dissimulation play in statecraft. Such statements are also often concocted with domestic political, not foreign audiences in mind, or else are deliberate exercises in studied ambiguity. Motives are important in order to interpret actions, but neither actions nor words always clearly delineate motives.

It is, moreover, especially difficult to distinguish defensive from compellent actions and deterrent from swaggering ones unless we know the reasons for which they were undertaken. Peaceful defensive preparations often look largely the same as peaceful compellent ones. Defensive attacks are nearly indistinguishable from compellent ones. Is he who attacks first the defender or the compeller? Deterrence and swaggering both involve the acquisition and display of an era's prestigious weapons. Are such weapons acquired to enhance prestige or to dissuade an attack?

Second, to make matters worse, consider the following example. Germany launched an attack upon France and Russia at the end of July 1914 and thereby began World War I. There are two schools of thought as to why Germany did this.

One holds that its motives were aggressive—territorial aggrandizement, economic gain, and elevation to the status of a world empire. Another holds that her motives were preventive and hence defensive. She struck first because she feared encirclement, slow strangulation, and then inevitable attack by her two powerful neighbors, foes whom she felt were daily increasing their military might faster than she was. She struck while she had the chance to win.

It is not simple to decide which school is the more nearly correct because both can marshall evidence to build a powerful case. Assume for the moment, though, that the second is closer to the truth. There are then two possibilities to consider: (1) Germany launched an attack because it *was* the case that her foes were planning to attack her ultimately, and Germany had the evidence to prove it; or (2) Germany felt she had reasonable evidence of her foes' *intent* to attack her eventually, but in fact her evidence was wrong because she misperceived their intent from their actions. If the first was the case, then we must ask this question: How responsible was Germany's diplomacy in the fifteen years before 1914, aggressive and blundering as it was, in breeding hostility in her neighbors? Germany attacked in the knowledge that they would eventually have struck her, but if her fifteen-year diplomatic record was a significant factor in causing them to lay these plans, must we conclude that Germany in 1914 was merely acting defensively? Must we confine our judgment about the defensive or aggressive nature of the act to the month or even the year in which it occurred? If not, how many years back in history do we go in order to make a judgment? If the second was the case, then we must ask this question: If Germany attacked in the belief, mistakenly as it turns out, that she would be attacked, must we conclude that Germany was acting defensively? Must we confine our judgment about the defensive or aggressive nature of the act simply to Germany's beliefs about others' intent, without reference to their actual intent?

It is not easy to answer these questions. Fortunately, we do not have to. Asking them is enough because it illustrates that an assessment of the *legitimacy* of a state's motives in using force is integral to the task of determining what its motives are. One cannot, that is, specify motives without at the same time making judgments about their legitimacy. The root cause of this need lies in the nature of state action. In anarchy every state is a valid judge of the legitimacy of its goals because there is no supranational authority to enforce agreed upon rules. Because of the lack of universal standards, we are forced to examine each case within its given context and to make individual judgments about the meaning of the particulars. When individual judgment is exercised, individuals may well differ. Definitive answers are more likely to be the exception rather than the rule.

Where does all of this leave us? Our four categories tell us what are the four possible purposes for which states can employ military power. The attributes of each alert us to the types of evidence for which to search. But because the context of an action is crucial in order to judge its ultimate purpose, these four categories cannot be applied mindlessly and ahistorically. Each state's purpose in using force in a given instance must fall into one of these four categories. We know *a priori* what the possibilities are. Which one it is, is an exercise in judgment, an exercise that depends as much upon the particulars of the given case as it does upon the general features of the given category . . . (See Table 1).

TABLE 1 ■ THE PURPOSES OF FORCE

| Type | Purpose | Mode | Targets | Characteristics |
|------|---------|------|---------|-----------------|
| Defensive | Fend off attacks and/or reduce damage of an attack | Peaceful and physical | Primarily military<br>Secondarily industrial | Defensive preparations can have dissuasion value;<br>Defensive preparations can look aggressive;<br>First strikes can be taken for defense. |
| Deterrent | Prevent adversary from initiating an action | Peaceful | Primarily civilian<br>Tertiarily military | Threats of retaliation made as not to have to be carried out;<br>Second strike preparations can be viewed as first strike preparations. |
| Compellent | Get adversary to stop doing something or start doing something | Peaceful and physical | All three with no clear ranking | Easy to recognize but hard to achieve;<br>Competent actions can be justified on defensive grounds. |
| Swaggering | Enhance prestige | Peaceful | None | Difficult to describe because of instrumental and irrational nature;<br>Swaggering can be threatening. |

# The Diplomacy of Violence

## THOMAS C. SCHELLING

The usual distinction between diplomacy and force is not merely in the instruments, words or bullets, but in the relation between adversaries—in the interplay of motives and the role of communication, understandings, compromise, and restraint. Diplomacy is bargaining; it seeks outcomes that, though not ideal for either party, are better for both than some of the alternatives. In diplomacy each party somewhat controls what the other wants, and can get more by compromise, exchange, or collaboration than by taking things in his own hands and ignoring the other's wishes. The bargaining can be polite or rude, entail threats as well as offers, assume a status quo or ignore all rights and privileges, and assume mistrust rather than trust. But whether polite or impolite, constructive or aggressive, respectful or vicious, whether it occurs among friends or antagonists and whether or not there is a basis for trust and goodwill, there must be some common interest, if only in the avoidance of mutual damage, and an awareness of the need to make the other party prefer an outcome acceptable to oneself.

With enough military force a country may not need to bargain. Some things a country wants it can take, and some things it has it can keep, by sheer strength, skill, and ingenuity. It can do this *forcibly*, accommodating only to opposing strength, skill, and ingenuity and without trying to appeal to an enemy's wishes. Forcibly a country can repel and expel, penetrate and occupy, seize, exterminate, disarm and disable, confine, deny access, and directly frustrate intrusion or attack. It can, that is, if it has enough strength. "Enough" depends on how much an opponent has.

There is something else, though, that force can do. It is less military, less heroic, less impersonal, and less unilateral; it is uglier, and has received less attention in Western military strategy. In addition to seizing and holding, disarming and confining, penetrating and obstructing, and all that, military force can be used to *hurt*. In addition to taking and protecting things of value it can destroy value. In addition to weakening an enemy militarily it can cause an enemy plain suffering. . . .

## THE CONTRAST OF BRUTE FORCE WITH COERCION

There is a difference between taking what you want and making someone give it to you, between fending off assault and making someone afraid to assault you, between holding what people are trying to take and making them afraid to take it, between losing what someone can forcibly take and giving it up to avoid risk or damage. It is the difference between defense and deterrence, between brute force and intimidation, between conquest and blackmail, between action and threats. It is the difference between the unilateral, "undiplomatic" recourse to strength, and coercive diplomacy based on the power to hurt.

The contrasts are several. The purely "military" or "undiplomatic" recourse to forcible action is concerned with enemy strength, not enemy interests; the coercive use of the power to hurt, though, is the very exploitation of enemy wants and fears. And brute strength is usually measured relative to enemy strength, the one directly opposing the other, while the power to hurt is typically not reduced by the enemy's power to hurt in return. Opposing strengths may cancel each other, pain and grief do not. The willingness to hurt, the credibility of a threat, and the ability to exploit the power to hurt will indeed depend on how much the adversary can hurt in return but there is little or nothing about an adversary's pain or grief that directly reduces one's own. Two sides cannot both overcome each other with superior strength; they may both be able to hurt each other. With strength they can dispute objects of value; with sheer violence they can destroy them.

And brute force succeeds when it is used, whereas the power to hurt is most successful when held in reserve. It is the *threat* of damage, or of more damage to come, that can make someone yield or comply. It is *latent* violence that can influence someone's choice—violence that can still be withheld or inflicted or that a victim believes can be withheld or inflicted. The threat of pain tries to structure someone's motives, while brute force tries to overcome his strength. Unhappily, the power to hurt is often communicated by some performance of it. Whether it is sheer terroristic violence to induce an irrational response, or cool premeditated violence to persuade somebody that you mean it and may do it again, it is not the pain and damage itself but its influence on somebody's behavior that matters. It is the expectation of *more* violence that gets the wanted behavior, if the power to hurt can get it at all.

To exploit a capacity for hurting and inflicting damage one needs to know what an adversary treasures and what scares him and one needs the adversary to understand what behavior of his will cause the violence to be inflicted and what will cause it to be withheld. The victim has to know what is wanted, and he may have to be assured of what is not wanted. The pain and suffering have to appear *contingent* on his behavior; it is not the threat alone that is effective—the threat of pain or loss if he fails to comply—but the corresponding assurance, possibly an implicit one, that he can avoid the pain or loss if he does comply. The prospect of certain death may stun him, but it gives him no choice.

Coercion by threat of damage also requires that our interests and our opponent's not be absolutely opposed. If his pain were our greatest delight and our satisfaction his great woe, we would just proceed to hurt and to frustrate each other. It is when his pain gives us little or no satisfaction compared with what he can do for us, and the action or inaction that satisfies us costs him less than the pain we can cause, that there is room for coercion. Coercion requires finding a bargain, arranging for him to be better off doing what we want—worse off not . . . doing what we want—when he takes the threatened penalty into account. . . .

This difference between coercion and brute force is as often in the intent as in the instrument. To hunt down Comanches and to exterminate them was brute force; to raid their villages to make them behave was coercive diplomacy, based on the power to hurt. The pain and loss to the Indians might have looked much the same one way as the other; the difference was one of purpose and effect. If Indians were killed because they were in the way, or somebody wanted their land, or the authorities despaired of making them behave and could not confine them and decided to exterminate them, that was pure unilateral force. If *some* Indians were killed to make *other* Indians behave, that was coercive violence—or intended to be, whether or not it was effective. The Germans at Verdun perceived themselves to be chewing up hundreds of thousands of French soldiers in a gruesome "meatgrinder." If the purpose was to eliminate a military obstacle—the French infantryman, viewed as a military "asset" rather than as a warm human being—the offensive at Verdun was a unilateral exercise of military force. If instead the object was to make the loss of young men—not of impersonal "effectives," but of sons, husbands, fathers and the pride of French manhood—so anguishing as to be unendurable, to make surrender a welcome relief and to spoil the foretaste of an Allied victory, then it was an exercise in coercion, in applied violence, intended to offer relief upon accommodation. And of course, since any use of force tends to be brutal, thoughtless, vengeful, or plain obstinate, the motives themselves can be mixed and confused. The fact that heroism and brutality can be either coercive diplomacy or a contest in pure strength does not promise that the distinction will be made, and the strategies enlightened by the distinction, every time some vicious enterprise gets launched. . . .

War appears to be, or threatens to be, not so much a contest of strength as one of endurance, nerve, obstinacy, and pain. It appears to be, and threatens to be, not so much a contest of military strength as a bargaining process—dirty, extortionate, and often quite reluctant bargaining on one side or both—nevertheless a bargaining process.

The difference cannot quite be expressed as one between the *use* of force and the *threat* of force. The actions involved in forcible accomplishment, on the one hand, and in fulfilling a threat, on the other, can be quite different. Sometimes the most effective direct action inflicts enough cost or pain on the enemy to serve as a threat, sometimes not. The United States threatens the Soviet Union with virtual destruction of its society in the event of a surprise attack on the United States; a hundred million deaths are awesome as pure damage, but they are useless in stopping the Soviet attack—especially if the threat is to do it all afterward anyway. So it is worthwhile to keep the concepts distinct—to distinguish forcible action from the threat of pain—recognizing that some actions serve as both a means of forcible accomplishment and a means of inflicting pure damage; some do not. Hostages tend to entail almost pure pain and damage, as do all forms of reprisal after the fact. Some modes of self-defense may exact so little in blood or treasure as to entail negligible violence; and some forcible actions entail so much violence that their threat can be effective by itself.

The power to hurt, though it can usually accomplish nothing directly, is potentially more versatile than a straightforward capacity for forcible accomplishment. By force alone we cannot even lead a horse to water—we have to drag him—much less make him drink. Any affirmative action, any collaboration, almost anything but physical exclusion, expulsion, or extermination, requires that an opponent or a victim do something, even if only to stop or get out. The threat of pain and damage may make him want to do it, and anything he can do is potentially susceptible to inducement. Brute force can only accomplish what requires no collaboration. The principle is illustrated by a technique of unarmed combat: One can disable a man by various stunning, fracturing, or killing blows, but to take him to jail one has to exploit the man's own efforts. "Come-along" holds are those that threaten pain or disablement, giving relief as long as the victim complies, giving him the option of using his own legs to get to jail. . . .

The fact that violence—pure pain and damage—can be used or threatened to coerce and to deter, to intimidate and to blackmail, to demoralize and to paralyze, in a conscious process of dirty bargaining, does not by any means imply that violence is not often wanton and meaningless or, even when purposive, in danger of getting out of hand. Ancient wars were often quite "total" for the loser, the men being put to death, the women sold as slaves, the boys castrated, the cattle slaughtered, and the buildings leveled, for the sake of revenge, justice, personal gain, or merely custom. If an enemy bombs a city, by design or by carelessness, we usually bomb his if we can. In the excitement and fatigue of warfare, revenge is one of the few satisfactions that can be savored. . . . Pure violence, like fire, can be harnessed to a purpose; that does not mean that behind every holocaust is a shrewd intention successfully fulfilled.

But if the occurrence of violence does not always bespeak a shrewd purpose, the absence of pain and destruction is no sign that violence was idle. Violence is most purposive and most successful when it is threatened and not used. Successful threats are those that do not have to be carried out. . . .

## THE STRATEGIC ROLE OF PAIN AND DAMAGE

Pure violence, nonmilitary violence, appears most conspicuously in relations between unequal countries, where there is no substantial military challenge and the outcome of military engagement is not in question: Hitler could make his threats contemptuously and brutally against Austria; he could make them, if he wished, in a more refined way against Denmark. It is noteworthy that it was Hitler, not his generals, who used this kind of language; proud military establishments do not like to think of themselves as extortionists. Their favorite job is to deliver victory, to dispose of opposing military force and to leave most of the civilian violence to politics and diplomacy. But if there is no room for doubt how a contest in strength will come out, it may be possible to bypass the military stage altogether and to proceed at once to the coercive bargaining.

A typical confrontation of unequal forces occurs at the *end* of a war, between victor and vanquished. Where Austria was vulnerable before a shot was fired, France was vulnerable after its military shield had collapsed in 1940. Surrender negotiations are the place where the threat of civil violence can come to the fore. Surrender negotiations are often so one-sided, or the potential violence so unmistakable, that bargaining succeeds and the violence remains in reserve. But the fact that most of the actual damage was done during the military stage of the war, prior to victory and defeat, does not mean that violence was idle in the aftermath, only that it was latent and the threat of it successful. . . .

The Russians crushed Budapest in 1956 and cowed Poland and other neighboring countries. There was a lag of ten years between military victory and this show of violence, but the principle was the one [just] explained. . . . Military victory is often the prelude to violence, not the end of it, and the fact that successful violence is usually held in reserve should not deceive us about the role it plays.

What about pure violence during war itself, the infliction of pain and suffering as a military technique? Is the threat of pain involved only in the political use of victory, or is it a decisive technique of war itself?

Evidently between unequal powers it has been part of warfare. Colonial conquest has often been a matter of "punitive expeditions" rather than genuine military engagements. If the tribesmen escape into the brush you can burn their villages without them until they assent to receive what, in strikingly modern language, used to be known as the Queen's "protection.". . .

Pure hurting, as a military tactic, appeared in some of the military actions against the plains Indians. In 1868, during the war with the Cheyennes, General Sheridan decided that his best hope was to attack the Indians in their winter camps. His reasoning was that the Indians could maraud as they pleased during the seasons when their ponies could subsist on grass, and in the winter hide away in remote places. "To disabuse their minds from the idea that they were secure from punishment, and to strike at a period when they were helpless to move their stock and villages, a winter campaign was projected against the large bands hiding away in the Indian territory."[1]

These were not military engagements; they were punitive attacks on people. They were an effort to subdue by the use of violence, without a futile attempt to draw the enemy's military forces into decisive battle. They were "massive retaliation" on a diminutive scale, with local effects not unlike those of Hiroshima. The Indians themselves totally lacked organization and discipline, and typically could not afford enough ammunitions for target practice and were no military match for the calvary; their own rudimentary strategy was at best one of harassment and reprisal. Half a century of Indian fighting in the West left us a legacy of cavalry tactics; but it is hard to find a serious treatise on American strategy against the Indians or Indian strategy against the whites. The twentieth is not the first century in which "retaliation" has been part of our strategy, but it is the first in which we have systematically recognized it. . . .

Making it "terrible beyond endurance" is what we associate with Algeria and Palestine, the crushing of Budapest, and the tribal warfare in Central Africa. But in the great wars of the last hundred years it was usually military victory, not the hurting of the people, that was decisive; General Sherman's attempt to make war hell for the Southern people did not come to epitomize military strategy for the century to follow. To seek out and destroy the enemy's military force, to achieve a crushing victory over enemy armies, was still the avowed purpose and the central aim of American strategy in both world wars. Military action was seen as an *alternative* to bargaining, not a *process* of bargaining.

The reason is not that civilized countries are so averse to hurting people that they prefer "purely military" wars. (Nor were all of the participants in these wars entirely civilized.) The reason is apparently that the technology and geography of warfare, at least for a war between anything like equal powers during the century ending in World War II, kept coercive violence from being decisive before military victory was achieved. Blockade indeed was aimed at the whole enemy nation, not concentrated on its military forces; the German civilians who died of influenza in the First World War were victims directed at the whole country. It has never been quite clear whether blockade—of the South in the Civil War or of the Central Powers in both world wars, or submarine warfare against Britain—was expected to make war unendurable for the people or just to weaken the enemy forces by denying economic support. Both arguments were made, but there was no need to be clear about the purpose as long as either purpose was regarded as legitimate and either might be served. "Strategic bombing" of enemy homelands was also occasionally rationalized in terms of the pain and privation it could inflict on people and the civil damage it could do to the nation, as an effort to display either to the population or to the enemy leadership that surrender was better than persistence in view of the damage that could be done. It was also rationalized in more "military" terms, as a way of selectively denying war material to the troops or as a way of generally weakening the economy on which the military effort rested.

But terrorism—as violence intended to coerce the enemy rather than to weaken him militarily—blockade and strategic bombing by themselves were not quite up to the job in either world war in Europe. (They might have been sufficient in the war with Japan after straightforward military action had brought American aircraft into range.) Airplanes could not quite make punitive, coercive violence decisive in Europe, at least on a tolerable time schedule, and preclude the need to defeat or to destroy enemy forces as long as they had nothing but conventional explosives and incendiaries to carry. Hitler's V–1 buzz bomb and his V–2 rocket are fairly pure cases of weapons whose purpose was to intimidate, to hurt Britain itself rather than Allied military forces. What the V–2 needed was a punitive payload worth carrying, and the Germans did not have it. Some of the expectations in the 1920s and the 1930s that another major war would be one of pure civilian violence, of shock and terror from the skies, were not borne out by the available technology. The threat of punitive violence kept occupied countries quiescent; but the wars were won in Europe on the basis of brute strength and skill and not by intimidation, not by the threat of civilian violence but by the application of military force. Military victory was still the price of admission. Latent violence against people was reserved for the politics of surrender and occupation.

The great exception was the two atomic bombs on Japanese cities. These were weapons of terror and shock. They hurt, and promised more hurt, and that was their purpose. The few "small" weapons we had were undoubtedly of some direct military value but their enormous advantage was in pure violence. In a military sense the United States could gain a little by destruction of two Japanese industrial cities; in a civilian sense, the Japanese could lose much. The bomb that hit Hiroshima was a threat aimed at all of Japan. The political target of the bomb was not the dead of Hiroshima or the factories they worked in, but the survivors of

Tokyo. The two bombs were in the tradition of Sheridan against the Comanches and Sherman in Georgia. Whether in the end those two bombs saved lives or wasted them, Japanese lives or American lives; whether punitive coercive violence is uglier than straightforward military force or more civilized; whether terror is more or less humane than military destruction; we can at least perceive that the bombs on Hiroshima and Nagasaki represented violence against the country itself and not mainly an attack on Japan's material strength. The effect of the bombs, and their purpose, was not mainly the military destruction they accomplished but the pain and the shock and the promise of more.

## THE NUCLEAR CONTRIBUTION TO TERROR AND VIOLENCE

Man has, it is said, for the first time in history enough military power to eliminate his species from the earth, weapons against which there is no conceivable defense. War has become, it is said, so destructive and terrible that it ceases to be an instrument of national power. "For the first time in human history," says Max Lerner in a book whose title, *The Age of Overkill,* conveys the point, "men have bottled up a power . . . which they have thus far not dared to use." And Soviet military authorities, whose party dislikes having to accommodate an entire theory of history to a single technological event, have had to re-examine a set of principles that had been given the embarrassing name of "permanently operating factors" in warfare. Indeed, our era is epitomized by words like "the first time in human history," and by the abdication of what was "permanent."

For dramatic impact these statements are splendid. Some of them display a tendency, not at all necessary, to belittle the catastrophe of earlier wars. They may exaggerate the historical novelty of deterrence and the balance of terror.[2] More important, they do not help to identify just what is new about war when so much destructive energy can be packed in warheads at a price that permits advanced countries to have them in large numbers. Nuclear warheads are incomparably more devastating than anything packaged before. What does that imply about war?

It is not true that for the first time in history man has the capability to destroy a large fraction, even the major part, of the human race. Japan was defenseless by August 1945. With a combination of bombing and blockade, eventually invasion, and if necessary the deliberate spread of disease, the United States could probably have exterminated the population of the Japanese islands without nuclear weapons. . . .

It is a grisly thing to talk about. We did not do it and it is not imaginable that we would have done it. We had no reason; if we had had a reason, we would not have the persistence of purpose once the fury of war had been dissipated in victory and we had taken on the task of the executioner. If we and our enemies might do such a thing to each other now, and to others as well, it is not because nuclear weapons have for the first time made it feasible.

Nuclear weapons can do it quickly. . . . To compress a catastrophic war within the span of time that a man can stay awake drastically changes the politics of war, the process of decision, the possibility of central control and restraint, the motivations of people in charge, and the capacity to think and reflect while war is in progress. It *is* imaginable that we might destroy 200,000,000 Russians in a war of the present, though not 80,000,000 Japanese in a war of the past. It is not only imaginable, it is imagined. It is imaginable because it could be done "in a moment, in the twinkling of an eye, at the last trumpet."

This may be why there is so little discussion of how an all-out war might be brought to a close. People do not expect it to be "brought" to a close, but just to come to an end when everything has been spent. It is also why the idea of "limited war" has become so explicit in recent years. Earlier wars, like the World Wars I and II or the Franco-Prussian War, were limited by *termination,* by an ending that occurred before the period of greatest potential violence, by negotiation that brought the *threat* of pain and privation to bear but often precluded the massive *exercise* of civilian violence. With nuclear weapons available, the restraint of violence cannot await the outcome of a contest of military strength; restraint, to occur at all, must occur during war itself.

This is a difference between nuclear weapons and bayonets. It is not in the number of people they can eventually kill but in the speed with which it can be done, in the centralization of decision, in the divorce of the war from political process, and in computerized programs that threaten to take the war out of human hands once it begins.

That nuclear weapons make it *possible* to compress the fury of global war into a few hours does not mean that they make it *inevitable.* We have still to ask whether that is the way a major nuclear war would be fought, or ought to be fought. Nevertheless, that the whole war might go off like one big string of firecrackers makes a critical difference between our conception of nuclear war and the world wars we have experienced. . . .

There is another difference. In the past it has usually been the victors who could do what they pleased to the enemy. War has often been "total war" for the loser. With deadly monotony the Persians, Greeks and Romans "put to death all men of military age, and sold the women and children into slavery," leaving the defeated territory nothing but its name until new settlers arrived sometime later. But the defeated could not do the same to their victors. The boys could be castrated and sold only after the war had been won, and only on the side that lost it. The power to hurt could be brought to bear only after military strength had achieved victory. The same sequence characterized the great wars of this century; for reasons of technology and geography, military force has usually had to penetrate, to exhaust, or to collapse opposing military force—to achieve military victory—before it could be brought to bear on the enemy nation itself. The Allies in World War I could not inflict coercive pain and suffering directly on the Germans in a decisive way until they could defeat the German army; and the Germans could not coerce the French people with bayonets unless they first beat the Allied troops that stood in their way. With two-dimensional warfare, there is a tendency for troops to confront each other, shielding their own lands while attempting to press into each other's. Small penetrations could not do major damage to the people; large penetrations were so destructive of military organization that they usually ended the military phase of the war.

Nuclear weapons make it possible to do monstrous violence to the enemy without first achieving victory. With nuclear weapons and today's means of delivery, one expects to penetrate an enemy homeland without first collapsing his military force. What nuclear weapons have done, or appear to do, is to promote this kind of warfare to first place. Nuclear weapons threaten to make war less military, and are responsible for the lowered status of "military victory" at the present time. *Victory is no longer a prerequisite for hurting the enemy.* And it is no assurance against being terribly hurt. One need not wait until he has won the war before inflicting "unendurable" damages on his enemy. One need not wait until he has lost the war. There was a time when the assurance of victory—false or genuine assurance—could make national leaders not just willing but sometimes enthusiastic about war. Not now.

Not only *can* nuclear weapons hurt the enemy before the war has been won, and perhaps hurt decisively enough to make the military engagement academic, but it is widely assumed that in a major war that is *all* they can do. Major war is often discussed as though it would be only a contest in national destruction. If this is indeed the case—if the destruction of cities and their populations has become, with nuclear weapons, the primary object in an all-out war—the sequence of war has been reversed. Instead of destroying enemy forces as a prelude to imposing one's will on the enemy nation, one would have to destroy the nation as a means or a prelude to destroying the enemy forces. If one cannot disable enemy forces without virtually destroying the country, the victor does not even have the option of sparing the conquered nation. He has already destroyed it. Even with blockade and strategic bombing it could be supposed that a country would be defeated before it was destroyed, or would elect surrender before annihilation had gone far. In the Civil War it could be hoped that the South would become too weak to fight before it became too weak to survive. For "all-out" war, nuclear weapons threaten to reverse this sequence.

So nuclear weapons do make a difference, marking an epoch in warfare. The difference is not just in the amount of destruction that can be accomplished but in the role of destruction and in the decision process. Nuclear weapons can change the speed of events, the control of events, the sequence of events, the relation of victor to vanquished, and the relation of homeland to fighting front. Deterrence rests today on the threat of pain and extinction, not just on the threat of military defeat. We may argue about the wisdom of announcing "unconditional surrender" as an aim in the last major war, but seem to expect "unconditional destruction" as a matter of course in another one.

Something like the same destruction always *could* be done. With nuclear weapons there is an expectation that it would be done. . . . What is new is . . . the idea that major war might be just a contest in the killing of countries, or not even a contest but just two parallel exercises in devastation.

That is the difference nuclear weapons make. At least they *may* make the difference. They also may not. If the weapons themselves are vulnerable to attack, or the machines that carry them, a successful surprise might eliminate the opponent's means of retribution. That an enormous explosion can be packaged in a single bomb does not by itself guarantee that the victor will receive deadly punishment.

Two gunfighters facing each other in a Western town had an unquestioned capacity to kill one another; that did not guarantee that both would die in a gunfight—only the slower of the two. Less deadly weapons, permitting an injured one to shoot back before he died, might have been more conducive to a restraining balance of terror, or of caution. The very efficiency of nuclear weapons could make them ideal for starting war, if they can suddenly eliminate the enemy's capability to shoot back.

And there is a contrary possibility: that nuclear weapons are not vulnerable to attack and prove not to be terribly effective against each other, posing no need to shoot them quickly for fear they will be destroyed before they are launched, and with no task available but the systematic destruction of the enemy country and no necessary reason to do it fast rather than slowly. Imagine that nuclear destruction had to go slowly—that the bombs could be dropped only one per day. The prospect would look very different, something like the most terroristic guerilla warfare on a massive scale. It happens that nuclear war does not have to go slowly; but it may also not have to go speedily. The mere existence of nuclear weapons does not itself determine that everything must go off in a blinding flash, any more than that it must go slowly. Nuclear weapons do not simplify things quite that much. . . .

In World Wars I and II one went to work on enemy military forces, not his people, because until the enemy's military forces had been taken care of there was typically not anything decisive that one could do to the enemy nation itself. The Germans did not, in World War I, refrain from bayoneting French citizens by the millions in the hopes that the Allies would abstain from shooting up the German population. They could not get at the French citizens until they had breached the Allied lines. Hitler tried to terrorize London and did not make it. The Allied air forces took the war straight to Hitler's territory, with at least some thought of doing in Germany what Sherman recognized he was doing in Georgia; but with the bombing technology of World War II one could not afford to bypass the troops and go exclusively for enemy populations—not, anyway, in Germany. With nuclear weapons one has that alternative.

To concentrate on the enemy's military installations while deliberately holding in reserve a massive capacity for destroying his cities, for exterminating his people and eliminating his society, on condition that the enemy observe similar restraint with respect to one's own society is not the "conventional approach." In World Wars I and II the first order of business was to destroy enemy armed forces because that was the only promising way to make him surrender. To fight a purely military engagement "all-out" while holding in reserve a decisive capacity for violence, on condition the enemy do likewise, is not the way military operations have traditionally been approached.

. . . In the present era noncombatants appear to be not only deliberate targets but primary targets. . . . In fact, noncombatants appeared to be primary targets at both ends of the scale of warfare; thermonuclear war threatened to be a contest in the destruction of cities and populations; and, at the other end of the scale, insurgency is almost entirely terroristic. We live in an era of dirty war.

Why is this so? Is war properly a military affair among combatants, and is it a depravity peculiar to the twentieth century that we cannot keep it within decent bounds? Or is war inherently dirty?

To answer this question it is useful to distinguish three stages in the involvement of noncombatants—of plain people and their possessions—in the fury of war. These stages are worth distinguishing; but their sequence is merely descriptive of Western Europe during the past three hundred years, not a historical generalization. The first stage is that in which the people may get hurt by inconsiderate combatants. This is the status that people had during the period of "civilized warfare" that the International Committee had in mind.

From about 1648 to the Napoleonic era, war in much of Western Europe was something superimposed on society. It was a contest engaged in by monarchies for stakes that were measured in territories, and, occasionally, money or dynastic claims. The troops were mostly mercenaries and the motivation for war was confined to the aristocratic elite. Monarchs fought for bits of territory, but the residents of disputed terrain were more concerned with protecting their crops and their daughters from marauding troops than with whom they owed allegiance to. They were, as Quincy Wright remarked in his classic *Study of War,* little concerned that the territory in which they lived had a new sovereign.[3] Furthermore, as far as the King of Prussia and the Emperor of Austria were concerned, the loyalty and enthusiasm of the Bohemian farmer were not decisive considerations. It is an exaggeration to refer to European war during this period as a sport of kings, but not a gross exaggeration. And the military logistics of those days confined military operations to a scale that did not require the enthusiasm of a multitude.

Hurting people was not a decisive instrument in warfare. Hurting people or destroying property only reduced the value of things that were being fought over, to the disadvantage of both sides. Furthermore, the monarchs who conducted wars often did not want to discredit the social institutions they shared with their enemies. Bypassing an enemy monarch and taking the war straight to his people would have had revolutionary implications. Destroying the opposing monarchy was often not in the interest of either side; opposing sovereigns had much more in common with each other than with their own subjects, and to discredit the claims of a monarchy might have produced a disastrous backlash. It is not surprising—or, if it is surprising, not altogether astonishing—that on the European continent in that particular era war was fairly well confined to military activity.

One could still, in those days and in that part of the world, be concerned for the rights of noncombatants and hope to devise rules that both sides in the war might observe. The rules might well be observed because both sides had something to gain from preserving social order and not destroying the enemy. Rules might be a nuisance, but if they restricted both sides the disadvantages might cancel out.

This was changed during the Napoleonic wars. In Napoleon's France, people cared about the outcome. The nation was mobilized. The war was a national effort, not just an activity of the elite. It was both political and military genius on the part of Napoleon and his ministers that an entire nation could be mobilized for war. Propaganda became a tool of warfare, and war became vulgarized.

Many writers deplored this popularization of war, this involvement of the democratic masses. In fact, the horrors we attribute to thermonuclear war were already foreseen by many commentators, some before the First World War and more after it, but the new "weapon" to which these terrors were ascribed was people, millions of people, passionately engaged in national wars, spending themselves in a quest for total victory and desperate to avoid total defeat. Today we are impressed that a small number of highly trained pilots can carry enough energy to blast and burn tens of millions of people and the buildings they live in; two or three generations ago there was concern that tens of millions of people using bayonets and barbed wire, machine guns and shrapnel, could create the same kind of destruction and disorder.

That was the second stage in the relation of people to war, the second in Europe since the middle of the seventeenth century. In the first stage people had been neutral but their welfare might be disregarded; in the second stage people were involved because it was *their* war. Some fought, some produced materials of war, some produced food, and some took care of children; but they were all part of a war-making nation. When Hitler attacked Poland in 1939, the Poles had reason to care about the outcome. When Churchill said the British would fight on the beaches, he spoke for the British and not for a mercenary army. The war was about something that mattered. If people would rather fight a dirty war than lose a clean one, the war will be between nations and not just between governments. If people have an influence on whether the war is continued or on the terms of a truce, making the war hurt people serves a purpose. It is a dirty purpose, but war itself is often about something dirty. The Poles and the Norwegians, the Russians and the British, had reason to believe that if they lost the war the consequences would be dirty. This is so evident in modern civil wars—civil wars that involve popular feelings—that we expect them to be bloody and violent. To hope that they would be fought cleanly with no violence to people would be a little like hoping for a clean race riot.

There is another way to put it that helps to bring out the sequence of events. If a modern war were a clean one, the violence would not be ruled out but merely saved for the postwar period. Once the army has been defeated in the clean war, the victorious enemy can be as brutally coercive as he wishes. A clean war would determine which side gets to use its power to hurt coercively after victory, and it is likely to be worth some violence to avoid being the loser.

"Surrender" is the process following military hostilities in which the power to hurt is brought to bear. If surrender negotiations are successful and not followed by overt violence, it is because the capacity to inflict pain and damage was successfully used in the bargaining process. On the losing side, prospective pain and damage were averted by concessions; on the winning side, the capacity for inflicting further harm was traded for concessions. The same is true in a successful kidnapping. It only reminds us that the purpose of pure pain and damage is extortion; it is *latent* violence that can be used to advantage. A well-behaved occupied country is not one in which violence plays no part; it may be one in which latent violence is used so skillfully that it need not be spent in punishment.

This brings us to the third stage in the relation of civilian violence to warfare. If the pain and damage can be inflicted during war itself, they need not wait for the surrender negotiation that succeeds a military decision. If one can coerce people and their governments while war is going on, one does not need to wait until he has achieved victory or risk losing that coercive power by spending it all in a losing war. General Sherman's march through Georgia might have made as much sense, possibly more, had the North been losing the war, just as the German buzz bombs and

V–2 rockets can be thought of as coercive instruments to get the war stopped before suffering military defeat.

In the present era, since at least the major East-West powers are capable of massive civilian violence during war itself beyond anything available during the Second World War, the occasion for restraint does not await the achievement of military victory or truce. The principal restraint during the Second World War was a temporal boundary, the date of surrender. In the present era we find the violence dramatically restrained during war itself. The Korean War was furiously "all-out" in the fighting, not only on the peninsular battlefield but in the resources used by both sides. It was "all-out," though, only within some dramatic restraints; no nuclear weapons, no Russians, no Chinese territory, no Japanese territory, no bombing of ships at sea or even airfields on the United Nations side of the line. It was a contest in military strength circumscribed by the threat of unprecedented civilian violence. Korea may or may not be a good model for speculation on limited war in the age of nuclear violence, but it was dramatic evidence that the capacity for violence can be consciously restrained even under the provocation of war that measures its military dead in tens of thousands and that fully preoccupies two of the largest countries in the world.

A consequence of this third stage is that "victory" inadequately expresses what a nation wants from its military forces. Mostly it wants, in these times, the influence that resides in latent force. It wants the bargaining power that comes from its capacity to hurt, not just the direct consequence of successful military action. Even total victory over an enemy provides at best an opportunity for unopposed violence against the enemy population. How to use that opportunity in the national interest, or in some wider interest, can be just as important as the achievement of victory itself; but traditional military science does not tell us how to use that capacity for inflicting pain. And if a nation, victor or potential loser, is going to use its capacity for pure violence to influence the enemy, there may be no need to await the achievement of total victory.

Actually, this third stage can be analyzed into two quite different variants. In one, sheer pain and damage are primary instruments of coercive warfare and may actually be applied, to intimidate or to deter. In the other, pain and destruction *in* war are expected to serve little or no purpose but *prior threats* of sheer violence, even of automatic and uncontrolled violence, are coupled to military force. The difference is in the all-or-none character of deterrence and intimidation. Two acute dilemmas arise. One is the choice of making prospective violence as frightening as possible or hedging with some capacity for reciprocated restraint. The other is the choice of making retaliation as automatic as possible or keeping deliberate control over the fateful decisions. The choices are determined partly by governments, partly by technology. Both variants are characterized by the coercive role of pain and destruction—of threatened (not inflicted) pain and destruction. But in one the threat either succeeds or fails altogether, and any ensuing violence is gratuitous; in the other, progressive pain and damage may actually be used to threaten more. The present era, for countries possessing nuclear weapons, is a complex and uncertain blend of the two. . . .

The power to hurt is nothing new in warfare, but for the United States modern technology has drastically enhanced the strategic importance of pure, unconstructive, unacquisitive pain and damage, whether used against us or in our own defense. This in turn enhances the importance of war and threats of war as techniques of influence, not of destruction; of coercion and deterrence, not of conquest and defense; of bargaining and intimidation. . . .

War no longer looks like just a contest of strength. War and the brink of war are more a contest of nerve and risk-taking, of pain and endurance. Small wars embody the threat of a larger war; they are not just military engagements but "crisis diplomacy." The threat of war has always been somewhere underneath international diplomacy, but for Americans it is now much nearer the surface. Like the threat of a strike in industrial relations, the threat of divorce in a family dispute, or the threat of bolting the party at a political convention, the threat of violence continuously circumscribes international politics. Neither strength nor goodwill procures immunity.

Military strategy can no longer be thought of, as it could for some countries in some eras, as the science of military victory. It is now equally, if not more, the art of coercion, of intimidation and deterrence. The instruments of war are more punitive than acquisitive. Military strategy, whether we like it or not, has become the diplomacy of violence.

## NOTES

1. Paul I. Wellman, *Death on the Prairie* (New York: Macmillan, 1934), p. 82.
2. Winston Churchill is often credited with the term, "balance of terror," and the following quotation succinctly expresses the familiar notion of nuclear mutual deterrence. This, though, is from a speech in Commons in November 1934. "The fact remains that when all is said and done as regards defensive methods, pending some new discovery the only direct measure of defense upon a great scale is the certainty of being able to inflict simultaneously upon the enemy as great damage as he can inflict upon ourselves. Do not let us undervalue the efficiency of this procedure. It may well prove in practice— I admit I cannot prove it in theory—capable of giving complete immunity. If two Powers show themselves equally capable of inflicting damage upon each other by some particular process of war, so that neither gains an advantage from its adoption and both suffer the most hideous reciprocal injuries, it is not only possible but it seems probable that neither will employ that means . . . "
3. (Chicago: University of Chicago Press), 1942, p. 296.

# Coercive Diplomacy

## ROBERT J. ART

Coercive diplomacy is, in Alexander George's words, "forceful persuasion": the attempt to get a target—a state, a group (or groups) within a state, or a nonstate actor—to change its objectionable behavior through either the threat to use force or the actual use of limited force. It is a strategy that "seeks to *persuade* an opponent to cease his aggression rather than bludgeon him into stopping." Coercive diplomacy can include, but need not include, positive inducements, and these inducements can involve either a transfer of resources to the target or the offer of things that do not involve resource transfer but that are nonetheless of tangible benefit to the target. Coercive diplomacy is intended to be an alternative to war, even though it involves some employment of military power to achieve a state's desired objective. It is a technique for achieving objectives "on the cheap" and has allure because it promises big results with small costs (to the coercer). Next to outright war, however, coercive diplomacy represents the most dangerous way to use a state's military power because, if coercive diplomacy fails, the state that tries it then faces two stark choices: back down or wage war. The first risks loss of face and future bargaining power; the second, loss of life and military defeat. Because both outcomes are possible, a state should never undertake coercive diplomacy lightly. . . we distinguish between coercive diplomacy and coercive attempts. The feature that distinguishes the two is the presence or absence of the employment of force. Coercive diplomacy has as one of its essential features, and often its only feature, the threat or the limited use of force. Coercive attempts utilize levers over a target, but these levers do not involve the threat or use of force. Therefore, we have excluded from our cases of coercive diplomacy those coercive attempts that involve only the use of economic sanctions, only the withholding of benefits to a target, only the cessation of benefits that a target currently enjoys, or more generally any coercive attempt that does not entail some employment of military power. Clearly, all these actions are coercive in nature, but they do not constitute coercive diplomacy as we have defined it. In distinguishing between coercive attempts and coercive diplomacy, we follow the convention set by George: coercive diplomacy must involve the threat or limited use of force, even though it can also include some of these other types of coercive actions.

Because it entails coercion, coercive diplomacy is a form of compellence—a term first coined by Thomas Schelling in order to distinguish it from deterrence. For Schelling, the distinction between compellence and deterrence is the difference between an action "intended to make an adversary do something"—compellence—

From *The United States and Coercive Diplomacy* edited by Robert J. Art and Patrick M. Cronin. Copyright © by the Endowment of the United States Institute of Peace. Used with permission by the United States Institute of Peace Press, Washington, D.C.

and an action "intended to keep him from starting something"—deterrence. The change in behavior sought by compellence can be manifested in one of two ways: either the adversary starts doing something it is not now doing, or the adversary stops doing something it is now doing. Either way, the adversary changes its behavior. Deterrence, in contrast, is a strategy designed to prevent an adversary from changing its behavior by dissuading it from initiating an action. Deterrence seeks to get the adversary not to change its behavior—that is, to continue "not doing what it is not doing." Thus, compellence aims to alter an adversary's behavior; deterrence, to keep it the same. Deterrence generally involves only threats to use force, whereas compellence can involve both the threat to use force and the actual use of force. In a deterrent situation, if the threat has to be carried out, then, by definition, the adversary has changed its behavior and deterrence has failed. In contrast, because compellence can entail both threats and actual use of force, compellence has not necessarily failed if the threats are carried out.

Although deterrence and compellence are analytically distinct strategies, they usually become conflated when disputing parties contest the legitimacy of the status quo, which they generally do. The deterrer defends the status quo because of the benefits it confers; the target tries to overthrow the status quo because of the injury it inflicts. The target views the deterrer's attempt to maintain the status quo as compellence: "You are coercing me (the target) to accept a situation that benefits you but not me." If the target attempts to alter the status quo, however, then the deterrer will view that attempt as compellence: "You are attempting to coerce me (the deterrer) to stop defending the status quo and accept a revision in it that is less beneficial to me." In such a situation, deterrence and compellence become intermingled. Similarly, deterrent threats can become transformed into compellent actions in situations where deterrence has failed, for in that case the would-be deterrer must decide whether to carry out its threat. If it does so, not for purposes of revenge but to get the adversary to stop its objectionable behavior, then, by definition, execution of the deterrent threat becomes a compellent action. Finally, the deterrer may calculate that deterrence is weakening, even though it has not totally failed, and may decide to bolster deterrence by engaging in actions that are compellent in nature. In that case, compellence is exercised to deter.

Compellence can come in three doses or forms: (1) diplomatic use—the issuance of threats to use force against an adversary if it does not change its behavior, (2) demonstrative use—the exemplary and limited uses of force, and (3) full-scale use, or war—the use of whatever amount of force it takes to get the adversary to change its behavior. The first form of compellence does not use force physically against the target state but only threatens use. The second form uses "just enough force of an appropriate kind to demonstrate resolution to protect one's interests and to establish the credibility of one's determination to use more force if necessary." The third form is to be understood as war—the large-scale use of military power to make the adversary change its behavior. In this volume we follow Alexander George and define coercive diplomacy to encompass only the first two forms of compellence—the diplomatic and demonstrative uses of force. The third form—war—is coercion but not coercive diplomacy, even though diplomacy is never totally absent from war.

The meanings of threat and war are clear. Threat can involve mobilizing and moving large amounts of military force to make the coercer's seriousness of purpose as credible as possible to the target state, or it can simply mean the issuance of verbal warnings. The one thing threat does not mean is the actual physical use of force against the target. War involves sustained, large-scale combat operations against the target, with the goal of either militarily defeating it or bringing about its surrender short of achieving a complete victory over it. Either way, war involves the use of force that is massive, at least to the target.

The meaning of demonstrative use is more difficult to pin down. Although George argues that demonstrative should mean only the "quite limited" use of force, we have used a somewhat broader meaning of demonstrative use. How much is "just enough force" to demonstrate resolution and establish credibility can vary enormously from one situation to another and depends on the nature of the coercer's goals, on the one hand, and on the military capabilities and intensity of interests of the target, on the other. We have therefore defined demonstrative use to include both exemplary and limited use. Exemplary use serves as both a model and a warning of what can or will come: "You did not believe my threat; here is an example for you to chew on of what I can do to you if you do not change your ways." Exemplary use can encompass a one-time employment of force, or a few instances of use, but the major constraint is that it is at the low end of force employment, close to the boundary between threat and use. Exemplary use means moving just beyond the border of threat to make clear by the actions taken that the coercer is deadly serious about escalating the use of force if the target does not comply. In this volume limited use can mean anything from one to several steps beyond exemplary use. The meaning of limited use is this: "You failed to take both my threat and my exemplary use seriously; you obviously need more persuading; let me now give you a better idea of the consequences that your continued noncompliance will bring." More force is used, but not so much such that the boundary to war has been crossed.

A central point follows when coercive diplomacy is conceived to encompass only threat and demonstrative use, but not full-scale use: coercive diplomacy has failed when full-scale use occurs. Wherever one draws the line between limited and full-scale use, if the coercer has to cross that line to achieve its objectives, then, by definition, coercive diplomacy has failed. In this case, war, not coercive diplomacy, produced the change. Any employment of force beyond threat, exemplary use, or limited use signals the failure of coercive diplomacy, even though the subsequent full-scale use of force may succeed in accomplishing the original objectives. As a consequence, exactly where the boundary between limited and full-scale use is drawn becomes crucial for coding cases in which limited use involves escalatory steps that skirt the boundary. Such cases can be coded as either successes or failures of coercive diplomacy, depending on which side of the boundary it is placed. Categorizing such cases becomes an exercise in qualitative judgment. . . .

## WHY IS COERCIVE DIPLOMACY DIFFICULT?

There are good theoretical reasons why coercive diplomacy is difficult. In particular, four factors, which stem from the inherent nature of coercive diplomacy and which therefore operate in every such attempt, explain why this technique is hard to pull off. In addition, depending on the specific situation, two other factors can manifest themselves, and when they are present, they make the successful exercise of coercive diplomacy even more difficult.

## Compellence Is Difficult

First, coercive diplomacy is a form of compellence and, as Thomas Schelling observed, compellence is harder to pull off than deterrence. It is intrinsically more difficult to get a target to change its behavior than to keep its behavior as is. Compellent actions require that the target alter its behavior in a manner quite visible to all in response to an equally visible initiative taken by the coercer. In contrast, deterrent threats are easier for the target to appear to have ignored or to acquiesce in without great loss of face. In deterrent situations the target can claim plausible deniability, maintaining that it had no intention of changing its behavior in the first place, or it can simply appear to ignore the deterrent threats while not changing its behavior. The target has no such plausible deniability in the case of compellence because its overt submission is required. Greater face is thus lost when a target, under pressure, reverses a course of action to which it has committed its prestige and devoted resources than when it simply persists in the same behavior. Finally, compellence more directly engages the passions of the target state than does deterrence because of the pain and humiliation inflicted upon it, but passions, once engaged, are dangerous and produce boomerang effects: they cause the government to mobilize domestic opinion against the coercer, and they increase domestic support for the target government. Both effects perversely make the government more popular after it becomes subject to coercive action than it was before, with the ironic result that the target becomes less susceptible to coercive diplomacy. For these reasons, compellence is harder than deterrence.

## Denial, Punishment, and Risk Strategies Are Hard with Diplomatic and Demonstrative Uses of Force

Coercive diplomacy is a form of coercion, and coercion, as Robert Pape has argued, can be applied in a denial, punishment, or risk fashion.[1] Denial strategies seek to change an adversary's behavior by thwarting its military strategy. Denial takes aim at the target's military forces in order to undercut their effectiveness, seeking to stalemate these forces rather than bring outright military victory over them. A successful denial strategy is one that prevents the target from achieving its political objectives with its military strategy. Punishment strategies seek to change an adversary's behavior by raising the costs of its continued resistance. Punishment imposes pain, either directly to the target's population or to those assets that are important for the population's or the leadership's quality of life. A successful punishment strategy is one that causes the target to give way, not because its military strategy has been thwarted, but because the costs to its population have become too great. Risk strategies seek to change an adversary's behavior by raising the probability that it will suffer ever-greater punishment in the future if it fails to comply. Risk means escalation, and risk threatens more pain to the population or to its valuable assets. A successful risk strategy is one that causes the target to give way because it becomes convinced that the pain it will suffer from looming punishment is not worth the objectives it seeks.

To the extent that it is applied to produce risk, coercive diplomacy is inherently difficult to pull off because risk strategies, Pape tells us, are inherently difficult. They fail for several reasons. For starters, risk strategies are successful to the extent that they create in the target's mind fear of future punishment sufficiently costly that the target changes its behavior. As Pape points out, however, the pain suffered from damage done in the present is greater than the pain imagined from damage done in the future. This happens because human beings discount the future, which means they value the present more. Risk should be conceived as future punishment, and imagined future pain hurts less than present pain. Moreover, because of political considerations, risk strategies are generally applied incrementally, with the coercer gradually ratcheting up the pain inflicted. This produces more perverse effects: the target has time to adapt its tactics to reduce the damage done, time to get used to the pain being inflicted, and time to mobilize domestic opinion against the foreign intruder—all of which make the target better able to tolerate the pain being doled out by the coercer. Finally, when the pain is only threatened or is severely limited when inflicted, as is the case, by definition, with coercive diplomacy, then a coercive risk strategy becomes all the more difficult.

For similar reasons, punishment and denial strategies are difficult to execute with coercive diplomacy. After all, it is hard to inflict much punishment with coercive diplomacy: the limited use of force produces only limited punishment. Delivering limited punishment is not likely to cause a target that cares a great deal about its objectives to change course. Similarly, the threat to deny is not denial, and the limited use of force can produce only limited denial. Strictly speaking, coercive diplomacy cannot employ denial in the sense that it cannot use enough force to stalemate a target. Instead, to the extent that coercive diplomacy aims at denial, it employs "demonstrative denial." Through limited military action the coercer demonstrates to the target that the coercer can, if it so chooses, undercut the effectiveness of the target's military strategy but without actually undercutting it.

Whether the coercer intends to employ its military power to manipulate risk, inflict punishment, or execute denial, all three are hard to bring off when the employment of military power is severely constricted, as it is with coercive diplomacy. To the coercer, its threats and limited use are intended to signal its firm resolve to escalate the use of force—for risk, punishment, or denial purposes—unless the target knuckles under, but the target, especially a highly motivated one, can just as easily see threats and limited use as signaling weak resolve. After all, if the coercer cares that much about its objective, why pull its punches in the first place? What looks to the coercer as steely determination can appear to the target as an unwillingness or inability to employ large-scale use of force to attain its goal. Threats and limited use are not unequivocal in their meaning; they can be interpreted to signify both firmness and weakness in resolve, depending on the perspective of the viewer.

Some of these dynamics appear to have been at work in the Kosovo War. Before the war, the NATO allies thought that Slobodan Milosevic would cave in after a few days of bombing, because they concluded, incorrectly, that he had done so once before—in September 1995, after a period of short intensive bombing strikes against Serbian forces in Bosnia. In 1999, however, Milosevic proved them wrong. Apparently, he believed that he could ride out a few days of bombing and calculated that the alliance could not hold together if it engaged in a sustained, heavy bombing campaign against him. Believing he could outlast the alliance, he forced NATO to resort to an extensive air campaign and ultimately to threaten a ground campaign in order to win the war.

In sum, neither significant punishment nor significant denial is possible with coercive diplomacy. Therefore, what coercive diplomacy can most easily communicate to the target is the increasing probability of more punishment to come if it fails to comply, which is risk, and also some indication of the denial powers of the coercer.

## Estimating Resolve Is Difficult

The third reason that coercive diplomacy is hard to execute lies in the fact that estimating resolve both before and during a coercive diplomatic attempt is a tricky affair and therefore easy to get wrong. Resolve refers to the strength of a party's will to prevail, and the balance of resolve refers to whose will—the target's or the coercer's—is the stronger. Before the fact, the coercer can never know for certain whose resolve is the stronger—its own or the target's. Indeed, this is the function of the crisis produced by the resort to coercive diplomacy: to test the relative strength of the two parties' resolves. Coercive diplomatic attempts are games of chicken that reveal to the target and the coercer which one cares more about something and just how much more. After all, if the relative strength of the parties' resolves were known before coercive diplomacy began, then there would be no reason to begin it. If the target knew, for example, that it cared much less than the coercer and knew that the coercer was intent on getting its way no matter what, and if the coercer also knew that the target cared less than it did, then the target would most likely relent at the first signs of serious intent by the coercer. In serious disputes, however, this does not happen because each party cares intensely about its respective goals. Hence, the resulting crisis serves the function of demonstrating who cares more.

Even if the coercer accurately estimates the relative strength of the two parties' resolves before the crisis gets under way, this is no guarantee that their resolves will remain the same once the crisis begins. Indeed, once it begins, resolves can change and usually do, but generally in the direction of greater firmness by both parties. Each party digs in, in order to see how strongly the other cares. Moreover, when threats are made, and especially when some force is used, both sides are likely to harden their initial positions even more, because the use of force engages passions and almost always causes both the target and the coercer to stiffen their wills. As a consequence, both will bear more sacrifice in order to justify the pain already suffered.

Economists argue that sunk costs should be ignored when making current decisions. Their motto is, "Never throw good money after bad." Statesmen, however, cannot ignore sunk costs because of political considerations: the costs already incurred impel them to pour in even more resources. Their motto is, "Sacrifices already borne justify those currently being made." As a consequence, initial resolves are likely to harden, not weaken, under the impact of a coercive attempt; threats to use force are likely to lead to exemplary use; and exemplary use is likely to lead to full-scale use of force. Therefore, as Glenn Snyder and Paul Diesing have demonstrated, crises that look like games of chicken have an inherent dynamic toward escalation before they are resolved because neither party will give way at the outset.[2] None of this is to argue that coercive diplomacy is inevitably doomed to fail, only that the odds are not in its favor when the resulting crisis hardens the initial resolves of the parties.

## Credibility and Power Are at Stake

Fourth, coercive diplomacy is difficult because the target has to worry about the effects of a confrontation not only on its credibility stakes but also on its power stakes. Credibility stakes concern reputation; power stakes, capabilities. Both are involved in the target's calculations about whether to stand firm or give way to the coercer. Credibility considerations make compromise difficult enough for the target because they involve the following sorts of issues: if the target gives way on this matter, will this be the coercer's last demand, or is it only the first in a series of demands? Even if the coercer will not demand more, what effects will giving way to this coercer have on other would-be coercers? In this regard a target is in the same situation that British leaders were in when dealing with Hitler in the late 1930s: will appeasement satiate Hitler, or will it only whet his appetite and that of other potential coercers as well? Actions in the present always set precedents for the future, and the target can never ignore how its reactions to pressures from others will affect its reputation.

Power stakes are equally, if not more, important. Giving way to the coercer is usually not cost free for the target's power. For example, when the United Nations began to push for representative councils in Somalia in March 1993, Mohammed Farah Aideed, the most powerful of the Somali warlords, understood that he would lose a lot of territory and hence power if representative councils were to emerge in a reconstructed Somalia. He therefore resisted the establishment of these councils. Similarly, both Iraq and North Korea would have faced a significant weakening in their military power if they had acceded to U.S. demands to give up their programs to acquire weapons of mass destruction. North Korea demanded a great deal in return, and Iraq tried to do everything to thwart UN inspectors. Hence, when giving way means that the target's future capacity to resist is significantly diminished, its incentives to stand firm go up dramatically. In these situations a coercive diplomatic demand looks to the target like unilateral disarmament: actions that are being demanded of the target weaken its future power. Thus, giving way represents a double whammy for the target because both its reputation for resolve and its ability to stand firm are undercut.

The inherent difficulty of both compellent and risk strategies, the formidable task of estimating resolves before and during crises, and the target's concern for its power and credibility stakes—all make every attempt at coercive diplomacy hard, not easy, to bring off. Two other factors can complicate the task even further when they are present.

## Multiple Coercers and Multiple Targets Complicate Coercive Diplomacy

Coercive diplomacy becomes even more demanding in situations in which more than a single coercer and a single target are present. If there is a coalition of coercers, it may be united in its overall goal, but more often than not, the coalition will be divided over the means to achieve the goal. Sometimes the coalition will even be divided on the goal itself. If either is the case, then actions are required to keep the members united in their effort. The rub lies here: actions taken to hold the coalition together can degrade the military and diplomatic effectiveness of the coercive attempt. If several targets are present, it becomes more difficult to design actions that coerce them all. Sometimes steps that coerce one of the parties can actually encourage the others to resist. Other times it may be necessary to favor one of the targets in order to induce the others to cooperate. The presence of two or more targets thus requires that the coercer devise actions that ultimately induce all the targets to change their behavior. Neither holding together a coalition while maintaining its military effectiveness nor devising actions to alter the behavior of all the targets is an easy task to accomplish, and success in such situations requires finesse, diplomacy, patience, compromise, and, oftentimes, duplicity. Thus, two or more parties at either the target or the coercer end, or both, complicate what is already an inherently difficult task.

Five of our cases—Bosnia, Kosovo, Iraq, Somalia, and even North Korea— involved more than two parties, and complications ensued as a consequence. Steven Burg and Paul Shoup report that NATO's bombing in late August and early September 1995, which helped end the Bosnian War, was a two-edged sword. It helped bring the Serbs to the negotiating table, but it also encouraged the Muslims and Croats, who were allied at that time, to continue to resist and achieve all their goals through continued battle, using NATO as their air force. As a consequence NATO had to walk a fine line between bombing the Serbs enough to bring them to the negotiating table and bombing them not so much that it pushed the Croatian-Muslim alliance away from the negotiating table.[3] The Kosovo War witnessed serious conflicts among the NATO members over the selection of targets for the bombing campaign. The United States wanted to escalate both the scope and the intensity of the bombing more quickly than did many of its European allies, and these conflicts threatened the cohesiveness of the coalition and probably the efficiency of the bombing campaign, even if they did not ultimately degrade the campaign's military effectiveness. The coalition against Iraq, united during the war, began to fall apart during the 1990s as members became more and more disaffected with the continuing costs of the sanctions. The intervention in Somalia had to deal with dozens of factions vying for power, with two of them, one led by Ali Mahdi Mohammed and the other by Mohammed Farah Aideed, being the most important. Ali Mahdi cooperated more with the United Nations than did Aideed, who viewed the United Nations and the actions it took as hurting his interests and benefiting Ali Mahdi's. This set the stage for the armed confrontation that led to the collapse of the United Nations' mission in Somalia. Finally, even though the United States was the only coercer of North Korea, it could not ignore the views and interests of both South Korea and Japan, its close allies in the region. Their views made U.S. air strikes on North Korea's nuclear facilities difficult because of the fear they would release radioactive material that could disperse over both Japan and South Korea as well as re-ignite the Korean War.

## Belief in "Counter-Coercion" Techniques Can Foil Coercive Diplomacy

Finally, if the target believes that it has the ability to counter the coercer's diplomatic and military pressures, then coercive diplomacy becomes so difficult that it will generally fail. The task for the coercer is to convince the target that sufficient pain and suffering will ensue if the target does not cease its actions. If the target believes that it can foil or significantly mitigate the coercer's measures or in turn impose risks on the coercer, through what are called "counter-coercion" techniques, which can be political, economic, or military in nature, then the target is much less likely to give way. Milosevic must have made such calculations when contemplating NATO's air war against him, because in the months before the war, Serbian military figures visited Iraq to see if they could learn how to thwart U.S. airpower. One device the Serbs hit upon was not to fire most of their surface-to-air missiles (SAMs) but instead to hold them back. This forced NATO pilots to fly at high altitudes over Kosovo and impeded their ability to knock out Serbian armor placed there. Thus, believing that he had the means to ride out an air war, Milosevic did not back down under NATO's threats.

Matters become especially vexing in those situations in which the target will not reveal its counter-coercion techniques for fear that doing so will negate their effectiveness. Not all counter-coercion techniques are undermined if the target makes them known beforehand to the coercer. Indeed, there are often strong incentives to make such measures known ahead of time if doing so will deter the coercer from undertaking his actions. For example, before the onset of the Persian Gulf War, Saddam Hussein argued that Americans could not suffer heavy casualties the way that Iraqis could, thereby attempting to make Iraqi willingness to suffer more than the Americans a counter-coercion tool for deterrence. In the Kosovo conflict there is credible evidence that Milosevic believed his threat to expel large numbers of Albanians from Kosovo to surrounding states in order to destabilize them would deter the NATO alliance from launching the air war against him. The counter-coercion measures that the target must conceal are those that the coercer can quickly design around once they become known, thereby enabling it to make the threat of significant punishment once again credible. In these cases the target has no incentive to forewarn the coercer of its counter-coercion techniques because such foreknowledge would degrade the target's defenses against the coercer's attack, not enhance deterrence of it.

The target's failure to reveal its counter-coercion techniques produces a perverse result: not only does it make the coercer's resort to coercive diplomacy more likely; it also raises the probability that the attempt will fail. Ignorant that its initial measures might be thwarted, the coercer will begin its coercive diplomatic maneuver. Confident that it can defend itself, the target then applies its counter-coercion methods to undermine the coercer's gambit once it begins. The coercer then works furiously to devise its own counters to the target's counters; the target responds in kind; both persist in their respective actions, pouring more into their respective efforts. In short, the dynamics of crisis behavior take over, and the confrontation escalates from threats and exemplary use to the third stage of coercion—war. Thus, when a target believes that it possesses effective counter-coercion techniques that cannot be revealed, it will not find the coercer's threats or exemplary use of force credible, and full-scale use of force will be required if the coercer wants to get its way.

In sum, these six factors explain why coercive diplomacy is difficult. The first four are "permanently operating factors" and explain why, even if executed well, coercive diplomacy often fails. The last two are occasional factors, present or absent depending on the exact nature of the coercive diplomatic attempt. The first five factors make coercive diplomacy inherently hard but not impossible. The last factor—the target's belief that it has effective counter-coercion techniques—makes it highly likely, if not guaranteed, that coercive diplomacy will fail.

## CONCLUSION: WHAT POLICY GUIDELINES CAN BE OFFERED?

Based on the logic and evidence presented, what guidelines can we give to policy-makers who are contemplating resort to coercive diplomacy? Six seem in order.

- *First, coercive diplomacy is difficult and has a relatively low success rate.*
- *Second, it is difficult to estimate the likely outcome of any given coercive diplomatic gambit.*
- *Third, possession of military superiority over the target does not guarantee success at coercive diplomacy.*
- *Fourth, positive inducements seem to enhance the likelihood of success, but only if they are offered after the threatened or actual use of exemplary or limited force.*
- *Fifth, demonstrative denial works better than limited punishment for coercive diplomacy.*
- *Sixth, never resort to coercive diplomacy unless you are prepared to go to war should it fail, or unless you have devised a suitable political escape hatch if war is not acceptable.*

Because the fourth and fifth guidelines have already been discussed at length in the preceding section, I deal here with only the other four.

## 1. Coercive Diplomacy Is Difficult

As I argued earlier, coercive diplomacy is difficult because coercion in general is difficult and because coercive diplomacy is the most difficult form of coercion. The case studies [examined] . . . show that coercive diplomacy has a success rate of 32 percent. Even that figure may be too high because two of our cases (Bosnia 1995 and Haiti 1994) were borderline successes and because one (Iraq 1993) may not be a success at all. A tougher coding could easily rank all three as failures, driving the success rate down significantly.

Standing alone, this 32 percent figure lacks context, but fortunately we have some statistics on how other instruments and strategies compare—not as much as we would like but enough to provide some context within which to place the record of coercive diplomacy. The evidence concerning economic sanctions provides a useful starting point, because the imposition of sanctions is roughly analogous to what happens in coercive diplomacy: something is done to try to force a change in a target's behavior without going to war against it. Although the primary instrument of each differs (military versus economic), the objectives and general method of procedure of both are roughly the same. The evidence on sanctions is remarkably similar to our coercive diplomacy data. Gary Hufbauer, Jeffrey Schott, and Kimberly Elliot have produced the most comprehensive study to date of economic sanctions, having reviewed 120 cases in the twentieth century when sanctions were imposed. They concluded that sanctions worked 33 percent of the time to produce a modest change in the target's policies and 25 percent of the time to produce a major policy change. These figures are not identical to the upper and lower bounds of the success rate for our coercive diplomacy cases, but they are close enough to support the proposition that coercion short of war through either economic or economic-military means is difficult and fails more than it succeeds.

Still, the data on sanctions do not provide sufficient context because it could be the case that most other types of diplomatic gambits also fail more than they succeed. Fortunately, we have one other evidentiary benchmark that shows this does not have to be the case and that helps put into comparative perspective the success rate of coercion short of war. It concerns extended deterrence—a diplomatic gambit wherein one state (the defender) tries to protect another (the protégé) from attack by a third party (the attacker). Paul Huth and Bruce Russett studied the universe of cases of extended deterrence—fifty-four such instances—from 1900 to 1980. They found that extended deterrence was successful in thirty-one of these cases, for a success rate of 57 percent. The Huth-Russett study not only shows that some political-military uses of force can succeed more than they fail but also provides empirical support for the proposition that deterrence is easier than compellence.

Table 5 displays the success rates for these three data sets. Taken together, the evidence about economic sanctions, coercive diplomacy, and extended deterrence gives us greater confidence that coercive diplomacy's success rate is not due simply to flawed execution and, therefore, that coercion short of war is indeed an inherently difficult enterprise. . . .

TABLE 5 ■ COMPARATIVE SUCCESS RATES

| Type of Strategy or Instrument | Success Rate |
| --- | --- |
| Coercive diplomacy | 32% |
| Economic sanctions | 25–33% |
| Extended deterrence | 57% |

## 2. Estimating Outcomes is Difficult

We have seen that positive inducements and denial strategies enhance the likelihood of success at coercive diplomacy, but they alone cannot guarantee success because the size of the disparity in resolve between the coercer and the target plays a significant role in determining the outcome. Therefore, determining before the fact whether any given coercive diplomatic attempt will be successful is also hard, and again the problem derives from the inherent difficulty of estimating relative resolves.

First, before the coercive diplomatic crisis begins, the coercer cannot know the strength of the target's resolve compared with its own, nor can it fully know how strongly the target is attached to the interest it is trying to defend. Oftentimes in such situations, the coercer may not be fully certain about the strength of its own resolve and how firmly it is committed to the interests it is defending. The same may be true for the target. To complicate matters, the coercer will find it difficult to credibly communicate to the target just how strong its resolve is, because only resort to war will reveal the full lengths to which it is prepared to go to prevail. War, however, is generally not desired by the coercer since it has chosen coercive diplomacy in the hope of avoiding war. It is therefore inherently hard for the coercer to persuade the target that it is prepared to wage war if coercive diplomacy fails when the coercer has chosen a step short of war to signify the seriousness of its intent. Furthermore, for its part, the target will, more often than not, believe that it has effective counter-coercion instruments available to it, some of which it will want to hide and some or all of which will cause it to believe that it can persevere and ultimately prevail in the test of wills. If the coercer cannot fully reveal its resolve and if the target believes it can counter the coercer, then accurately predicting the outcome of the encounter is difficult. Finally, under the impact of events, wills can change, standing interests can take on different values, and new interests can be formed.

All these factors make *ex ante* estimation of outcomes extraordinarily difficult. As a consequence, the United States should be wary of putting high confidence in estimates about the likely outcome of any given coercive diplomatic attempt. This also means that it should put little confidence in the notion that the less demanding changes in a target's behavior are easier to bring about than the more demanding ones.

## 3. Military Superiority Is No Guarantee of Success

In every one of our cases, the United States possessed military capabilities far superior to the target's. If military superiority alone guaranteed success, then the United States should have had a 100 percent success rate. The fact that it had only a 32 percent success rate shows that the militarily stronger adversary does not necessarily prevail at coercive diplomacy.

The reason why is clear. Compare coercive diplomatic gambits to war. In war, if the wills (resolves) and skills of the opponents are equally matched, then the outcome is decided by relative military capabilities, and the party with superior military strength prevails. If the weaker party has the stronger will, it still cannot prevail against a stronger adversary unless that adversary cares so little about what is at stake that it will quit the fight, which is usually not the case once the war begins. After all, states do not wage war over things that one or both care little about; they wage war only over things that they both care a great deal about.

In coercive diplomacy, in contrast, will counts more heavily than capability. Clearly, capability counts to a degree. Both parties do make estimates of each other's power, calculating how much it can hurt the other, how well it can defend itself from the blows of the other, and to what extent it can foil the other's military strategy. These power estimates do affect resolve, especially when the target believes it possesses effective counter-coercion techniques that can thwart or mitigate the coercer's military power. However, military capability still takes second place to will in coercive diplomacy situations because estimates about the efficacy of military power are different from the actual use of military power. In a coercive diplomatic gambit the coercer employs only threats and limited force, not the full panoply of its military capabilities. Its purpose is to signal to the target just how far it is willing to go in its use of force without having to use much force. With military power partly sheathed, it is the value that each party puts on the objectives at stake that largely determines how many risks each will take and how many costs each will bear. True, confidence about its military capability can strengthen a target's resolve, but the target must have a strong resolve to begin with because it can never be certain that its counter-coercion techniques will work as envisioned. It must therefore value the objective highly enough to take the risk that its counter-coercion techniques may well not work. At their core, then, coercive diplomatic crises are akin to games of chicken in which wills more than capabilities are being tested. In such situations the more the target values its objectives, the more pain it is willing to bear to achieve them, and hence the less likely the coercer is to succeed.

In all the cases we studied, the United States faced targets that, although militarily inferior, were initially more highly motivated than the United States. After all, in the bulk of our cases, the issues at stake between the United States and the target were vital for the target, but not for the United States, with the 1994 North Korean, 1990–91 Iraqi, and 2001 Afghanistan cases being the clear exceptions. How much military power the United States is prepared to commit, and therefore how far it is willing to go in signaling its intent to commit its vast resources, depends on how much the United States values the interests at stake. The United States can always militarily overwhelm such a target, but to win at coercive diplomacy, it must convince the target that the United States cares more about winning than does the target, and that the United States will use a sufficient portion of its superior strength to prevail. This is not easy to accomplish in situations in which the target views the issues at stake as vital. As a consequence, targets with strong wills but inferior military capabilities may well believe that their superior determination will offset their capabilities' deficit.

For all these reasons, the United States should never bank on the fact that being militarily stronger automatically brings victory in coercive diplomatic encounters the way it can in wars. Were that the case, the United States could dispense with war and do only coercive diplomacy.

## 4. Do Not Resort to Coercive Diplomacy Unless, Should It Fail, You Are Prepared to Go Down the Path of War or You Have Prepared a Suitable Political Escape Hatch

This advice does not imply that policymakers should eschew coercive diplomacy. Indeed, it is reasonable for U.S. national security decision makers to use it in order to achieve their objectives because coercion short of war, if it works, is cheaper than waging war. Because the odds are against success, however, the United States should not start down the road of coercive diplomacy unless it is willing to resort to war, or unless it has devised a political strategy that will enable it to back down without too much loss of face, should coercive diplomacy fail. To resort to coercive diplomacy and then to abandon pursuit of the objective when coercive diplomacy fails, if done too much, weakens the technique for future use and may well discredit it. Although it is true that the objectives at hand determine to a great degree how both the target and the coercer view the coercer's determination, repeated use of coercive diplomacy, followed by hasty retreats when strong resistance is encountered, cannot but have a negative effect on the coercer's reputation and, by extension, on its use of this technique. For this reason, if for no other, resort to coercive diplomacy should be undertaken only when the objectives sought are worth going to war for, or can somehow be easily discounted politically to the U.S. public and its external audiences, should coercive diplomacy fail. There is obviously a tension here, however, because if the objective is worth going to war for, it is more difficult to discount politically. Thus, although the temptation to try coercion on the cheap is great, the United States should not try it unless it is prepared to go the expensive route or can find a suitable escape hatch.

## NOTES

1. Robert P. Pape, *Bombing to Win: Airpower and Coercion* (Ithaca, N.Y.: Cornell University Press, 1996), pp. 18–19.
2. Glenn Snyder and Paul Diesing, *Conflict among Nations: Bargaining, Decision Making, and System Structure in International Crises* (Princeton, N.J.: Princeton University Press, 1977), pp. 118–122.
3. Steven L. Burg and Paul S. Sharp, *The War in Bosnia-Herzegovina: Ethnic Conflict and International Intervention* (Armonk, N.Y.: M. E. Sharpe, 1991), pp. 354–355.

# Offense, Defense, and the Security Dilemma

## ROBERT JERVIS

Another approach starts with the central point of the security dilemma—that an increase in one state's security decreases the security of others—and examines the conditions under which this proposition holds. Two crucial variables are involved: whether defensive weapons and policies can be distinguished from offensive ones, and whether the defense or the offense has the advantage. The definitions are not always clear, and many cases are difficult to judge, but these two variables shed a great deal of light on the question of whether status-quo powers will adopt compatible security policies. All the variables discussed so far leave the heart of the problem untouched. But when defensive weapons differ from offensive ones, it is possible for a state to make itself more secure without making others less secure. And when the defense has the advantage over the offense, a large increase in one state's security only slightly decreases the security of the others, and status-quo powers can all enjoy a high level of security and largely escape from the state of nature.

## OFFENSE-DEFENSE BALANCE

When we say that the offense has the advantage, we simply mean that it is easier to destroy the other's army and take its territory than it is to defend one's own. When the defense has the advantage, it is easier to protect and to hold than it is to move forward, destroy, and take. If effective defenses can be erected quickly, an attacker may be able to keep territory he has taken in an initial victory. Thus, the dominance of the defense made it very hard for Britain and France to push Germany out of France in World War I. But when superior defenses are difficult for an aggressor to improvise on the battlefield and must be constructed during peacetime, they provide no direct assistance to him.

The security dilemma is at its most vicious when commitments, strategy, or technology dictate that the only route to security lies through expansion. Status-quo powers must then act like aggressors: the fact that they would gladly agree to forego the opportunity for expansion in return for guarantees for their security has no implications for their behavior. Even if expansion is not sought as a goal in itself, there will be quick and drastic changes in the distribution of territory and influence. Conversely,

From "Cooperation Under the Security Dilemma" from *World Politics*, Vol. 30, No. 2 (January 1978), pp. 186–214 by Robert Jervis. Reprinted with permission of Johns Hopkins University Press. Portions of the text and some footnotes have been omitted.

when the defense has the advantage, status-quo states can make themselves more secure without gravely endangering others.[1] Indeed, if the defense has enough of an advantage and if the states are of roughly equal size, not only will the security dilemma cease to inhibit status-quo states from cooperating, but aggression will be next to impossible, thus rendering international anarchy relatively unimportant. If states cannot conquer each other, then the lack of sovereignty, although it presents problems of collective goods in a number of areas, no longer forces states to devote their primary attention to self-preservation. Although, if force were not usable, there would be fewer restraints on the use of nonmilitary instruments, these are rarely powerful enough to threaten the vital interests of a major state.

Two questions of the offense-defense balance can be separated. First, does the state have to spend more or less than one dollar on defensive forces to offset each dollar spent by the other side on forces that could be used to attack? If the state has one dollar to spend on increasing its security, should it put it into offensive or defensive forces? Second, with a given inventory of forces, is it better to attack or to defend? Is there an incentive to strike first or to absorb the other's blow? These two aspects are often linked: If each dollar spent on offense can overcome each dollar spent on defense, and if both sides have the same defense budgets, then both are likely to build offensive forces and find it attractive to attack rather than to wait for the adversary to strike.

These aspects affect the security dilemma in different ways. The first has its greatest impact on arms races. If the defense has the advantage, and if the status-quo powers have reasonable subjective security requirements, they can probably avoid an arms race. Although an increase in one side's arms and security will still decrease the other's security, the former's increase will be larger than the latter's decrease. So if one side increases its arms, the other can bring its security back up to its previous level by adding a smaller amount to its forces. And if the first side reacts to this change, its increase will also be smaller than the stimulus that produced it. Thus a stable equilibrium will be reached. Shifting from dynamics to statics, each side can be quite secure with forces roughly equal to those of the other. Indeed, if the defense is much more potent than the offense, each side can be willing to have forces much smaller than the other's, and can be indifferent to a wide range of the other's defense policies.

The second aspect—whether it is better to attack or to defend—influences short-run stability. When the offense has the advantage, a state's reaction to international tension will increase the chances of war. The incentives for preemption and the "reciprocal fear of surprise attack" in this situation have been made clear by analyses of the dangers that exist when two countries have first-strike capabilities.[2] There is no way for the state to increase its security without menacing, or even attacking, the other. Even Bismarck, who once called preventive war "committing suicide from fear of death," said that "no government, if it regards war as inevitable even if it does not want it, would be so foolish as to leave to the enemy the choice of time and occasion and to wait for the moment which is most convenient for the enemy."[3] In another arena, the same dilemma applies to the policeman in a dark alley confronting a suspected criminal who appears to be holding a weapon. Though racism may indeed be present, the security dilemma can account for many of the tragic shootings of innocent people in the ghettos.

Beliefs about the course of a war in which the offense has the advantage further deepen the security dilemma. When there are incentives to strike first, a successful attack will usually so weaken the other side that victory will be relatively quick, bloodless, and decisive. It is in these periods when conquest is possible and attractive that states consolidate power internally—for instance, by destroying the feudal barons—and expand externally. There are several consequences that decrease the chance of cooperation among status-quo states. First, war will be profitable for the winner. The costs will be low and the benefits high. Of course, losers will suffer; the fear of losing could induce states to try to form stable cooperative arrangements, but the temptation of victory will make this particularly difficult. Second, because wars are expected to be both frequent and short, there will be incentives for high levels of arms, and quick and strong reaction to the other's increases in arms. The state cannot afford to wait until there is unambiguous evidence that the other is building new weapons. Even large states that have faith in their economic strength cannot wait, because the war will be over before their products can reach the army. Third, when wars are quick, states will have to recruit allies in advance.[4] Without the opportunity for bargaining and realignments during the opening stages of hostilities, peacetime diplomacy loses a degree of the fluidity that facilitates balance-of-power policies. Because alliances must be secured during peacetime, the international system is more likely to become bipolar. It is hard to say whether war therefore becomes more or less likely, but this bipolarity increases tension between the two camps and makes it harder for status-quo states to gain the benefits of cooperation. Fourth, if wars are frequent, statesmen's perceptual thresholds will be adjusted accordingly and they will be quick to perceive ambiguous evidence as indicating that others are aggressive. Thus, there will be more cases of status-quo powers arming against each other in the incorrect belief that the other is hostile.

When the defense has the advantage, all the foregoing is reversed. The state that fears attack does not preempt—since that would be a wasteful use of its military resources—but rather prepares to receive an attack. Doing so does not decrease the security of others, and several states can do it simultaneously; the situation will therefore be stable, and status-quo powers will be able to cooperate. When Herman Kahn argues that ultimatums "are vastly too dangerous to give because . . . they are quite likely to touch off a pre-emptive strike,"[5] he incorrectly assumes that it is always advantageous to strike first.

More is involved than short-run dynamics. When the defense is dominant, wars are likely to become stalemates and can be won only at enormous cost. Relatively small and weak states can hold off larger and stronger ones, or can deter attack by raising the costs of conquest to an unacceptable level. States then approach equality in what they can do to each other. Like the .45-caliber pistol in the American West, fortifications were the "great equalizer" in some periods. Changes in the status quo are less frequent and cooperation is more common wherever the security dilemma is thereby reduced.

Many of these arguments can be illustrated by the major powers' policies in the periods preceding the two world wars. Bismarck's wars surprised statesmen by showing that the offense had the advantage, and by being quick, relatively cheap, and quite decisive. Falling into a common error, observers projected this pattern into the future.[6] The resulting expectations had several effects. First, states sought semi-permanent allies. In the early stages of the Franco-Prussian War, Napoleon III had thought that there would be plenty of time to recruit Austria to his side. Now, others were not going to repeat this mistake. Second, defense budgets were high and reacted quite sharply to increases on the other side. It is not surprising that Richardson's theory of arms races fits this period well. Third, most decision makers thought that the next European war would not cost much blood and treasure.[7] That is one reason why war was generally seen as inevitable and why mass opinion was so bellicose. Fourth, once war seemed likely, there were strong pressures to preempt. Both sides believed that whoever moved first could penetrate the other deep enough to disrupt mobilization and thus gain an insurmountable advantage. (There was no such belief about the use of naval forces. Although Churchill made an ill-advised speech saying that if German ships "do not come out and fight in time of war they will be dug out like rats in a hole,"[8] everyone knew that submarines, mines and coastal fortifications made this impossible. So at the start of the war each navy prepared to defend itself rather than attack, and the short-run destabilizing forces that launched the armies toward each other did not operate.)[9] Furthermore, each side knew that the other saw the situation the same way, thus increasing the perceived danger that the other would attack, and giving each added reasons to precipitate a war if conditions seemed favorable. In the long and the short run, there were thus both offensive and defensive incentives to strike. This situation casts light on the common question about German motives in 1914: "Did Germany unleash the war deliberately to become a world power or did she support Austria merely to defend a weakening ally," thereby protecting her own position?[10] To some extent, this question is misleading. Because of the perceived advantage of the offense, war was seen as the best route both to gaining expansion and to avoiding drastic loss of influence. There seemed to be no way for Germany merely to retain and safeguard her existing position.

Of course the war showed these beliefs to have been wrong on all points. Trenches and machine guns gave the defense an overwhelming advantage. The fighting became deadlocked and produced horrendous casualties. It made no sense for the combatants to bleed themselves to death. If they had known the power of the defense beforehand, they would have rushed for their own trenches rather than for the enemy's territory. Each side could have done this without increasing the other's incentives to strike. War might have broken out anyway; but at least the pressures of time and the fear of allowing the other to get the first blow would not have contributed to this end. And, had both sides known the costs of the war, they would have negotiated much more seriously. The obvious question is why the states did not seek a negotiated settlement as soon as the shape of the war became clear. Schlieffen had said that if his plan failed, peace should be sought.[11] The answer is complex, uncertain, and largely outside of the scope of our concerns. But part of the reason was the hope and sometimes the expectation that break-throughs could be made and the dominance of the offensive restored. Without that hope, the political and psychological pressures to fight to a decisive victory might have been overcome.

The politics of the interwar period were shaped by the memories of the previous conflict and the belief that any future war would resemble it. Political and military lessons reinforced each other in ameliorating the security dilemma. Because it was believed that the First World War had been a mistake that could have been avoided by skillful conciliation, both Britain and, to a lesser extent, France were highly sensitive to the possibility that interwar Germany was not a real threat to peace, and alert to the danger that reacting quickly and strongly to her arms could create unnecessary conflict. And because Britain and France expected the defense to continue to dominate, they concluded that it was safe to adopt a more relaxed and nonthreatening military posture.[12] Britain also felt less need to maintain tight alliance bonds. The Allies' military posture then constituted only a slight danger to Germany; had the latter been content with the status quo, it would have been easy for both sides to have felt secure behind their lines of fortifications. Of course the Germans were not content, so it is not surprising that they devoted their money and attention to finding ways out of a defense-dominated stalemate. *Blitzkrieg* tactics were necessary if they were to use force to change the status quo.

The initial stages of the war on the Western Front also contrasted with the First World War. Only with the new air arm were there any incentives to strike first, and these forces were too weak to carry out the grandiose plans that had been both dreamed and feared. The armies, still the main instrument, rushed to defensive positions. Perhaps the allies could have successfully attacked while the Germans were occupied in Poland.[13] But belief in the defense was so great that this was never seriously contemplated. Three months after the start of the war, the French Prime Minister summed up the view held by almost everyone but Hitler: on the Western Front there is "deadlock. Two Forces of equal strength and the one that attacks seeing such enormous casualties that it cannot move without endangering the continuation of the war or of the aftermath."[14] The Allies were caught in a dilemma they never fully recognized, let alone solved. On the one hand, they had very high war aims; although unconditional surrender had not yet been adopted, the British had decided from the start that the removal of Hitler was a necessary condition for peace.[15] On the other hand, there were no realistic plans or instruments for allowing the Allies to impose their will on the other side. The British Chief of the Imperial General Staff noted, "The French have no intention of carrying out an offensive for years, if at all"; the British were only slightly bolder.[16] So the Allies looked to a long war that would wear the Germans down, cause civilian suffering through shortages, and eventually undermine Hitler. There was little analysis to support this view—and indeed it probably was not supportable—but as long as the defense was dominant and the numbers on each side relatively equal, what else could the Allies do?

To summarize, the security dilemma was much less powerful after World War I than it had been before. In the later period, the expected power of the defense allowed status-quo states to pursue compatible security policies and avoid arms races. Furthermore, high tension and fear of war did not set off short-run dynamics by which each state, trying to increase its security, inadvertently acted to make war more likely. The expected high costs of war, however, led the Allies to believe that no sane German leader would run the risks entailed in an attempt to dominate the Continent, and discouraged them from risking war themselves.

## Technology and Geography

Technology and geography are the two main factors that determine whether the offense or the defense has the advantage. As Brodie notes, "On the tactical level, as a rule, few physical factors favor the attacker but many favor the defender. The defender usually has the advantage of cover. He characteristically fires from behind some form of shelter while his opponent crosses open ground."[17] Anything that increases the amount of ground the attacker has to cross, or impedes his progress across it, or makes him more vulnerable while crossing, increases the advantage accruing to the defense. When states are separated by barriers that produce these effects, the security dilemma is eased, since both can have forces adequate for defense without being able to attack. Impenetrable barriers would actually prevent war; in reality, decision makers have to settle for a good deal less. Buffer zones slow the attacker's progress; they thereby give the defender time to prepare, increase problems of logistics, and reduce the number of soldiers available for the final assault. At the end of the nineteenth century, Arthur Balfour noted Afghanistan's "non-conducting" qualities. "So long as it possesses few roads, and no railroads, it will be impossible for Russia to make effective use of her great numerical superiority at any point immediately vital to the Empire." The Russians valued buffers for the same reasons; it is not surprising that when Persia was being divided into Russian and British spheres of influence some years later, the Russians sought assurances that the British would refrain from building potentially menacing railroads in their sphere. Indeed, since railroad construction radically altered the abilities of countries to defend themselves and to attack others, many diplomatic notes and much intelligence activity in the late nineteenth century centered on this subject.[18]

Oceans, large rivers, and mountain ranges serve the same function as buffer zones. Being hard to cross, they allow defense against superior numbers. The defender has merely to stay on his side of the barrier and so can utilize all the men he can bring up to it. The attacker's men, however, can cross only a few at a time, and they are very vulnerable when doing so. If all states were self-sufficient islands, anarchy would be much less of a problem. A small investment in shore defenses and a small army would be sufficient to repel invasion. Only very weak states would be vulnerable, and only very large ones could menace others. As noted above, the United States, and to a lesser extent Great Britain, have partly been able to escape from the state of nature because their geographical positions approximated this ideal.

Although geography cannot be changed to conform to borders, borders can and do change to conform to geography. Borders across which an attack is easy tend to be unstable. States living within them are likely to expand or be absorbed. Frequent wars are almost inevitable since attacking will often seem the best way to protect what one has. This process will stop, or at least slow down, when the state's borders reach—by expansion or contraction—a line of natural obstacles. Security without attack will then be possible. Furthermore, these lines constitute salient solutions to bargaining problems and, to the extent that they are barriers to migration, are likely to divide ethnic groups, thereby raising the costs and lowering the incentives for conquest.

Attachment to one's state and its land reinforce one quasi-geographical aid to the defense. Conquest usually becomes more difficult the deeper the attacker pushes into the other's territory. Nationalism spurs the defenders to fight harder; advancing not only lengthens the attacker's supply lines, but takes him through unfamiliar and often devastated lands that require troops for garrison duty. These stabilizing dynamics will not operate, however, if the defender's war matériel is situated near its borders, or if the people do not care about their state, but only about being on the winning side. In such cases, positive feedback will be at work and initial defeats will be insurmountable.[19]

Imitating geography, men have tried to create barriers. Treaties may provide for demilitarized zones on both sides of the border, although such zones will rarely be deep enough to provide more than warning. Even this was not possible in Europe, but the Russians adopted a gauge for their railroads that was broader than that of the neighboring states, thereby complicating the logistics problems of any attacker—including Russia.

Perhaps the most ambitious and at least temporarily successful attempts to construct a system that would aid the defenses of both sides were the interwar naval treaties, as they affected Japanese-American relations. As mentioned earlier, the problem was that the United States could not defend the Philippines without denying Japan the ability to protect her home islands.[20] (In 1941 this dilemma became insoluble when Japan sought to extend her control to Malaya and the Dutch East Indies. If the Philippines had been invulnerable, they could have provided a secure base from which the United States could interdict Japanese shipping between the homeland and the areas she was trying to conquer.) In the 1920s and early 1930s each side would have been willing to grant the other security for its possessions in return for a reciprocal grant, and the Washington Naval Conference agreements were designed to approach this goal. As a Japanese diplomat later put it, their country's "fundamental principle" was to have "a strength insufficient for attack and adequate for defense."[21] Thus Japan agreed in 1922 to accept a navy only three-fifths as large as that of the United States, and the United States agreed not to fortify its Pacific islands.[22] (Japan had earlier been forced to agree not to fortify the islands she had taken from Germany in World War I.) Japan's navy would not be large enough to defeat America's anywhere other than close to the home islands. Although the Japanese could still take the Philippines, not only would they be unable to move farther, but they might be weakened enough by their efforts to be vulnerable to counterattack. Japan, however, gained security. An American attack was rendered more difficult because the American bases were unprotected and because, until 1930, Japan was allowed unlimited numbers of cruisers, destroyers, and submarines that could weaken the American fleet as it made its way across the ocean.[23]

The other major determinant of the offense-defense balance is technology. When weapons are highly vulnerable, they must be employed before they are attacked. Others can remain quite invulnerable in their bases. The former characteristics are embodied in unprotected missiles and many kinds of bombers. (It should be noted that it is not vulnerability *per se* that is crucial, but the location of the vulnerability. Bombers and missiles that are easy to destroy only after having been launched toward their targets do not create destabilizing dynamics.) Incentives to strike first are usually absent for naval forces that are threatened by a naval attack.

Like missiles in hardened silos, they are usually well protected when in their bases. Both sides can then simultaneously be prepared to defend themselves successfully.

In ground warfare under some conditions, forts, trenches, and small groups of men in prepared positions can hold off large numbers of attackers. Less frequently, a few attackers can storm the defenses. By and large, it is a contest between fortifications and supporting light weapons on the one hand, and mobility and heavier weapons that clear the way for the attack on the other. As the erroneous views held before the two world wars show, there is no simple way to determine which is dominant. "[T]hese oscillations are not smooth and predictable like those of a swinging pendulum. They are uneven in both extent and time. Some occur in the course of a single battle or campaign, others in the course of a war, still others during a series of wars." Longer-term oscillations can also be detected:

> The early Gothic age, from the twelfth to the late thirteenth century, with its wonderful cathedrals and fortified places, was a period during which the attackers in Europe generally met serious and increasing difficulties, because the improvement in the strength of fortresses outran the advance in the power of destruction. Later, with the spread of firearms at the end of the fifteenth century, old fortresses lost their power to resist. An age ensued during which the offense possessed, apart from short-term setbacks, new advantages. Then, during the seventeenth century, especially after about 1660, and until at least the outbreak of the War of the Austrian Succession in 1740, the defense regained much of the ground it had lost since the great medieval fortresses had proved unable to meet the bombardment of the new and more numerous artillery.[24]

Another scholar has continued the argument: "The offensive gained an advantage with new forms of heavy mobile artillery in the nineteenth century, but the stalemate of World War I created the impression that the defense again had an advantage; the German invasion in World War II, however, indicated the offensive superiority of highly mechanized armies in the field."[25]

The situation today with respect to conventional weapons is unclear. Until recently it was believed that tanks and tactical air power gave the attacker an advantage. The initial analyses of the 1973 Arab-Israeli war indicated that new anti-tank and anti-aircraft weapons have restored the primacy of the defense. These weapons are cheap, easy to use, and can destroy a high proportion of the attacking vehicles and planes that are sighted. It then would make sense for a status-quo power to buy lots of $20,000 missiles rather than buy a few half-million dollar fighter-bombers. Defense would be possible even against a large and well-equipped force; states that care primarily about self-protection would not need to engage in arms races. But further examinations of the new technologies and the history of the October War cast doubt on these optimistic conclusions and leave us unable to render any firm judgment.[26]

Concerning nuclear weapons, it is generally agreed that defense is impossible—a triumph not of the offense, but of deterrence. Attack makes no sense, not because it can be beaten off, but because the attacker will be destroyed in turn. In terms of the questions under consideration here, the result is the equivalent of the primacy of the defense. First, security is relatively cheap. Less than one percent of the G.N.P. is devoted to deterring a direct attack on the United States; most of it is spent on acquiring redundant systems to provide a lot of insurance against the worst conceivable contingencies. Second, both sides can simultaneously gain security in the form of second-strike capability. Third, and related to the foregoing, second-strike capability can be maintained in the face of wide variations in the other side's military posture. There is no purely military reason why each side has to react quickly and strongly to the other's increases in arms. Any spending that the other devotes to trying to achieve first-strike capability can be neutralized by the state's spending much smaller sums on protecting its second-strike capability. Fourth, there are no incentives to strike first in a crisis.

Important problems remain, of course. Both sides have interests that go well beyond defense of the homeland. The protection of these interests creates conflicts even if neither side desires expansion. Furthermore, the shift from defense to deterrence has greatly increased the importance and perceptions of resolve. Security now rests on each side's belief that the other would prefer to run high risks of total destruction rather than sacrifice its vital interests. Aspects of the security dilemma thus appear in a new form. Are weapons procurements used as an index of resolve? Must they be so used? If one side fails to respond to the other's buildup, will it appear weak and thereby invite predation? Can both sides simultaneously have images of high resolve or is there a zero-sum element involved? Although these problems are real, they are not as severe as those in the prenuclear era: There are many indices of resolve, and states do not so much judge images of resolve in the abstract as ask how likely it is that the other will stand firm in a particular dispute. Since states are most likely to stand firm on matters which concern them most, it is quite possible for both to demonstrate their resolve to protect their own security simultaneously.

## OFFENSE-DEFENSE DIFFERENTIATION

The other major variable that affects how strongly the security dilemma operates is whether weapons and policies that protect the state also provide the capability for attack. If they do not, the basic postulate of the security dilemma no longer applies. A state can increase its own security without decreasing that of others. The advantage of the defense can only ameliorate the security dilemma. A differentiation between offensive and defensive stances comes close to abolishing it. Such differentiation does not mean, however, that all security problems will be abolished. If the offense has the advantage, conquest and aggression will still be possible. And if the offense's advantage is great enough, status-quo powers may find it too expensive to protect themselves by defensive forces and decide to procure offensive weapons even though this will menace others. Furthermore, states will still have to worry that even if the other's military posture shows that it is peaceful now, it may develop aggressive intentions in the future.

Assuming that the defense is at least as potent as the offense, the differentiation between them allows status-quo states to behave in ways that are clearly different from those of aggressors. Three beneficial consequences follow. First, status-quo powers can identify each other, thus laying the foundations for cooperation. Conflicts growing out of the mistaken belief that the other side is expansionist will be less frequent. Second, status-quo states will obtain advance warning when others plan aggression. Before a state can attack, it has to develop and deploy offensive weapons. If procurement of these weapons cannot be disguised and takes a fair amount of time, as it almost always does, a status-quo state will have the time to take counter-measures. It need not maintain a high level of defensive arms as long as its potential adversaries are adopting a peaceful posture. (Although being so armed should not, with the one important exception noted below, alarm other status-quo powers.) States do, in fact, pay special attention to actions that they believe would not be taken by a status-quo state because they feel that states exhibiting such behavior are aggressive. Thus the seizure or development of transportation facilities will alarm others more if these facilities have no commercial value, and therefore can only be wanted for military reasons. In 1906, the British rejected a Russian protest about their activities in a district of Persia by claiming that this area was "only of [strategic] importance [to the Russians] if they wished to attack the Indian frontier, or to put pressure upon us by making us think that they intend to attack it."[27]

The same inferences are drawn when a state acquires more weapons than observers feel are needed for defense. Thus, the Japanese spokesman at the 1930 London naval conference said that his country was alarmed by the American refusal to give Japan a 70 percent ratio (in place of a 60 percent ratio) in heavy cruisers: "As long as America held that ten percent advantage, it was possible for her to attack. So when America insisted on sixty percent instead of seventy percent, the idea would exist that they were trying to keep that possibility, and the Japanese people could not accept that."[28] Similarly, when Mussolini told Chamberlain in January 1939 that Hitler's arms program was motivated by defensive considerations, the Prime Minister replied that "German military forces were now so strong as to make it impossible for any Power or combination of Powers to attack her successfully. She could not want any further armaments for defensive purposes; what then did she want them for?"[29]

Of course these inferences can be wrong—as they are especially likely to be because states underestimate the degree to which they menace others.[30] And when they are wrong, the security dilemma is deepened. Because the state thinks it has received notice that the other is aggressive, its own arms building will be less restrained and the chances of cooperation will be decreased. But the dangers of incorrect inferences should not obscure the main point: When offensive and defensive postures are different, much of the uncertainty about the other's intentions that contributes to the security dilemma is removed.

The third beneficial consequence of a difference between offensive and defensive weapons is that if all states support the status quo, an obvious arms control agreement is a ban on weapons that are useful for attacking. As President Roosevelt put it in his message to the Geneva Disarmament Conference in 1933: "If all nations will agree wholly to eliminate from possession and use the weapons which make possible a successful attack, defenses automatically will become impregnable, and the frontiers and independence of every nation will become secure."[31] The fact that such treaties have been rare—the Washington naval agreements discussed above and the anti-ABM treaty can be cited as examples—shows either that states are not always willing to guarantee the security of others, or that it is hard to distinguish offensive from defensive weapons.

Is such a distinction possible? Salvador de Madariaga, the Spanish statesman active in the disarmament negotiations of the interwar years, thought not: "A weapon is either offensive or defensive according to which end of it you are looking at." The French Foreign Minister agreed (although French policy did not always follow this view): "Every arm can be employed offensively or defensively in turn. . . . The only way to discover whether arms are intended for purely defensive purposes or are held in a spirit of aggression is in all cases to enquire into the intentions of the country concerned." Some evidence for the validity of this argument is provided by the fact that much time in these unsuccessful negotiations was devoted to separating offensive from defensive weapons. Indeed, no simple and unambiguous definition is possible and in many cases no judgment can be reached. Before the American entry into World War I, Woodrow Wilson wanted to arm merchantmen only with guns in the back of the ship so they could not initiate a fight, but this expedient cannot be applied to more common forms of armaments.[32]

There are several problems. Even when a differentiation is possible, a status-quo power will want offensive arms under any of three conditions: (1) If the offense has a great advantage over the defense, protection through defensive forces will be too expensive. (2) Status-quo states may need offensive weapons to regain territory lost in the opening stages of war. It might be possible, however, for a state to wait to procure these weapons until war seems likely, and they might be needed only in relatively small numbers, unless the aggressor was able to construct strong defenses quickly in the occupied areas. (3) The state may feel that it must be prepared to take the offensive either because the other side will make peace only if it loses territory or because the state has commitments to attack if the other makes war on a third party. As noted above, status-quo states with extensive commitments are often forced to behave like aggressors. Even when they lack such commitments, status-quo states must worry about the possibility that if they are able to hold off an attack, they will still not be able to end the war unless they move into the other's territory to damage its military forces and inflict pain. Many American naval officers after the Civil War, for example, believed that "only by destroying the commerce of the opponent could the United States bring him to terms."[33]

A further complication is introduced by the fact that aggressors as well as status-quo powers require defensive forces as a prelude to acquiring offensive ones, to protect one frontier while attacking another, or for insurance in case the war goes badly. Criminals as well as policemen can use bulletproof vests. Hitler as well as Maginot built a line of forts. Indeed, Churchill reports that in 1936 the German Foreign Minister said: "As soon as our fortifications are constructed [on our western borders] and the countries in Central Europe realize that France cannot enter German territory, all these countries will begin to feel very differently about their foreign policies, and a new constellation will develop."[34] So a state may not necessarily be reassured if its neighbor constructs strong defenses.

More central difficulties are created by the fact that whether a weapon is offensive or defensive often depends on the particular situation—for instance, the geographical setting and the way in which the weapon is used. "Tanks. . . . spearheaded the fateful German thrust through the Ardennes in 1940, but if the French had disposed of a properly concentrated armored reserve, it would have provided the best means for their cutting off the penetration and turning into a disaster for the Germans what became instead an overwhelming victory."[35] Anti-aircraft weapons seem obviously defensive—to be used, they must wait for the other side to come to them. But the Egyptian attack on Israel in 1973 would have been impossible without effective air defenses that covered the battlefield. Nevertheless, some distinctions are possible. Sir John Simon, then the British Foreign Secretary, in response to the views cited earlier, stated that just because a fine line could not be drawn, "that was no reason for saying that there were not stretches of territory on either side which all practical men and women knew to be well on this or that side of the line." Although there are almost no weapons and strategies that are useful only for attacking, there are some that are almost exclusively defensive. Aggressors could want them for protection, but a state that relied mostly on them could not menace others. More frequently, we cannot "determine the absolute character of a weapon, but [we can] make a comparison . . . [and] discover whether or not the offensive potentialities predominate, whether a weapon is more useful in attack or in defense."[36]

The essence of defense is keeping the other side out of your territory. A purely defensive weapon is one that can do this without being able to penetrate the enemy's land. Thus a committee of military experts in an interwar disarmament conference declared that armaments "incapable of mobility by means of self-contained power," or movable only after long delay, were "only capable of being used for the defense of a State's territory."[37] The most obvious examples are fortifications. They can shelter attacking forces, especially when they are built right along the frontier,[38] but they cannot occupy enemy territory. A state with only a strong line of forts, fixed guns, and a small army to man them would not be much of a menace. Anything else that can serve only as a barrier against attacking troops is similarly defensive. In this category are systems that provide warning of an attack, the Russian's adoption of a different railroad gauge, and nuclear land mines that can seal off invasion routes.

If total immobility clearly defines a system that is defensive only, limited mobility is unfortunately ambiguous. As noted above, short-range fighter aircraft and anti-aircraft missiles can be used to cover an attack. And, unlike forts, they can advance with the troops. Still, their inability to reach deep into enemy territory does make them more useful for the defense than for the offense. Thus, the United States and Israel would have been more alarmed in the early 1970s had the Russians provided the Egyptians with long-range instead of short-range aircraft. Naval forces are particularly difficult to classify in these terms, but those that are very short-legged can be used only for coastal defense.

Any forces that for various reasons fight well only when on their own soil in effect lack mobility and therefore are defensive. The most extreme example would be passive resistance. Noncooperation can thwart an aggressor, but it is very hard for large numbers of people to cross the border and stage a sit-in on another's territory. Morocco's recent march on the Spanish Sahara approached this tactic, but its success depended on special circumstances. Similarly, guerrilla warfare is defensive to the extent to which it requires civilian support that is likely to be forthcoming only in opposition to a foreign invasion. Indeed, if guerrilla warfare were easily exportable and if it took ten defenders to destroy each guerrilla, then this weapon would not only be one which could be used as easily to attack the other's territory as to defend one's own, but one in which the offense had the advantage: so the security dilemma would operate especially strongly.

If guerrillas are unable to fight on foreign soil, other kinds of armies may be unwilling to do so. An army imbued with the idea that only defensive wars were just would fight less effectively, if at all, if the goal were conquest. Citizen militias may lack both the ability and the will for aggression. The weapons employed, the short term of service, the time required for mobilization, and the spirit of repelling attacks on the homeland, all lend themselves much more to defense than to attacks on foreign territory.[39]

Less idealistic motives can produce the same result. A leading student of medieval warfare has described the armies of that period as follows: "Assembled with difficulty, insubordinate, unable to maneuver, ready to melt away from its standard the moment that its short period of service was over, a feudal force presented an assemblage of unsoldierlike qualities such as have seldom been known to coexist. Primarily intended to defend its own borders from the Magyar, the Northman, or the Saracen . . . , the institution was utterly unadapted to take the offensive."[40] Some political groupings can be similarly described. International coalitions are more readily held together by fear than by hope of gain. Thus Castlereagh was not being entirely self-serving when in 1816 he argued that the Quadruple Alliance "could only have owed its origin to a sense of common danger; in its very nature it must be conservative; it cannot threaten either the security or the liberties of other States."[41] It is no accident that most of the major campaigns of expansion have been waged by one dominant nation (for example, Napoleon's France and Hitler's Germany), and that coalitions among relative equals are usually found defending the status quo. Most gains from conquest are too uncertain and raise too many questions of future squabbles among the victors to hold an alliance together for long. Although defensive coalitions are by no means easy to maintain—conflicting national objectives and the free-rider problem partly explain why three of them dissolved before Napoleon was defeated—the common interest of seeing that no state dominates provides a strong incentive for solidarity.

Weapons that are particularly effective in reducing fortifications and barriers are of great value to the offense. This is not to deny that a defensive power will want some of those weapons if the other side has them: Brodie is certainly correct to argue that while their tanks allowed the Germans to conquer France, properly used French tanks could have halted the attack. But France would not have needed these weapons if Germany had not acquired them, whereas even if France had no tanks, Germany could not have foregone them since they provided the only chance of breaking through the French lines. Mobile heavy artillery is, similarly, especially useful in destroying fortifications. The defender, while needing artillery to fight off attacking troops or to counterattack, can usually use lighter guns since they do not need to penetrate such massive obstacles. So it is not surprising that one of the few things that most nations at the interwar disarmament conferences were able to agree on was that heavy tanks and mobile heavy guns were particularly valuable to a state planning an attack.[42]

Weapons and strategies that depend for their effectiveness on surprise are almost always offensive. That fact was recognized by some of the delegates to the interwar disarmament conferences and is the principle behind the common national ban on concealed weapons. An earlier representative of this widespread view was the mid-nineteenth-century Philadelphia newspaper that argued: "As a measure of defense, knives, dirks, and sword canes are entirely useless. They are fit only for attack, and all such attacks are of murderous character. Whoever carries such a weapon has prepared himself for homicide."[43]

It is, of course, not always possible to distinguish between forces that are most effective for holding territory and forces optimally designed for taking it. Such a distinction could not have been made for the strategies and weapons in Europe during most of the period between the Franco-Prussian War and World War I. Neither naval forces nor tactical air forces can be readily classified in these terms. But the point here is that when such a distinction is possible, the central characteristic of the security dilemma no longer holds, and one of the most troublesome consequences of anarchy is removed.

## Offense-Defense Differentiation and Strategic Nuclear Weapons

In the interwar period, most statesmen held the reasonable position that weapons that threatened civilians were offensive.[44] But when neither side can protect its civilians, a counter-city posture is defensive because the state can credibly threaten to retaliate only in response to an attack on itself or its closest allies. The costs of this strike are so high that the state could not threaten to use it for the less-than-vital interest of compelling the other to abandon an established position.

In the context of deterrence, offensive weapons are those that provide defense. In the now familiar reversal of common sense, the state that could take its population out of hostage, either by active or passive defense or by destroying the other's strategic weapons on the ground, would be able to alter the status quo. The desire to prevent such a situation was one of the rationales for the anti-ABM agreements; it explains why some arms controllers opposed building ABMs to protect cities, but favored sites that covered ICBM fields. Similarly, many analysts wanted to limit warhead accuracy and favored multiple re-entry vehicles (MRVs), but opposed multiple independently targetable re-entry vehicles (MIRVs). The former are more useful than single warheads for penetrating city defenses, and ensure that the state has a second-strike capability. MIRVs enhance counterforce capabilities. . . .

What is most important for the argument here is that land-based ICBMs are both offensive and defensive, but when both sides rely on Polaris-type systems (SLBMs), offense and defense use different weapons. ICBMs can be used either to destroy the other's cities in retaliation or to initiate hostilities by attacking the other's strategic missiles. Some measures—for instance, hardening of missile sites and warning systems—are purely defensive, since they do not make a first strike easier. Others are predominantly offensive—for instance, passive or active city defenses, and highly accurate warheads. But ICBMs themselves are useful for both purposes. And because states seek a high level of insurance, the desire for protection as well as the contemplation of a counterforce strike can explain the acquisition of extremely large numbers of missiles. So it is very difficult to infer the other's intentions from its military posture. Each side's efforts to increase its own security by procuring more missiles decreases, to an extent determined by the relative efficacy of the offense and the defense, the other side's security. That is not the case when both sides use SLBMs. The point is not that sea-based systems are less vulnerable than land-based ones (this bears on the offense-defense ratio) but that SLBMs are defensive, retaliatory weapons. . . . SLBMs are not the main instrument of attack against other SLBMs. The hardest problem confronting a state that wants to take its cities out of hostage is to locate the other's SLBMs, a job that requires not SLBMs but anti-submarine weapons. A state might use SLBMs to attack the other's submarines (although other weapons would probably be more efficient), but without anti-submarine warfare (ASW) capability the task cannot be performed. A status-quo state that wanted to forego offensive capability could simply forego ASW research and procurement. . . .

When both sides rely on ICBMs, one side's missiles can attack the other's, and so the state cannot be indifferent to the other's building program. But because one side's SLBMs do not menace the other's, each side can build as many as it wants and the other need not respond. Each side's decision on the size of its force depends on technical questions, its judgment about how much destruction is enough to deter, and the amount of insurance it is willing to pay for—and these considerations are independent of the size of the other's strategic force. Thus the crucial nexus in the arms race is severed. . . .

## FOUR WORLDS

The two variables we have been discussing—whether the offense or the defense has the advantage, and whether offensive postures can be distinguished from defensive ones—can be combined to yield four possible worlds.

The first world is the worst for status-quo states. These is no way to get security without menacing others, and security through defense is terribly difficult to obtain. Because offensive and defensive postures are the same, status-quo states acquire the same kind of arms that are sought by aggressors. And because the offense has the advantage over the defense, attacking is the best route to protecting what you have; status-quo states will therefore behave like aggressors. The situation will be unstable. Arms races are likely. Incentives to strike first will turn crises into wars. Decisive victories and conquests will be common. States will grow and shrink rapidly, and it will be hard for any state to maintain its size and influence without trying to increase them. Cooperation among status-quo powers will be extremely hard to achieve.

There are no cases that totally fit this picture, but it bears more than a passing resemblance to Europe before World War I. Britain and Germany, although in many respects natural allies, ended up as enemies. Of course much of the explanation lies in Germany's ill-chosen policy. And from the perspective of our theory, the powers' ability to avoid war in a series of earlier crises cannot be easily explained.

TABLE 1 ■

|  | Offense has the advantage | Defense has the advantage |
|---|---|---|
|  | 1 | 2 |
| Offensive posture not distinguishable from defensive one | Doubly dangerous | Security dilemma, but security requirements may be compatible |
|  | 3 | 4 |
| Offensive posture distinguishable from defensive one | No security dilemma, but aggression possible<br>Status-quo states can follow different policy than aggressors<br>Warning given | Doubly stable |

Nevertheless, much of the behavior in this period was the product of technology and beliefs that magnified the security dilemma. Decision makers thought that the offense had a big advantage and saw little difference between offensive and defensive military postures. The era was characterized by arms races. And once war seemed likely, mobilization races created powerful incentives to strike first.

In the nuclear era, the first world would be one in which each side relied on vulnerable weapons that were aimed at similar forces and each side understood the situation. In this case, the incentives to strike first would be very high—so high that status-quo powers as well as aggressors would be sorely tempted to preempt. And since the forces could be used to change the status quo as well as to preserve it, there would be no way for both sides to increase their security simultaneously. Now the familiar logic of deterrence leads both sides to see the dangers in this world. Indeed, the new understanding of this situation was one reason why vulnerable bombers and missiles were replaced. Ironically, the 1950s would have been more hazardous if the decision makers had been aware of the dangers of their posture and had therefore felt greater pressure to strike first.

In the second world, the security dilemma operates because offensive and defensive postures cannot be distinguished; but it does not operate as strongly as in the first world because the defense has the advantage, and so an increment in one side's strength increases its security more than it decreases the other's. So, if both sides have reasonable subjective security requirements, are of roughly equal power, and the variables discussed earlier are favorable, it is quite likely that status-quo states can adopt compatible security policies. Although a state will not be able to judge the other's intentions from the kinds of weapons it procures, the level of arms spending will give important evidence. Of course a state that seeks a high level of arms might be not an aggressor but merely an insecure state, which if conciliated will reduce its arms, and if confronted will reply in kind. To assume that the apparently excessive level of arms indicates aggressiveness could therefore lead to a response that would deepen the dilemma and create needless conflict. But empathy and skillful statesmanship can reduce this danger. Furthermore, the advantageous position of the defense means that a status-quo state can often maintain a high degree of security with a level of arms lower than that of its expected adversary. Such a state demonstrates that it lacks the ability or desire to alter the status quo, at least at the present time. The strength of the defense also allows states to react slowly and with restraint when they fear that others are menacing them. So, although status-quo powers will to some extent be threatening to others, that extent will be limited.

This world is the one that comes closest to matching most periods in history. Attacking is usually harder than defending because of the strength of fortifications and obstacles. But purely defensive postures are rarely possible because fortifications are usually supplemented by armies and mobile guns which can support an attack. In the nuclear era, this world would be one in which both sides relied on relatively invulnerable ICBMs and believed that limited nuclear war was impossible. Assuming no MIRVs, it would take more than one attacking missile to destroy one of the adversary's. Preemption is therefore unattractive. If both sides have large inventories, they can ignore all but drastic increases on the other side. A world of either ICBMs or SLBMs in which both sides adopted the policy of limited nuclear war would probably fit in this category too. The means of preserving the status quo would also be the means of changing it, as we discussed earlier. And the defense usually would have the advantage, because compellence is more difficult than deterrence. Although a state might succeed in changing the status quo on issues that matter much more to it than to others, status-quo powers could deter major provocations under most circumstances.

In the third world there may be no security dilemma, but there are security problems. Because states can procure defensive systems that do not threaten others, the dilemma need not operate. But because the offense has the advantage, aggression is possible, and perhaps easy. If the offense has less of an advantage, stability and cooperation are likely because the status-quo states will procure defensive forces. They need not react to others who are similarly armed, but can wait for the warning they would receive if others started to deploy offensive weapons. But each state will have to watch the others carefully, and there is room for false suspicions. The costliness of the defense and the allure of the offense can lead to unnecessary mistrust, hostility, and war, unless some of the variables discussed earlier are operating to restrain defection.

A hypothetical nuclear world that would fit this description would be one in which both sides relied on SLBMs, but in which ASW techniques were very effective. Offense and defense would be different, but the former would have the advantage. This situation is not likely to occur; but if it did, a status-quo state could show its lack of desire to exploit the other by refraining from threatening its submarines. The desire to have more protecting you than merely the other side's fear of retaliation is a strong one, however, and a state that knows that it would not expand even if its cities were safe is likely to believe that the other would not feel threatened by its ASW program. It is easy to see how such a world could become unstable, and how spirals of tensions and conflict could develop.

The fourth world is doubly safe. The differentiation between offensive and defensive systems permits a way out of the security dilemma; the advantage of the defense disposes of the problems discussed in the previous paragraphs. There is no reason for a status-quo power to be tempted to procure offensive forces, and aggressors give notice of their intentions by the posture they adopt. Indeed, if the advantage of the defense is great enough, there are no security problems. The loss of the ultimate form of the power to alter the status quo would allow greater scope for the exercise of nonmilitary means and probably would tend to freeze the distribution of values.

This world would have existed in the first decade of the twentieth century if the decision makers had understood the available technology. In that case, the European powers would have followed different policies both in the long run and in the summer of 1914. Even Germany, facing powerful enemies on both sides, could have made herself secure by developing strong defenses. France could also have made her frontier almost impregnable. Furthermore, when crises arose, no one would have had incentives to strike first. There would have been no competitive mobilization races reducing the time available for negotiations.

In the nuclear era, this world would be one in which the superpowers relied on SLBMs, ASW technology was not up to its task, and limited nuclear options were not taken seriously. . . . Because the problem of violence below the nuclear threshold would remain, on issues other than defense of the homeland, there would still be security dilemmas and security problems. But the world would nevertheless be safer than it has usually been.

## NOTES

1. Thus, when Wolfers argues that a status-quo state that settles for rough equality of power with its adversary, rather than seeking preponderance, may be able to convince the other to reciprocate by showing that it wants only to protect itself, not menace the other, he assumes that the defense has an advantage. See Arnold Wolfers, *Discord and Collaboration* (Baltimore: Johns Hopkins Press, 1962), p. 126.
2. Thomas Schelling, *The Strategy of Conflict* (New York: Oxford University Press, 1963), chap. 9.
3. Quoted in Fritz Fischer, *War of Illusions* (New York: Norton, 1975), pp. 377, 461.
4. George Quester, *Offense and Defense in the International System* (New York: John Wiley, 1977), p. 105.
5. Herman Kahn, *On Thermonuclear War* (Princeton, N.J.: Princeton University Press, 1960), p. 211 (also see p. 144).
6. For a general discussion of such mistaken learning from the past, see Jervis, *Perception and Misperception in International Relations* (Princeton, N.J.: Princeton University Press, 1976), chap. 6. The important and still not completely understood question of why this belief formed and was maintained throughout the war is examined in Bernard Brodie, *War and Politics* (New York: Macmillan, 1973), pp. 262–70; Brodie, "Technological Change, Strategic Doctrine, and Political Outcomes," in Klaus Knorr, ed., *Historical Dimensions of National Security Problems* (Lawrence: University Press of Kansas, 1976), pp. 290–92; and Douglas Porch, "The French Army and the Spirit of the Offensive, 1900–14," in Brian Bond and Ian Roy, eds., *War and Society* (New York: Holmes & Meier, 1975), pp. 117–43.

7. Some were not so optimistic. Grey's remark is well-known: "The lamps are going out all over Europe; we shall not see them lit again in our life-time." The German Prime Minister, Bethmann Hollweg, also feared the consequences of the war. But the controlling view was that it would certainly pay for the winner.

8. Quoted in Martin Gilbert, *Winston S. Churchill*, III, *The Challenge of War, 1914–1916* (Boston: Houghton Mifflin, 1971), p. 84.

9. Quester (fn. 4), pp. 98–99. Robert Art, *The Influence of Foreign Policy on Seapower*, II (Beverly Hills: Sage Professional Papers in International Studies Series, 1973), pp. 14–18, 26–28.

10. Konrad Jarausch, "The Illusion of Limited War: Chancellor Bethmann Hollweg's Calculated Risk, July 1914," *Central European History*, II (March 1969): p. 50.

11. Brodie, *War and Politics* (New York: Macmillan, 1973), p. 58.

12. President Roosevelt and the American delegates to the League of Nations Disarmament Conference maintained that the tank and the mobile heavy artillery had reestablished the dominance of the offensive, thus making disarmament more urgent (Marion Boggs, *Attempts to Define and Limit "Aggressive" Armament in Diplomacy and Strategy* [Columbia: University of Missouri Studies, XVI, No. 1, 1941]: pp. 31, 108), but this was a minority position and may not even have been believed by the Americans. The reduced prestige and influence of the military, and the high pressures to cut government spending throughout this period also contributed to the lowering of defense budgets.

13. Jon Kimche, *The Unfought Battle* (New York: Stein, 1968); Nicholas William Bethell, *The War Hitler Won: The Fall of Poland, September 1939* (New York: Holt, 1972); Alan Alexandroff and Richard Rosecrance, "Deterrence in 1939," *World Politics*, XXIX (April 1977): pp. 404–24.

14. Roderick Macleod and Denis Kelly, eds., *Time Unguarded: The Ironside Diaries, 1937–1940* (New York: McKay, 1962), p. 173.

15. For a short time, as France was falling, the British Cabinet did discuss reaching a negotiated peace with Hitler. The official history downplays this, but it is covered in P. M. H. Bell, *A Certain Eventuality* (Farnborough, England: Saxon House, 1974), pp. 40–48.

16. MacLeod and Kelly (fn. 14), 174. In flat contradiction to common sense and almost everything they believed about modern warfare, the Allies planned an expedition to Scandinavia to cut the supply of iron ore to Germany and to aid Finland against the Russians. But the dominant mood was the one described above.

17. Brodie (fn. 11), p. 179.

18. Arthur Balfour, "Memorandum," Committee on Imperial Defence, April 30, 1903, pp. 2–3; see the telegrams by Sir Arthur Nicolson, in G. P. Gooch and Harold Temperley, eds., *British Documents on the Origins of the War*, Vol. 4 (London: H.M.S.O., 1929), pp. 429, 524. These barriers do not prevent the passage of long-range aircraft; but even in the air, distance usually aids the defender.

19. See, for example, the discussion of warfare among Chinese warlords in Hsi-Sheng Chi, "The Chinese Warlord System as an International System," in Morton Kaplan, ed., *New Approaches to International Relations* (New York: St. Martin's, 1968), pp. 405–25.

20. Some American decision makers, including military officers, thought that the best way out of the dilemma was to abandon the Philippines.

21. Quoted in Elting Morrison, *Turmoil and Tradition: A Study of the Life and Times of Henry L. Stimson* (Boston: Houghton Mifflin, 1960), p. 326.

22. The U.S. "refused to consider limitations on Hawaiian defenses, since these works posed no threat to Japan." William Braisted, *The United States Navy in the Pacific, 1909–1922* (Austin: University of Texas Press, 1971), p. 612.

23. That is part of the reason why the Japanese admirals strongly objected when the civilian leaders decided to accept a seven-to-ten ratio in lighter craft in 1930. Stephen Pelz, *Race to Pearl Harbor* (Cambridge, Mass.: Harvard University Press, 1974), p. 3.

24. John Nef, *War and Human Progress* (New York: Norton, 1963), p. 185. Also see *ibid.*, pp. 237, 242–43, and 323; C. W. Oman, *The Art of War in the Middle Ages* (Ithaca, N.Y.: Cornell University Press, 1953), pp. 70–72; John Beeler, *Warfare in Feudal Europe, 730–1200* (Ithaca, N.Y.: Cornell University Press, 1971), pp. 212–14; Michael Howard, *War in European History* (London: Oxford University Press, 1976), pp. 33–37.

25. Quincy Wright, *A Study of War* (abridged ed.; Chicago: University of Chicago Press, 1964), p. 142. Also see pp. 63–70, 74–75. There are important exceptions to these generalizations—the American Civil War, for instance, falls in the middle of the period Wright says is dominated by the offense.

26. Geoffrey Kemp, Robert Pfaltzgraff, and Uri Ra'anan, eds., *The Other Arms Race* (Lexington, Mass.: D.C. Heath, 1975); James Foster, "The Future of Conventional Arms Control," *Policy Sciences*, No. 8 (Spring 1977): pp. 1–19.

27. Richard Challener, *Admirals, Generals, and American Foreign Policy, 1898–1914* (Princeton, N.J.: Princeton University Press, 1973); Grey to Nicolson, in Gooch and Temperley (fn. 18), p. 414.

28. Quoted in James Crowley, *Japan's Quest for Autonomy* (Princeton, N.J.: Princeton University Press, 1966), p. 49. American naval officers agreed with the Japanese that a ten-to-six ratio would endanger Japan's supremacy in her home waters.

29. E. L. Woodward and R. Butler, ed., *Documents on British Foreign Policy, 1919–1939.* 3d ser. III (London: H.M.S.O., 1950), p. 526.

30. Jervis (fn. 6), pp. 69–72, 352–55.

31. Quoted in Merze Tate, *The United States and Armaments* (Cambridge, Mass.: Harvard University Press, 1948), p. 108.

32. Boggs (fn. 12), pp. 15, 40.

33. Kenneth Hagan, *American Gunboat Diplomacy and the Old Navy, 1877–1899* (Westport, Conn.: Greenwood Press, 1973), p. 20.

34. Winston Churchill, *The Gathering Storm* (Boston: Houghton, 1948), p. 206.

35. Brodie, *War and Politics* (fn. 6), p. 325.

36. Boggs (fn. 12), pp. 42, 83. For a good argument about the possible differentiation between offensive and defensive weapons in the 1930s, see Basil Liddell Hart, "Aggression and the Problem of Weapons," *English Review*, 55 (July 1932): pp. 71–78.

37. Quoted in Boggs (fn. 12), p. 39.

38. On these grounds, the Germans claimed in 1932 that the French forts were offensive (*ibid.*, p. 49). Similarly, fortified forward naval bases can be necessary for launching an attack; see Braisted (fn. 22), p. 643.

39. The French made this argument in the interwar period; see Richard Challener, *The French Theory of the Nation in Arms* (New York: Columbia University Press, 1955), pp. 181–82. The Germans disagreed; see Boggs (fn. 12), pp. 44–45.

40. Oman (fn. 24), pp. 57–58.

41. Quoted in Charles Webster, *The Foreign Policy of Castlereagh*, II, *1815–1822* (London: G. Bell and Sons, 1963), p. 510.
42. Boggs (fn. 12), pp. 14–15, 47–48, 60.
43. Quoted in Philip Jordan, *Frontier Law and Order* (Lincoln: University of Nebraska Press, 1970), p. 7; also see pp. 16–17.
44. Boggs (fn. 12), pp. 20, 28.

# *What Is Terrorism?*

## BRUCE HOFFMAN

What is terrorism? Few words have so insidiously worked their way into our everyday vocabulary. Like "Internet"—another grossly over-used term that has similarly become an indispensable part of the argot of the late twentieth century—most people have a vague idea or impression of what terrorism is, but lack a more precise, concrete and truly explanatory definition of the word. This imprecision has been abetted partly by the modern media, whose efforts to communicate an often complex and convoluted message in the briefest amount of airtime or print space possible have led to the promiscuous labelling of a range of violent acts as "terrorism." Pick up a newspaper or turn on the television and—even within the same broadcast or on the same page—one can find such disparate acts as the bombing of a building, the assassination of a head of state, the massacre of civilians by a military unit, the poisoning of produce on supermarket shelves or the deliberate contamination of over-the-counter medication in a chemist's shop all described as incidents of terrorism. Indeed, virtually any especially abhorrent act of violence that is perceived as directed against society—whether it involves the activities of anti-government dissidents or governments themselves, organized crime syndicates or common criminals, rioting mobs or persons engaged in militant protest, individual psychotics or lone extortionists—is often labelled "terrorism." . . .

Terrorism, in the most widely accepted contemporary usage of the term, is fundamentally and inherently political. It is also ineluctably about power: the pursuit of power, the acquisition of power, and the use of power to achieve political change. Terrorism is thus violence—or, equally important, the threat of violence—used and directed in pursuit of, or in service of, a political aim. With this vital point clearly illuminated, one can appreciate the significance of the additional definition of "terrorist" provided by the *[Oxford English Dictionary]*: "Any one who attempts to further his views by a system of coercive intimidation." This definition underscores clearly the other fundamental characteristic of terrorism: that it is a planned, calculated, and indeed systematic act.

Given this relatively straightforward elucidation, why, then, is terrorism so difficult to define? The most compelling reason perhaps is because the meaning of the term has changed so frequently over the past two hundred years. . . .

# WHY IS TERRORISM SO DIFFICULT TO DEFINE?

Not surprisingly, as the meaning and usage of the word have changed over time to accommodate the political vernacular and discourse of each successive era, terrorism has proved increasingly elusive in the face of attempts to construct one consistent definition. At one time, the terrorists themselves were far more cooperative in this endeavour than they are today. The early practitioners didn't mince their words or hide behind the semantic camouflage of more anodyne labels such as "freedom fighter" or "urban guerrilla." The nineteenth-century anarchists, for example, unabashedly proclaimed themselves to be terrorists and frankly proclaimed their tactics to be terrorism. The members of Narodnaya Volya similarly displayed no qualms in using these same words to describe themselves and their deeds. However, such frankness did not last. The Jewish terrorist group of the 1940s known as Lehi (the Hebrew acronym for Lohamei Herut Yisrael, the Freedom Fighters for Israel, more popularly known simply as the Stern Gang after their founder and first leader, Abraham Stern) is thought to be one of the last terrorist groups actually to describe itself publicly as such. It is significant, however, that even Lehi, while it may have been far more can did than its latter-day counterparts, chose as the name of the organization not "Terrorist Fighters for Israel," but the far less pejorative "Freedom Fighters for Israel." Similarly, although more than twenty years later the Brazilian revolutionary Carlos Marighela displayed few compunctions about openly advocating the use of "terrorist" tactics, he still insisted on depicting himself and his disciples as "urban guerrillas" rather than "urban terrorists." Indeed, it is clear from Marighela's writings that he was well aware of the word's undesirable connotations, and strove to displace them with positive resonances. "The words 'aggressor' and 'terrorist,'" Marighela wrote in his famous *Handbook of Urban Guerrilla War* (also known as the "Mini-Manual"), "no longer mean what they did. Instead of arousing fear or censure, they are a call to action. To be called an aggressor or a terrorist in Brazil is now an honour to any citizen, for it means that he is fighting, with a gun in his hand, against the monstrosity of the present dictatorship and the suffering it causes."

This trend towards ever more convoluted semantic obfuscations to side-step terrorism's pejorative overtones has, if anything, become more entrenched in recent decades. Terrorist organizations almost without exception now regularly select names for themselves that consciously eschew the word "terrorism" in any of its forms. Instead these groups actively seek to evoke images of:

- Freedom and liberation (e.g. the National Liberation Front, the Popular Front for the Liberation of Palestine, Freedom for the Basque Homeland, etc.);
- Armies or other military organizational structures (e.g. the National Military Organization, the Popular Liberation Army, the Fifth Battalion of the Liberation Army, etc.);
- Actual self-defence movements (e.g. the Afrikaner Resistance Movement, the Shankhill Defence Association, the Organization for the Defence of the Free People, the Jewish Defense Organization, etc.);

- Righteous vengeance (the Organization for the Oppressed on Earth, the Justice Commandos of the Armenian Genocide, the Palestinian Revenge Organization, etc.);

—or else deliberately choose names that are decidedly neutral and therefore bereft of all but the most innocuous suggestions or associations [e.g. the Shining Path, Front Line, al-Dawa ("The Call"), Alfaro Lives—Damn It!, Kach ("Thus"), al-Gamat al-Islamiya ("The Islamic Organization"), the Lantero Youth Movement, etc.].

What all these examples suggest is that terrorists clearly do not see or regard themselves as others do. "Above all I am a family man," the archterrorist Carlos, "The Jackal," described himself to a French newspaper following his capture in 1994. Cast perpetually on the defensive and forced to take up arms to protect themselves and their real or imagined constituents only, terrorists perceive themselves as reluctant warriors, driven by desperation—and lacking any viable alternative—to violence against a repressive state, a predatory rival ethnic or nationalist group, or an unresponsive international order. This perceived characteristic of self-denial also distinguishes the terrorist from other types of political extremists as well as from persons similarly involved in illegal, violent avocations. A communist or a revolutionary, for example, would likely readily accept and admit that he is in fact a communist or a revolutionary. Indeed, many would doubtless take particular pride in claiming either of those appellations for themselves. Similarly, even a person engaged in illegal, wholly disreputable or entirely selfish violent activities, such as robbing banks or carrying out contract killings, would probably admit to being a bank robber or a murderer for hire. The terrorist, by contrast, will *never* acknowledge that he is a terrorist and moreover will go to great lengths to evade and obscure any such inference or connection. . . . The terrorist will always argue that it is society or the government or the socio-economic "system" and its laws that are the *real* "terrorists," and moreover that if it were not for this oppression, he would not have felt the need to defend either himself or the population he claims to represent. . . .

On one point, at least, everyone agrees: terrorism is a pejorative term. It is a word with intrinsically negative connotations that is generally applied to one's enemies and opponents, or to those with whom one disagrees and would otherwise prefer to ignore. "What is called terrorism," Brian Jenkins has written, "thus seems to depend on one's point of view. Use of the term implies a moral judgement; and if one party can successfully attach the label *terrorist* to its opponent, then it has indirectly persuaded others to adopt its moral viewpoint." Hence the decision to call someone or label some organization "terrorist" becomes almost unavoidably subjective, depending largely on whether one sympathizes with or opposes the person/group/cause concerned. If one identifies with the victim of the violence, for example, then the act is terrorism. If, however, one identifies with the perpetrator, the violent act is regarded in a more sympathetic, if not positive (or, at the worst, an ambivalent) light; and it is not terrorism. . . .

The approach where identification with the victim determines the classification of a violent act as terrorism is evident in the conclusions of a parliamentary working group of NATO (an organization comprised of long-established, status quo Western states). The final report of the 1989 North Atlantic Assembly's Subcommittee on

Terrorism states: "Murder, kidnapping, arson and other felonious acts constitute criminal behavior, but many non-Western nations have proved reluctant to condemn as terrorist acts what they consider to be struggles of national liberation." In this reasoning, the defining characteristic of terrorism is the act of violence itself, not the motivations or justification for or reasons behind it. . . . But this is not an entirely satisfactory solution either, since it fails to differentiate clearly between violence perpetrated by states and by non-state entities, such as terrorists. Accordingly, it plays into the hands of terrorists and their apologists who would argue that there is no difference between the "low-tech" terrorist pipe-bomb placed in the rubbish bin at a crowded market that wantonly and indiscriminately kills or maims everyone within a radius measured in tens of feet and the "high-tech" precision-guided ordnance dropped by air force fighter-bombers from a height of 20,000 feet or more that achieves the same wanton and indiscriminate effects on the crowded marketplace far below. This rationale thus equates the random violence inflicted on enemy population centres by military forces—such as the Luftwaffe's raids on Warsaw and Coventry, the Allied fire-bombings of Dresden and Tokyo, and the atomic bombs dropped by the United States on Hiroshima and Nagasaki during the Second World War, and indeed the countervalue strategy of the post-war superpowers' strategic nuclear policy, which deliberately targeted the enemy's civilian population—with the violence committed by substate entities labelled "terrorists," since both involve the infliction of death and injury on non-combatants. . . .

It is a familiar argument. Terrorists, as we have seen, deliberately cloak themselves in the terminology of military jargon. They consciously portray themselves as bona fide (freedom) fighters, if not soldiers, who—though they wear no identifying uniform or insignia—are entitled to treatment as prisoners of war (POWs) if captured and therefore should not be prosecuted as common criminals in ordinary courts of law. Terrorists further argue that, because of their numerical inferiority, far more limited firepower and paucity of resources compared with an established nation-state's massive defence and national security apparatus, they have no choice but to operate clandestinely, emerging from the shadows to carry out dramatic (in other words, bloody and destructive) acts of hit-and-run violence in order to attract attention to, and ensure publicity for, themselves and their cause. . . .

But rationalizations such as these ignore the fact that, even while national armed forces have been responsible for far more death and destruction than terrorists might ever aspire to bring about, there nonetheless is a fundamental qualitative difference between the two types of violence. . . . In theory, if not always in practice, the rules of war—as observed from the early seventeenth century when they were first proposed by the Dutch jurist Hugo Grotius and subsequently codified in the famous Geneva and Hague Conventions on Warfare of the 1860s, 1899, 1907, and 1949—not only grant civilian non-combatants immunity from attack, but also

- Prohibit taking civilians as hostages;
- Impose regulations governing the treatment of captured or surrendered soldiers (POWs);
- Outlaw reprisals against either civilians or POWs;
- Recognize neutral territory and the rights of citizens of neutral states; and

- Uphold the inviolability of diplomats and other accredited representatives.

Even the most cursory review of terrorist tactics and targets over the past quarter-century reveals that terrorists have violated all these rules. They not infrequently have

- Taken hostage civilians, whom in some instances they have then brutally executed (e.g. the former Italian prime minister Aldo Moro and the German industrialist Hans Martin Schleyer, who were respectively taken captive and later murdered by the Red Brigades and the Red Army Faction);
- Similarly abused and murdered kidnapped military officers—even when they were serving on UN-sponsored peacekeeping or truce supervisory missions (e.g. the American Marine Lieutenant–Colonel William Higgins, the commander of a UN truce monitoring detachment, who was abducted by Lebanese Shi'a terrorists in 1989 and subsequently hanged);
- Undertaken reprisals against wholly innocent civilians, often in countries far removed from the terrorists' ostensible "theatre of operation," thus disdaining any concept of neutral states or the rights of citizens of neutral countries (e.g. the brutal 1986 machine-gun and hand-grenade attack on Turkish Jewish worshippers at an Istanbul synagogue carried out by the Palestinian Abu Nidal Organization in retaliation for a recent Israeli raid on a guerrilla base in southern Lebanon); and
- Repeatedly attacked embassies and other diplomatic installations (e.g. the bombings of the US embassies in Beirut and Kuwait City in 1983 and 1984, and the mass hostage-taking at the Japanese ambassador's residence in Lima, Peru, in 1996–7), as well as deliberately targeting diplomats and other accredited representatives (e.g. the British ambassador to Uruguay, Sir Geoffrey Jackson, who was kidnapped by leftist terrorists in that country in 1971, and the fifty-two American diplomats taken hostage at the Tehran legation in 1979).

Admittedly, the armed forces of established states have also been guilty of violating some of the same rules of war. However, when these transgressions do occur — when civilians are deliberately and wantonly attacked in war or taken hostage and killed by military forces—the term "war crime" is used to describe such acts and, imperfect and flawed as both international and national judicial remedies may be, steps nonetheless are often taken to hold the perpetrators accountable for these crimes. By comparison, one of the fundamental *raisons d'être* of international terrorism is a refusal to be bound by such rules of warfare and codes of conduct. International terrorism disdains any concept of delimited areas of combat or demarcated battlefields, much less respect of neutral territory. Accordingly, terrorists have repeatedly taken their often parochial struggles to other, sometimes geographically distant, third party countries and there deliberately enmeshed persons completely unconnected with the terrorists' cause or grievances in violent incidents designed to generate attention and publicity. . . .

Are we to conclude that terrorism is impervious to precise, much less accurate definition? Not entirely. If we cannot define terrorism, then we can at least usefully distinguish it from other types of violence and identify the characteristics that make terrorism the distinct phenomenon of political violence that it is.

## DISTINCTIONS AS A PATH TO DEFINITION

Guerrilla warfare is a good place to start. Terrorism is often confused or equated with, or treated as synonymous with, guerrilla warfare. This is not entirely surprising, since guerrillas often employ the same tactics (assassination, kidnapping, bombings of public gathering-places, hostage-taking, etc.) for the same purposes (to intimidate or coerce, thereby affecting behaviour through the arousal of fear) as terrorists. In addition, both terrorists and guerrillas wear neither uniform nor identifying insignia and thus are often indistinguishable from non-combatants. However, despite the inclination to lump both terrorists and guerrillas into the same catch-all category of "irregulars," there are nonetheless fundamental differences between the two. "Guerrilla," for example, in its most widely accepted usage, is taken to refer to a numerically larger group of armed individuals, who operate as a military unit, attack enemy military forces, and seize and hold territory (even if only ephemerally during daylight hours), while also exercising some form of sovereignty or control over a defined geographical area and its population. Terrorists, however, do not function in the open as armed units, generally do not attempt to seize or hold territory, deliberately avoid engaging enemy military forces in combat and rarely exercise any direct control or sovereignty either over territory or population.

It is also useful to distinguish terrorists from ordinary criminals. Like terrorists, criminals use violence as a means to attaining a specific end. However, while the violent act itself may be similar—kidnapping, shooting, arson, for example—the purpose or motivation clearly is not. Whether the criminal employs violence as a means to obtain money, to acquire material goods, or to kill or injure a specific victim for pay, he is acting primarily for selfish, personal motivations (usually material gain). Moreover, unlike terrorism, the ordinary criminal's violent act is not designed or intended to have consequences or create psychological repercussions beyond the act itself. The criminal may of course use some short-term act of violence to "terrorize" his victim, such as waving a gun in the face of a bank clerk during a robbery in order to ensure the clerk's expeditious compliance. In these instances, however, the bank robber is conveying no "message" (political or otherwise) through his act of violence beyond facilitating the rapid handing over of his "loot." The criminal's act therefore is not meant to have any effect reaching beyond either the incident itself or the immediate victim. Further, the violence is neither conceived nor intended to convey any message to anyone other than the bank clerk himself, whose rapid cooperation is the robber's only objective. Perhaps most fundamentally, the criminal is not concerned with influencing or affecting public opinion: he simply wants to abscond with his money or accomplish his mercenary task in the quickest and easiest way possible so that he may reap his reward and enjoy the fruits of his labours. By contrast, the fundamental aim of the terrorist's violence is ultimately to change "the system"—about which the ordinary criminal, of course, couldn't care less. . . .

We may therefore now attempt to define terrorism as the deliberate creation and exploitation of fear through violence or the threat of violence in the pursuit of political change. All terrorist acts involve violence or the threat of violence.

Terrorism is specifically designed to have far-reaching psychological effects beyond the immediate victim(s) or object of the terrorist attack. It is meant to instil fear within, and thereby intimidate, a wider "target audience" that might include a rival ethnic or religious group, an entire country, a national government or political party, or public opinion in general. Terrorism is designed to create power where there is none or to consolidate power where there is very little. Through the publicity generated by their violence, terrorists seek to obtain the leverage, influence, and power they otherwise lack to effect political change on either a local or an international scale.

# THE POLITICAL UTILITY OF FORCE TODAY

## The Fungibility of Force

### ROBERT J. ART

There are two fundamental reasons why military power remains more essential to statecraft than is commonly thought. First, in an anarchic realm (one without a central government), force is integral to political interaction. Foreign policy cannot be divorced from military power. Second, force is "fungible." It can be used for a wide variety of tasks and across different policy domains; it can be employed for both military and nonmilitary purposes. . . .

## POWER ASSETS: COMPARISONS AND CONFUSIONS

. . . I have argued that force is integral to statecraft because international politics is anarchic. By itself, that fact makes force fungible to a degree. Exactly how fungible an instrument is military power, however, and how does it compare in this regard to the other power assets a state wields? In this section, I answer these questions. First, I make a rough comparison as to the fungibility of the main instruments of statecraft. Second, I present a counterargument that force has little fungibility and then critique it.

### Comparing Power Assets

Comparing the instruments of statecraft according to their fungibility is a difficult task. We do not have a large body of empirical studies that systematically analyze the comparative fungibility of a state's power assets. The few studies we do have, even though they are carefully done, focus on only one or two instruments and are more concerned with looking at assets within specific issue areas than with comparing

From Robert J. Art, "American Foreign Policy and the Fungibility of Force," *Security Studies*, Vol. 5, No. 4 (Summer 1996), pp. 7–42. Copyright 1996. Reproduced by permission of Taylor & Francis Group, LLC, http://www.taylorandfrancis.com.

assets across issue areas. As a consequence, we lack sufficient evidence to compare power assets according to their fungibility. Through a little logic, however, we can provide some ballpark estimates.

Consider what power assets a state owns. They include population—the size, education level, and skills of its citizenry; geography—the size, location, and natural resource endowment of the state; governance—the effectiveness of its political system; values—the norms a state lives by and stands for, the nature of its ideology, and the extent of its appeal to foreigners; wealth—the level, sources, and nature of its productive economy; leadership—the political skill of its leaders and the number of skillful leaders it has; and military power—the nature, size, and composition of its military forces. Of all these assets, wealth and political skill look to be the most versatile, geography and governance the least versatile, because both are more in the nature of givens that set the physical and political context within which the other assets operate; values and population are highly variable, depending, respectively, on the content of the values and on the education and skill of the populace; and military power lies somewhere between wealth and skill on the one hand, and geography and governance on the other hand, but closer to the former than to the latter. In rank order, the three most fungible power assets appear to be wealth, political skill, and military power.

Economic wealth has the highest fungibility. It is the easiest to convert into the most liquid asset of all, namely, money, which in turn can be used to buy many different things—such as a good press, topflight international negotiators, smart lawyers, cutting-edge technology, bargaining power in international organizations, and so on. Wealth is also integral to military power. A rich state can generate more military power than a poor one. A state that is large and rich can, if it so chooses, generate especially large amounts of military power. The old mercantilist insight that wealth generates power (and vice-versa) is still valid.

Political skill is a second power asset that is highly fungible. By definition, skilled political operators are ones who can operate well in different policy realms because they have mastered the techniques of persuasion and influence. They are equally adept at selling free trade agreements, wars, or foreign aid to their citizens. Politically skillful statesmen can roam with ease across different policy realms. Indeed, that is what we commonly mean by a politically skillful leader—one who can lead in many different policy arenas. Thus, wealth and skill are resources that are easily transferable from one policy realm to another and are probably the two most liquid power assets.

Military power is a third fungible asset. It is not as fungible as wealth or skill, but that does not make it illiquid. Military power possesses versatility because force is integral to politics, even when states are at peace. If force is integral to international politics, it must be fungible. It cannot have pervasive effects and yet be severely restricted in its utility. Its pervasive effects, however, can be uniformly strong, uniformly weak, or variable in strength. Which is the case depends on how military power affects the many domains, policy arenas, and disparate issues that come within its field. At the minimum, however, military power is fungible to a degree because its physical use, its threatened use, or simply its mere presence structure expectations and influence the political calculations of actors. The gravitational effects of military power mean that its influence pervades the other policy realms, even if it is not dominant in most of them. Pervasiveness implies fungibility.

In the case of military power, moreover, greater amounts of it increase its fungibility. Up to a reasonable point, more of it is therefore better than less. It is more desirable to be militarily powerful than militarily weak. Militarily powerful states have greater clout in world politics than militarily weak ones. Militarily strong states are less subject to the influence of other states than militarily weak ones. Militarily powerful states can better offer protection to other states, or more seriously threaten them, in order to influence their behavior than can militarily weak ones. Finally, militarily powerful states are more secure than militarily weak ones. To have more clout, to be less subject to the will of others, to be in a stronger position to offer protection or threaten harm, and to be secure in a world where others are insecure—these are political advantages that can be diplomatically exploited, and they can also strengthen the will, resolve, and bargaining stance of the state that has them. Thus, although military power ranks behind wealth and skill in terms of its versatility, it can be a close third behind those two, at least for those great powers that choose to generate large amounts of it and then to exploit it.

## Conflating Sufficiency and Fungibility

The view argued here—that military power possesses a relatively high degree of fungibility—is not the conventional wisdom. Rather, the commonly accepted view is that put forward by David Baldwin, who argues that military power is of restricted utility. Baldwin asserts:

> Two of the most important weaknesses in traditional theorizing about international politics have been the tendency to exaggerate the effectiveness of military power resources and the tendency to treat military power as the ultimate measuring rod to which other forms of power should be compared.[1]

Baldwin's view of military power follows from his more general argument that power assets tend to be situationally specific. By that he means: "What functions as a power resource in one policy-contingency framework may be irrelevant in another." If assets are situationally or domain-specific, then they are not easily transferable from one policy realm to another. In fact, as Baldwin argues: "Political power resources . . . tend to be much less liquid than economic resources"; and although power resources vary in their degree of fungibility, "no political power resource begins to approach the degree of fungibility of money."[2]

For Baldwin, two consequences flow from the domain-specific nature of power resources. First, we cannot rely on a gross assessment of a state's overall power assets in order to determine how well it will do in any specific area. Instead, we must assess the strength of the resources that it wields in that specific domain. Second, the generally low fungibility of political power resources explains what Baldwin calls the "paradox of unrealized power": the fact that a strong state can prevail in one policy area and lose in another. The reason for this, he tells us, is simple: The state at issue has strong assets in the domain where it prevails and weak ones where it does not.

On the face of it, Baldwin's argument is reasonable. It makes intuitive sense to argue, for example, that armies are better at defeating armies than they are at promoting stable exchange rates. It also makes good sense to take the position that the more carefully we assess what specific assets a state can bring to bear on a specific issue, the more fine-tuned our feel will be of what the state can realistically accomplish on that issue. To deny that all power assets are domain-specific to a degree is therefore absurd. Equally absurd, however, are the positions that all assets are domain-specific to the same degree, and that a gross inventory of a state's overall power assets is not a reliable, even if only a rough, guide to how well the state is likely to do in any given domain. Assets are not equal in fungibility, and fine-tuning does not mean dramatically altering assessments.

What does all this mean for the fungibility of military power? Should we accept Baldwin's view about it? I argue that we should not. To see why, let us look in greater detail at what else he has to say.

Baldwin adduces four examples that purport to demonstrate the limited versatility of military power.[3] The examples are hypothetical, but are nonetheless useful to analyze because they are equivalent to thought experiments. These are the examples:

> Possession of nuclear weapons is not just irrelevant to securing the election of a U.S. citizen as UN secretary-general; it is a hindrance.
> . . . The owner of a political power resource, such as the means to deter atomic attack, is likely to have difficulty converting this resource into another resource that would, for instance, allow his country to become the leader of the Third World.
> Planes loaded with nuclear weapons may strengthen a state's ability to deter nuclear attacks but may be irrelevant to rescuing the *Pueblo* [a U.S. destroyer seized by the North Koreans in early 1968] on short notice.
> The ability to get other countries to refrain from attacking one's homeland is not the same as the ability to "win the hearts and minds of the people" in a faraway land [the reference is to the Vietnam War].[4]

Seemingly persuasive at first glance, the examples are, in fact, highly misleading. A little reflection about each will show how Baldwin has committed the cardinal error of conflating the insufficiency of an instrument with its low fungibility, and, therefore, how he has made military power look more domain-specific in each example than it really is.

Consider first the United Nations case. Throughout the United Nations' history, the United States never sought, nor did it ever favor, the election of an American as secretary-general. If it had, money and bribes would have been of as little use as a nuclear threat. The Soviet Union would have vetoed it, just as the United States would have vetoed a Soviet national as secretary-general. Neither state would have countenanced the appointment of a citizen from the other, or from one of its client states. The reason is clear: The Cold War polarized the United Nations between East and West, and neither superpower was willing to allow the other to gain undue influence in the institution if they could prevent it. Therefore, because neither superpower would have ever agreed on a national from the other camp, both sought a secretary-general from the ranks of the unaligned, neutral nations. This explains why cold war secretaries-general came from the unaligned Scandinavian or Third World nations (Dag Hammarskjold from Sweden; U Thant from Burma, for example), particularly during the heyday of the Cold War. This arrangement, moreover, served both superpowers' interest. At those rare times when they both agreed that the

United Nations could be helpful, UN mediation was made more effective because it had a secretary-general that was neutral, not aligned.

Finally, even if America's military power had nothing to do with electing secretaries-general, we should not conclude that it has nothing to do with America's standing within the institution. America's preeminence within the United Nations has been clear. So, too, is the fact that this stems from America's position as the world's strongest nation, a position deriving from both its economic and military strength. Thus, although nuclear weapons cannot buy secretary-general elections, great military power brings great influence in an international organization, one of whose main purposes, after all, is to achieve collective security through the threat or use of force.

The Third World example is equally misleading. To see why, let us perform a simple "thought experiment." Although a Third World leader that had armed his state with nuclear weapons might not rise automatically to the top of the Third World pack, he or she would become a mighty important actor nonetheless. Think of how less weighty China and India, which have nuclear weapons, would appear to other states if they did not possess them; and think of how Iraq, Iran, or Libya, which do not have them, would be viewed if they did. For the former set of states, nuclear weapons add to their global political standing; for the latter set, their mere attempts to acquire them have caused their prominence to rise considerably. By themselves, nuclear weapons cannot buy the top slot in the Third World or elsewhere. Neither economic wealth, nor military power, nor any other power asset alone, can buy top dog. That slot is reserved for the state that surpasses the others in all the key categories of power. Although they do not buy the top position, nuclear weapons nevertheless do significantly enhance the international influence of any state that possesses them, if influence is measured by how seriously a state is taken by others. In this particular case, then, Baldwin is correct to argue that nuclear weapons are not readily convertible into another instrument asset. Although true, the point is irrelevant: They add to the ultimate resource for which all the other assets of a state are mustered—political influence.

The *Pueblo* example is the most complex of the cases, and the one, when reexamined, that provides the strongest support for Baldwin's general argument.[5] Even when reexamined, this strong case falls far short of demonstrating that military power has little fungibility.

The facts of the *Pueblo* case are straightforward. On 23 January 1968, North Korea seized the USS *Pueblo*, an intelligence ship that was fitted with sophisticated electronic eavesdropping capabilities and that was listening in on North Korea, and did not release the ship's crew members until 22 December 1968, almost a year after they had been captured. North Korea claimed the ship was patrolling inside its twelve-mile territorial waters limit; the United States denied the claim because its radio "fix" on the *Pueblo* showed that it was patrolling fifteen and a half nautical miles from the nearest North Korean land point. Immediately after the seizure, the United States beefed up its conventional and nuclear forces in East Asia, sending 14,000 Navy and Air Force reservists and 350 additional aircraft to South Korea, as well as moving the aircraft carrier USS *Enterprise* and its task force within a few minutes' flying time of Wonsan, North Korea. Some of the aircraft sent to South Korean bases and those on the *Enterprise* were nuclear capable. According to President Johnson, several military options were considered but ultimately rejected:

> mining Wonsan harbor; mining other North Korean harbors; interdicting coastal shipping; seizing a North Korean ship; striking selected North Korean targets by air and naval gunfire. In each case we decided that the risk was too great and the possible accomplishment too small. "I do not want to win the argument and lose the sale," I consistently warned my advisers.[6]

The American government's denial, its military measures, and its subsequent diplomatic efforts, were to no avail. North Korea refused to release the crew. In fact, right from the outset of the crisis, the North Korean negotiators made clear that only an American confession that it had spied on North Korea and had intruded into its territorial waters would secure the crew's release. For eleven months the United States continued to insist that the *Pueblo* was not engaged in illegal activity, and that it had not violated North Korea's territorial waters. Only on 22 December, when General Gilbert Woodward, the U.S. representative to the negotiations, signed a statement in which the U.S. government apologized for the espionage and the intrusion, did North Korea release the crew. The American admission of guilt, however, was made under protest: Immediately before signing the statement, the government disavowed what it was about to sign; and immediately after the signing, the government disavowed what it had just admitted.

Although the facts of the *Pueblo* case are straightforward, the interpretation to be put on them is not. This much is clear: Neither nuclear weapons, nor any of America's other military assets, appear to have secured the crew's release. Equally clear, however, is that none of its other assets secured the crew's release either. Should we then conclude from this case that military power, diplomacy, and whatever other assets were employed to secure the crew's release have low fungibility? Clearly, that would be a foolish conclusion to draw. There was only one thing that secured the crew's release: the public humiliation of the United States. If nothing but humiliation worked, it is reasonable to conclude that humiliation either was, or more likely, quickly became North Korea's goal. When an adversary is firmly fixed on humiliation, military posturing, economic bribes, diplomatic pressure, economic threats, or any other tool used in moderation is not likely to succeed. Only extreme measures, such as waging war or economic blockade, are likely to be successful. At that point, the costs of such actions must be weighed against the benefits. One clear lesson we can draw from the *Pueblo* case is that sometimes there are tasks for which none of the traditional tools of statecraft are sufficient. These situations are rare, but they do on occasion occur. The *Pueblo* was one of them.

There is, however, a second and equally important point to be drawn from this example. Although it is true that America's military power did not secure the crew's release, nevertheless, there were other reasons to undertake the military buildup the United States subsequently engaged in. Neither the United States nor South Korea knew why the North had seized the *Pueblo*. President Johnson and his advisors, however, speculated that the seizure was related to the Tet offensive in Vietnam that began eight days after the *Pueblo*'s capture. They reasoned that the *Pueblo*'s seizure was deliberately timed to distract the United States and to frighten the South Koreans. Adding weight to this reasoning was the fact that the *Pueblo* was not an isolated incident. Two days earlier, thirty-one special North Korean agents infiltrated into Seoul and got within one-half mile of the presidential palace before they were overcome in battle. Their mission was to kill President Park. The United States feared that through these two incidents, and perhaps others to come, North Korea was trying to divert American military resources from Vietnam to Korea and to make the South Koreans sufficiently nervous that they would bring their two divisions fighting in Vietnam back home.[7]

The *Pueblo*'s seizure thus raised three problems for the United States: how to get its crew and ship back; how to deter the North from engaging in further provocative acts; and how to reassure the South Koreans sufficiently so that they would keep their troops in South Vietnam. A strong case could be made that the last two tasks, not the first, were the primary purposes for the subsequent American military buildup in East Asia. After all, the United States did not need additional forces there to pressure the North militarily to release the crew. There were already about 100,000 American troops in East Asia. A military buildup, however, would be a useful signal for deterrence of further provocations and reassurance of its ally. Until (or if) North Korea's archives are opened up, we cannot know whether deterrence of further provocation worked, because we do not know what additional plans the North had. What we do know is that the reassurance function of the buildup did work: South Korea kept its divisions in South Vietnam. Thus, America's military buildup had three purposes. Of those, one was achieved, another was not, and the third we cannot be certain about. In sum, it is wrong to draw the conclusion that the *Pueblo* case shows that force has little fungibility, even though military posturing appears not to have gotten the crew released.

Baldwin's final example is equally problematic if the point is to show that military power has little fungibility. Yes, it is true that preventing an attack on one's homeland is a different task than winning the hearts and minds of a people in a distant land. Presumably, however, the point of the example is to argue that the latter task is not merely different from the former, but also more difficult. If this is the assertion, it is unexceptionable: Compelling another government to change its behavior has always been an inherently more difficult task than deterring a given government from attacking one's homeland. Not only is interstate compellence more difficult than interstate deterrence, but intrastate compellence is more difficult than interstate compellence. Forcing the adversaries in a civil war to lay down their arms and negotiate an end to their dispute is a notoriously difficult task, as the Chinese civil war in the 1940s, the Vietnamese civil war in the 1960s, and the Bosnian civil war in the 1990s all too tragically show. It is an especially difficult task in a situation like Vietnam, where the outside power's internal ally faces an adversary that has the force of nationalism on its side. (Ho Chi Minh was Vietnam's greatest nationalist figure of the twentieth century and was widely recognized as such within Vietnam.) It is hard to prevail in a civil war when the adversary monopolizes the appeal of nationalism. Equally important, however, it is hard to prevail in a civil war without resort to force. The United States could not have won in Vietnam by force alone, but it would have had no chance at all to win without it.

No thoughtful analyst of military power would therefore disagree with the following propositions that can be teased out of the fourth example: (1) military power works better for defense than for conquest; (2) military power alone cannot guarantee pacification once conquest has taken place; (3) military power alone is not sufficient to compel a populace to accept the legitimacy of its government; and (4) compellence is more difficult than deterrence. These are reasonable statements. There is, however, also a fifth that should be drawn from this example: (5) when an outside power arrays itself in a civil war on the wrong side of nationalism, not only will force be insufficient to win, but so, too, will nearly all the other tools of statecraft—money, political skill, propaganda, and so on. In such cases military power suffers from the same insufficiency as the other instruments. That makes it no more, but no less, fungible than they are.

All four of Baldwin's examples demonstrate an important fact about military power: Used alone, it cannot achieve many things. Surely, this is an important point to remember, but is it one that is peculiar to military power alone or that proves that it has little fungibility? Surely not. Indeed, no single instrument of statecraft is ever sufficient to attain any significant foreign policy objective—a fact I shall term "task insufficiency."[8] There are two reasons for this. First, a statesman must anticipate the counteractions that will be undertaken by the states he is trying to influence. They will attempt to counter his stratagems with those of their own; they will use different types of instruments to offset the ones he is using; and they will attempt to compensate for their weakness in one area with their strength in another. A well-prepared influence attempt therefore requires a multi-instrumental approach to deal with the likely counters to it. Second, any important policy itself has many facets. A multifaceted policy by necessity requires many instruments to implement it. For both reasons, all truly important matters require a statesman to muster several, if not all, the instruments at his disposal, even though he may rely more heavily on some than on others. In sum, in statecraft no tool can stand alone.

For military power, then, as for the other instruments of statecraft, fungibility should not be equated with sufficiency, and insufficiency should not be equated with low fungibility. A given instrument can carry a state part of the way to a given goal, even though it cannot carry the state all the way there. At one and the same time, an instrument of statecraft can usefully contribute to attaining many goals and yet by itself be insufficient to attain any one of them. Thus, careful consideration of Baldwin's examples demonstrates the following: (1) military power was not sufficient to achieve the defined task; (2) none of the other traditional policy instruments were sufficient either; and (3) military power was of some value, either for the defined task or for another task closely connected to it. What the examples did not demonstrate is that states are unable to transfer military power from one policy task to another. Indeed, to the contrary: Each showed that military power can be used for a variety of tasks, even though it may not be sufficient, by itself, to achieve any of them.

## HOW FORCE ACHIEVES FUNGIBILITY

If military power is a versatile instrument of statecraft, then exactly how does it achieve its fungibility? What are the paths through which it can influence events in other domains?

There are two paths. The first is through the spill-over effects that military power has on other policy domains; the second, through the phenomenon of "linkage politics." In the first case, military power encounters military power, but from this military encounter ensues an outcome with significant consequences for nonmilitary matters. In the second case, military power is deliberately linked to a non-military issue, with the purpose of strengthening a state's bargaining leverage on that issue. In the first case, force is used against force; in the second, force is linked with another issue. In both cases, military power becomes fungible because it produces effects outside the strictly military domain. I explain how each path works and illustrate both with examples.

## Spill-Over Effects

A military encounter, whether peaceful or forceful, yields a result that can be consequential to the interactions and the outcomes that take place in other domains. This result, which I term the "spill-over effect," is too often forgotten.[9] Military-to-military encounters do not produce only military results—cities laid waste, armies defeated, enemies subdued, attacks prevented, allies protected. They also bring about political effects that significantly influence events in other domains. Military power achieves much of its fungibility through this effect: The political shock waves of a military encounter reverberate beyond the military domain and extend into the other policy domains as well. The exercise of successful deterrence, compellence, or defense affects the overall political framework of relations between two states. Because all policy domains are situated within this overarching framework, what happens in the latter affects what happens in these domains. Spill-over effects define with more precision why force acts akin to a gravitational field.

A spill-over effect can be understood either as a prerequisite or a by-product. As a prerequisite, the result produced by the act of force checking force creates something that is deliberate and viewed as essential in order to reach a given outcome in another domain. As a by-product, the encounter produces something in another domain that may be beneficial but is incidental or even unintended. Of course, what is by-product and what is prerequisite hangs on what outcomes are valued in that other domain. Two examples will illustrate how the spill-over effect works and how it manifests itself either as a prerequisite or a by-product.

### Examples: Banking and Cold War Interdependence

The first example has to do with banks; the second with recent history. The banking example demonstrates the role force plays in solvency; the historical example, the role that U.S. military power played in creating today's economic interdependence.

First, the banking example. Begin with this question, Why do we deposit our money in a bank? The answer is we put our money in a bank because we think we can take it out whenever we want. We believe the money is there when we want it. In short, we believe the bank to be solvent.

Solvency is usually thought of solely in economic terms: A bank is solvent because it has enough assets to meet its financial liabilities if they are called.[10] Solvency, however, is a function, not simply of finances, but of physical safety. A bank's solvency depends on the fact both that its assets exceed its liabilities (its balance sheet is in the black) and that its assets are physically secure (not easily stolen). Physical security is therefore as important to a bank's solvency as its liquidity, even though we generally take the former for granted when we reside in a stable domestic order. If the banks within a state could be robbed at will, then its citizens would not put their money in them. A state makes banks physically secure by using its military power to deter and defend against would-be robbers and to compel them to give back the funds if a robbery takes place (assuming they are caught and the funds recovered). Through its use of its legitimate monopoly on the use of force, a state seeks to neutralize the threat of forcible seizure. If the state succeeds in establishing the physical security of its banks, it produces one of the two prerequisites required for a bank's solvency.

In sum, in a well-ordered state, public force suppresses private force. The effect of this suppression is to create a generalized stability that sets the context within which all societal interactions take place. This effect spills over into numerous other domains and produces many manifestations, one of which is confidence about the physical security of banks. This confidence can be viewed as a by-product of the public suppression of private force, as a prerequisite to banking solvency, or, more sensibly, as both.

A good historical example of the spill-over effect of military power is the economic interdependence produced among the free world's economies during the Cold War. In a fundamental sense, this is the banking analogy writ large. The bank is the free world economies, the potential robber is the Soviet Union, and the provider of physical safety is the United States.

During the Cold War era, the United States used its military power to deter a Soviet attack on its major allies, the Western Europeans and the Japanese. American military power checked Soviet military power. This military-to-military encounter yielded a high degree of military security for America's allies, but it also produced several by-products, one of the most important of which was the creation of an open and interdependent economic order among the United States, Western Europe, and Japan. Today's era of economic interdependence is in no small part due to the exercise of American military power during the Cold War. A brief discussion will show how American military power helped create the economic interdependence from which much of today's world benefits.

America's forty-year struggle with the Soviets facilitated economic integration within Western Europe and among Western Europe, North America, and Japan. Obviously, American military power was not the sole factor responsible for today's interdependence among the major industrialized nations. Also crucial were the conversion of governments to Keynesian economics; their overwhelming desire to avoid the catastrophic experience of the Great Depression and the global war it brought in its wake; the lesson they learned from the 1930s about how noncooperative, beggar-thy-neighbor policies ultimately redound to the disadvantage of all; the willingness of the United States to underwrite the economic costs of setting up the system and of sustaining it for a time; the acceptance by its allies of the legitimacy of American leadership; the hard work of the peoples involved; and so on. Important as all these factors were, however, we must remember where economic openness first began and where it subsequently flourished most: among the great powers that were allied with the United States against the Soviet Union.

How, then, did the Soviet threat and the measures taken to counter it help produce the modern miracle of economic interdependence among America's industrial allies? And how, exactly, did America's military power and its overseas military presence contribute to it? There were four ways.

First, the security provided by the United States created a political stability that was crucial to the orderly development of trading relations. As I discussed at the outset of this article, markets do not exist in political vacuums; rather, they work best when embedded in political frameworks that yield predictable expectations. American military power deployed in the Far East and on the European continent brought these stable expectations, first, by providing the psychological reassurance that the Europeans and the Japanese needed to rebuild themselves and, second, by continuing to provide them thereafter with a sense of safety that enabled their economic energies to work their will. Indeed, we should remember that the prime reason NATO was formed was psychological, not military: to make the Europeans feel secure enough against the Soviets so that they would have the political will to rebuild themselves economically. The initial purpose of NATO is the key to its (and to the U.S.-Japan defense treaty's) long-lasting function: the creation of a politically stable island amidst a turbulent international sea.

Second, America's provision of security to its allies in Europe and in the Far East dampened their respective concerns about German and Japanese military rearmament. The United States presence protected its allies not only from the Soviets, but also from the Germans and the Japanese. Because German and Japanese military power was contained in alliances that the United States dominated, and especially because American troops were visibly present and literally within each nation, Germany's and Japan's neighbors, while they did not forget the horrors they suffered at the hands of these two during the Second World War, nevertheless, were not paralyzed from cooperating with them. The success of the European Common Market owes as much to the presence of American military power on the continent of Europe as it does to the vision of men like Monnet. The same can be said for the Far East. America's military presence has helped "oil the waters" for Japan's economic dominance there.

Third, America's military presence helped to dampen concerns about disparities in relative economic growth and about vulnerabilities inherent in interdependence, both of which are heightened in an open economic order. Freer trade benefits all nations, but not equally. The most efficient benefit the most; and economic efficiencies can be turned to military effect. Interdependence brings dependencies, all the greater the more states specialize economically. Unequal gains from trade and trade dependencies all too often historically have had adverse political and military effects. Through its provision of military protection to its allies, the United States mitigated the security externalities of interdependence and enabled the Germans and the Japanese to bring their neighbors (America's allies) into their economic orbits without those neighbors fearing that German or Japanese military conquest or political domination would follow. With the security issue dealt with, the economic predominance of the Germans and Japanese was easier for their neighbors to swallow.

Finally, America's military presence fostered a solidarity that came by virtue of being partners against a common enemy. That sense of solidarity, in turn, helped develop the determination and the good will necessary to overcome the inevitable economic disputes that interdependencies bring. The "spill-over" effects of military cooperation against the Soviets on the political will to sustain economic openness should not be underestimated, though they are difficult to pinpoint and quantify. Surely, however, the sense of solidarity and good will that alliance in a common cause bred must have had these spill-over effects. Finally, the need to preserve a united front against the common enemy put limits on how far the allies, and the United States, would permit their economic disputes to go. The need to maintain a united political-military front bounded the inevitable economic disputes and prevented them from escalating into a downward-spiraling economic nationalism. Political stability, protection from potential German and Japanese military resurgence, the dampening of concerns about relative gains and dependencies, and the sense of solidarity—all of these were aided by the American military presence in Europe and the Far East.

## Linkage Politics

The second way force exerts influence on other domains of policy is through the power of linkage politics. In politics, whether domestic or foreign, issues are usually linked to one another. The link can be either functional or artificial. If two issues are linked functionally, then there is a causal connection between them: A change in one produces a change in the other. The price of the dollar (its exchange rate value) and the price of oil imports, for example, are functionally linked, because the global oil market is priced in dollars. (Not only that, oil can only be bought with dollars.) A decline in the value of the dollar will increase the cost of a given amount of oil imported to the United States. Similarly, a rise in the value of the dollar will decrease the cost of a given amount of imported oil. As long as oil remains priced in dollars, the functional tie between exchange rates and energy cannot be delinked. Moreover, as the oil-dollar example illustrates, functional linkages generally have corresponding spill-over effects. That is, weakness on one issue (a weaker dollar) produces more weakness on the other (more money spent on energy imports); and strength on one (a stronger dollar) produces greater strength on the other (cheaper energy imports). Thus, functional linkages produce causal effects that either magnify a state's weakness or add to its strength.

When two issues are linked artificially, there is no causal connection between them. A change in one does not automatically produce a change in the other. Instead, the two issues become linked because a statesman has made a connection where none before existed. Usually, but not always, this will be done to gain bargaining leverage. By making a link between two heretofore unconnected issues, statesmen try to bring about politically what is not produced functionally. They make a link in order to compensate for weakness on a given issue. Their method is to tie an issue where they are weak to an issue where they are strong. Their goal is to produce a more desirable outcome in the weak area either by threatening to do something undesirable in the strong area, or by promising to do something beneficial there. If they can make the connection stick, then the result of an artificial linkage is a strengthening of a state's overall position. Unlike a functional linkage, where weakness begets weakness and strength begets strength, in an artificial linkage, strength offsets weakness. Thus, an artificial linkage is a bargaining connection that is made in the head of a statesman, but it is not any less real or any less effective as a result. I provide an example of a bargaining linkage below.

Whether functional or artificial, issue linkages have a crucial consequence for both the analysis and the exercise of state power. We can put the point more strongly: Because issues are connected, domains cannot be wholly delinked from one another. If they cannot be delinked, then we should not view them in isolation from one another. Therefore, any explanation of an outcome in a given domain that is based only on what goes on in that domain will always be incomplete, if not downright wrong. In sum, issue linkages limit the explanatory power of a domain-restricted analysis.

Bargaining linkages in particular make state assets more fungible than they might otherwise be. Linkage politics is a fact of international political life. We should not expect otherwise. Statesmen are out to make the best deals they can by compensating for weakness in one area with strength in others. Powerful states can better engage in these compensatory linkages than can weak ones. They are stronger in more areas than they are weak; consequently, they can more easily utilize their leverage in the strong areas to make up for their deficit in the weak ones. Great powers are also better able to shift assets among issue areas in order to build positions of bargaining strength when necessary. They can, for example, more easily generate military power when they need to in order to link it to nonmilitary tasks. Therefore, because powerful states can link issues more easily than can weaker ones, can compensate for deficiencies better, can generate more resources and do so more quickly when needed, and can shift assets around with greater ease, how powerful a state is overall remains an essential determinant to how successful it is internationally, irrespective of how weak it may be at any given moment on any specific issue in any particular domain. In sum, linkage politics enhances the advantages of being powerful and boosts the fungibility of force by enabling it to cross domains. . . .

### Examples: Deficits, Petrodollars, and Oil Prices

Three . . . brief examples show the range of state goals that can be served by constructing such linkages.

The first involves the relation between America's large and continuing balance of payments deficits and its global alliance system. Throughout most of the Cold War era, the United States ran an annual large balance of payments deficits. Historically, no nation has been able to buy more abroad than it sells abroad (import more than it exports) in as huge a volume and for as long a period as has the United States. There were many reasons why it was able to, ranging from the liquidity that deficit dollars provided, which enabled world trade to grow, to general confidence in the American economy, which caused foreigners to invest their dollar holdings in the United States. Part of the reason that foreigners continued to take America's continuing flow of dollars, however, was an implicit, if not explicit, tradeoff: In return for their acceptance of American IOU's (deficit dollars), the United States provided the largest holders of them (the Germans, the Japanese, and the Saudis) military protection against their enemies. America's military strength compensated for its lack of fiscal discipline.[11]

A second example involves the recycling of petrodollars.[12] After the oil price hikes of the 1970s, the OPEC producers, especially the Persian Gulf members, were accumulating more dollars than they could profitably invest at home. Where to put those dollars was an important financial decision, especially for the Saudis, who were generating the largest dollar surpluses. There is strong circumstantial evidence that the Saudis agreed to park a sizable portion of their petrodollars in U.S. Treasury bills (T-bills) in part because of an explicit American proposal "to provide a security umbrella for the Gulf."[13] As David Spiro notes: "By the fourth quarter of 1977, Saudi Arabia accounted for twenty percent of all holdings of Treasury notes and bonds by foreign central banks."[14] The Saudis also continued to agree to price oil in dollars rather than peg it to a basket of currencies. Although there were clear financial incentives for both Saudi decisions, the incentives are not sufficient to explain Saudi actions. The Kuwaitis, for example, never put as many of their petrodollars in the United States, nor as many in T-bills, as did the Saudis. Moreover, an internal U.S. Treasury study concluded that the Saudis would have done better if oil had been pegged to a basket of currencies than to dollars. Indeed, OPEC had decided in 1975 to price oil in such a basket, but never followed through.[15] America's provision of security to the Saudis was an important, even if not sufficient, ingredient in persuading them both to price oil in dollars and then to park the dollars in the United States. Both decisions were of considerable economic benefit to the United States. Parking Saudi dollars in T-bills gave the American government "access to a huge pool of foreign capital"; pricing oils in dollars meant that the United States "could print money to buy oil."[16] Military power bought economic benefits.

A third example, again involving the Saudis, concerns the link between American military protection and the price of oil. The Saudis have a long-term economic interest that dictates moderation in oil prices. With a relatively small population and with the world's largest proven oil reserves, their strategy lies in maximizing revenue from oil over the long term. It is therefore to their advantage to keep the price of oil high enough to earn sizable profits, but not so high as to encourage investment in alternative energy sources. Periodically, Saudi Arabia has faced considerable pressure from the price hawks within OPEC to push prices higher than its interest dictates. American military protection has strengthened Saudi willingness to resist the hawks.

A specific instance of this interaction between U.S. protection and Saudi moderation, for example, occurred in the fall of 1980, with the onset of the Iran-Iraq war. Iraq attacked Iran in September, and the two countries proceeded to bomb one another's oil facilities. The initial stages of the war removed about four million barrels of oil per day from world markets and drove the price of oil to its highest level ever ($42 per barrel).[17] As part of their balancing strategy in the Gulf, this time the Saudis had allied themselves with Iraq and, fearing Iranian retaliation against their oil fields, asked for American military intervention to deter Iranian attacks on their oil fields and facilities. The United States responded by sending AWACS aircraft to Saudi Arabia and by setting up a joint Saudi-American naval task force to guard against Iranian attacks on oil tankers in the Gulf.[18] In return, the Saudis increased their oil production from 9.7 million barrels per day (mbd) to 10.3, which was the highest level it could sustain, and kept it there for the next ten months. Saudi actions had a considerable effect on oil prices, as Safran argues:

> Physically, the Saudi increase of 0.5 mbd was hardly enough to make up for the shortfall caused by the war. . . . Psychologically, however, the Saudi action was crucial in preventing

the development of the kind of panic that had sent oil prices soaring after the fall of the shah and the Saudis' April 1979 decision to cut production by 1 mbd.[19]

As in the other cases, in this instance, American military power alone was not sufficient to cause Saudi actions to lower oil prices, but it was essential because during this turbulent period Saudi decisions on how much oil they would pump were not determined solely by economic factors. True, the Saudis, against the desires of the price hawks, which included the Iranians, had been pumping more oil since 1978 in order to lower oil prices. The Saudis had also violated their long-term strategy in March 1979, however, when they decided to cut oil production by 1 mbd, primarily to appease Iran, a move that triggered a rapid increase in oil prices. This pumping decision followed a political decision to move diplomatically away from the United States. Only a few months later, however, the conflict within the Saudi ruling family between an American- versus an Arab-oriented strategy was resolved in a compromise that led to a political reconciliation with the United States; and this political decision was followed by another to increase oil production by 1 mbd, starting 1 July 1979.[20] Before the Iran-Iraq war, then, Saudi pumping decisions were affected by political calculations about their security, in which the strategic connection with the Americans played a prominent role. If this was true in peacetime, surely it was so in wartime, too. The military protection announced by the Americans on 30 September 1980 was a necessary condition for the Saudi increase in oil production that followed in October. Again, military power had bought an economic benefit.

In sum, these . . . examples— . . . America's ability to run deficits, petrodollar recycling, and moderate oil prices—all illustrate just how pervasive bargaining linkages are in international politics and specifically how military power can be linked politically to produce them. In all cases, military power was not sufficient. Without it, however, the United States could not have produced the favorable economic outcomes it achieved.

## NOTES

1. David Baldwin, *Paradoxes of Power* (New York: Blackwell, 1989), 151–52. Baldwin first developed his argument in his "Power Analysis and World Politics," *World Politics* 31, 1 (January 1979), 161–94, which is reprinted in *Paradoxes of Power.*
2. Quotes from Baldwin, *Paradoxes of Power,* 134–35, 135, and 136, respectively.
3. In fairness to Baldwin, these examples were not fully developed, but consist of only a sentence or two. Nevertheless, they are fair game because Baldwin used them as illustrations of his more general point about the limits to the utility of military power. The fact that he did not develop them further led him astray, in my view. He was trying to show with them that military power is less effective than commonly thought. I reinterpret these examples to show how versatile military power in fact is. Neither Baldwin nor I, however, can put a number on the fungibility of military power, and I certainly agree with him that "no political power resource begins to approach the degree of fungibility of money" (Baldwin, *Paradoxes of Power,* 135).
4. Baldwin, *Paradoxes of Power,* 134, 135, 133.
5. For the facts and interpretation of this case, I have relied on Lyndon Baines Johnson, *The Vantage Point: Perspectives of the Presidency, 1963–1969* (New York: Holt, Rinehart,

Winston, 1971), 385, 387, and 532–37; Barry M. Blechman and Stephen S. Kaplan, *Force Without War: U.S. Armed Forces as a Political Instrument* (Washington, D.C.: Brookings, 1978), 48 and 71–72; Richard P. Stebbins and Elaine P. Adam, *Documents on American Foreign Relations, 1968–69* (New York: Simon & Schuster, 1972), 292–302; and the *New York Times Index,* 1968, 732–36.

6. Johnson, 536.

7. Johnson, 535; Blechman and Kaplan, 72.

8. Baldwin, of course, agrees with this point. He has written: "Actually, any technique of statecraft works poorly in isolation from the others." See David A. Baldwin, *Economic Statecraft* (Princeton: Princeton University Press, 1985), 143.

9. I have borrowed this term from Ernst Haas, even though I am using it differently than he does. He used the phrase to describe the effects that cooperation on economic matters among the states of Western Europe could have on their political relations. He argued that cooperation on economic matters would spill over into their political relations, induce greater cooperation there, and lead ultimately to the political integration of Western Europe. See Ernst Haas, *Beyond the Nation State: Functionalism and International Organization* (Stanford: Stanford University Press, 1964), 48. For Haas's later assessment of how effective spill-over effects were, see Ernst Haas, *The Obsolescence of Regional Integration Theory* (Berkeley: Institute of International Studies, University of California, 1974).

10. Solvency is to be distinguished from liquidity. A bank can be solvent but not liquid. Liquidity refers to the ability of a bank to meet all its liabilities upon demand. Most banks are not able to do so if all the demands are called at the same time. The reason is that many assets of any given bank are tied up in investments that cannot be called back on short notice but take time to convert into cash. The function of a central bank is to solve the liquidity problem of a nation's banking system by providing the liquidity in the short term in order to prevent runs on a bank.

11. As Gilpin put it: "Partially for economic reasons, but more importantly for political and strategic ones, Western Europe (primarily West Germany) and Japan agreed to finance the American balance of payments deficit." See Robert Gilpin, *U.S. Power and the Multinational Corporation: The Political Economy of Direct Investment* (New York: Basic Books, 1975), 154.

12. For this example, I have relied exclusively on David Spiro's original and thorough research. See David E. Spiro, *Hegemony Unbound: Petrodollar Recycling and the De-Legitimation of American Power* (Ithaca: Cornell University Press, forthcoming), chap. 4.

13. The quote is from an interview conducted by Spiro in Boston in 1984 with a former American ambassador to the Middle East. See Spiro, 271. (All page references are for the manuscript version.)

14. Spiro, 261.

15. Spiro, 263–66, 281–83.

16. Spiro, 259, 287.

17. Daniel Yergin, *The Prize: The Epic Quest for Oil, Money and Power* (New York: Simon & Schuster, 1992), 711.

18. Nadar Safran, *Saudi Arabia: The Ceaseless Quest for Security* (Ithaca: Cornell University Press, 1988), 322, 410–11.

19. Safran, 411.

20. Safran, 237.

# The Strategic Logic of Suicide Terrorism

## ROBERT A. PAPE

Terrorist organizations are increasingly relying on suicide attacks to achieve major political objectives. For example, spectacular suicide terrorist attacks have recently been employed by Palestinian groups in attempts to force Israel to abandon the West Bank and Gaza, by the Liberation Tigers of Tamil Eelam to compel the Sri Lankan government to accept an independent Tamil homeland, and by Al Qaeda to pressure the United States to withdraw from the Saudi Arabian Peninsula. Moreover, such attacks are increasing both in tempo and location. Before the early 1980s, suicide terrorism was rare but not unknown. However, since the attack on the U.S. embassy in Beirut in April 1983, there have been at least 188 separate suicide terrorist attacks worldwide, in Lebanon, Israel, Sri Lanka, India, Pakistan, Afghanistan, Yemen, Turkey, Russia and the United States. The rate has increased from 31 in the 1980s, to 104 in the 1990s, to 53 in 2000–2001 alone. The rise of suicide terrorism is especially remarkable, given that the total number of terrorist incidents worldwide fell during the period, from a peak of 666 in 1987 to a low of 274 in 1998, with 348 in 2001.

What accounts for the rise in suicide terrorism, especially, the sharp escalation from the 1990s onward? Although terrorism has long been part of international politics, we do not have good explanations for the growing phenomenon of suicide terrorism. Traditional studies of terrorism tend to treat suicide attack as one of many tactics that terrorists use and so do not shed much light on the recent rise of this type of attack. The small number of studies addressed explicitly to suicide terrorism tend to focus on the irrationality of the act of suicide from the perspective of the individual attacker. As a result, they focus on individual motives—either religious indoctrination (especially Islamic Fundamentalism) or psychological predispositions that might drive individual suicide bombers.

The first-wave explanations of suicide terrorism were developed during the 1980s and were consistent with the data from that period. However, as suicide attacks mounted from the 1990s onward, it has become increasingly evident that these initial explanations are insufficient to account for which individuals become suicide terrorists and, more importantly, why terrorist organizations are increasingly relying on this form of attack. First, although religious motives may matter, modern

From Robert A. Pape, "The Strategic Logic of Suicide Terrorism," *American Political Science Review,* Vol. 97, No. 3 (August 2003), pp. 343–361. Copyright © 2003 by The American Political Science Association. Reprinted with the permission of Cambridge University Press.

suicide terrorism is not limited to Islamic Fundamentalism. Islamic groups receive the most attention in Western media, but the world's leader in suicide terrorism is actually the Liberation Tigers of Tamil Eelam (LTTE), a group who recruits from the predominantly Hindu Tamil population in northern and eastern Sri Lanka and whose ideology has Marxist/Leninist elements. The LTTE alone accounts for 75 of the 186 suicide terrorist attacks from 1980 to 2001. Even among Islamic suicide attacks, groups with secular orientations account for about a third of these attacks.

Second, although study of the personal characteristics of suicide attackers may someday help identify individuals terrorist organizations are likely to recruit for this purpose, the vast spread of suicide terrorism over the last two decades suggests that there may not be a single profile. Until recently, the leading experts in psychological profiles of suicide terrorists characterized them as uneducated, unemployed, socially isolated, single men in their late teens and early 20s. Now we know that suicide terrorists can be college educated or uneducated, married or single, men or women, socially isolated or integrated, from age 13 to age 47. In other words, although only a tiny number of people become suicide terrorists, they come from a broad cross section of lifestyles, and it may be impossible to pick them out in advance.

In contrast to the first-wave explanations, this article shows that suicide terrorism follows a strategic logic. Even if many suicide attackers are irrational or fanatical, the leadership groups that recruit and direct them are not. Viewed from the perspective of the terrorist organization, suicide attacks are designed to achieve specific political purposes: to coerce a target government to change policy, to mobilize additional recruits and financial support, or both. Crenshaw has shown that terrorism is best understood in terms of its strategic function; the same is true for suicide terrorism. In essence, suicide terrorism is an extreme form of what Thomas Schelling calls "the rationality of irrationality," in which an act that is irrational for individual attackers is meant to demonstrate credibility to a democratic audience that still more and greater attacks are sure to come. As such, modern suicide terrorism is analogous to instances of international coercion. For states, air power and economic sanctions are often the preferred coercive tools. For terrorist groups, suicide attacks are becoming the coercive instrument of choice.

To examine the strategic logic of suicide terrorism, this article collects the universe suicide terrorist attacks worldwide from 1980 to 2001, explains how terrorist organizations have assessed the effectiveness of these attacks, and evaluates the limits on their coercive utility.

Five principal findings follow. First, suicide terrorism is strategic. The vast majority of suicide terrorist attacks are not isolated or random acts by individual fanatics but, rather, occur in clusters as part of a larger campaign by an organized group to achieve a specific political goal. Groups using suicide terrorism consistently announce specific political goals and stop suicide attacks when those goals have been fully or partially achieved.

Second, the strategic logic of suicide terrorism is specifically designed to coerce modern democracies to make significant concessions to national self-determination. In general, suicide terrorist campaigns seek to achieve specific territorial goals, most often the withdrawal of the target state's military forces from what the terrorists see as national homeland. From Lebanon to Israel to Sri Lanka to Kashmir to Chechnya, every suicide terrorist campaign from 1980 to 2001 has been waged by terrorist groups whose main goal has been to establish or maintain self-determination for their community's homeland by compelling an enemy to withdraw. Further, every suicide terrorist campaign since 1980 has been targeted against a state that had a democratic form of government.

Third, during the past 20 years, suicide terrorism has been steadily rising because terrorists have learned that it pays. Suicide terrorists sought to compel American and French military forces to abandon Lebanon in 1983, Israeli forces to leave Lebanon in 1985, Israeli forces to quit the Gaza Strip and the West Bank in 1994 and 1995, the Sri Lankan government to create an independent Tamil state from 1990 on, and the Turkish government to grant autonomy to the Kurds in the late 1990s. Terrorist groups did not achieve their full objectives in all these cases. However, in all but the case of Turkey, the terrorist political cause made more gains after the resort to suicide operations than it had before. . . .

Fourth, although moderate suicide terrorism led to moderate concessions, these more ambitious suicide terrorist campaigns are not likely to achieve still greater gains and may well fail completely. In general, suicide terrorism relies on the threat to inflict low to medium levels of punishment on civilians. In other circumstances, this level of punishment has rarely caused modern nation states to surrender significant political goals, partly because modern nation states are often willing to countenance high costs for high interests and partly because modern nation states are often able to mitigate civilian costs by making economic and other adjustments. Suicide terrorism does not change a nation's willingness to trade high interests for high costs, but suicide attacks can overcome a country's efforts to mitigate civilian costs. Accordingly, suicide terrorism may marginally increase the punishment that is inflicted and so make target nations somewhat more likely to surrender modest goals, but it is unlikely to compel states to abandon important interests related to the physical security or national wealth of the state. National governments have in fact responded aggressively to ambitious suicide terrorist campaigns in recent years, events which confirm these expectations.

Finally, the most promising way to contain suicide terrorism is to reduce terrorists' confidence in their ability to carry out such attacks on the target society. States that face persistent suicide terrorism should recognize that neither offensive military action nor concessions alone are likely to do much good and should invest significant resources in border defenses and other means of homeland security.

## THE LOGIC OF SUICIDE TERRORISM

Most suicide terrorism is undertaken as a strategic effort directed toward achieving particular political goals; it is not simply the product of irrational individuals or an expression of fanatical hatreds. The main purpose of suicide terrorism is to use the threat of punishment to coerce a target government to change policy, especially to cause democratic states to withdraw forces from territory terrorists view as their homeland. The record of suicide terrorism from 1980 to 2001 exhibits tendencies in the timing, goals, and targets of attack that are consistent with this strategic logic but not with irrational or fanatical behavior: (1) *timing*—nearly all suicide attacks occur in organized, coherent campaigns, not as isolated or randomly timed incidents; (2) *nationalist goals*—suicide terrorist campaigns are directed at gaining control of what the terrorists see as their national homeland territory, specifically at ejecting foreign forces from that territory; and (3) *target selection*—all suicide terrorist campaigns in the last two decades have been aimed at democracies, which make more suitable targets from the terrorists' point of view.

## Defining Suicide Terrorism

Terrorism involves the use of violence by an organization other than a national government to cause intimidation or fear among a target audience. Although one could broaden the definition of terrorism so as to include the actions of a national government to cause terror among an opposing population, adopting such a broad definition would distract attention from what policy makers would most like to know: how to combat the threat posed by subnational groups to state security. Further, it could also create analytic confusion. Terrorist organizations and state governments have different levels of resources, face different kinds of incentives, and are susceptible to different types of pressures. Accordingly, the determinants of their behavior are not likely to be the same and, thus, require separate theoretical investigations.

In general, terrorism has two purposes—to gain supporters and to coerce opponents. Most terrorism seeks both goals to some extent, often aiming to affect enemy calculations while simultaneously mobilizing support for the terrorists cause and, in some cases, even gaining an edge over rival groups in the same social movement. However, there are trade-offs between these objectives and terrorists can strike various balances between them. These choices represent different forms of terrorism, the most important of which are demonstrative, destructive, and suicide terrorism.

*Demonstrative terrorism* is directed mainly at gaining publicity, for any or all of three reasons: to recruit more activists, to gain attention to grievances from soft-liners on the other side, and to gain attention from third parties who might exert pressure on the other side. Groups that emphasize ordinary, demonstrative terrorism include the Orange Volunteers (Northern Ireland), National Liberation Army (Columbia), and Red Brigades (Italy). Hostage taking, airline hijacking, and explosions announced in advance are generally intended to use the possibility of harm to bring issues to the attention of the target audience. In these cases, terrorists often avoid doing serious harm so as not to undermine sympathy for the political cause. Brian Jenkins captures the essence of demonstrative terrorism with his well-known remark, "Terrorists want a lot of people watching, not a lot of people dead."

*Destructive terrorism* is more aggressive, seeking to coerce opponents as well as mobilize support for the cause. Destructive terrorists seek to inflict real harm on members of the target audience at the risk of losing sympathy for their cause. Exactly how groups strike the balance between harm and sympathy depends on the nature of the political goal. For instance, the Baader-Meinhoft group selectively assassinated rich German industrialists, which alienated certain segments of German society but not others. Palestinian terrorists in the 1970s often sought to kill as many Israelis as possible, fully alienating Jewish society but still evoking sympathy from Muslim communities. Other groups that emphasize destructive terrorism include the Irish Republican Army, the Revolutionary Armed Forces of Colombia (FARC), and the nineteenth-century Anarchists.

*Suicide terrorism* is the most aggressive form of terrorism, pursuing coercion even at the expense of losing support among the terrorists' own community. What distinguishes a suicide terrorist is that the attacker does not expect to survive a mission and often employs a method of attack that requires the attacker's death in order to succeed (such as planting a car bomb, wearing a suicide vest, or ramming an airplane into a building). In essence, a suicide terrorist kills others at the same time that he kills himself. In principle, suicide terrorists could be used for demonstrative purposes or could be limited to targeted assassinations. In practice, however, suicide terrorists often seek simply to kill the largest number of people. Although this maximizes the coercive leverage that can be gained from terrorism, it does so at the greatest cost to the basis of support for the terrorist cause. Maximizing the number of enemy killed alienates those in the target audience who might be sympathetic to the terrorists cause, while the act of suicide creates a debate and often loss of support among moderate segments of the terrorists' community, even if also attracting support among radical elements. Thus, while coercion is an element in all terrorism, coercion is the paramount objective of suicide terrorism.

## The Coercive Logic of Suicide Terrorism

At its core, suicide terrorism is a strategy of coercion, a means to compel a target government to change policy. The central logic of this strategy is simple: Suicide terrorism attempts to inflict enough pain on the opposing society to overwhelm their interest in resisting the terrorists demands and, so, to cause either the government to concede or the population to revolt against the government. The common feature of all suicide terrorist campaigns is that they inflict punishment on the opposing society, either directly by killing civilians or indirectly by killing military personnel in circumstances that cannot lead to meaningful battlefield victory. As we shall see, suicide terrorism is rarely a one time event but often occurs in a series of suicide attacks. As such, suicide terrorism generates coercive leverage both from the immediate panic associated with each attack and from the risk of civilian punishment in the future.

Suicide terrorism does not occur in the same circumstances as military coercion used by states, and these structural differences help to explain the logic of the strategy. In virtually all instances of international military coercion, the coercer is the stronger state and the target is the weaker state; otherwise, the coercer would likely be deterred or simply unable to execute the threatened military operations. In these circumstances, coercers have a choice between two main coercive strategies, punishment and denial. Punishment seeks to coerce by raising the costs or risks to the target society to a level that overwhelms the value of the interests in dispute. Denial seeks to coerce by demonstrating to the target state that it simply cannot win the dispute regardless of its level of effort, and therefore fighting to a finish is pointless—for example, because the coercer has the ability to conquer the disputed territory. Hence, although coercers may initially rely on punishment, they often have the resources to create a formidable threat to deny the opponent victory in battle and, if necessary, to achieve a brute force military victory if the target government refuses to change its behavior. The Allied bombing of Germany in World War II, American bombing of North Vietnam in 1972, and Coalition attacks against Iraq in 1991 all fit this pattern.

Suicide terrorism (and terrorism in general) occurs under the reverse structural conditions. In suicide terrorism, the coercer is the weaker actor and the target is the stronger. Although some elements of the situation remain the same, flipping the stronger and weaker sides in a coercive dispute has a dramatic change on the relative feasibility of punishment and denial. In these circumstances, denial is impossible, because military conquest is ruled out by relative weakness. Even though some groups using suicide terrorism have received important support from states and some have been strong enough to wage guerrilla military campaigns as well as terrorism, none have been strong enough to have serious prospects of achieving their political goals by conquest. The suicide terrorist group with the most significant military capacity has been the LTTE, but it has not had a real prospect of controlling the whole of the homeland that it claims, including Eastern and Northern Provinces of Sri Lanka.

As a result, the only coercive strategy available to suicide terrorists is punishment. Although the element of "suicide" is novel and the pain inflicted on civilians is often spectacular and gruesome, the heart of the strategy of suicide terrorism is the same as the coercive logic used by states when they employ air power or economic sanctions to punish an adversary: to cause mounting civilian costs to overwhelm the target state's interest in the issue in dispute and so to cause it to concede the terrorists' political demands. What creates the coercive leverage is not so much actual damage as the expectation of future damage. Targets may be economic or political, military or civilian, but in all cases the main task is less to destroy the specific targets than to convince the opposing society that they are vulnerable to more attacks in the future. These features also make suicide terrorism convenient for retaliation, a tit-for-tat interaction that generally occurs between terrorists and the defending government (Crenshaw 1981). . . .

Suicide terrorists' willingness to die magnifies the coercive effects of punishment in three ways. First, suicide attacks are generally more destructive than other terrorist attacks. An attacker who is willing to die is much more likely to accomplish the mission and to cause maximum damage to the target. Suicide attackers can conceal weapons on their own bodies and make last-minute adjustments more easily than ordinary terrorists. They are also better able to infiltrate heavily guarded targets because they do not need escape plans or rescue teams. Suicide attackers are also able to use certain especially destructive tactics such as wearing "suicide vests" and ramming vehicles into targets. The 188 suicide terrorist attacks from 1980 to 2001 killed an average of 13 people each, not counting the unusually large number of fatalities on September 11 and also not counting the attackers themselves. During the same period, there were about 4,155 total terrorist incidents worldwide, which killed 3,207 people (also excluding September 11), or less than one person per incident. Overall, from 1980 to 2001, suicide attacks amount to 3% of all terrorist attacks but account for 48% of total deaths due to terrorism, again excluding September 11.

Second, suicide attacks are an especially convincing way to signal the likelihood of more pain to come, because suicide itself is a costly signal, one that suggests that the attackers could not have been deterred by a threat of costly retaliation. Organizations that sponsor suicide attacks can also deliberately orchestrate the circumstances around the death of a suicide attacker to increase further expectations of future attacks. This can be called the "art of martyrdom." The more suicide terrorists justify their actions on the basis of religious or ideological motives that match the beliefs of a broader national community, the more the status of terrorist martyrs is elevated, and the more plausible it becomes that others will follow in their footsteps. Suicide terrorist organizations commonly cultivate "sacrificial myths" that include elaborate sets of symbols and rituals to mark an individual attacker's death as a contribution to the nation. Suicide attackers' families also often receive material rewards both from the terrorist organizations and from other supporters. As a result, the art of martyrdom elicits popular support from the terrorists' community, reducing the moral backlash that suicide attacks might otherwise produce, and so establishes the foundation for credible signals of more attacks to come.

Third, suicide terrorist organizations are better positioned than other terrorists to increase expectations about escalating future costs by deliberately violating norms in the use of violence. They can do this by crossing thresholds of damage, by breaching taboos concerning legitimate targets, and by broadening recruitment to confound expectations about limits on the number of possible terrorists. The element of suicide itself helps increase the credibility of future attacks, because it suggests that attackers cannot be deterred. Although the capture and conviction of Timothy McVeigh gave reason for some confidence that others with similar political views might be deterred, the deaths of the September 11 hijackers did not, because Americans would have to expect that future Al Qaeda attackers would be equally willing to die.

## The Record of Suicide Terrorism, 1980 to 2001

To characterize the nature of suicide terrorism, this study identified every suicide terrorist attack from 1980 to 2001 that could be found in Lexis Nexis's on-line database of world news media. Examination of the universe shows that suicide terrorism has three properties that are consistent with the above strategic logic but not with irrational or fanatical behavior: (1) *timing*—nearly all suicide attacks occur in organized, coherent campaigns, not as isolated or randomly timed incidents; (2) *nationalist goals*—suicide terrorist campaigns are directed at gaining control of what the terrorists see as their national homeland territory, specifically at ejecting foreign forces from that territory; and (3) *target selection*—all suicide terrorist campaigns in the last two decades have been aimed at democracies, which make more suitable targets from the terrorists' point of view. Nationalist movements that face nondemocratic opponents have not resorted to suicide attack as a means of coercion.

### Timing.

As Table 1 indicates, there have been 188 separate suicide terrorist attacks between 1980 and 2001. Of these, 179, or 95%, were parts of organized, coherent campaigns, while only nine were isolated or random events. Seven separate disputes

TABLE 1 ■ SUICIDE TERRORIST CAMPAIGNS, 1980–2001

| Date | Terrorist Group | Terrorist's Goal | No. of Attacks | No. Killed | Target Behavior |
|---|---|---|---|---|---|
| | | *Completed Campaigns* | | | |
| 1. Apr-Dec 1983 | Hezboliah | U.S./France out of Lebanon | 6 | 384 | Complete withdrawal |
| 2. Nov 1983– Apr 1985 | Hezbollah | Israel out of Lebanon | 6 | 96 | Partial withdrawal |
| 3. June 1985– June 1986 | Hezbollah | Israel out of Lebanon security zone | 16 | 179 | No change |
| 4. July 1990– Nov 1994 | LTTE | Sri Lanka accept Tamil state | 14 | 164 | Negotiations |
| 5. Apr 1995– Oct 2000 | LTTE | Sri Lanka accept Tamil state | 54 | 629 | No change |
| 6. Apr 1994 | Hamas | Israel out of Palestine | 2 | 15 | Partial withdrawal Gaza |
| 7. Oct 1994– Aug 1995 | Hamas | Israel out of Palestine | 7 | 65 | Partial withdrawal from West Bank |
| 8. Feb–Mar 1996 | Hamas | Retaliation for Israeli assassination | 4 | 58 | No change |
| 9. Mar–Sept 1997 | Hamas | Israel out of Palestine | 3 | 24 | Hamas leader released |
| 10. June–Oct 1996 | PKK | Turkey accept Kurd autonomy | 3 | 17 | No change |
| 11. Mar–Aug 1999 | PKK | Turkey release jailed leader | 6 | 0 | No change |
| | | *Ongoing Campaigns, as of December 2001* | | | |
| 12. 1996– | Al Qaeda | U.S. out of Saudi Peninsula | 5 | 3,329 | TBD[*] |
| 13. 2000– | Chechnen Rebels | Russia out of Chechnya | 4 | 53 | TBD |
| 14. 2000– | Kashmir Rebels | India out of Kashmir | 3 | 45 | TBD |
| 15. 2001– | LTTE | Sri Lanka accept Tamil state | 6 | 51 | TBD |
| 16. 2000– | Several | Israel out of Palestine | 39 | 177 | TBD |
| Total incidents | 188 | | | | |
| No. of campaigns | 179 | | | | |
| No. isolated | 9 | | | | |

*Source:* Robert Pape, "The Universe of Suicide Terrorist Attacks Worldwide, 1980–2001," University of Chicago, Typescript.

[*]To be determined.

have led to suicide terrorist campaigns: the presence of American and French forces in Lebanon, Israeli occupation of West Bank and Gaza, the independence of the Tamil regions of Sri Lanka, the independence of the Kurdish region of Turkey, Russian occupation of Chechnya, Indian occupation of Kashmir, and the presence of American forces on the Saudi Arabian Peninsula. Overall, however, there have been 16 distinct campaigns, because in certain disputes the terrorists elected to suspend operations one or more times either in response to concessions or for other reasons. Eleven of the campaigns have ended and five were ongoing as of the end of 2001. The attacks comprising each campaign were organized by the same terrorist group (or, sometimes, a set of cooperating groups as in the ongoing "second *intifada*" in Israel/Palestine), clustered in time, publically justified in terms of a specified political goal, and directed against targets related to that goal.

The most important indicator of the strategic orientation of suicide terrorists is the timing of the suspension of campaigns, which most often occurs based on a strategic decision by leaders of the terrorist organizations that further attacks would be counterproductive to their coercive purposes—for instance, in response to full or partial concessions by the target state to the terrorists' political goals. Such suspensions are often accompanied by public explanations that justify the decision to opt for a "cease-fire." Further, the terrorist organizations' discipline is usually fairly good; although there are exceptions, such announced cease-fires usually do stick for a period of months at least, normally until the terrorist leaders take a new strategic decision to resume in pursuit of goals not achieved in the earlier campaign. This pattern indicates that both terrorist leaders and their recruits are sensitive to the coercive value of the attacks.

As an example of a suicide campaign, consider Hamas's suicide attacks in 1995 to compel Israel to withdraw from towns in the West Bank. Hamas leaders deliberately withheld attacking during the spring and early summer in order to give PLO negotiations with Israel an opportunity to finalize a withdrawal. However, when in early July, Hamas leaders came to believe that Israel was backsliding and delaying withdrawal, Hamas launched a series of suicide attacks. Israel accelerated the pace of its withdrawal, after which Hamas ended the campaign. . . .

If suicide terrorism were mainly irrational or even disorganized, we would expect a much different pattern in which either political goals were not articulated (e.g., references in news reports to "rogue" attacks) or the stated goals varied considerably even within the same conflict. We would also expect the timing to be either random or, perhaps, event-driven, in response to particularly provocative or infuriating actions by the other side, but little if at all related to the progress of negotiations over issues in dispute that the terrorists want to influence.

### Nationalist Goals.

Suicide terrorism is a high-cost strategy, one that would only make strategic sense for a group when high interests are at stake and, even then, as a last resort. The reason is that suicide terrorism maximizes coercive leverage at the expense of support among the terrorists' own community and so can be sustained over time only when there already exists a high degree of commitment among the potential pool of recruits. The most important goal that a community can have is the independence of its homeland

TABLE 2  ■  MOTIVATION AND TARGETS OF SUICIDE TERRORIST CAMPAIGNS, 1980–2001

| Region Dispute | Homeland Status | Terrorist Goal | Target a Democracy? |
|---|---|---|---|
| Lebanon, 1983–86 | U.S./F/IDF military presence | U.S./F/IDF withdrawal | Yes |
| West Bank/ Gaza, 1994– | IDF military presence | IDF withdrawal | Yes |
| Tamils in Sri Lanka, 1990– | SL military presence | SL withdrawal | Yes (1950) |
| Kurds in Turkey, 1990s | Turkey military presence | Turkey withdrawal | Yes (1983) |
| Chechnya, 2000– | Russia military presence | Russian withdrawal | Yes (1993) |
| Kashmir, 2000– | Indian military presence | Indian withdrawal | Yes |
| Saudi Peninsula, 1996– | U.S. military presence | U.S. withdrawal | Yes |

(population, property, and way of life) from foreign influence or control. As a result, a strategy of suicide terrorism is most likely to be used to achieve nationalist goals, such as gaining control of what the terrorists see as their national homeland territory and expelling foreign military forces from that territory.

In fact, every suicide campaign from 1980 to 2001 has had as a major objective—or as its central objective—coercing a foreign government that has military forces in what they see as their homeland to take those forces out. Table 2 summarizes the disputes that have engendered suicide terrorist campaigns. Since 1980, there has not been a suicide terrorist campaign directed mainly against domestic opponents or against foreign opponents who did not have military forces in the terrorists homeland. Although attacks against civilians are often the most salient to Western observers, actually every suicide terrorist campaign in the past two decades has included attacks directly against the foreign military forces in the country, and most have been waged by guerrilla organizations that also use more conventional methods of attack against those forces.

Even Al Qaeda fits this pattern. Although Saudi Arabia is not under American military occupation per se and the terrorists have political objectives against the Saudi regime and others, one major objective of Al Qaeda is the expulsion of U.S. troops from the Saudi Peninsula and there have been attacks by terrorists loyal to Osama Bin Laden against American troops in Saudi Arabia. To be sure, there is a major debate among Islamists over the morality of suicide attacks, but within Saudi Arabia there is little debate over Al Qaeda's objection to American forces in the region and over 95% of Saudi society reportedly agrees with Bin Laden on this matter.

Still, even if suicide terrorism follows a strategic logic, could some suicide terrorist campaigns be irrational in the sense that they are being waged for unrealistic goals? The answer is that some suicide terrorist groups have not been realistic in expecting the full concessions demanded of the target, but this is normal for disputes involving overlapping nationalist claims and even for coercive attempts in general.

Rather, the ambitions of terrorist leaders are realistic in two other senses. First, suicide terrorists' political aims, if not their methods, are often more mainstream than observers realize; they generally reflect quite common, straight-forward nationalist self-determination claims of their community. Second, these groups often have significant support for their policy goals versus the target state, goals that are typically much the same as those of other nationalists within their community. Differences between the terrorists and more "moderate" leaders usually concern the usefulness of a certain level of violence and—sometimes—the legitimacy of attacking additional targets besides foreign troops in the country, such as attacks in other countries or against third parties and civilians. Thus, it is not that the terrorists pursue radical goals and then seek others' support. Rather, the terrorists are simply the members of their societies who are the most optimistic about the usefulness of violence for achieving goals that many, and often most, support.

The behavior of Hamas illustrates the point. Hamas terrorism has provoked Israeli retaliation that has been costly for Palestinians, while pursuing the—apparently unrealistic—goal of abolishing the state of Israel. Although prospects of establishing an Arab state in all of "historic Palestine" may be poor, most Palestinians agree that it would be desirable if possible. Hamas's terrorist violence was in fact carefully calculated and controlled. In April 1994, as its first suicide campaign was beginning, Hamas leaders explained that "martyrdom operations" would be used to achieve intermediate objectives, such as Israeli withdrawal from the West Bank and Gaza, while the final objective of creating an Islamic state from the Jordan River to the Mediterranean may require other forms of armed resistance.

### Democracies as the Targets.

Suicide terrorism is more likely to be employed against states with democratic political systems than authoritarian governments for several reasons. First, democracies are often thought to be especially vulnerable to coercive punishment. Domestic critics and international rivals, as well as terrorists, often view democracies as "soft," usually on the grounds that their publics have low thresholds of cost tolerance and high ability to affect state policy. Even if there is little evidence that democracies are easier to coerce than other regime types, this image of democracy matters. Since terrorists can inflict only moderate damage in comparison to even small interstate wars, terrorism can be expected to coerce only if the target state is viewed as especially vulnerable to punishment. Second, suicide terrorism is a tool of the weak, which means that, regardless of how much punishment the terrorists inflict, the target state almost always has the capacity to retaliate with far more extreme punishment or even by exterminating the terrorists' community. Accordingly, suicide terrorists must not only have high interests at stake, they must also be confident that their opponent will be at least somewhat restrained. While there are infamous exceptions, democracies have generally been more restrained in their use of force against civilians, at least since World War II. Finally, suicide attacks may also be harder to organize or publicize in authoritarian police states, although these possibilities are weakened by the fact that weak authoritarian states are also not targets.

In fact, the target state of every modern suicide campaign has been a democracy. The United States, France, Israel, India, Sri Lanka, Turkey, and Russia were all democracies when they were attacked by suicide terrorist campaigns, even though the last three became democracies more recently than the others. . . .

The Kurds, which straddle Turkey and Iraq, illustrate the point that suicide terrorist campaigns are more likely to be targeted against democracies than authoritarian regimes. Although Iraq has been far more brutal toward its Kurdish population than has Turkey, violent Kurdish groups have used suicide attacks exclusively against democratic Turkey and not against the authoritarian regime in Iraq. There are plenty of national groups living under authoritarian regimes with grievances that could possibly inspire suicide terrorism, but none have. Thus, the fact that rebels have resorted to this strategy only when they face the more suitable type of target counts against arguments that suicide terrorism is a nonstrategic response, motivated mainly by fanaticism or irrational hatreds.

## TERRORISTS' ASSESSMENTS OF SUICIDE TERRORISM

The main reason that suicide terrorism is growing is that terrorists have learned that it works. Even more troubling, the encouraging lessons that terrorists have learned from the experience of 1980s and 1990s are not, for the most part, products of wild-eyed interpretations or wishful thinking. They are, rather, quite reasonable assessments of the outcomes of suicide terrorist campaigns during this period.

To understand how terrorists groups have assessed the effectiveness of suicide terrorism requires three tasks: (1) explanation of appropriate standards for evaluating the effectiveness of coercion from the standpoint of coercers; (2) analysis of the 11 suicide terrorist campaigns that have ended as of 2001 to determine how frequently target states made concessions that were, or at least could have been, interpreted as due to suicide attack; and (3) close analysis of terrorists' learning from particular campaigns. Because some analysts see suicide terrorism as fundamentally irrational, it is important to assess whether the lessons that the terrorists drew were reasonable conclusions from the record. The crucial cases are the Hamas and Islamic Jihad campaigns against Israel during the 1990s, because they are most frequently cited as aimed at unrealistic goals and therefore as basically irrational.

### Standards of Assessment

Terrorists, like other people, learn from experience. Since the main purpose of suicide terrorism is coercion, the learning that is likely to have the greatest impact on terrorists' future behavior is the lessons that they have drawn from past campaigns about the coercive effectiveness of suicide attack.

Most analyses of coercion focus on the decision making of target states, largely to determine their vulnerability to various coercive pressures. The analysis here, however, seeks to determine why terrorist coercers are increasingly attracted to a specific coercive strategy. For this purpose, we must develop a new set of standards, because assessing the value of coercive pressure for the coercer is not the same problem as assessing its impact on the target.

From the perspective of a target state, the key question is whether the value of the concession that the coercer is demanding is greater than the costs imposed by the coercive pressure, regardless of whether that pressure is in the form of lives at risk, economic hardship, or other types of costs. However, from the perspective of the coercer, the key question is whether a particular coercive strategy promises to be more effective than alternative methods of influence and, so, warrants continued (or increased) effort. This is especially true for terrorists who are highly committed to a particular goal and so willing to exhaust virtually any alternative rather than abandoning it. In this search for an effective strategy, coercers' assessments are likely to be largely a function of estimates of the success of past efforts; for suicide terrorists, this means assessments of whether past suicide campaigns produced significant concessions.

A glance at the behavior of suicide terrorists reveals that such trade-offs between alternative methods are important in their calculations. All of the organizations that have resorted to suicide terrorism began their coercive efforts with more conventional guerrilla operations, nonsuicide terrorism, or both. Hezbollah, Hamas, Islamic Jihad, the PKK, the LTTE, and Al Qaeda all used demonstrative and destructive means of violence long before resorting to suicide attack. Indeed, looking at the trajectory of terrorist groups over time, there is a distinct element of experimentation in the techniques and strategies used by these groups and distinct movement toward those techniques and strategies that produce the most effect. Al Qaeda actually prides itself for a commitment to even tactical learning over time— the infamous "terrorist manual" stresses at numerous points the importance of writing "lessons learned" memoranda that can be shared with other members to improve the effectiveness of future attacks. . . .

## The Apparent Success of Suicide Terrorism

Perhaps the most striking aspect of recent suicide terrorist campaigns is that they are associated with gains for the terrorists' political cause about half the time. As Table 1 shows, of the 11 suicide terrorist campaigns that were completed during 1980–2001, six closely correlate with significant policy changes by the target state toward the terrorists' major political goals. In one case, the terrorists' territorial goals were fully achieved (Hezbollah v. US/F, 1983); in three cases, the terrorists territorial aims were partly achieved (Hezbollah v. Israel, 1983–85; Hamas v. Israel, 1994; and Hamas v. Israel, 1994–95); in one case, the target government entered into sovereignty negotiations with the terrorists (LTTE v. Sri Lanka, 1993–94); and in one case, the terrorist organization's top leader was released from prison (Hamas v. Israel, 1997). Five campaigns did not lead to noticeable concessions (Hezbollah's second effort against Israel in Lebanon, 1985–86; a Hamas campaign in 1996 retaliating for an Israeli assassination; the LTTE v. Sri Lanka, 1995–2002; and both PKK campaigns). Coercive success is so rare that even a 50% success rate is significant, because international military and economic coercion, using the same standards as above, generally works less than a third of the time.

There were limits to what suicide terrorism appeared to gain in the 1980s and 1990s. Most of the gains for the terrorists' cause were modest, not involving interests central to the target countries' security or wealth, and most were potentially revocable. For the United States and France, Lebanon was a relatively minor foreign policy interest. Israel's apparent concessions to the Palestinians from 1994 to 1997 were more modest than they might appear. Although Israel withdrew its forces from parts of Gaza and the West Bank and released Sheikh Yassin, during the same period Israeli settlement in the occupied territories almost doubled, and recent events have shown that Israel is not deterred from sending force back in when necessary. In two disputes, the terrorists achieved initial success but failed to reach greater goals. Although Israel withdrew from much of Lebanon in June 1985, it retained a six-mile security buffer zone along the southern edge of the country for another 15 years from which a second Hezbollah suicide terrorist campaign failed to dislodge it. The Sri Lankan government did conduct apparently serious negotiations with the LTTE from November 1994 to April 1995, but did not concede the Tamil's main demand for independence, and since 1995, the government has preferred to prosecute the war rather than consider permitting Tamil secession.

Still, these six concessions, or at least apparent concessions, help to explain why suicide terrorism is on the rise. In three of the cases, the target government policy changes are clearly due to coercive pressure from the terrorist group. The American and French withdrawal was perhaps the most clear-cut coercive success for suicide terrorism. In his memoirs, President Ronald Reagan explained the U.S. decision to withdraw from Lebanon:

> The price we had to pay in Beirut was so great, the tragedy at the barracks was so enormous. . . . We had to pull out. . . . We couldn't stay there and run the risk of another suicide attack on the Marines.

The IDF withdrawal from most of southern Lebanon in 1985 and the Sri Lankan government decision to hold negotiations with the LTTE were also widely understood to be a direct result of the coercive punishment imposed by Hezbollah and LTTE respectively. In both cases, the concessions followed periods in which the terrorists had turned more and more to suicide attacks, but since Hezbollah and the LTTE employed a combination of suicide attack and conventional attack on their opponents, one can question the relative weight of suicide attack in coercing these target states. However, there is little question in either case that punishment pressures inflicted by these terrorist organizations were decisive in the outcomes. For instance, as a candidate in the November 9, 1994, presidential election of Sri Lanka, Mrs. Chandrika Kumaratunga explicitly asked for a mandate to redraw boundaries so as to appease the Tamils in their demand for a separate homeland in the island's northeast provinces, often saying, "We definitely hope to begin discussions with the Tamil people, with their representatives—including the Tigers—and offer them political solutions to end the war . . . [involving] extensive devolution." This would, Kumaratunga said, "create an environment in which people could live without fear."

The other three concessions, or arguable concessions, are less clear-cut. All three involve Hamas campaigns against Israel. Not counting the ongoing second intifada, Hamas waged four separate suicide attack campaigns against Israel, in 1994, 1995, 1996, and 1997. One, in 1996, did not correspond with Israeli concessions. This campaign was announced as retaliation for Israel's assassination of a Hamas leader; no particular coercive goal was announced, and it was suspended by Hamas after four attacks in two weeks. The other three all do correspond with

Israeli concessions. In April 1994, Hamas began a series of suicide bombings in relation to the Hebron Massacre. After two attacks, Israel decided to accelerate its withdrawal from Gaza, which was required under the Oslo Agreement but which had been delayed. Hamas then suspended attacks for five months. From October 1994 to August 1995, Hamas (and Islamic Jihad) carried out a total of seven suicide attacks against Israel. In September 1995, Israel agreed to withdraw from certain West Bank towns that December, which it earlier had claimed could not be done before April 1996 at the soonest. Hamas then suspended attacks until its retaliation campaign during the last week of February and first week of March 1996. Finally, in March 1997, Hamas began a suicide attack campaign that included an attack about every two months until September 1997. In response Israeli Prime Minister Netanyahu authorized the assassination of a Hamas leader. The attempt, in Amman, Jordan, failed and the Israeli agents were captured. To get them back Israel agreed to release Sheikh Ahmed Yassin, spiritual leader of Hamas. While this was not a concession to the terrorists' territorial goals, there is no evidence that Hamas interpreted this in any way different from the standard view that this release was the product of American and Jordanian pressure. . . .

## THE LIMITS OF SUICIDE TERRORISM

Despite suicide terrorists' reasons for confidence in the coercive effectiveness of this strategy, there are sharp limits to what suicide terrorism is likely to accomplish in the future. During the 1980s and 1990s, terrorist leaders learned that moderate punishment often leads to moderate concessions and so concluded that more ambitious suicide campaigns would lead to greater political gains. However, today's more ambitious suicide terrorist campaigns are likely to fail. Although suicide terrorism is somewhat more effective than ordinary coercive punishment using air power or economic sanctions, it is not drastically so.

### Suicide Terrorism Is Unlikely to Achieve Ambitious Goals

In international military coercion, threats to inflict military defeat often generate more coercive leverage than punishment. Punishment, using anything short of nuclear weapons, is a relatively weak coercive strategy because modern nation states generally will accept high costs rather than abandon important national goals, while modern administrative techniques and economic adjustments over time often allow states to minimize civilian costs. The most punishing air attacks with conventional munitions in history were the American B-29 raids against Japan's 62 largest cities from March to August 1945. Although these raids killed nearly 800,000 Japanese civilians—almost 10% died on the first day, the March 9, 1945, fire-bombing of Tokyo, which killed over 85,000—the conventional bombing did not compel the Japanese to surrender.

Suicide terrorism makes adjustment to reduce damage more difficult than for states faced with military coercion or economic sanctions. However, it does not affect the target state's interests in the issues at stake. As a result, suicide terrorism can coerce states to abandon limited or modest goals, such as withdrawal from territory of low strategic importance or, as in Israel's case in 1994 and 1995, a temporary and partial withdrawal from a more important area. However, suicide terrorism is unlikely to cause targets to abandon goals central to their wealth or security, such as a loss of territory that would weaken the economic prospects of the state or strengthen the rivals of the state.

Suicide terrorism makes punishment more effective than in international military coercion. Targets remain willing to countenance high costs for important goals, but administrative, economic, or military adjustments to prevent suicide attack are harder, while suicide attackers themselves are unlikely to be deterred by the threat of retaliation. Accordingly, suicide attack is likely to present a threat of continuing limited civilian punishment that the target government cannot completely eliminate, and the upper bound on what punishment can gain for coercers is recognizably higher in suicidal terrorism than in international military coercion.

The data on suicide terrorism from 1980 to 2001 support this conclusion. While suicide terrorism has achieved modest or very limited goals, it has so far failed to compel target democracies to abandon goals central to national wealth or security. When the United States withdrew from Lebanon in 1984, it had no important security, economic, or even ideological interests at stake. Lebanon was largely a humanitarian mission and not viewed as central to the national welfare of the United States. Israel withdrew from most of Lebanon in June 1985 but remained in a security buffer on the edge of southern Lebanon for more than a decade afterward, despite the fact that 17 of 22 suicide attacks occurred in 1985 and 1986. Israel's withdrawals from Gaza and the West Bank in 1994 and 1995 occurred at the same time that settlements increased and did little to hinder the IDF's return, and so these concessions were more modest than they may appear. Sri Lanka has suffered more casualties from suicide attack than Israel but has not acceded to demands that it surrender part of its national territory. Thus, the logic of punishment and the record of suicide terrorism suggests that, unless suicide terrorists acquire far more destructive technologies, suicide attacks for more ambitious goals are likely to fail and will continue to provoke more aggressive military responses.

## POLICY IMPLICATIONS FOR CONTAINING SUICIDE TERRORISM

While the rise in suicide terrorism and the reasons behind it seem daunting, there are important policy lessons to learn. The current policy debate is misguided. Offensive military action or concessions alone rarely work for long. For over 20 years, the governments of Israel and other states targeted by suicide terrorism have engaged in extensive military efforts to kill, isolate, and jail suicide terrorist leaders and operatives, sometimes with the help of quite good surveillance of the terrorists' communities. Thus far, they have met with meager success. Although decapitation of suicide terrorist organizations can disrupt their operations temporarily, it rarely yields long-term gains. Of the 11 major suicide terrorist campaigns that had ended as of 2001, only one—the PKK versus Turkey—did so as a result of leadership decapitation, when the leader, in Turkish custody, asked his followers to stop. So far, leadership decapitation has also not ended Al Qaeda's campaign. Although the United States successfully toppled the Taliban in Afghanistan in December 2001, Al Qaeda launched seven successful suicide terrorist attacks from April to December 2002, killing some 250 Western civilians, more than in the three years before September 11, 2001, combined.

Concessions are also not a simple answer. Concessions to nationalist grievances that are widely held in the terrorists' community can reduce popular support for further terrorism, making it more difficult to recruit new suicide attackers and improving the standing of more moderate nationalist elites who are in competition with the terrorists. Such benefits can be realized, however, only if the concessions really do substantially satisfy the nationalist or self-determination aspirations of a large fraction of the community.

Partial, incremental, or deliberately staggered concessions that are dragged out over a substantial period of time are likely to become the worst of both worlds. Incremental compromise may appear—or easily be portrayed—to the terrorists' community as simply delaying tactics and, thus, may fail to reduce, or actually increase, their distrust that their main concerns will ever be met. Further, incrementalism provides time and opportunity for the terrorists to intentionally provoke the target state in hopes of derailing the smooth progress of negotiated compromise in the short term, so that they can reradicalize their own community and actually escalate their efforts toward even greater gains in the long term. Thus, states that are willing to make concessions should do so in a single step if at all possible.

Advocates of concessions should also recognize that, even if they are successful in undermining the terrorist leaders' base of support, almost any concession at all will tend to encourage the terrorist leaders further about their own coercive effectiveness. Thus, even in the aftermath of a real settlement with the opposing community, some terrorists will remain motivated to continue attacks and, for the medium term, may be able to do so, which in term would put a premium on combining concessions with other solutions.

Given the limits of offense and of concessions, homeland security and defensive efforts generally must be a core part of any solution. Undermining the feasibility of suicide terrorism is a difficult task. After all, a major advantage of suicide attack is that it is more difficult to prevent than other types of attack. However, the difficulty of achieving perfect security should not keep us from taking serious measures to prevent would-be terrorists from easily entering their target society. As Chaim Kaufmann has shown, even intense ethnic civil wars can often be stopped by demographic separation because it greatly reduces both means and incentives for the sides to attack each other. This logic may apply with even more force to the related problem of suicide terrorism, since, for suicide attackers, gaining physical access to the general area of the target is the only genuinely demanding part of an operation, and as we have seen, resentment of foreign occupation of their national homeland is a key part of the motive for suicide terrorism.

The requirements for demographic separation depend on geographic and other circumstances that may not be attainable in all cases. For example, much of

Israel's difficulty in containing suicide terrorism derives from the deeply intermixed settlement patterns of the West Bank and Gaza, which make the effective length of the border between Palestinian and Jewish settled areas practically infinite and have rendered even very intensive Israeli border control efforts ineffective. As a result, territorial concessions could well encourage terrorist leaders to strive for still greater gains while greater repression may only exacerbate the conditions of occupation that cultivate more recruits for terrorist organizations. Instead, the best course to improve Israel's security may well be a combined strategy: abandoning territory on the West Bank along with an actual wall that physically separates the populations.

Similarly, if Al Qaeda proves able to continue suicide attacks against the American homeland, the United States should emphasize improving its domestic security. In the short term, the United States should adopt stronger border controls to make it more difficult for suicide attackers to enter the United States. In the long term, the United States should work toward energy independence and, thus, reduce the need for American troops in the Persian Gulf countries where their presence has helped recruit suicide terrorists to attack America. These measures will not provide a perfect solution, but they may make it far more difficult for Al Qaeda to continue attacks in the United States, especially spectacular attacks that require elaborate coordination.

Perhaps most important, the close association between foreign military occupations and the growth of suicide terrorist movements in the occupied regions should give pause to those who favor solutions that involve conquering countries in order to transform their political systems. Conquering countries may disrupt terrorist operations in the short term, but it is important to recognize that occupation of more countries may well increase the number of terrorists coming at us.

# THE SPREAD OF NUCLEAR WEAPONS

## Nuclear Instability in South Asia

### SCOTT D. SAGAN

The emerging nuclear history of India and Pakistan strongly supports the pessimistic predictions of organizational theorists. Military organizational behavior has led to serious problems in meeting all three requirements for stable nuclear deterrence—prevention of preventive war during periods of transition when one side has a temporary advantage, the development of survivable second-strike forces, and avoidance of accidental nuclear war. . . . These problems have now appeared in India and Pakistan.

It should be acknowledged from the start that there are important differences between the nuclear relationship emerging between India and Pakistan and the cold war system that developed over time between the United States and the Soviet Union. While the differences are clear, however, the significance of these differences is not. For example, the nuclear arsenals in South Asia are, and are likely to remain, much smaller and less sophisticated than were the U.S. and Soviet arsenals. This should make each arsenal both more vulnerable to a counterforce attack (an attack on the adversary's own nuclear forces) and less capable of mounting counterforce attacks, and thus the net effect is uncertain. There are also important differences in civil-military relations in the two cases, but these differences, too, are both stabilizing and potentially destabilizing. The Soviets and the Americans both eventually developed an "assertive" command system with tight high-level civilian control over their nuclear weapons. Also India has an extreme system of assertive civilian control of the military, with (at least until recently) very little direct military influence on any aspect of nuclear weapons policy. Pakistan, however, is at the other end of the spectrum, with the military in complete control of the nuclear arsenal, and with only marginal influence from civilian political leaders, even during the periods when there was a civilian-led government in Islamabad. There are, finally, important differences in mutual understanding, proximity, and hostility. India and Pakistan share a common colonial and pre-colonial history, have some common cultural roots, and share a common border; they also have engaged in four wars against each other, and are involved in a violent fifty-year dispute about the status of Kashmir. In contrast, the Americans and Soviets were on opposite sides of the globe and viewed each other as mysterious, often unpredictable adversaries. The cold war superpowers were involved in a deep-seated ideological rivalry, but held no disputed territory between them and had no enduring history of armed violence against each other.

There is also, however, a crucially important similarity between the nuclear conditions that existed in cold war and those that exist in South Asia today. In both cases, the parochial interests and routine behaviors of the organizations that manage nuclear weapons limit the stability of nuclear deterrence. The newest nuclear weapons will not make exactly the same mistakes with nuclear weapons as did their superpower predecessors. They are, however, also unlikely to meet with complete success in the difficult effort to control these weapons and maintain nuclear peace.

## THE PROBLEM OF PREVENTIVE WAR

Pakistan has been under direct military rule for almost half of its existence, and some analysts have argued that the organizational biases of its military leaders had strong effects on strategic decisions concerning the initiation and conduct of the 1965 and 1971 wars with India. In contrast, India has a sustained tradition of strict civilian control over the military since its independence. These patterns of civil-military relations influence nuclear weapons doctrine and operations. In India, the military has traditionally not been involved in decisions concerning nuclear testing, design, or even command and control. In Pakistan, the military largely runs the nuclear weapons program; even during the periods in which civilian prime ministers have held the reins of government, they have neither been told the full details of the nuclear weapons program nor been given direct control over the operational arsenal.

An organizational theory lens suggests that it is very fortunate that it was India, not Pakistan, that was the first to develop nuclear weapons in South Asia. Military rule in Islamabad (and military influence during periods of civilian rule) certainly has played an important role in Pakistani decision making concerning the use of force (see the discussion of the Kargil conflict below). But the Pakistani military did not possess nuclear weapons before India tested in 1974, and thus was not in a position to argue that preventive war now was better than war later after India developed a rudimentary arsenal.

The preventive war problem in South Asia is a complex one, however, and new evidence suggests that military influence in India produced serious risks of preventive war in the 1980s, despite strong institutionalized civilian control. The government of Prime Minister Indira Gandhi considered, but then rejected, plans to attack Pakistan's Kahuta nuclear facility in the early 1980s, a preventive attack plan that was recommended by senior Indian military leaders. Yet, as occurred in the United States, the preferences of senior officers did not suddenly change when civilian leaders ruled against preventive war. Instead, the beliefs went underground, only to resurface later in a potentially more dangerous form.

These beliefs emerged from the shadows during the 1986–87 "Brasstacks" crisis. This serious crisis began in late 1986 when the Indian military initiated a massive military exercise in Rajasthan, involving an estimated 250,000 troops and 1,500 tanks, including the issuance of live ammunition to troops and concluding with a simulated "counter-offensive" attack, including Indian Air Force strikes, into Pakistan. The Pakistani military, fearing that the exercise might turn into a large-scale attack, alerted military forces and conducted exercises along the border, which led to Indian military counter-movements closer to the border and an operational Indian Air Force alert. The resulting crisis produced a flurry of diplomatic activity and was resolved only after direct intervention by the highest political authorities.

The traditional explanation for the Brasstacks crisis has been that it was an accidental crisis, caused by Pakistan's misinterpretation of an inadvertently provocative Indian Army exercise. For example, Devin Hagerty's detailed examination of "New Delhi's intentions in conducting Brasstacks" concludes that "India's conduct of 'normal' exercises rang alarm bells in Pakistan; subsequently, the logic of the security dilemma structured both sides' behavior, with each interpreting the other's defensive moves as preparations for offensive action.[1] A stronger explanation, however, unpacks "New Delhi's intentions" to look at what different Indian decision makers in the capital wanted to do before and during the crisis.

The key is to understand the preventive-war thinking of the then-Indian chief of the Army Staff, General Krishnaswami Sundarji. Sundarji apparently believed that India's security would be greatly eroded by Pakistani development of a usable nuclear arsenal and thus deliberately designed the Brasstacks exercise in hopes of provoking a Pakistani military response. He hoped that this would then provide India with an excuse to implement existing contingency plans to go on the offensive against Pakistan and to take out its nuclear program in a preventive strike. According to the memoirs of Lieutenant General P. N. Hoon, the commander in chief of the Western Army during Brasstacks:

> Brasstacks was no military exercise. It was a plan to build up a situation for a fourth war with Pakistan. And what is even more shocking is that the Prime Minister, Mr. Rajiv Gandhi, was not aware of these plans for war.

The preventive war motivation behind Sundarji's plans helps to explain why the Indian military did not provide full notification of the exercise to the Pakistanis and then failed to use the special hotline to explain their operations when information was requested by Pakistan during the crisis. A final piece of evidence confirms that Sundarji advocated a preventive strike against Pakistan during the crisis. Considerations of an attack on Pakistani nuclear facilities went all the way up to the most senior decision makers in New Delhi in January 1987:

> [Prime Minister] Rajiv [Gandhi] now considered the possibility that Pakistan might initiate war with India. In a meeting with a handful of senior bureaucrats and General Sundarji, he contemplated beating Pakistan to the draw by launching a preemptive attack on the Army Reserve South. This would have included automatically an attack on Pakistan's nuclear facilities to remove the potential for a Pakistani nuclear riposte to

India's attack. Relevant government agencies were not asked to contribute analysis or views to the discussion. Sundarji argued that India's cities could be protected from a Pakistani counterattack (perhaps a nuclear one), but, upon being probed, could not say how. One important advisor from the Ministry of Defense argued eloquently that 'India and Pakistan have already fought their last war, and there is too much to lose in contemplating another one.' This view ultimately prevailed.

## THE KARGIL CONFLICT AND FUTURE PROBLEMS

Optimists cannot accept that the Brasstacks crisis may have been a deliberate attempt to spark a preventive attack, but they might be reassured by the final outcome, as senior political leaders stepped in to stop further escalation. The power of nuclear deterrence to prevent war in South Asia, optimists insist, has been demonstrated in repeated crises: the Indian preventive attack discussions in 1984; the Brasstacks crisis; and the 1990 Kashmir crisis. "There is no more ironclad law in international relations theory than this," Devin Hagerty's detailed study concludes, "nuclear states do not fight wars with each other."[2]

In the spring and summer of 1999, however, one year after the exchange of nuclear tests, India and Pakistan did fight a war in the mountains along the line of control separating the portions of Kashmir controlled by each country, near the Indian town of Kargil. The conflict began in May, when the Indian intelligence services discovered what appeared to be Pakistani regular forces lodged in mountain redoubts on the Indian side of the line of control. For almost two months, Indian Army units attacked the Pakistani forces and Indian Air Force jets bombed their bases high in the Himalayan peaks. Although the Indian forces carefully stayed on their side of the line of control in Kashmir, Indian prime minister Atal Bihari Vajpayee informed the U.S. government that he might have to order attacks into Pakistan. U.S. spy satellites revealed that Indian tanks and heavy artillery were being prepared for a counter-offensive in Rajasthan. The fighting ended in July, when Pakistani prime minister Nawaz Sharif flew to Washington and, after receiving "political cover" in the form of statement that President Bill Clinton would "take a personal interest" in resolving the Kashmir problem, pledged to withdraw forces to the Pakistani side of the line of control. Over one thousand Indian and Pakistani soldiers died in the conflict, and Sharif's decision to pull out was one of the major causes of the coup that overthrew his regime in October 1999.

The 1999 Kargil conflict is disturbing not only because it demonstrates that nuclear-armed states can fight wars, but also because the organizational biases of the Pakistani military were a major cause of the conflict. Moreover, such biases continue to exist and could play a role in starting crises in the future. This increases the dangers of both a preventive and preemptive strike if war is considered inevitable, as well as the risk of a deliberate, but limited, use of nuclear weapons on the battlefield.

Three puzzling aspects of the Kargil conflict are understandable from an organizational perspective. First, in late 1998, the Pakistani military planned the Kargil operation, paying much more attention, as organization theory would predict, to the tactical effects of the surprise military maneuver than to the broader strategic consequences. Ignoring the likely international reaction and the predictable domestic consequences of the military incursion in India, however, proved to be a significant factor in the ultimate failure of the Kargil operation.

Second, the Pakistani Army also started the operation with the apparent belief—following the logic of what has been called the "stability/instability paradox"—that a "stable nuclear balance" between India and Pakistan permitted more offensive actions to take place with impunity in Kashmir. It is important to note that this belief was more strongly held by senior military officers than by civilian leaders. For example, at the height of the fighting near Kargil, Pakistani Army leaders stated that "there is almost a red alert situation," but they nevertheless insisted "there is no chance of the Kargil conflict leading to a full-fledged war between the two sides."[3] Although Prime Minister Nawaz Sharif apparently approved the plan to move forces across the line of control, it is not clear that he was fully briefed on the nature, scope, or potential consequences of the operation. The prime minister's statement that he was "trying to avoid nuclear war" and his suggestion that he feared "that India was getting ready to launch a full-scale military operation against Pakistan" provide a clear contrast to the confident military assessment that there was virtually no risk of an Indian counterattack or escalation to nuclear war.

Third, the current Pakistani military government's interpretation of the Kargil crisis, at least in public, is that Nawaz Sharif lost courage and backed down unnecessarily. This view is not widely shared by Pakistani scholars and journalists, but such a "stab in the back" thesis does serve the parochial self-interests of the Pakistani army, which does not want to acknowledge its errors or those of the current Musharraf regime. The New Delhi government's interpretation, however, is that the Indian threats that military escalation—a counterattack across the international border—would be ordered, if necessary, forced Pakistan to retreat. These different "lessons learned" could produce ominous outcomes in future crises: each side believes that the Kargil conflict proved that if its government displays resolve and threatens to escalate to new levels of violence, the other side will exhibit restraint and back away from the brink.

Future military crises between India and Pakistan are likely to be nuclear crises. Proliferation optimists are not concerned about this likelihood, however, since they argue that the danger of preventive war, if it ever existed at all, has been eliminated by the development of deliverable nuclear weapons in both countries after May 1998. The problem of preventive war during periods of transition in South Asia is only of historical interest now, optimists would insist.

I am not convinced by this argument for two basic reasons. First, there is an arms race looming on the horizon in South Asia. The Indian government has given strong support to the Bush administration's plans to develop missile defense technology and has expressed interest in eventually procuring or developing its own missile defense capability. I believe that the Indian nuclear program is strongly influenced by the fact that hawkish nuclear policies are popular among Indian voters and thus serve the domestic political interests of Indian politicians. China is likely to respond to the U.S. decision to build national missile defenses by increasing the size and readiness of its own missile force. This will in turn encourage the Indian government to increase its own missile deployments and develop defense technology.

These deployments in India, however, will threaten the smaller nuclear deterrent forces in Pakistan, and this would inevitably reopen the window of opportunity for preventive war considerations. Military biases, under the preventive war logic of "better now than later," could encourage precipitous action in either country if the government had even a fleeting moment of superiority in this new kind of arms race.

The second reason to be pessimistic is that, in serious crises, attacks might be initiated based on the belief that an enemy's use of nuclear weapons is imminent and unavoidable. While it is clear that the existence of nuclear weapons in South Asia made both governments cautious in their use of conventional military force in 1999, it is also clear that Indian leaders were prepared to escalate the conflict if necessary. Pakistani political authorities, however, made nuclear threats during the crisis, suggesting that nuclear weapons would be used precisely under such conditions. Moreover, according to U.S. officials the Pakistani military, apparently without the Prime Minister's knowledge took initial steps to alert its nuclear forces during the Kargil conflict.

This dangerous alerting pattern was repeated in the South Asian crises that occurred after the September 11, 2001, terrorist attacks in the United States and the December 13, 2001, terrorist attack on the Parliament in New Delhi. In both cases, the Pakistani government feared that its nuclear forces would be attacked and therefore took alert measures to disperse the nuclear weapons and missiles to new locations away from their storage sites. Pakistani fears that attacks on their nuclear arsenal were being planned may not have been entirely fanciful.

After the September 11 Pentagon and World Trade Center attacks, President Bush warned Islamabad that Pakistan would either side with the United States in the new war against terrorism or else be treated as a terrorist state. The development of military plans for U.S. commando raids against the Pakistani nuclear weapons sites was soon widely reported. President Musharraf defused the crisis by deciding to abandon support for the Taliban regime in Afghanistan and to provide logistical and intelligence support for the U.S. war there.

After the December 13 terrorist attack against the Indian Parliament, the Indian government sent massive military forces to the Pakistani border and threatened to attack unless Musharraf cracked down on the radical Islamic groups that supported terrorist operations in Kashmir and New Delhi. Before Musharraf could respond, General S. Padmanabhan, the Indian Army chief, issued a bellicose statement announcing that the military buildup "was not an exercise": "A lot of viable options (beginning from a strike on the camps to a full conventional war) are available. We can do it. . . . If we go to war, jolly good."[4] Senior Indian political authorities criticized the Army chief for making the statement, and diplomats in New Delhi speculated that General Padmanabhan had deliberately made it more difficult for the Pakistanis to back down in this crisis, thus increasing the likelihood of war. Again, President Musharraf defused the crisis, at least temporarily, by initiating a crackdown on Islamic Jihadi groups promoting terrorism in Kashmir and the rest of India.

What lessons should be drawn from these dangerous crises? Optimists will look at only the final result and assume that it was inevitable: Deterrence and coercion worked; as serious threats were issued, the Pakistani president compromised and no war occurred. At a deeper level, however, two more ominous lessons should be learned. First, President Musharraf's decision to back down was by no means inevitable, and he was subject to significant criticism from Islamic parties and some military circles for his conciliatory stance. Other Pakistani leaders could have gone the other way, and, indeed, Musharraf may be less prone to compromise in the future precisely because he was forced to change policies under the threat of attack in these crises. Second, the Pakistani fear that a preventive or preemptive strike against its nuclear arsenal was imminent forced it to take very dangerous military alerting steps in both crises. Taking nuclear weapons and missiles out of their more secure storage locations and deploying them into the field may make the forces less vulnerable to an enemy attack, but it makes the weapons more vulnerable to theft or internal attacks by terrorist organizations. Given the number of al Qaeda members and supporters in Pakistan, this hidden terrorist problem may well have been the most serious nuclear danger of the crises. In short, the crises of 2001 and 2002 demonstrate that nuclear weapons in South Asia may well produce a modicum of restraint, but also momentous dangers.

In future crises in South Asia, the likelihood of either a preventive or preemptive attack will be strongly influenced by a complex mixture of perceptions of the adversary's intent, estimates about its future offensive and defensive capabilities, and estimates of the vulnerability of its current nuclear arsenal. Organizational biases could encourage worst-case assumptions about the adversary's intent and pessimistic beliefs about the prospects for successful strategic deterrence over the long term. Unfortunately, as will be seen below, inherent organizational characteristics can also produce vulnerabilities to an enemy strike.

## SURVIVABILITY OF NUCLEAR FORCES IN SOUTH ASIA

The fear of retaliation is central to successful deterrence, and the second requirement for stability with nuclear weapons is therefore the development of secure, second-strike forces. Unfortunately, there are strong reasons to be concerned about the ability of the Indian and Pakistani military to maintain survivable forces. Two problems can already be seen to have reduced (at least temporarily) the survivability of nuclear forces in Pakistan. First, there is evidence that the Pakistani military, as was the case in the cold war examples cited earlier, deployed its missile forces, following standard operating procedures, in ways that produce signatures giving away their deployment locations. Indian intelligence officers, for example, identified the locations of planned Pakistani deployments of M-11 missiles by spotting the placement of "secret" defense communication terminals nearby. A second, and even more dramatic, example follows a cold war precedent quite closely. Just as the road engineers in the Soviet Union inadvertently gave away the location of their ICBMs because construction crews built roads with wide-radius turns next to the missile silos, Pakistani road construction crews have inadvertently signaled the location of the "secret" M-11 missiles by placing wide-radius roads and roundabouts outside newly constructed garages at the Sargodha military base.

Finally, analysts should also not ignore the possibility that Indian or Pakistani intelligence agencies could intercept messages revealing the "secret" locations of otherwise survivable military forces, an absolutely critical issue with small or opaque nuclear arsenals. The history of the 1971 war, for example, demonstrates that both states' intelligence agencies were able to intercept critical classified messages sent by and to the other side. . . .

Perhaps most dramatically, on December 12, 1971, the Indians intercepted a radio message scheduling a meeting of high-level Pakistani officials at Government House in Dacca, which led to an air attack on the building in the middle of the meeting. . . .

## NORMAL ACCIDENTS AND UNAUTHORIZED USE IN NUCLEAR SOUTH ASIA

Will the Indian and Pakistani nuclear arsenals be more safe and secure than were the U.S. and Soviet arsenals during the cold war? It is clear that the emerging South Asian nuclear deterrence system is both smaller and less complex today than was the case in the United States or Soviet Union at the height of the cold war. It is also clear, however, that the South Asian nuclear relationship is inherently more tightly coupled because of geographical proximity. With inadequate warning systems in place and with weapons with short flight times emerging in the region, the time-lines for decision making are highly compressed and the danger that one accident could lead to another and then lead to a catastrophic accidental war is high and growing. The proximity of New Delhi and Islamabad to their potential adversary's border poses particular concerns about rapid "decapitation" attacks on national capitals. Moreover, there are legitimate concerns about social stability and support for terrorists inside Pakistan, problems that could compromise nuclear weapons safety and security.

Proliferation optimists will cite the small sizes of India and Pakistan's nuclear arsenals as a reason to be less worried about these problems. Yet the key from a normal accidents perspective is not the numbers, but rather the structure of the arsenal. Here there is both good and bad news. The good news is that under normal peacetime conditions, neither the Indians, nor the Pakistanis regularly deploy nuclear forces mated with delivery systems in the field. The bad news, however, is two-fold. First, Pakistani nuclear weapons do not have PALs (Permissive Action Links, the advanced electronic locks on U.S. nuclear weapons that require a special code for the weapons' activation) on them. Second, Pakistan has started to alert its nuclear weapons in crises; it did so in 1999 during the Kargil crisis and then again in September and December of 2001, in response to fears of Indian (and maybe U.S.) military action after the terrorist attacks in New York, Washington, and New Delhi.

From an organizational perspective, it is not surprising to find evidence of serious accidents emerging in the Indian nuclear and missile programs. . . . The false warning incident that occurred just prior to the Pakistani nuclear tests in May 1998 . . . demonstrat[es] the dangers of accidental war in South Asia. During the crucial days just prior to Prime Minister Sharif's decision to order the tests of Pakistani nuclear weapons, senior military intelligence officers informed him that the Indian and Israeli air forces were about to launch a preventive strike on the test site. The incident is shrouded in mystery, and the cause of this warning message is not clear. Although it is certainly possible that Pakistani intelligence officers simply misidentified aircraft in the region, a more likely explanation is that Inter-Service Intelligence (ISI) officials did not believe there was any threat of an imminent Indian-Israeli attack in 1998, but deliberately concocted (or exaggerated) the warning of a preventive strike to force the prime minister, who was wavering under U.S. pressure, to test the weapons immediately. It is not clear which of these is the more worrisome interpretation of the incident: false warnings could be catastrophic in a crisis whether they are deliberate provocations by rogue intelligence officers, or genuinely believed, but inaccurate, reports of imminent or actual attack.

It is important to note that the possibility of a false warning producing an accidental nuclear war in South Asia is reduced, but is by no means eliminated, by India's adoption of a nuclear no-first-use policy. Not only might the Pakistani government, following its stated first-use doctrine, respond to intelligence (in this case false) that India was about to attack successfully a large portion of Pakistani nuclear forces, but either government could misidentify an accidental nuclear detonation occurring during transport and alert activities at one of their own military bases as the start of a counterforce attack by the other state. Pakistani officials should be particularly sensitive to this possibility because of the 1988 Ojheri incident, in which a massive conventional munitions explosion at a secret ammunition dump near Rawalpindi caused fears among some decision makers that an Indian attack had begun. The possibility of this kind of accident producing a false warning of an attack cannot, however, be ruled out in India, either, as long as the government plans to alert forces or mate nuclear weapons to delivery vehicles during crises.

In addition, there should be serious concern about whether both countries can maintain centralized control over their nuclear weapons. Although government policy in this regard is, for obvious reasons, kept classified, it is known that Pakistan has no personnel reliability program (PRP) for the officers who control the arsenal or the guards who protect the weapons storage sites. In the United States, the program is a set of psychological tests and organizational checks; each year, between 2.5 percent and 5.0 percent of previously PRP certified individuals have been decertified, that is, deemed unsuitable for nuclear weapons related duties. Presumably, similarly low, but still significant, percentages of officers, soldiers, and civilians in other countries would be of questionable reliability as guardians of the arsenal. This personnel reliability problem is serious in India, where civilian custodians maintain custody of the nuclear weapons; it is particularly worrisome in Pakistan, where the weapons are controlled by a professional military organization facing the difficult challenge of maintaining discipline while dealing with a failing economy, serious social problems, and growing religious fundamentalism. This situation increases the risk of accidents and of unauthorized use, such as theft or use by terrorists groups.

Finally, there is evidence that neither the Indian nor the Pakistani military has focused sufficiently on the danger that a missile test launch during a crisis could be misperceived as the start of a nuclear attack. There was an agreement, as part of the Lahore accords in January 1999, to provide advance notification of missile tests, but even such an agreement is not a fool-proof solution, as the Russians discovered in January 1995 when a bureaucratic snafu in Moscow led to a failure to pass on advance notification of a Norwegian weather rocket launch, that resulted in serious false warning of a missile attack. Moreover, both the Pakistanis and the Indians appear to be planning to use their missile test facilities for actual nuclear weapons launches in war. In India, Wheeler Island is reportedly being used like Vandenberg air force base, a test site in peacetime and crises, and a launch site in war. During Kargil, according to the Indian Army chief of staff, nuclear alert activities were also detected at "some of Pakistan's launch areas—some of the areas where they carried out tests earlier of one of their missiles."[5]

Nuclear South Asia will be a dangerous place, not because of ill will or irrationality among government leaders, nor because of any unique cultural inhibitions against strategic thinking in both countries. India and Pakistan face a dangerous nuclear future because they have become like other nuclear powers. Their leaders seek security through nuclear deterrence, but imperfect humans inside imperfect organizations control their nuclear weapons. If my theories are right, these organizations will someday fail to produce secure nuclear deterrence. Unfortunately the evidence from these first years of South Asia's nuclear history suggests that the pessimistic predictions of organization theory are likely to come true, even though I cannot predict the precise pathway by which deterrence will break down.

The organizational perspective suggests that there are more similarities than differences between nuclear powers in the way they manage, or at least try to manage, nuclear weapons operations. There is, however, one important structural difference between the new nuclear powers and their cold war predecessors Just as each new child is born into a different family, each new nuclear power is born into a different nuclear system in which nuclear states influence each other's behavior. Some observers believe that the possibility that other nuclear powers—such as the United States or China—can intervene in future crises in South Asia may be a major constraint on undesired escalation. I fear the opposite: the possibility of intervention may encourage the governments of India and Pakistan to engage in risky behavior, initiating crises or making limited uses of force, precisely because they anticipate (correctly or incorrectly) that other nuclear powers may bail them out diplomatically if the going gets rough.

The possibility that other nuclear states might be able to influence nuclear behavior in South Asia does, however, lead to one final optimistic note. There are many potential unilateral steps and bilateral agreements that could be instituted to reduce the risk of nuclear war between India and Pakistan, and the U.S. government can play a useful role in helping to facilitate such agreements. Many, though not all, of the problems identified in this article can be reduced if nuclear weapons in both countries are maintained in a de-alerted state, with warheads removed from delivery vehicles. U.S. assistance could be helpful in providing the arms verification technology that could permit such de-alerting (or non-alerting in this case) to take place within a cooperative framework. The United States could also be helpful in providing intelligence and warning information, on a case-by-case basis, in peacetime or in crises to reduce the danger of false alarms. Finally, increased security of storage sites and safer management of nuclear weapons operations can be encouraged by sharing better security devices for storage sites and discussing organizational "best practices."

There will be no progress on any of these issues, however, unless Indians, Pakistanis, and Americans stop denying that serious problems exist. A basic awareness of nuclear command and control problems exists in New Delhi and Islamabad, but unfortunately Indian and Pakistani leaders too often trivialize them. The United States, in turn, refused to assist the Indians and Pakistanis in developing improved safety and security for their nuclear weapons until after the terrorist attacks on September 11, 2001. Washington officials argued before the September 11 attacks that any assistance in this area would 'reward' Islamabad and New Delhi for testing, and signal to other potential nuclear weapons states that the United States was not serious about its nonproliferation goals. The September 11 attacks led the U.S. government to switch its position, and Pakistani officials accepted, at least in principle, that some assistance with their nuclear weapons security could be useful. It is crucial that such efforts to improve Pakistani nuclear security measures be fully implemented and eventually be extended to India.

Nuclear weapons will remain in Pakistan and India for the foreseeable future, and the conflict over Kashmir will continue to smolder, threatening to erupt into a wider and more dangerous war. The deep political problems between the two South Asian nuclear states may someday be resolved, and the U.S. government should encourage progress toward that end. In the meantime, the U.S. government should do whatever it can to reduce the risk that India and Pakistan will use nuclear weapons against each other.

## NOTES

1. Devin T. Hagerty, *The Consequences of Nuclear Proliferation* (Cambridge, Mass., MIT Press, 1998), p. 92, 106.
2. Hagerty, *The Consequences of Nuclear Proliferation*, p. 184.
3. Ihtashamul Haque, "Peace Linked to Kashmir Solution," *Dawn Wire Service*, June 26, 1999.
4. "Army Ready for War, Says Chief," *The Statesman* (India), January 12, 2002.
5. Raj Chenagappa, "Pakistan Tried Nuclear Blackmail," *The Newspaper Today*, - January 12, 2000. www.thenewspapertoday.com/interview/index.phtml? INTER-VIEWINT_PADCOUNT.

# Nuclear Stability in South Asia

## KENNETH N. WALTZ

The American government and most American journalists look on the blossoming of nuclear forces in South Asia as an ominous event, different in implication and effect from all the similar events that we worried about throughout the cold war. A 1998 New York Times headline, for example, proclaimed that "India's Arms Race Isn't Safe Like the Cold War." Few thought the American-Soviet arms race safe at the time, and for good reasons few Indians and Pakistanis expect an arms race now. Most of the alarmist predictions about the fate of the subcontinent display forgetfulness about the past and confusion over the effects of nuclear weapons. In the same New York Times article, Joseph Cirincione, director of the Non-Proliferation Project at the Carnegie Endowment, reports that Pentagon war games between Pakistan and India always end with a nuclear exchange. Has everyone in that building forgotten that deterrence works precisely because nuclear states fear that conventional military engagements may escalate to the nuclear level, and therefore they draw back from the brink? Admiral David E. Jeremiah, once vice-chairman of the Joint Chiefs of Staff, laments the cultural mindset that leads Americans to believe that "everybody thinks like us," and a longtime president of the Henry L. Stimson Center, Michael Krepon, worries that because of the Pressler Amendment, which cut off aid to nations developing nuclear weapons, Pakistani officers have not had the benefit of attending our military schools. One's reaction to both statements may well be "thank goodness."

The Brookings Institution totaled up the cost of American nuclear weapons over the decades and arrived at the figure of 5.5 trillion dollars. Strobe Talbott, when he was deputy secretary of state, implied that military competition between Pakistan and India will cause them to spend on a proportionate scale. When asked why we should not provide India and Pakistan with advice about, and equipment for safe deterrence, he retorted that "if they locked themselves into the mentality of MAD (Mutual Assured Destruction), they will then be tempted into—like us— a considerable escalation of the arms race."[1] Yet nuclear states need race only to the second-strike level, which is easy to achieve and maintain. Indian and Pakistani leaders have learned from our folly. A minimal deterrent deters as well as a maximal one. Homi Jehangar Bhabha, father of the Indian bomb, called this "absolute deterrence." K. Subrahmanyam, a foremost strategist, emphasizes that Indians have learned that to build large forces is wasteful and foolish. An arsenal of about sixty weapons, he believes, will deter either Pakistan or China; and Pakistan might need, say, twenty to deter India. Some have claimed that no nuclear country has been satisfied with having only a minimum deterrent. Yet China, with even today only about twenty ICBMs, has been content with small numbers; and India and Pakistan would follow its example were it not for the disruptive effects of American missile defenses on the strategic arms balance in Asia. Political as well as economic constraints on both countries ensure this. Talbott has discerned a global trend away from reliance on nuclear weapons."[2] The United States does rely less on nuclear weapons now because it is the world's dominant conventional power, spending as much on its armed forces in the year 2000 as the next eight big spenders combined. Partly for that reason, some other countries rely more on their nuclear weapons— Russia, for example, with its conventional forces in shambles. Countries that once counted on one of the two great powers for military assistance are now concerned to provide security for themselves: Pakistan, India, Iraq, Japan, and North Korea are all examples.

India tested its "peaceful bomb" in 1974. Its next tests came twenty-four years later. The United States complained loudly both times. Yet the United States tested nuclear weapons many times yearly for many years on end—more than a thousand above and below ground, which is more than the tests of all other countries combined. America's excuse was, at first, that it anticipated a mortal threat from the Soviet Union and, later, that it actually faced such a threat. America's nonproliferation policy denies that such reasoning can legitimate other countries' entering the tight circle of nuclear powers. Nevertheless, the reasoning the United States applied to itself applies to India and to Pakistan as well. Does anyone believe that testing nuclear warheads is something that, in their place, we would not have done?

The question raised by India's and Pakistan's nuclear tests is not whether they should have been conducted, but whether their security requires their becoming nuclear powers. Some countries need nuclear weapons; some do not. Brazil and Argentina set themselves on course to become nuclear states. Both decided to abandon the effort. Neither posed a threat to the other. South Africa became a nuclear state and then, finding no commensurate threat, reversed its policy.

Pakistan obviously needs nuclear weapons. When asked why nuclear weapons are so popular in Pakistan, former prime minister Benazir Bhutto answered, "It's our history. A history of three wars with a larger neighbor. India is five times larger than we are. Their military strength is five times larger. In 1971, our country was disintegrated. So the security issue for Pakistan is an issue of survival." From the other side, Shankar Bajpai, former Indian ambassador to Pakistan, China, and the United States, has said that "Pakistan's quest for a nuclear capability steams from its fear of its larger neighbor, removing that fear should open up immense possibilities"— possibilities for a less worried and more relaxed life. Shamshad Ahmad, Pakistan's foreign secretary, has echoed their thoughts: "In South Asia nuclear deterrence may . . . usher in an era of durable peace between Pakistan and India providing the requisite incentives for resolving all outstanding issues, especially Jammu and Kashmir."[3] In recent years, some Indians and Pakistanis have begun to talk about a peaceful accommodation, and according to a *New York Times* reporter, "just about everybody" in Kashmir "cites the two countries' possession of nuclear weapons as a factor pushing towards peace."[4]

In the 1980s, after the Soviet occupation of Afghanistan, the United States, knowing of Pakistan's nuclear progress, nevertheless continued to supply Pakistan with sophisticated conventional weapons. The United States did not care much about Pakistan's nuclear progress as long as Soviet worries dominated American policy. Once the Soviet Union went into steep decline and then disappeared, America dropped Pakistan, with a speed that surprised not only Pakistan but India as well. For Pakistan to compete conventionally with India was economically impossible. Nuclear weapons linked to a sensible strategy are a low cost way of leveling the playing field. Understandably Pakistan felt itself pressed to follow the nuclear course.

Can India be seen in a similar light? With its superior conventional forces, it needed no nuclear weapons to protect itself against a Pakistan that lacked them, but what about China? Americans think of India as the dominant power in South Asia. India feels differently. India is part of a hostile world. With a Muslim minority of about 150 million, it adjoins Muslim Pakistan, and beyond lies a Muslim world becoming more fundamentalist and more hostile. To the north is an increasingly nationalist, steadily more powerful, and potentially unstable China. The United States has reinforced India's worries about a Chinese-Pakistani-American axis, notably when America "tilted" toward Pakistan in the 1971 war with India. In the middle of the war, Henry Kissinger told Mao Zedong, "We want to keep the pressure on India both militarily and politically," adding that if China "took measures to protect its security, the US would oppose efforts of others to interfere."[5] In a show of support for Pakistan, the American navy moved the aircraft carrier *Enterprise* into the Indian Ocean. To this day, Indians consider this an attempt to hold them in nuclear awe. They call it blackmail. India continues to believe that America favors China over India. A professor at Jawaharlal Nehru University found nuclear cooperation between Beijing and Islamabad "unprecedented in the history of international relations."[6] And an Indian minister of defense wondered, as many Indians do, "why India and Pakistan should be seen as blowing each other up when nuclear weapons in the hands of the United States and China are seen as stabilizing factors."[7] That the United States seems to trust China as an old nuclear power, and not India as a new one, is a cause of bitter resentment.

The decision to make nuclear weapons was a momentous one for India. The tests of May 1998 were overwhelmingly popular with the public at large, but the decision emerged over decades, with much opposition along the way. Even today, Indians who view nuclear deterrence as a difficult and demanding task believe that India will be unable to develop and deploy a nuclear force sufficient for the deterrence of China. In their view, the main effect of India's developing nuclear capabilities was to cause Pakistan to develop its own. India is therefore worse off with nuclear weapons than it would have been without them. The Indian view that carried the day rests on the contrary argument: namely, that it does not take much to deter.

Is it farfetched for India to worry about a Chinese threat to its security? Any country has trouble seeing the world as others do. Let's try. If the United States shared a two-thousand-mile border with a country that was more populous, more prosperous, more heavily armed, and in possession of nuclear weapons, we would react militarily and, judging from our response to the Soviet Union, more vigorously than India has done. What *is* farfetched is for the United States to worry about a Chinese threat to its security and then wonder why India does too.

Kanti Bajpai, a professor at Nehru University, strongly opposes India's nuclear armament. He doubts that India's nuclear deterrent would dissuade China from seizing Arunachal Pradesh in the northeast or Pakistan from seizing Kashmir in the northwest. This is comparable to the worry, dreamt up in the 1960s, about a "Hamburg grab." Some American military commentators worried that the Soviet Union might suddenly seize Hamburg, which jutted into East Germany, and then in effect: ask, "Is NATO's fighting to regain Hamburg worth risking a nuclear conflagration?" Similarly, Kanti Bajpai imagines "a quick grabbing thrust into the two states, backed by nuclear weapons, in the hope of presenting India with a fait accompli."[8] Such worries are as fanciful as American worries were in the cold war. The invader would have to assemble troops near the border. India would then alert its forces, including nuclear ones. With the potential crisis easily foreseeable, why would China or Pakistan run such risks?

One answer to the question is that Pakistan did move troops across the line of control into Kashmir and fight for a time at a fairly high level in the engagement known as Kargil. Joseph Cirincione voices widespread fears when, with the Kashmir conflict in mind, he says, "Just assemble all the risk factors and multiply it out. . . . This is the most dangerous and unstable military situation in the world."[9] His pronouncement repeats the tired old error of inferring from the conventional past what the nuclear future holds, a mistake made almost every time another country gets nuclear weapons. With nuclear weapons added, conventionally dangerous and unstable situations become safer and stabler ones. Nuclear weapons produce what Joseph Nye calls the "crystal ball" effect. Everyone knows that if force gets out of hand all the parties to a conflict face catastrophe. With conventional weapons, the crystal ball is clouded. With nuclear weapons, it is perfectly clear.

What reasons do we have to believe that India's and Pakistan's crystal balls are clouded? Well, again, Kargil. Some observers worry that Pakistan may believe that it can safely raise the level of conventional violence since nuclear weapons limit the extent of India's response. But, of course, they also limit the size and scope of Pakistan's attack, since Pakistan knows it could face nuclear retaliation. And the same reasoning applies to India. It's the same old story: In the presence of nuclear weapons, a country can achieve a significant victory only by risking devastating retaliation.

Sagan calls Kargil the fourth Indian-Pakistani war because it fits the social science definition holding that a military encounter is a war if it produces more than one thousand battle-related deaths. If Kargil is called a war, then the definition of war requires revision; and now that both countries have nuclear weapons the fifth "war" will be no worse than the so-called fourth one. The late Pakistani chief of the army staff, General Mirza Aslam Beg, remarked that India and Pakistan can no longer fight even a conventional war over Kashmir, and his counterpart, the chief of the Indian army staff, General Krishnaswami Sundarji concurred. Kargil showed once again that deterrence does not firmly protect disputed areas but does limit the extent of the violence. Indian rear admiral Raja Menon put the larger point simply: "The Kargil crisis demonstrated that the subcontinental nuclear threshold probably lies territorially in the heartland of both countries, and not on the Kashmir cease-fire line."[10]

The obvious conclusion to draw from Kargil is that the presence of nuclear weapons prevented escalation from major skirmish to full-scale war. This contrasts starkly with the bloody 1965 war, in which both parties were armed only with conventional weapons.

Another question is whether India and Pakistan can firmly control and safely deploy nuclear forces sufficient to deter. Because I said enough about the ease of deterrence in chapter 8, I shall concentrate on questions of safety and control. Sagan claims that "the emerging history of nuclear India and nuclear Pakistan strongly supports the pessimistic predictions of organizational theorists." Yet the evidence, accumulated over five decades, shows that nuclear states fight with nuclear states only at low levels, that accidents seldom occur, and that when they do they never have bad effects. If nuclear pessimists were right, nuclear deterrence would have failed again and again. Nuclear pessimists deal with the potential causes of catastrophe; optimists, with the effects the causes do *not* produce. Since the evidence fails to support the predictions of pessimists, one wonders why the spread of nuclear weapons to South Asia should have bad rather than good effects. What differences in the situation of India and Pakistan may cause their fates to depart from the nuclear norm? If they and their situations are different, then the happy history of the nuclear past does not forecast their futures. American commentators dwell on the differences between the United States and the Soviet Union earlier and India and Pakistan today. Among the seeming differences, these are given prominence: differences in the states involved, differences in their histories of conflict, and differences in the distance between the competing parties. I consider them in turn.

## DOES DETERRENCE DEPEND ON WHO IS DETERRING WHOM?

For decades we believed that we were trying to deter two monstrous countries—one an "evil empire" and the other a totalitarian country ruled by a megalomaniac. Now we learn that deterrence worked in the past because the United States, the Soviet Union, and China were settled and sensible societies. Karl Kaiser, of the Research Institute of the German Society for Foreign Affairs, and Arthur G. Rubinoff of the University of Toronto, for example, argue that the success of deterrence depends on its context, that is, on who the countries are and on how they relate to each other. In Kaiser's view, "the stability of nuclear deterrence between East and West rest[ed] on a multitude of military and political factors which in other regions are either totally missing or are only partially present." In Rubinoff's view, it is foolish to compare the American-Soviet conflict with South Asia, where the dynamics are "reminiscent of the outbreak of the First World War." Reminiscence flickers, however, since no one then had nuclear weapons. With a Hindu chauvinist in power in New Delhi and an Islamic party governing India, Rubinoff finds "no resemblance to the deterrent situation that characterized the U.S.-Soviet conflict."[11] That statement may once have applied to India and Pakistan, but only until they armed themselves with nuclear weapons. The history of the cold war shows that what matters is not the character of the countries that have nuclear weapons but the fact that they have them. Differences among nuclear countries abound, but for keeping the peace what difference have they made?

Whatever the identity of rulers, and whatever the characteristics of their states, the national behaviors they produce are strongly conditioned by the world outside. With conventional weapons, a defensive country has to ask itself how much power it must harness to its policy in order to dissuade an aggressive state from striking. Countries willing to run high risks are hard to dissuade. The characteristics of governments and the temperaments of leaders have to be carefully weighed. With nuclear weapons, any state will be deterred by another state's second-strike forces, one need not be preoccupied with the qualities of the state that is to be deterred or scrutinize its leaders. In a nuclear world, any state—whether ruled by a Stalin, a Mao Zedong, a Saddam Hussein, or a Kim Jong Il—will be deterred by the knowledge that aggressive actions may lead to its own destruction.

## DOES DETERRENCE DEPEND ON THE DETERRERS' RECENT HISTORY?

India and Pakistan have fought three wars in little more than fifty years and Kashmir is a bone in the throat of Pakistan. In contrast, America and Russia have never fought a war against each other. Yet some other nuclear countries look more like India and Pakistan, and nuclear weapons have kept the peace between them. Russia and China have suffered numerous military invasions by one another over the centuries. In the 1960s, when both had nuclear weapons, skirmishes broke out from time to time along the Siberian frontier, and the fighting was on a fairly large scale. The bitterness of the antagonists rivalled that between India and Pakistan fueled by ethnic resentments and ideological differences.

Clashes between nuclear countries over peripheral areas are hardly the exception. Of today's eight nuclear countries, five have fought their neighbors in the past half century: Russia, China, Israel, Pakistan, and India. Those who believe that the South Asian situation is without parallel often ignore the Middle East. The parallel is not exact, but it is instructive. The Middle East is unrivalled for long-standing conflict, irreconcilable disputes, feelings of distrust and hatred, and recurrent wars. In 1973, two nonnuclear Arab countries, Egypt and Syria, attacked Israel and fought what by anyone's definition was a war. Limited in extent by one side's nuclear weapons, it nonetheless did not spiral out of control.

## DOES DETERRENCE DEPEND ON DISTANCE?

Proximity is a constantly emphasized difference between the relations of India and Pakistan and that of the United States and the Soviet Union. America and Russia are separated by vast distances; Pakistan and India live cheek by jowl. They continually rub against each other in irritating and dangerous ways. George Perkovich had this in mind when he expressed his fear that "Somebody blows up something big and India says, 'That's it, and takes out targets. Then you're on your way. Who's going to back down?'"[12] Much the same fears in much the same words were expressed during the cold war. The two antagonists might "go to the brink"; one would slip over the edge, and once the exchange of warheads began neither side would be willing to stop it by giving in to the other. In actuality, however, backing down in times of crisis proved not to be such a big problem. Never do two countries share a common interest more completely than when they are locked in death's embrace. Each may want something else as well, but both want most of all to get out of the dire situation they are in. During the Kargil fighting, India went to "Readiness State 3," which means that warheads were prepared for placement on delivery vehicles, and Pakistan apparently took similar steps. These were seen as rash and dangerous moves, but what does one expect? The United States and the Soviet Union alerted their forces a number of times. Doing so is a way of saying, "This is getting serious, and we both had better calm down." Despite the pessimism engendered by the history of South Asia, Indian-Pakistani wars have been, as wars go, quite restrained. As Admiral Menon has written, "Any analysis of the three wars fought often refers to the rather gentlemanly manner in which they were fought with care taken to avoid civilian casualties."[13] Pakistan's 1999 thrust into Kashmir may have been rash, yet as Menon has rightly said, "Subsequent Pakistani attempts to signal an unwillingness to escalate were mature and sober."[14] And in the Kargil campaign, India never sent its troops across the line of control.

History tells us only what we want to know. A pair of *New York Times* journalists contrasts then with now by claiming that, except in Cuba, "the Americans and Soviets took care not to place their troops in direct military confrontation."[15] What, then, were NATO and Warsaw Treaty Organization troops doing in the middle of Europe, where confrontation was a constant and serious business?

Proximity does make warning time short. Missiles can fly between Islamabad and New Delhi in less than five minutes. Yet nuclear countries in the past have often been close militarily if not geographically. Cuba is only ninety miles from American shores, and that is proximity enough. The United States flew planes at the Soviet Union's borders and across them, believing its radars would not spot them. American bravado continues. In April 2001, an American surveillance plane was struck by a Chinese plane over waters near China. Close surveillance is provocative even if international legalities are nicely observed. As President Dwight D. Eisenhower said when an American plane went down thirty-two miles from the Chinese coast in August 1956, "If planes were flying 20 to 50 miles from our shores, we would be very likely to shoot them down if they came in closer, whether through error or not."[16]

Operation Brasstacks was an all-service Indian operation staged in 1987. As Sagan says, it is widely believed that General Sundarji intended it to be a prelude to a war in which India would destroy Pakistan's nuclear facilities. Sundarji may have thought that even if Pakistan had a few bombs, India would be able to destroy them on the ground. In retrospect, Brasstacks looks more like a typical instance of Indian failure to coordinate policies among the Prime Minister's Office, the External Affairs Ministry, the Defense Ministry, and the military services.

Brasstacks is not something new in the nuclear annals. It pales in comparison to provocative acts by the United States and the Soviet Union. In 1983, for example, Able Archer—a recurrent NATO military exercise—was more extensive than ever before. It was held at a time of extraordinary tension. The Soviets believed that surprise was the key to American war plans. During the exercise, the simulated alert of NATO nuclear forces was thought by the Soviets to be a real one. American Pershing II missiles were to be deployed in Europe soon. The Soviets believed that some of them, with their fifty-kiloton payload, fifty-meter accuracy, and ten-minute delivery time to Moscow, had already arrived. Early in the Reagan administration, Defense Secretary Caspar Weinberger and other officials proclaimed that it was our aim to be able to fight, sustain, and win a nuclear war. With some reason, Soviet leaders believed it was about to begin.

Vast distances lie between the United States and Russia. What difference do these distances make when American troops and missiles are stationed in Europe and Northeast Asia? Those who believe that the Indian-Pakistani confrontation is without precedent have either little knowledge of cold war history or oddly defective memories.

Proximity shortens the time between launch and landing. With little warning time, quick decisions would seem to be required. Acting on early warnings of incoming missiles that may turn out to be false could be fatal to both sides. The notion that deterrence demands the threat of swift retaliation was ingrained in American and Russian thinking, and it remains so today, with both forces still on hair-trigger alert. Yet deterrence of a would-be attacker does not depend on the belief that retaliation will be prompt, but only on the belief that the attacked may in due course retaliate. As K. Subrahmanyam has put it, "The strike back need not be highly time-critical."[17] A small force may be a vulnerable force, but smaller is worse than bigger only if the attacker believes he can destroy *all* of the force before *any* of it can be launched.

Students of organizations rightly worry about complex and tightly-coupled systems because they are susceptible to damaging accidents. They wrongly believe that conflicting nuclear states should be thought of as a tightly-coupled system. Fortunately, nuclear weapons loosen the coupling of states by lessening the effects of proximity and by cutting through the complexities of conventional confrontations. Organizational theorists fail to distinguish between the technical complexities of nuclear-weapons systems and the simplicity of the situations they create.

Sagan points out that the survival of Indian and Pakistani forces cannot be guaranteed. But neither can their complete destruction, and that is what matters. Oddly, many pessimists believe that countries with small and technologically limited nuclear forces may be able to accomplish the difficult feat of making a successful first strike but not the easy one of making their own nuclear force appear to be invulnerable. They overlook a basic nuclear truth: If some part of a force is invulnerable, all of the force is invulnerable. Destroying even a major portion of a nuclear force does no good because of the damage a small number of surviving warheads can do. Conventional weapons put a premium on striking first to gain the initial advantage and set the course of the war. Nuclear weapons eliminate this premium. The initial advantage is insignificant if the cost of gaining it is half a dozen cities.

More important than the size of arsenals, the sophistication of command and control, the proximity of competitors, and the history of the relations, are the sensibilities of leaders. Fortunately, nuclear weapons make leaders behave sensibly even though under other circumstances they might be brash and reckless.

The South Asian situation, said so often to be without precedent, finds precedents galore. Rather than assuming that the present differs significantly from the past, we should emphasize the similarities and learn from them. Fortunately, India and Pakistan have learned from their nuclear predecessors. . . .

Sagan believes that future Indian-Pakistani crises may be nuclear. Once countries have nuclear weapons any confrontation that merits the term "crisis" is a nuclear one. With conventional weapons, crises tend toward instability. Because of the perceived, or misperceived, advantage of striking first, war may be the outcome. Nuclear weapons make crises stable, which is an important reason for believing that India and Pakistan are better off with than without them.

Yet because nuclear weapons limit escalation, they may tempt countries to fight small wars. Glenn Snyder long ago identified the strategic stability/tactical instability paradox. Benefits carry costs in the nuclear business just as they do in other endeavors. The possibility of fighting at low levels is not a bad price to pay for the impossibility of fighting at high levels. This impossibility becomes obvious, since in the presence of nuclear weapons no one can score major gains, and all can lose catastrophically.

Sagan carries Snyder's logic a step farther by arguing that Pakistan and India may nevertheless fight to a higher level of violence, believing that if one side or the other begins to lose control, a third party will step in to prevent the use of nuclear weapons. The idea is a hangover from cold war days when the United States and the Soviet Union thought they had compelling reasons to intervene in other countries' conflicts. The end of the cold war reduced the incentives for such intervention. As K. Subrahmanyam has said, "In a world dominated by the Cold War, there was a certain predictability that any Chinese nuclear threat to India would be countervailed by one or the other super power or both. In the aftermath of the Cold War that predictability has disappeared."[18] Intervention by a third party during low-level fighting would still be possible, but neither side could count on it.

Kanti Bajpai spotted another consequence of nuclear weapons that may be harmful: They may drive the antagonists apart by removing the need to agree. Since deterrence works, Bajpai wonders why countries would try to settle their differences. India and Pakistan, however, did not reach agreement on Kashmir or on other issues when neither had nuclear weapons; now both sides have at least an incentive to discuss their problems.

Crises on the subcontinent recur, and when they do, voices of despair predict a conventional clash ending in nuclear blasts. On December 13, 2001, five gunmen attacked the Indian Parliament. Fourteen people died, including the gunmen. India, blaming Pakistani terrorists, mounted its largest mobilization in the past thirty years and massed troops and equipment along the India-Pakistan border. As in the crisis of 1990, the United States deployed its diplomats, this time dispatching Secretary of State Colin Powell to calm the contestants. Tempers on both sides flared, bombast filled the air, and an American commentator pointed out once again that all of the American military's war games show that a conventional Indian-Pakistani war will end in a nuclear conflagration. Both India and Pakistan claimed that they could fight conventionally in the face of nuclear weapons. What reason do we have to believe that military and civilian leaders on either side fail to understand the dangers of fighting a conventional war against a nuclear neighbor? The statements of Pakistan's leader, General Musharraf, were mainly conciliatory. Indian military leaders emphasized that any military engagements would have to be limited to such targets as guerrilla training camps and military facilities used by extremists. As an astute analyst put it, "India's way of looking at this is that we're not threatening Pakistan's core interests, so they would have no incentive to launch their weapons."[19] Indian leaders made it clear that they intended to pressure Pakistan to control military intrusions by irregular forces. Pakistan made it clear that its pressure for a Kashmiri settlement would be unremitting. Except to alarmist observers, mainly American, neither side looked as though it would cross or even approach the nuclear threshold. The proposition that nuclear weapons limit the extent of fighting and ultimately preserve peace again found vindication.

Are India and Pakistan worse or better off now that they have nuclear weapons? Are their futures dimmer or brighter? I will surprise no one by saying "brighter." I have looked in vain for important differences between the plight of India and Pakistan and that of other nuclear countries. Nuclear weapons put all countries that possess them in the same boat. South Asia is said to be the "acid test" for deterrence optimists. So far, nuclear deterrence has passed all of the many tests it has faced.

## NOTES

1. Quoted in Steven Erlanger, "India's Arms Race Isn't Safe Like the Cold War," *New York Times,* July 12, 1998, section 4, p. 18.
2. Strobe Talbott, "Dealing with the Bomb in South Asia," *Foreign Affairs* 78, No. 2 (March/April 1999), p. 117.
3. Claudia Dreifus, "Benazir Bhutto," *New York Times Magazine,* May 15, 1994, p. 39; K. Shankar Bajpai, "Nuclear Exchange," *Far Eastern Economic Review,* June 24, 1993, p. 24; Shamshad Ahmad, "The Nuclear Subcontinent: Bringing Stability to South Asia," *Foreign Affairs* 78, No. 4 (July/August 1999), p. 125.
4. John F. Burns, "War-Weary Kashmiris Contemplate the Price of Peace," *New York Times,* July 11, 2001, p. A3.
5. Quoted in Jonathan Spence, "Kissinger and the Emperor," *New York Review of Books,* March 4, 1999, p. 21.
6. Amitabh Maltoo, "India's Nuclear Policy in an Anarchic World," in Mattoo, ed., *India's Nuclear Deterrent: Pokhran II and Beyond* (New Delhi: Har-Anand, 1999), p. 22.
7. George Fernandes, quoted in John F. Burns, "Indian Defense Chief Calls U.S. Hypocritical," *New York Times,* June 18, 1998, p. A6.
8. Kanti Bajpai, "The Fallacy of an Indian Deterrent," in Amitabh Mattoo, ed., *India's Nuclear Deterrent,* p. 183. China does not recognize Arunachal Pradesh or Sikkim as parts of India.
9. Quoted in Erlanger, "India's Arms Race Isn't Safe Like the Cold War."
10. Raja Menon, *A Nuclear Strategy for India* (New Delhi: Sage, 2000), p. 116.
11. Karl Kaiser, "Nonproliferation and Nuclear Deterrence, *Survival* 31, No. 2 (March/April, 1989), p. 125; Arthur G. Rubinoff, "The Failure of Nuclear Deterrence in South Asia," *Toronto Globe and Mail,* June 1, 1998, p. A17.
12. Quoted in Celia W. Dugger and Barry Bearak, "You've Got the Bomb. So Do I. Now I Dare You to Fight," *New York Times,* January 16, 2000. sec. 4, p. 1.

13. Menon, *A Nuclear Strategy for India*, p. 293.

14. *Ibid.*, p. 197.

15. Celia W. Dugger and Barry Bearak, "You've Got the Bomb. So Do I. Now I Dare You to Fight," *New York Times*, January 16, 2000, section 4, p. 1.

16. James Bamford, "The Dangers of Spy Planes," *New York Times*, April 5, 2001, p. A21.

17. K. Subrahmanyan, "Nuclear Force Design and Minimum Deterrence Strategy," in Bharat Kamad, ed., *Future Imperiled: India's Security in the 1990s and Beyond* (New Delhi: Viking, 1994).

18. *Ibid.*, p. 186.

19. The analyst is Commodore Uday Bhaskar, deputy directory of the Institute for Defense Studies and Analysis, quoted in Rajiv Chandrasekaran "For India, Deterrence May Not Prevent War," *Washington Post Foreign Service*, January 17, 2002, p. A1.

# PART 3

# The International Political Economy

In Part One, we examined the meaning of anarchy and saw the consequences for state behavior that flowed from it. In Part Two, we analyzed in more detail one of the primary instruments that states can and must use, namely, military power. In Part Three, we are concerned with the other primary instrument of state action, economic power.

Disparities in power, as we saw earlier, have important effects on state behavior. Such disparities occur not simply because of the differences in the military power that states wield but also because of the differences in economic resources that they generate. In the first instance, the force that a nation can wield is dependent in part on the economic wealth that it can muster to support and sustain its military forces. Wealth is therefore a component of state power. But the generation of wealth, unlike the generation of military power, is also an end of state action. Except in the rarest of circumstances, military power is never sought as an end in itself, but rather is acquired as a means to attain security or the other ends that a state pursues. By contrast, wealth is both a component of state power and a good that can be consumed by its citizenry. Force is mustered primarily for the external arena. Wealth is sought for both the external and the domestic arena. Moreover, wealth and power differ in the degree to which states can pursue each without detriment to the positions and interests of other nations. No situation in international politics is ever totally cooperative or conflictual, but the potential for cooperative behavior is greater in the realm of wealth than in the realm of power.

It is the duality of economic power (as a component and end of state action) and its greater potential for common gains that makes the analysis of the role it plays in state behavior and international interactions complex and elusive. The study of international political economy, as it has been traditionally understood, encompasses both these aspects of economic power.

## PERSPECTIVES ON POLITICAL ECONOMY

"The science of economics presupposes a given political order, and cannot be profitably studied in isolation from politics." So wrote E. H. Carr in his seminal work,

*The Twenty Years' Crisis*, in 1939. Fifty years earlier, in an essay entitled "Socialism: Utopian or Scientific" Karl Marx's coauthor, Friedrich Engels asserted: "The materialist conception of history starts from the proposition that the production of the means to support human life. . . is the basis of all social structure. . . ." These two views—that economic processes are not autonomous but require political structures to support them and that economic factors determine the social and political structures of states—represent the polar extremes on the relationship of politics and economics.

Which view is correct? To this question there is no simple or single answer. Any reply is as much philosophical as it is empirical. The economic interests of individuals in a state and of states within the international arena do powerfully affect the goals that are sought and the degree of success with which they are attained. But the political structure of international action is also a constraint. Anarchy makes cooperative actions more difficult to attain than would otherwise be the case and requires that statesmen consider both relative and absolute positions when framing actions in the international economic realm. And often in international politics the imperatives of security and survival override the dictates of economic interests. War, after all, almost never pays in a strict balance-sheet sense, particularly when waged between states of roughly equal power. The economic wealth lost in fighting is usually not recouped in the peace that follows.

The best answers to the question, what is the relation between politics and economics in international affairs, have been given by the classical theorists of international politics. Robert Gilpin examines three schools of thought—the liberals, the Marxists, and the mercantilists. Unlike the other two, liberal political economists have stressed the cooperative, not the conflictual, nature of international economic relations. They have extended Adam Smith's arguments about the domestic economy to the international economy. Smith argued that the specialization of function by individuals within a state, together with their unfettered pursuit of their own self-interests, would increase the wealth of a nation and thereby benefit all. Collective harmony and national wealth could thus be the product of self-interested behavior, if only the government would provide as little restraint on individual action as was necessary. The eighteenth-century philosophers and the nineteenth- and twentieth-century free traders argued that what was good for individuals within a state would also be good for states in the international arena. By trading freely with one another, states could specialize according to their respective comparative advantages and the wealth of all nations would, as a consequence, increase. "Make trade not war" has been the slogan of the liberal free traders.

By contrast, both mercantilists and Marxists have seen state relations as inherently conflictual. For Marxists, this is so because capitalists within and among states compete fiercely with one another to maximize their profits. Driven by their greed, they are incapable of cooperating with one another. Because a state's policy is determined by the capitalist ruling class, states will wage wars for profit and, under Lenin's dictum, will wage wars to redivide the world's wealth. Imperialism as the highest stage of capitalism is a classic zero-sum situation. Mercantilists also argue that economic factors make relations among states conflictual. Their analysis, however, rests not on the externalization of class conflict, but on the nature of political and economic power. For eighteenth-century mercantilists, the world's wealth was fixed and could only be redivided. For nineteenth- and twentieth-century mercantilists, wealth could be increased for all, but because wealth contributes to national power and power is relative, not absolute, conflict would continue.

All three schools of thought are motivated by their views on the relation of politics to economics. Mercantilists stress the primacy of politics and the consequent pursuit of national power and relative position in the international arena. Both liberals and Marxists stress the primacy of economics. For the former, the potential for economic harmony can override the forces of nationalism if only free trade is pursued. For the latter, economic interests determine political behavior and, since the first is conflictual, the second must be also. Both liberals and Marxists want to banish politics from international relations, the former through free trade, the latter through the universal spread of communism. Mercantilists, like realists, view these prescriptions as naive and believe that the national interests of every state are only partly determined by their economic interests.

Contemporary writers continue to wrestle with the relation between politics and economics in international affairs. Robert O. Keohane analyzes what types of international political structures are conducive to economic cooperation among nations. He finds the theory of hegemonic stability—that a dominant power is necessary to create and sustain a stable international economic order—a suggestive but not definitive way to understand the last one hundred years. A hegemonic power can foster economic cooperation among states, as the United States did after World War II, but cooperation can occur in the absence of such a power. A hegemonic power is neither a necessary nor a sufficient condition for interstate cooperation.

Bruce R. Scott looks at the political-economic relations between rich and poor states, and asks why the gap between these two has increased during the globalization era of the last twenty years, when, in fact, neoclassical economic theory predicts that the gap should have decreased. According to this theory, in a free global market poor states lessen the gap because they are supposed to grow faster than rich states. That this has not happened is due, according to Scott, to the barriers imposed by the rich states on immigration and agriculture from the poorer states, and to the inadequate government structures in the poor states that make them less than ideal outlets for capital investments from the rich states. Thus, the reasons are political-economic in nature, and the fault lies with both the rich and the poor states.

## THE MEANING OF GLOBALIZATION

At the beginning of the twenty-first century, which way will the international political economy go? Can the nations of the world muster the political will necessary to preserve a relatively open international system that has benefited them all, even if they have benefited unequally? Or, have the political costs of severe economic dislocations, which the open system of the last two decades has produced, been too great? Will states lapse into protectionism? Does free trade still make sense when factor endowments (land, labor, capital, and technology) are no longer fixed and when, therefore, comparative advantages are no longer static but perhaps can be created behind protectionist barriers?

These are difficult questions to answer. How they are answered depends heavily on how economically interdependent one sees the nations of the world today. "Interdependence" is one of those terms that has developed a myriad of meanings. The most fruitful way to use the term, when considering the relationship between this concept and peaceful cooperation among states, is as follows: Interdependence is the size of the stake that a state believes it has in seeing other states' economies prosper so as to help its own economy prosper too. Interdependence can be high or low. The more highly perceived interdependence is, the larger a state's stake in the economic well-being of the countries with which it heavily interacts; the less interdependence, the smaller is its stake. High levels of interdependence should facilitate cooperation among states for their mutual gain.

After World War II, the United States used its considerable economic and military power to create an open international economic order by working to lower the barriers among nations to the flow of manufactured goods, raw materials other than agriculture, and capital. The result of this international economic openness was a rise in the level of interdependence, particularly among the industrialized nations of the world, but also, to a considerable degree, among the industrializing nations in East Asia and Latin America. But interdependence has its costs as well as its benefits. High levels of participation in the international economy can bring the benefits of efficiency that flow from specialization, but also the destruction of national industries that can no longer compete internationally. States today must reconcile the imperatives of what Robert Gilpin has called "Keynes at home" with "Smith abroad": maintenance of full employment domestically and competitive participation in the international economy. Through exports and capital inflows, interdependence can help a state increase its wealth, but it also brings vulnerabilities that derive from the need to rely partially on others for one's own prosperity. Balancing the two imperatives is a difficult political act.

Interdependence can exist between pairs of countries and can be generated by important but narrow flows of goods. Globalization, as the term indicates, involves most if not all countries and a wide range of economic transactions. The potential loss of autonomy is broader because the nature of national economies, the abilities of states to direct their individual economic and even social policies, and the stability of governments are affected by the movement toward a truly worldwide economy.

The readings in this section explore various aspects of interdependence and globalization. Jeffrey Frankel provides several benchmarks by which to measure the globalization and integration of the world economy today and then provides a tentative balance sheet on the economic and social effects of globalization. Martin Wolf analyzes the factors that have produced globalization and assesses the threats to it. Finally, Kenneth N. Waltz argues that the worldwide nature of globalization has been exaggerated and that states—especially powerful ones like the United States—continue to play leading roles and to be guided by political calculations.

# THE PROS AND CONS OF GLOBALIZATION

Today's globalization should not only be measured and compared, however; it must also be assessed. Does it benefit all states that become entangled in it, or do a few benefit at the expense of the many? Is heavy participation in the global economy a prerequisite to economic development, or can such participation actually harm development? Does globalization hasten the degradation of the environment, weaken protection of worker rights in both the rich and poor countries, and give too much power to multinational corporations? Globalization may be a fact of today's world, but it is no longer seen as an unalloyed good, as the protests in Seattle in 1999 and in Genoa in 2001 demonstrate.

The three readings in this section take differing stands on these questions. Dani Rodrik asserts that globalization can be a false promise to developing states. He challenges free-trade orthodoxy by showing that high tariff and nontarrif barriers do not necessarily bring with them low growth, and argues that the preparations that poorer states must take to open themselves up to international trade and investment divert precious and scarce resources from the task of economic development. Geoffrey Garrett argues that globalization may have benefited the rich and poor countries, but it has hurt both the middle income countries and the industrial middle classes in the wealthy countries. This "middle" has missed the benefits of globalization because neither the middle income countries nor the middle classes within the rich countries can compete in either the global knowledge economy or the global low wage economy. The only hope for both parts of the "missing middle" is to enter the global knowledge economy. John Mickelthwait and Adrian Wooldridge take an opposing view to both Rodrik and Garrett. Global economic growth, they argue, has been aided significantly by the growth in world trade. Globalization can also be a force for protecting the environment because the wealthier states become, the more they tend to clean up their environment. Finally, globalization aids workers because multinational companies generally pay better wages and provide better working conditions than their local competitors.

# PERSPECTIVES ON
# POLITICAL ECONOMY

## *The Nature of Political Economy*

### ROBERT GILPIN

> *The international corporations have evidently declared ideological war on the "antiquated" nation state. . . . The charge that materialism, modernization and internationalism is the new liberal creed of corporate capitalism is a valid one. The implication is clear: The nation state as a political unit of democratic decision-making must, in the interest of "progress," yield control to the new mercantile mini-powers.*[1]
> *While the structure of the multinational corporation is a modern concept, designed to meet the requirements of a modern age, the nation state is a very old-fashioned idea and badly adapted to serve the needs of our present complex world.*[2]

These two statements—the first by Kari Levitt, a Canadian nationalist, the second by George Ball, a former United States undersecretary of state—express a dominant theme of contemporary writings on international relations. International society, we are told, is increasingly rent between its economic and its political organization. On the one hand, powerful economic and technological forces are creating a highly interdependent world economy, thus diminishing the traditional significance of national boundaries. On the other hand, the nation-state continues to command men's loyalties and to be the basic unit of political decision making. As one writer has put the issue, "The conflict of our era is between ethnocentric nationalism and geocentric technology."[3]

Ball and Levitt represent two contending positions with respect to this conflict. Whereas Ball advocates the diminution of the power of the nation-state in order to give full rein to the productive potentialities of the multinational corporation, Levitt argues for a powerful nationalism which could counterbalance American corporate domination. What appears to one as the logical and desirable consequence of economic rationality seems to the other to be an effort on the part of American imperialism to eliminate all contending centers of power.

Although the advent of the multinational corporation has put the question of the relationship between economics and politics in a new guise, it is an old issue. In the nineteenth century, for example, it was this issue that divided classical liberals like John Stuart Mill from economic nationalists, represented by Georg Friedrich List. Whereas the former gave primacy in the organization of society to economics and the production of wealth, the latter emphasized the political determination of economic relations. As this issue is central both to the contemporary debate on the multinational corporation and to the argument of this study, this chapter analyzes the three major treatments of the relationship between economics and politics— that is, the three major ideologies of political economy.

## THE MEANING OF POLITICAL ECONOMY

The argument of this study is that the relationship between economics and politics, at least in the modern world, is a reciprocal one. On the one hand, politics largely determines the framework of economic activity and channels it in directions intended to serve the interests of dominant groups; the exercise of power in all its forms is a major determinant of the nature of an economic system. On the other hand, the economic process itself tends to redistribute power and wealth; it transforms the power relationships among groups. This in turn leads to a transformation of the political system, thereby giving rise to a new structure of economic relationships. Thus, the dynamics of international relations in the modern world is largely a function of the reciprocal interaction between economics and politics.

First of all, what do I mean by "politics" or "economics"? Charles Kindleberger speaks of economics and politics as two different methods of allocating scarce resources: the first through a market mechanism, the latter through a budget.[4] Robert O. Keohane and Joseph Nye, in an excellent analysis of international political economy, define economics and politics in terms of two levels of analysis: those of structure and of process.[5] Politics is the domain "having to do with the establishment of an order of relations, a structure. . . ."[6] Economics deals with "short-term allocative behavior (i.e., holding institutions, fundamental assumptions, and expectations constant). . . ."[7] Like Kindleberger's definition, however, this definition tends to isolate economic and political phenomena except under certain conditions, which Keohane and Nye define as the "politicization" of the economic system. Neither formulation comes to terms adequately with the dynamic and intimate nature of the relationship between the two.

In this study, the issue of the relationship between economics and politics translates into that between wealth and power. According to this statement of the problem, economics takes as its province the creation and distribution of wealth; politics is the realm of power. I shall examine their relationship from several ideological perspectives, including my own. But what is wealth? What is power?

In response to the question, What is wealth?, an economist-colleague responded, "What do you want, my thirty-second or thirty-volume answer?" Basic concepts are elusive in economics, as in any field of inquiry. No unchallengeable definitions are possible. Ask a physicist for his definition of the nature of space, time, and matter, and you will not get a very satisfying response. What you will get is an *operational* definition, one which is usable: It permits the physicist to build an intellectual edifice whose foundations would crumble under the scrutiny of the philosopher.

Similarly, the concept of wealth, upon which the science of economics ultimately rests, cannot be clarified in a definitive way. Paul Samuelson, in his textbook, doesn't even try, though he provides a clue in his definition of economics as "the study of how men and society *choose* . . . to employ *scarce* productive resources . . . to produce various commodities . . . and distribute them for consumption."[8] Following this lead, we can say that wealth is anything (capital, land, or labor) that can generate future income; it is composed of physical assets and human capital (including embodied knowledge).

The basic concept of political science is power. Most political scientists would not stop here; they would include in the definition of political science the purpose for which power is used, whether this be the advancement of the public welfare or the domination of one group over another. In any case, few would dissent from the following statement of Harold Lasswell and Abraham Kaplan:

> The concept of power is perhaps the most fundamental in the whole of political science: The political process is the shaping, distribution, and exercise of power (in a wider sense, of all the deference values, or of influence in general).[9]

Power as such is not the sole or even the principal goal of state behavior. Other goals or values constitute the objectives pursued by nation-states: welfare, security, prestige. But power in its several forms (military, economic, psychological) is ultimately the necessary means to achieve these goals. For this reason, nation-states are intensely jealous of and sensitive to their relative power position. The distribution of power is important because it profoundly affects the ability of states to achieve what they perceive to be their interests.

The nature of power, however, is even more elusive than that of wealth. The number and variety of definitions should be an embarrassment to political scientists. Unfortunately, this study cannot bring the intradisciplinary squabble to an end. Rather, it adopts the definition used by Hans J. Morgenthau in his influential *Politics Among Nations:* "man's control over the minds and actions of other men."[10] Thus, power, like wealth, is the capacity to produce certain results.

Unlike wealth, however, power cannot be quantified; indeed, it cannot be overemphasized that power has an important psychological dimension. Perceptions of power relations are of critical importance; as a consequence, a fundamental task of statesmen is to manipulate the perceptions of other statesmen regarding the distribution of power. Moreover, power is relative to a specific situation or set of circumstances; there is no single hierarchy of power in international relations. Power may take many forms—military, economic, or psychological—though, in the final analysis, force is the ultimate form of power. Finally, the inability to predict the behavior of others or the outcome of events is of great significance. Uncertainty regarding the distribution of power and the ability of the statesmen to control events plays an important role in international relations. Ultimately, the determination of the distribution of power can be made only in retrospect as a consequence of war. It is precisely for this reason that war has had, unfortunately, such a central place in the history of international relations. In short, power is an elusive concept indeed upon which to erect a science of politics.

Such mutually exclusive definitions of economics and politics as these run counter to much contemporary scholarship by both economists and political scientists, for both disciplines are invading the formerly exclusive jurisdictions of the other. Economists, in particular, have become intellectual imperialists; they are applying their analytical techniques to traditional issues of political science with great success. These developments, however, really reinforce the basic premise of this study, namely, the inseparability of economics and politics.

The distinction drawn above between economics as the science of wealth and politics as the science of power is essentially an analytical one. In the real world, wealth and power are ultimately joined. This, in fact, is the basic rationale for a political economy of international relations. But in order to develop the argument of this study, wealth and power will be treated, at least for the moment, as analytically distinct.

To provide a perspective on the nature of political economy, the next section will discuss the three prevailing conceptions of political economy: liberalism, Marxism, and mercantilism. Liberalism regards politics and economics as relatively separable and autonomous spheres of activities; I associate most professional economists as well as many other academics, businessmen, and American officials with this outlook. Marxism refers to the radical critique of capitalism identified with Karl Marx and his contemporary disciples; according to this conception, economics determines politics and political structure. Mercantilism is a more questionable term because of its historical association with the desire of nation-states for a trade surplus and for treasure (money). One must distinguish, however, between the specific form mercantilism took in the seventeenth and eighteenth centuries and the general outlook of mercantilistic thought. The essence of the mercantilistic perspective, whether it is labeled economic nationalism, protectionism, or the doctrine of the German Historical School, is the subservience of economy to the state and its interests—interests that range from matters of domestic welfare to those of international security. It is this more general meaning of mercantilism that is implied by the use of the term in this study.

Following the discussion of these three schools of thought, I shall elaborate my own, more eclectic, view of political economy and demonstrate its relevance for understanding the phenomenon of the multinational corporation.

## THREE CONCEPTIONS OF POLITICAL ECONOMY

The three prevailing conceptions of political economy differ on many points. Several critical differences will be examined in this brief comparison. (See Table 1.)

### The Nature of Economic Relations

The basic assumption of liberalism is that the nature of international economic relations is essentially harmonious. Herein lay the great intellectual innovation of

TABLE 1  ■  COMPARISON OF THE THREE CONCEPTIONS OF POLITICAL ECONOMY

|  | Liberalism | Marxism | Mercantilism |
|---|---|---|---|
| Nature of economic relations | Harmonious | Conflictual | Conflictual |
| Nature of the actors | Households and firms | Economic classes | Nation-states |
| Goal of economic activity | Maximization of global welfare | Maximization of class interests | Maximization of national interest |
| Relationship between economics and politics | Economics *should* determine politics | Economics *does* determine politics | Politics determines economics |
| Theory of change | Dynamic equilibrium | Tendency toward disequilibrium | Shifts in the distribution of power |

Adam Smith. Disputing his mercantilist predecessors, Smith argued that international economic relations could be made a positive-sum game; that is to say, everyone could gain, and no one need lose, from a proper ordering of economic relations, albeit the distribution of these gains may not be equal. Following Smith, liberalism assumes that there is a basic harmony between true national interest and cosmopolitan economic interest. Thus, a prominent member of this school of thought has written, in response to a radical critique, that the economic efficiency of the sterling standard in the nineteenth century and that of the dollar standard in the twentieth century serve "the cosmopolitan interest in a national form."[11] Although Great Britain and the United States gained the most from the international role of their respective currencies, everyone else gained as well.

Liberals argue that, given this underlying identity of national and cosmopolitan interests in a free market, the state should not interfere with economic transactions across national boundaries. Through free exchange of commodities, removal of restrictions on the flow of investment, and an international division of labor, everyone will benefit in the long run as a result of a more efficient utilization of the world's scarce resources. The national interest is therefore best served, liberals maintain, by a generous and cooperative attitude regarding economic relations with other countries. In essence, the pursuit of self-interest in a free, competitive economy achieves the greatest good for the greatest number in international no less than in the national society.

Both mercantilists and Marxists, on the other hand, begin with the premise that the essence of economic relations is conflictual. There is no underlying harmony; indeed, one group's gain is another's loss. Thus, in the language of game theory, whereas liberals regard economic relations as a non-zero-sum game, Marxists and mercantilists view economic relations as essentially a zero-sum game.

## The Goal of Economic Activity

For the liberal, the goal of economic activity is the optimum or efficient use of the world's scarce resources and the maximization of world welfare. While most liberals refuse to make value judgments regarding income distribution, Marxists and mercantilists stress the distributive effects of economic relations. For the Marxist the distribution of wealth among social classes is central; for the mercantilist it is the distribution of employment, industry, and military power among nation-states that is most significant. Thus, the goal of economic (and political) activity for both Marxists and mercantilists is the redistribution of wealth and power.

## The State and Public Policy

These three perspectives differ decisively in their view regarding the nature of the economic actors. In Marxist analysis, the basic actors in both domestic and international relations are economic classes; the interests of the dominant class determine the foreign policy of the state. For mercantilists, the real actors in international economic relations are nation-states; national interest determines foreign policy. National interest may at times be influenced by the peculiar economic interests of classes, elites, or other subgroups of the society; but factors of geography, external configurations of power, and the exigencies of national survival are primary in determining foreign policy. Thus, whereas liberals speak of world welfare and Marxists of class interests, mercantilists recognize only the interests of particular nation-states.

Although liberal economists such as David Ricardo and Joseph Schumpeter recognized the importance of class conflict and neoclassical liberals analyze economic growth and policy in terms of national economies, the liberal emphasis is on the individual consumer, firm, or entrepreneur. The liberal ideal is summarized in the view of Harry Johnson that the nation-state has no meaning as an economic entity.[12]

Underlying these contrasting views are differing conceptions of the nature of the state and public policy. For liberals, the state represents an aggregation of private interests: public policy is but the outcome of a pluralistic struggle among interest groups. Marxists, on the other hand, regard the state as simply the "executive committee of the ruling class," and public policy reflects its interests. Mercantilists, however, regard the state as an organic unit in its own right: the whole is greater than the sum of its parts. Public policy, therefore, embodies the national interest or Rousseau's "general will" as conceived by the political elite.

## The Relationship between Economics and Politics: Theories of Change

Liberalism, Marxism, and mercantilism also have differing views on the relationship between economics and politics. And their differences on this issue are directly relevant to their contrasting theories of international political change.

Although the liberal ideal is the separation of economics from politics in the interest of maximizing world welfare, the fulfillment of this ideal would have important political implications. The classical statement of these implications was that of Adam Smith in *The Wealth of Nations*.[13] Economic growth, Smith argued, is primarily a function of the extent of the division of labor, which in turn is dependent upon the scale of the market. Thus he attacked the barriers erected by feudal principalities and mercantilistic states against the exchange of goods and the enlargement of markets. If men were to multiply their wealth, Smith argued, the contradiction between political organization and economic rationality had to be resolved in favor of the latter. That is, the pursuit of wealth should determine the nature of the political order.

Subsequently, from nineteenth-century economic liberals to twentiethcentury writers on economic integration, there has existed "the dream . . . of a great republic of world commerce, in which national boundaries would cease to have any great economic importance and the web of trade would bind all the people of the world in the prosperity of peace."[14] For liberals the long-term trend is toward world integration, wherein functions, authority, and loyalties will be transferred from "smaller units to larger ones; from states to federalism; from federalism to supranational unions and from these to superstates."[15] The logic of economic and technological development, it is argued, has set mankind on an inexorable course toward global political unification and world peace.

In Marxism, the concept of the contradiction between economic and political relations was enacted into historical law. Whereas classical liberals—although Smith less than others—held that the requirements of economic rationality *ought* to determine political relations, the Marxist position was that the mode of production does in fact determine the superstructure of political relations. Therefore, it is argued, history can be understood as the product of the dialectical process—the contradiction between the evolving techniques of production and the resistant sociopolitical system.

Although Marx and Engels wrote remarkably little on international economics, Engels, in his famous polemic, *Anti-Duhring*, explicitly considers whether economics or politics is primary in determining the structure of international relations.[16] E. K. Duhring, a minor figure in the German Historical School, had argued, in contradiction to Marxism, that property and market relations resulted less from the economic logic of capitalism than from extraeconomic political factors: "The basis of the exploitation of many by man was an historical act of force which created an exploitative economic system for the benefit of the stronger man or class."[17] Since Engels, in his attack on Duhring, used the example of the unification of Germany through the Zollverein or customs union of 1833, his analysis is directly relevant to this discussion of the relationship between economics and political organization.

Engels argued that when contradictions arise between economic and political structures, political power adapts itself to the changes in the balance of economic forces; politics yields to the dictates of economic development. Thus, in the case of nineteenth-century Germany, the requirements of industrial production had become incompatible with its feudal, politically fragmented structure. "Though political reaction was victorious in 1815 and again in 1848," he argued, "it was unable to prevent the growth of large-scale industry in Germany and the growing participation of German commerce in the world market."[18] In summary, Engels wrote, "German unity had become an economic necessity."[19]

In the view of both Smith and Engels, the nation-state represented a progressive stage in human development, because it enlarged the political realm of economic activity. In each successive economic epoch, advances in technology and an increasing scale of production necessitate an enlargement of political organization. Because the city-state and feudalism restricted the scale of production and the division of labor made possible by the Industrial Revolution, they prevented the efficient utilization of resources and were, therefore, superseded by larger political units. Smith considered this to be a desirable objective; for Engels it was an historical necessity. Thus, in the opinion of liberals, the establishment of the Zollverein was a movement toward maximizing world economic welfare;[20] for Marxists it was the unavoidable triumph of the German industrialists over the feudal aristocracy.

Mercantilist writers from Alexander Hamilton to Frederich List to Charles de Gaulle, on the other hand, have emphasized the primacy of politics; politics, in this view, determines economic organization. Whereas Marxists and liberals have pointed to the production of wealth as the basic determinant of social and political organization, the mercantilists of the German Historical School, for example, stressed the primacy of national security, industrial development, and national sentiment in international political and economic dynamics.

In response to Engels's interpretation of the unification of Germany, mercantilists would no doubt agree with Jacob Viner that "Prussia engineered the customs union primarily for political reasons, in order to gain hegemony or at least influence over the lesser German states. It was largely in order to make certain that the hegemony should be Prussian and not Austrian that Prussia continually opposed Austrian entry into the Union, either openly or by pressing for a customs union tariff lower than highly protectionist Austria could stomach."[21] In pursuit of this strategic interest, it was "Prussian might, rather than a common zeal for political unification arising out of economic partnership, [that] . . . played the major role."[22]

In contrast to Marxism, neither liberalism nor mercantilism has a developed theory of dynamics. The basic assumption of orthodox economic analysis (liberalism) is the tendency toward equilibrium; liberalism takes for granted the existing social order and given institutions. Change is assumed to be gradual and adaptive—a continuous process of dynamic equilibrium. There is no necessary connection between such political phenomena as war and revolution and the evolution of the economic system, although they would not deny that misguided statesmen can blunder into war over economic issues or that revolutions are conflicts over the distribution of wealth; but neither is inevitably linked to the evolution of the productive system. As for mercantilism, it sees change as taking place owing to shifts in the balance of power; yet, mercantilist writers such as members of the German Historical School and contemporary political realists have not developed a systematic theory of how this shift occurs.

On the other hand, dynamics is central to Marxism; indeed Marxism is essentially a theory of social *change*. It emphasizes the tendency toward *dis*equilibrium owing to changes in the means of production and the consequent effects on the ever-present class conflict. When these tendencies can no longer be contained, the sociopolitical system breaks down through violent upheaval. Thus war and revolution are seen as an integral part of the economic process. Politics and economics are intimately joined.

## Why an International Economy?

From these differences among the three ideologies, one can get a sense of their respective explanations for the existence and functioning of the international economy.

An interdependent world economy constitutes the normal state of affairs for most liberal economists. Responding to technological advances in transportation and communications, the scope of the market mechanism, according to this analysis, continuously expands. Thus, despite temporary setbacks, the long-term trend is toward global economic integration. The functioning of the international economy is determined primarily by considerations of efficiency. The role of the dollar as the basis of the international monetary system, for example, is explained by the preference for it among traders and nations as the vehicle of international commerce.[23] The system is maintained by the mutuality of the benefits provided by trade, monetary arrangements, and investment.

A second view—one shared by Marxists and mercantilists alike—is that every interdependent international economy is essentially an imperial or hierarchical system. The imperial or hegemonic power organizes trade, monetary, and investment relations in order to advance its own economic and political interests. In the absence of the economic and especially the political influence of the hegemonic power, the system would fragment into autarkic economies or regional blocs. Whereas for liberalism maintenance of harmonious international market relations is the norm, for Marxism and mercantilism conflicts of class or national interests are the norm.

## PERSPECTIVE OF THE AUTHOR

My own perspective on political economy rests on what I regard as a fundamental difference in emphasis between economics and politics; namely, the distinction between absolute and relative gains. The emphasis of economic science—or, at least, of liberal economics—is on *absolute* gains; the ultimate defense of liberalism is that over the long run everyone gains, albeit in varying degrees, from a liberal economic regime. Economics, according to this formulation, need not be a zero-sum game. Everyone can gain in wealth through a more efficient division of labor; moreover, everyone can lose, in absolute terms, from economic inefficiency. Herein lies the strength of liberalism.

This economic emphasis on absolute gains is in fact embodied in what one can characterize as the ultimate ideal of liberal economics: the achievement of a "Pareto optimum" world. Such a properly ordered world would be one wherein "by improving the position of one individual (by adding to his possessions) no one else's position is deteriorated." As Oskar Morgenstern has observed, "[e]conomic literature is replete with the use of the Pareto optimum thus formulated or in equivalent language."[24] It is a world freed from "interpersonal comparisons of utility," and thus a world freed from what is central to politics, i.e., ethical judgment and conflict regarding the just and relative distribution of utility. That the notion of a Pareto optimum is rife with conceptual problems and is utopian does not detract from its centrality as the implicit objective of liberal economics. And this emphasis of economics on absolute gains for all differs fundamentally from the nature of political phenomena as studied by political scientists: viz., struggles for power as a goal itself or as a means to the achievement of other goals.

The essential fact of politics is that power is always relative; one state's gain in power is by necessity another's loss. Thus, even though two states may be gaining absolutely in wealth, in political terms it is the effect of these gains on relative power positions which is of primary importance. From this *political* perspective, therefore, the mercantilists are correct in emphasizing that in power terms, international relations is a zero-sum game.

In a brilliant analysis of international politics, the relativity of power and its profound implications were set forth by Jean-Jacques Rousseau:

> The state, being an artificial body is not limited in any way. . . . It can always increase; it always feels itself weak if there is another that is stronger. Its security and preservation demand that it make itself more powerful than its neighbors. It can increase, nourish and exercise its power only at their expense . . . while the inequality of man has natural limits that between societies can grow without cease, until one absorbs all the others. . . . Because the grandeur of the state is purely relative it is forced to compare itself with that of the others. . . . It is in vain that it wishes to keep itself to itself; it becomes small or great, weak or strong, according to whether its neighbor expands or contracts, becomes stronger or declines. . . .
>
> The chief thing I notice is a patent contradiction in the condition of the human race. . . . Between man and man we live in the condition of the civil state, subjected to laws; between people and people we enjoy natural liberty, which makes the situation worse. Living at the same time in the social order and in the state of nature, we suffer from the inconveniences of both without finding . . . security in either. . . . We see men united by artificial bonds, but united to destroy each other; and all the horrors of war take birth from the precautions they have taken in order to prevent them. . . . War is born of peace, or at least of the precautions which men have taken for the purpose of achieving durable peace.[25]

Because of the relativity of power, therefore, nation-states are engaged in a neverending struggle to improve or preserve their relative power positions.

This rather stark formulation obviously draws too sharp a distinction between economics and politics. Certainly, for example, liberal economists may be interested in questions of distribution; the distributive issue was, in fact, of central concern to Ricardo and other classical writers. However, when economists stop taking the system for granted and start asking questions about distribution, they have really ventured into what I regard as the essence of politics, for distribution is really a political issue. In a world in which power rests on wealth, changes in the relative distribution of wealth imply changes in the distribution of power and in the political system itself. This, in fact, is what is meant by saying that politics is about relative gains. Politics concerns the efforts of groups to redistribute gains to their own advantage.

Similarly, to argue that politics is about relative gains is not to argue that it is a constant-sum game. On the contrary, man's power over nature and his fellow man has grown immensely in absolute terms over the past several centuries. It is certainly the case that everyone's absolute capabilities can increase due to the development of new weaponry, the expansion of productive capabilities, or changes in the political system itself. Obviously such absolute increases in power are important politically.

Who can deny, for example, that the advent of nuclear weapons has profoundly altered international politics? Obviously, too, states can negotiate disarmament and other levels of military capability.

Yet recognition of these facts does not alter the prime consideration that changes in the relative distribution of power are of fundamental significance politically. Though all may be gaining or declining in absolute capability, what will concern states principally are the effects of these absolute gains or losses on relative positions. How, for example, do changes in productive capacity or military weaponry affect the ability of one state to impose its will on another? It may very well be that in a particular situation absolute gains will not affect relative positions. But the efforts of groups to cause or prevent such shifts in the relative distribution of power constitute the critical issue of politics.

This formulation of the nature of politics obviously does not deny that nations may cooperate in order to advance their mutual interest. But even cooperative actions may have important consequences for the distribution of power in the system. For example, the Strategic Arms Limitation Talks (SALT) between the United States and the Soviet Union are obviously motivated by a common interest in preventing thermonuclear war. Other states will also benefit if the risk of war between the superpowers is reduced. Yet, SALT may also be seen as an attempt to stabilize the international distribution of power to the disadvantage of China and other third powers. In short, in terms of the system as a whole, political cooperation can have a profound effect on the relative distribution of power among nation-states.

The point may perhaps be clarified by distinguishing between two aspects of power. When one speaks of absolute gains in power, such as advances in economic capabilities or weapons development, one is referring principally to increases in physical or material capabilities. But while such capabilities are an important component of power, power, as we have seen, is more than physical capability. Power is also a psychological relationship: Who can influence whom to do what? From this perspective, what may be of most importance is how changes in capability affect this psychological relationship. Insofar as they do, they alter the relative distribution of power in the system.

In a world in which power rests increasingly on economic and industrial capabilities, one cannot really distinguish between wealth (resources, treasure, and industry) and power as national goals. In the short run there may be conflicts between the pursuit of power and the pursuit of wealth; in the long run the two pursuits are identical. Therefore, the position taken in this study is similar to Viner's interpretation of classical mercantilism:

> What then is the correct interpretation of mercantilist doctrine and practice with respect to the roles of power and plenty as ends of national policy? I believe that practically all mercantilists, whatever the period, country, or status of the particular individual, would have subscribed to all of the following propositions: (1) wealth is an absolutely essential means to power, whether for security or for aggression; (2) power is essential or valuable as a means to the acquisition or retention of wealth; (3) wealth and power are each proper ultimate ends of national policy; (4) there is long-run harmony between these ends, although in particular circumstances it may be necessary for a time to make economic sacrifices in the interest of military security and therefore also of long-run prosperity.[26]

This interpretation of the role of the economic motive in international relations is substantially different from that of Marxism. In the Marxist framework of analysis, the economic factor is reduced to the profit motive, as it affects the behavior of individuals or firms. Accordingly, the foreign policies of capitalist states are determined by the desire of capitalists for profits. This is, in our view, far too narrow a conception of the economic aspect of international relations. Instead, in this study we label "economic" those sources of wealth upon which national power and domestic welfare are dependent.

Understood in these broader terms, the economic motive and economic activities are fundamental to the struggle for power among nation-states. The objects of contention in the struggles of the balance of power include the centers of economic power. As R. G. Hawtrey has expressed it, "the political motives at work can only be expressed in terms of the economic. Every conflict is one of power and power depends on resources."[27] In pursuit of wealth *and* power, therefore, nations (capitalist, socialist, or fascist) contend over the territorial division and exploitation of the globe.

Even at the level of peaceful economic intercourse, one cannot separate out the political element. Contrary to the attitude of liberalism, international economic relations are in reality political relations. The interdependence of national economies creates economic power, defined as the capacity of one state to damage another through the interruption of commercial and financial relations.[28] The attempts to create and to escape from such dependency relationships constitute an important aspect of international relations in the modern era.

The primary actors in the international system are nation-states in pursuit of what they define as their national interest. This is not to argue, however, that nation-states are the only actors, nor do I believe that the "national interest" is something akin to Rousseau's "general will"—the expression of an organic entity separable from its component parts. Except in the abstract models of political scientists, it has never been the case that the international system was composed solely of nation-states. In an exaggerated acknowledgment of the importance of nonstate or transnational actors at an earlier time, John A. Hobson asked rhetorically whether "a great war could be undertaken by any European state, or a great state loan subscribed, if the House of Rothschild and its connexions set their face against it."[29] What has to be explained, however, are the economic and political circumstances that enable such transnational actors to play their semi-independent role in international affairs. The argument of this study is that the primary determinants of the role played by these non-state actors are the larger configurations of power among nation-states. What is determinant is the interplay of national interests.

As for the concept of "national interest," the national interest of a given nation-state is, of course, what its political and economic elite determines it to be. In part, as Marxists argue, this elite will define it in terms of its own group or class interests. But the national interest comprehends more than this. More general influences, such as cultural values and considerations relevant to the security of the state itself—geographical position, the evolution of military technology, and the international distribution of power—are of greater importance. There is a sense, then, in which the factors that determine the national interest are objective. A ruling elite that fails to take these factors into account does so at its peril. In short, then, there is a basis for considering the nation-state itself as an actor pursuing its own set of security, welfare, and status concerns in competition or cooperation with other nation-states.

Lastly, in a world of conflicting nation-states, how does one explain the existence of an interdependent international economy? Why does a liberal international economy—that is, an economy characterized by relatively free trade, currency convertibility, and freedom of capital movement—remain intact rather than fragment into autarkic national economies and regional or imperial groupings? In part, the answer is provided by liberalism: economic cooperation, interdependence, and an international division of labor enhance efficiency and the maximization of aggregate wealth. Nation-states are induced to enter the international system because of the promise of more rapid growth; greater benefits can be had than could be obtained by autarky or a fragmentation of the world economy. The historical record suggests, however, that the existence of mutual economic benefits is not always enough to induce nations to pay the costs of a market system or to forgo opportunities of advancing their own interests at the expense of others. There is always the danger that a nation may pursue certain short-range policies, such as the imposition of an optimum tariff, in order to maximize its own gains at the expense of the system as a whole.

For this reason, a liberal international economy requires a power to manage and stabilize the system. As Charles Kindleberger has convincingly shown, this governance role was performed by Great Britain throughout the nineteenth century and up to 1931, and by the United States after 1945.[30] The inability of Great Britain in 1929 to continue running the system and the unwillingness of the United States to assume this responsibility led to the collapse of the system in the "Great Depression." The result was the fragmentation of the world economy into rival economic blocs. Both dominant economic powers had failed to overcome the divisive forces of nationalism and regionalism.

The argument of this study is that the modern world economy has evolved through the emergence of great national economies that have successively become dominant. In the words of the distinguished French economist François Perroux, "the economic evolution of the world has resulted from a succession of dominant economies, each in turn taking the lead in international activity and influence. . . . Throughout the nineteenth century the British economy was the dominant economy in the world. From the [eighteen] seventies on, Germany was dominant in respect to certain other Continental countries and in certain specified fields. In the twentieth century, the United States economy has clearly been and still is the internationally dominant economy."[31]

An economic system, then, does not arise spontaneously owing to the operation of an invisible hand and in the absence of the exercise of power. Rather, every economic system rests on a particular political order; its nature cannot be understood aside from politics. This basic point was made some years ago by E. H. Carr when he wrote that "the science of economics presupposes a given political order, and cannot be profitably studied in isolation from politics."[32] Carr sought to convince his fellow Englishmen that an international economy based on free trade was not a natural and inevitable state of affairs but rather one that reflected the economic and political interests of Great Britain. The system based on free trade had come into existence through, and was maintained by, the exercise of British economic and military power. With the rise after 1880 of new industrial and military powers with contrasting economic interests—namely, Germany, Japan, and the United States—an international economy based on free trade and British power became less and less viable. Eventually this shift in the locus of industrial and military power led to the collapse of the system in World War I. Following the interwar period, a liberal international economy was revived through the exercise of power by the world's newly emergent dominant economy—the United States.

Accordingly, the regime of free investment and the preeminence of the multinational corporation in the contemporary world have reflected the economic and political interests of the United States. The multinational corporation has prospered because it has been dependent on the power of, and consistent with the political interests of, the United States. This is not to deny the analyses of economists who argue that the multinational corporation is a response to contemporary technological and economic developments. The argument is rather that these economic and technological factors have been able to exercise their profound effects because the United States—sometimes with the cooperation of other states and sometimes over their opposition—has created the necessary political framework. As former Secretary of the Treasury Henry Fowler stated several years ago, "it is . . . impossible to overestimate the extent to which the efforts and opportunities for American firms abroad depend upon the vast presence and influence and prestige that America holds in the world."[33]

By the mid-1970s, however, the international distribution of power and the world economy resting on it were far different from what they had been when Fowler's words were spoken. The rise of foreign economic competitors, America's growing dependence upon foreign sources of energy and other resources, and the expansion of Soviet military capabilities have greatly diminished America's presence and influence in the world. One must ask if, as a consequence, the reign of the American multinationals over international economic affairs will continue into the future.

In summary, although nation-states, as mercantilists suggest, do seek to control economic and technological forces and channel them to their own advantage, this is impossible over the long run. The spread of economic growth and industrialization cannot be prevented. In time the diffusion of industry and technology undermines the position of the dominant power. As both liberals and Marxists have emphasized, the evolution of economic relations profoundly influences the nature of the international political system. The relationship between economics and politics is a reciprocal one.

Although economic and accompanying political change may well be inevitable, it is not inevitable that the process of economic development and technological advance will produce an increasingly integrated world society. In the 1930s, Eugene Staley posed the issue:

> A conflict rages between technology and politics. Economics, so closely linked to both, has become the major battlefield. Stability and peace will reign in the world economy only when, somehow, the forces on the side of technology and the forces on the side of politics have once more become accommodated to each other.[34]

Staley believed, as do many present-day writers, that politics and technology must ultimately adjust to one another. But he differed with contemporary writers with regard to the inevitability with which politics would adjust to technology. Reflecting the intense economic nationalism of the period in which he wrote, Staley pointed out that the adjustment may very well be the other way around. As he reminds us, in his own time and in earlier periods economics has had to adjust to political realities: "In the 'Dark Ages' following the collapse of the Roman Empire, technology adjusted itself to politics. The magnificent Roman roads fell into disrepair, the baths and aqueducts and amphitheatres and villas into ruins. Society lapsed back to localism in production and distribution, forgot much of the learning and the technology and the governmental systems of earlier days."[35]

## CONCLUSION

The purpose of this chapter has been to set forth the analytical framework that will be employed in this study. This framework is a statement of what I mean by "political economy." In its eclecticism it has drawn upon, while differing from, the three prevailing perspectives of political economy. It has incorporated their respective strengths and has attempted to overcome their weaknesses. In brief, political economy in this study means the reciprocal and dynamic interaction in international relations of the pursuit of wealth and the pursuit of power. In the short run, the distribution of power and the nature of the political system are major determinants of the framework within which wealth is produced and distributed. In the long run, however, shifts in economic efficiency and in the location of economic activity tend to undermine and transform the existing political system. This political transformation in turn gives rise to changes in economic relations that reflect the interests of the politically ascendant state in the system.

## NOTES

1. Kari Levitt, "The Hinterland Economy," *Canadian Forum* 50 (July–August 1970): p. 163.
2. George W. Ball, "The Promise of the Multinational Corporation," *Fortune*, June 1, 1967, p. 80.
3. Sidney Rolfe, "Updating Adam Smith," *Interplay* (November 1968): p. 15.
4. Charles Kindleberger, *Power and Money: The Economics of International Politics and the Politics of International Economics* (New York: Basic Books, 1970), p. 5.
5. Robert Keohane and Joseph Nye, "World Politics and the International Economic System," in C. Fred Bergsten, ed., *The Future of the International Economic Order: An Agenda for Research* (Lexington, Mass.: D.C. Heath, 1973), p. 116.
6. Ibid.
7. Ibid., p. 117.
8. Paul Samuelson, *Economics: An Introductory Analysis* (New York: McGraw-Hill, 1967), p. 5.
9. Harold Lasswell and Abraham Kaplan, *Power and Society: A Framework for Political Inquiry* (New Haven, Conn.: Yale University Press, 1950), p. 75.
10. Hans Morgenthau, *Politics Among Nations* (New York: Alfred A. Knopf), p. 26. For a more complex but essentially identical view, see Robert Dahl, *Modern Political Analysis* (Englewood Cliffs, N.J.: Prentice-Hall, 1963).

11. Kindleberger, *Power and Money*, p. 227.

12. For Johnson's critique of economic nationalism, see Harry Johnson, ed., *Economic Nationalism in Old and New States* (Chicago: University of Chicago Press, 1967).

13. Adam Smith, *The Wealth of Nations* (New York: Modern Library, 1937).

14. J. B. Condliffe, *The Commerce of Nations* (New York: W. W. Norton, 1950), p. 136.

15. Amitai Etzioni, "The Dialectics of Supernational Unification" in *International Political Communities* (New York: Doubleday, 1966), p. 147.

16. The relevant sections appear in Ernst Wangerman, ed., *The Role of Force in History: A Study of Bismarck's Policy of Blood and Iron*, trans. Jack Cohen (New York: International Publishers, 1968).

17. Ibid., p. 12.

18. Ibid., p. 13.

19. Ibid., p. 14.

20. Gustav Stopler, *The German Economy* (New York: Harcourt, Brace and World, 1967), p. 11.

21. Jacob Viner, *The Customs Union Issue*, Studies in the Administration of International Law and Organization, No. 10 (New York: Carnegie Endowment for International Peace, 1950), pp. 98–99.

22. Ibid., p. 101.

23. Richard Cooper, "Eurodollars, Reserve Dollars, and Asymmetrics in the International Monetary System," *Journal of International Economics* 2 (September 1972): pp. 325–44.

24. Oskar Morgenstern, "Thirteen Critical Points in Contemporary Economic Theory: An Interpretation," *Journal of Economic Literature* 10 (December 1972): p. 1169.

25. Quoted in F. H. Hinsley, *Power and the Pursuit of Peace* (Cambridge: Cambridge University Press, 1963), pp. 50–51.

26. Jacob Viner, "Power versus Plenty as Objectives of Foreign Policy in the Seventeenth and Eighteenth Centuries," in *The Long View and the Short: Studies in Economic Theory and Practice* (Glencoe, Ill.: The Free Press, 1958), p. 286.

27. R. G. Hawtrey, *Economic Aspects of Sovereignty* (London: Longmans, Green, 1952), p. 120.

28. Albert Hirshman, *National Power and the Structure of Foreign Trade* (Berkeley: University of California Press, 1969), p. 16.

29. John A. Hobson, *Imperialism: A Study* (1902; 3rd ed., rev., London: G. Allen and Unwin, 1938), p. 57.

30. Charles Kindleberger, *The World in Depression 1929–1939* (Berkeley: University of California Press, 1973), p. 293.

31. François Perroux, "The Domination Effect and Modern Economic Theory," in *Power in Economics*, ed. K. W. Rothschild (London: Penguin, 1971), p. 67.

32. E. H. Carr, *The Twenty Years' Crisis, 1919–1939* (New York: Macmillan, 1951), p. 117.

33. Quoted in Kari Levitt, *Silent Surrender: The American Economic Empire in Canada* (New York: Liveright Press, 1970), p. 100.

34. Eugene Staley, *World Economy in Transition: Technology vs. Politics, Laissez Faire vs. Planning, Power vs. Welfare* (New York: Council on Foreign Relations [under the auspices of the American Coordinating Committee for International Studies], 1939), pp. 51–52.

35. Ibid., p. 52.

# Hegemony in the World Political Economy

## ROBERT O. KEOHANE

It is common today for troubled supporters of liberal capitalism to look back with nostalgia on British preponderance in the nineteenth century and American dominance after World War II. Those eras are imagined to be simpler ones in which a single power, possessing superiority of economic and military resources, implemented a plan for international order based on its interests and its vision of the world. As Robert Gilpin has expressed it, "the *Pax Britannica* and *Pax Americana*, like the *Pax Romana*, ensured an international system of relative peace and security. Great Britain and the United States created and enforced the rules of a liberal international economic order."

Underlying this statement is one of the two central propositions of the theory of hegemonic stability:[1] that order in world politics is typically created by a single dominant power. Since regimes constitute elements of an international order, this implies that the formation of international regimes normally depends on hegemony. The other major tenet of the theory of hegemonic stability is that the maintenance of order requires continued hegemony. As Charles P. Kindleberger has said, "For the world economy to be stabilized, there has to be a stabilizer, one stabilizer."[2] This implies that cooperation, . . . [the] mutual adjustment of state policies to one another, also depends on the perpetuation of hegemony.

I discuss hegemony before elaborating my definitions of cooperation and regimes because my emphasis on how international institutions such as regimes facilitate cooperation only makes sense if cooperation and discord are not determined simply by interests and power. In this chapter I argue that a deterministic version of the theory of hegemonic stability, relying only on the realist concepts of interests and power, is indeed incorrect. There is some validity in a modest version of the first proposition of the theory of hegemonic stability—that hegemony can facilitate a certain type of cooperation—but there is little reason to believe that hegemony is either a necessary or a sufficient condition for the emergence of cooperative relationships. Furthermore, and even more important for the argument presented here, the second major proposition of the theory is erroneous: Cooperation does not necessarily require the existence of a hegemonic leader after international regimes have been established. Post-hegemonic cooperation is also possible. . . .

The task of the present chapter is to explore in a preliminary way the value and limitations of the concept of hegemony for the study of cooperation. The first section analyzes the claims of the theory of hegemonic stability; the second section briefly addresses the relationship between military power and hegemony in the world political economy; and the final section seeks to enrich our understanding of the concept by considering Marxian insights. Many Marxian interpretations of hegemony turn out to bear an uncanny resemblance to Realist ideas, using different language to make similar points. Antonio Gramsci's conception of ideological hegemony, however, does provide an insightful supplement to purely materialist arguments, whether Realist or Marxist.

## EVALUATING THE THEORY OF HEGEMONIC STABILITY

The theory of hegemonic stability, as applied to the world political economy, defines hegemony as preponderance of material resources. Four sets of resources are especially important. Hegemonic powers must have control over raw materials, control over sources of capital, control over markets, and competitive advantages in the production of highly valued goods.

The importance of controlling sources of raw materials has provided a traditional justification for territorial expansion and imperialism, as well as for the extension of informal influence. . . . [S]hifts in the locus of control over oil affected the power of states and the evolution of international regimes. Guaranteed access to capital, though less obvious as a source of power, may be equally important. Countries with well-functioning capital markets can borrow cheaply and may be able to provide credit to friends or even deny it to adversaries. Holland derived political and economic power from the quality of its capital markets in the seventeenth century; Britain did so in the eighteenth and nineteenth centuries; and the United States has similarly benefited during the last fifty years.

Potential power may also be derived from the size of one's market for imports. The threat to cut off a particular state's access to one's own market, while allowing other countries continued access, is a "potent and historically relevant weapon of economic 'power'."[3] Conversely, the offer to open up one's own huge market to other exporters, in return for concessions or deference, can be an effective means of influence. The bigger one's own market, and the greater the government's discretion in opening it up or closing it off, the greater one's potential economic power.

The final dimension of economic preponderance is competitive superiority in the production of goods. Immanuel Wallerstein has defined hegemony in economic terms as "a situation wherein the products of a given core state are produced so efficiently that they are by and large competitive even in other core states, and therefore the given core state will be the primary beneficiary of a maximally free world market."[4] As a definition of economic preponderance this is interesting but poorly worked out, since under conditions of overall balance of payments equilibrium each unit—even the poorest and least developed—will have some comparative advantage. The fact that in 1960 the United States had a trade deficit in textiles and apparel and in basic manufactured goods (established products not, on the whole, involving the use of complex or new technology) did not indicate that it had lost predominant economic status.[5] Indeed, one should expect the economically preponderant state to import products that are labor-intensive or that are produced with well-known production techniques. Competitive advantage does not mean that the leading economy exports *everything*, but that it produces and exports the most profitable products and those that will provide the basis for producing even more advanced goods and services in the future. In general, this ability will be based on the technological superiority of the leading country, although it may also rest on its political control over valuable resources yielding significant rents.

To be considered hegemonic in the world political economy, therefore, a country must have access to crucial raw materials, control major sources of capital, maintain a large market for imports, and hold comparative advantages in goods with high value added, yielding relatively high wages and profits. It must also be stronger, on these dimensions taken as a whole, than any other country. The theory of hegemonic stability predicts that the more one such power dominates the world political economy, the more cooperative will interstate relations be. This is a parsimonious theory that relies on . . . a "basic force model," in which outcomes reflect the tangible capabilities of actors.

Yet, like many such basic force models, this crude theory of hegemonic stability makes imperfect predictions. In the twentieth century it correctly anticipates the relative cooperativeness of the twenty years after World War II. It is at least partially mistaken, however, about trends of cooperation when hegemony erodes. Between 1900 and 1913 a decline in British power coincided with a decrease rather than an increase in conflict over commercial issues. . . . [R]ecent changes in international regimes can only partially be attributed to a decline in American power. How to interpret the prevalence of discord in the interwar years is difficult, since it is not clear whether any country was hegemonic in material terms during those two decades. The United States, though considerably ahead in productivity, did not replace Britain as the most important financial center and lagged behind in volume of trade. Although American domestic oil production was more than sufficient for domestic needs during these years, Britain still controlled the bulk of major Middle Eastern oil fields. Nevertheless, what prevented American leadership of a cooperative world political economy in these years was less lack of economic resources than an absence of political willingness to make and enforce rules for the system. Britain, despite its efforts, was too weak to do so effectively. The crucial factor in producing discord lay in American politics, not in the material factors to which the theory points.

Unlike the crude basic force model, a refined version of hegemonic stability theory does not assert an automatic link between power and leadership. Hegemony is defined as a situation in which "one state is powerful enough to maintain the essential rules governing interstate relations, and willing to do so."[6] This interpretive framework retains an emphasis on power but looks more seriously than the crude power theory at the internal characteristics of the strong state. It does not assume that strength automatically creates incentives to project one's power abroad. Domestic attitudes, political structures, and decision making processes are also important.

This argument's reliance on state decisions as well as power capabilities puts it into the category of what March calls "force activation models." Decisions to exercise leadership are necessary to "activate" the posited relationship between power capabilities and outcomes. Force activation models are essentially *post hoc* rather than *a priori*, since one can always "save" such a theory after the fact by thinking of reasons why an actor would not have wanted to use all of its available potential power. In effect, this modification of the theory declares that states with preponderant resources will be hegemonic except when they decide not to commit the necessary effort to the tasks of leadership, yet it does not tell us what will determine the latter decision. As a causal theory this is not very helpful, since whether a given configuration of power will lead the potential hegemon to maintain a set of rules remains indeterminate unless we know a great deal about its domestic politics.

Only the cruder theory generates predictions. When I refer without qualification to the theory of hegemonic stability, therefore, I will be referring to this basic force model. We have seen that the most striking contention of this theory—that hegemony is both a necessary and a sufficient condition for cooperation—is not strongly supported by the experience of this century. Taking a longer period of about 150 years, the record remains ambiguous. International economic relations were relatively cooperative both in the era of British hegemony during the mid-to-late nineteenth century and in the two decades of American dominance after World War II. But only in the second of these periods was there a trend toward the predicted disruption of established rules and increased discord. And a closer examination of the British experience casts doubt on the causal role of British hegemony in producing cooperation in the nineteenth century.

Both Britain in the nineteenth century and the United States in the twentieth met the material prerequisites for hegemony better than any other states since the Industrial Revolution. In 1880 Britain was the financial center of the world, and it controlled extensive raw materials, both in its formal empire and through investments in areas not part of the Imperial domain. It had the highest per capita income in the world and approximately double the share of world trade and investment of its nearest competitor, France. Only in the aggregate size of its economy had it already fallen behind the United States.[7] Britain's share of world trade gradually declined during the next sixty years, but in 1938 it was still the world's largest trader, with 14 percent of the world total. In the nineteenth century Britain's relative labor productivity was the highest in the world, although it declined rather precipitously thereafter. As Table 1 shows, Britain in the late nineteenth century and the United States after World War II were roughly comparable in their proportions of world trade, although until 1970 or so the United States had maintained much higher levels of relative productivity than Britain had done three-quarters of a century earlier.

Yet, despite Britain's material strength, it did not always enforce its preferred rules. Britain certainly did maintain freedom of the seas. But it did not induce major continental powers, after the 1870s, to retain liberal trade policies. A recent investigation of the subject has concluded that British efforts to make and enforce rules were less extensive and less successful than hegemonic stability theory would lead us to believe they were.[8]

TABLE 1  ■  MATERIAL RESOURCES OF BRITAIN AND THE UNITED STATES AS HEGEMONS: PROPORTIONS OF WORLD TRADE AND RELATIVE LABOR PRODUCTIVITY

|  | Proportion of world trade | Relative labor productivity* |
|---|---|---|
| Britain, 1870 | 24.0 | 1.63 |
| Britain, 1890 | 18.5 | 1.45 |
| Britain, 1913 | 14.1 | 1.15 |
| Britain, 1938 | 14.0 | .92 |
| United States, 1950 | 18.4 | 2.77 |
| United States, 1960 | 15.3 | 2.28 |
| United States, 1970 | 14.4 | 1.72 |
| United States, 1977 | 13.4 | 1.45 |

* As compared with the average rate of productivity in the other members of the world economy.
*Source:* David A. Lake, "International Economic Structures and American Foreign Economic Policy, 1887–1934," *World Politics,* vol. 35, no. 4 (July 1983), table 1 (p. 525) and table 3 (p. 541).

Attempts by the United States after World War II to make and enforce rules for the world political economy were much more effective than Britain's had ever been. America after 1945 did not merely replicate earlier British experience; on the contrary, the differences between Britain's "hegemony" in the nineteenth century and America's after World War II were profound. As we have seen, Britain had never been as superior in productivity to the rest of the world as the United States was after 1945. Nor was the United States ever as dependent on foreign trade and investment as Britain. Equally important, America's economic partners—over whom its hegemony was exercised, since America's ability to make the rules hardly extended to the socialist camp—were also its military allies; but Britain's chief trading partners had been its major military and political rivals. In addition, one reason for Britain's relative ineffectiveness in maintaining a free trade regime is that it had never made extensive use of the principle of reciprocity in trade.[9] It thus had sacrificed potential leverage over other countries that preferred to retain their own restrictions while Britain practiced free trade. The policies of these states might well have been altered had they been confronted with a choice between a closed British market for their exports on the one hand and mutual lowering of barriers on the other. Finally, Britain had an empire to which it could retreat, by selling less advanced goods to its colonies rather than competing in more open markets. American hegemony, rather than being one more instance of a general phenomenon, was essentially unique in the scope and efficacy of the instruments at the disposal of a hegemonic state and in the degree of success attained.

That the theory of hegemonic stability is supported by only one or at most two cases casts doubt on its general validity. Even major proponents of the theory refrain from making such claims. In an article published in 1981, Kindleberger seemed to entertain the possibility that two or more countries might "take on the task of providing leadership together, thus adding to legitimacy, sharing the burdens, and reducing the danger that leadership is regarded cynically as a cloak for domination and exploitation."[10] In *War and Change in World Politics,* Gilpin promulgated what appeared to be a highly deterministic conception of hegemonic cycles: "the conclusion of one hegemonic war is the beginning of another cycle of growth, expansion, and eventual decline."[11] Yet he denied that his view was deterministic, and he asserted that "states can learn to be more enlightened in their definitions of their interests and can learn to be more cooperative in their behavior."[12] Despite the erosion of hegemony, "there are reasons for believing that the present disequilibrium in the international system can be resolved without resort to hegemonic war."[13]

The empirical evidence for the general validity of hegemonic stability theory is weak, and even its chief adherents have doubts about it. In addition, the logical underpinnings of the theory are suspect. Kindleberger's strong claim for the necessity of a single leader rested on the theory of collective goods. He argued that "the danger we face is not too much power in the international economy, but too little, not an excess of domination, but a superfluity of would-be free riders, unwilling to mind the store, and waiting for a storekeeper to appear."[14] . . . [S]ome of the "goods" produced by hegemonic leadership are not genuinely collective in character, although the implications of this fact are not necessarily as damaging to the theory as might be imagined at first. More critical is the fact that in international economic systems a few actors typically control a preponderance of resources. This point is especially telling, since the theory of collective goods does not properly imply that cooperation among a few countries should be impossible. Indeed, one of the original purposes of Olson's use of the theory was to show that in systems with only a few participants these actors "can provide themselves with collective goods without relying on any positive inducements apart from the good itself."[15] Logically, hegemony should not be a necessary condition for the emergence of cooperation in an oligopolistic system.

The theory of hegemonic stability is thus suggestive but by no means definitive. Concentrated power alone is not sufficient to create a stable international economic order in which cooperation flourishes, and the argument that hegemony is necessary for cooperation is both theoretically and empirically weak. If hegemony is redefined as the ability and willingness of a single state to make and enforce rules, furthermore, the claim that hegemony is sufficient for cooperation becomes virtually tautological.

The crude theory of hegemonic stability establishes a useful, if somewhat simplistic, starting-point for an analysis of changes in international cooperation and discord. Its refined version raises a looser but suggestive set of interpretive questions for the analysis of some eras in the history of the international political economy. Such an interpretive framework does not constitute an explanatory systemic theory, but it can help us think of hegemony in another way—less as a concept that helps to explain outcomes in terms of power than as a way of describing an international system in which leadership is exercised by a single state. Rather than being a component of a scientific generalization—that power is a necessary or sufficient condition for cooperation—the concept of hegemony, defined in terms of willingness as well as ability to lead, helps us think about the incentives facing the potential hegemon. Under what conditions, domestic and international, will such a country decide to invest in the construction of rules and institutions?

Concern for the incentives facing the hegemon should also alert us to the frequently neglected incentives facing other countries in the system. What calculus do they confront in considering whether to challenge or defer to a would-be leader? Thinking about the calculations of secondary powers raises the question of deference. Theories of hegemony should seek not only to analyze dominant powers' decisions to engage in rule-making and rule-enforcement, but also to explore why secondary states defer to the leadership of the hegemon. That is, they need to account for the legitimacy of hegemonic regimes and for the coexistence of cooperation, . . . with hegemony. We will see later that Gramsci's notion of "ideological hegemony" provides some valuable clues helping us understand how cooperation and hegemony fit together.

## MILITARY POWER AND HEGEMONY IN THE WORLD POLITICAL ECONOMY

Before taking up these themes, we need to clarify the relationship between this analysis of hegemony in the world political economy and the question of military power. A hegemonic state must possess enough military power to be able to protect the international political economy that it dominates from incursions by hostile adversaries. This is essential because economic issues, if they are crucial enough to basic national values, may become military-security issues as well. For instance, Japan attacked the United States in 1941 partly in response to the freezing of Japanese assets in the United States, which denied Japan "access to all the vitally needed supplies outside her own control, in particular her most crucial need, oil."[16] During and after World War II the United States used its military power to assure itself access to the petroleum of the Middle East; and at the end of 1974 Secretary of State Henry A. Kissinger warned that the United States might resort to military action if oil-exporting countries threatened "some actual strangulation of the industrialized world."[17]

Yet the hegemonic power need not be militarily dominant worldwide. Neither British nor American power ever extended so far. Britain was challenged militarily during the nineteenth century by France, Germany, and especially Russia; even at the height of its power after World War II the United States confronted a recalcitrant Soviet adversary and fought a war against China. The military conditions for economic hegemony are met if the economically preponderant country has sufficient military capabilities to prevent incursions by others that would deny it access to major areas of its economic activity.

The sources of hegemony therefore include sufficient military power to deter or rebuff attempts to capture and close off important areas of the world political economy. But in the contemporary world, at any rate, it is difficult for a hegemon to use military power directly to attain its economic policy objectives with its military partners and allies. Allies cannot be threatened with force without beginning to question the alliance; nor are threats to cease defending them unless they conform to the hegemon's economic rules very credible except in extraordinary circumstances. Many of the relationships within the hegemonic international political economy dominated by the United States after World War II approximated more closely the ideal type of "complex interdependence"—with multiple issues, multiple channels of contact among societies, and inefficacy of military force for most policy objectives—than the converse ideal type of realist theory.[18]

This does not mean that military force has become useless. It has certainly played an indirect role even in U.S. relations with its closest allies, since Germany and Japan could hardly ignore the fact that American military power shielded them from Soviet pressure. It has played a more overt role in the Middle East, where American military power has occasionally been directly employed and has always cast a shadow and where U.S. military aid has been conspicuous. Yet changes in relations of military power have not been the major factors affecting patterns of cooperation and discord among the advanced industrialized countries since the end of World War II. Only in the case of Middle Eastern oil have they been highly significant as forces contributing to changes in international economic regimes, and even in that case . . . shifts in economic interdependence, and therefore in economic power, were more important. Throughout the period between 1945 and 1983 the United States remained a far stronger military power than any of its allies and the only country capable of defending them from the Soviet Union or of intervening effectively against serious opposition in areas such as the Middle East. . . .

Some readers may wish to criticize this account by arguing that military power has been more important than claimed here. By considering military power only as a background condition for postwar American hegemony rather than as a variable, I invite such a debate. Any such critique, however, should keep in mind what I am trying to explain [here] . . . not the sources of hegemony (in domestic institutions, basic resources, and technological advances any more than in military power), but rather the effects of changes in hegemony on cooperation among the advanced industrialized countries. I seek to account for the impact of American dominance on the creation of international economic regimes and the effects of an erosion of that preponderant position on those regimes. Only if *these* problems—not other questions that might be interesting—could be understood better by exploring more deeply the impact of changes in relations of military power would this hypothetical critique be damaging to my argument.

## MARXIAN NOTIONS OF HEGEMONY

For Marxists, the fundamental forces affecting the world political economy are those of class struggle and uneven development. International history is dynamic and dialectical rather than cyclical. The maneuvers of states reflect the stages of capitalist development and the contradictions of that development. For a Marxist, it is futile to discuss hegemony, or the operation of international institutions, without understanding that they operate, in the contemporary world system, within a capitalist context shaped by the evolutionary patterns and functional requirements of capitalism. Determinists may call these requirements laws. Historicists may see the patterns as providing some clues into a rather open-ended process that is nevertheless affected profoundly by what has gone before: people making their own history, but not just as they please.

Any genuinely Marxian theory of world politics begins with an analysis of capitalism. According to Marxist doctrine, no smooth and progressive development of productive forces within the confines of capitalist relations of production can persist for long. Contradictions are bound to appear. It is likely that they will take the form of tendencies toward stagnation and decline in the rate of profit, but they may also be reflected in crises of legitimacy for the capitalist state, even in the absence of economic crises.[19] Any "crisis of hegemony" will necessarily be at the same time—and more fundamentally—a crisis of capitalism.

For Marxists, theories of hegemony are necessarily partial, since they do not explain changes in the contradictions facing capitalism. Nevertheless, Marxists have often used the concept of hegemony, implicitly defined simply as dominance, as a way of analyzing the surface manifestations of world politics under capitalism. For Marxists as well as mercantilists, wealth and power are complementary; each depends on the other. . . . [T]he analyses of the Marxist Fred Block and the Realist Robert Gilpin are quite similar: both emphasize the role of U.S. hegemony in creating order after the Second World War and the disturbing effects of the erosion of American power.

Immanuel Wallerstein's work also illustrates this point. He is at pains to stress that modern world history should be seen as the history of capitalism as a world system. Apart from "relatively minor accidents" resulting from geography, peculiarities of history, or luck, "it is the operations of the world-market forces which accentuate the differences, institutionalize them, and make them impossible to surmount over the long run."[20] Nevertheless, when considering particular epochs, Wallerstein emphasizes hegemony and the role of military force. Dutch economic hegemony in the seventeenth century was destroyed not by the operation of the world-market system or contradictions of capitalism, but by the force of British and French arms.[21]

The Marxian adoption of mercantilist categories raises analytical ambiguities having to do with the relationship between capitalism and the state. Marxists who adopt this approach have difficulty maintaining a class focus, since their unit of analysis shifts to the country, rather than the class, for purposes of explaining international events. This is a problem for both Block and Wallerstein, as it often appears that their embrace of state-centered analysis has relegated the concept of class to the shadowy background of political economy. The puzzle of the relationship between the state and capitalism is also reflected in the old debate between Lenin and Kautsky about "ultra-imperialism."[22] Lenin claimed that contradictions among the capitalist powers were fundamental and could not be resolved, against Kautsky's view that capitalism could go through a phase in which capitalist states could maintain unity for a considerable period of time.

The successful operation of American hegemony for over a quarter-century after the end of World War II supports Kautsky's forecast that ultra-imperialism could be stable and contradicts Lenin's thesis that capitalism made inter-imperialist war inevitable. It does not, however, resolve the issue of whether ultra-imperialism could be maintained in the absence of hegemony. An analysis of the contemporary situation in Marxian terminology would hold that one form of ultra-imperialism—American hegemony—is now breaking down, leading to increased disorder, and that the issue at present is "whether all this will ultimately result in a new capitalist world order, in a revolutionary reconstitution of world society, or in the common ruin of the contending classes and nations."[23] The issue from a Marxian standpoint is whether ultra-imperialism could be revived by new efforts at inter-capitalist collaboration or, on the contrary, whether fundamental contradictions in capitalism or in the coexistence of capitalism with the state system prevent any such recovery.

The key question of this book—how international cooperation can be maintained among the advanced capitalist states in the absence of American hegemony—poses essentially the same problem. The view taken here is similar to that of Kautsky and his followers, although the terminology is different. My contention is that the common interests of the leading capitalist states, bolstered by the effects of existing international regimes (mostly created during a period of American hegemony), are strong enough to make sustained cooperation possible, though not inevitable. One need not go so far as . . . the "internationalization of capital" to understand the strong interests that capitalists have in maintaining some cooperation in the midst of rivalry. Uneven development in the context of a state system maintains rivalry and ensures that cooperation will be incomplete and fragile . . . but it does not imply that the struggle must become violent or that compromises that benefit all sides are impossible.

Despite the similarities between my concerns and those of many Marxists, I do not adopt their categories in this study. Marxian explications of the "laws of capitalism" are not sufficiently well established that they can be relied upon for inferences about relations among states in the world political economy or for the analysis of future international cooperation. Insofar as there are fundamental contradictions in capitalism, they will surely have great impact on future international cooperation; but the existence and nature of these contradictions seem too murky to justify incorporating them into my analytical framework.

As this discussion indicates, Marxian insights into international hegemony derive in part from combining Realist conceptions of hegemony as dominance with arguments about the contradictions of capitalism. But this is not the only Marxian contribution to the debate. In the thought of Antonio Gramsci and his followers, hegemony is distinguished from sheer dominance. As Robert W. Cox has expressed it:

> Antonio Gramsci used the concept of hegemony to express a unity between objective material forces and ethico-political ideas—in Marxian terms, a unity of structure and superstructure—in which power based on dominance over production is rationalized through an ideology incorporating compromise or consensus between dominant and subordinate groups. A hegemonial structure of world order is one in which power takes a primarily consensual form, as distinguished from a non-hegemonic order in which there are manifestly rival powers and no power has been able to establish the legitimacy of its dominance.[24]

The value of this conception of hegemony is that it helps us understand the willingness of the partners of a hegemon to defer to hegemonial leadership. Hegemons require deference to enable them to construct a structure of world capitalist order. It is too expensive, and perhaps self-defeating, to achieve this by force; after all, the key distinction between hegemony and imperialism is that a hegemon, unlike an empire, does not dominate societies through a cumbersome political superstructure, but rather supervises the relationships between politically independent societies through a combination of hierarchies of control and the operation of markets.[25] Hegemony rests on the subjective awareness by elites in secondary states that they are benefiting, as well as on the willingness of the hegemon itself to sacrifice tangible short-term benefits for intangible long-term gains.

Valuable as the conception of ideological hegemony is in helping us understand deference, it should be used with some caution. First, we should not assume that leaders of secondary states are necessarily the victims of "false consciousness" when they accept the hegemonic ideology, or that they constitute a small, parasitical elite that betrays the interests of the nation to its own selfish ends. It is useful to remind ourselves, as Robert Gilpin has, that during both the *Pax Britannica* and the *Pax Americana* countries other than the hegemon prospered, and that indeed many of them grew faster than the hegemon itself.[26] Under some conditions—not necessarily all—it may be not only in the self-interest of peripheral elites, but conducive to the economic growth of their countries, for them to defer to the hegemon.[27]

We may also be permitted to doubt that ideological hegemony is as enduring internationally as it is domestically. The powerful ideology of nationalism is not available for the hegemon, outside of its own country, but rather for its enemies. Opponents of hegemony can often make nationalism the weapon of the weak and may also seek to invent cosmopolitan ideologies that delegitimize hegemony, such as the current ideology of a New International Economic Order, instead of going along with legitimating ones. Thus the potential for challenges to hegemonic ideology always exists.

## CONCLUSIONS

Claims for the general validity of the theory of hegemonic stability are often exaggerated. The dominance of a single great power may contribute to order in world politics, in particular circumstances, but it is not a sufficient condition and there is little reason to believe that it is necessary. But Realist and Marxian arguments about hegemony both generate some important insights.

Hegemony is related in complex ways to cooperation and to institutions such as international regimes. Successful hegemonic leadership itself depends on a certain form of asymmetrical cooperation. The hegemon plays a distinctive role, providing its partners with leadership in return for deference; but, unlike an imperial power, it cannot make and enforce rules without a certain degree of consent from other sovereign states. As the interwar experience illustrates, material predominance alone does not guarantee either stability or effective leadership. Indeed, the hegemon may have to invest resources in institutions in order to ensure that its preferred rules will guide the behavior of other countries.

Cooperation may be fostered by hegemony, and hegemons require cooperation to make and enforce rules. Hegemony and cooperation are not alternatives; on the contrary, they are often found in symbiotic relationships with one another. To analyze the relationships between hegemony and cooperation, we need a conception of cooperation that is somewhat tart rather than syrupy-sweet. It must take into account the facts that coercion is always possible in world politics and that conflicts of interest never vanish even when there are important shared interests. . . . [C]ooperation should be defined not as the absence of conflict—which is always at least a potentially important element of international relations—but as a process that involves the use of discord to stimulate mutual adjustment.

## NOTES

1. Robert O. Keohane, "The Theory of Hegemonic Stability and Changes in International Economic Regimes, 1967–1977," in Ole Holsti et al., *Change in the International System* (Boulder, Colo.: Westview Press, 1980), pp. 131–162.
2. Charles P. Kindleberger, *The World in Depression, 1929–1939* (Berkeley: University of California Press, 1973), p. 305.
3. Timothy J. McKeown, "Hegemonic Stability Theory and Nineteenth Century Tariff Levels in Europe," *International Organization*, Vol. 37, No. 1 (Winter 1980), p. 78.
4. Immanuel Wallerstein, *The Modern World-System II: Mercantilism and the Consolidation of the European World-Economy. 1600–1750* (New York: Academic Press, 1980), p. 38.
5. Stephen D. Krasner, "United States Commercial and Monetary Policy: Unravelling the Paradox of External Strength and Internal Weakness," in Peter J. Katzenstein, ed., *Between Power and Plenty: Foreign Economic Policies of Advanced Industrial States* (Madison: University of Wisconsin Press, 1978), pp. 68–69.
6. Robert O. Keohane and Joseph S. Nye, *Power and Interdependence: World Politics in Transition* (Boston: Little, Brown), p. 44.
7. Stephen D. Krasner, "State Power and the Structure of International Trade," *World Politics*, Vol. 28, No. 3 (April 1976), p. 333.
8. McKeown, p. 88.
9. Ibid.
10. Charles P. Kindleberger, "Dominance and Leadership in the International Economy," *International Studies Quarterly*, Vol. 25, No. 3 (June 1981), p. 252.
11. Robert Gilpin, *War and Change in World Politics* (Cambridge: Cambridge University Press, 1981), p. 210.
12. Ibid., p. 227.
13. Ibid., p. 234.
14. Ibid., p. 253.
15. Mancur Olson, quoted in McKeown, p. 79.
16. Paul Schroeder, *The Axis Alliance and Japanese-American Relations* (Ithaca, N.Y.: Cornell University Press, 1958), p. 53.
17. Seyom Brown, *The Faces of Power: Constancy and Change in United States Foreign Policy from Truman to Reagan* (New York: Columbia University Press, 1983), p. 428.
18. Keohane and Nye, chap. 2.
19. Jurgen Haberman, *Legitimation Crisis* (London: Heinemann, 1976).
20. Immanuel Wallerstein, *The Capitalist World Economy* (Cambridge: Cambridge University Press, 1979), p. 21.
21. Wallerstein, *The Modern World-System II*, pp. 38–39.

22. V. I. Lenin, *Imperialism: The Highest Stage of Capitalism* (New York: International Publishers, 1939), pp. 93–94.

23. Giovanni Arrighi, "A Crisis of Hegemony," in Samir Amin, Giovanni Arrighi, Andre Gunder Frank, and Immanuel Wallerstein, *Dynamics of Global Crisis* (New York: Monthly Review Press, 1982), p. 108.

24. Robert W. Cox, "Social Forces, States, and World Orders: Beyond International Relations Theory," *Journal of International Studies, Millennium*, vol. 10, no. 2 (Summer 1981), p. 153, note 27.

25. Immanuel Wallerstein, *The Modern World System: Capitalist Agriculture and the Origins of the European World-Economy in the Sixteenth Century* (New York: Academic Press, 1974), pp. 15–17.

26. Robert Gilpin, pp. 175–185.

27. This is not to say that hegemony in general benefits small or weak countries. There certainly is no assurance that this will be the case. Hegemons may prevent middle-sized states from exploiting small ones and may construct a structure of order conducive to world economic growth; but they may also exploit smaller states economically or distort their patterns of autonomous development through economic, political, or military intervention. The issue of whether hegemony helps poor countries cannot be answered unconditionally, because too many other factors intervene. Until a more complex and sophisticated theory of the relationships among hegemony, other factors, and welfare is developed, it remains an empirically open question.

# The Great Divide in the Global Village

## BRUCE R. SCOTT

## INCOMES ARE DIVERGING

Mainstream economic thought promises that globalization will lead to a widespread improvement in average incomes. Firms will reap increased economies of scale in a larger market, and incomes will converge as poor countries grow more rapidly than rich ones. In this "win-win" perspective, the importance of nation-states fades as the "global village" grows and market integration and prosperity take hold.

But the evidence paints a different picture. Average incomes have indeed been growing, but so has the income gap between rich and poor countries. Both trends have been evident for more than 200 years, but improved global communications have led to an increased awareness among the poor of income inequalities and heightened the pressure to emigrate to richer countries. In response, the industrialized nations have erected higher barriers against immigration, making the world economy seem more like a gated community than a global village. And although international markets for goods and capital have opened up since World War II and multilateral organizations now articulate rules and monitor the world economy, economic inequality among countries continues to increase. Some two billion people earn less than $2 per day.

At first glance, there are two causes of this divergence between economic theory and reality. First, the rich countries insist on barriers to immigration and agricultural imports. Second, most poor nations have been unable to attract much foreign capital due to their own government failings. These two issues are fundamentally linked: by forcing poor people to remain in badly governed states, immigration barriers deny those most in need the opportunity to "move up" by "moving out." In turn, that immobility eliminates a potential source of pressure on ineffective governments, thus facilitating their survival.

Since the rich countries are unlikely to lower their agricultural and immigration barriers significantly, they must recognize that politics is a key cause of economic inequality. And since most developing countries receive little foreign investment, the wealthy nations must also acknowledge that the "Washington consensus," which assumes that free markets will bring about economic convergence, is mistaken. If they at least admit these realities, they will abandon the notion that their own particular

Bruce R. Scott, "The Great Divide in the Global Village." Reprinted by permission of *Foreign Affairs*, Vol. 80, No. 1 (January/February 2001), pp. 160–177. Copyright 2001 by the Council on Foreign Relations, Inc.

strategies are the best for all countries. In turn, they should allow poorer countries considerable freedom to tailor development strategies to their own circumstances. In this more pragmatic view, the role of the state becomes pivotal.

Why have economists and policymakers not come to these conclusions sooner? Since the barriers erected by rich countries are seen as vital to political stability, leaders of those countries find it convenient to overlook them and focus instead on the part of the global economy that has been liberalized. The rich countries' political power in multilateral organizations makes it difficult for developing nations to challenge this self-serving world-view. And standard academic solutions may do as much harm as good, given their focus on economic stability and growth rather than on the institutions that underpin markets. Economic theory has ignored the political issues at stake in modernizing institutions, incorrectly assuming that market-based prices can allocate resources appropriately.

The fiasco of reform in Russia has forced a belated reappraisal of this blind trust in markets. Many observers now admit that the transition economies needed appropriate property rights and an effective state to enforce those rights as much as they needed the liberalization of prices. Indeed, liberalization without property rights turned out to be the path to gangsterism, not capitalism. China, with a more effective state, achieved much greater success in its transition than did Russia, even though Beijing proceeded much more slowly with liberalization and privatization.

Economic development requires the transformation of institutions as well as the freeing of prices, which in turn requires political and social modernization as well as economic reform. The state plays a key role in this process; without it, developmental strategies have little hope of succeeding. The creation of effective states in the developing world will not be driven by familiar market forces, even if pressures from capital markets can force fiscal and monetary discipline. And in a world still governed by "states rights," real progress in achieving accountable governments will require reforms beyond the mandates of multilateral institutions.

## GO WITH THE FLOW

In theory, globalization provides an opportunity to raise incomes through increased specialization and trade. This opportunity is conditioned by the size of the markets in question, which in turn depends on geography, transportation costs, communication networks, and the institutions that underpin markets. Free trade increases both the size of the market and the pressure to improve economic performance. Those who are most competitive take advantage of the enhanced market opportunities to survive and prosper.

Neoclassical economic theory predicts that poor countries should grow faster than rich ones in a free global market. Capital from rich nations in search of cheaper labor should flow to poorer economies, and labor should migrate from low-income areas toward those with higher wages. As a result, labor and capital costs—and eventually income—in rich and poor areas should eventually converge.

The U.S. economy demonstrates how this theory can work in a free market with the appropriate institutions. Since the 1880s, a remarkable convergence of incomes among the country's regions has occurred. The European Union has witnessed a similar phenomenon, with the exceptions of Greece and Italy's southern half, the *Mezzogiorno*. What is important, however, is that both America and the EU enjoy labor and capital mobility as well as free internal trade.

But the rest of the world does not fit this pattern. The most recent *World Development Report* shows that real per capita incomes for the richest one-third of countries rose by an annual 1.9 percent between 1970 and 1995, whereas the middle third went up by only 0.7 percent and the bottom third showed no increase at all. In the Western industrial nations and Japan alone, average real incomes have been rising about 2.5 percent annually since 1950—a fact that further accentuates the divergence of global income. These rich countries account for about 60 percent of world GDP but only 15 percent of world population.

Why is it that the poor countries continue to fall further behind? One key reason is that most rich countries have largely excluded the international flow of labor into their markets since the interwar period. As a result, low-skilled labor is not free to flow across international boundaries in search of more lucrative jobs. From an American or European perspective, immigration appears to have risen in recent years, even approaching its previous peak of a century ago in the United States. Although true, this comparison misses the central point. Billions of poor people could improve their standard of living by migrating to rich countries. But in 1997, the United States allowed in only 737,000 immigrants from developing nations, while Europe admitted about 665,000. Taken together, these flows are only 0.04 percent of all potential immigrants.

The point is not that the rich countries should permit unfettered immigration. A huge influx of cheap labor would no doubt be politically explosive; many European countries have already curtailed immigration from poor countries for fear of a severe backlash. But the more salient issue is that rich nations who laud liberalism and free markets are rejecting those very principles when they restrict freedom of movement. The same goes for agricultural imports. Both Europe and Japan have high trade barriers in agriculture, while the United States remains modestly protectionist.

Mainstream economic theory does provide a partial rationalization for rich-country protectionism: Immigration barriers need not be a major handicap to poor nations because they can be offset by capital flows from industrialized economies to developing ones. In other words, poor people need not demand space in rich countries because the rich will send their capital to help develop the poor countries. This was indeed the case before World War I, but it has not been so since World War II.

But the question of direct investment, which typically brings technologies and know-how as well as financial capital, is more complicated than theories would predict. The total stock of foreign direct investment did rise almost sevenfold from 1980 to 1997, increasing from 4 percent to 12 percent of world GDP during that period. But very little has gone to the poorest countries. In 1997, about 70 percent went from one rich country to another, 8 developing countries received about 20 percent, and the remainder was divided among more than 100 poor nations. According to the World Bank, the truly poor countries received less than 7 percent of the foreign direct investment to all developing countries in 1992–98. At the same time, the unrestricted opening of capital markets in developing countries gives larger firms from rich countries the opportunity for takeovers that are reminiscent of colonialism. It is not accidental that rich countries insist on open markets where they have an advantage and barriers in agriculture and immigration, where they would be at a disadvantage.

As for the Asian "tigers," their strong growth is due largely to their high savings rate, not foreign capital. Singapore stands out because it has enjoyed a great deal of foreign investment, but it has also achieved one of the highest domestic-savings rates in the world, and its government has been a leading influence on the use of these funds. China is now repeating this pattern, with a savings rate of almost 40 percent of GDP. This factor, along with domestic credit creation, has been its key motor of economic growth. China now holds more than $100 billion in low-yielding foreign-exchange reserves, the second largest reserves in the world.

In short, global markets offer opportunities for all, but opportunities do not guarantee results. Most poor countries have been unable to avail themselves of much foreign capital or to take advantage of increased market access. True, these countries have raised their trade ratios (exports plus imports) from about 35percent of their GDP in 1981 to almost 50 percent in 1997. But without the Asian tigers, developing-country exports remain less than 25 percent of world exports.

Part of the problem is that the traditional advantages of poor countries have been in primary commodities (agriculture and minerals), and these categories have shrunk from about 70 percent of world trade in 1900 to about 20 percent at the end of the century. Opportunities for growth in the world market have shifted from raw or semiprocessed commodities toward manufactured goods and services—and, within these categories, toward more knowledge-intensive segments. This trend obviously favors rich countries over poor ones, since most of the latter are still peripheral players in the knowledge economy. (Again, the Asian tigers are the exception. In 1995, they exported as much in high-technology goods as did France, Germany, Italy, and Britain combined—which together have three times the population of the tigers.)

## ONE COUNTRY, TWO SYSTEMS

Why is the performance of poor countries so uneven and out of sync with theoretical forecasts? Systemic barriers at home and abroad inhibit the economic potential of poorer nations, the most formidable of these obstacles being their own domestic political and administrative problems. These factors, of course, lie outside the framework of mainstream economic analysis. A useful analogy is the antebellum economy of the United States, which experienced a similar set of impediments.

Like today's "global village," the U.S. economy before the Civil War saw incomes diverge as the South fell behind the North. One reason for the Confederacy's secession and the resulting civil war was Southern recognition that it was falling behind in both economic and political power, while the richer and more populous North was attracting more immigrants. Half of the U.S. population lived in the North in 1780; by 1860, this share had climbed to two-thirds. In 1775, incomes in the five original

Southern states equaled those in New England, even though wealth (including slaves) was disproportionately concentrated in the South. By 1840, incomes in the northeast were about 50 percent higher than those in the original Southern states; the North's railroad mileage was about 40 percent greater (and manufacturing investment four times higher) than the South's. As the economist Robert Fogel has pointed out, the South was not poor—in 1860 it was richer than all European states except England—but Northern incomes were still much higher and increasing.

Why had Southern incomes diverged from those in the North under the same government, laws, and economy? Almost from their inception, the Southern colonies followed a different path from the North—specializing in plantation agriculture rather than small farms with diversified crops—due to geography and slavery. Thanks to slave labor, Southerners were gaining economies of scale and building comparative advantage in agriculture, exporting their goods to world markets and the North. Gang labor outproduced "free" (paid) labor. But the North was building even greater advantages by developing a middle class, a manufacturing sector, and a more modern social and political culture. With plans to complete transcontinental railroads pending, the North was on the verge of achieving economic and political dominance and the capacity to shut off further expansion of slavery in the West. The South chose war over Northern domination—and modernization.

Although the Constitution guaranteed free trade and free movement of capital and labor, the institution of slavery meant that the South had much less factor mobility than the North. It also ensured less development of its human resources, a less equal distribution of income, a smaller market for manufactures, and a less dynamic economy. It was less attractive to both European immigrants and external capital. With stagnant incomes in the older states, it was falling behind. In these respects, it was a forerunner of many of today's poor countries, especially those in Latin America.

What finally put the South on the path to economic convergence? Four years of civil war with a total of 600,000 deaths and vast destruction of property were only a start. Three constitutional amendments and twelve years of military "reconstruction" were designed to bring equal rights and due process to the South. But the reestablishment of racial segregation following Reconstruction led to sharecropping as former slaves refused to return to the work gangs. Labor productivity dropped so much that Southern incomes fell to about half of the North's in 1880. In fact, income convergence did not take off until the 1940s, when a wartime boom in the North's industrial cities attracted Southern migrants in search of better jobs. At the same time, the South began drawing capital as firms sought lower wages, an anti-union environment, and military contracts in important congressional districts. But this process did not fully succeed until the 1960s, as new federal laws and federal troops brought full civil rights to the South and ensured that the region could finally modernize.

## THE GREAT DIVIDE

Although slavery is a rarity today, the traditional U.S. divide between North and South provides a good model for understanding contemporary circumstances in many developing countries. In the American South, voter intimidation, segregated housing, and very unequal schooling were the rule, not the exception—and such tactics are repeated today by the elites in today's poor countries. Brazil, Mexico, and Peru had abundant land relative to population when the Europeans arrived, and their incomes roughly approximated those in North America, at least until 1700. The economists Stanley Engerman and Kenneth Sokoloff have pointed out that these states, like the Confederacy, developed agricultural systems based on vast landholdings for the production of export crops such as sugar and coffee. Brazil and many Caribbean islands also adopted slavery, while Peru and Mexico relied on forced indigenous labor rather than African slaves.

History shows that the political development of North America and developing nations—most of which were colonized by Europeans at some point—was heavily influenced by mortality. In colonies with tolerable death rates (Australia, Canada, New Zealand, and the United States), the colonists soon exerted pressure for British-style protections of persons and property. But elsewhere (most of Africa, Latin America, Indonesia, and to a lesser degree, India), disease caused such high mortality rates that the few resident Europeans were permitted to exploit a disenfranchised laboring class, whether slave or free. When the colonial era ended in these regions, it was followed by "liberationist" regimes (often authoritarian and incompetent) that maintained the previous system of exploitation for the advantage of a small domestic elite. Existing inequalities within poor countries continued; policies and institutions rarely protected individual rights or private initiative for the bulk of the population and allowed elites to skim off rents from any sectors that could bear it. The economist Hernando de Soto has shown how governments in the developing world fail to recognize poor citizens' legal titles to their homes and businesses, thereby depriving them of the use of their assets for collateral. The losses in potential capital to these countries have dwarfed the cumulative capital inflows going to these economies in the last century.

The legacy of these colonial systems also tends to perpetuate the unequal distribution of income, wealth, and political power while limiting capital mobility. Thus major developing nations such as Brazil, China, India, Indonesia, and Mexico are experiencing a divergence of incomes by province within their economies, as labor and capital fail to find better opportunities. Even in recent times, local elites have fought to maintain oppressive conditions in Brazil, El Salvador, Guatemala, Mexico, Nicaragua, and Peru. Faced with violent intimidation, poor people in these countries have suffered from unjust law enforcement similar to what was once experienced by black sharecroppers in the American South.

Modernization and economic development inevitably threaten the existing distribution of power and income, and powerful elites continue to protect the status quo—even if it means that their society as a whole falls further behind. It takes more than a constitution, universal suffrage, and regular elections to achieve governmental accountability and the rule of law. It may well be that only the right of exit—emigration—can peacefully bring accountability to corrupt and repressive regimes. Unlike the U.S. federal government, multilateral institutions lack the legitimacy to intervene in the internal affairs of most countries. Europe's economic takeoff in the second half of the nineteenth century was aided by the emigration of 60 million people to North America, Argentina, Brazil, and Australia. This emigration—about 10 percent of the labor force—helped raise European wages while depressing inflated wages in labor-scarce areas such as Australia and the United States. A comparable out-migration of labor from today's poor countries would involve hundreds of millions of people.

Of course, Latin America has seen some success. Chile has received the most attention for its free market initiatives, but its reforms were implemented by a brutally repressive military regime—hardly a model for achieving economic reform through democratic processes. Costa Rica would seem to be a much better model for establishing accountability, but its economic performance has not been as striking as Chile's.

Italy, like the United States in an earlier era, is another good example of "one country, two systems." Italy's per capita income has largely caught up with that of its European neighbors over the past 20 years, even exceeding Britain's and equaling France's in 1990, but its *Mezzogiorno* has failed to keep up. Whereas overall Italian incomes have been converging toward those of the EU, *Mezzogiorno* incomes have been diverging from those in the north. Southern incomes fell from 65 percent of the northern average in 1975 to 56 percent 20 years later; in Calabria, they fell to 47 percent of the northern average. Southern unemployment rose from 8 percent in 1975 to 19 percent in 1995—almost three times the northern average. In short, 50 years of subsidies from Rome and the EU have failed to stop the *Mezzogiorno* from falling further behind. Instead, they have yielded local regimes characterized by greatly increased public-sector employment, patronage, dependency, and corruption—not unlike the results of foreign aid for developing countries. And the continuing existence of the Mafia further challenges modernization.

Democracy, then, is not enough to ensure that the governed are allowed to reap the gains of their own efforts. An effective state requires good laws as well as law enforcement that is timely, even-handed, and accessible to the poor. In many countries, achieving objective law enforcement means reducing the extralegal powers of vested interests. When this is not possible, the only recourse usually available is emigration. But if the educated elite manages to emigrate while the masses remain trapped in a society that is short of leaders, the latter will face even more formidable odds as they try to create effective institutions and policies. Although Italians still emigrate from south to north, the size of this flow is declining, thanks in part to generous transfer payments that allow them to consume almost as much as northerners. In addition, policymaking for the *Mezzogiorno* is still concentrated in Rome.

The immigration barriers in rich countries not only foreclose opportunities in the global village to billions of poor people, they help support repressive, pseudo-democratic governments by denying the citizens of these countries the right to vote against the regime with their feet. In effect, the strict dictates of sovereignty allow wealthy nations to continue to set the rules in their own favor while allowing badly governed poor nations to continue to abuse their own citizens and retard economic development. Hence the remedy for income divergence must be political as well as economic.

## GETTING INSTITUTIONS RIGHT

According to economic theory, developing nations will create and modernize the institutions needed to underpin their markets so that their markets and firms can gradually match the performance of rich countries. But reality is much more complex than theory. For example, de Soto's analysis makes clear that effectively mobilizing domestic resources offers a much more potent source of capital for most developing nations than foreign inflows do. Yet mainstream economists and their formal models largely ignore these resources. Western economic advisers in Russia were similarly blindsided by their reliance on an economic model that had no institutional context and no historical perspective. Economists have scrambled in recent years to correct some of these shortcomings, and the Washington consensus now requires the "right" institutions as well as the "right" prices. But little useful theory exists to guide policy when it comes to institutional analysis, and gaps in the institutional foundations in most developing countries leave economic models pursuing unrealistic solutions or worse.

The adjustment of institutions inevitably favors certain actors and disadvantages others. As a result, modernization causes conflict that must be resolved through politics as well as economics. At a minimum, successful development signifies that the forces for institutional change have won out over the status quo. Achieving a "level playing field" signifies that regulatory and political competition is well governed.

Economists who suggest that all countries must adopt Western institutions to achieve Western levels of income often fail to consider the changes and political risks involved. The experts who recommended that formerly communist countries apply "shock therapy" to markets and democracy disregarded the political and regulatory issues involved. Each change requires a victory in the "legislative market" and successful persuasion within the state bureaucracy for political approval. Countries with lower incomes and fewer educated people than Russia face even more significant developmental challenges just to achieve economic stability, let alone attract foreign investment or make effective use of it. Institutional deficiencies, not capital shortages, are the major impediment to development, and as such they must be addressed before foreign investors will be willing to send in capital.

Although price liberalization can be undertaken rapidly, no rapid process (aside from revolution) exists for an economy modernizing its institutions. Boris Yeltsin may be credited with a remarkable turnover, if not a coup d'état, but his erratic management style and the lack of parliamentary support ensured that his government would never be strong. In these circumstances, helping the new Russian regime improve law enforcement should have come ahead of mass privatization. Launching capitalism in a country where no one other than apparatchiks had access to significant amounts of capital was an open invitation to gangsterism and a discredited system. Naive economic models made for naive policy recommendations.

## HOW THE WEST WON

The state's crucial role is evident in the West's economic development. European economic supremacy was forged not by actors who followed a "Washington consensus" model but by strong states. In the fifteenth century, European incomes were not much higher than those in China, India, or Japan. The nation-state was a European innovation that replaced feudalism and established the rule of law; in turn, a legal framework was formed for effective markets. Once these countries were in the lead, they were able to continuously increase their edge through technological advances. In addition, European settlers took their civilization with them to North America and the South Pacific, rapidly raising these areas to rich-country status as well. Thus Europe's early lead became the basis for accumulating further advantages with far-reaching implications.

Europe's rise to economic leadership was not rapid at first. According to the economist Angus Maddison, Europe's economy grew around 0.07 percent a year until 1700; only after 1820 did it reach one percent. But the pace of technological and institutional innovation accelerated thereafter. Meanwhile, discovery of new markets in Africa, Asia, and the Americas created new economic opportunities. Secular political forces overthrew the hegemony of the Catholic Church. Feudalism was eroded by rising incomes and replaced by a system that financed government through taxes, freeing up land and labor to be traded in markets. Markets permitted a more efficient reallocation of land and labor, allowing further rises in incomes. Effective property rights allowed individuals to keep the fruits of their own labor, thereby encouraging additional work. And privatization of common land facilitated the clearing of additional acreage.

The nation-state helped forge all these improvements. It opened up markets by expanding territory; reduced transaction costs; standardized weights, measures, and monetary units; and cut transport costs by improving roads, harbors, and canals. In addition, it was the state that established effective property rights. The European state system thrived on flexible alliances, which constantly changed to maintain a balance of power. Military and economic rivalries prompted states to promote development in agriculture and commerce as well as technological innovation in areas such as shipping and weaponry. Absent the hegemony of a single church or state, technology was diffused and secularized. Clocks, for instance, transferred timekeeping from the monastery to the village clock tower; the printing press did much the same for the production and distribution of books.

Europe's development contrasts sharply with Asia's. In the early modern era, China saw itself as the center of the world, without real rivals. It had a much larger population than Europe and a far bigger market as well. But though the Chinese pioneered the development of clocks, the printing press, gunpowder, and iron, they did not have the external competitive stimulus to promote economic development. Meanwhile, Japan sealed itself off from external influences for more than 200 years, while India, which had continuous competition within the subcontinent, never developed an effective national state prior to the colonial era.

The Europeans also led in establishing accountable government, even though it was achieved neither easily nor peacefully. Most European states developed the notion that the sovereign (whether a monarch or a parliament) had a duty to protect subjects and property in return for taxes and service in the army. Rulers in the Qing, Mughal, and Ottoman Empires, in contrast, never recognized a comparable responsibility to their subjects. During the Middle Ages, Italy produced a number of quasi-democratic city-states, and in the seventeenth century Holland created the first modern republic after a century of rebellion and warfare with Spain. Britain achieved constitutional monarchy in 1689, following two revolutions. After a bloody revolution and then dictatorship, France achieved accountable government in the nineteenth century.

Europe led the way in separating church and state—an essential precursor to free inquiry and adoption of the scientific method—after the Thirty Years' War. The secular state in turn paved the way for capitalism and its "creative destruction." Creative destruction could hardly become the norm until organized religion lost its power to execute as heretics those entrepreneurs who would upset the status quo. After the Reformation, Europeans soon recognized another fundamental tenet of capitalism: the role of interest as a return for the use of capital. Capitalism required that political leaders allow private hands to hold power as well as wealth; in turn, power flowed from the rural nobility to merchants in cities. European states also permitted banks, insurance firms, and stock markets to develop. The "yeast" in this recipe lay in the notion that private as well as state organizations could mobilize and reallocate society's resources—an idea with profound social, political, and economic implications today.

Most of Europe's leading powers did not rely on private initiative alone but adopted mercantilism to promote their development. This strategy used state power to create a trading system that would raise national income, permitting the government to enhance its own power through additional taxes. Even though corruption was sometimes a side effect, the system generally worked well. Venice was the early leader, from about 1000 to 1500; the Dutch followed in the sixteenth and seventeenth centuries; Britain became dominant in the eighteenth century. In Britain, as in the other cases, mercantilist export promotion was associated with a dramatic rise in state spending and employment (especially in the navy), as well as "crony capitalism." After World War II, export-promotion regimes were adopted by Japan, South Korea, Singapore, and Taiwan with similar success. Today, of course, such strategies are condemned as violations of global trade rules, even for poor countries.

Finally, geography played a pivotal role in Europe's rise, providing a temperate climate, navigable rivers, accessible coastline, and defensible boundaries for future states. In addition, Europe lacked the conditions for the production of labor-intensive commodities such as coffee, cotton, sugar, or tobacco—production that might have induced the establishment of slavery. Like in the American North, European agriculture was largely rain-fed, diversified, and small-scale.

Europe's rise, then, was partly due to the creation and diffusion of technological innovations and the gradual accumulation of capital. But the underlying causes were political and social. The creation of the nation-state and institutionalized state rivalry fostered government accountability. Scientific enlightenment and upward social mobility, spurred by healthy competition, also helped Europe achieve such transformations. But many of today's developing countries still lack these factors crucial for economic transformation.

## PLAYING CATCH-UP

Globalization offers opportunities for all nations, but most developing countries are very poorly positioned to capitalize on them. Malarial climates, limited access to navigable water, long distances to major markets, and unchecked population growth are only part of the problem. Such countries also have very unequal income structures inherited from colonial regimes, and these patterns of income distribution are hard to change unless prompted by a major upheaval such as a war or a revolution. But as serious as these disadvantages are, the greatest disadvantage has been the poor quality of government.

If today's global opportunities are far greater and potentially more accessible than at any other time in world history, developing countries are also further behind than ever before. Realistic political logic suggests that weak governments need to show that they can manage their affairs much better before they pretend to have strategic ambitions. So what kind of catch-up models could they adopt?

Substituting domestic goods for imports was the most popular route to economic development prior to the 1980s. But its inward orientation made those who adopted it unable to take advantage of the new global opportunities and ultimately it led to a dead end. Although the United States enjoyed success with such a strategy from 1790 until 1940, no developing country has a home market large enough to support a modern economy today. The other successful early growth model was European mercantilism, namely export promotion, as pioneered by Venice, the Dutch republic, Britain, and Germany. Almost all of the East Asian success stories, China included, are modern versions of the export-oriented form of mercantilism.

For its part, free trade remains the right model for rich countries because it provides decentralized initiatives to search for tomorrow's market opportunities. But it does not necessarily promote development. Britain did not adopt free trade until the 1840s, long after it had become the world's leading industrial power. The prescription of lower trade barriers may help avoid even worse strategies at the hands of bad governments, but the Washington-consensus model remains best suited for those who are ahead rather than behind.

Today's shareholder capitalism brings additional threats to poor countries, first by elevating compensation for successful executives, and second by subordinating all activities to those that maximize shareholder value. Since 1970, the estimated earnings of an American chief executive have gone from 30 times to 450 times that of the average worker. In the leading developing countries, this ratio is still less than 50. Applying a similar "market-friendly" rise in executive compensation within the developing world would therefore only aggravate the income gap, providing new ammunition for populist politicians. In addition, shareholder capitalism calls for narrowing the managerial focus to the interests of shareholders, even if this means dropping activities that offset local market imperfections. A leading South African bank has shed almost a million small accounts—mostly held by blacks—to raise its earnings per share. Should this bank, like its American counterparts, have an obligation to serve its community, including its black members, in return for its banking license?

Poor nations must improve the effectiveness of their institutions and bureaucracies in spite of entrenched opposition and poorly paid civil servants. As the journalist Thomas Friedman has pointed out, it is true that foreign-exchange traders can dump the currencies of poorly managed countries, thereby helping discipline governments to restrain their fiscal deficits and lax monetary policies. But currency pressures will not influence the feudal systems in Pakistan and Saudi Arabia, the theocracies in Afghanistan and Iran, or the kleptocracies in Kenya or southern Mexico. The forces of capital markets will not restrain Brazilian squatters as they take possession of "public lands" or the slums of Rio de Janeiro or São Paulo, nor will they help discipline landlords and vigilantes in India's Bihar as they fight for control of their state. Only strong, accountable government can do that.

## LOOKING AHEAD

Increased trade and investment have indeed brought great improvements in some countries, but the global economy is hardly a win-win situation. Roughly one billion people earn less than $1 per day, and their numbers are growing. Economic resources to ameliorate such problems exist, but the political and administrative will to realize the potential of these resources in poor areas is lacking. Developing-nation governments need both the pressure to reform their administrations and institutions, and the access to help in doing so. But sovereignty removes much of the external pressure, while immigration barriers reduce key internal motivation. And the Washington consensus on the universality of the rich-country model is both simplistic and self-serving.

The world needs a more pragmatic, country-by-country approach, with room for neomercantilist regimes until such countries are firmly on the convergence track. Poor nations should be allowed to do what today's rich countries did to get ahead, not be forced to adopt the laissez-faire approach. Insisting on the merits of comparative advantage in low-wage, low-growth industries is a sure way to stay poor. And continued poverty will lead to rising levels of illegal immigration and low-level violence, such as kidnappings and vigilante justice, as the poor take the only options that remain. Over time, the rich countries will be forced to pay more attention to the fortunes of the poor—if only to enjoy their own prosperity and safety.

Still, the key initiatives must come from the poor countries, not the rich. In the last 50 years, China, India, and Indonesia have led the world in reducing poverty. In China, it took civil war and revolution, with tens of millions of deaths, to create a strong state and economic stability; a de facto coup d'état in 1978 brought about a very fortunate change of management. The basic forces behind Chinese reform were political and domestic, and their success depended as much on better using resources as opening up markets. Meanwhile, the former Soviet Union and Africa lie at the other extreme. Their economic decline stems from their failure to maintain effective states and ensure the rule of law.

It will not be surprising if some of today's states experience failure and economic decline in the new century. Argentina, Colombia, Indonesia, and Pakistan will be obvious cases to watch, but other nations could also suffer from internal regional failures—for example, the Indian state of Bihar. Income growth depends heavily on the legal, administrative, and political capabilities of public actors in sovereign states. That is why, in the end, external economic advice and aid must go beyond formal models and conform to each country's unique political and social context.

# THE MEANING OF GLOBALIZATION

# Globalization of the Economy

## JEFFREY FRANKEL

Economic globalization is one of the most powerful forces to have shaped the post-war world. In particular, international trade in goods and services has become increasingly important over the past fifty years, and international financial flows over the past thirty years. This chapter documents quantitatively the process of globalization for trade and finance. It then briefly goes beyond the causes of international economic integration to consider its effects, concluding that globalization is overall a good thing, not just for economic growth but also when noneconomic goals are taken into account.

The two major drivers of economic globalization are reduced costs to transportation and communication in the private sector and reduced policy barriers to trade and investment on the part of the public sector. Technological progress and innovation have long been driving the costs of transportation and communication steadily lower. In the postwar period we have seen major further cost-saving advances, even within ocean shipping: supertankers, roll-on-roll-off ships, and containerized cargo. Between 1920 and 1990 the average ocean freight and port charges per short ton of U.S. import and export cargo fell from $95.00 to $29.00 (in 1990 dollars). An increasing share of cargo goes by air. Between 1930 and 1990, average air transport revenue per passenger mile fell from $0.68 to $0.11. Jet air shipping and refrigeration have changed the status of goods that had previously been classified altogether as not tradable internationally. Now fresh-cut flowers, perishable broccoli and strawberries, live lobsters, and even ice cream are sent between continents. Communications costs have fallen even more rapidly. Over this period the cost of a three-minute telephone call from New York to London fell from $244.65 to $3.32. Recent inventions such as faxes and the Internet require no touting.

Jeffrey Frankel, "Globalization of the Economy," in Joseph S. Nye and John D. Donahue, eds. *Governance in a Globalizing World*. Washington, DC: Brookings Institution, 2000, pp. 45–69. Portions of the text and footnotes have been omitted.

**309**

It is easy to exaggerate the extent of globalization. Much excited discussion of the topic makes it sound as though the rapid increase in economic integration across national borders is unprecedented. Some commentators imply that it has now gone so far that it is complete; one hears that distance and national borders no longer matter, that the nation-state and geography are themselves no longer relevant for economic purposes, and that it is now as easy to do business with a customer across the globe as across town. After all, has not the World Wide Web reduced cross-border barriers to zero?

It would be a mistake for policymakers or private citizens to base decisions on the notion that globalization is so new that the experience of the past is not relevant, or that the phenomenon is now irreversible, or that national monetary authorities are now powerless in the face of the global marketplace, or that the quality of life of Americans—either economic or noneconomic aspects—is determined more by developments abroad than by American actions at home.

It is best to recognize that at any point in history many powerful forces are working to drive countries apart, at the same time as other powerful forces are working to shrink the world. In the 1990s, for example, at the same time that forces such as the Internet and dollarization have led some to proclaim the decline of the nation-state, more new nations have been created (out of the ruins of the former Soviet bloc) than in any decade other than the decolonizing 1960s, each with its own currencies and trade policies. The forces of shrinkage have dominated in recent decades, but the centrifugal forces are important as well.

## TWO BENCHMARKS FOR MEASURING ECONOMIC INTEGRATION

The overall post–World War II record of economic integration across national borders, powerful as it has been, is, in two respects, not as striking as widely believed. The first perspective is to judge by the standard of 100 years ago. The second is to judge by the standard of what it would mean to have truly perfect global integration.

### Judging Globalization 2000 by the Standard of 1900

The globalization that took place in the nineteenth century was at least as impressive as the current episode. The most revolutionary breakthroughs in transportation and communication had already happened by 1900—for example, the railroad, steamship, telegraph, and refrigeration. Freight rates had fallen sharply throughout the century. An environment of political stability was provided by the Pax Britannica, and an environment of monetary stability was provided by the gold standard. Kevin O'Rourke and Jeffrey Williamson show that, as a result of rapidly growing trade, international differences in commodity prices narrowed dramatically.

It is inescapable to invoke a particularly famous quote from John Maynard Keynes: "What an extraordinary episode in the progress of man that age was which came to an end in August 1914! . . . The inhabitant of London could order by telephone, sipping his morning tea in bed, the various products of the whole earth . . . he could at the same time and by the same means adventure his wealth in the natural resources and new enterprise of any quarter of the world."[1]

The world took a giant step back from economic globalization during the period 1914–1944. Some of the causes of this retrogression were isolationist sentiments in the West that followed World War I, the monetary instability and economic depression that plagued the interwar period, increases in tariffs and other trade barriers including most saliently the adoption by the U.S. Congress of the Smoot-Hawley tariff of 1930, the rise of the fascist bloc in the 1930s, and the rise of the communist bloc in the 1940s. All of these factors pertain to barriers that were created by governments, in contrast to the forces of technology and the private marketplace, which tend to reduce barriers. As a result, the world that emerged in 1945 was far more fragmented economically than the world that had turned to war in 1914.

The victors, however, were determined not to repeat the mistakes they had made at the time of the first world war. This time, they would work to promote economic integration in large part to advance long-term political goals. To govern international money, investment, and trade, they established multilateral institutions—the International Monetary Fund, World Bank, and General Agreement on Tariffs and Trade. The United States initially led the way by reducing trade barriers and making available gold-convertible dollars.

By one basic measure of trade, exports or imports of merchandise as a fraction of total output, it took more than twenty-five years after the end of World War II before the United States around 1970 reached the same level of globalization that it had experienced on the eve of World War I. This fraction continued to increase rapidly between 1971 and 1997—reaching about 9 percent today, still far lower than that in Britain throughout the late and early twentieth centuries. By other measures, some pertaining to the freedom of factor movements, the world even by the turn of the millennium was no more integrated than that of the preceding turn of the century.

Most people find it surprising that trade did not reattain its pre–World War I importance until the early 1970s. The significance of the comparison with 100 years ago goes well beyond factoids that economic historians enjoy springing on the uninitiated. Because technological know-how is irreversible—or was irreversible over the second millennium, if not entirely over the first—there is a tendency to see globalization as irreversible. But the political forces that fragmented the world for thirty years (1914–44) were evidently far more powerful than the accretion of technological progress in transport that went on during that period. The lesson is that nothing is inevitable about the process of globalization. For it to continue, world leaders must make choices of the sort made in the aftermath of World War II, instead of those made in the aftermath of World War I.

## Judging by the Globalization 2000 Standard of Perfect International Integration

Perhaps perfect economic integration across national borders is a straw man. . . . But straw men have their purposes, and in this case ample rhetoric exists to justify the interest. A good straw man needs to be substantial enough to impress the crows and yet not so substantial that he can't be knocked flat. On both scores the proposition of complete international integration qualifies admirably.

Consider again the basic statistics of trade integration—a country's total exports of goods and services, or total imports, as a fraction of GDP. With the rapid increase in services included, these ratios now average 12 percent for the United States. The current level of trade likely represents a doubling from 100 years ago. As remarkable as is this evidence of declining transportation costs, tariffs, and other barriers to trade, it is still very far from the condition that would prevail if these costs and barriers were zero. More sophisticated statistics below will document this claim. But a very simple calculation is sufficient to make the point. U.S. output is about one-fourth of gross world product. The output of producers in other countries is thus about three-fourths of gross world product. If Americans were prone to buy goods and services from foreign producers as easily as from domestic producers, then foreign products would constitute a share of U.S. spending equal to that of the spending of the average resident of the planet. The U.S. import-GDP ratio would equal .75. The same would be true of the U.S. export-GDP ratio. And yet these ratios are only about one-sixth of this hypothetical level (12 percent/75 percent=one-sixth). In other words, globalization would have to increase another sixfold, as measured by the trade ratio, before it would literally be true that Americans did business as easily across the globe as across the country.

Other countries are also a long way from perfect openness in this sense. The overall ratio of merchandise trade to output worldwide is about twice the U.S. ratio. This is to be expected, as other countries are smaller. For the other two large economies—Japan and the European Union considered as a whole—the ratio is closer to the U.S. level. In almost all cases, the ratio falls far short of the level that would prevail in a perfectly integrated world. In Figure 1, the vertical dimension represents the share of a country's output that is sold to its fellow citizens, rather than exported. The downward movement for most countries illustrates that they have become more open over the past 130 years. (One can also see that the integration trend was interrupted during the interwar period.) The United States is still far from perfect openness: the share of output sold at home is disproportionate to the share of world output. Other countries have a higher ratio of trade to GDP than the United States as a result of being smaller and less self-sufficient. Nonetheless, they are similarly far from perfect openness.

Why is globalization still so far from complete? To get an idea of the combination of transportation costs, trade barriers, and other frictions that remains yet to be dismantled, we must delve more deeply into the statistics.

## STATISTICAL MEASURES OF ECONOMIC INTEGRATION

It can be instructive to look at direct measures of how some of the barriers to transborder integration have changed during the twentieth century—the level of tariffs on manufactures as an illustration of trade policy, or the price of a trans-Atlantic telephone call as an illustration of technological change in communications and transportation. Nevertheless, the political and physical determinants are too numerous and varied to be aggregated into a few key statistics that are capable of

Share of output sold at home

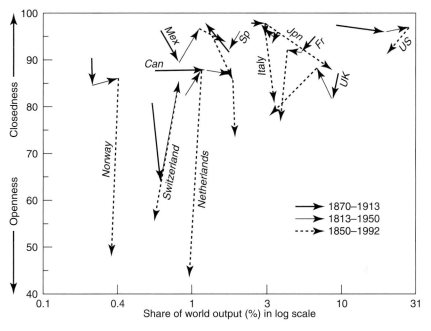

**FIGURE 1** ■ Country Size (Share of World Output) versus Closedness (Sales at Home/Total Output)

*Source: Author's calculations and data from Angus Maddison, Monitoring the World Economy (Paris: Development Center of the Organization for Economic Cooperation and Development, 1995). Note: Closedness = (1 − (x/GDP))\*100.*

measuring the overall extent of integration in trade or finance. Tariff rates, for example, differ tremendously across commodities, and there is no single sensible way to aggregate them. The situation is even worse for nontariff barriers. Alternative possible measures of the importance of tariffs and other trade barriers have very low correlation with each other. . . .

It is more rewarding to look at summary measures of the *effects* of cross-border barriers on the patterns of trade and investment than to look at measures of the barriers themselves. Two sorts of measures are in use: those pertaining to quantities and those pertaining to prices.

Measures of quantities might appear more direct: "just how big are international flows?" But economists often prefer to look at price measures. In the first place, the quality of the data is often higher for prices than quantities. (This is particularly true of data on international financial markets—the data on the prices of foreign securities are extremely good, the data on aggregate international trade in securities are extremely bad.) In the second place, even at a conceptual level, international differentials in the prices of specific goods or specific assets, which measure the ability of international arbitrage to hold these prices in line, are more useful indicators of the extent of integration in a causal sense. Consider the example of U.S. trade in petroleum products. It is not especially large as a percentage of total

U.S. output or consumption of petroleum products. And yet arbitrage ties the price of oil within the United States closely to the price in the world market. Even a pair of countries that records no bilateral oil trade whatsoever will find that their prices move closely together. It is the absence of barriers and the *potential* for large-scale trade that keeps prices in line and makes the markets integrated in the most meaningful sense, not the magnitude of trade that takes place.

## The Ability of Arbitrage to Eliminate International Differentials in Goods Prices

According to basic economic theory, arbitrage, defined as the activity of buying an item in a place where it is cheap and simultaneously selling the same item where it is expensive, should drive prices into equality. Its failure to do so perfectly is a source of repeated surprise to economists (though perhaps to nobody else). Often the explanation is that the commodities in question are not in fact identical. Brand names matter, if for no other reason than matters of retailing, warranty, and customer service. A BMW is certainly not the same automobile as a Lexus, and even a BMW sold in Germany is not the same as a BMW sold in the United States (different air pollution control equipment, for example). When the comparison across countries uses aggregate price indexes, as in standard tests of "purchasing power parity," it is no surprise to find only weak evidence of arbitrage. The finding of international price differentials is more surprising in the case of nondifferentiated non-brand-name commodities such as standardized ball bearings. Tests find that price differentials for specific goods are far larger across national borders than they are within countries. Exchange rate variability is a likely culprit.

Even more surprising is the paucity of evidence of a tendency for price differentials to diminish over the long sweep of history. Kenneth Froot, Michael Kim, and Kenneth Rogoff have obtained data on prices in England and Holland since the year 1273 for eight commodities (barley, butter, cheese, eggs, oats, peas, silver, and wheat).[2] Deviations from the so-called Law of One Price across the English Channel are no smaller or less persistent now than they were in the past, even though technological progress has certainly reduced the cost of shipping these products dramatically. Evidently other forces have counteracted the fall in transport costs; candidates are trade barriers under Europe's Common Agricultural Policy and volatility in the exchange rate between the guilder and the pound.

## Factors Contributing to Home-Country Bias in Trade

Geography in general—and distance in particular—remain far more important inhibitions to trade than widely believed.

### Distance

Distance is still an important barrier to trade and not solely because of physical shipping costs. The effects of informational barriers are observed to decrease with proximity and with linguistic, cultural, historical, and political links. We might call it social distance. Hans Linnemann called it "psychic distance," and Peter Drysdale and Ross Garnaut named it "subjective resistance."[3]

Among many possible proofs that distance is still important, one of the simplest is the observed tendency toward geographical agglomeration of industries. The tendency for industry to concentrate regionally is evidence both of costs to transportation and communication and of increasing returns to scale in production.

The agglomeration occurs even in sectors where physical transport costs are negligible, as in financial services or computer software. Financial firms concentrate in Manhattan and information technology firms concentrate in Silicon Valley. The reason they choose to locate near each other is not because they are trading physical commodities with each other and wish to save on shipping costs. Rather, face-to-face contact is important for exchanging information and negotiating deals.

The importance of distance is also revealed by analysis of data on prices of goods in different locations. If transport costs and other costs of doing business at a distance are important, then arbitrage should do a better job of keeping prices of similar goods in line when they are sold at locations close together rather than far apart. Charles Engel and John Rogers study prices in fourteen consumption categories for twenty-three Canadian and U.S. cities. They find that the distance between two North American cities significantly affects the variability of their relative prices. . . .

Statistical estimates find highly significant effects of distance on bilateral trade. When the distance between two countries is increased by 1 percent, trade between them falls by 0.7 to 1.0 percent. This statistic, like the others that follow, pertains to the effect in isolation, holding constant other effects on trade, such as the size of the trading partners. . . .

## Other Geographical Variables

Other physical attributes of location also have statistically significant effects. Landlocked countries engage in less trade by a factor of about one-third, holding other factors equal. Two countries that are adjacent to each other trade about 80 percent more than two otherwise similar countries.

## Linguistic and Colonial Factors

Linguistic barriers remain an impediment to trade. Two countries that speak the same language trade about 50 percent more than two otherwise similar countries. The multitude of languages is one of the reasons why economic integration remains far from complete in the European Union.

Colonial links have also been important historically. In 1960, the year when the break-up of the largest colonial empires began in earnest, trade between colonies and the colonial power was on average two to four times greater than for otherwise similar pairs of countries. This effect, already reduced from an earlier peak in the colonial era, has continued to decline in the 1970s and 1980s. But it has not disappeared. Indeed, if small dependencies are included in the sample, then two units that share the same colonizer still trade on average an estimated 80 percent more with each other than two otherwise similar countries (as recently as 1990). In addition, if one of the pair is the colonial mother country, trade is five to nine times greater than it would otherwise be.

### Military Factors
The effects on bilateral trade of politico-military alliances, wars, have also been examined. Theoretically and empirically (in the gravity framework) trade is generally higher among countries that are allies and lower among countries that are actual or potential adversaries. Understandably, if two countries are currently at war, there is usually a negative effect on trade. It runs as high as a 99 percent reduction in 1965. More typical is an 82 percent reduction in 1990.[4]

### Free Trade Areas
Regional trading arrangements reduce tariffs and other trade barriers within a group of countries, though there is a range from mild preferential trading arrangements to full-fledged economic unions. Often the members of such groups are already tightly linked through proximity, common language, or other ties. But even holding constant for such factors, in the gravity model, the formation of a free trade area is estimated on average to raise trade by 70 to 170 percent. A serious common market, such as the European Union, can have a bigger effect. Nevertheless, in each of the EU member countries, a large bias toward trade within that country remains.

### Political Links
A naive economist's view would be that once tariffs and other explicit trade barriers between countries are removed, and geographic determinants of transportation costs are held constant, trade should move as easily across national boundaries as within them. But this is far from the case in reality. If two geographic units belong to the same sovereign nation, such as France and its overseas departments, trade is roughly tripled. Thus political relationships among geographic units have larger effects on trade than such factors as explicit trade policies or linguistic barriers.

### Common Country
Even after adjusting for distance (including noncontiguity) and linguistic barriers, all countries still exhibit a substantial bias toward buying domestic goods rather than foreign. . . .

There would be some great advantages of having data at the level of states or provinces within countries. We would be able to ascertain how trade between two geographical entities is affected by their common membership in a political union. We have learned that when two geographical units share such links as speaking a common language, their bilateral trade is clearly boosted. It stands to reason that when two units share a common cultural heritage or legal system, their trade will be enhanced by even more. Data are not generally available on trade among U.S. states, Japanese prefectures, German länder, British counties, or French departments. But there do exist data on trade undertaken by Canadian provinces, among one another and with major American states. They show a strong intranational bias to trade. Ontario exports three times as much to British Columbia as to California, even though the latter has ten times as many people. (The figures are for 1988.) . . .

## Currencies

There has long been reason to suspect that the existence of different currencies, and especially the large fluctuation in the exchange rates between currencies since the break-up of the Bretton Woods monetary system in 1971, has been a barrier to international trade and investment. Exchange rate fluctuations are clearly related to the failures of the law of one price observed in goods markets. When it is observed that, for example, Canadians and Americans trade far more with their countrymen than with each other, in a context where trade barriers, geography, and linguistic barriers have been eliminated, the currency difference is one of the prime suspects. . . .

Promoting trade and finance is one of several motivations for the recent adoption of common currencies or currency boards by roughly twenty countries over the past decade (including the eleven members of the European Economic and Monetary Union in 1999). At the same time, however, approximately the same number of new currencies have come into existence, as a result of the breakup of the former Soviet bloc.

## Measures of Financial Market Integration

The delegates who met at Bretton Woods in 1944 had a design for the world monetary system that explicitly did not accord financial markets the presumption that was accorded trade in goods, the presumption that international integration was unambiguously good and that barriers should be liberalized as rapidly as possible. Although economic theory can make as elegant a case in favor of free trade in assets as for free trade in goods and services, the delegates had been persuaded by the experience of the 1930s that some degree of controls on international capital movements was desirable. It was not until the final 1973 breakdown of the system of fixed exchange rates that Germany and the United States removed their capital controls. Japan and the United Kingdom kept theirs until the end of the 1970s, and most other European countries did not liberalize until the end of the 1980s. Many emerging-market countries also opened up to large-scale international capital movements in the 1990s (though the subsequent crises have convinced some observers that those delegates at Bretton Woods might have had it right in the first place).

Tests regarding financial markets show international integration that has increased tremendously over the past thirty years but that is less complete than often supposed. This generalization applies to quantity-based tests as well as to price-based tests.

It is true that the gross volume of cross-border capital flows has grown very large. Perhaps the most impressive and widely cited statistic is the gross volume of turnover in foreign exchange markets: $1.5 trillion per day worldwide, by April 1998, which is on the order of a hundred times greater than the volume of trade in goods and services. *Net* capital flows are for most purposes more interesting than gross flows, however. Net capital flows today are far smaller as a share of GDP than were pre-World War I net flows out of Great Britain and into such land-abundant countries as Argentina, Australia, and Canada. Furthermore, Martin Feldstein and Charles Horioka argued in a very influential paper that net capital flows are far smaller than one would expect them to be in a world of perfect international capital mobility: a country that suffers a shortfall in national saving tends to experience an almost commensurate fall in investment, rather than making up the difference by borrowing from abroad. Similarly, investors in every country hold far lower proportions of their portfolios in the form of other countries' securities than they would in a well-diversified portfolio, a puzzle known as home country bias. Evidently, imperfect information and transactions costs are still important barriers to cross-country investment.

The ability of arbitrage to equate asset prices or rates of return across countries has been widely tested. One would expect that in the absence of barriers to cross-border financial flows, arbitrage would bring interest rates into equality. But the answer depends on the precise condition tested. Interest rates that have had the element of exchange risk removed by forward market cover are indeed virtually equated across national borders among industrialized countries, showing that they have few controls on international capital movements. But interest rates seem not to be equalized across countries when they are adjusted for expectations of exchange rate changes rather than for forward exchange rates, and interest rates are definitely not equalized when adjusted for expected inflation rates. Evidently, currency differences are important enough to drive a wedge between expected rates of return. Furthermore, residual transactions costs or imperfect information apparently affects cross-border investment in equities. They discourage investors altogether from investing in some information-intensive assets, such as mortgages, across national borders. Furthermore, country risk still adds a substantial penalty wedge to all investments in developing countries.

In short, though international financial markets, much like goods markets, have become far more integrated in recent decades, they have traversed less of the distance to perfect integration than is widely believed. Globalization is neither new, nor complete, nor irreversible.

## The Impact of Economic Globalization

What are the effects of globalization and its merits? We must acknowledge a lower degree of certainty in our answers. It becomes harder to isolate cause and effect. Moreover, once we extend the list of objectives beyond maximizing national incomes, value judgments come into play. Nevertheless, economic theory and empirical research still have much to contribute.

## The Effect of Trade on the Level and Growth of Real Income

Why do economists consider economic integration so important? What are the benefits of free trade for the economy?

### The Theoretical Case for Trade
Classical economic theory tells us that there are national gains from trade, associated with the phrase "comparative advantage." Over the past two decades, scholars have developed a "new trade theory." It suggests the existence of additional benefits from trade, which are termed dynamic. We consider each theory in turn.

The classical theory goes back to Adam Smith and David Ricardo. Adam Smith argued that specialization—the division of labor—enhances productivity. David Ricardo extended this concept to trade between countries. The notion is that trade allows each country to specialize in what it does best, thus maximizing the value of its output. If a government restricts trade, resources are wasted in the production of goods that could be imported more cheaply than they can be produced domestically.

What if one country is better than anyone else at producing *every* good? The argument in favor of free trade still carries the day. All that is required is for a country to be *relatively* less skilled than another in the production of some good in order for it to benefit from trade. This is the doctrine of comparative advantage—the fundamental (if perhaps counterintuitive) principle that underlies the theory of international trade. It makes sense for Michael Jordan to pay someone else to mow his lawn, even if Jordan could do it better himself, because he has a comparative advantage at basketball over lawn mowing. Similarly, it makes sense for the United States to pay to import certain goods that can be produced more efficiently abroad (apparel, shoes, tropical agriculture, consumer electronics), because the United States has a comparative advantage in other goods (aircraft, financial services, wheat, and computer software).

This is the classical view of the benefits of free trade in a nutshell. Two key attributes of the classical theory are worth flagging. First, it assumes perfect competition, constant returns to scale, and fixed technology, assumptions that are not very realistic. Second, the gains from trade are primarily static in nature—that is, they affect the *level* of real income. The elimination of trade barriers raises income, but this is more along the lines of a one-time increase.

What of the "new trade theory"? It is more realistic than the classical theory, in that it takes into account imperfect competition, increasing returns to scale, and changing technology. It can be viewed as providing equally strong, or stronger, support for the sort of free trade policies that the United States has followed throughout the postwar period, that is, multilateral and bilateral negotiations to reduce trade barriers, than did the classical theory.

To be sure, these theories say that, under certain very special conditions, one country can get ahead by interventions (for example, subsidies to strategic sectors), provided the government gets it exactly right and provided the actions of other countries are taken as given. But these theories also tend to have the property that a world in which everyone is subsidizing at once is a world in which everyone is worse off, and that we are all better off if we can agree to limit subsidies or other interventions.

Bilateral or multilateral agreements where other sides make concessions to U.S. products, in return for whatever concessions the United States makes, are virtually the only sorts of trade agreements the United States has made. Indeed, most recent trade agreements (like the North American Free Trade Agreement and China's accession to the WTO) have required much larger reductions in import barriers by U.S. trading partners than by the United States. The reason is that their barriers were higher than those of the United States to start with. But the natural implication is that such agreements raise foreign demand for U.S. products by more than they raise U.S. demand for imports. Hence the United States is likely to benefit from a positive "terms of trade effect." This just adds to the usual benefits of increased efficiency of production and gains to consumers from international trade.

Furthermore, even when a government does not fear retaliation from abroad for trade barriers, intervention in practice is usually based on inadequate knowledge and is corrupted by interest groups. Seeking to rule out all sector-specific intervention is the most effective way of discouraging rent-seeking behavior. Globalization increases the number of competitors operating in the economy. Not only does this work to reduce distortionary monopoly power in the marketplace (which is otherwise exercised by raising prices), it can also reduce distortionary corporate power in the political arena (which is exercised by lobbying).

Most important, new trade theory offers reason to believe that openness can have a permanent effect on a country's rate of growth, not just the level of real GDP. A high rate of economic interaction with the rest of the world speeds the absorption of frontier technologies and global management best practices, spurs innovation and cost-cutting, and competes away monopoly.

These dynamic gains come from a number of sources. They include the benefits of greater market size and enhanced competition. Other sources include technological improvements through increased contact with foreigners and their alternative production styles. Such contact can come, for example, from direct investment by foreign firms with proprietary knowledge or by the exposure to imported goods that embody technologies developed abroad. Each of these elements of international trade and interactions has the effect of promoting growth in the domestic economy. When combined with the static effects, there is no question that the efforts to open markets, when successful, can yield significant dividends.

### The Empirical Case for Trade

Citing theory is not a complete answer to the question, "how do we know that trade is good?" We need empirical evidence. Economists have undertaken statistical tests of the determinants of countries' growth rates. Investment in physical capital and investment in human capital are the two factors that emerge the most strongly. But other factors matter. Estimates of growth equations have found a role for openness, measured, for example, as the sum of exports and imports as a share of GDP. David Romer and I look at a cross-section of 100 countries during the period since 1960. The study sought to address a major concern about simultaneous causality between growth and trade: does openness lead to growth, or does growth lead to openness? We found that the effect of openness on growth is even stronger when we correct for the simultaneity compared with standard estimates.

The estimate of the effect of openness on income per capita ranges from 0.3 to 3.0. Consider a round middle number such as 1.0. The increase in U.S. openness since the 1950s is 0.12. Multiplying the two numbers together implies that the increased integration has had effect of 12 percent on U.S. income. More dramatically, compare a stylized Burma, with a ratio close to zero, versus a stylized Singapore, with a ratio close to 100 percent. Our ballpark estimate, the coefficient of 1.0, implies that Singapore's income is 100 percent higher than Burma's as a result of its openness. The fact that trade can affect a country's growth rate—as opposed to affecting the level of its GDP in a "one-shot" fashion—makes the case for trade liberalization even more compelling. . . .

### Macroeconomic Interdependence

Trade and financial integration generally increase the transmission of business cycle fluctuations among countries. Floating exchange rates give countries some insulation against one another's fluctuations. When capital markets are highly integrated, floating rates do not give complete insulation, as the post-1973 correlation among major industrialized economies shows. But international transmission can be good for a country as easily as bad, as happens when adverse domestic developments are in part passed off to the rest of the world. The trade balance can act as an important automatic stabilizer for output and employment, improving in recessions and worsening in booms.

Contagion of financial crises is more worrying. The decade of the 1990s alone abounds with examples: the 1992–93 crises in the European exchange rate mechanism, the "tequila crisis" that began with the December 1994 devaluation of the Mexican peso, and the crises in East Asia and emerging markets worldwide from July 1997 to January 1999. Evidently when one country has a crisis it affects others. There is now a greater consensus among economists than before that not all of the observed volatility, or its cross-country correlation, can be attributed to efficient capital markets punishing or rewarding countries based on a rational evaluation of the economic fundamentals. It is difficult to do justice in one paragraph to a discussion that is as voluminous and vigorous as the debate over the welfare implications of the swelling international capital flows. Still, the majority view remains that countries are overall better off with modern globalized financial markets than without them.

## The Effect of Trade on Other Social Goals

Many who fear globalization concede that trade has a positive effect on aggregate national income but suspect that it has adverse effects on other highly valued goals such as labor rights, food safety, culture, and so forth. Here we consider only two major values—equality and the environment—and briefly at that.

### Income Distribution

International trade and investment can be a powerful source of growth in poor countries, helping them catch up with those who are ahead in endowments of capital and technology. This was an important component of the spectacular growth of East Asian countries between the 1960s and the 1990s, which remains a miracle even in the aftermath of the 1997–98 currency crises. By promoting convergence, trade can help reduce the enormous worldwide inequality in income. Most of those who are concerned about income distribution, however, seem more motivated by within-country equality than global equality.

A standard textbook theory of international trade, the Heckscher-Ohlin-Samuelson model, has a striking prediction to make regarding within-country income distribution. It is that the scarce factors of production will lose from trade, and the abundant factors will benefit. This means that in rich countries, those who have capital and skills will benefit at the expense of unskilled labor, whereas in poor countries it will be the other way around. The same prediction holds for international capital mobility (or, for that matter, for international labor mobility). It has been very difficult, however, to find substantial direct evidence of the predictions of the model during the postwar period, including distribution effects within either rich or poor countries. Most likely the phenomena of changing technology, intraindustry trade, and worker ties to specific industries are more important today than the factor endowments at the heart of the Heckscher-Ohlin-Samuelson model.

In the United States, the gap between wages paid to skilled workers and wages paid to unskilled workers rose by 18 percentage points between 1973 and 1995 and then leveled off. The fear is that trade is responsible for some of the gap, by benefiting skilled workers more than unskilled workers. Common statistical estimates—which typically impose the theoretical framework rather than testing it—are that between 5 and 30 percent of the increase is attributable to trade. Technology, raising the demand for skilled workers faster than the supply, is the major factor responsible for the rest. One of the higher estimates is that trade contributes one-third of the net increase in the wage gap.

On a sample of seventy-three countries, Chakrabarti finds that trade actually reduces inequality, as measured by the Gini coefficient. This relationship also holds for each income class.

Clearly, income distribution is determined by many factors beyond trade. One is redistribution policies undertaken by the government. In some cases such policies are initiated in an effort to compensate or "buy off" groups thought to be adversely affected by trade. But a far more important phenomenon is the tendency for countries to implement greater redistribution as they grow richer.

A long-established empirical regularity is the tendency for income inequality to worsen at early stages of growth and then to improve at later stages. The original explanation for this phenomenon, known as the Kuznets curve, had to do with rural-urban migration. But a common modern interpretation is that income redistribution is a "superior good"—something that societies choose to purchase more of, even though at some cost to aggregate income, as they grow rich enough to be able to afford to do so. If this is right, then trade can be expected eventually to raise equality, by raising aggregate income.

## Environment

Similar logic holds that trade and growth can also be good for the environment, once the country gets past a certain level of per capita income. Gene Grossman and Alan Krueger found what is called the environmental Kuznets curve: growth is bad for air and water pollution at the initial stages of industrialization but later on reduces pollution as countries become rich enough to pay to clean up their environments. . . . A key point is that popular desires need not translate automatically into environmental quality; rather government intervention is usually required to address externalities.

The idea that trade can be good for environment is surprising to many. The pollution-haven hypothesis instead holds that trade encourages firms to locate production of highly polluting sectors in low-regulation countries in order to stay competitive. But economists' research suggests that environmental regulation is not a major determinant of firms' ability to compete internationally. Furthermore, running counter to fears of a "race to the bottom," is the Pareto-improvement point: trade allows countries to attain more of whatever their goals are, including higher market-measured income for a given level of environmental quality or a better environment for a given level of income. . . .

The econometric studies of the effects of trade and growth on the environment get different results depending on what specific measures of pollution they use. There is a need to look at other environmental criteria as well. It is difficult to imagine, for example, that trade is anything but bad for the survival of tropical hardwood forests or endangered species, without substantial efforts by governments to protect them.

The argument that richer countries will take steps to clean up their environments holds only for issues when the effects are felt domestically—where the primary "bads," such as smog or water pollution, are external to the firm or household but internal to the country. Some environmental externalities that have received increased attention in recent decade, however, are global. Biodiversity, overfishing, ozone depletion, and greenhouse gas emissions are four good examples. A ton of carbon dioxide has the same global warming effect regardless of where in the world it is emitted. In these cases, individual nations can do little to improve the environment on their own, no matter how concerned their populations or how effective their governments. For each of the four examples, governments have negotiated international treaties in an attempt to deal with the problem. But only the attempt to address ozone depletion, the Montreal Protocol, can be said as yet to have met with much success.

Is the popular impression then correct, that international trade and finance exacerbates these global environmental externalities? Yes, but only in the sense that trade and finance promote economic growth. Clearly if mankind were still a population of a few million people living in preindustrial poverty, greenhouse gas emissions would not be a big issue. Industrialization leads to environmental degradation, and trade is part of industrialization. But virtually everyone wants industrialization, at least for themselves. Deliberate self-impoverishment is not a promising option. Once this point is recognized, there is nothing special about trade compared with the other sources of economic growth: capital accumulation, rural-urban migration, and technological progress. . . .

## SUMMARY OF CONCLUSIONS

This chapter gives confident answers to questions about the extent and sources of economic globalization and moderately confident answers to some questions about its effects.

The world has become increasingly integrated with respect to trade and finance since the end of World War II, owing to declining costs to transportation and communication and declining government barriers. The phenomenon is neither new nor complete, however. Globalization was more dramatic in the half-century preceding World War I, and much of the progress during the last half-century has merely reversed the closing off that came in between. In the second regard, globalization is far from complete. Contrary to popular impressions, national borders and geography still impede trade and investment substantially. A simple calculation suggests that the ratio of trade to output would have to increase at least another sixfold before it would be true that Americans trade across the globe as readily as across the country. Such barriers as differences in currencies, languages, and political systems each have their own statistically estimated trade-impeding influences, besides the remaining significant effects of distance, borders, and other geographical and trade policy variables.

The chapter's discussion of the impacts of economic globalization has necessarily been exceedingly brief. Both theory and evidence are read as clearly supportive of the proposition that trade has a positive effect on real incomes. This is why economists believe it is important that the process of international integration be allowed to continue, especially for the sake of those countries that are still poor.

Effects on social values other than aggregate incomes can be positive or negative, depending on the details, and the statistical evidence does not always give clear-cut answers about the bottom line. In the two most studied cases, income distribution and environmental pollution, there seems to be a pattern whereby things get worse in the early stages of industrialization but then start to get better at higher levels of income. Societies that become rich in terms of market-measured output choose to improve their quality of life in other ways as well. It is possible that the same principle extends to noneconomic values such as safety, human rights, and democracy. In short, there is reason to hope that, aside from the various more direct effects of trade on noneconomic values, there is a general indirect beneficial effect that comes through the positive effect of trade on income. . . .

## NOTES

1. John Maynard Keynes, *The Economic Consequences of The Peace* (Harcourt Brace, and Howe (1920).
2. Kenneth Froot, Michael Kim, and Kenneth Rogoff, "The Law of One Price over 700 Years," Working Paper 5132 (Cambridge, Mass.: National Bureau of Economic Research, May 1995).
3. Hans Linnemann, *An Econometric Study of International Trade Flows* (Amsterdam: North-Holland, 1960); and Peter Drysdale and Ross Garnaut, "Trade Intensities and the Analysis of Bilateral Trade Flows in a Many-Country World," *Hitotsubashi Journal of Economics*, Vol. 22 (1982), pp. 62–84.
4. Edward Mansfield, "Effects of International Politics on Regionalism in International Trade," in Kym Anderson and Richard Blackhurst, eds., *Regional Integration and the Global Trading System* (Harvester Wheatsheaf, 1993); Edward Mansfield and Rachel Bronson, "The Political Economy of Major-Power Trade Flows," in Edward Mansfield and Helen Milner, eds., *The Political Economy of Regionalism* (Columbia University Press 1997); and Joanne Gowa and Edward Mansfield, "Power Politics and International Trade," *American Political Science Review*, Vol. 87 (June 1993), pp. 408–20.

# Will Globalization Survive?

## MARTIN WOLF

Ours is not the first age of globalization. The decades before the First World War were remarkably similar to our own era. Under the aegis of the United Kingdom and stimulated by a host of technological advances, the world enjoyed an era of liberal trade, remarkably free movement of people, and almost entirely free movement of capital. The world also enjoyed an unprecedented rise in prosperity. According to the economic historian, Angus Maddison, real [Gross Domestic Product] per head rose at a rate of 1.3 percent a year in the world as a whole between 1870 and 1913.[1] This is not far short of the improvement of the past three decades. Only Asia and Africa, both victims of colonialism, failed to share in the rising prosperity.

Then came the war. Norman Angell, in his notorious book, *The Great Illusion*, published in 1910, argued persuasively that war was a ruinous folly. He hoped to persuade people that nothing could come from a European war but mutual ruin. His hopes failed. Many have since condemned him for his innocence. But if one reads his book, one will find not that he thought war impossible, but that he thought it insane. He hoped people would prove rational. People, as is their wont, disappointed him.

That war began the ruin of the first globalization. The economic disarray of the interwar years, the failure of the United States to assume the responsibilities of power, the weariness and weakness of the United Kingdom and France, the bitterness of the Germans, and the Bolshevik triumph in Russia completed the job. The failure of the first liberal order—that of the 19th century—led to 30 years of catastrophe. "Never again" was the motto under which I wrote my book, *Why Globalization Works*.[2]

Since then, we have recreated a better liberal international order—one that extends opportunities to the world as a whole. It is our duty to our descendants not to throw away this golden opportunity once again. Yet the fact that we should not do something does not mean that we will not do so. Globalization is fragile, for a simple reason: A global market economy depends on the support of states. States provide the security of property and person on which all complex exchange depends. But states are necessarily territorial. The loyalties they create, evoke, or reflect are steeped in humanity's characteristic tribalism.

In the remarks that follow, I wish to extend this argument by first analysing the driving forces of globalization and then looking at its achievements and failures before examining the risks that lie ahead. I conclude with what we can do to minimize those risks. But when I say "we," I really mean you: the United States.

---

Martin Wolf, "Will Globalization Survive?" The Third Whitman Lecture, Institute for International Economics, Washington, DC., April 5, 2005. Reprinted by permission of the author.

## WHAT DRIVES GLOBALIZATION

I define globalization as the integration of economies through markets across frontiers. It is driven, in turn, by two forces: the reduction in the costs of transportation and communications and economic liberalization. The reduction in the costs of transportation and communications is a consistent tendency in human history, though one that has accelerated over the past two centuries. Economic liberalization, however, is far from consistent. On the contrary, the last two centuries have seen two upswings and one huge downswing.

### Falling Costs of Transportation and Communications

Changes in transportation and communications technology create opportunities for increased commerce and are, in turn, created by them. This is *not* a new phenomenon.[3] The railway, the steamship, the refrigerator, and the telegraph created the opportunities for the integration of the 19th and early 20th centuries. The railway made the shipping of commodities in bulk over land feasible for the first time in history. With the steamship, tens of millions of people could cross the oceans with ease—and did so.

The first transatlantic cable was laid in 1866. This, argues professor Kevin O'Rourke, was "the most important breakthrough of the last 200 years" for the capital markets. "No other innovation," he writes, "including the late nineteenth-century invention, the telephone, or its late twentieth-century equivalent, the Internet, has had comparable impact on the speed of information flows and capital market integration."[4]

The 20th century added the container ship, the giant tanker, and the airliner. It also added radio, television, transcontinental telephony, the satellite, the computer, and the Internet. New opportunities have been created and, again, they have been exploited. They are to be seen in 24-hour financial markets, mass tourism, and the global interconnection of production that has spawned the multinational corporations of today.

### Economic Liberalization

In the long run, then, the world seems bound to become more globalized because opportunities have grown enormously. But history tells us that this does not mean a never-ending rise in integration. In the 19th century, a rising ride of liberalism reached its highest point in the last one or two decades of the century. Thereupon a combination of powerful forces reversed the tide. I define those forces as the four "I's": geopolitical insecurity—the rivalry among the great powers that culminated in two world wars; macroeconomic instability—above all the Great Depression; protectionist interests—particularly important in the United States in 1930, when the Smoot-Hawley tariff was enacted; and collectivist ideas—nationalism, imperialism, socialism, and communism. By 1945, the integrated world economy had disappeared.

After World War II, liberalization began anew, though haltingly, in Western Europe and across the Atlantic under the wise leadership of the United States. By the late 1960s, the success of a small number of relatively outward-looking east Asian economies was becoming more visible. By the late 1970s, the failures of state planning and nationalization were also becoming evident. This set the stage for what must be the most dramatic period of economic liberalization there has ever been—a process that has, in a quarter of a century, brought something like four billion additional people within the purview of the global market.

Think of the headlines alone: the transformation of Mao Zedong's China into what is, almost certainly, the most internationally open large country in history; the collapse of the Soviet empire; and the end of India's "license raj." These events alone transformed the economic lives of about 2.8 billion people. But this was not all. Economic liberalization also swept across much of Latin America.

In all these cases, moreover, what happened was not just liberalization at the border. As has usually been the case, the move towards the market has been simultaneously internal and external. There have been exceptions: The United States was one in the 19th century, when it combined high protection against imports with laissez-faire at home. But when countries decide to adopt the logic of the market, they normally do so both domestically and internationally. Once one has accepted that market relations make sense among domestic residents, it is hard to argue that foreigners must be excluded. A country's international transactions are, after all, just the aggregate of the individual transactions by its residents. Moreover, because the motivation for such transactions is the same as for transactions with fellow residents, they are just as likely to contribute to the welfare of those who undertake them. This is the logic of international integration.

It is impossible in a short space to examine this liberalization in detail. But let us take one example: China. Between 1992 and 2002, the weighted average tariff on Chinese imports fell from 40.6 percent to 6.4 percent. In effect, China, within just ten years, moved from having import barriers comparable to those of today's high income countries in the early 1950s to levels close to the current ones of the high-income countries. And, since a tax on imports is also a tax on exports, China's exports exploded: Between 1999 and last year, exports rose from $200 billion to not much short of $600 billion. What we are seeing here is nothing short of a global market revolution.

## GLOBALIZATION'S RECORD

What has been the result of the interaction of these twin forces, the declining costs of communications and the move to the market? Summarized briefly, two big things have happened over the past two and a half decades: The first is a huge rise in the integration of the goods-producing sectors of economies, and the second is a still bigger increase in foreign direct investment. These are two aspects of one thing: the integration of production across frontiers by transnational companies. They have, in the process, created something quite new: specialization of production within manufacturing on the basis of specific sources of comparative advantage.

Yet it is also important to be clear about what has not happened. Two things, in particular, are almost certainly less globalized than a century ago: labor markets and long-term capital markets.

The former is shown by the fact that the proportion of the world's population living in countries other than the country of birth is about 3 percent now, against about 10 percent in the late 19th century. It is also shown by the historically unprecedented gaps in real wages across the planet for people with much the same skills.

The latter is shown by the failure to generate consistent large net capital flows from rich countries to poorer ones. In fact, over the past seven years, the net flows have gone in the opposite direction, from the developing world to the world's richest country. The failure to create the basis for stable net flows of capital from the rich world to the poor one is, I would argue, the greatest single failure of the second age of globalization.

If we turn to human welfare, what is our assessment?

- Globalization has brought large economic gains to many parts of the world, above all to Asia, which has successfully exploited the ladder of development created by labor-intensive manufactures.
- Globalization has brought about huge reductions in the number of people in extreme poverty. According to the latest World Bank data, the proportion of the east Asian population living on less than a dollar a day at purchasing power parity fell from 56 percent in 1981 to 16 percent in 2001. This is the biggest and fastest reduction in extreme poverty in world history.
- The relatively rapid growth of Asian developing countries has almost certainly reduced global inequality among households for the first time since the 1820s.
- Globalization has brought big gains to the developed countries as well. Recent work by the Institute for International Economics suggests that the gains to the United States alone amount to $1,000 billion—almost 10 percent of GDP. For the United Kingdom, the gains must be far greater.[5]
- Globalization has not worked well for Africa or much of Latin America. For this there are three reasons: the resource curse, persistent protectionism in agriculture, and the weak supply conditions in these countries. In addition, for these countries, the entry of China into the world economy is a massive shock, both positive and, in some cases, negative.

My conclusion then is that we have done quite well, but we must do better. For this reason, I strongly support the idea of a big push on Africa. It is also why we must do what we can to encourage the rest of Latin America to learn from Chile's success, not Argentina's failure.

## THREATS TO GLOBALIZATION

Doing better would be excellent. But we can also do far worse. The international economic integration of the late 19th century went into reverse. Is the present move towards integration likely to suffer the same fate? To answer this question, one needs to take account of the differences and similarities between these two epochs. The breakdown last time was the consequence of the combined force of protectionist interests, antiliberal ideas, economic instability, and international rivalry. How likely are the same four horsemen of the apocalypse to return?

## Protectionist Interests

The first force underlying the disintegration of the earlier form of globalization was protectionist interests, shown most decisively in the United States in the interwar years. The highly protectionist policies of the world's biggest and most successful economy undermined liberalism elsewhere.

Yet these forces have happily been significantly modified and ameliorated by contemporary economic developments.

The rise of the internationally integrated transnational company has reduced the ability (and willingness) of producers to wrap themselves in national flags. It is no accident that protectionist interests are strongest in predominantly nationally owned and operated industries—such as steel and agriculture. Is a Toyota factory in the United States less or more American than a General Motors factory in China? Is Goldman Sachs in Frankfurt less or more American than HSBC in New York? The answer to such questions is: Who knows? Modern companies have global interests. The same is true for many of their most valued employees. Nationalists find the cosmopolitan attitudes of companies and many top-level employees objectionable. A significant consequence, however, is the breakdown in the ability and willingness of companies to collaborate with trades unions on their demand for protection. Developing countries have been affected by the same trends. Inward foreign direct investment and intraindustry trade diffuse traditional protectionist interests. The concept of a purely national business sector has become increasingly irrelevant and, just as in industrial countries, this diffuses protectionist lobbying.

The increase in service sector employment and the decline in employment in manufacturing has, along with the rise in the portion of the population in retirement, reduced the share of the voters whose jobs are directly vulnerable to import competition. Consumers have also become accustomed to foreign products. They may, as workers, complain about imports. But they still like the products foreign companies provide. Many in high-income countries express concern about the decline in relative wages and employment opportunities of the unskilled. But the political power of unskilled workers has diminished. Moreover, the consensus of economists, disputed by only a minority of politicians, is that this decline in opportunities reflects changes in technology, not in trade.

In addition, the existence of multilateral institutions and a web of strong international commitments makes it far more difficult for protectionist interests to capture legislatures, as they once did. There is too much at stake for countries to reverse the commitments they have made. Even the Bush administration, wedded though it is to unilateralism, has never said that it should ignore its obligations under the World Trade Organization (WTO), even though it is the most binding multilateral economic commitment the United States has.

## Collectivist Ideas

A second element in the 20th century collapse of the liberal international order began, at home, with the rise of antiliberal ideas. There are parallels today between groups then and now, particularly with what the former chief economist of the OECD, David Henderson, has called "new millennium collectivists"—the groups who unite to protest against global capitalism.[6] But this group of protesters is very different—and much less intellectually coherent—than the opponents of liberalism of a century ago. The antagonists of liberalism then converged around two ideas: radical socialism and racially-defined nationalism. Both groups called for control of the state over the economy and primacy of the collective over the self-seeking individual. Both sought power—and knew what they wanted to do with it. That made them extraordinarily dangerous.

The intellectual origins of today's antiliberal movement are far more diverse. They include environmentalists, development lobbies, populists, socialists, communists, and anarchists. These groups are united only in what they oppose. They are rooted in no cohesive social force, such as the organized working class. They largely reject party politics. They offer no alternative way of running an economy. They are split in their objectives. Part of what some protesters say—notably on the hypocrisy of the advanced countries and the plight of the poor—is valid. But a political movement cannot beat something with nothing. A movement that offers only protest is unlikely to triumph.

## Economic Instability

The decisive event in the collapse of the integrated economy of the late 19th and early 20th centuries was the Great Depression in the United States and the financial and exchange rate crises that rolled across the world in the 1930s. In developing countries, financial and exchange rate crises have come with depressing frequency over the past two decades. Substantial financial and exchange rate crises also erupted among the other advanced economies in the 1980s and early 1990s. Japan is still struggling with the aftermath of its bubble economy, while the United States has also suffered a huge stock market bubble, which reached its maximum extent in 2000.

All these are signs of significant financial instability. Yet it is almost impossible to believe that the outcome will be another 1930s. The move to floating rates has, as Max Corden foresaw, significantly reduced the risk of such crises.[7] The woes inflicted upon Argentina by the collapse of its currency board at the end of 2001 should, therefore, be viewed as the end of an era rather than as the beginning of a new one. Its crisis has also had remarkably little effect on other emerging-market economies. Much of the transfer of resources to developing countries is now taking place in the longer-term, more sustainable form of foreign direct investment. For all these reasons, the likelihood of massive waves of financial crises in emerging-market economies has declined. It is also striking that, despite these crises, no significant country has reversed its commitment to liberal trade or even to freedom from exchange controls. That even includes Argentina. Today, such policies are seen as a dead end—the quickest way to join Castro's Cuba or Kim Jong-il's North Korea in far from splendid isolation.

Yet I cannot leave the question of global economic instability without touching upon what is both the strangest and most disturbing feature of the world economy— its dependence for macroeconomic stability on explosive rises in U.S. current account deficits. The United States has, in essence, become the world's borrower of last resort. Since it is the world's most creditworthy debtor and the issuer of the world's most trusted currency, it is better placed to play this role than any other country. In the process, the United States is making it possible for the world to run at tolerably high levels of economic activity, by absorbing the excess savings of Japan and continental Europe and accommodating the mercantilism of emerging Asia. In addition, it has been substituting its own excellent credit for the poor credit of weak emerging-market economies, which would otherwise have surely been the world's principal borrowers. That has eliminated the big financial crises of the 1990s.

Yet this "solution" to the adding-up problem for the world economy itself carries two big risks: rising protectionist sentiment in the United States, and, at some point, a brutal and sudden correction, as the rest of the world decides that its holdings of dollar claims are excessive and, not least, too vulnerable to the depreciation that must occur if the U.S. current account deficit is to fall sharply as a share of GDP. The chance of a hard landing, with unpredictable political consequences in the United States and among the creditors, though not 100 percent, is not zero either, and, as I have frequently argued, the odds increase with each passing year.

## International Rivalry

Yet the most important cause of the 20th century breakdown was the collapse of harmonious international relations, as rivalries among the great powers and the rise of communism and fascism fragmented the globe.

. . . [Niall] Ferguson, too, emphasizes the geopolitical dangers, pointing to five parallels between the United States today and the United Kingdom a century ago: overstretched, physically and financially; great power rivalry, with China now in Germany's role; an unstable alliance system, with the disintegration of the transatlantic relationship; rogue regimes (then Serbia, now Iran and North Korea); and revolutionary organizations (then the Bolsheviks, now Al Qaeda).[8] I believe he is right: the breakdown in economics starts from a breakdown in global politics.

For the moment, however, the situation is different, in four fundamental respects:

- There is a single undisputed hegemon, the United States, and little chance of a war among the great powers in the near future, except just conceivably between the United States and China over Taiwan. Yet China is not, at present, powerful enough to be a rival of the United States.
- Second, all the great powers have largely abandoned the atavistic notion that prosperity derives from territorial gains and plunder rather than internal economic development and peaceful exchange. One of the striking features of today's war against terrorism is that all the world's great powers are on the same side.
- Third, all the great powers share a commitment to market-led economic development and international economic and political integration.

- Fourth, global institutions and habits of close cooperation reinforce the commitment to cooperation.

All these are powerful differences between the world of nearly a century ago and today's world. Against this, we must note two obvious parallels.

The breakdown of the early 20th century occurred, in part, because of the pressures to accommodate rising powers in the global economic and political order. The rise of China will, in time, create comparable pressures. If the United States remains wedded to notions of global primacy rather than of a shared global order, conflict with a rising China would seem virtually inevitable. Indeed, John Mearsheimer, professor of political science at the University of Chicago, argues that conflict (though not war) is inevitable *tout court*: the United States, he argues, will not tolerate a strategic rival.[9] War would then ensue for exactly the same reason that Thucydides thought it arose between Athens and Sparta: The status quo powers feared the rise of a rival, while the rising power resented the pretensions of the incumbents.

In addition, China's rise will force uncomfortable economic adjustments on the rest of the world. These are already creating protectionist pressures, notably so in the United States. It is not, alas, impossible to envisage a spiral of mutual hostility that undermines the commitment to a liberal international economic order.

Today, however, instead of such a breakdown in relations among the world's most important powers, we confront an alternative threat: mega-terrorism. Some fear that terrorist outrages on the scale of the attacks on New York and Washington of September 11, 2001—or even bigger ones—will end the commitment to open borders. It is not difficult to envisage the devastating impact the smuggling of a nuclear device into a country on a container ship would have on confidence in open borders. Closely related fears concern the development of weapons of mass destruction by regimes hostile to the liberal world order in general and the United States in particular. At worst, such regimes might collaborate with terrorists to inflict vast, and virtually untraceable, damage on civilized states.

Fear of what might come across borders must act as a tax on globalization. If countries had to be sure of the safety of every shipment and person that crosses their borders, much of today's globalization would become impossible. Yet that would also hand the victory to the terrorists and their sponsors. At present, it does not appear that the world's response to September 11 will be to close borders. That would only exacerbate the desperation in the world's less economically successful countries. Global cooperation to control terrorists and improved security measures seem a more appropriate and effective route. But the danger is a genuine one. It cannot be ignored.

## Resource Insufficiency

Power is not the only asset whose availability creates a zero-sum relationship. So does the supply of finite resources. While most countries now understand that wealth is created by production and exchange, not plunder, that is not so obviously true of access to raw materials, particularly fossil fuels. If one accepts that the supply is, indeed, finite, then more demand by new consumers makes other consumers unambiguously worse off. In recent years, incremental demand for oil from Asia has exceeded incremental demand from North America by two to one. This is one of the explanations for today's high prices. If one combines this with the fact that the politically unstable Gulf region seems set to become an ever more important source of this vital fuel, the potential for disruption and even conflict is not small. Why, Americans might reasonably ask, should they bear the price of ensuring oil to China at the same (high) price as the one they pay themselves? The search for vital raw materials was a motivating force behind territorial expansion in the first half of the 20th century. It could easily become so again in the years ahead.

## SO WHAT IS TO BE DONE?

Globalization is not inevitable. It depends on politics. In today's world, it depends above all on U.S. politics. Without successful U.S. leadership at a time of huge upheavals, the present globalization may founder, just as the last one did. I suggest three priorities:

First, a big effort must be made to ensure that the weakest and poorest countries are in a position to share at least some of the benefits of the global economy and advancing technologies. It is too easy to imagine that, by the middle of this century, as many as 1.5 billion to 2 billion people will live in countries whose real incomes per head are less than a hundredth of those in the richest. Such a world cannot possibly be stable.

Second, an equally big effort must be made to fix the sources of global macro-economic instability. In the long run, it will be important for emerging-market economies to pursue policies that allow them to borrow in their own currencies. More importantly, China must be told firmly that the Asian mercantilist strategy will not work for a country of its scale. At the very least, it should run a current account deficit equal to the net inflow of foreign direct investment.

Third and most important, the United States must find a way to deal with the three principal long-term sources of geopolitical instability: dependency on oil from the Gulf region; Islamic fundamentalism; and a rising China. In none of these cases will the United States be able to achieve what it wants on its own. In all cases, however, the outcome will depend on U.S. leadership.

Progress or relapse—the choice is largely, but not entirely, the United States'. History will judge. We can only warn. Peace, prosperity, and harmonious international relations are neither normal nor natural. They must be worked for by every generation. Ours is no exception.

## NOTES

1. Angus Maddison, *The World Economy: Historical Statistics* (Paris: Organisation for Economic Co-operation and Development, 2003).
2. Martin Wolf, *Why Globalization Works* (New Haven and London: Yale University Press, 2004), x–xviii.

3. Kevin O'Rourke, "Europe and the Causes of Globalization, 1790 to 2000" in Henryk Kierzkowski, ed., *Europe and Globalization* (Basingstoke: Palgrave Macmillan, 2002) chap. 3, 74–6.

4. Ibid., 76.

5. Institute for International Economics, "A New Foreign Economic Policy for the United States" (Washington: Institute for International Economics, February 9, 2005), http://www.iie.com/publications/newsreleases/feppr.htm.

6. See David Henderson, *Anti-Liberalism 2000: the Rise of New Millennium Collectivism* (London: The Institute of Economic Affairs, 2001).

7. See W. Max Corden, *Economic Policy, Exchange Rates, and the International System* (Oxford: Oxford University Press and Chicago: University of Chicago Press, 1994).

8. Niall Ferguson, "Sinking Globalization," *Foreign Affairs* (March/April 2005), 64–77.

9. John J. Mearsheimer, "Better to Be Godzilla than Bambi," *Foreign Policy* (January/February 2005).

# Globalization and Governance

## KENNETH N. WALTZ

In 1979 I described the interdependence of states as low but increasing. It has increased, but only to about the 1910 level if measured by trade or capital flows as a percentage of GNP; lower if measured by the mobility of labor, and lower still if measured by the mutual military dependence of states. Yet one feels that the world has become a smaller one. International travel has become faster, easier, and cheaper; music, art, cuisines, and cinema have all become cosmopolitan in the world's major centers and beyond. The *Peony Pavilion* was produced in its entirety for the first time in 400 years, and it was presented not in Shanghai or Beijing, but in New York. Communication is almost instantaneous, and more than words can be transmitted, which makes the reduced mobility of labor of less consequence. High-technology jobs can be brought to the workers instead of the workers to the jobs; foreigners can become part of American design teams without leaving their homelands. Before World War I, the close interdependence of states was thought of as heralding an era of peace among nations and democracy and prosperity within them. Associating interdependence, peace, democracy, and prosperity is nothing new. In his much translated and widely read book, *The Great Illusion* (1933), Norman Angell summed up the texts of generations of classical and neo-classical economists and drew from them the dramatic conclusion that wars would no longer be fought because they would not pay. World War I instead produced the great disillusion, which reduced political optimism to a level that remained low almost until the end of the Cold War. I say "almost" because beginning in the 1970s a new optimism, strikingly similar in content to the old, began to resurface. Inter-dependence was again associated with peace and peace increasingly with democracy, which began to spread wonderfully to Latin America, to Asia, and with the Soviet Union's collapse, to Eastern Europe. Francis Fukuyama (1992) foresaw a time when all states would be liberal democracies and, more recently, Michael Doyle (1997) projected the year for it to happen as lying between 2050 and 2100. John Mueller (1989), heralding the disappearance of war among the world's advanced countries, argued that Norman Angell's premises were right all along, but that he had published his book prematurely.

Robert Keohane and Joseph Nye in their 1977 book, *Power and Interdependence,* strengthened the notion that interdependence promotes peace and limits the use of force by arguing that simple interdependence had become complex

From Kenneth N. Waltz, "Globalization and Governance," *PS: Political Science & Politics,* Vol. 32, No. 4 (December 1999), pp. 693–700 with minor revisions. Copyright © 1999 by The American Political Science Association. Reprinted with the permission of Cambridge University Press.

interdependence, binding the economic and hence the political interests of states ever more tightly together. Now, we hear from many sides that interdependence has reached yet another height, transcending states and making *The Borderless World*, which is the title and theme of Kenichi Ohmae's 1990 book. People, firms, markets matter more; states matter less. Each tightening of the economic screw raises the benefits of economic exchange and makes war among the more advanced states increasingly costly. The simple and plausible propositions are that as the benefits of peace rise, so do the costs of war. When states perceive wars to be immensely costly, they will be disinclined to fight them. War becomes rare, but is not abolished because even the strongest economic forces cannot conquer fear or eliminate concern for national honor (Friedman 1999, 196–97).

Economic interests become so strong that markets begin to replace politics at home and abroad. That economics depresses politics and limits its significance is taken to be a happy thought. The first section of this paper examines its application domestically; the second, internationally.

## THE STATE OF THE STATE

Globalization is the fad of the 1990s, and globalization is made in America. Thomas Friedman's *The Lexus and the Olive Tree* is a celebration of the American way, of market capitalism and liberal democracy. Free markets, transparency, and flexibility are the watchwords. The "electronic herd" moves vast amounts of capital in and out of countries according to their political and economic merits. Capital moves almost instantaneously into countries with stable governments, progressive economies, open accounting, and honest dealing, and out of countries lacking those qualities. States can defy the "herd," but they will pay a price, usually a steep one, as did Thailand, Malaysia, Indonesia, and South Korea in the 1990s. Some countries may defy the herd inadvertently (the countries just mentioned); others, out of ideological conviction (Cuba and North Korea); some, because they can afford to (oil-rich countries); others, because history has passed them by (many African countries).

Countries wishing to attract capital and to gain the benefits of today's and tomorrow's technology have to don the "golden straitjacket," a package of policies including balanced budgets, economic deregulation, openness to investment and trade, and a stable currency. The herd decides which countries to reward and which to punish, and nothing can be done about its decisions. In September 1997, at a World Bank meeting, Malaysia's prime minister, Dr. Mahathir Mohammad, complained bitterly that great powers and international speculators had forced Asian countries to open their markets and had manipulated their currencies in order to destroy them. Friedman (1999, 93) wonders what Robert Rubin, then-U.S. treasury secretary, might have said in response. He imagines it would have been something like this: "What planet are you living on? . . . Globalization isn't a choice, it's a reality, . . . and the only way you can grow at the speed that your people want to grow is by tapping into the global stock and bond markets, by seeking out multinationals to invest in your country, and by selling into the global trading system what your factories produce. And the most basic truth about globalization is this: *No one is in charge.*"

The herd has no telephone number. When the herd decides to withdraw capital from a country, there is no one to complain to or to petition for relief. Decisions of the herd are collective ones. They are not made; they happen, and they happen because many investors individually make decisions simultaneously and on similar grounds to invest or to withdraw their funds. Do what displeases the herd, and it will trample you into the ground. Globalization is shaped by markets, not by governments.

Globalization means homogenization. Prices, products, wages, wealth, and rates of interest and profit tend to become the same all over the world. Like any powerful movement for change, globalization encounters resistance—in America, from religious fundamentalists; abroad, from anti-Americanists; everywhere from cultural traditionalists. And the resisters become bitter because consciously or not they know they are doomed. Driven by technology, international finance sweeps all before it. Under the protection of American military power, globalization proceeds relentlessly. As Friedman proclaims: "America truly is the ultimate benign hegemony" (375).

The "end of the Cold War and the collapse of communism have discredited all models other than liberal democracy." The statement is by Larry Diamond, and Friedman repeats it with approval. There is one best way, and America has found it. "It's a post-industrial world, and America today is good at everything that is post-industrial" (145, 303). The herd does not care about forms of government as such, but it values and rewards "stability, predictability, transparency, and the ability to transfer and protect its private property." Liberal democracies represent the one best way. The message to all governments is clear: Conform or suffer.

There is much in what Friedman says, and he says it very well. But how much? And, specifically, what is the effect of closer interdependence on the conduct of the internal and external affairs of nations?

First, we should ask how far globalization has proceeded? As everyone knows, much of the world has been left aside: most of Africa and Latin America, Russia, all of the Middle East except Israel, and large parts of Asia. Moreover, for many countries, the degree of participation in the global economy varies by region. Northern Italy, for example, is in; southern Italy is out. In fact, globalization is not global but is mainly limited to northern latitudes. Linda Weiss points out that, as of 1991, 81% of the world stock of foreign direct investment was in high-wage countries of the north: mainly the United States, followed by the United Kingdom, Germany, and Canada. She adds that the extent of concentration has grown by 12 points since 1967 (Weiss 1998; cf., Hirst and Thompson 1996, 72).

Second, we should compare the interdependence of nations now with interdependence earlier. The first paragraph of this paper suggests that in most ways we have not exceeded levels reached in 1910. The rapid growth of international trade and investment from the middle 1850s into the 1910s preceded a prolonged period of war, internal revolution, and national insularity. After World War II, protectionist policies lingered as the United States opened its borders to trade while taking a relaxed attitude toward countries that protected their markets during the years of recovery from war's devastation. One might say that from 1914 into the 1960s an interdependence deficit developed, which helps to explain the steady growth of interdependence thereafter. Among the richest 24 industrial economies (the OECD countries), exports grew at about twice the rate of GDP after 1960. In 1960, exports were 9.5% of their GDPs; in 1900, 20.5% (Wade 1996, 62; cf., Weiss 1998, 171). Finding that 1999 approximately equals 1910 in extent of interdependence is hardly surprising. What is true of trade also holds for capital flows, again as a percentage of GDP (Hirst and Thompson 1996, 36).

Third, money markets may be the only economic sector one can say has become truly global. Finance capital moves freely across the frontiers of OECD countries and quite freely elsewhere (Weiss 1998, xii). Robert Wade notes that real interest rates within northern countries and between northern and southern countries vary by no more than 5%. This seems quite large until one notices variations across countries of 10 to 50 times in real wages, years of schooling, and numbers of working scientists. Still, with the movement of financial assets as with commodities, the present remains like the past. Despite today's ease of communication, financial markets at the turn of the previous century were at least as integrated as they are now (Wade 1996, 73–75).

Obviously, the world is not one. Sadly, the disparities of the North and South remain wide. Perhaps surprisingly, among the countries that are thought of as being in the zone of globalization, differences are considerable and persistent. To take just one example, financial patterns differ markedly across countries. The United States depends on capital imports, Western Europe does not, and Japan is a major capital exporter. The more closely one looks, the more one finds variations. That is hardly surprising. What looks smooth, uniform, and simple from a distance, on closer inspection proves to be pockmarked, variegated, and complex. Yet here, the variations are large enough to sustain the conclusion that globalization, even within its zone, is not a statement about the present, but a prediction about the future.

Many globalizers underestimate the extent to which the new looks like the old. In any competitive system the winners are imitated by the losers, or they continue to lose. In political as in economic development, latecomers imitate the practices and adopt the institution of the countries who have shown the way. Occasionally, someone finds a way to outflank, to invent a new way, or to ingeniously modify an old way to gain an advantage; and then the process of imitation begins anew. That competitors begin to look like one another if the competition is close and continuous is a familiar story. Competition among states has always led some of them to imitate others politically, militarily, and economically; but the apostles of globalization argue that the process has now sped up immensely and that the straitjacket allows little room to wiggle. In the old political era, the strong vanquished the weak; in the new economic era, "the fast eat the slow" (Klaus Schwab quoted in Friedman 1999, 171). No longer is it "Do what the strong party says or risk physical punishment"; but instead "Do what the electronic herd requires or remain impoverished." But then, in a competitive system there are always winners and losers. A few do exceptionally well, some get along, and many bring up the rear.

States have to conform to the ways of the more successful among them or pay a stiff price for not doing so. We then have to ask what is the state of the state?

What becomes of politics within the coils of encompassing economic processes? The message of globalizers is that economic and technological forces impose near uniformity of political and economic forms and functions on states. They do so because the herd is attracted only to countries with reliable, stable, and open governments—that is, to liberal democratic ones.

Yet a glance at just the past 75 years reveals that a variety of political-economic systems have produced impressive results and were admired in their day for doing so. In the 1930s and again in the 1950s, the Soviet Union's economic growth rates were among the world's highest, so impressive in the '50s that America feared being overtaken and passed by. In the 1960s President Kennedy got "the country moving again," and America's radically different system gained world respect. In the '70s, Western European welfare states with managed and directed economics were highly regarded. In the late '70s and through much of the '80s, the Japanese brand of neomercantilism was thought to be the wave of the future; and Western Europe and the United States worried about being able to keep up. Imitate or perish was the counsel of some; pry the Japanese economy open and make it compete on our grounds was the message of others. America did not succeed in doing much of either. Yet in the 1990s, its economy has flourished. Globalizers offer it as the ultimate political-economic model—and so history again comes to an end. Yet it is odd to conclude from a decade's experience that the one best model has at last appeared. Globalization, if it were realized, would mean a near uniformity of conditions across countries. Even in the 1990s, one finds little evidence of globalization. The advanced countries of the world have enjoyed or suffered quite different fates. Major Western European countries were plagued by high and persistent unemployment; Northeast and Southeast Asian countries experienced economic stagnation or collapse while China continued to do quite well; and we know about the United States.

Variation in the fortunes of nations underlines the point: The country that has done best, at least lately, is the United States. Those who have fared poorly have supposedly done so because they have failed to conform to the American Way. Globalizers do not claim that globalization is complete, but only that it is in process and that the process is irreversible. Some evidence supports the conclusion; some does not. Looking at the big picture, one notices that nations whose economies have faltered or failed have been more fully controlled, directed, and supported governmentally than the American economy. Soviet-style economies failed miserably; in China, only the free-market sector flourishes; the once much-favored Swedish model has proved wanting. One can easily add more examples. From them it is tempting to leap to the conclusion that America has indeed found, or stumbled onto, the one best way.

Obviously, Thomas Friedman thinks so. Tip O'Neill, when he was a congressman from Massachusetts, declared that all politics are local. Wrong, Friedman says, all politics have become global. "The electronic herd," he writes, "turns the whole world into a parliamentary system, in which every government lives under the fear of a no-confidence vote from the herd" (1999, 62, 115).

I find it hard to believe that economic processes direct or determine a nation's policies, that spontaneously arrived at decisions about where to place resources reward or punish a national economy so strongly that a government either does what pleases the "herd" or its economy fails to prosper or even risks collapse. We all recall recent cases, some of them mentioned above, that seem to support Friedman's thesis. Mentioning them both makes a point and raises doubts.

First, within advanced countries at similar levels of development that are closely interrelated, one expects uniformities of form and function to be most fully displayed. Yet Stephen Woolcock, looking at forms of corporate governance within the European community, finds a "spectrum of approaches" and expects it to persist for the foreseeable future (1996, 196). Since the 1950s, the economies of Germany and France have grown more closely together as each became the principal trading partner of the other. Yet a study of the two countries concludes that France has copied German policies but has been unwilling or unable to copy institutions (Boltho 1996). GDP per work hour among seven of the most prosperous countries came close together between the 1950s and the 1980s (Boyer 1996, 37). Countries at a high level of development do tend to converge in productivity, but that is something of a tautology.

Second, even if all politics have become global, economies remain local perhaps to a surprising extent. Countries with large economies continue to do most of their business at home. Americans produce 88% of the goods they buy. Sectors that are scarcely involved in international trade, such as government, construction, nonprofit organizations, utilities, and wholesale and retail trade employ 82% of Americans (Lawrence 1997, 21). As Paul Krugman says, "The United States is still almost 90% an economy that produces goods and services for its own use" (1997, 166). For the world's three largest economies—the United States, Japan, and the European Union—taken as a unit, exports are 12% or less of GDP (Weiss 1998, 176). What I found to be true in 1970 remains true today: The world is less interdependent than is usually supposed (Waltz 1970). Moreover, developed countries, oil imports aside, do the bulk of their external business with one another, and that means that the extent of their dependence on commodities that they could not produce for themselves is further reduced.

Reinforcing the parochial pattern of productivity, the famous footloose corporations in fact turn out to be firmly anchored in their home bases. One study of the world's 100 largest corporations concludes that not one of them could be called truly "global" or "footloose." Another study found one multinational corporation that seemed to be leaving its home base: Britain's chemical company, ICI (Weiss 1998, 18, 22; cf., Hirst and Thompson 1996, 82–93, 90, 95ff.). On all the important counts—location of most assets, site of research and development, ownership, and management—the importance of a corporation's home base is marked. And the technological prowess of corporations corresponds closely to that of the countries in which they are located.

Third, the *"transformative capacity"* of states, as Linda Weiss emphasizes, is the key to their success in the world economy (Weiss 1998, xii). Because technological innovation is rapid, and because economic conditions at home and abroad change often, states that adapt easily have considerable advantages. International politics remains inter-national. As the title of a review by William H. McNeill

(1997) puts it, "Territorial States Buried Too Soon." Global or world politics has not taken over from national politics. The twentieth century was the century of the nation-state. The twenty-first will be too. Trade and technology do not determine a single best way to organize a polity and its economy. National systems display a great deal of resilience. States still have a wide range of choice. Most states survive, and the units that survive in competitive systems are those with the ability to adapt. Some do it well, and they grow and prosper. Others just manage to get along. That's the way it is in competitive systems. In this spirit, Ezra Taft Benson, when he was President Eisenhower's secretary of agriculture, gave this kindly advice to America's small farmers: "Get big or get out." Success in competitive systems requires the units of the system to adopt ways they would prefer to avoid.

States adapt to their environment. Some are light afoot, and others are heavy. The United States looked to be heavy afoot in the 1980s when Japan's economy was booming. Sometimes it seemed that MITI (Ministry of International Trade and Industry) was manned by geniuses who guided Japan's economy effortlessly to its impressive accomplishments. Now it is the United States that appears light afoot, lighter than any other country. Its government is open: Accurate financial information flows freely, most economic decisions are made by private firms. These are the characteristics that make for flexibility and for quick adaptation to changing conditions.

Competitive systems select for success. Over time, the qualities that make for success vary. Students of American government point out that one of the advantages of a federal system is that the separate states can act as laboratories for social-economic experimentation. When some states succeed, others may imitate them. The same thought applies to nations. One must wonder who the next winner will be.

States adapt; they also protect themselves. Different nations, with distinct institutions and traditions, protect themselves in different ways. Japan fosters industries, defends them, and manages its trade. The United States uses its political, economic, and military leverage to protect itself and manipulate international events to promote its interests. Thus, as David E. Spiro elaborately shows, international markets and institutions did not recycle petrodollars after 1974. The United States did. Despite many statements to the contrary, the United States worked effectively through different administrations and under different cabinet secretaries to undermine markets and thwart international institutions. Its leverage enabled it to manipulate the oil crisis to serve its own interests (1999, chap. 6).

Many of the interdependers of the 1970s expected the state to wither and fade away. Charles Kindleberger wrote in 1969 that "the nation-state is just about through as an economic unit" (207). Globalizers of the 1990s believe that this time it really is happening. The state has lost its "monopoly over internal sovereignty," Wolfgang H. Reinecke writes, and as "an externally sovereign actor" it "will become a thing of the past" (1997, 137; cf., Thurow 1999). Internally, the state's monopoly has never been complete, but it seems more nearly so now than earlier, at least in well-established states. The range of governmental functions and the extent of state control over society and economy has seldom been fuller than it is now. In many parts of the world the concern has been not with the state's diminished internal powers but with their increase. And although state control has lessened somewhat recently, does anyone believe that the United States and Britain, for example, are back to a 1930s level, let alone to a nineteenth-century level of governmental regulation?

States perform essential political social-economic functions, and no other organization appears as a possible competitor to them. They foster the institutions that make internal peace and prosperity possible. In the state of nature, as Kant put it, there is "no mine and thine." States turn possession into property and thus make saving, production, and prosperity possible. The sovereign state with fixed borders has proved to be the best organization for keeping peace and fostering the conditions for economic well being.1 We do not have to wonder what happens to society and economy when a state begins to fade away. We have all too many examples. A few obvious ones are China in the 1920s and '30s and again in the 1960s and '70s, post-Soviet Russia, and many African states since their independence. The less competent a state, the likelier it is to dissolve into component parts or to be unable to adapt to transnational developments. Challenges at home and abroad test the mettle of states. Some states fail, and other states pass the tests nicely. In modern times, enough states always make it to keep the international system going as a system of states. The challenges vary; states endure. They have proved to be hardy survivors.

Having asked how international conditions affect states, I now reverse the question and ask how states affect the conduct of international political affairs.

## THE STATE IN INTERNATIONAL POLITICS

Economic globalization would mean that the world economy, or at least the globalized portion of it, would be integrated and not merely interdependent. The difference between an interdependent and an integrated world is a qualitative one and not a mere matter of proportionately more trade and a greater and more rapid flow of capital. With integration, the world would look like one big state. Economic markets and economic interests cannot perform the functions of government. Integration requires or presumes a government to protect, direct, and control. Interdependence, in contrast to integration, is "the mere mutualism" of states, as Émile Durkheim put it. It is not only less close than usually thought but also politically less consequential. Interdependence did not produce the world-shaking events of 1989–91. A political event, the failure of one of the world's two great powers, did that. Had the configuration of international politics not fundamentally changed, neither the unification of Germany nor the war against Saddam Hussein would have been possible. The most important events in international politics are explained by differences in the capabilities of states, not by economic forces operating across states or transcending them. Interdependers, and globalizers even more so, argue that the international economic interests of states work against their going to war. True, they do. Yet if one asks whether economic interests or nuclear weapons inhibit war more strongly, the answer obviously is nuclear weapons. European great powers prior to World War I were tightly tied together economically. They nevertheless fought a long and bloody war. The United States and the Soviet Union were not even loosely connected economically. They co-existed peacefully through the four-and-a-half decades of the Cold War. The most important causes of peace, as of war, are found in international-political conditions, including the weaponry available to states. Events following the Cold War dramatically demonstrate the political weakness of economic forces. The integration (not just the interdependence) of the parts of the Soviet Union and of Yugoslavia, with all of their entangling economic interests, did not prevent their disintegration. Governments and people sacrifice welfare and even security to nationalism, ethnicity, and religion.

Political explanations weigh heavily in accounting for international-political events. National *politics*, not international markets, account for many international *economic* developments. A number of students of politics and of economics believe that blocs are becoming more common internationally. Economic interests and market forces do not create blocs; governments do. Without governmental decisions, the Coal and Steel Community, the European Economic Community, and the European Union would not have emerged. The representatives of states negotiate regulations in the European Commission. The Single-Market Act of 1985 provided that some types of directives would require less than a unanimous vote in the Council of Ministers. This political act cleared the way for passage of most of the harmonization standards for Europe (Dumez and Jeunemaître 1996, 229). American governments forged NAFTA; Japan fashioned an East and Southeast Asian producing and trading area. The decisions and acts of a country, or a set of countries arriving at political agreements, shape international political and economic institutions. Governments now intervene much more in international economic matters than they did in the earlier era of interdependence. Before World War I, foreign-ministry officials were famed for their lack of knowledge of, or interest in, economic affairs. Because governments have become much more active in economic affairs at home and abroad, interdependence has become less of an autonomous force in international politics.

The many commentators who exaggerate the closeness of interdependence, and even more so those who write of globalization, think in unit rather than in systemic terms. Many small states import and export large shares of their gross domestic products. States with large GDPs do not. They are little dependent on others, while a number of other states heavily depend on them. The terms of political, economic, and military competition are set by the larger units of the international-political system. Through centuries of multipolarity, with five or so great powers of comparable size competing with one another, the international system was quite closely interdependent. Under bi- and unipolarity the degree of interdependence declined markedly.

States are differentiated from one another not by function but primarily by capability. For two reasons, inequalities across states have greater political impact than inequalities across income groups within states. First, the inequalities of states are larger and have been growing more rapidly. Rich countries have become richer while poor countries have remained poor. Second, in a system without central governance, the influence of the units of greater capability is disproportionately large because there are no effective laws and institutions to direct and constrain them. They are able to work the system to their advantage, as the petrodollar example showed. I argued in 1970 that what counts are states' capacity to adjust to external conditions and their ability to use their economic leverage for political advantage. The United States was then and is still doubly blessed. It remains highly important in the international economy, serving as a principal market for a number of countries and as a major supplier of goods and services, yet its dependence on others is quite low. Precisely because the United States is relatively little dependent on others, it has a wide range of policy choices and the ability both to bring pressure on others and to assist them. The "herd" with its capital may flee from countries when it collectively decides that they are politically and economically unworthy, but some countries abroad, like some firms at home, are so important that they cannot be allowed to fail. National governments and international agencies then come to the rescue. The United States is the country that most often has the ability and the will to step in. The agency that most often acts is the IMF, and most countries think of the IMF as the enforcement arm of the U.S. Treasury (Strange 1996, 192). Thomas Friedman believes that when the "herd" makes its decisions, there is no appeal; but often there is an appeal, and it is for a bail out organized by the United States.

The international economy, like national economies, operates within a set of rules and institutions. Rules and institutions have to be made and sustained. Britain, to a large extent, provided this service prior to World War I; no one did between the wars, and the United States has done so since. More than any other state, the United States makes the rules and maintains the institutions that shape the international political economy.

Economically, the United States is the world's most important country; militarily, it is not only the most important country, it is the decisive one. Thomas Friedman puts the point simply: The world is sustained by "the presence of American power and America's willingness to use that power against those who would threaten the system of globalization. . . . The hidden hand of the market will never work without a hidden fist" (1999, 373). But the hidden fist is in full view. On its military forces, the United States outspends the next six or seven big spenders combined. When force is needed to keep or to restore the peace, either the United States leads the way or the peace is not kept. The Cold War militarized international politics. Relations between the United States and the Soviet Union, and among some other countries as well, came to be defined largely in a single dimension, the military one. As the German sociologist Erich Weede has remarked, "National security decision making in some . . . democracies (most notably in West Germany) is actually penetrated by the United States" (1989, 225). . . .

Many globalizers believe that the world is increasingly ruled by markets. Looking at the state among states leads to a different conclusion. The main difference between international politics now and earlier is not found in the increased interdependence of states but in their growing inequality. With the end of bipolarity, the distribution of capabilities across states has become extremely lopsided. Rather than elevating economic forces and depressing political ones, the inequalities of international politics enhance the political role of one country. Politics, as usual, prevails over economics.[1]

# NOTE

1. The picture of the purpose and the performance of states is especially clear in Thomson and Krasner (1989).

# REFERENCES

Angell, Norman. 1933. *The Great Illusion.* New York: G.P. Putnam's Sons.

Boltho, Andrea. 1996. "Has France Converged on Germany?" In *National Diversity and Global Capitalism,* ed. Suzanne Berger and Ronald Dore. Ithaca: Cornell University Press.

Bover, Robert. 1996. "The Convergence Hypothesis Revisited: Globalization But Still the Century of Nations." In *National Diversity and Global Capitalism,* ed. Suzanne Berger and Ronald Dore. Ithaca: Cornell University Press.

Carter, Ashton B., and William J. Perry. 1999. *Preventive Defense: A New Security Strategy for America.* Washington, DC: The Brookings Institution.

_____, and John D. Steinbruner. 1992. *A New Concept of Cooperative Security.* Washington, DC: The Brookings Institution.

Doyle, Michael W. 1997. *Ways of War and Peace: Realism, Liberalism, and Socialism.* New York: W.W. Norton.

Dumez, Hervé, and Alain Jeunemaître. 1996. "The Convergence of Competition Policies in Europe: Internal Dynamics and External Imposition." In *National Diversity and Global Capitalism,* ed. Suzanne Berger and Ronald Dore. Ithaca: Cornell University Press.

Fukuyama, Francis. 1992. *The End of History and the Last Man.* New York: Free Press.

Friedman, Thomas L. 1999. *The Lexus and the Olive Tree.* New York: Farrar, Straus, Giroux.

Gardner, Lloyd. 1995. *Pay Any Price: Lyndon Johnson and the Wars for Vietnam.* Chicago: I.R. Dee.

Hist, Paul, and Grahame Thompson. 1996. *Globalization in Question: The International Economy and the Possibilities of Governance.* Cambridge, UK: Polity Press.

Huntington, Samuel P. 1999. "The Lonely Superpower." *Foreign Affairs* 78 (March/April).

Ikenberry, John. 1998/99. "Institutions, Strategic Restraint, and the Persistence of American Postwar Order." *International Security* 23 (Winter): 77–78.

Keohane, Robert O., and Joseph S. Nye. 1977. *Power and Interdependence: World Politics in Transition.* Boston: Little, Brown.

Kindleberger, Charles P. 1969. *American Business Abroad.* New Haven: Yale University Press.

Krugman, Paul. 1997. "Competitiveness: A Dangerous Obsession." In *The New Shape of World Politics.* New York: W.W. Norton and *Foreign Affairs.*

Lawrence, Robert Z. 1997. "Workers and Economists II: Resist the Binge." In *The New Shape of Politics.* New York: W.W. Norton and *Foreign Affairs.*

Mueller, John. 1989. *Retreat from Doomsday: The Obsolescence of Major War.* New York: Basic Books.

McNeill, William H. 1997. "Territorial States Buried Too Soon." *Mershon International Studies Review.*

Nye, Joseph Jr. 1999. "Redefining the National Interest." *Foreign Affairs* 78 (July/August).

Ohmae, Kenichi. 1990. *The Borderless World: Power and Strategy in the Interlinked Economy.* New York: HarperBusiness.

Reinecke, Wolfgang H. 1997. "Global Public Policy." *Foreign Affairs* 76 (November/December).

Spiro, David E. 1999. *The Hidden Hand of American Hegemony: Petrodollar Recycling and International Markets.* Ithaca: Cornell University Press.

Strange, Susan. 1996. *The Retreat of the State: The Diffusion of Power in the World Economy.* Cambridge: Cambridge University Press.

Thomson, Janice E., and Stephen D. Krasner. 1989. "Global Transactions and the Consolidation of Sovereignty." In *Global Changes and Theoretical Challenges: Approaches to World Politics for the 1990s,* ed. Ernst-Otto Czempiel and James N. Rosenau. Lexington, MA: Lexington Books.

Thurow, Lester C. 1999. *Building Wealth: The New Rules for Individuals, Companies, and Nations in a Knowledge-Based Economy.* New York: HarperCollins.

Wade, Robert. 1996. "Globalization and Its Limits: Reports of the Death of the National Economy Are Grossly Exaggerated." In *National Diversity and Global Capitalism,* ed. Suzanne Berger and Ronald Dore. Ithaca: Cornell University Press.

Waltz, Kenneth N. 1970. "The Myth of National Interdependence." In *The International Corporation,* ed. Charles P. Kindleberger. Cambridge, MA: MIT Press.

_____. "Structural Realism after the Cold War." Presented at the Annual Meeting of the American Political Science Association, Boston.

Weede, Erich. 1989. "Collective Goods in an Interdependent World: Authority and Order as Determinants of Peace and Prosperity." In *Global Changes and Theoretical Challenges: Approaches to World Politics for the 1990s,* ed. Ernst-Otto Czempiel and James N. Rosenau. Lexington, MA: Lexington Books.

Weiss, Linda. 1998. *The Myth of the Powerless State: Governing the Economy in a Global Era.* Cambridge, UK: Polity Press.

Woolcock, Stephen. 1996. "Competition among Forms of Corporate Governance in the European Community: The Case of Britain." In *National Diversity and Global Capitalism,* ed. Suzanne Berger and Ronald Dore. Ithaca: Cornell University Press.

# THE PROS AND CONS OF GLOBALIZATION

## Trading in Illusions

### DANI RODRIK

A senior U.S. Treasury official recently urged Mexico's government to work harder to reduce violent crime because "such high levels of crime and violence may drive away foreign investors." This admonition nicely illustrates how foreign trade and investment have become the ultimate yardstick for evaluating the social and economic policies of governments in developing countries. Forget the slum dwellers or *campesinos* who live amidst crime and poverty throughout the developing world. Just mention "investor sentiment" or "competitiveness in world markets" and policymakers will come to attention in a hurry.

Underlying this perversion of priorities is a remarkable consensus on the imperative of global economic integration. Openness to trade and investment flows is no longer viewed simply as a component of a country's development strategy; it has mutated into the most potent catalyst for economic growth known to humanity. Predictably, senior officials of the World Trade Organization (WTO), International Monetary Fund (IMF), and other international financial agencies incessantly repeat the openness mantra. In recent years, however, faith in integration has spread quickly to political leaders and policymakers around the world.

Joining the world economy is no longer a matter simply of dismantling barriers to trade and investment. Countries now must also comply with a long list of admission requirements, from new patent rules to more rigorous banking standards. The apostles of economic integration prescribe comprehensive institutional reforms that took today's advanced countries generations to accomplish, so that developing countries can, as the cliché goes, maximize the gains and minimize the risks of participation in the world economy. Global integration has become, for all practical purposes, a substitute for a development strategy.

From Dani Rodrik, "Trading in Illusions," *Foreign Policy*, issue #123 (March/April 2001), pp. 54–62.

This trend is bad news for the world's poor. The new agenda of global integration rests on shaky empirical ground and seriously distorts policymakers' priorities. By focusing on international integration, governments in poor nations divert human resources, administrative capabilities, and political capital away from more urgent development priorities such as education, public health, industrial capacity, and social cohesion. This emphasis also undermines nascent democratic institutions by removing the choice of development strategy from public debate.

World markets are a source of technology and capital; it would be silly for the developing world not to exploit these opportunities. But globalization is not a short-cut to development. Successful economic growth strategies have always required a judicious blend of imported practices with domestic institutional innovations. Policymakers need to forge a domestic growth strategy by relying on domestic investors and domestic institutions. The costliest downside of the integrationist faith is that it crowds out serious thinking and efforts along such lines.

## EXCUSES, EXCUSES

Countries that have bought wholeheartedly into the integration orthodoxy are discovering that openness does not deliver on its promise. Despite sharply lowering their barriers to trade and investment since the 1980s, scores of countries in Latin America and Africa are stagnating or growing less rapidly than in the heyday of import substitution during the 1960s and 1970s. By contrast, the fastest growing countries are China, India, and others in East and Southeast Asia. Policymakers in these countries have also espoused trade and investment liberalization, but they have done so in an unorthodox manner—gradually, sequentially, and only after an initial period of high growth—and as part of a broader policy package with many unconventional features.

The disappointing outcomes with deep liberalization have been absorbed into the faith with remarkable aplomb. Those who view global integration as the prerequisite for economic development now simply add the caveat that opening borders is insufficient. Reaping the gains from openness, they argue, also requires a full complement of institutional reforms.

Consider trade liberalization. Asking any World Bank economist what a successful trade-liberalization program requires will likely elicit a laundry list of measures beyond the simple reduction of tariff and nontariff barriers: tax reform to make up for lost tariff revenues; social safety nets to compensate displaced workers; administrative reform to bring trade practices into compliance with WTO rules; labor market reform to enhance worker mobility across industries; technological assistance to upgrade firms hurt by import competition; and training programs to ensure that export-oriented firms and investors have access to skilled workers. As the promise of trade liberalization fails to materialize, the prerequisites keep expanding. For example, Clare Short, Great Britain's secretary of state for international development, recently added universal provision of health and education to the list.

In the financial arena, integrationists have pushed complementary reforms with even greater fanfare and urgency. The prevailing view in Washington and other Group of Seven (G-7) capitals is that weaknesses in banking systems, prudential regulation, and corporate governance were at the heart of the Asian financial crisis of the late 1990s. Hence the ambitious efforts by the G-7 to establish international codes and standards covering fiscal transparency, monetary and financial policy, banking supervision, data dissemination, corporate governance, and accounting _standards. The Financial Stability Forum (FSF)—a G-7 organization with minimal representation from developing nations—has designated 12 of these standards as essential for creating sound financial systems in developing countries. The full FSF compendium includes an additional 59 standards the agency considers "relevant for sound financial systems," bringing the total number of codes to 71. To fend off speculative capital movements, the IMF and G-7 also typically urge developing countries to accumulate foreign reserves and avoid exchange-rate regimes that differ from a "hard peg" (tying the value of one's currency to that of a more stable currency, such as the U.S. dollar) or a "pure float" (letting the market determine the appropriate exchange rate).

A cynic might wonder whether the point of all these prerequisites is merely to provide easy cover for eventual failure. Integrationists can conveniently blame disappointing growth performance or a financial crisis on "slippage" in the implementation of complementary reforms rather than on a poorly designed liberalization. So if Bangladesh's freer trade policy does not produce a large enough spurt in growth, the World Bank concludes that the problem must involve lagging reforms in public administration or continued "political uncertainty" (always a favorite). And if Argentina gets caught up in a confidence crisis despite significant trade and financial liberalization, the IMF reasons that structural reforms have been inadequate and must be deepened.

## FREE TRADE-OFFS

Most (but certainly not all) of the institutional reforms on the integrationist agenda are perfectly sensible, and in a world without financial, administrative, or political constraints, there would be little argument about the need to adopt them. But in the real world, governments face difficult choices over how to deploy their fiscal resources, administrative capabilities, and political capital. Setting institutional priorities to maximize integration into the global economy has real opportunity costs.

Consider some illustrative trade-offs. World Bank trade economist Michael Finger has estimated that a typical developing country must spend $150 million to implement requirements under just three WTO agreements (those on customs valuation, sanitary and phytosanitary measures, and trade-related intellectual property rights). As Finger notes, this sum equals a year's development budget for many least-developed countries. And while the budgetary burden of implementing financial codes and standards has never been fully estimated, it undoubtedly entails a substantial diversion of fiscal and human resources as well. Should governments in developing countries train more bank auditors and accountants, even if those investments mean fewer secondary-school teachers or reduced spending on primary education for girls?

In the area of legal reform, should governments focus their energies on "importing" legal codes and standards or on improving existing domestic legal institutions?

In Turkey, a weak coalition government spent several months during 1999 gathering political support for a bill providing foreign investors the protection of international arbitration. But wouldn't a better long-run strategy have involved reforming the existing legal regime for the benefit of foreign and domestic investors alike?

In public health, should governments promote the reverse engineering of patented basic medicines and the importation of low-cost generic drugs from "unauthorized" suppliers, even if doing so means violating WTO rules against such practices? When South Africa passed legislation in 1997 allowing imports of patented AIDS drugs from cheaper sources, the country came under severe pressure from Western governments, which argued that the South African policy conflicted with WTO rules on intellectual property.

How much should politicians spend on social protection policies in view of the fiscal constraints imposed by market "discipline"? Peru's central bank holds foreign reserves equal to 15 months of imports as an insurance policy against the sudden capital outflows that financially open economies often experience. The opportunity cost of this policy amounts to almost 1 percent of gross domestic product annually— more than enough to fund a generous antipoverty program.

How should governments choose their exchange-rate regimes? During the last four decades, virtually every growth boom in the developing world has been accompanied by a controlled depreciation of the domestic currency. Yet financial openness makes it all but impossible to manage the exchange rate.

How should policymakers focus their anticorruption strategies? Should they target the high-level corruption that foreign investors often decry or the petty corruption that affects the poor the most? Perhaps, as the proponents of permanent normal trade relations with China argued in the recent U.S. debate, a government that is forced to protect the rights of foreign investors will become more inclined to protect the rights of its own citizens as well. But this is, at best, a trickledown strategy of institutional reform. Shouldn't reforms target the desired ends directly—whether those ends are the rule of law, improved observance of human rights, or reduced corruption?

The rules for admission into the world economy not only reflect little awareness of development priorities, they are often completely unrelated to sensible economic principles. For instance, WTO agreements on anti-dumping, subsidies and countervailing measures, agriculture, textiles, and trade-related intellectual property rights lack any economic rationale beyond the mercantilist interests of a narrow set of powerful groups in advanced industrial countries. Bilateral and regional trade agreements are typically far worse, as they impose even tighter prerequisites on developing countries in return for crumbs of enhanced "market access." For example, the African Growth and Opportunity Act signed by U.S. President Clinton in May 2000 provides increased access to the U.S. market only if African apparel manufacturers use U.S.-produced fabric and yarns. This restriction severely limits the potential economic spillovers in African countries.

There are similar questions about the appropriateness of financial codes and standards. These codes rely heavily on an Anglo-American style of corporate governance and an arm's-length model of financial development. They close off alternative paths to financial development of the sort that have been followed by many of today's rich countries (for example, Germany, Japan, or South Korea).

In each of these areas, a strategy of "globalization above all" crowds out alternatives that are potentially more development-friendly. Many of the institutional reforms needed for insertion into the world economy can be independently desirable or produce broader economic benefits. But these priorities do not necessarily coincide with the priorities of a comprehensive development agenda.

## ASIAN MYTHS

Even if the institutional reforms needed to join the international economic community are expensive and preclude investments in other crucial areas, pro-globalization advocates argue that the vast increases in economic growth that invariably result from insertion into the global marketplace will more than compensate for those costs. Take the East Asian tigers or China, the advocates say. Where would they be without international trade and foreign capital flows?

That these countries reaped enormous benefits from their progressive integration into the world economy is undeniable. But look closely at what policies produced those results, and you will find little that resembles today's rule book.

Countries like South Korea and Taiwan had to abide by few international constraints and pay few of the modern costs of integration during their formative growth experience in the 1960s and 1970s. At that time, global trade rules were sparse and economies faced almost none of today's common pressures to open their borders to capital flows. So these countries combined their outward orientation with unorthodox policies: high levels of tariff and non-tariff barriers, public ownership of large segments of banking and industry, export subsidies, domestic-content requirements, patent and copyright infringements, and restrictions on capital flows (including on foreign direct investment). Such policies are either precluded by today's trade rules or are highly frowned upon by organizations like the IMF and the World Bank.

China also followed a highly unorthodox two-track strategy, violating practically every rule in the guidebook (including, most notably, the requirement of private property rights). India, which significantly raised its economic growth rate in the early 1980s, remains one of the world's most highly protected economies.

All of these countries liberalized trade gradually, over a period of decades, not years. Significant import liberalization did not occur until after a transition to high economic growth had taken place. And far from wiping the institutional slate clean, all of these nations managed to eke growth out of their existing institutions, imperfect as they may have been. Indeed, when some of the more successful Asian economies gave in to Western pressure to liberalize capital flows rapidly, they were rewarded with the Asian financial crisis.

That is why these countries can hardly be considered poster children for today's global rules. South Korea, China, India, and the other Asian success cases had the freedom to do their own thing, and they used that freedom abundantly. Today's globalizers would be unable to replicate these experiences without running afoul of the IMF or the WTO.

The Asian experience highlights a deeper point: A sound overall development strategy that produces high economic growth is far more effective in achieving integration with the world economy than a purely integrationist strategy that relies on openness to work its magic. In other words, the globalizers have it exactly backwards. Integration is the result, not the cause, of economic and social development. A relatively protected economy like Vietnam is integrating with the world economy much more rapidly than an open economy like Haiti because Vietnam, unlike Haiti, has a reasonably functional economy and polity.

Integration into the global economy, unlike tariff rates or capital-account regulations, is not something that policymakers control directly. Telling finance ministers in developing nations that they should increase their "participation in world trade" is as meaningful as telling them that they need to improve technological capabilities—and just as helpful. Policymakers need to know which strategies will produce these results, and whether the specific prescriptions that the current orthodoxy offers are up to the task.

## TOO GOOD TO BE TRUE

Do lower trade barriers spur greater economic progress? The available studies reveal no systematic relationship between a country's average level of tariff and nontariff barriers and its subsequent economic growth rate. If anything, the evidence for the 1990s indicates a positive relationship between import tariffs and economic growth [see chart]. The only clear pattern is that countries dismantle their trade restrictions as they grow richer. This finding explains why today's rich countries, with few exceptions, embarked on modern economic growth behind protective barriers but now display low trade barriers.

The absence of a strong negative relationship between trade restrictions and economic growth may seem surprising in view of the ubiquitous claim that trade liberalization promotes higher growth. Indeed, the economics literature is replete with cross-national studies concluding that growth and economic dynamism are strongly linked to more open trade policies. A particularly influential study finds that economies that are "open," by the study's own definition, grew 2.45 percentage points faster annually than closed ones—an enormous difference.

Upon closer look, however, such studies turn out to be unreliable. In a detailed review of the empirical literature, University of Maryland economist Francisco Rodríguez and I found a major gap between the results that economist have actually obtained and the policy conclusions they have typically drawn. For example, in many cases economists blame poor growth on the government's failure to liberalize trade policies, when the true culprits are ineffective institutions, geographic determinants (such as location in a tropical region), or inappropriate macroeconomic policies (such as an overvalued exchange rate). Once these misdiagnoses are corrected, any meaningful relationship across countries between the level of trade barriers and economic growth evaporates.

The evidence on the benefits of liberalizing capital flows is even weaker. In theory, the appeal of capital mobility seems obvious: If capital is free to enter (and leave) markets based on the potential return on investment, the result will be an efficient allocation of global resources. But in reality, financial markets are inherently unstable, subject to bubbles (rational or otherwise), panics, shortsightedness, and self-fulfilling prophecies. There is plenty of evidence that financial liberalization is often followed by financial crash—just ask Mexico, Thailand, or Turkey—while there is little convincing evidence to suggest that higher rates of economic growth follow capital-account liberalization.

Perhaps the most disingenuous argument in favor of liberalizing international financial flows is that the threat of massive and sudden capital movements serves to discipline policymakers in developing nations who might otherwise manage their economies irresponsibly. In other words, governments might be less inclined to squander their societies' resources if such actions would spook foreign lenders. In practice, however, the discipline argument falls apart. Behavior in international capital markets is dominated by mood swings unrelated to fundamentals. In good times, a government with a chronic fiscal deficit has an easier time financing its spending when it can borrow funds from investors abroad; witness Russia prior to

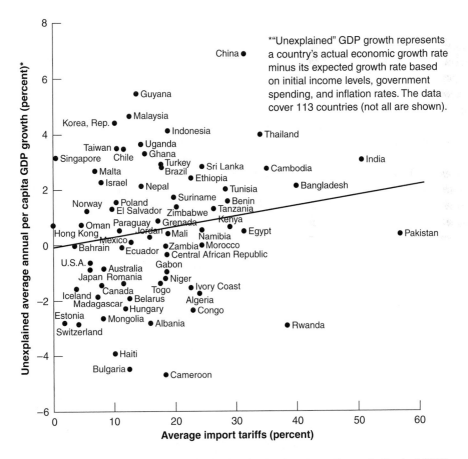

**FIGURE 1** ■ HIGH TARIFFS DON'T MEAN LOW GROWTH Gross Domestic Product (GDP) Growth and Tariff Rates, 1990s

*Source: Author's calculations based on World Bank data.*

1998 or Argentina in the 1990s. And in bad times, governments may be forced to adopt inappropriate policies in order to conform to the biases of foreign investors; witness the excessively restrictive monetary and fiscal policies in much of East Asia in the immediate aftermath of the Asian financial crisis. A key reason why Malaysia was able to recover so quickly after the imposition of capital controls in September 1998 was that Prime Minister Mahathir Mohamad resisted the high interest rates and tight fiscal policies that South Korea, Thailand, and Indonesia adopted at the behest of the International Monetary Fund.

## GROWTH BEGINS AT HOME

Well-trained economists are justifiably proud of the textbook case in favor of free trade. For all the theory's simplicity, it is one of our profession's most significant achievements. However, in their zeal to promote the virtues of trade, the most ardent proponents are peddling a cartoon version of the argument, vastly overstating the effectiveness of economic openness as a tool for fostering development. Such claims only endanger broad public acceptance of the real article because they unleash unrealistic expectations about the benefits of free trade. Neither economic theory nor empirical evidence guarantees that deep trade liberalization will deliver higher economic growth. Economic openness and all its accouterments do not deserve the priority they typically receive in the development strategies pushed by leading multilateral organizations.

Countries that have achieved long-term economic growth have usually combined the opportunities offered by world markets with a growth strategy that mobilizes the capabilities of domestic institutions and investors. Designing such a growth strategy is both harder and easier than implementing typical integration policies. It is harder because the binding constraints on growth are usually country specific and do not respond well to standardized recipes. But it is easier because once those constraints are targeted, relatively simple policy changes can yield enormous economic payoffs and start a virtuous cycle of growth and additional reform.

Unorthodox innovations that depart from the integration rule book are typically part and parcel of such strategies. Public enterprises during the Meiji restoration in Japan; township and village enterprises in China; an export processing zone in Mauritius; generous tax incentives for priority investments in Taiwan; extensive credit subsidies in South Korea; infant-industry protection in Brazil during the 1960s and 1970s—these are some of the innovations that have been instrumental in kick-starting investment and growth in the past. None came out of a Washington economist's tool kit.

Few of these experiments have worked as well when transplanted to other settings, only underscoring the decisive importance of local conditions. To be effective, development strategies need to be tailored to prevailing domestic institutional strengths. There is simply no alternative to a homegrown business plan. Policymakers who look to Washington and financial markets for the answers are condemning themselves to mimicking the conventional wisdom du jour, and to eventual disillusionment.

# Globalization's Missing Middle

## GEOFFREY GARRETT

### SQUEEZED

The polarized debate over the effects of free trade and international capital flows has become a fixture of world politics. Boosters of globalization assert that it is a win-win proposition for the rich and the poor, developed and developing countries alike. President George W. Bush has said that "a world that trades in freedom . . . grows in prosperity," reiterating a theme Bill Clinton championed in the 1990s. But critics see a small global elite lining its pockets at the expense of everyone else. John Kerry's decrying of outsourcing by "Benedict Arnold CEOs" is this year's version of Ross Perot's 1992 forecast that the North Atlantic Free Trade Agreement (NAFTA) would make a "giant sucking sound" by drawing jobs out of the United States.

All this good-versus-evil rhetoric obscures one key fact: while globalization has benefited many, it has squeezed the middle class, both within societies and in the international system. In today's global markets, there are only two ways to get ahead. People and countries must be competitive in either the knowledge economy, which rewards skills and institutions that promote cutting-edge technological innovation, or the low-wage economy, which uses widely available technology to do routine tasks at the lowest possible cost. Those who cannot compete in either include not only the erstwhile industrial middle class in wealthy nations, but also most countries in the middle of the worldwide distribution of income, notably in Latin America and eastern and central Europe. . . .

The question is, how can they be helped? Displaced American manufacturing workers would probably rather get jobs at Microsoft or Genentech than at McDonald's or Wal-Mart. But for most of them this just is not a realistic option. On the global stage, countries such as Mexico and Poland would similarly like to compete with Japan and Germany in the U.S. market for high-value-added goods and services. But their work forces are not skilled enough and their economic institutions not sufficiently supportive of investment or innovation to take advantage of the knowledge workers they do have. As a result, the middle-income countries have been forced into unwinnable battles with China for market share in standardized manufacturing and, increasingly, with India for low-wage service-sector exports.

In the United States and the rest of the Western world, the challenge of helping the disaffected middle class "tech up" (rather than dumb down) is well understood.

From Geoffrey Garrett, "Globalization's Missing Middle." Reprinted by permission of *Foreign Affairs*, Vol. 83, No. 6 (November/December 2004), pp. 84–96. Copyright 2004 by the Council on Foreign Relations, Inc.

People must be given access to the education and training that can transform them into successful knowledge workers. Likewise, middle-income countries must be helped up the global skill chain. Meaningful educational reform is long overdue, but it is only the beginning. Middle-income countries need broad and deep institutional reforms in government, banking, and law to transform economies that stifle innovation into ones that foster it with strong property-rights regimes, effective financial systems, and good governance. . . .

## ANOTHER COUNTRY

Princeton economist Paul Krugman lamented in *The New York Times* two years ago that "the middle-class America of my youth was another country." He was right. According to the Bureau of Labor Statistics, manufacturing employment, the quintessential American middle-class occupation, has fallen from one-fifth to one-tenth of total American jobs in just the last two decades. Meanwhile, employment in "professional and business services," which pay higher salaries to more skilled workers, has more than doubled, overtaking manufacturing in the process. At the same time, the number of low-paying jobs in "leisure and hospitality" industries has also essentially doubled and now rivals total manufacturing employment. Jobs on the American factory floor have thus been replaced, in more or less equal measure, by "junk" jobs such as flipping burgers and cleaning floors and by the new glamour professions of writing software and managing money. The result is that the distribution of income in the United States has been stretched at both the high and low ends, significantly increasing social inequality.

A similar process has been taking place at the global level. The world's wealthiest countries have grown richer in recent decades as a result of dramatic advances in technology, and the rate of economic advance has been even faster in the new manufacturing dynamos among the world's poorest countries. Squeezed between these two success stories, the countries in the middle have floundered.

One easy way to measure these changes is to track per capita national income worldwide according to the three major country groupings created by the World Bank. The top 25 percent of countries are labeled "high income," a category that comprises the nations in the Organization for Economic Cooperation and Development, plus a few small Middle Eastern oil exporters and trading states such as Singapore. The bottom 30 percent are labeled "low income." This group includes more than half of the world's six billion people, chiefly in the countries of Asia and sub-Saharan Africa. The remaining 45 percent of countries—almost all of Latin America and the former Soviet bloc as well as the Asian tigers and much of the Middle East—are "middle income."

In 1980 (a useful ending date for the pre-globalization period), the differences in per capita income among these three groups of countries were enormous: roughly 1,000 percent both between the low- and middle-income countries and between the middle- and high-income countries. Average GDP per capita was less than $300 in the low-income group, roughly $2,500 in the middle-income group, and more than $20,000 in the high-income group (in 1995 dollars at market exchange rates and adjusted for inflation). After two decades of integration of national economies into international markets, by 2000, per capita incomes in the countries categorized as high income in 1980 had increased by roughly 50 percent in real terms, due in no small part to innovation fueled by advances in biotech and information and communications technology.

At the other end of the spectrum, the world's poorest countries fared even better—indeed much better. During the 1980s and 1990s, their real per capita income increased by more than 160 percent. This growth miracle was spurred not by sales of agricultural products (the focus of ongoing debate over the future of the World Trade Organization), but by large-scale exports of standardized manufactured goods, ranging from steel to shoes to computer hardware. Exports of all goods and services increased in the low-income countries from less than 15 percent of GDP in 1980 to 28 percent in 2000. Over the same period, the share of manufacturing in total exports tripled, rising from 15 percent to more than 45 percent.

To be sure, profound inequalities remain in the cross-national distribution of income (even if one uses comparisons based on purchasing-power parity, which substantially increase estimates of per capita income in developing countries, rather than comparisons based on market exchange rates). But the big story of the past two decades is that the income ratio between the countries characterized as high and low income in 1980 has essentially been cut in half. Moreover, the growth led by manufacturing exports seems to have benefited wide cross-sections of the population in low-income countries . . .

Although proponents of globalization can point to record growth in low-income countries as proof of their wisdom, they should be troubled by the economic stagnation in middle-income countries. Supporters of NAFTA are wont to label the treaty a success for middle-income Mexico because it has stimulated trade and manufacturing across the border from the United States. And it is true that exports in the middle-income world increased from less than 20 percent of GDP in 1980 to more than 30 percent in 2000, while the share of manufacturing in total exports increased from under 30 percent to more than 50 percent. But despite the export growth, this group of nations has fallen even further behind the West, defying the age-old logic of "catch up," by which poorer countries reap the rewards of technology developed in richer nations. Real per capita income in the middle-income group grew by less than 20 percent during the 1980s and 1990s, less than half of the growth rate achieved in the high-income world and less than one-eighth of that in low-income countries. As a result, the ratio of per capita incomes of high- and middle-income countries actually increased by about 20 percent during the past two decades, while the ratio between high- and low-income countries dropped by 50 percent. These figures are all the more troubling because middle-income countries tend to have better-developed economic and political institutions and more educated labor forces—which development economists consider key drivers of growth—than their low-income counterparts.

Why has globalization been disappointing for countries in the middle? The answer seems to be that they have not found a niche in world markets. They have been unable to compete in high-value-added markets dominated by wealthy economies because their work forces are not sufficiently skilled and their legal and banking systems are not sophisticated enough. As a result, they have had little choice but to try to compete with China and other low-income economies in markets for standardized products made with widely available and relatively old technologies. But because of their higher wages, the middle-income nations are bound to lose the battle. . . .

## SEARCHING FOR EXPLANATIONS

The success of globalization in both high- and low-income countries can be readily explained by mainstream economics. Technological change and the international integration of markets have spurred growth in high-income nations, reversing the slowdown of the 1970s. Low-income countries have exploited their comparative advantage in cheap labor to gain large shares of the global marketplace.

The failure of middle-income countries to compete in global markets for either knowledge or low-wage products is decidedly less well understood, however. It flies in the face of many economists' core belief that all countries should gain from opening their markets to the outside world by doing what they do best, even if they do not do it as well as their competitors. As a result, supporters of "free trade for all" try to explain the poor performance of middle-income nations by pointing to causes other than their inability to find a productive niche in the global economy. These true believers argue that the integration of the middle tier into international markets is not at fault for these countries' recent dire economic record and that freer trade has ameliorated, not exacerbated, their problems. . . .

## FROM MISSING TO MODERNIZED

Counter to mainstream economic expectations, middle-income countries have struggled economically in the last two decades, and those that have opened their markets more have fared even worse. Yet a return to protectionism is unlikely to do any good. The pace and pervasiveness of technological change make it difficult, if not impossible, to put the globalization genie back in its bottle. But the formula of "more free-trade agreements"—bilaterally, regionally, and multilaterally—is unlikely to work, either.

The challenge for the middle-income world is to find ways to "tech up" and enter the global knowledge economy, so as to escape the trap of having to dumb down to compete in standardized manufacturing and, increasingly, standardized services. This will require educational reforms geared toward producing a large pool of skilled and creative labor, as well as good government, secure property rights, and strong financial systems to fight corruption and inefficiency. Such reforms would give entrepreneurs incentives to take advantage of newly minted knowledge workers, fostering innovation. But such a transformation will be expensive and difficult to execute, and the countries of Latin America and eastern Europe are not likely to be able to achieve it on their own. The transition to democracy has not itself proved the necessary catalyst. Instead, it has raised popular expectations that politicians find increasingly difficult to satisfy.

What can the West do to help? For much of eastern Europe, entry into the European Union, long and drawn out as the process of accession has been, may well be the answer. Poland, Hungary, and the other formerly communist countries that were admitted this year hope that membership will bring to them what it has brought to Greece, Portugal, and Spain over the past 20 years: access to western European markets, capital, and development assistance, as well as other, less tangible, but equally important advantages. New members must adopt the *acquis communautaire* of the EU: the full range of its laws, regulations, and institutions. Although it has often been derided as overly bureaucratic and sclerotic, over time, the *acquis* has aligned the domestic institutions of these nations with common European practice, bringing the EU's poorest members stability, predictability, and credibility—and an environment conducive to the emergence of the knowledge economy—far more quickly than they could otherwise have expected. . . .

Latin American nations have aggressively pursued closer economic relations with the EU, but membership is obviously not an option for them, and they have no analogous organization on the continent. NAFTA is more than a mere free trade agreement, but its rules and regulations are rudimentary compared with the EU's. . . .

If unalloyed free-trade agreements alone cannot do the job and an EU-like organization is a pipe dream, what can be done for Latin America? The World Bank has been promoting smart development assistance, focusing on the creation of knowledge economies. So far, however, it has remained largely ineffective as an agent of change in the middle-income world. The United States recently launched the Middle East Partnership Initiative to foster educational, financial, and judicial reform in the middle-income countries of that region. Such efforts should be replicated in Latin America and all middle-income countries to counteract the economic stagnation and rising popular frustration that threaten these nations' openness and stability.

The problem today is that U.S. policymakers have more pressing things on their mind than Latin America's economic woes. In the early Cold War era, the Marshall Plan advanced U.S. foreign policy by creating democratic and capitalist bulwarks against communism in Europe. Bailing out Russia and Mexico also made sense in the years following the Cold War, when traditional security issues receded into the background. But since the September 11, 2001, attacks, achieving political goals through economic means has been given a much lower priority than the war on terrorism. And if a new Marshall Plan is created, it will focus on the Middle East.

The ultimate irony facing globalization's missing middle may be that the more the free trade project founders in Latin America, the greater will be the pressure on people in the region to migrate to the United States. Migration will, in turn, squeeze employment and wages for the American manufacturing middle class even more and force the U.S. government to think creatively about growing economic problems south of its border. After all, the flow of former East Germans into western Germany motivated Chancellor Helmut Kohl to invest massively in the formerly communist part of the newly unified country. Rapid increases in the number of eastern Europeans looking to live and work in western Europe also strengthened the case for the EU's eastern expansion. Much like East Germans did, eastern Europeans will benefit because western European investment will speed their transition to the knowledge economy. Perhaps, then, migration into the United States from Mexico and the rest of Latin America will ultimately help the continent move into the knowledge economy.

Before September 11, the disagreement over globalization was the principal fault line in world politics. Even today, ensuring that globalization's benefits reach all parts of the world would provide a bedrock upon which peace and prosperity in the twenty-first century can be built. Unfortunately, so far the middle-income nations have been left out. The United States and the EU must help Latin America and eastern Europe develop competitive knowledge economies. This project may seem banal compared with the war on terrorism, but over time, ignoring those pushed aside by globalization will have immense implications—economically and politically.

# Why the Globalization Backlash
# Is Stupid

## JOHN MICKLETHWAIT AND
## ADRIAN WOOLDRIDGE

### "GLOBALIZATION MEANS THE TRIUMPH OF GIANT COMPANIES"

*Nonsense.* If you listen to antiglobalists, we live in a world of "Disneyfication" and "Coca-Colonization" in which giant companies simultaneously trample over their smaller commercial rivals and turn national governments into helpless lackeys. They are wrong on both counts.

The proportion of output from big companies has declined, not increased. Globalization radically shifts the balance of advantage from incumbents to challengers. Incumbents could once protect themselves behind lofty barriers such as the high cost of capital, the difficulty of acquiring new technology, or the importance of close relationships with national governments. Globalization reduces the importance of all these things. Lower barriers make capital easier to raise, technology easier to buy, markets easier to reach, and ties with national governments ever less important. You no longer have to be a multinational to have the reach of one.

By all rights, Motorola Inc. ought to be the undisputed ruler of the wireless world. The company was the first to mass-produce car phones. It also sits in the heart of the world's biggest market for them. But it has been humbled by Nokia Corp., a relatively small company from Finland that only a decade ago was more interested in bathroom tissue than mobile phones. Nokia's only weapons were better phones and better management. Against these, mere size proved a puny defense—which helps explain why giants such as AT&T Corp. and General Motors Corp. (GM) now look so vulnerable.

The idea that companies are now more important than governments is equally misleading. Far from getting smaller, governments in most Western countries remain colossal, consuming more than 40 percent of Western Europe's gross domestic product (GDP), for example. They continue to expand their influence over corporate behavior through regulatory policy. Bill Gates rapidly discovered that a rather obscure Justice Department antitrust lawyer, Joel Klein, was a much more fearsome

From John Micklethwait and Adrian Wooldridge, "The Globalization Backlash," *Foreign Policy*, issue #126 (September/October 2001), pp. 16–28. © 2001 by the Carnegie Endowment for International Peace. Reprinted with permission.

opponent than any mere company. Jack Welch, the face of American Big Business, met his Waterloo in Belgium when the similarly anonymous bureaucrats of the European Commission blocked what would have been the biggest merger in history, that between General Electric and Honeywell.

As for the oft-quoted "statistics" about so many companies being bigger than countries—the idea that GM is as big as Denmark—these compare sales figures with GDP. Since GDP measures value added, the correct corporate comparison is profits. As Martin Wolf of the *Financial Times* has pointed out, GM then slides from being as large as the 23rd biggest country to the 55th, about the same size as a basket case like Ukraine.

## "GLOBALIZATION IS DESTROYING THE ENVIRONMENT"

*Not really.*    Myth provides a prime example of a conceit that underlies a great deal of antiglobal thinking. Take one self-evident truth that all sensible people can agree upon—business of all sorts tends to despoil the environment. Then repeat that observation in highly emotive language, ignoring all other mitigating factors. Then heap all the blame on global companies, global regulators, and indeed globalization itself, when the bulk of the damage is done by local governments, local companies, and even local voters. And, whatever happens, keep running away from the really hard question: How much is greenery worth?

A good starting point is that almost all business that produces a physical product tends to be dirty. Until relatively recently, businesspeople were reluctant to admit this reality. That not only made them look shifty, it also meant that they never made arguments about the choices involved. For instance, during the furor in 1995 over the offshore disposal of its Brent Spar oil rig, Shell failed to argue with any force that Greenpeace's demand that the rig be disposed of on land was by no means the greener solution.

Nowadays, business, particularly multinational business, is better behaved. Businesspeople have not become softer. They have simply wised up to two things. The first is that dirty factories lose them consumers. The second is that environmental regulations are not prohibitively expensive, particularly for multinationals. A 1990 study by the U.S. Environmental Protection Agency, for instance, found that even the most polluting industries don't have to spend more than 2 percent of their revenues on being good environmental citizens. Go to a ghastly eyesore in the Third World, such as Cubatão, the capital of Brazil's chemical business (once dubbed the most polluted city on earth), and you find that multinational companies tend to be cleaner than their Brazilian counterparts—and keener to abide by international standards.

What about the idea that trade, by increasing business activity generally, harms the environment? This is certainly true in the short term. If open borders increase the market for a chemical factory in Lagos, the factory will create more chemicals. But as countries grow richer, they also tend to clean up their act: An elaborate index of environmental sustainability in 122 countries prepared for the World Economic Forum this year showed a strong correlation between a country's greenness and wealth (though, to be fair, an even stronger one with its lack of corruption). More generally, although environmentalism is a good thing, it must be balanced against other virtues, including, from a developing country's point of view, economic growth. It is patronizing for rich-world greens to decide that Africans should not tolerate dirtier air and water in exchange for more wealth.

Alas, the cost of the environment is nearly always tabulated incorrectly. In China, according to the World Bank, air and water pollution cost $54 billion a year—8 percent of the country's GDP. But it is not the polluting companies that bear this price. For that matter, what incentive do Indian polluters have to stop throwing rubbish into the Ganges that then wrecks Bangladesh's rice paddies? One reason why fish stocks are alarmingly low globally is because the seas of the world provide a textbook example of the "tragedy of the commons." Because nobody owns them, nobody feels responsible for them. If a Norwegian fisherman does not pillage them, then his British rival will. This dynamic is also dramatically evident in the current impasse over global warming.

But blaming these things on globalization seems a spurious way to let local politicians off the hook. The right way to protest, say, George W. Bush's decision to junk the Kyoto Protocol is not to blame "the market," but Bush himself. And how exactly would a less interlinked world help? Global warming would not go away if trade barriers went up. Far from being caused by unfettered capitalism, environmental damage is often caused by exactly the opposite. One reason fishing fleets can continue to ravage the oceans is because governments spend $21 billion a year supporting them. Brazil's government initially spurred on the despoliation of the rain forest. The World-watch Institute reckons that there are $650 billion worth of subsidies going to environmentally destructive activities. On the other hand, globalization sometimes directly benefits the environment by promoting things such as trade in pollution-control technology and the privatization of state-owned companies, which become less polluting as they are restructured.

## "GLOBALIZATION MAKES GEOGRAPHY IRRELEVANT"

*Wrong again.* You might think that the death of distance also means the death of geography. The truth is probably the opposite. If most tangible resources are within anyone's reach, then what matters are the intangible things, which in turn means proximity to people.

The world economy is visibly organizing itself around various clusters of excellence, most obviously Hollywood, Silicon Valley, and Wall Street. The main challenge for companies in a global economy is to situate themselves in various centers of excellence and weave together different centers of excellence into a global production network. The main challenge for communities is to invest in their comparative advantage. Look at the way that Miami has exploited its connections with Latin America. Or the way that the energy cluster in Houston has used its expertise in oil to move into gas, electricity, and energy trading.

The idea that businesses can simply up-sticks and move is also rubbish. Considerable publicity has been given to the few Swedish and German companies that have eventually moved some operations out of their highly taxed homelands; the real story is how long those firms stuck it out. Wander around Los Angeles, America's main manufacturing center, and you will find squadrons of low-tech factories churning out toys, furniture, and clothes, all of which could probably be made cheaper elsewhere. They stay partly for personal reasons (many are family-owned), partly because they can compensate for high labor costs by using more machines, but mostly because Los Angeles is a hub for all three industries—a place where designers, suppliers, and distributors are just around the corner.

Finally, borders remain much more important than many people imagine. Canada and the United States are both English-speaking countries and members of the North American Free Trade Agreement. But the average Canadian province does 12 times as much trade in goods and 40 times as much trade in services with another Canadian province as it does with an American state of the same size and proximity. Similar figures exist for the European Union (EU) countries.

## "GLOBALIZATION MEANS AMERICANIZATION"

*Not necessarily.* True, globalization certainly tilts the playing field in favor of liberal virtues such as accountability, transparency, and individual rights that are often deemed to be American.

Yet does this mean Americanization? Foreign dictators who want to use xenophobia to prop up their positions would no doubt argue that it does. But the United States has no monopoly on liberal virtues. Classical liberalism was first developed by a group of British thinkers—John Locke, David Hume, and Adam Smith. We still use a French phrase, laissez faire, when we invoke the ideal of a free market economy. The first joint stock company was developed in Britain rather than the United States. Indeed, American democracy was arguably the product of British corporations such as the Virginia Company. For all its bureaucracy, the EU now enshrines liberal values such as democratic representation and individual rights every bit as firmly as the U.S. Constitution.

Certainly, Europe is now moving closer to the Anglo-American shareholder model of capitalism than it had in the immediate postwar years. A popular share-owning culture is slowly putting down roots in Europe. The euro, like the single market before it, is forcing European companies to slim. But these developments do not mean that European companies or European society will become mere facsimiles of America. Europeans will probably continue to put much more emphasis on social solidarity than the United States. France's tight labor laws (including a relatively new 35-hour week) have not stopped its global companies from being competitive, though they have arguably kept its unemployment rate unnecessarily high. The Nordic countries, whose economic performance has matched America's, argue that their well-developed welfare states make their economies more flexible because people are not afraid to change jobs. There are growing signs that Europe (with a potential internal market of 500 million people) is beginning to flex its muscles against the United States, whether it be through vetoing mergers, building its own army, or generally disagreeing with American foreign policy in areas such as the Middle East.

Nor does globalization necessarily mean the Americanization of popular culture. True, American films can be seen almost all over the world, the Big Mac™ is the closest thing we have to a universal food, and Britney Spears is hard to avoid, even if you are in Tibet. But cultural trade is a two-way process. If you look at popular musicals (Andrew Lloyd Webber's) or the bestseller lists (the *Harry Potter* series), Britain continues to exercise a powerful influence on the United States. The most successful programs on American television at the moment are "reality" programs imported from Europe. Foreigners own half of America's top 20 book-publishing houses and half of its film studios. On the whole, consumers have a marked taste for local products, something that is becoming easier to satisfy as technology makes economies of scale less important. The most popular television program in European countries is nearly always a local production. A few years ago hardly any self-respecting European teenager would have been caught listening to local groups. Now France has Air and Sweden has The Cardigans.

But there is a more important reason why globalization does not mean the triumph of a particular nationality. The essence of globalization is that it increases choice. And this includes the choice to live life according to your own lights. A nice example of this is the Bruderhof, a religious group that is rather like the Amish. The Bruderhof reject many features of the modern world. They don't have radios or televisions; they don't approve of feminism and homosexuality. But they have established a highly successful global toy business using a mixture of Japanese management techniques and American technology. The result: They have all the money that they need to keep their community flourishing, but they have not had to abandon their way of life.

## "GLOBALIZATION MEANS A RACE TO THE BOTTOM IN LABOR STANDARDS"

*No.* This argument rests on four misconceptions.

The first is that employers are concerned, above all, with the price of labor. In fact, what really interests them is the value of labor. Some companies will undoubtedly move routine tasks to parts of the world where hourly wages are lower. But in general what employers want is not cheap workers but productive ones. And the most productive workers are usually those with the best education, access to the best machinery, and a support system that includes things like good infrastructure.

If the "race to the bottom" argument were correct, you would expect foreign direct investment (FDI) to be pouring into countries with the lowest wages and the weakest labor standards. Nothing could be further from the truth. The United States is the world's largest recipient of FDI. Year after year the United States has run a net surplus in its capital account (and the inflow of foreign capital has helped to keep interest rates low, build new factories, and bring new production methods to bear on the economy). About 80 percent of U.S. FDI goes to other rich countries. American investment in countries like Mexico and China is a mere fragment of U.S. investment at home.

The second is that globalization is weakening the ties of companies to their home regions. But companies depend on the environment that first created them in all sorts of ways, some obvious, some more subtle. During the Justice Department's investigation of Microsoft, Bill Gates could not have threatened to move his operation to the Bahamas, even though Microsoft has relatively few fixed assets. Microsoft depends not just on a supply of educated workers (who would have refused to move) but also on its close relationship with American universities.

The third idea—that global companies are hostile to "worker protection" such as trade-union rights and labor standards—contains a half-truth. Companies rarely react favorably to unions (or indeed to governments) that want to shackle their freedom of maneuver with inflexible rules about, say, hiring and firing. But, by and large, multinationals are much less hostile to things such as safe working environments, on-the-job training, and opportunities for promotion. Once again, the key factor for companies is boosting productivity rather than lowering the price they pay for labor, so a well-trained and healthy workforce is important. Survey after survey shows multinationals providing higher wages and better working conditions for their employees than their local competitors.

The fourth and largest misconception is that globalization is a zero-sum game: that if the rich are getting richer as a result of globalization, then the poor must be getting poorer. But the argument in favor of globalization is that it can improve the lot of everybody by leading to a more efficient use of resources.

Of course, globalization does not always achieve this goal, and of course it cannot impose efficiency without a certain amount of pain, but in general, globalization improves the living standards of the vast majority of people. In the half century since the foundation of the General Agreement on Tariffs and Trade (GATT), the world economy has grown sixfold, in part because trade has expanded 16-fold. The Organisation for Economic Co-operation and Development calculates that nations that are relatively open to trade grow about twice as fast as those that are relatively closed. Despite the Asian crisis, the World Bank calculates that some 800 million people moved out of absolute poverty in the past decade. And the people left behind still tend to suffer from too little globalization (be it trade barriers to the goods that they produce or restraints on the information they can get at home) rather than too much.

## "GLOBALIZATION CONCENTRATES POWER IN UNDEMOCRATIC INSTITUTIONS LIKE THE WTO"

*No.*   Organizations like the World Trade Organization (WTO) and the International Monetary Fund (IMF) are not quite paper tigers. But they are much less powerful than their detractors (and a few of their inmates) imagine. The WTO is essentially an arbitration mechanism: It deals with issues that clashing governments refer to it. The IMF is a crisis management agency. True, it can impose stringent requirements for structural reforms on its clients, and it has often done so with breathtaking arrogance and insensitivity. But governments only resort to the IMF if they are already in serious trouble.

By any conceivable measure, national governments are far more important players in the international order than global institutions. During the Asian crisis, it was the U.S. Treasury Department that decided whether to bail out countries, not the IMF. (And why not? It was writing the checks.) For all the fears in the American heartland about the U.N.'s black helicopters, national governments decide whether to send peacekeeping troops. And now the international institutions face a new constraint. The number of international nongovernmental organizations (NGOs) increased from 6,000 in 1990 to 26,000 by the end of the decade. Visit any old-fashioned multilateral institution and you will find it surrounded by NGOs monitoring it. There are 1,700 clustered around the United Nations' offices in Geneva, for example.

Membership of the WTO suggests that globalization is a bottom-up process. When GATT was founded in 1948, it only had 23 contracting parties, most of them industrialized nations; today the WTO has 142 members, more than three quarters of them developing nations, and 20 more countries are eagerly waiting to join. It may be true that the global civil servants who run most international institutions are not directly elected (just as the heads of civil service departments are not directly elected). But they are accountable to national governments, the majority of which are now democracies.

Indeed, you could argue that the real democratic deficit in global institutions is to be found not in the IMF and the WTO but in the NGOs that protest against them. NGOs claim to represent global civil society (whatever that is). But nobody elects them. They are not accountable to democratic governments. They represent nobody but their members and their activist cadres, which in some of the noisiest cases means a few hundred people.

# PART 4

# Contemporary World Politics

With the end of the Cold War, the start of the "War on Terrorism," and the war in Iraq, we are in a new era of international politics. In Part Four we have picked five features of this era that we believe are the most important for understanding its major contours and challenges for more systematic analysis. They are: the future of war (both conventional and unconventional), the uses to which American power should be put and the reactions of others to that power, the causes and ways of dealing with domestic collapse and civil wars, the protection of the global environment, especially the gargantuan task of coping with likely climate change, and the effects on world politics being wrought by the rise of new actors and new forces, such as the European Union, nongovernmental organizations (NGOs), transnational corporations, and a more activist commitment to the rule of international law.

## CONFLICT, WAR, AND TERRORISM

War is as old as the time when human beings first organized themselves into groups. In the modern era, it has been the great powers that have fought most, and that have always conducted their policies with the possibility of war in mind. Will the world be as ravaged by war in the decades to come as it has been since the dawn of civilization? Or are we now entering a new era when war will disappear or be transformed? If war continues, will it still be waged between the kind of actors who were most prominent in the past?

Robert Jervis, Samuel P. Huntington, and Fareed Zakaria address the future nature of war and the likely sources of conflict. Jervis argues that war among the rich democracies of North America, Western Europe, and Japan is not only a thing of the past but is no longer even contemplated. Since war among the leading powers has been the motor of traditional international politics, the coming era will be radically different. The rest of the world is not likely to remain at peace, however, and the United States may continue to intervene abroad. In much of the Third World conflicts between, but especially within, states rage and disputes over borders and natural resources provide proximate reasons for conflict. Huntington argues that the fault lines of future conflicts will be more civilizational than state-centered in nature. He identifies seven major world civilizations and explains the reasons why political conflicts, and sometimes wars, are more likely to occur among states belonging to different civilizations rather than among states of the same civilization.

The obvious new elements of conflict are the War on Terrorism and the war in Iraq triggered by al Qaeda's attack on the World Trade Center and the Pentagon. Many of the consequences of the American response are discussed in the next section. Fareed Zakaria looks at the question so often asked after September 11, 2001, "Why do they hate us?" Is there something wrong with Arab countries, Muslim countries, or the West? The answers are not simple, and include a combination of the desire to be like the West and yet to be different from it, with religion playing a role but the conflict not being centrally about religion.

## THE USES OF, AND REACTIONS TO, AMERICAN POWER

Since the collapse of the Soviet Union in 1991, the United States has been the world's strongest economic and military power, and, as a consequence, analysts have argued that we live in a "unipolar" world—one dominated by a single state. Immediately following the end of the Cold War, America's economic and military strength was an important feature of international political life: American military power deployed abroad was a stabilizing influence in key regions, and America's remarkable economic growth in the 1990s helped other states to prosper as well. For many of the conflicts that have erupted since 1991, the United States has been the "911" of the world.

But 9/11 now obviously has an additional meaning, and the use of American power since the terrorist attacks raises a host of new issues. How will the United States pursue its war on terror? To what extent is this largely an American struggle? Is the invasion/liberation of Iraq a unique event or the first of many such adventures? What is the role of other states, how will they react to the highly assertive American policy, and how heavily should the United States weigh their preferences and interests? These issues are sharply raised by what can be called the "Bush Doctrine" outlined in numerous official documents and presidential speeches and embodied in many American actions, especially the ouster of Saddam Hussein. Many people have attributed the new American policy and the sharp shift in President Bush's policy to a combination of factors, most obviously the terrorist attacks, but also Bush's unilateralist predispositions, his religious beliefs, and the role of neo-conservatives in his administration. While not denying the relevance of these factors, Robert Jervis looks to the structure of the international system for much of the explanation. Realists like Morgenthau and Waltz have stressed that power is checked only by counter-balancing power. A unipolar system will be highly conducive to unilateralism on the part of the leading state as it sees both that no other states can block it and that countries which share its interests are not sufficiently powerful enough to act on their own, but rather will wait for the leading power to shoulder the burden of action.

Many Americans agree with President Bush that the best way to fight terrorism and secure American interests is to spread democracy. Terrorism cannot thrive in a free and open society, it is often said. Gregory Gause sharply challenges this comfortable conclusion. Terrorism can have widespread support in the general population; indeed, the Irish Republican Army received moral, organizational, and financial support from communities within the United States. Furthermore, free elections in Islamic countries may well produce governments hostile to the United States.

Much of the fate of American policy will be determined by how others react to it, and for many countries how to react to the rise of American power and assertiveness is the most important question they have to answer. Traditional balance of power thinking would imply that others would try to thwart the United States and rein in its power. But current circumstances are unusual and it is far from clear that such attempts would succeed or be in others' interests. Thus Stephen Walt argues that we are likely to see a variety of responses aimed at guiding, influencing, and sometimes thwarting United States policies. He argues that to most effectively serve its own interests, the United States should consider the interests and likely responses of others.

## FAILED STATES, CIVIL WARS, AND NATION-BUILDING

Although civil strife and domestic collapse are as old as history, they have become more prominent after the Cold War and have become even more important recently through the perceived links to terrorism. State failure and civil war are fed by both internal and external causes, which makes them particularly hard to understand and deal with. Because of the growth in the number of states and because of the heightened consequences for regions, if not for the entire world, of disturbance in one area, these subjects are now high on the agenda of both scholars and policymakers. Because we live in a well-established country with a high degree of public order, most of us too easily forget that this situation is not a natural one, but rather the hard-won result of a broad concatenation of political, economic, and social forces. Under some circumstances, central authority can not only be subject to violent dispute, but can also be so torn apart that it simply disappears, resulting in the national government being replaced by local warlords, roving bands of thugs, and chaos.

Robert Rotberg looks at strong, weak, and collapsing states. He details many of the paths that lead to state collapse, as well as examining states that seemed headed in this direction but have saved themselves. State failure and civil war are often reciprocally related, of course. One prominent explanation for domestic disorder, violence, and disintegration is the power of deep grievances and divisions within a state, often along ethnic lines. Chaim Kaufmann analyzes the nature of ethnic civil wars, shows why they are so intractable, and surveys the various methods of intervening in them. He concludes that physical separation of the warring ethnic groups, either by creating safe areas within a state or by partitioning the state, offers the best long-term hope to stop the killing. Most current discussion focuses not on dividing countries but on rebuilding them. James Dobbins extracts the lessons we can learn from outsiders' attempts at nation-building and democratization since World War II. He looks at the efforts of the United States and the UN, arguing that while they operate somewhat differently, each has done fairly well considering the obstacles. Focusing more directly on democratization, James Payne is more pessimistic. Of course the results from several attempts, most obviously in Iraq, are not yet in, but it is clear that beliefs about whether interventions can produce stability and democracy will strongly influence the future course of American policy.

## THE ENVIRONMENT AND CLIMATE CHANGE

Protection of the global environment is not a new issue, but its importance has increased within the last two decades, with the greater damage in the form of depletion of the world's fisheries, degradation of the ozone layer, and the threat of global warming and attendant climate change. The United Nations Conference on the Environment held in Rio in 1992 marked a watershed in international awareness of the increasing threat to the global environment.

Truly global environmental threats, as opposed to strictly national ones, are especially difficult to deal with because they are a "commons" problem. In such cases, concertation of state action does not come easily because the situation looks as follows: No single state owns the resource being consumed (or abused), but all use it (or abuse it), and none can be prevented from using and abusing it. A commons (or public) good is therefore one that no single individual or entity owns, but that all need and can use. For such goods, no individual or state has an incentive to minimize its exploitation unless it is persuaded that all others will act in a similar fashion. This represents a collective action problem: uncoordinated individual action produces collective disaster. This is the "tragedy of the commons" and the message of Garrett Hardin's article.

Environmental degradation is not only bad in itself but can lead to international and domestic conflicts. The ways in which this can happen are complex, however. Thomas Homer-Dixon explores many of them. Economic and social changes put great pressure on political systems and the coming years will test our foresight, discipline, and skill. Both the policy and the intellectual questions are of course contested, and part of the dispute pivots on whether one should be optimistic or pessimistic about the ability of market forces to bring about appropriate behavior.

Climate change induced by man-made global warming, or what is termed "the enhanced greenhouse effect," may be humankind's greatest challenge. Widespread and growing use of fossil fuels to develop and sustain modern economies has added enough carbon dioxide to the world's atmosphere to cause the average global temperature to increase by nearly one degree centigrade since the onset of the Industrial Revolution. This may sound insignificant, but it is not. The overall change in global temperature from the depths of the last Ice Age until now can be measured within the range of four to nine degrees centigrade. The best estimates of climatologists are that at present and projected rates of fossil fuel burning, the average global temperature will increase from two to six degrees centigrade by the end of the twenty-first century. At the high end of this estimate, we will be in the range within which severe climate change occurred in the past. Climate change raises dangers not only of widespread dislocations but also of catastrophic climate change if warming feeds on itself (positive feedback in which warming produces more warming).

Climate change is the biggest commons problem of them all. Every nation contributes to it, although some much more than others. The United States, for example, contributes about one-fifth of the greenhouse gases produced each year. China is also a big contributor, but so, too, are nations that cut down their forests because trees absorb carbon dioxide. Slowing greenhouse gas emissions, and preferably stabilizing them a safe level, will require a degree of international cooperation not yet achieved in humankind's history. It also will likely involve massive transfers of resources from the rich nations to the poor, adoption of clean and environmentally-friendly energy technologies, novel political-economic schemes like emissions trading rights, and sacrifice by both rich and poor.

The nations of the world have been wrestling with this extremely complex problem for about 15 years. At the Rio Conference in 1992, they committed themselves to a framework convention on dealing with global warming, but they made no specific commitments. Rio was more an exhortation to act than a specific plan for action. At the Kyoto Conference in 1997, the rich developed states did lay out a plan of action that committed them to reduce by 2010 their greenhouse gas emissions from six to eight percent below their 1990 levels. The world's poorer developing states, however, refused to make similar binding commitments, arguing that the developed states had created the problem and therefore should solve it, first by reducing their own emissions and then by giving the developing states the financial resources and technology to build environmentally safe energy industries. The parties to the Kyoto Treaty have subsequently been engaged in negotiating the specific measures and mechanisms necessary to put the Kyoto commitments into effect, and most of them have ratified the Kyoto Protocol, but the United States decided not to be part of this process. If the world is to deal effectively with global warming, then Third World nations, China, and the United States must be convinced to do their share. Indeed, Third World nations are not likely to agree to help until the United States takes serious action to reduce its greenhouse gas emissions. John Browne looks at the mix of market and political measures that states must take if they are to tackle this problem seriously.

## NEW ACTORS AND NEW FORCES

The state system we live in today dates roughly from the Peace of Westphalia, which ended the Thirty Years War, one of the bloodiest in human history. Consequently, the modern international system of states has recently celebrated its 350th anniversary. Will it accommodate the rise of newly powerful states? Will the state system itself continue? That is, will the state remain the most important, although not the only important, actor in world politics?

China is not a new actor in world politics, but it is an increasingly important one. Within the United States there is a sharp debate about whether the "rise of China" will inevitably lead to conflict with the United States. Richard K. Betts and Thomas Christensen analyze the contrasting reasons for optimism and for pessimism and produce a mixed answer that straightens out many of the tendentious arguments. Europe in the form of the European Union is a new actor in world politics, if a partial or incomplete one. As Andrew Moravscik argues, the importance of the defeat of the EU constitution should not be exaggerated; the EU is not about to fade away. Neither does the lack of directly-elected institutions mean that the EU is undemocratic. Rather, it is a creative way of moving some decisions to a supranational level while keeping many others within national borders.

The six final selections of this book analyze the growing importance of non-state actors. Margaret E. Keck and Kathryn Sikkink provide a more systematic analysis of NGOs and show how transnational networks operate and increasingly affect state action. Sebastian Mallaby takes the unconventional if not perverse position that while NGOs often do great good in the world, we must not forget that they have their own interests and their own views of the interests of those they claim to speak for, and these may not correspond to what is best for those populations. Many NGOs are deeply concerned about human rights, and at bottom, the most fundamental units in the world are not states but individuals. Rhoda E. Howard and Jack Donnelly argue that, although cultures and systems differ, each individual still has a set of rights by virtue of being human. In the absence of effective international government, there is no choice but to rely on states for the enforcement of human rights. So states are both strengthened because they have assumed new responsibilities and weakened because their sovereignty is challenged by universal norms and outside actors. States are also challenged by the flow of commodities and people that illegally flow across their borders, especially drugs, arms, terrorists, money derived from crime, migrants, and refugees. Moisés Naím examines these and the limited responses available to state authorities. Daniel Drezner looks at another important area–the regulation of the internet – and argues that far from undermining the state power, this new technology and the forms of politics it calls up strengthen the state in many ways. Steven R. Ratner argues that international law is having greater effect on state action, and by implication, that international politics are becoming more regulated and domestic-like. More international law is being written, and enforcement is being improved.

Whether the forces and actors described above will eventually subvert the state system or instead remain subservient to it, or whether some new patterns now difficult to imagine will emerge, is something we will be able to answer only several decades from now.

# CONFLICT, WAR, AND TERRORISM

# *The Era of Leading Power Peace*

## ROBERT JERVIS

War and the possibility of war among the great powers has been the motor of international politics, not only strongly influencing the boundaries and distribution of values among them, but deeply affecting their internal arrangements and shaping the fates of the smaller ones. Being seen as an ever-present possibility produced by deeply-rooted factors such as human nature and the lack of world government, this force was expected to continue indefinitely. But I would argue that war among the leading great powers—the most developed states of the United States, West Europe, and Japan—will not occur in the future, and indeed is no longer a source of concern for them (Mueller 1989).

Now, however, the leading states form what Karl Deutsch called a pluralistic security community, a group among whom war is literally unthinkable—i.e., neither the publics nor the political elites nor even the military establishments expect war with each other (Deutsch et al. 1957). No official in the Community would advocate a policy on the grounds that it would improve the state's position in the event of war with other members or allow the state to more effectively threaten them.

Although no one state can move away from the reliance on war by itself lest it become a victim, they can collectively do so if each forsakes the resort to force. This development challenges many of our theories and raises the question of what international politics will be like in the future.

Security communities are not unprecedented. But what is unprecedented is that the states that constitute this one are the leading members of the international system and so are natural rivals who in the past were central to the violent struggle

From Robert Jervis, "Theories of War in an Era of Leading-Power Peace: Presidential Address, American Political Science Association, 2001," *American Political Science Review,* Vol. 96, No. 1 (March 2002), pp. 1–14. Copyright © 2002 by The American Political Science Association. Reprinted with the permission of Cambridge University Press. Portions of the text and some footnotes have been omitted.

for security, power, and contested values. Winston Churchill exaggerated only slightly when he declared that "people talked a lot of nonsense when they said nothing was ever settled by war. Nothing in history was ever settled *except* by wars" (quoted in Gilbert 1983, 860–61). Even cases of major change without war, such as Britain yielding hegemony in the Western hemisphere to the United States at the turn of the twentieth century, were strongly influenced by security calculations. Threatening war, preparing for it, and trying to avoid it have permeated all aspects of politics, and so a world in which war among the most developed states is unthinkable will be very different from the history with which we are familiar. To paraphrase and extend a claim made by Evan Luard (1986, 77), given the scale and frequency of war among the great powers in the preceding millennia, this is a change of spectacular proportions, perhaps the single most striking discontinuity that the history of international politics has anywhere provided.

Two major states, Russia and China, might fight each other or a member of the Community. But, as I will discuss below, such a conflict would be different from traditional wars between great powers. Furthermore, these countries lack many of the attributes of great powers: their internal regimes are shaky, they are not at the forefront of any advanced forms of technology or economic organization, they can pose challenges only regionally, and they have no attraction as models for others. They are not among the most developed states and I think it would be fair to put them outside the ranks of the great powers as well. But their military potential, their status as nuclear powers, and the size of their economies renders that judgment easily debatable and so I will not press it but rather will argue that the set of states that form the Community are not all the great powers, but all the most developed ones.

## CENTRAL QUESTIONS

Five questions arise. First, does the existence of the Community mean the end of security threats to its members, and more specifically to the United States? Second, will the Community endure? Third, what are the causes of its construction and maintenance? Fourth, what are the implications for this transformation for the conduct of international affairs? Finally, what does this say about theories of the causes of war?

## CONTINUED THREATS

The fact that the United States is not menaced by the most developed countries does not mean that it does not face any military threats at all. Indeed, some see the United States as no more secure than it was during the Cold War, being imperiled by terrorists and "rogue" states, in addition to Russia and China. But even if I am wrong to believe that these claims are greatly exaggerated, these conflicts do not have the potential to drive world politics the way that clashes among the leading powers did in the past. They do not permeate all facets of international politics and structure state–society relations; they do not represent a struggle for dominance in the international system or a direct challenge to American vital interests.

Recent terrorist attacks are of unprecedented magnitude and will have a significant impact on domestic and international politics, but I do not think they have the potential to be a functional substitute for great power war—i.e., to be the driving force of politics. Despite rhetoric to the contrary, there is little chance that all the countries will unite to combat terrorism; the forms of this scourge are too varied and indeed often are a useful tool for states, and states have many other interests that are at least as important as combating terrorism. Similarly, although the events of September 11 have triggered significant changes in American foreign policy and international alignments, I believe that in a fairly short period of time previous outlooks and conflicts of interest will reassert themselves. Even if this is not the case and if combating terrorism becomes the most important goal for most or all states, the move away from leading power war is still both important and puzzling.

## WILL THE SECURITY COMMUNITY LAST?

Predictions about the maintenance of the Community are obviously disputable (indeed, limitations on people's ability to predict could undermine it), but nothing in the short period since the end of the Cold War points to an unraveling. We could make a long list of disputes, but there were at least as many in the earlier period. The Europeans' effort to establish an independent security force is aimed at permitting them to intervene when the United States chooses not to (or perhaps by threatening such action, to trigger American intervention), not at fighting the United States. Even if Europe were to unite either to balance against the United States or because of its own internal dynamics and the world were to become bipolar again, it is very unlikely that suspicions, fears for the future, and conflicts of interest would be severe enough to break the Community.

A greater threat would be the failure of Europe to unite coupled with an American withdrawal of forces, which could lead to "security competition" within Europe (Art 1996a; Mearsheimer 2001, 385–96). Partly general, the fears would focus on Germany. Their magnitude is hard to gauge and it is difficult to estimate what external shocks or kinds of German behavior would activate them. The fact that Thatcher and Mitterrand opposed German unification is surely not forgotten in Germany and is an indication that concerns remain. But this danger is likely to constitute a self-denying prophecy in two ways. First, many Germans are aware of the need not only to reassure others by tying themselves closely to Europe, but also to seek to make it unlikely that future generations of Germans would want to break these bonds even if they could. Second, Americans who worry about the residual danger will favor keeping some troops in Europe as the ultimate intra-European security guarantee.

Expectations of peace close off important routes to war. The main reason for Japanese aggression in the 1930s was the desire for a self-sufficient sphere that would permit Japan to fight the war with the Western powers that was seen as inevitable, not because of particular conflicts, but because it was believed that great powers always fight each other. By contrast, if states believe that a security community will last they will not be hypersensitive to threats from within it and will not feel the need to undertake precautionary measures that could undermine the security of other members. Thus the United States is not disturbed that British and French nuclear missiles could destroy American cities and while those two countries object to American plans for missile defense, they do not feel the need to increase their forces in response. As long as peace is believed to be very likely, the chance of inadvertent spirals of tension and threat is low.

Nevertheless, the point with which I began this section is unavoidable. World politics can change rapidly and saying that nothing foreseeable will dissolve the Community is not the same as saying that it will not dissolve (Betts 1992). To the extent that it rests on democracy and prosperity (see below), anything that would undermine these would also undermine the Community. Drastic climate change could also shake the foundations of much that we have come to take for granted. But it is hard to see how dynamics at the international level (i.e., the normal trajectory of fears, disputes, and rivalries) could produce war among the leading states. In other words, the Community does not have within it the seeds of its own destruction.

Our faith in the continuation of this peace is increased to the extent that we think we understand its causes and have reason to believe that they will continue. This is our next topic.

## EXPLANATIONS FOR THE SECURITY COMMUNITY

There are social constructivist, liberal, and realist explanations for the Community which, although proceeding from different assumptions and often using different terms, invoke overlapping factors.

### Social Constructivism

Social constructivist accounts stress the role of norms of non-violence and shared identities that, through an interactive process of reciprocal behaviors and expectations, have led the advanced democracies to assume the role of each other's friend. In contradistinction to the liberal and realist explanations, this downplays the importance of material factors and elevates ideas, images of oneself and others, and conceptions of appropriate conduct. The roots of the changes that have produced this enormous shift in international politics among some countries but not others is not specified in detail, but the process is a self-reinforcing one—a benign cycle of behavior, beliefs, and expectations.

People become socialized into attitudes, beliefs, and values that are conducive to peace. Individuals in the Community may see their own country as strong and good—and even better than others—but they rarely espouse the virulent nationalism that was common in the past. Before World War I, one German figure could proclaim that the Germans were "the greatest civilized people known to history" while another declared that the Germans were "the chosen people of this century," which explains "why other people hate us. They do not understand us but they fear our tremendous spiritual superiority." Thomas Macaulay similarly wrote that the British were "the greatest and most highly civilized people that ever the world saw" and were "the acknowledged leaders of the human race in the causes of political improvement," while Senator Albert Beveridge proclaimed that "God has made us the master organizers of the world" (quoted in Van Evera 1984, 27). These sentiments are shocking today because they are so at variance from what we have been taught to think about others and ourselves. We could not adopt these views without rejecting a broad set of beliefs and values. An understanding of the effects of such conceptions led the Europeans, and to an unfortunately lesser extent the Japanese, to de-nationalize and harmonize their textbooks after World War II and has similarly led countries with remaining enemies to follow a different path: The goals for the education of a 12-year-old child in Pakistan include the "ability to know all about India's evil designs about Pakistan; acknowledge and identify forces that may be working against Pakistan; understand the Kashmir problem" (quoted in Kumar 2001, 29).

The central objection to constructionism is that it mistakes effect for cause: its description is correct, but the identities, images, and self-images are superstructure, being the product of peace and of the material incentives discussed below. What is crucial is not people's thinking, but the factors that drive it. The validity of this claim is beyond the reach of current evidence, but it points to a critique of the constructivist argument that the Community will last, which places great faith in the power of socialization and the ability of ideas to replicate and sustain themselves. This conception may betray an excessive faith in the validity of ideas that seem self-evident today, but that our successors might reject. Constructivism may present us with actors who are "over-socialized" (Wrong 1976, ch. 2) and leave too little role for agency in the form of people who think differently, perhaps because their material conditions are different.

## Liberalism

The liberal explanation has received most attention. Although it comes in several variants, the central strands are the pacifying effects of democracy and economic interdependence.

### Democracy

The members of the Community are democracies, and many scholars argue that democracies rarely if ever fight each other. Although the statistical evidence is, as usual, subject to debate, Jack Levy is correct to claim that it is "as close as anything we have to an empirical law in international politics" (Levy 1989, 88).

Less secure, however, is our understanding of why this is the case. We have numerous explanations, which can be seen as competing or complementary. Democracies are systems of dispersed power, and dispersed power means multiple veto points and groups that could block war. (This seems true almost by definition, but if the accounts of former Soviet leaders are to be trusted, Brezhnev was more constrained by his colleagues than was Nixon, at least where arms control was concerned.) Related are the norms of these regimes: democracies function through compromise, non-violence, and respect for law. To the extent that these values and habits govern foreign policy, they are conducive to peace, especially in relations with other democracies who reciprocate.

Other scholars have argued that the key element lies in the realm of information. By having a relatively free flow of intelligence and encouraging debate, democracies are less likely to make egregious errors in estimating what courses of action will maintain the peace. The other side of the informational coin is that democracies can more effectively telegraph their own intentions, and so avoid both unnecessary spirals of conflict and wars that stem from others' incorrect beliefs that the democracy is bluffing (although an obvious cost is an inability to bluff).

Finally, in a recasting of the traditional argument that democracies are less likely to go to war because those who hold ultimate authority (i.e., the general public) will pay the price for conflict, some argue that the institutional and coalitional nature of democratic regimes requires their leaders to pursue successful policies if they are to stay in office. Thus democracies will put greater efforts into winning wars and be careful to choose to fight only wars they can win. Autocracies have a much narrower base and so can stay in power by buying off their supporters even if their foreign policies are unnecessarily costly. These arguments, while highly suggestive, share with earlier liberal thinking quite stylized assumptions about the preferences of societal actors and pay little attention to how each country anticipates the behavior of others and assesses how others expect it to behave.

These explanations for the democratic peace are thoughtful and often ingenious, but not conclusive. Many of them lead us to expect not only dyadic effects, but monadic ones as well—i.e., democracies should be generally peaceful, not only peaceful toward each other, a finding that most scholars deny. They would also lead us to expect that one democracy would not seek to overthrow another, a proposition that is contradicted by American behavior during the Cold War. Furthermore, most of the arguments are built around dyads but it is not entirely clear that the posited causes would apply as well to multilateral groupings like the Community.

The causal role of democracy is hard to establish because these regimes have been relatively rare until recently, much of the democratic peace can be explained by the Soviet threat, and the same factors that lead countries to become democratic (e.g., being relatively rich and secure) are conducive to peace between them. It is particularly important and difficult to control for the role of common interest, which loomed so large during the Cold War. But interests are not objective and may be strongly influenced by the country's internal regime. Thus the democracies may have made common cause during the Cold War in part because they were democracies; common interest may be a mechanism by which the democratic peace is sustained as much as it is a competing explanation for it (for this and related issues, see Farber and Gowa 1995, 1997; Gartzke 1998, 2000; Maoz 1997; Oneal and Russett 1999; Schweller 2000). Moreover, if democracies are more likely to become economically interdependent with one another, additional common interest will be created. But to bring up the importance of interest is to highlight an ambiguity and raise a question. The ambiguity is whether the theory leads us to expect democracies *never* to fight each other or "merely" to fight *less* than do other dyads. (Most scholars take the latter view, but this does not mean that this is what most versions of the theory actually imply.) The related hypothetical question is: Is it impossible for two democracies to have a conflict of interest so severe that it leads to war? This troubles the stronger version of the argument because it is hard to answer in the affirmative.

But would democracies let such a potent conflict of interest develop? At least as striking as the statistical data is the fact—or rather, the judgment—that the regimes that most disturbed the international order in the twentieth century also devastated their own peoples—the USSR, Germany under the Nazis and, perhaps, under Kaiser Wilhelm. One reason for this connection may be the desire to remake the world (but because the international order was established by countries that were advanced democracies, it may not be surprising that those who opposed it were not). Not all murderous regimes are as ambitious (e.g., Idi Amin's Uganda), and others with both power and grand designs may remain restrained (e.g., Mao's China), but it is hard to understand the disruptive German and Soviet foreign policy without reference to their domestic regimes.

## Interdependence

The second leg of the liberal explanation for the Community is the high level of economic interdependence. The basic argument was developed by Cobden, Bright, and the other nineteenth-century British liberals. As the former put it: "Free Trade is God's diplomacy and there is no other certain way of uniting people in bonds of peace." (Quoted in Bourne 1970, 85. For a general treatment of Cobden's views, see Cain 1979. For the most recent evidence, see McMillan 1997; Russett and Oneal 2001, ch. 4; for arguments that interdependence has been exaggerated and misunderstood, see Waltz 1970, 1979 ch. 7, 1999. Most traditional liberal thinking and the rest of my brief discussion assumes symmetry; as Hirschman 1945 showed, asymmetric dependence can provide the basis for exploitative bargaining.) Although the evidence for this proposition remains in dispute, the causal argument is relatively straightforward. "If goods cannot cross borders, armies will" is the central claim, in the words of the nineteenth-century French economist Frederick Bastiat which were often repeated by Secretary of State Cordell Hull (perhaps excessively influenced by the experience of the 1930s). Extensive economic intercourse allows states to gain by trade the wealth that they would otherwise seek through fighting. Relatedly, individuals and groups who conduct these economic relations develop a powerful stake in keeping the peace and maintaining good relations. Thus it is particularly significant that in the contemporary world many firms have important ties abroad and that direct foreign investment holds the fates of important actors hostage to continued good relations. There can be a benign cycle here as increasing levels of trade strengthen the political power of actors who have a stake in deepening these ties.

The liberal view assumes that actors place a high priority on wealth, that trade is a better route to it than conquest, and that actors who gain economically from the exchange are politically powerful. These assumptions are often true, especially in the modern world, but are not without their vulnerabilities. At times honor and glory, in addition to more traditional forms of individual and national interest, can be more salient than economic gain. Thus as the Moroccan crisis of 1911 came to its climax, General von Moltke wrote to his wife: "If we again slip away from this affair with our tail between our legs . . . I shall despair of the future of the German Empire. I shall then retire. But before handing in my resignation I shall move to abolish the Army and to place ourselves under Japanese protectorate; we shall then be in a position to make money without interference and to develop into ninnies" (quoted in Berghahn 1973, 97). Traditional liberal thought understood this well and stressed that economic activity was so potent not only because it gave people an interest in maintaining peace, but because it reconstructed social values to downgrade status and glory and elevate material well-being. It follows that the stability of the Community rests in part upon people giving priority to consumption. Critics decry modern society's embodiment of individualistic, material values, but one can easily imagine that others could generate greater international conflict.

There are four general arguments against the pacific influence of interdependence. First, if it is hard to go from the magnitude of economic flows to the costs that would be incurred if they were disrupted, it is even more difficult to estimate how much political impact these costs will have, which depends on the other considerations in play and the political context. This means that we do not have a theory that tells us the expected magnitude of the effect. Second, even the sign of the effect can be disputed: interdependence can increase conflict as states gain bargaining leverage over each other, fear that others will exploit them, and face additional sources of disputes. These effects might not arise if states expect to remain at peace with each other, however. Third, it is clear that interdependence does not guarantee peace. High levels of economic integration did not prevent World War I, and nations that were much more unified than any security community have peacefully dissolved or fought civil wars. But this does not mean that interdependence is not conducive to peace. Fourth, interdependence may be more an effect than a cause, more the product than a generator of expectations of peace and cooperation.

## Realist Explanations

The crudest realist explanation for the Community would focus on the rise of the common threat from Russia and China. While not entirely implausible, this argument does not fit the views espoused by most elites in Japan and Europe, who are relatively unconcerned about these countries and believe that whatever dangers emanate from them would be magnified rather than decreased by a confrontational policy.

### American Hegemony

Two other realist accounts are stronger. The first argues that the Community is largely caused by the other enormous change in world politics—the American dominance of world politics. U.S. defense spending, to take the most easily quantifiable indicator, is now greater than that of the next 8 countries combined (O'Hanlon 2001, 4–5). Furthermore, thanks to the Japanese constitution and the integration of armed forces within NATO, America's allies do not have to fear attacks from each other: their militaries (especially Germany's) are so truncated that they could not fight a major war without American assistance or attack each other without undertaking a military buildup that would give others a great deal of warning. American dominance also leads us to expect that key outcomes, from the expansion of NATO, to the American-led wars in Kosovo and the Persian Gulf, to the IMF bailouts of Turkey and Argentina in the spring of 2001, will conform to American preferences.

But closer examination reveals differences between current and past hegemonies. The United States usually gives considerable weight to its partners' views and indeed its own preferences are often influenced by theirs, as was true in Kosovo. For their parts, the other members of the Community seek to harness and constrain American power, not displace it. The American hegemony will surely eventually decay but increased European and Japanese strength need not lead to war, contrary to the expectations of standard theories of hegemony and great power rivalry. Unlike previous eras of hegemony, the current peace seems uncoerced and accepted by most states, which does not fit entirely well with realism.

### Nuclear Weapons

The second realist argument was familiar during the Cold War but receives less attention now. This is the pacifying effect of nuclear weapons, which, if possessed in sufficient numbers and invulnerable configurations, make victory impossible and war a feckless option. An immediate objection is that not all the major states in the Community have nuclear weapons. But this is only technically correct: Germany and Japan could produce nuclear weapons if a threat loomed, as their partners fully understand. The other factors discussed in the previous pages may or may not be important; nuclear weapons by themselves would be sufficient to keep the great powers at peace.

While there is a great deal to this argument, it is not without its problems. First, because this kind of deterrence rests on the perceived possibility of war, it may explain peace, but not a security community. Second, mutual deterrence can be used as a platform for hostility, coercion, and even limited wars. In what Glenn Snyder (1965; also see Jervis 1989, 19–23, 74–106) calls the stability-instability paradox, the common realization that all-out war would be irrational provides a license for threats and the use of lower levels of violence. Under some circumstances a state could use the shared fear of nuclear war to exploit others. If the state thinks that the other is preoccupied with the possibility of war and does not anticipate that the state will make the concessions needed to reduce this danger, it will expect the other to retreat and so can stand firm. In other words, the fact that war would be the worst possible outcome for both sides does not automatically lead to uncoerced peace, let alone to a security community.

## A Synthetic Interactive Explanation

I think the development and maintenance of the Community is best explained by a combination and reformulation of several factors discussed previously. Even with the qualifications just discussed, a necessary condition is the belief that conquest is difficult and war is terribly costly. When conquest is easy, aggression is encouraged and the security dilemma operates with particular viciousness as even defensive states need to prepare to attack (Van Evera 1999). But when states have modern armies with extensive firepower and, even more, nuclear weapons, it is hard for anyone to believe that war could make sense.

Statesmen must consider the gains that war might bring as well as the costs. Were they to be very high, they might outweigh great expected costs. But, if anything, the expected benefits of war within the Community have declined, in part because the developed countries, including those that lost World War II, are generally satisfied with the status quo. Even in the case that shows the greatest strain—U.S.–Japanese relations—no one has explained how a war could provide either side much gross, let alone net, benefit. It is then hard to locate a problem for which war among the Community members would provide a solution. Furthermore, as liberals have stressed, peace within the Community brings many gains, especially economic.

Of course costs and benefits are subjective, depending as they do on what the actors value, and changes in values are the third leg of my explanation. Most political analysis takes the actors' values for granted because they tend to be widely shared and to change slowly. Their importance and variability becomes clear only when we confront a case like Nazi Germany which, contrary to standard realist conceptions of national interest and security, put everything at risk in order to seek the domination of the Aryan race.

The changes over the last 50–75 years in what the leaders and publics in the developed states value drive some of the calculations of costs and benefits. To start with, war is no longer seen as good in itself; no great power leader today would agree with Theodore Roosevelt that "no triumph of peace is quite so great as the supreme triumph of war" (quoted in Harbaugh 1961, 99). In earlier eras it was commonly believed that war brought out the best in individuals and nations and that the virtues of discipline, risk-taking, and self-sacrifice that war required were central to civilization. Relatedly, honor and glory used to be central values. In a world so constituted, the material benefits of peace would be much less important; high levels of trade, the difficulty of making conquest pay, and even nuclear weapons might not produce peace.

Democracy and identity also operate through what actors value, and may in part be responsible for the decline in militarism just noted. Compromise, consideration for the interests of others, respect for law, and a shunning of violence outside this context all are values that underpin democracy and are reciprocally cultivated by it. The Community also is relatively homogeneous in that its members are all democracies and have values that are compatibly similar. One impulse to war is the desire to change the other country, and this disappears if values are shared. The United States could conquer Canada, for example, but what would be the point when so much of what it wants to see there is already in place?

Central to the rise of the Community is the decline in territorial disputes among its members. Territory has been the most common cause and object of conflicts in the past, and we have become so accustomed to their absence that it is easy to lose sight of how drastic and consequential this change is. Germans no longer care that Alsace and Lorraine are French; the French are not disturbed by the high level of German presence in these provinces. The French furthermore permitted the Saar to return to Germany and are not bothered by this loss, and indeed do not feel it as a loss at all. Although for years the Germans refused to renounce their claims to the "lost territories" to the east, they did so upon unification and few voices were raised in protest.

The causes of these changes in values in general and nationalism and concern with territory in particular are subject to dispute, as are the developments that could reverse them. In particular, it is unclear how much they are rooted in material changes, most obviously the increased destructiveness of war and the unprecedented prosperity that is seen as linked to good political relations, and to what extent they are more autonomous, following out perhaps a natural progression and building on each other. They may be linked (inextricably?) to high levels of consumption, faith in rationality, and the expectation of progress, although it is not unreasonable to argue that this describes Europe in 1914 as well. The decreased salience of territory and decline of territorial disputes is almost surely produced in part by the decoupling of territorial control and national prosperity, and most of the other relationships between material structures and ideational patterns are complex and reciprocal. Just as capitalism is built and sustained by pre-capitalist values and post-materialism may grow from prosperity so the values that sustain the Community can neither be separated nor simply deduced from changes in the means and levels of production and potential destruction.

The increased destructiveness of war, the benefits of peace, and the changes in values interact and reinforce each other. If war were not so dreadful, it could be considered as an instrument for national enrichment; if peace did not seem to bring prosperity and national well-being, violence would at least be contemplated; that military victory is no longer seen as a positive value both contributes to and is in part explained by the high perceived costs of war. Similarly, expectations of peace allow states to value each other's economic and political successes. Although these may incite envy, they no longer produce strong security fears, as they did in the past. The Community may then contain within it the seeds of its own growth through the feedbacks among its elements.

Another dynamic element is crucial as well: the progress of the Community is path-dependent in that without the Cold War it is unlikely that the factors we have discussed could have overcome prevalent fears and rivalries. The conflict with the Soviet Union produced American security guarantees and an unprecedented sense of common purpose among the states that now form the Community. Since the coalition could be undermined by social unrest or political instability, each country sought to see that the others were well off and resisted the temptation to solve its own problems by exporting them to its neighbors. Since the coalition would have been disrupted had any country developed strong grievances against other members, each had reason to moderate its demands and mediate when conflicts developed between others. To cultivate better relations in the future, leaders consciously portrayed the others as partners and sponsored the socialization practices discussed above. The American willingness to engage in extensive cooperation abroad, the European willingness to go far down the road of integration, the Japanese willingness to tie itself closely to the United States were improbable without the Cold War. But having been established, these forms of cooperation set off positive feedback and are now self-sustaining.

## IMPLICATIONS

What are the implications of the existence of the security community for how these states will carry out relations among themselves and for general theories of war and peace?

## International Politics Within the Community

In previous eras, no aspect of international politics and few aspects of domestic politics were untouched by the anticipation of future wars among the leading powers. Much will then change in the Community. In the absence of these states amalgamating—a development that is out of the question outside of Europe and unlikely within it—they will neither consider using force against one another nor lose their sovereignty. There will then be significant conflicts of interest without clear means of resolving them. They will continue to be rivals in some respects, and to bargain with each other. Indeed, the stability-instability paradox implies that the shared expectation that disputes will remain peaceful will remove some restraints on vituperation and competitive tactics. The dense network of institutions within the Community should serve to provide multiple means for resolving conflicts, but will also provide multiple ways for a dissatisfied country to show its displeasure and threaten disruption.

The fact that the situation is a new one poses challenges and opportunities for states. What goals will have highest priority? How important will considerations of status be? Will non-military alliances form? Bargaining will continue, and this means that varieties of power, including the ability to help and hurt others, will remain relevant. Threats, bluffs, warnings, the mobilization of resources for future conflicts, intense diplomatic negotiations, and shifting patterns of working with and against others all will remain. But the content of these forms will differ from those of traditional international politics.

Politics within the Community may come to resemble the relations between the United States and Canada and Australia that Keohane and Nye (1977) described as complex interdependence: extensive transnational and transgovernmental relations, bargains carried out across different issue areas, and bargaining power gained through asymmetric dependence but limited by overall common interests. Despite this path-breaking study, however, we know little about how this kind of politics will be conducted. As numerous commentators have noted, economic issues and economic resources will play large roles, but the changed context will matter. Relative economic advantage was sought in the past in part because it contributed to military security. This no longer being the case, the possibilities for cooperation are increased.

Even though force will not be threatened within the Community, it will remain important in relations among its members. During the Cold War the protection the United States afforded to its allies gave it an important moral claim and significant bargaining leverage. Despite the decreased level of threat, this will be true for the indefinite future because militarily Japan and Europe need the United States much more than the United States needs them. While the unique American ability to lead military operations like those in the Persian Gulf and Kosovo causes resentments and frictions with its allies, it also gives it a resource that is potent even—or especially—if it is never explicitly brought to the table.

### Four Possible Futures

Even within the contours of a Community, there is a significant range of patterns of relations that are possible, four of which can be briefly sketched.

The greatest change would be a world in which national autonomy would be further diminished and the distinctions between domestic and foreign policy would continue to erode. Medieval Europe, with its overlapping forms of sovereignty rather than compartmentalized nation-states, which might dissolve because they are no longer needed to provide security and can no longer control their economies, is one model here. Although most scholars see the reduction of sovereignty and the growth of the power of non-governmental organizations as conducive to peace and harmony, one can readily imagine sharp conflicts, for example among business interests, labor, and environmentalists (many Marxists see class conflicts as increasingly important); between those with different views of the good life; between those calling for greater centralization to solve common problems and those advocating increased local control. But state power and interest would in any case be greatly decreased. The notion of "national interest," always contested, would become even more problematic.

A second world, not completely incompatible with the first, would be one in which states in the Community play a large role, but with more extensive and intensive cooperation. Relations would be increasingly governed by principles and laws, a change that could benignly spill over into relations outside the Community. Although bargaining would not disappear, there would be more joint efforts to solve common problems and the line between "high" and "low" politics would become even more blurred.

In this world, the United States would share more power and responsibility with the rest of the Community than is true today. While popular with scholars at least as likely is a continuation of the present trajectory in which the United States maintains hegemony and rejects significant limitations on its freedom of action. National interests would remain distinct and the United States would follow the familiar pattern in which ambitions and perceived interests expand as power does. Both conflicts of interest and the belief that hegemony best produces collective goods would lead the United States to oppose the efforts of others to become a counterweight if not a rival to it. In effect, the United States would lead an empire, but probably a relatively benign one. Doing so would be rendered more difficult by the fact that the American self-image precludes seeing its role for what it is, in part because of the popularity of values of equality and supranationalism. Other members of the Community would resent seeing their interests overridden by the United States on some occasions, but the exploitation would be limited by their bargaining power and the American realization that excessive discontent would have serious long-term consequences. Others might accept these costs in return for the U.S. security guarantee and the ability to keep their own defense spending very low, especially because the alternative to American-dominated stability might be worse.

The fourth model also starts with the American attempt to maintain hegemony, but this time the costs and dangers of American unilateralism become sufficient to lead others to form a counter-balancing coalition, one that might include Russia and China as well. Europe and Japan might also become more assertive because they fear that the United States will eventually withdraw its security guarantee, thereby accelerating if not creating a rift within the Community. Much that realism stresses—the clash of national interests, the weakness of international institutions, maneuvering for advantage, and the use of power and threats—would come to the fore, but with the vital difference that force would not be contemplated and the military balance would enter in only indirectly, as discussed above. This would be a strange mixture of the new and the familiar, and the central question is what *ultima ratio* will replace cannons. What will be the final arbiter of disputes? What kinds of threats will be most potent? How fungible will the relevant forms of power be?

Outlining these possibilities raises two broad questions that I cannot answer. First, is the future essentially determined, as many structural theories would imply, or does it depend on national choices strongly influenced by variable domestic politics, leaders, and accidents? Second, if the future is not determined, how much depends on choices the United States has yet to make, and what will most influence these choices?

## IMPLICATIONS FOR THEORIES OF THE CAUSES OF WAR

Whatever its explanation, the very existence of a security community among the leading powers refutes many theories of the causes of war, or at least indicates they are not universally valid. Thus human nature and the drive for dominance, honor, and glory may exist and contribute to a wide variety of human behaviors but they are not fated to lead to war.

The obvious rebuttal is that war still exists outside the Community and that civil wars continue unabated. But only wars fought by members of the Community have the potential to undermine the argument that, under some conditions, attributes of humans and societies that were seen as inevitably producing wars in fact do not do so. The cases that could be marshalled are the Gulf War and the operation in Kosovo, but they do not help these theories. These wars were provoked by others, gained little honor and glory for the Community, and were fought in a manner that minimized the loss of life on the other side. It would be hard to portray them as manifestations of brutal or evil human nature. Indeed, it is more plausible to see the Community's behavior as consistent with a general trend toward its becoming less violent generally: the abolition of official torture and the decreased appeal of capital punishment, to take the most salient examples (Mueller 1989).

The existence of the Community also casts doubt on theories that argue that the leading powers always struggle for dominance for gain, status, or security, and are willing to use force to this end. Traditional Marxist theories claim that capitalists could never cooperate; proponents of the law of uneven growth see changes in the relative power of major states as producing cycles of domination, stability, challenge, and war. Similarly, "power transitions" in which rising powers catch up with dominant ones are seen to be very difficult to manage peacefully. These theories, like the version of hegemonic stability discussed above, have yet to be tested because the United States has not yet declined. But if the arguments made here are correct, transitions will not have the same violent outcome that they had in the past, leading us to pay greater attention to the conditions under which these theories do and do not hold.

For most scholars, the fundamental cause of war is international anarchy, compounded by the security dilemma. These forces press hardest on the leading powers because while they may be able to guarantee the security of others, no one can provide this escape from the state of nature for them. As we have seen, different schools of thought propose different explanations for the rise of the Community and so lead to somewhat different propositions about the conditions under which anarchy can be compatible with peace. Constructivism stresses the importance of identities and ideas; liberalism argues for the power of material incentives for peace; realism looks at the costs of war and the details of the payoff structure; my composite explanation stresses the interaction among several factors of costs, benefits, values, and path-dependence. But what is most important is that the Community constitutes a proof by existence of uncoerced peace without central authority. Because these countries are the most powerful ones and particularly war-prone, the Community poses a fundamental challenge to our understanding of world politics and our expectations of future possibilities.

# REFERENCES

Art, Robert J. 1996. "Why Western Europe Needs the United States and NATO." *Political Science Quarterly* 111 (Spring): 1–39.

Berghahn, V. R. 1973. *Germany and the Approach of War in 1914.* New York: St. Martin's Press.

Betts, Richard. 1992. "Systems of Peace or Causes of War? Collective Security, Arms Control, and the New Europe." *International Security* 17 (Summer): 5–43.

Bourne, Kenneth. 1970. *The Foreign Policy of Victorian England: 1830–1902.* Oxford: Clarendon Press.

Cain, Peter. 1979. "Capitalism, War and Internationalism in the Thought of Richard Cobden." *British Journal of International Studies* 5 (October): 229–47.

Deutsch, Karl W., et al. 1957. *Political Community and the North Atlantic Area: International Organizations in the Light of Historical Experience.* Princeton, NJ: Princeton University Press.

Farber, Henry, and Joanne Gowa. 1995. "Polities and Peace." *International Security* 20 (Fall): 123–46.

Farber, Henry and Joanne Gowa. 1997. "Common Interests or Common Polities?" *Journal of Politics* 59 (May): 123–46.

Gartzke, Erik. 1998. "Kant We All Get Along? Motive, Opportunity, and the Origins of the Democratic Peace." *American Journal of Political Science* 42 (1): 1–27.

Gartzke, Erik. 2000. "Preferences and Democratic Peace." *International Studies Quarterly* 44 (June): 191–212.

Gilbert, Martin. 1983. *Winston S. Churchill,* Volume VI, *Finest Hour 1939–1941.* London: Heinemann.

Harbaugh, William Henry. 1961. *The Life and Times of Theodore Roosevelt.* New York: Collier Books.

Hirschman, Albert O. 1945. *National Power and the Structure of Foreign Trade.* Berkeley and Los Angeles: University of California Press.

Jervis, Robert. 1989. *The Meaning of Nuclear Revolution: Statecraft and the Prospect of Armageddon.* Ithaca, NY: Cornell University Press.

Keohane, Robert O., and Joseph Nye, eds. 1977. *Power and Interdependence: World Politics in Transition.* Boston, MA: Little Brown.

Kumar, Amitava. 2001. "Bristling on the Subcontinent." *The Nation.* April 23, 2001, 29–30.

Levy, Jack S. 1989. "Domestic Politics and War." In *The Origins and Prevention of Major Wars,* eds. Robert I. Rotberg and Theodore K. Rabb. Cambridge: Cambridge University Press. pp. 79–100.

Luard, Evan. 1986. *War in International Society: A Study in International Sociology.* London: I.B. Tauris.

Maoz, Zeev. 1997. "The Controversy Over the Democratic Peace: Rearguard Action or Cracks in the Wall?" *International Security* 22 (Summer): 162–98.

McMillan, Susan M. 1997. "Interdependence and Conflict." *Mershon International Studies Review* 41, supplement 1 (May): 33–58.

Mearsheimer, John J. 2001. *The Tragedy of Great Power Politics.* New York: Norton.

Mueller, John. 1989. *Retreat from Doomsday: The Obsolescence of Major War.* New York: Basic Books.

O'Hanlon, Michael E. 2001. *Defense Policy Choices for the Bush Administration.* Washington, DC: Brookings Institution Press.

Oneal, John R., and Bruce Russett. 1999. "Is the Liberal Peace Just an Artifact of Cold War Interests? Assessing Recent Critiques." *International Interactions* 25 (3): 213–41.

Russett, Bruce, and John R. Oneal. 2001. *Triangulating Peace: Democracy, Interdependence, and International Organizations.* New York: Norton.

Schweller, Randall L. 2000. "Democracy and the Post–Cold War Era." In *The New World Order,* eds. Birthe Hansen and Bertel Heurlin. New York: St. Martin's Press. pp. 46–80.

Snyder, Glenn. 1965. "The Balance of Power and the Balance of Terror." In *The Balance of Power,* ed. Paul Seabury. San Francisco: Chandler. pp. 184–201.

Van Evera, Stephen. 1984. "The Cult of the Offensive and the Origins of the First World War." *International Security* 9 (Summer): 58–107.

Van Evera, Stephen. 1999. *Causes of War: Power and the Roots of Conflict.* Ithaca, NY: Cornell University Press.

Waltz, Kenneth N. 1970. "The Myth of National Interdependence." In *The International Corporation,* ed. Charles P. Kindleberger. Cambridge, MA: MIT Press. pp. 205–23.

Waltz, Kenneth N. 1979. *Theory of International Politics.* Reading, MA: Addison-Wesley Publishing.

Waltz, Kenneth N. 1999. "Globalization and Governance." *PS: Political Science & Politics* 32 (December): 693–700.

Wrong, Dennis H. 1976. *Skeptical Sociology.* New York: Columbia University Press.

# The Clash of Civilizations?

## SAMUEL P. HUNTINGTON

### THE NEXT PATTERN OF CONFLICT

World politics is entering a new phase, and intellectuals have not hesitated to proliferate visions of what it will be—the end of history, the return of traditional rivalries between nation-states, and the decline of the nation-state from the conflicting pulls of tribalism and globalism, among others. Each of these visions catches aspects of the emerging reality. Yet they all miss a crucial, indeed a central, aspect of what global politics is likely to be in the coming years.

It is my hypothesis that the fundamental source of conflict in this new world will not be primarily ideological or primarily economic. The great divisions among humankind and the dominating source of conflict will be cultural. Nation states will remain the most powerful actors in world affairs, but the principal conflicts of global politics will occur between nations and groups of different civilizations. The clash of civilizations will dominate global politics. The fault lines between civilizations will be the battle lines of the future.

Conflict between civilizations will be the latest phase in the evolution of conflict in the modern world. For a century and a half after the emergence of the modern international system with the Peace of Westphalia, the conflicts of the Western world were largely among princes—emperors, absolute monarchs, and constitutional monarchs attempting to expand their bureaucracies, their armies, their mercantilist economic strength, and, most important, the territory they ruled. In the process they created nation-states, and beginning with the French Revolution the principal lines of conflict were between nations rather than princes. In 1793, as R. R. Palmer put it, "The wars of kings were over; the wars of peoples had begun." This nineteenth-century pattern lasted until the end of World War I. Then, as a result of the Russian Revolution and the reaction against it, the conflict of nations yielded to the conflict of ideologies, first among communism, fascism-Nazism, and liberal democracy, and then between communism and liberal democracy. During the Cold War, this latter conflict became embodied in the struggle between the two superpowers, neither of which was a nation-state in the classical European sense and each of which defined its identity in terms of its ideology.

These conflicts between princes, nation-states, and ideologies were primarily conflicts within Western civilization, "Western civil wars," as William Lind has

From Samuel P. Huntington, "The Clash of Civilizations?" Reprinted by permission of *Foreign Affairs*, Vol. 72, No. 3 (Summer 1993), pp. 22–49. Copyright 1993 by the Council on Foreign Relations, Inc.

labeled them. This was as true of the Cold War as it was of the world wars and the earlier wars of the seventeenth, eighteenth, and nineteenth centuries. With the end of the Cold War, international politics moves out of its Western phase, and its centerpiece becomes the interaction between the West and non-Western civilizations and among non-Western civilizations. In the politics of civilizations, the peoples and governments of non-Western civilizations no longer remain the objects of history as targets of Western colonialism but join the West as movers and shapers of history.

## THE NATURE OF CIVILIZATIONS

During the Cold War the world was divided into the First, Second, and Third worlds. Those divisions are no longer relevant. It is far more meaningful now to group countries not in terms of their political or economic systems or in terms of their level of economic development but rather in terms of their culture and civilization.

What do we mean when we talk of a civilization? A civilization is a cultural entity. Villages, regions, ethnic groups, nationalities, religious groups, all have distinct cultures at different levels of cultural heterogeneity. The culture of a village in southern Italy may be different from that of a village in northern Italy, but both will share in a common Italian culture that distinguishes them from German villages. European communities, in turn, will share cultural features that distinguish them from Arab or Chinese communities. Arabs, Chinese, and Westerners, however, are not part of any broader cultural entity. They constitute civilizations. A civilization is thus the highest cultural grouping of people and the broadest level of cultural identity people have short of that which distinguishes humans from other species. It is defined both by common objective elements, such as language, history, religion, customs, institutions, and by the subjective self-identification of people. People have levels of identity: A resident of Rome may define himself with varying degrees of intensity as a Roman, an Italian, a Catholic, a Christian, a European, a Westerner. The civilization to which he belongs is the broadest level of identification with which he intensely identifies. People can and do redefine their identities and, as a result, the composition and boundaries of civilizations change.

Civilizations may involve a large number of people, as with China ("a civilization pretending to be a state," as Lucian Pye put it), or a very small number of people, such as the Anglophone Caribbean. A civilization may include several nation-states, as is the case with Western, Latin American, and Arab civilizations, or only one, as is the case with Japanese civilization. Civilizations obviously blend and overlap, and may include subcivilizations. Western civilization has two major variants, European and North American, and Islam has its Arab, Turkic, and Malay subdivisions. Civilizations are nonetheless meaningful entities, and while the lines between them are seldom sharp, they are real. Civilizations are dynamic; they rise and fall; they divide and merge. And, as any student of history knows, civilizations disappear and are buried in the sands of time.

Westerners tend to think of nation-states as the principal actors in global affairs. They have been that, however, for only a few centuries. The broader reaches of human history have been the history of civilizations. In *A Study of History*, Arnold Toynbee identified 21 major civilizations; only six of them exist in the contemporary world.

## WHY CIVILIZATIONS WILL CLASH

Civilization identity will be increasingly important in the future, and the world will be shaped in large measure by the interactions among seven or eight major civilizations. These include Western, Confucian, Japanese, Islamic, Hindu, Slavic-Orthodox, Latin American, and possibly African civilization. The most important conflicts of the future will occur along the cultural fault lines separating these civilizations from one another.

Why will this be the case?

First, differences among civilizations are not only real; they are basic. Civilizations are differentiated from each other by history, language, culture, tradition, and, most important, religion. The people of different civilizations have different views on the relations between God and man, the individual and the group, the citizen and the state, parents and children, husband and wife, as well as differing views of the relative importance of rights and responsibilities, liberty and authority, equality and hierarchy. These differences are the product of centuries. They will not soon disappear. They are far more fundamental than differences among political ideologies and political regimes. Differences do not necessarily mean conflict, and conflict does not necessarily mean violence. Over the centuries, however, differences among civilizations have generated the most prolonged and the most violent conflicts.

Second, the world is becoming a smaller place. The interactions between peoples of different civilizations are increasing; these increasing interactions intensify civilization-consciousness and awareness of differences between civilizations and commonalities within civilizations. North African immigration to France generates hostility among Frenchmen and at the same time increased receptivity to immigration by "good" European Catholic Poles. Americans react far more negatively to Japanese investment than to larger investments from Canada and European countries. . . . The interactions among peoples of different civilizations enhance the civilization-consciousness of people that, in turn, invigorates differences and animosities stretching or thought to stretch back deep into history.

Third, the processes of economic modernization and social change throughout the world are separating people from longstanding local identities. They also weaken the nation-state as a source of identity. In much of the world religion has moved in to fill this gap, often in the form of movements that are labeled "fundamentalist." Such movements are found in Western Christianity, Judaism, Buddhism, and Hinduism, as well as in Islam. In most countries and most religions the people active in fundamentalist movements are young, college-educated, middle-class technicians, professionals, and business persons. . . . The revival of religion . . . provides a basis for identity and commitment that transcends national boundaries and unites civilizations.

Fourth, the growth of civilization-consciousness is enhanced by the dual role of the West. On the one hand, the West is at a peak of power. At the same time, however, and perhaps as a result, a return to the roots phenomenon is occurring among non-Western civilizations. Increasingly one hears references to trends toward a turning inward and "Asianization" in Japan, the end of the Nehru legacy and the "Hinduization" of India, the failure of Western ideas of socialism and nationalism and hence "re-Islamization" of the Middle East. . . . A West at the peak of its power confronts non-Wests that increasingly have the desire, the will, and the resources to shape the world in non-Western ways.

In the past, the elites of non-Western societies were usually the people who were most involved with the West, had been educated at Oxford, the Sorbonne, or Sandhurst, and had absorbed Western attitudes and values. At the same time, the populace in non-Western countries often remained deeply imbued with the indigenous culture. Now, however, these relationships are being reversed. A de-Westernization and indigenization of elites is occurring in many non-Western countries at the same time that Western, usually American, cultures, styles, and habits become more popular among the mass of the people.

Fifth, cultural characteristics and differences are less mutable and hence less easily compromised and resolved than political and economic ones. In the former Soviet Union, communists can become democrats, the rich can become poor and the poor rich, but Russians cannot become Estonians and Azeris cannot become Armenians. In class and ideological conflicts, the key question was "Which side are you on?" and people could and did choose sides and change sides. In conflicts between civilizations, the question is "What are you?" That is a given that cannot be changed. . . . Even more than ethnicity, religion discriminates sharply and exclusively among people. A person can be half-French and half-Arab and simultaneously even a citizen of two countries. It is more difficult to be half-Catholic and half-Muslim.

Finally, economic regionalism is increasing. The proportions of total trade that were intraregional rose between 1980 and 1989 from 51 percent to 59 percent in Europe, 33 percent to 37 percent in East Asia, and 32 percent to 36 percent in North America. The importance of regional economic blocs is likely to continue to increase in the future. On the one hand, successful economic regionalism will reinforce civilization-consciousness. On the other hand, economic regionalism may succeed only when it is rooted in a common civilization. The European Community rests on the shared foundation of European culture and Western Christianity. The success of the North American Free Trade Area depends on the convergence now underway of Mexican, Canadian, and American cultures. Japan, in contrast, faces difficulties in creating a comparable economic entity in East Asia because Japan is a society and civilization unique to itself. However strong the trade and investment links Japan may develop with other East Asian countries, its cultural differences with those countries inhibit and perhaps preclude its promoting regional economic integration like that in Europe and North America.

Common culture, in contrast, is clearly facilitating the rapid expansion of the economic relations between the People's Republic of China and Hong Kong, Taiwan, Singapore, and the overseas Chinese communities in other Asian countries. With the Cold War over, cultural commonalities increasingly overcome ideological differences, and mainland China and Taiwan move closer together. If cultural commonality is a prerequisite for economic integration, the principal East

Asian economic bloc of the future is likely to be centered on China. This bloc is, in fact, already coming into existence. . . .

Culture and religion also form the basis of the Economic Cooperation Organization, which brings together ten non-Arab Muslim countries: Iran, Pakistan, Turkey, Azerbaijan, Kazakhstan, Kyrgyzstan, Turkmenistan, Tadjikistan, Uzbekistan, and Afghanistan. One impetus to the revival and expansion of this organization, founded originally in the 1960s by Turkey, Pakistan, and Iran, is the realization by the leaders of several of these countries that they had no chance of admission to the European Community. Similarly, Caricom, the Central American Common Market, and Mercosur rest on common cultural foundations. Efforts to build a broader Caribbean–Central American economic entity bridging the Anglo-Latin divide, however, have to date failed.

As people define their identity in ethnic and religious terms, they are likely to see an "us" versus "them" relation existing between themselves and people of different ethnicity or religion. . . . Most important, the efforts of the West to promote its values of democracy and liberalism as universal values, to maintain its military predominance, and to advance its economic interests engender countering responses from other civilizations. Decreasingly able to mobilize support and form coalitions on the basis of ideology, governments and groups will increasingly attempt to mobilize support by appealing to common religion and civilization identity.

The clash of civilizations thus occurs at two levels. At the micro-level, adjacent groups along the fault lines between civilizations struggle, often violently, over the control of territory and each other. At the macro-level, states from different civilizations compete for relative military and economic power, struggle over the control of international institutions and third parties, and competitively promote their particular political and religious values.

## THE FAULT LINES BETWEEN CIVILIZATIONS

The fault lines between civilizations are replacing the political and ideological boundaries of the Cold War as the flash points for crisis and bloodshed. The Cold War began when the Iron Curtain divided Europe politically and ideologically. The Cold War ended with the end of the Iron Curtain. As the ideological division of Europe has disappeared, the cultural division of Europe between Western Christianity, on the one hand, and Orthodox Christianity and Islam, on the other, has reemerged. The most significant dividing line in Europe, as William Wallace has suggested, may well be the eastern boundary of Western Christianity in the year 1500. This line runs along what are now the boundaries between Finland and Russia and between the Baltic states and Russia, cuts through Belarus and Ukraine separating the more Catholic western Ukraine from Orthodox eastern Ukraine, swings westward separating Transylvania from the rest of Romania, and then goes through Yugoslavia almost exactly along the line now separating Croatia and Slovenia from the rest of Yugoslavia. In the Balkans this line, of course, coincides with the historic boundary between the Hapsburg and Ottoman empires. The peoples to the north and west of this line are Protestant or Catholic; they shared the common experiences of European history—feudalism, the Renaissance, the Reformation, the Enlightenment, the French Revolution, the Industrial Revolution; they are generally economically better off than the peoples to the east; and they may now look forward to increasing involvement in a common European economy and to the consolidation of democratic political systems. The peoples to the east and south of this line are Orthodox or Muslim; they historically belonged to the Ottoman or Tsarist empires and were only lightly touched by the shaping events in the rest of Europe; they are generally less advanced economically; they seem much less likely to develop stable democratic political systems. The Velvet Curtain of culture has replaced the Iron Curtain of ideology as the most significant dividing line in Europe. As the events in Yugoslavia show, it is not only a line of difference; it is also at times a line of bloody conflict. . . .

After World War II, the West . . . began to retreat; the colonial empires disappeared; first Arab nationalism and then Islamic fundamentalism manifested themselves; the West became heavily dependent on the Persian Gulf countries for its energy; the oil-rich Muslim countries became money-rich and, when they wished to, weapons-rich. Several wars occurred between Arabs and Israel (created by the West). France fought a bloody and ruthless war in Algeria for most of the 1950s; British and French forces invaded Egypt in 1956; American forces went into Lebanon in 1958; subsequently American forces returned to Lebanon, attacked Libya, and engaged in various military encounters with Iran; Arab and Islamic terrorists, supported by at least three Middle Eastern governments, employed the weapon of the weak and bombed Western planes and installations and seized Western hostages. This warfare between Arabs and the West culminated in 1990, when the United States sent a massive army to the Persian Gulf to defend some Arab countries against aggression by another. In its aftermath NATO planning is increasingly directed to potential threats and instability along its "southern tier."

This centuries-old military interaction between the West and Islam is unlikely to decline. It could become more virulent. The Gulf War left some Arabs feeling proud that Saddam Hussein had attacked Israel and stood up to the West. It also left many feeling humiliated and resentful of the West's military presence in the Persian Gulf, the West's overwhelming military dominance, and their apparent inability to shape their own destiny. Many Arab countries, in addition to the oil exporters, are reaching levels of economic and social development where autocratic forms of government become inappropriate and efforts to introduce democracy become stronger. Some openings in Arab political systems have already occurred. The principal beneficiaries of these openings have been Islamist movements. In the Arab world, in short, Western democracy strengthens anti-Western political forces. This may be a passing phenomenon, but it surely complicated relations between Islamic countries and the West. . . .

On both sides the interaction between Islam and the West is seen as a clash of civilizations. The West's "next confrontation," observes M. J. Akbar, an Indian Muslim author, "is definitely going to come from the Muslim world. It is in the sweep of the Islamic nations from the Maghreb to Pakistan that the struggle for a new world order will begin.". . .

Historically, the other great antagonistic interaction of Arab Islamic civilization has been with the pagan, animist, and now increasingly Christian black peoples to the south. In the past, this antagonism was epitomized in the image of Arab slave dealers and black slaves. It has been reflected in the ongoing civil war in the Sudan between Arabs and blacks, the fighting in Chad between Libyan-supported insurgents and the government, the tensions between Orthodox Christians and Muslims in the Horn of Africa, and the political conflicts, recurring riots, and communal violence between Muslims and Christians in Nigeria. The modernization of Africa and the spread of Christianity are likely to enhance the probability of violence along this fault line. Symptomatic of the intensification of this conflict was Pope John Paul II's speech in Khartoum in February 1993 attacking the actions of the Sudan's Islamist government against the Christian minority there.

On the northern border of Islam, conflict has increasingly erupted between Orthodox and Muslim peoples, including the carnage of Bosnia and Sarajevo, the simmering violence between Serb and Albanian, the tenuous relations between Bulgarians and their Turkish minority, the violence between Ossetians and Ingush, the unremitting slaughter of each other by Armenians and Azeris, the tense relations between Russians and Muslims in Central Asia, and the deployment of Russian troops to protect Russian interests in the Caucasus and Central Asia. Religion reinforces the revival of ethnic identities and restimulates Russian fears about the security of their southern borders. . . .

The conflict of civilizations is deeply rooted elsewhere in Asia. The historic clash between Muslim and Hindu in the subcontinent manifests itself now not only in the rivalry between Pakistan and India but also in intensifying religious strife within India between increasingly militant Hindu groups and India's substantial Muslim minority. The destruction of the Ayodhya mosque in December 1992 brought to the fore the issue of whether India will remain a secular democratic state or become a Hindu one. In East Asia, China has outstanding territorial disputes with most of its neighbors. It has pursued a ruthless policy toward the Buddhist people of Tibet, and it is pursuing an increasingly ruthless policy toward its Turkic-Muslim minority. With the Cold War over, the underlying differences between China and the United States have reasserted themselves in areas such as human rights, trade, and weapons proliferation. These differences are unlikely to moderate. . . .

The same phrase has been applied to the increasingly difficult relations between Japan and the United States. Here cultural difference exacerbates economic conflict. People on each side allege racism on the other, but at least on the American side the antipathies are not racial but cultural. The basic values, attitudes, behavioral patterns of the two societies could hardly be more different. The economic issues between the United States and Europe are no less serious than those between the United States and Japan, but they do not have the same political salience and emotional intensity because the differences between American culture and European culture are so much less than those between American civilization and Japanese civilization.

The interactions between civilizations vary greatly in the extent to which they are likely to be characterized by violence. Economic competition clearly predominates between the American and European subcivilizations of the West and between both of them and Japan. On the Eurasian continent, however, the proliferation of ethnic conflict, epitomized at the extreme in "ethnic cleansing," has not been totally random. It has been most frequent and most violent between groups belonging to different civilizations. In Eurasia the great historic fault lines between civilizations are once more aflame. This is particularly true along the boundaries of the crescent-shaped Islamic bloc of nations from the bulge of Africa to central Asia. Violence also occurs between Muslims, on the one hand, and Orthodox Serbs in the Balkans, Jews in Israel, Hindus in India, Buddhists in Burma, and Catholics in the Philippines. Islam has bloody borders.

## CIVILIZATION RALLYING: THE KIN-COUNTRY SYNDROME

Groups or states belonging to one civilization that become involved in war with people from a different civilization naturally try to rally support from other members of their own civilization. As the post–Cold War world evolves, civilization commonality, what H. D. S. Greenway has termed the "kin-country" syndrome, is replacing political ideology and traditional balance of power considerations as the principal basis for cooperation and coalitions. It can be seen gradually emerging in the post–Cold War conflicts in the Persian Gulf, the Caucasus and Bosnia. None of these was a full-scale war between civilizations, but each involved some elements of civilizational rallying, which seemed to become more important as the conflict continued and which may provide a foretaste of the future.

First, in the Gulf War one Arab state invaded another and then fought a coalition of Arab, Western, and other states. While only a few Muslim governments overtly supported Saddam Hussein, many Arab elites privately cheered him on, and he was highly popular among large sections of the Arab publics. Islamic fundamentalist movements universally supported Iraq rather than the Western-backed governments of Kuwait and Saudi Arabia. Forswearing Arab nationalism, Saddam Hussein explicitly invoked an Islamic appeal. He and his supporters attempted to define the war as a war between civilizations. "It is not the world against Iraq," as Safar Al-Hawali, dean of Islamic Studies at the Umm Al-Qura University in Mecca, put it in a widely circulated tape. "It is the West against Islam." Ignoring the rivalry between Iran and Iraq, the chief Iranian religious leader, Ayatollah Ali Khamenei, called for a holy war against the West: "The struggle against American aggression, greed, plans, and policies will be counted as a jihad, and anybody who is killed on that path is a martyr." "This is a war," King Hussein of Jordan argued, "against all Arabs and all Muslims and not against Iraq alone.". . .

Second, the kin-country syndrome also appeared in conflicts in the former Soviet Union. Armenian military successes in 1992 and 1993 stimulated Turkey to become increasingly supportive of its religious, ethnic, and linguistic brethren in Azerbaijan. "We have a Turkish nation feeling the same sentiments as the Azerbaijanis," said one Turkish official in 1992. "We are under pressure. Our newspapers are full of the photos of atrocities and are asking us if we are still serious about pursuing our neutral policy. Maybe we should show Armenia that there's a big Turkey in the region." President Turgut Özal agreed, remarking that Turkey should at least "scare the Armenians a little bit." Turkey, Özal threatened again in 1993, would "show its fangs." Turkish Air Force jets flew reconnaissance flights along the Armenian border; Turkey suspended food shipments and air flights to Armenia; and Turkey and Iran announced they would not accept dismemberment of Azerbaijan. In the last years of its existence, the Soviet government supported Azerbaijan because its government was dominated by former communists. With the end of the Soviet Union, however, political considerations gave way to religious ones. Russian troops fought on the side of the Armenians, and Azerbaijan accused the "Russian government of turning 180 degrees" toward support for Christian Armenia.

Third, with respect to the fighting in the former Yugoslavia, Western publics manifested sympathy and support for the Bosnian Muslims and the horrors they suffered at the hands of the Serbs. Relatively little concern was expressed, however, over Croatian attacks on Muslims and participation in the dismemberment of Bosnia-Herzegovina. In the early stages of the Yugoslav breakup, Germany, in an unusual display of diplomatic initiative and muscle, induced the other 11 members of the European Community to follow its lead in recognizing Slovenia and Croatia. As a result of the pope's determination to provide strong backing to the two Catholic countries, the Vatican extended recognition even before the Community did. The United States followed the European lead. Thus the leading actors in Western civilization rallied behind their coreligionists. Subsequently Croatia was reported to be receiving substantial quantities of arms from Central European and other Western countries. Boris Yeltsin's government, on the other hand, attempted to pursue a middle course that would be sympathetic to the Orthodox Serbs but not alienate Russia from the West. Russian conservative and nationalist groups, however, including many legislators, attacked the government for not being more forthcoming in its support for the Serbs. By early 1993 several hundred Russians apparently were serving with the Serbian forces, and reports circulated of Russian arms being supplied to Serbia.

Islamic governments and groups, on the other hand, castigated the West for not coming to the defense of the Bosnians. Iranian leaders urged Muslims from all countries to provide help to Bosnia; in violation of the U.N. arms embargo, Iran supplied weapons and men for the Bosnians; Iranian-supported Lebanese groups sent guerrillas to train and organize the Bosnian forces. In 1993 up to 4,000 Muslims from over two dozen Islamic countries were reported to be fighting in Bosnia. The governments of Saudi Arabia and other countries felt under increasing pressure from fundamentalist groups in their own societies to provide more vigorous support for the Bosnians. By the end of 1992, Saudi Arabia had reportedly supplied substantial funding for weapons and supplies for the Bosnians, which significantly increased their military capabilities vis-à-vis the Serbs. . . .

Civilization rallying to date has been limited, but it has been growing, and it clearly has the potential to spread much further. As the conflicts in the Persian Gulf, the Caucasus, and Bosnia continued, the positions of nations and the cleavages between them increasingly were along civilizational lines. Populist politicians, religious leaders, and the media have found it a potent means of arousing mass support and of pressuring hesitant governments. In the coming years, the local conflicts most likely to escalate into major wars will be those, as in Bosnia and the Caucasus, along the fault lines between civilizations. The next world war, if there is one, will be a war between civilizations.

## THE WEST VERSUS THE REST

The West is now at an extraordinary peak of power in relation to other civilizations. Its superpower opponent has disappeared from the map. Military conflict among Western states is unthinkable, and Western military power is unrivaled. Apart from Japan, the West faces no economic challenge. It dominates international political and security institutions and with Japan international economic institutions. Global political and security issues are effectively settled by a directorate of the United States, Britain, and France, world economic issues by a directorate of the United States, Germany, and Japan, all of which maintain extraordinarily close relations with each other to the exclusion of lesser and largely non-Western countries. Decisions made at the U.N. Security Council or in the International Monetary Fund that reflect the interests of the West are presented to the world as reflecting the desires of the world community. The very phrase "the world community" has become the euphemistic collective noun (replacing "the Free World") to give global legitimacy to actions reflecting the interests of the United States and other western powers. Through the IMF and other international economic institutions, the West promotes its economic interests and imposes on other nations the economic policies it thinks appropriate. In any poll of non-Western peoples, the IMF undoubtedly would win the support of finance ministers and a few others, but get an overwhelmingly unfavorable rating from just about everyone else, who would agree with Georgy Arbatov's characterization of IMF officials as "neo-Bolsheviks who love expropriating other people's money, imposing undemocratic and alien rules of economic and political conduct and stifling economic freedom."

Western domination of the U.N. Security Council and its decisions, tempered only by occasional abstention by China, produced U.N. legitimation of the West's use of force to drive Iraq out of Kuwait and its elimination of Iraq's sophisticated weapons and capacity to produce such weapons.... The West in effect is using international institutions, military power and economic resources to run the world in ways that will maintain Western predominance, protect Western interests, and promote Western political and economic values.

That at least is the way in which non-Westerners see the new world, and there is a significant element of truth in their view. Differences in power and struggles for military, economic, and institutional power are thus one source of conflict between the West and other civilizations. Differences in culture, that is basic values and beliefs, are a second source of conflict.... Western concepts differ fundamentally from those prevalent in other civilizations. Western ideas of individualism, liberalism, constitutionalism, human rights, equality, liberty, the rule of law, democracy, free markets, the separation of church and state, often have little resonance in Islamic, Confucian, Japanese, Hindu, Buddhist, or Orthodox cultures. Western efforts to propagate such ideas produce instead a reaction against "human rights imperialism" and a reaffirmation of indigenous values, as can be seen in the support for religious fundamentalism by the younger generation in non-Western cultures. The very notion that there could be a "universal civilization" is a Western idea, directly at odds with the particularism of most Asian societies and their emphasis on what distinguishes one people from another.... These differences are most manifest in the efforts of the United States and other Western powers to induce other peoples to adopt Western ideas concerning democracy and human rights. Modern democratic government originated in the West. When it has developed in non-Western societies it has usually been the product of Western colonialism or imposition.

The central axis of world politics in the future is likely to be, in Kishore Mahbubani's phrase, the conflict between "the West and the Rest" and the responses of non-Western civilizations to Western power and values.[1] Those responses generally take one or a combination of three forms. At one extreme, non-Western states can, like Burma and North Korea, attempt to pursue a course of isolation, to insulate their societies from penetration or "corruption" by the West, and, in effect, to opt out of participation in the Western-dominated global community. The costs of this course, however, are high, and few states have pursued it exclusively. A second alternative, the equivalent of "bandwagoning" in international relations theory, is to attempt to join the West and accept its values and institutions. The third alternative is to attempt to "balance" the West by developing economic and military power and cooperating with other non-Western societies against the West, while preserving indigenous values and institutions; in short, to modernize but not to Westernize.

## THE TORN COUNTRIES

In the future, as people differentiate themselves by civilization, countries with large numbers of peoples of different civilizations . . . are candidates for dismemberment. Some other countries have a fair degree of cultural homogeneity but are divided over whether their society belongs to one civilization or another. These are torn countries. Their leaders typically wish to pursue a bandwagoning strategy and to make their countries members of the West, but the history, culture, and traditions of their countries are non-Western. The most obvious and prototypical torn country is Turkey. The late twentieth-century leaders of Turkey have followed in the Attatürk tradition and defined Turkey as a modern, secular, Western nation-state. They allied Turkey with the West in NATO and in the Gulf War; they applied for membership in the European Community. At the same time, however, elements in Turkish society have supported an Islamic revival and have argued that Turkey is basically a Middle Eastern Muslim society. In addition, while the elite of Turkey has defined Turkey as a Western society, the elite of the West refuses to accept Turkey as such. Turkey will not become a member of the European Community, and the real reason, as President Özal said, "is that we are Muslim and they are Christian and they don't say that." Having rejected Mecca, and then being rejected by Brussels, where does Turkey look? Tashkent may be the answer. The end of the Soviet Union gives Turkey the opportunity to become the leader of a revived Turkic civilization involving seven countries from the borders of Greece to those of China. Encouraged by the West, Turkey is making strenuous efforts to carve out this new identity for itself.

During the past decade Mexico has assumed a position somewhat similar to that of Turkey. Just as Turkey abandoned its historic opposition to Europe and attempted to join Europe, Mexico has stopped defining itself by its opposition to the United States and is instead attempting to imitate the United States and to join it in the North American Free Trade Area. Mexican leaders are engaged in the great task of redefining Mexican identity and have introduced fundamental economic reforms that eventually will lead to fundamental political change. In 1991 a top adviser to President Carlos Salinas de Gortari described at length to me all the changes the Salinas government was making. When he finished, I remarked: "That's most impressive. It seems to me that basically you want to change Mexico from a Latin American country into a North American country." He looked at me with surprise and exclaimed: "Exactly! That's precisely what we are trying to do, but of course we could never say so publicly." As his remark indicates, in Mexico as in Turkey, significant elements in society resist the redefinition of their country's identity. In Turkey, European-oriented leaders have to make gestures to Islam (Özal's pilgrimage to Mecca); so also Mexico's North American-oriented leaders have to make gestures to those who hold Mexico to be a Latin American country (Salinas' Ibero-American Guadalajara summit).

Historically Turkey has been the most profoundly torn country. For the United States, Mexico is the most immediate torn country. Globally the most important torn country is Russia. The question of whether Russia is part of the West or the leader of a distinct Slavic-Orthodox civilization has been a recurring one in Russian history. That issue was obscured by the communist victory in Russia, which imported a Western ideology, adapted it to Russian conditions and then challenged the West in the name of that ideology. The dominance of communism shut off the historic debate over Westernization versus Russification. With communism discredited Russians once again face that question. . . .

To redefine its civilization identity, a torn country must meet three requirements. First, its political and economic elite has to be generally supportive of and enthusiastic about this move. Second, its public has to be willing to acquiesce in the redefinition. Third, the dominant groups in the recipient civilization have to be willing to embrace the convert. All three requirements in large part exist with respect to Mexico. The first two in large part exist with respect to Turkey. It is not clear that any of them exist with respect to Russia's joining the West. The conflict between liberal democracy and Marxism-Leninism was between ideologies which, despite their major differences, ostensibly shared ultimate goals of freedom, equality and prosperity. A traditional, authoritarian, nationalist Russia could have quite different goals. A Western democrat could carry on an intellectual debate with a Soviet Marxist. It would be virtually impossible for him to do that with a Russian traditionalist. If, as the Russians stop behaving like Marxists, they reject liberal democracy and begin behaving like Russians but not like Westerners, the relations between Russia and the West could again become distant and conflictual.

## THE CONFUCIAN-ISLAMIC CONNECTION

The obstacles to non-Western countries joining the West vary considerably. They are least for Latin American and East European countries. They are greater for the Orthodox countries of the former Soviet Union. They are still greater for Muslim,

Confucian, Hindu, and Buddhist societies. Japan has established a unique position for itself as an associate member of the West: It is in the West in some respects but clearly not of the West in important dimensions. Those countries that for reasons of culture and power do not wish to, or cannot, join the West compete with the West by developing their own economic, military, and political power. They do this by promoting their internal development and by cooperating with other non-Western countries. The most prominent form of this cooperation is the Confucian-Islamic connection that has emerged to challenge Western interests, values, and power.

Almost without exception, Western countries are reducing their military power. . . . China, North Korea, and several Middle Eastern states, however, are significantly expanding their military capabilities. They are doing this by the import of arms from Western and non-Western sources and by the development of indigenous arms industries. One result is the emergence of what Charles Krauthammer has called "Weapon States," and the Weapon States are not Western states. Another result is the redefinition of arms control, which is a Western concept and a Western goal. During the Cold War the primary purpose of arms control was to establish a stable military balance between the United States and its allies and the Soviet Union and its allies. In the post–Cold War world the primary objective of arms control is to prevent the development by non-Western societies of military capabilities that could threaten Western interests. The West attempts to do this through international agreements, economic pressure, and controls on the transfer of arms and weapons technologies.

The conflict between the West and the Confucian-Islamic states focuses largely, although not exclusively, on nuclear, chemical, and biological weapons, ballistic missiles, and other sophisticated means for delivering them, and the guidance, intelligence, and other electronic capabilities for achieving that goal. The West promotes nonproliferation as a universal norm and nonproliferation treaties and inspections as means of realizing that norm. It also threatens a variety of sanctions against those who promote the spread of sophisticated weapons and proposes some benefits for those who do not. The attention of the West focuses, naturally, on nations that are actually or potentially hostile to the West.

The non-Western nations, on the other hand, assert their right to acquire and to deploy whatever weapons they think necessary for their security. They also have absorbed, to the full, the truth of the response of the Indian defense minister when asked what lesson he learned from the Gulf War: "Don't fight the United States unless you have nuclear weapons." Nuclear weapons, chemical weapons, and missiles are viewed, probably erroneously, as the potential equalizer of superior Western conventional power. China, of course, already has nuclear weapons; Pakistan and India have the capability to deploy them. North Korea, Iran, Iraq, Libya, and Algeria appear to be attempting to acquire them. A top Iranian official has declared that all Muslim states should acquire nuclear weapons, and in 1988 the president of Iran reportedly issued a directive calling for development of "offensive and defensive chemical, biological, and radiological weapons."

Centrally important to the development of counter-West military capabilities is the sustained expansion of China's military power and its means to create military power. Buoyed by spectacular economic development, China is rapidly increasing its military spending and vigorously moving forward with the modernization of its armed forces. It is purchasing weapons from the former Soviet states; it is developing long-range missiles; in 1992 it tested a one-megaton nuclear device. It is developing power-projection capabilities, acquiring aerial refueling technology, and trying to purchase an aircraft carrier. Its military buildup and assertion of sovereignty over the South China Sea are provoking a multilateral regional arms race in East Asia. China is also a major exporter of arms and weapons technology. It has exported materials to Libya and Iraq that could be used to manufacture nuclear weapons and nerve gas. It has helped Algeria build a reactor suitable for nuclear weapons research and production. China has sold to Iran nuclear technology that American officials believe could only be used to create weapons and apparently has shipped components of 300-mile-range missiles to Pakistan. North Korea has had a nuclear weapons program under way for some while and has sold advanced missiles and missile technology to Syria and Iran. The flow of weapons and weapons technology is generally from East Asia to the Middle East. There is, however, some movement in the reverse direction; China has received Stinger missiles from Pakistan.

A Confucian-Islamic military connection has thus come into being, designed to promote acquisition by its members of the weapons and weapons technologies needed to counter the military power of the West. It may or may not last. At present, however, it is, as Dave McCurdy has said, "a renegades' mutual support pact, run by the proliferators and their backers." A new form of arms competition is thus occurring between Islamic-Confucian states and the West. In an old-fashioned arms race, each side developed its own arms to balance or to achieve superiority against the other side. In this new form of arms competition, one side is developing its arms and the other side is attempting not to balance but to limit and prevent that arms buildup while at the same time reducing its own military capabilities.

## IMPLICATIONS FOR THE WEST

This article does not argue that civilization identities will replace all other identities, that nation-states will disappear, that each civilization will become a single coherent political entity, that groups within a civilization will not conflict with and even fight each other. This paper does set forth the hypotheses that differences between civilizations are real and important; civilization-consciousness is increasing; conflict between civilizations will supplant ideological and other forms of conflict as the dominant global form of conflict; international relations, historically a game played out within Western civilization, will increasingly be de-Westernized and become a game in which non-Western civilizations are actors and not simply objects; successful political, security, and economic international institutions are more likely to develop within civilizations than across civilizations; conflicts between groups in different civilizations will be more frequent, more sustained, and more violent than conflicts between groups in the same civilization; violent conflicts between groups in different civilizations are the most likely and most dangerous source of escalation that could lead to global wars; the paramount axis of world politics will be the relations between "the West and the Rest"; the elites in some torn non-Western countries will try to make their countries part of the west, but in most cases face major obstacles to accomplishing this; a central focus of conflict for the immediate future will be between the West and several Islamic-Confucian states.

This is not to advocate the desirability of conflicts between civilizations. It is to set forth descriptive hypotheses as to what the future may be like. If these are plausible hypotheses, however, it is necessary to consider their implications for Western policy. These implications should be divided between short-term advantage and long-term accommodation. In the short term it is clearly in the interest of the West to promote greater cooperation and unity within its own civilization, particularly between its European and North American components; to incorporate into the West societies in Eastern Europe and Latin America whose cultures are close to those of the West; to promote and maintain cooperative relations with Russia and Japan; to prevent escalation of local inter-civilization conflicts into major inter-civilization wars; to limit the expansion of the military strength of Confucian and Islamic states; to moderate the reduction of Western military capabilities and maintain military superiority in East and Southwest Asia; to exploit differences and conflicts among Confucian and Islamic states; to support in other civilizations groups sympathetic to Western values and interests; to strengthen international institutions that reflect and legitimate Western interests and values; and to promote the involvement of non-Western states in those institutions.

In the longer term other measures would be called for. Western civilization is both Western and modern. Non-Western civilizations have attempted to become modern without becoming Western. To date only Japan has fully succeeded in this quest. Non-Western civilizations will continue to attempt to acquire the wealth, technology, skills, machines, and weapons that are part of being modern. They will also attempt to reconcile this modernity with their traditional culture and values. Their economic and military strength relative to the West will increase. Hence the West will increasingly have to accommodate those non-Western modern civilizations whose power approaches that of the West but whose values and interests differ significantly from those of the West. This will require the West to maintain the economic and military power necessary to protect its interests in relation to these civilizations. It will also, however, require the West to develop a more profound understanding of the basic religious and philosophical assumptions underlying other civilizations and the ways in which people in those civilizations see their interests. It will require an effort to identify elements of commonality between Western and other civilizations. For the relevant future, there will be no universal civilization, but instead a world of different civilizations, each of which will have to learn to coexist with the others.

## NOTE

1. Kishore Mahbubani, "The West and the Rest," *The National Interest* (Summer 1992), 3–13.

# Why Do They Hate Us?

## FAREED ZAKARIA

To the question "Why do the terrorists hate us?" Americans could be pardoned for answering, "Why should we care?" . . . Anger will not be enough to get us through what is sure to be a long struggle. For that we will need answers. The ones we have heard so far have been comforting but familiar. We stand for freedom and they hate it. We are rich and they envy us. We are strong and they resent this. All of which is true. But there are billions of poor and weak and oppressed people around the world. They don't turn planes into bombs. They don't blow themselves up to kill thousands of civilians. If envy were the cause of terrorism, Beverly Hills, Fifth Avenue and Mayfair would have become morgues long ago. There is something stronger at work here than deprivation and jealousy. Something that can move men to kill but also to die.

Osama bin Laden has an answer—religion. For him and his followers, this is a holy war between Islam and the Western world. Most Muslims disagree. Every Islamic country in the world has condemned the attacks of September 11. To many, bin Laden belongs to a long line of extremists who have invoked religion to justify mass murder and spur men to suicide. The words "thug," "zealot," and "assassin" all come from ancient terror cults—Hindu, Jewish, and Muslim, respectively—that believed they were doing the work of God. The terrorist's mind is its own place, and like Milton's Satan, can make a hell of heaven, a heaven of hell. Whether it is the Unabomber, Aum Shinrikyo or Baruch Goldstein (who killed scores of unarmed Muslims in Hebron), terrorists are almost always misfits who place their own twisted morality above mankind's.

## ADMIRATION FOR BIN LADEN

But bin Laden and his followers are not an isolated cult like Aum Shinrikyo or the Branch Davidians or demented loners like Timothy McVeigh and the Unabomber. They come out of a culture that reinforces their hostility, distrust, and hatred of the West—and of America in particular. This culture does not condone terrorism but fuels the fanaticism that is at its heart. To say that al Qaeda is a fringe group may be reassuring, but it is false. Read the Arab press in the aftermath of the attacks and you will detect a not-so-hidden admiration for bin Laden. Or consider this from the

Pakistani newspaper *The Nation*: "September 11 was not mindless terrorism for terrorism's sake. It was reaction and revenge, even retribution.". . . The problem is not that Osama bin Laden believes that this is a religious war against America. It's that millions of people across the Islamic world seem to agree.

This awkward reality has led some in the West to dust off old essays and older prejudices predicting a "clash of civilizations" between the West and Islam. The historian Paul Johnson has argued that Islam is intrinsically an intolerant and violent religion. Other scholars have disagreed, pointing out that Islam condemns the slaughter of innocents and prohibits suicide. Nothing will be solved by searching for "true Islam" or quoting the Quran. The Quran is a vast, vague book, filled with poetry and contradictions (much like the Bible). You can find in it condemnations of war and incitements to struggle, beautiful expressions of tolerance and stern strictures against unbelievers. Quotations from it usually tell us more about the person who selected the passages than about Islam. Every religion is compatible with the best and the worst of humankind. Through its long history, Christianity has supported inquisitions and anti-Semitism, but also human rights and social welfare.

Searching the history books is also of limited value. From the Crusades of the 11th century to the Turkish expansion of the 15th century to the colonial era in the early 20th century, Islam and the West have often battled militarily. This tension has existed for hundreds of years, during which there have been many periods of peace and even harmony. Until the 1950s, for example, Jews and Christians lived peaceably under Muslim rule. In fact, Bernard Lewis, the preeminent historian of Islam, has argued that for much of history religious minorities did better under Muslim rulers than they did under Christian ones. All that has changed in the past few decades. So surely the relevant question we must ask is, Why are we in a particularly difficult phase right now? What has gone wrong in the world of Islam that explains not the conquest of Constantinople in 1453 or the siege of Vienna of 1683 but September 11, 2001?

Let us first peer inside that vast Islamic world. Many of the largest Muslim countries in the world show little of this anti-American rage. The biggest, Indonesia, had, until the recent Asian economic crisis, been diligently following Washington's advice on economics, with impressive results. The second and third most populous Muslim countries, Pakistan and Bangladesh, have mixed Islam and modernity with some success. While both countries are impoverished, both have voted a woman into power as prime minister, before most Western countries have done so. Next is Turkey, the sixth largest Muslim country in the world, a flawed but functioning secular democracy and a close ally of the West (being a member of NATO).

Only when you get to the Middle East do you see in lurid colors all the dysfunctions that people conjure up when they think of Islam today. In Iran, Egypt, Syria, Iraq, Jordan, the occupied territories and the Persian Gulf, the resurgence of Islamic fundamentalism is virulent, and a raw anti-Americanism seems to be everywhere. This is the land of suicide bombers, flag-burners and fiery mullahs. . . .

But even the Arab rage at America is relatively recent. In the 1950s and 1960s it seemed unimaginable that the United States and the Arab world would end up locked in a cultural clash. Egypt's most powerful journalist, Mohamed Heikal, described the mood at the time: "The whole picture of the United States . . . was a glamorous one. Britain and France were fading, hated empires. The Soviet Union was 5,000 miles away and the ideology of communism was anathema to the Muslim religion. But America had emerged from World War II richer, more powerful and more appealing than ever." I first traveled to the Middle East in the early 1970s, and even then the image of America was of a glistening, approachable modernity: fast cars, Hilton hotels and Coca-Cola. Something happened in these lands. To understand the roots of anti-American rage in the Middle East, we need to plumb not the past 300 years of history but the past 30.

## CHAPTER 1: THE RULERS

It is difficult to conjure up the excitement in the Arab world in the late 1950s as Gamal Abdel Nasser consolidated power in Egypt. For decades Arabs had been ruled by colonial governors and decadent kings. Now they were achieving their dreams of independence, and Nasser was their new savior, a modern man for the postwar era. He was born under British rule, in Alexandria, a cosmopolitan city that was more Mediterranean than Arab. His formative years were spent in the Army, the most Westernized segment of the society. With his tailored suits and fashionable dark glasses, he cut an energetic figure on the world stage. "The Lion of Egypt," he spoke for all the Arab world.

Nasser believed that Arab politics needed to be fired by modern ideas like self-determination, socialism and Arab unity. And before oil money turned the Gulf states into golden geese, Egypt was the undisputed leader of the Middle East. So Nasser's vision became the region's. Every regime, from the Baathists in Syria and Iraq to the conservative monarchies of the Gulf, spoke in similar terms and tones. It wasn't that they were just aping Nasser. The Middle East desperately wanted to become modern. It failed. For all their energy these regimes chose bad ideas and implemented them in worse ways. Socialism produced bureaucracy and stagnation. Rather than adjusting to the failures of central planning, the economies never really moved on. The republics calcified into dictatorships. Third World "nonalignment" became pro-Soviet propaganda. Arab unity cracked and crumbled as countries discovered their own national interests and opportunities. Worst of all, Israel humiliated the Arabs in the wars of 1967 and 1973. When Saddam Hussein invaded Kuwait in 1990, he destroyed the last remnants of the Arab idea.

### Egypt's Quiet Nightmare

Look at Egypt today. The promise of Nasserism has turned into a quiet nightmare. The government is efficient in only one area: squashing dissent and strangling civil society. In the past 30 years Egypt's economy has sputtered along while its population has doubled. Unemployment is at 25 percent, and 90 percent of those searching for jobs hold college diplomas. Once the heart of Arab intellectual life, the country produces just 375 books every year (compared with Israel's 4,000). For all the angry protests to foreigners, Egyptians know all this.

Shockingly, Egypt has fared better than its Arab neighbors. Syria has become one of the world's most oppressive police states, a country where 25,000 people can be rounded up and killed by the regime with no consequences. (This in a land whose capital, Damascus, is the oldest continuously inhabited city in the world.) . . . In an almost unthinkable reversal of a global pattern, almost every Arab country today is less free than it was 30 years ago. There are few countries in the world of which one can say that. . . .

## Wealth's Negative Effects

The money that the gulf sheiks have frittered away is on a scale that is almost impossible to believe. Just one example: a favored prince of Saudi Arabia, at the age of 25, built a palace in Riyadh for $300 million and, as an additional bounty, was given a $1 billion commission on the kingdom's telephone contract with AT&T. Far from producing political progress, wealth has actually had some negative effects. It has enriched and empowered the gulf governments so that, like their Arab brethren, they, too, have become more repressive over time. The Bedouin societies they once ruled have become gilded cages, filled with frustrated, bitter and discontented young men—some of whom now live in Afghanistan and work with Osama bin Laden. (Bin Laden and some of his aides come from privileged backgrounds in Saudi Arabia.)

By the late 1980s, while the rest of the world was watching old regimes from Moscow to Prague to Seoul to Johannesburg crack, the Arabs were stuck with their aging dictators and corrupt kings. Regimes that might have seemed promising in the 1960s were now exposed as tired, corrupt kleptocracies, deeply unpopular and thoroughly illegitimate. One has to add that many of them are close American allies.

## CHAPTER II: FAILED IDEAS

How does a region that once yearned for modernity reject it so dramatically?

About a decade ago, in a casual conversation with an elderly Arab intellectual, I expressed my frustration that governments in the Middle East had been unable to liberalize their economies and societies in the way that the East Asians had done. "Look at Singapore, Hong Kong and Seoul," I said, pointing to their extraordinary economic achievements.

The man, a gentle, charming scholar, straightened up and replied sharply, "Look at them. They have simply aped the West. Their cities are cheap copies of Houston and Dallas. That may be all right for fishing villages. But we are heirs to one of the great civilizations of the world. We cannot become slums of the West."

This disillusionment with the West is at the heart of the Arab problem. It makes economic advance impossible and political progress fraught with difficulty. Modernization is now taken to mean, inevitably, uncontrollably, Westernization and, even worse, Americanization. This fear has paralyzed Arab civilization. In some ways the Arab world seems less ready to confront the age of globalization than even Africa, despite the devastation that continent has suffered from AIDS and economic and political dysfunction. At least the Africans want to adapt to the new global economy. The Arab world has not yet taken that first step.

## Past or Future?

The question is how a region that once yearned for modernity could reject it so dramatically. In the Middle Ages the Arabs studied Aristotle (when he was long forgotten in the West) and invented algebra. In the 19th century, when the West set ashore in Arab lands, in the form of Napoleon's conquest of Egypt, the locals were fascinated by this powerful civilization. In fact, as the historian Albert Hourani has documented, the 19th century saw European-inspired liberal political and social thought flourish in the Middle East.

The colonial era of the late 19th and early 20th centuries raised hopes of British friendship that were to be disappointed, but still Arab elites remained fascinated with the West. Future kings and generals attended Victoria College in Alexandria, learning the speech and manners of British gentlemen. Many then went on to Oxford, Cambridge and Sandhurst—a tradition that is still maintained by Jordan's royal family, though now they go to Hotchkiss or Lawrenceville. After World War I, a new liberal age flickered briefly in the Arab world, as ideas about opening up politics and society gained currency in places like Egypt, Lebanon, Iraq and Syria. But since they were part of a world of kings and aristocrats, these ideas died with those old regimes. The new ones, however, turned out to be just as Western.

Nasser thought his ideas for Egypt and the Arab world were modern. They were also Western. His "national charter" of 1962 reads as if it were written by left-wing intellectuals in Paris or London. (Like many Third World leaders of the time, Nasser was a devoted reader of France's *Le Monde* and Britain's *New Statesman*.) Even his most passionately held project, Pan-Arabism, was European. It was a version of the nationalism that had united Italy and Germany in the 1870s—that those who spoke one language should be one nation.

## One Failure After Another

America thinks of modernity as all good—and it has been almost all good for America. But for the Arab world, modernity has been one failure after another. Each path followed—socialism, secularism, nationalism—has turned into a dead end. While other countries adjusted to their failures, Arab regimes got stuck in their ways. And those that reformed economically could not bring themselves to ease up politically. The Shah of Iran, the Middle Eastern ruler who tried to move his country into the modern era fastest, reaped the most violent reaction in the Iranian revolution of 1979. But even the shah's modernization—compared, for example, with the East Asian approach of hard work, investment and thrift—was an attempt to buy modernization with oil wealth.

It turns out that modernization takes more than strongmen and oil money. Importing foreign stuff—Cadillacs, Gulfstreams and McDonald's—is easy. Importing the inner stuffings of modern society—a free market, political parties, accountability and the rule of law—is difficult and dangerous. The Gulf states, for example, have gotten modernization lite, with the goods and even the workers imported from abroad. Nothing was homegrown; nothing is even now. As for politics, the Gulf governments offered their people a bargain: we will bribe you with wealth, but in return let us stay in power. It was the inverse slogan of the American revolution—no taxation, but no representation either.

The new age of globalization has hit the Arab world in a very strange way. Its societies are open enough to be disrupted by modernity, but not so open that they can ride the wave. They see the television shows, the fast foods and the fizzy drinks. But they don't see genuine liberalization in the society, with increased opportunities and greater openness. Globalization in the Arab world is the critic's caricature of globalization—a slew of Western products and billboards with little else. For some in their societies it means more things to buy. For the regimes it is an unsettling, dangerous phenomenon. As a result, the people they rule can look at globalization but for the most part not touch it. . . .

## CHAPTER III: ENTER RELIGION

### The Origins of "Islamic Fundamentalism"

Nasser was a reasonably devout Muslim, but he had no interest in mixing religion with politics. It struck him as moving backward. This became apparent to the small Islamic parties that supported Nasser's rise to power. The most important one, the Muslim Brotherhood, began opposing him vigorously, often violently. Nasser cracked down on it in 1954, imprisoning more than a thousand of its leaders and executing six. One of those jailed, Sayyid Qutub, a frail man with a fiery pen, wrote a book in prison called "Signposts on the Road," which in some ways marks the beginnings of modern political Islam or what is often called "Islamic fundamentalism."

In his book, Qutub condemned Nasser as an impious Muslim and his regime as un-Islamic. Indeed, he went on, almost every modern Arab regime was similarly flawed. Qutub envisioned a better, more virtuous polity that was based on strict Islamic principles, a core goal of orthodox Muslims since the 1880s. As the regimes of the Middle East grew more distant and oppressive and hollow in the decades following Nasser, fundamentalism's appeal grew. It flourished because the Muslim Brotherhood and organizations like it at least tried to give people a sense of meaning and purpose in a changing world, something no leader in the Middle East tried to do.

In his seminal work, "The Arab Predicament," Fouad Ajami explains, "The fundamentalist call has resonance because it invited men to participate . . . [in] contrast to a political culture that reduces citizens to spectators and asks them to leave things to their rulers. At a time when the future is uncertain, it connects them to a tradition that reduces bewilderment." Fundamentalism gave Arabs who were dissatisfied with their lot a powerful language of opposition.

### Few Pathways for Dissent

On that score, Islam had little competition. The Arab world is a political desert with no real political parties, no free press, few path-ways for dissent. As a result, the mosque turned into the place to discuss politics. And fundamentalist organizations have done more than talk. From the Muslim Brotherhood to Hamas to Hizbullah, they actively provide social services, medical assistance, counseling and temporary housing. For those who treasure civil society, it is disturbing to see that in the Middle East these illiberal groups *are* civil society. . . .

Islamic fundamentalism got a tremendous boost in 1979 when Ayatollah Ruhollah Khomeini toppled the Shah of Iran. The Iranian revolution demonstrated that a powerful ruler could be taken on by groups within society. It also revealed how in a broken society even seemingly benign forces of progress—education and technology—can add to the turmoil. Until the 1970s most Muslims in the Middle East were illiterate and lived in villages and towns. They practiced a kind of street-Islam that had adapted itself to the local culture. Pluralistic and tolerant, these people often worshiped saints, went to shrines, sang religious hymns and cherished religious art, all technically disallowed in Islam. (This was particularly true in Iran.) By the 1970s, however, people had begun moving out of the villages and their religious experience was not rooted in a specific place. At the same time they were learning to read and they discovered that a new Islam was being preached by the fundamentalists, an abstract faith not rooted in historical experience but literal, puritanical and by the book. It was Islam of the High Church as opposed to Islam of the village fair.

## Against "Westoxification"

In Iran, Ayatollah Khomeini used a powerful technology—the audiocassette. His sermons were distributed throughout the country and became the vehicle of opposition to the shah's repressive regime. But Khomeini was not alone in using the language of Islam as a political tool. Intellectuals, disillusioned by the half-baked or overrapid modernization that was throwing their world into turmoil, were writing books against "Westoxification" and calling the modern Iranian man—half Western, half Eastern—rootless. Fashionable intellectuals, often writing from the comfort of London or Paris, would critique American secularism and consumerism and endorse an Islamic alternative. As theories like these spread across the Arab world, they appealed not to the poorest of the poor, for whom Westernization was magical (it meant food and medicine). They appealed to the half-educated hordes entering the cities of the Middle East or seeking education and jobs in the West.

The fact that Islam is a highly egalitarian religion for the most part has also proved an empowering call for people who felt powerless. At the same time it means that no Muslim really has the authority to question whether someone who claims to be a proper Muslim is one. The fundamentalists, from Sayyid Qutub on, have jumped into that void. They ask whether people are "good Muslims." It is a question that has terrified the Muslim world. And here we come to the failure not simply of governments but intellectual and social elites. Moderate Muslims are loath to criticize or debunk the fanaticism of the fundamentalists. Like the moderates in Northern Ireland, they are scared of what would happen to them if they speak their mind.

The biggest Devil's bargain has been made by the moderate monarchies of the Persian Gulf, particularly Saudi Arabia. The Saudi regime has played a dangerous game. It deflects attention from its shoddy record at home by funding religious schools (*madrasas*) and centers that spread a rigid, puritanical brand of Islam—

Wahhabism. In the past 30 years Saudi-funded schools have churned out tens of thousands of half-educated, fanatical Muslims who view the modern world and non-Muslims with great suspicion. America in this world view is almost always evil.

## Allied with Fundamentalism

This exported fundamentalism has in turn infected not just other Arab societies but countries outside the Arab world, like Pakistan. During the 11-year reign of Gen. Zia ul-Haq, the dictator decided that as he squashed political dissent he needed allies. He found them in the fundamentalists. With the aid of Saudi financiers and functionaries, he set up scores of *madrasas* throughout the country. They bought him temporary legitimacy but have eroded the social fabric of Pakistan.

If there is one great cause of the rise of Islamic fundamentalism, it is the total failure of political institutions in the Arab world. Muslim elites have averted their eyes from this reality. Conferences at Islamic centers would still rather discuss "Islam and the Environment" than examine the dysfunctions of the current regimes. But as the moderate majority looks the other way, Islam is being taken over by a small poisonous element, people who advocate cruel attitudes toward women, education, the economy and modern life in general. I have seen this happen in India, where I grew up. The rich, colorful, pluralistic and easygoing Islam of my youth has turned into a dour, puritanical faith, policed by petty theocrats and religious commissars. The next section deals with what the United States can do to help the Islamic world. But if Muslims do not take it upon themselves to stop their religion from falling prey to medievalists, nothing any outsider can do will save them.

## CHAPTER IV: WHAT TO DO

America's greatest sins toward the Arab world are sins of omission. If almost any Arab were to have read this essay so far, he would have objected vigorously by now. "It is all very well to talk about the failures of the Arab world," he would say, "but what about the failures of the West? You speak of long-term decline, but our problems are with specific, cruel American policies." For most Arabs, relations with the United States have been filled with disappointment.

While the Arab world has long felt betrayed by Europe's colonial powers, its disillusionment with America begins most importantly with the creation of Israel in 1948. As the Arabs see it, at a time when colonies were winning independence from the West, here was a state largely composed of foreign people being imposed on a region with Western backing. The anger deepened in the wake of America's support for Israel during the wars of 1967 and 1973, and ever since in its relations with the Palestinians. The daily exposure to Israel's iron-fisted rule over the occupied territories has turned this into the great cause of the Arab—and indeed the broader Islamic—world. Elsewhere, they look at American policy in the region as cynically geared to America's oil interests, supporting thugs and tyrants without any hesitation. . . .

There is substance to some of these charges, and certainly from the point of view of an Arab, American actions are never going to seem entirely fair. Like any country,

America has its interests. In my view, America's greatest sins toward the Arab world are sins of omission. We have neglected to press any regime there to open up its society. This neglect turned deadly in the case of Afghanistan. Walking away from that fractured country after 1989 resulted in the rise of bin Laden and the Taliban. This is not the gravest error a great power can make, but it is a common American one. . . . America has not been venal in the Arab world. But it has been careless.

## Explaining Arab Rage

Yet carelessness is not enough to explain Arab rage. After all, if concern for the Palestinians is at the heart of the problem, why have their Arab brethren done nothing for them? (They cannot resettle in any Arab nation but Jordan, and the aid they receive from the Gulf states is minuscule.) Israel treats its one million Arabs as second-class citizens, a disgrace on its democracy. And yet the tragedy of the Arab world is that Israel accords them more political rights and dignities than most Arab nations give to their own people. Why is the focus of Arab anger on Israel and not those regimes?

The disproportionate feelings of grievance directed at America have to be placed in the overall context of the sense of humiliation, decline, and despair that sweeps the Arab world. After all, the Chinese vigorously disagree with most of America's foreign policy and have fought wars with U.S. proxies. African states feel the same sense of disappointment and unfairness. But they do not work it into a rage against America. Arabs, however, feel that they are under siege from the modern world and that the United States symbolizes this world. Thus every action America takes gets magnified a thousandfold. And even when we do not act, the rumors of our gigantic powers and nefarious deeds still spread. Most Americans would not believe how common the rumor is throughout the Arab world that either the CIA or Israel's Mossad blew up the World Trade Center to justify attacks on Arabs and Muslims. This is the culture from which the suicide bombers have come.

America must now devise a strategy to deal with this form of religious terrorism. As is now widely understood, this will be a long war, with many fronts and battles small and large. Our strategy must be divided along three lines: military, political, and cultural. On the military front—by which I mean war, covert operations and other forms of coercion—the goal is simple: the total destruction of al Qaeda. Even if we never understand all the causes of apocalyptic terror, we must do battle against it. Every person who plans and helps in a terrorist operation must understand that he will be tracked and punished. Their operations will be disrupted, their finances drained, their hideouts destroyed. There will be associated costs to pursuing such a strategy, but they will all fade if we succeed. Nothing else matters on the military front.

## The New New World Order

The political strategy is more complex and more ambitious. At the broadest level, we now have a chance to reorder the international system around this pressing new danger. . . .

We can define a strategy for the post–Cold War era that addresses America's principal national-security need and yet is sustained by a broad international consensus. To do this we will have to give up some Cold War reflexes, such as an allergy to multilateralism, and stop insisting that China is about to rival us militarily or that Russia is likely to re-emerge as a new military threat. (For 10 years now, our defense forces have been aligned for everything but the real danger we face. This will inevitably change.)

The purpose of an international coalition is practical and strategic. Given the nature of this war, we will need the constant cooperation of other governments—to make arrests, shut down safe houses, close bank accounts and share intelligence. Alliance politics has become a matter of high national security. But there is a broader imperative. The United States dominates the world in a way that inevitably arouses envy or anger or opposition. That comes with the power, but we still need to get things done. If we can mask our power in—sorry, work with—institutions like the United Nations Security Council, U.S. might will be easier for much of the world to bear. Bush's father understood this, which is why he ensured that the United Nations sanctioned the Gulf War. The point here is to succeed, and international legitimacy can help us do that.

Now we get to Israel. It is obviously one of the central and most charged problems in the region. But it is a problem to which we cannot offer the Arab world support for its solution—the extinction of the state. We cannot in any way weaken our commitment to the existence and health of Israel. . . .

. . . On Israel we should make a clear distinction between its right to exist and its occupation of the West Bank and Gaza. On the first we should be as unyielding as ever; on the second we should continue trying to construct a final deal along the lines that Bill Clinton and Ehud Barak outlined. I suggest that we do this less because it will lower the temperature in the Arab world—who knows if it will?—than because it's the right thing to do. Israel cannot remain a democracy and continue to occupy and militarily rule three million people against their wishes. It's bad for Israel, bad for the Palestinians and bad for the United States.

But policy changes, large or small, are not at the heart of the struggle we face. The third, vital component to this battle is a cultural strategy. The United States must help Islam enter the modern world. It sounds like an impossible challenge, and it certainly is not one we would have chosen. But America—indeed the whole world—faces a dire security threat that will not be resolved unless we can stop the political, economic and cultural collapse that lies at the roots of Arab rage. During the Cold War the West employed myriad ideological strategies to discredit the appeal of communism, make democracy seem attractive, and promote open societies. We will have to do something on that scale to win this cultural struggle.

## Fresh Thinking in the Arab World

First, we have to help moderate Arab states, but on the condition that they embrace moderation. For too long regimes like Saudi Arabia's have engaged in a deadly dance with religious extremism. Even Egypt, which has always denounced fundamentalism, allows its controlled media to rant crazily about America and Israel. (That way they don't rant about the dictatorship they live under.) But more broadly, we must persuade Arab moderates to make the case to their people that Islam is compatible with modern society, that it does allow women to work, that it encourages education and that it has welcomed people of other faiths and creeds. . . . We can fund moderate Muslim groups and scholars and broadcast fresh thinking across the Arab world, all aimed at breaking the power of the fundamentalists. . . .

We have to press the nations of the Arab world—and others, like Pakistan, where the virus of fundamentalism has spread—to reform, open up and gain legitimacy. We need to do business with these regimes; yet, just as we did with South Korea and Taiwan during the Cold War, we can ally with these dictatorships and still push them toward reform. For those who argue that we should not engage in nation-building, I would say foreign policy is not theology. I have myself been skeptical of nation-building in places where our interests were unclear and it seemed unlikely that we would stay the course. In this case, stable political development is the key to reducing our single greatest security threat. We have no option but to get back into the nation-building business.

It sounds like a daunting challenge, but there are many good signs. . . . Al Qaeda is not more powerful than the combined force of many determined governments. . . . Islamic fundamentalism still does not speak to the majority of the Muslim people. In Pakistan, fundamentalist parties have yet to get more than 10 percent of the vote. In Iran, having experienced the brutal puritanism of the mullahs, people are yearning for normalcy. In Egypt, for all the repression, the fundamentalists are a potent force but so far not dominant. If the West can help Islam enter modernity in dignity and peace, it will have done more than achieved security. It will have changed the world.

# THE USES OF, AND REACTIONS TO, AMERICAN POWER

## Explaining the Bush Doctrine

### ROBERT JERVIS

The invasion of Iraq, although important in itself, is even more noteworthy as a manifestation of the Bush Doctrine. In a sharp break from the president's pre-September 11 views that saw American leadership, and especially its use of force, restricted to defending narrow and traditional vital interests, he has enunciated a far-reaching program that calls for something very much like an empire.

The Doctrine has four elements: a strong belief in the importance of a state's domestic regime in determining its foreign policy and the related judgment that this is a time of great opportunity to transform international politics, the perception of great threats that can be defeated only by new and vigorous policies (most notably preventive war), a willingness to act unilaterally when necessary, and as both a cause and a summary of these beliefs, an overriding sense that peace and stability requires the United States to assert its primacy in world politics. It is of course possible that I am exaggerating and that what we are seeing is mostly an elaborate rationale for the overthrow of Saddam Hussein that will have little relevance beyond that. I think the Doctrine is real, however. It is quite articulate and American policy since the end of the war has been consistent with it.

## DEMOCRACY AND LIBERALISM

This is not to say that the Doctrine is entirely consistent, and one component may not fit well with the rest despite receiving pride of place in the "The

Robert Jervis, "Understanding the Bush Doctrine." Reprinted by permission from *Political Science Quarterly*, 118 (Fall 2003): 365–388.

National Security Strategy of the U.S.," which starts thusly: "The great struggles of the twentieth century between liberty and totalitarianism ended with a decisive victory for the forces of freedom—and a single sustainable model for national success: freedom, democracy, and free enterprise." The spread of these values opens the path to "make the world not just safer but better," a "path [that] is not America's alone. It is open to all."[1] This taps deep American beliefs and traditions enunciated by Woodrow Wilson and echoed by Bill Clinton, and is linked to the belief, common among powerful states, that its values are universal and their spread will benefit the entire world. Just as Wilson sought to "teach [the countries of Latin America] to elect good men," so Bush will bring free markets and free elections to countries without them. This agenda horrifies Realists (and perhaps realists).[2] Some mid-level officials think this is window dressing; by contrast, John Gaddis sees it as the heart of the doctrine,[3] a view that is endorsed by other officials.

The administration's argument is that strong measures to spread democracy are needed and will be efficacious. Indeed, liberating Iraq will not only produce democracy there, but will encourage it in the rest of the Middle East. There is no incompatibility between Islam or any other culture and democracy; the example of political pluralism in one country will be emulated. The implicit belief is that democracy can take hold when the artificial obstacles to it are removed. Far from being the product of unusually propitious circumstances, a free and pluralist system is the natural order that will prevail unless something special intervenes. Furthermore, more democracies will mean greater stability, peaceful relations with neighbors, and less terrorism, comforting claims that evidence indicates is questionable at best.[4] Would a democratic Iraq be stable? Would an Iraq that reflected the will of its people recognize Israel or renounce all claims to Kuwait? Would a democratic Palestinian state be more willing to live at peace with Israel than an authoritarian one, especially if it did not gain all of the territory lost in 1967? Previous experience also calls into question the links between democracy and free markets, each of which can readily undermine the other. But such doubts do not cloud official pronouncements or even the off-the-record comments of top officials. The United States now appears to have a faith-based foreign policy.

This (or any other) administration may not act on it. No American government has been willing to sacrifice stability and support of U.S. policy to honor democracy in countries like Algeria, Egypt, Saudi Arabia, and Pakistan. But the current view does parallel Ronald Reagan's policy of not accepting a detente with the USSR that was limited to arms control and insisting on a larger agenda that included human rights within the Soviet Union, and thus implicitly called for new domestic regime. The Bush administration is heir to this tradition when it declares that any agreement with North Korea would have to address a range of problems in addition to nuclear weapons, including "the abominable way [the North] treats its people."[5] The argument is that, as in Iraq, regime change is necessary because tyrannical governments will always be prone to disregard agreements and coerce their neighbors just as they mistreat their own citizens. Notwithstanding their being Realists in their views about how states influence one another, Bush and his colleagues are Liberals in their beliefs about the sources of foreign policy.

Consistent with Liberalism, this perspective is highly optimistic in seeing the possibility of progress. A week after September 11, Bush is reported to have told one of his closest advisers: "We have an opportunity to restructure the world toward freedom, and we have to get it right." He expounded this theme in a formal speech marking the 6-month anniversary of the attack: "When the terrorists are disrupted and scattered and discredited, . . . we will see then that the old and serious disputes can be settled within the bounds of reason, and goodwill, and mutual security. I see a peaceful world beyond the war on terror, and with courage and unity, we are building that world together."[6] In February 2002 the president responded to a reporter's question about the predictable French criticism of his policy by saying that "history has given us a unique opportunity to defend freedom. And we're going to seize the moment, and do it."[7] One month later he declared, "We understand history has called us into action, and we are not going to miss that opportunity to make the world more peaceful and more free."[8]

## THREAT AND PREVENTIVE WAR

The second pillar of the Bush doctrine is that we live in a time not only of opportunity, but of great threat, posed primarily by terrorists and rogue states. Optimism and pessimism are linked in the belief that if the U.S. does not make the world better, it will grow more dangerous. As Bush said in his West Point address of June 1, 2002:

> Today our enemies see weapons of mass destruction as weapons of choice. For rogue states these weapons are tools of intimidation and military aggression against their neighbors. These weapons may also allow these states to attempt to blackmail the U.S. and our allies to prevent us from deterring or repelling the aggressive behavior of rogue states. Such states also see these weapons as their best means of overcoming the conventional superiority of the U.S.

These threats cannot be contained by deterrence. Terrorists are fanatics and there is nothing that they value that we can hold at risk; rogues like Iraq are risk-acceptant and accident prone. The heightened sense of vulnerability increases the dissatisfaction with deterrence, but it is noteworthy that this stance taps into the longstanding Republican critique of many American Cold War policies. One wing of the party always sought defense rather than deterrence (or, to be more precise, deterrence by denial instead of deterrence by punishment), and this was reflected in the search for escalation dominance, multiple nuclear options, and defense against ballistic missiles.[9]

Because even defense may not be possible against terrorists or rogues, the United States must be ready to wage preventive wars and to act "against . . . emerging threats before they are fully formed," as Bush puts it.[10] Prevention is not a new element in world politics, although Dale Copeland's important treatment exaggerates its previous centrality.[11] Israel launched a preventive strike against the Iraqi nuclear program in 1981, during the Cold War U.S. officials contemplated attacking the USSR and the PRC before they could develop robust nuclear capabilities,[12] and the Monroe Doctrine and westward expansion in the 19th century stemmed in part from the American desire to prevent any European power from establishing a presence that could menace it.

The United States was a weak country at that time; now the preventive war doctrine is based on strength, and on the associated desire to ensure the maintenance of American dominance. Critics argue that preventive wars are rarely necessary because deterrence can be effective and many threats are exaggerated or can be met with strong but less militarized policies. Libya, for example, once the leading rogue, now seems to be outside of the Axis of Evil. Bismarck called preventive wars "suicide for fear of death," and although the disparity of power between the United States and its adversaries means this is no longer the case, the argument for such wars implies a high degree of confidence that the future will be bleak unless they are undertaken, or at least a belief that this world will be worse than the likely one produced by the war.

This policy then faces three large obstacles. First, by definition, the relevant information is hard to obtain because it involves predictions about threats that reside sometime in the future. Thus while in retrospect it is easy to say that the Western allies should have stopped Hitler long before 1939, at the time it was far from clear that he would turn out to be such a menace. No one who reads Neville Chamberlain's speeches can believe that he was a fool. In some cases, a well-placed spy might be able to provide solid evidence that the other had to be stopped, but in many other cases—perhaps including Nazi Germany—even this would not be sufficient because leaders do not themselves know how they will act in the future. The Bush Doctrine implies that the problem is not so difficult because the state's foreign policy is shaped if not determined by its domestic political system. Thus knowing that North Korea, Iran, and Syria are brutal dictatorships tells us that they will seek to dominate their neighbors, sponsor terrorism, and threaten the United States. But while the generalization that states that oppress their own people will disturb the international system fits many cases, it is far from universal, which means that such short-cuts to the assessment process are fallible. Second and relatedly, even information on capabilities and past behavior may be difficult to come by, as the case of Iraq shows. Saddam's links to terrorists were murky and remain subject to debate, and while much remains unclear, it seems that the United States and Britain not only publicly exaggerated but also privately overestimated the extent of his WMD program.

Third, unless all challengers are deterred by the exercise of the Doctrine in Iraq, preventive war will have to be repeated as other threats reach a similar threshold. Doing so will require sustained domestic if not international support, which is made less likely by the first two complications. The very nature of a preventive war means that the evidence is ambiguous and the supporting arguments are subject to rebuttal. If Britain and France had gone to war with Germany before 1939, large segments of the public would have believed that the war was not necessary. If it had gone badly, the public would have wanted to sue for peace; if it had gone well, public opinion would have questioned its wisdom. While it is too early to say how American opinion will view Saddam's overthrow (and opinion is likely to change over time), a degree of skepticism that will inhibit the repetition of this policy seems probable.

National leaders are aware of these difficulties and generally hesitate to take strong actions in the face of such uncertainty. While one common motive for war has been the belief that the situation will deteriorate unless the state acts strongly now, and indeed this kind of fear drives the security dilemma, leaders usually put off decisions if they can. They know that many potential threats will never eventuate or will be made worse by precipitous military action, and they are predisposed to postpone, to await further developments and information, to kick the can down the road. In rejecting this approach (in Iraq, if not in North Korea), Bush and his colleagues are behaving unusually, although this does not mean they are wrong.

Part of the reason for their stance is the feeling of vulnerability and the consequent belief that the risks and costs of inaction are unacceptably high. Note one of the few lines that brought applause in Bush's Cincinnati speech of October 7, 2002 and that shows the powerful psychological link between September 11 and the drive to depose Saddam: "We will not live in fear." Taken literally, this makes no sense. Unfortunately, fear is often well-founded. What it indicates is an understandable desire for a safer world, despite that fact that the United States did live in fear throughout the Cold War and survived quite well. But if the sentence has little logical meaning, the emotion it embodies is an understandable fear of fear, a drive to gain certainty, an impulse to assert control by acting.

This reading of Bush's statement is consistent with my impression that many people who opposed invading Iraq before September 11, but altered their positions afterwards, had not taken terrorism terribly seriously before 9/11, a category that includes George Bush.[13] Those who had studied the subject were of course surprised by the timing and method of the attacks, but not that they took place, and so changed their beliefs only incrementally. But Bush frequently acknowledges, indeed stresses, that he was shocked by the assault, which greatly increased his feelings of danger and led him to feel that drastically different policies were necessary. As he put it in his Cincinnati speech: "On September 11th, 2001, America felt its vulnerability." It is no accident that this sentence comes between two paragraphs about the need to disarm Iraq. Three months later in response to an accusation that he always wanted to invade Iraq, Bush replied: "prior to September 11, we were discussing smart sanctions. . . . After September 11, the doctrine of containment just doesn't hold any water. . . . My vision shifted dramatically after September 11, because I now realize the stakes, I realize the world has changed."[14] Secretary of Defense Donald Rumsfeld similarly explained that the United States "did not act in Iraq because we had discovered dramatic new evidence of Iraq's pursuit of weapons of mass murder. We acted because we saw the existing evidence in a new light, through the prism of our experience on September 11."[15] The claim that some possibilities are unlikely enough to be put aside lost plausibility in face of the obvious retort: "What could be less likely than terrorists flying airplanes into the World Trade Center and the Pentagon?" During the Cold War, Bernard Brodie expressed his exasperation with wild suggestions about military actions the USSR might undertake: "All sorts of notions and propositions are churned out, and often presented for consideration with the prefatory words: 'It is conceivable that . . .' Such words establish their own truth, for the fact that someone has conceived of whatever proposition follows is enough to establish that it is conceivable. Whether it is worth a second thought, however, is another matter."[16] Worst case analysis is now hard to dismiss.

## UNILATERALISM

The perceived need for preventive wars is linked to the fundamental unilateralism of the Bush Doctrine since it is hard to get a consensus for such strong actions and other states have every reason to let the dominant power carry the full burden. Unilaterialism also has deep roots in the non-northeastern parts of the Republican Party, was well represented in the Reagan Administration, draws on long-standing American political traditions, and was part of Bush's outlook before September 11. Of course, assistance from others was needed in Afghanistan and solicited in Iraq. But these should not be mistaken for joint ventures as the United States did not bend its policy to meet others' preferences. In stressing that the United States is building coalitions in the plural rather than an alliance (the mission determines the coalition, in Rumsfeld's phrase), American leaders have made it clear that they will forego the participation of any particular country rather than compromise.

Even before September 11 Bush displayed little willingness to cater to world public opinion or to heed the cries of outrage from European countries as the United States interpreted its interests, and the interests of the world, in its own way. Thus the Bush administration walked away from the Kyoto Treaty, the International Criminal Court, and the protocol implementing the ban on biological weapons rather than trying to work within these frameworks and modify them. The United States also ignored European criticisms of its Middle Eastern policy. On a smaller scale, it forced out the heads of the Organization for the Prohibition of Chemical Weapons and the Intergovernmental Panel on Climate Change. In response to this kind of behavior, European diplomats can only say: "Big partners should consult with smaller partners."[17] The operative word is "should." When in the wake of the overthrow of Saddam, Chirac declares: "We are no longer in an era where one or two countries control the fate of another country," he describes the world as he would like it to be, not as it is.[18]

The administration has defended each of its actions, but not its general stance. The most principled, persuasive, and perhaps correct defense is built around the difficulty in procuring public goods. As long as leadership is shared, very little will happen because no one actor will be willing to shoulder the costs and the responsibilities. "At this moment in history, if there is a problem, we're expected to deal with it," is how Bush explains it; "We are trying to lead the world," is what one administration official said when the United States blocked language in a UN declaration on child health that might be read as condoning abortion.[19] This is not entirely hypocritical: many of the countries that endorsed the Kyoto protocol had grave reservations but were unwilling to stand up to strongly committed domestic groups.

Indeed, real consultation is likely to produce inaction, as was true in 1993 when Clinton called for "lift and strike" in Yugoslavia (i.e., lifting the arms embargo against Bosnia and striking Serbian forces). But because he believed in sharing power and was unwilling to move on his own, he sent Secretary of State Christopher to ascertain European views. This multilateral and democratic procedure did not work because the Europeans did not want to be put on the spot, and in the face of apparent American indecision they refused to endorse such a strong policy. If the United States had informed the Europeans rather than consulted them, they probably would have complained, but gone along; what critics call unilateralism often is effective leadership. Could Arafat have been moved from his central position if the United States had sought consensus rather than staking out its own position? Bush could also argue that just as Reagan's ignoring the sophisticated European counsels to moderate his rhetoric led to the delegitimation of the Soviet system, so his insistence on confronting tyrants has slowly brought others around to his general perspective, if not to his particular policies.

## AMERICAN HEGEMONY

The final element of the Doctrine, which draws together the others, is the establishment of American hegemony, primacy, or empire. In the Bush Doctrine there are no universal norms or rules governing all states. On the contrary, order can be maintained only if the dominant power behaves quite differently from the others. Thus the administration is not worried that its preventive war doctrine or attacking Iraq without Security Council endorsement will set a precedent for others because the dictates that apply to them do not bind the United States. Similarly, the United States sees no contradiction between expanding the ambit of nuclear weapons to threaten their employment even if others have not used WMD first on the one hand and a vigorous anti-proliferation policy on the other. American security, world stability, and the spread of liberalism require the United States to act in ways others cannot and must not. This is not a double standard, but is what world order requires.

Hegemony is implied when the Bush Nuclear Posture Review talks of dissuading future military competitors. At first glance this seems to refer to Russia and China, but the point applies to the countries of Western Europe as well, either individually or as a unit. This was clear in the draft defense guidance written by Paul Wolfowitz for Dick Cheney at the end of the first Bush administration and also was implied by President Bush when he declared to the graduating cadets at West Point: "America has, and intends to keep, military strengths beyond challenge—thereby making the destabilizing arms races of other eras pointless, and limiting rivalries to trade and other pursuits of peace."[20] This would mean not only sustaining such a high level of military spending that no other country or group of countries would be tempted to challenge it, but also using force on behalf of others so they will not need to develop potent military establishments of their own. In an implicit endorsement of hegemonic stability theory, the driving belief is that the world cannot afford to return to traditional multipolar balance of power politics, which would inevitably turn dangerous and destructive.

## HOW DID WE GET HERE?

Although many observers—myself included—were taken by surprise by this turn in American policy, we probably should not have been. It is consistent with standard patterns of international politics and with much previous American behavior in the Cold War. Until recently, however, it did not seem clear that the United States would in fact behave in a highly unilateral fashion and assert its primacy. The new American stance was precipitated if not caused by the interaction between the terrorist attacks and the election of George Bush, who brought to the office a more unilateral outlook than his predecessors and his domestic opponents. Bush's response to September 11 may parallel his earlier religious conversion and owe something to his religious beliefs, especially in his propensity to see the struggle as one between good and evil. There is reason to believe that just as his coming to Christ gave meaning to his previously aimless and dissolute personal life, so the war on terrorism has become not only the defining characteristic of his foreign policy, but also his sacred mission. An associate of the president reports: "I believe the president was sincere, after 9/11, thinking 'This is what I was put on this earth for.'"[21] We can only speculate on what President Gore would have done. My estimate is that he would have invaded Afghanistan, but not proceeded against Iraq, nor would he have moved away from treaties and other arrangements over a wide range of issues. To some extent, then, the current assertion of strong American hegemony may be an accident.

But it was an accident waiting to happen. To start with, there are structural reasons to have expected a large terrorist attack. Bin Laden had attacked American interests abroad and from early on sought to strike its homeland. His enmity stemmed primarily from the establishment of United States bases in Saudi Arabia, which was a product of America's world-wide responsibilities. (Ironically, the overthrow of Saddam is likely to permit the United States to greatly reduce its presence in Saudi Arabia, although I doubt if bin Laden expected this result to follow from his attack or that he will now be satisfied.) Furthermore, al Qaeda was not the only group targeting the United States; as Richard Betts has argued, terrorism is the obvious weapon of weak actors against the leading state.[22]

Even without terrorism, both internal and structural factors predisposed the United States to assert its dominance. I think the latter are more important, but it is almost a truism of the history of American foreign relations that the United States rarely if ever engages in deeply cooperative ventures with equals.[23] Unlike the European states who were surrounded by peers, once the United States had established its regional dominance, it had great choice about the terms on which it would work with others. Thus when the United States intervened in World War I, it insisted that the coalition be called the "Allied and Associated Powers"—i.e., it was an associate, with freedom of action, not an ally. The structure of the American government, its weak party system, its domestic diversity, and its political traditions, all make sustained cooperation difficult. It would be an exaggeration to say that unilateralism is the American way of foreign policy, but there certainly is a strong pull in this direction.

More importantly, the United States may be acting like a normal state that has gained a position of dominance. There are four facets to this argument. First and most general is the core of the Realist outlook that power is checked most effectively and often only by counter-balancing power. It follows that states that are not subject to external restraints tend to feel few restraints at all. As Edmund Burke put it, in a position endorsed by Hans Morgenthau: "I dread our *own* power and our *own* ambition; I dread our being too much dreaded. It is ridiculous to say that we are not men, and that, as men, we shall never wish to aggrandize ourselves."[24]

With this as one of his driving ideas, Waltz saw the likelihood of current behavior from the start of the post-Cold War era:

> The powerful state may, and the United States does, think of itself as acting for the sake of peace, justice, and well-being in the world. But these terms will be defined to the liking of the powerful, which may conflict with the preferences and the interests of others. In international politics, overwhelming power repels and leads others to try to balance against it. With benign intent, the United States has behaved, and until its power is brought into a semblance of balance, will continue to behave in ways that annoy and frighten others.[25]

Parts of the Bush Doctrine are unique to the circumstances, but it is the exception rather than the rule for states to stay on the path of moderation when others do not force them to do so.[26]

Second, states' definitions of their interests tend to expand as their power does. It then becomes worth pursuing a whole host of objectives that were out of reach when the state's security was in doubt and all efforts had to be directed to primary objectives. Under the new circumstances, states seek what Wolfers called "milieu goals."[27] The hope of spreading democracy and liberalism throughout the world has always been an American goal, but the lack of a peer competitor now makes it more realistic—although perhaps not very realistic—to actively strive for it. Seen in this light, the administration's perception that this is a time of great opportunity in the Middle East is the product not so much of the special circumstances in the region, but of the enormous resources at America's disposal.

More specifically, the quick American victory in Afghanistan probably contributed to the expansion of American goals, just as the easy military victory in Iraq will encourage the pursuit of a wider agenda, if not threatening force against other tyrants ("moving down the list," in the current phrase). Bush's initial speech after September 11 declared war on terrorists "with a global reach." This was ambitious, but at least the restriction to these kinds of terrorists meant that many others were not of concern. The modifier was dropped in the wake of Afghanistan, however. Not only did rhetoric shift to seeing terrorism in general as a menace to civilization and "the new totalitarian threat,"[28] but the United States sent first military trainers and then a combat unit to the Philippines to attack guerrillas who posed only a minimal threat to Americans and who have no significant links to al Qaeda. Furthermore, at least up to a point, the exercise of power can increase power as well as interests. I do not think that the desire to control a large supply of oil was significant motivation for the Iraqi war, but it will give the United States an additional instrument of influence.

A third structural explanation for American behavior is that increased relative power brings with it new fears. The reasons are both objective and subjective. As Wolfers notes in his classic essay on "National Security as Ambiguous Symbol," the latter can diverge from the former.[29] In one manifestation of this, as major threats disappear, people psychologically elevate ones that were previously seen as quite manageable. Indeed people now seem to be as worried as they were during the height of the Cold War despite the fact that a terrorist or rogue attack, even with WMD, could cause only a small fraction of World War III's devastation. But there is more to it than psychology. A dominant state acquires an enormous stake in the world order and interests spread throughout the globe. Most countries are primarily concerned with what happens in their immediate neighborhoods; the world is the hegemon's neighborhood, and it is not only hubris that leads it to be concerned with anything that happens anywhere. The result is a fusion of narrow and broad self-interest. At a point when most analysts were worried about the decline of American power, not its excesses, Waltz noted that for the United States, "like some earlier great powers. . . . the interest of the country in security came to be identified with the maintenance of a certain world order. For countries at the top, this is predictable behavior. . . . Once a state's interests reach a certain extent, they become self-reinforcing."[30]

The historian John S. Galbraith explored the related dynamic of the "turbulent frontier" that produced the unintended expansion of colonialism. As a European power gained an enclave in Africa or Asia, usually along the coast or river, it also gained an unpacified boundary that had to be policed. This led to further expansion of influence and often of settlement, and this in turn produced a new area that had to be protected and a new zone of threat.[31] There were few natural limits to this process. There are not likely to be many now. The wars in Afghanistan and Iraq have led to the establishment of United States bases and security commitments in central Asia, an area previously beyond reach. It is not hard to imagine how the United States could be drawn further into politics in the region, and to find itself using force to oppose terrorist or guerrilla movements that arise there, perhaps in part in reaction to the American presence. The same dynamic could play out in Colombia.

The fourth facet can be seen as a broader conception of the previous point. As Realists stress, even states that find the status quo acceptable have to worry about the future. Indeed, the more an actor sees the current situation as satisfactory, the more it will expect the future to be worse. Psychology plays a role here too: prospect theory argues that actors are prone to accept great risks when they believe they will suffer losses unless they act boldly. The adoption of a preventive war doctrine may be a mistake, especially if taken too far, but is not foreign to normal state behavior, as I noted earlier, and appeals to states that have a valued position to maintain. However secure states are, only rarely can they be secure enough, and if they are currently very powerful they will have strong reasons to act now to prevent a deterioration that could allow others to harm them in the future.

All this means that under the Bush Doctrine the United States is not a status quo power. Its motives may not be selfish, but the combination of power, fear, and perceived opportunity lead it to seek to reshape world politics and the societies of many of its members. This tracks with and extends traditional ideas in American foreign relations held by both liberals and conservatives that saw the United States as a revolutionary country. As the first modern democracy, the United States was founded on principles of equality, progress, and a government subordinate to civil society that, while initially being uniquely American, had universal applicability. Indeed, because a state's foreign policy is inseparable from its domestic regime, a safe and peaceful world required the spread of these arrangements. Under current conditions of terrorism and WMD, tyrannical governments pose too much of a potential if not actual danger to be tolerated. The world cannot stand still: without strong American intervention, the international environment will become more menacing to America and its values, but strong action can increase its security and produce a better world. In a process akin to the deep security dilemma,[32] in order to protect itself the United States is impelled to act in a way that will increase or at least bring to the surface conflicts with others. Even if the prevailing situation is satisfactory, it cannot be maintained by purely defensive measures. Making the world safe for American democracy is believed to require that dictatorial regimes be banished, or at least kept from weapons of mass destruction.

Although not mentioned in the pronouncements, the Bush Doctrine is made possible by the existence of a security community among the world's most powerful and developed states (the United States, Western Europe, and Japan).[33] The lack of fears of war among these countries allows the United States to focus on other dangers and to pursue other goals. Furthermore, the development of the security community gives the United States a position that it now wants to preserve.

## CONCLUSION

The war against Saddam marks out the path on which the United States is embarked, and illuminates the links between preventive war and hegemony, which was much of the reason for the opposition at home and abroad. Bush's goals are extraordinarily ambitious, involving remaking not only international politics but recalcitrant societies as well, which is seen as an end in itself and a means to American security. For better or (and?) for worse, the United States has set itself tasks that prudent states would shun. As a result, it will be infringing on what adversaries (if not allies) see as their vital interests. Coercion and especially deterrence may be insufficient for these tasks because these instruments share with traditional diplomacy the desire to minimize conflict by limiting one's own claims to interests that others can afford to respect. States that seek more need to be highly assertive if not aggressive (which provides additional reasons to question the goals themselves). The beliefs of Bush and his colleagues that Saddam's regime would have been an unacceptable menace to American interests if it had been allowed to obtain nuclear weapons not only tell us about their fears for the limits of United States influence that might have been imposed, but also speak volumes about the expansive definition of United States interests that they hold.[34]

Indeed, the war is hard to understand if the only object was to disarm Saddam or even to remove him from power. Even had the inflated estimates of his WMD capability been accurate, the danger was simply too remote to justify the effort. But if changing the Iraqi regime was expected to bring democracy and stability to the Middle East, discourage tyrants and energize reformers throughout the world, and demonstrate the American willingness to provide a high degree of what it considers world order whether others like it or not, then, as part of a larger project, the war makes sense. Those who find both the hopes and the fears excessive if not delusional agree with the great British statesman Lord Salisbury when he tried to bring some perspective to the Eastern Crisis of 1877–78: "It has generally been acknowledged to be madness to go to war for an idea, but if anything is more unsatisfactory, it is to go to war against a nightmare."[35]

We can only speculate about the crucial question of whether the Bush Doctrine will work. Contrary to the common impression, democracies, and especially the United States, do not find it easy to sustain a clear line of policy when the external environment is not compelling. Significant casualties will surely be corrosive, and when the going gets tough I think the United States will draw back.

Furthermore, while the United States is indeed the strongest country in the world, its power is still subject to two familiar limitations: it is harder to build than to destroy, and success depends on others' decisions because their cooperation is necessary for the state to reach its goals. The war in Iraq has increased the risks that others face in pursuing nuclear weapons, but it has also increased their incentives to do so. Amid the debate about what these weapons can accomplish, everyone agrees that they can deter invasion, which makes them very attractive to states who fear they might be in the American gun sights. Both Waltz's argument that proliferation will produce stability and the contrary and more common claim that it would make the world more dangerous imply that the spread of nuclear weapons will reduce American influence because others will have less need of its security guarantees and will be able to fend off its threats to their vital interests. The American attempt to minimize the ability of others to resist United States pressures is the mark of a country bent not on maintaining the status quo, but on fashioning a new and better order.

Russia and traditional American allies may see themselves better off with the United States as an assertive hegemon, allowing them to gain the benefits of world order while being spared the costs, and they may conclude that any challenge would fail or bring with it dangerous rivalry. Indeed, without the war in Iraq I doubt that the spring of 2003 would have seen the degree of cooperation that the United States obtained from Europe in combatting the Iranian nuclear program, and from Japan and the PRC in containing North Korea. But I suspect that much will depend on allies' answers to several questions: Can the American domestic political system sustain the Bush Doctrine over the long run? Will the United States be open to allied influence and values? Will it put pressure on Israel as well as on the Arabs to reach a settlement? More generally, will it seek to advance the broad interests of the diverse countries and people in the world or will it exploit its power for its own narrower political, economic, and social interests? Bush's world gives little place for other states—even democracies—except as members of a supporting cast. Conflating broader with narrower interests and believing that one has a monopoly on wisdom are familiar patterns for dominant powers, and ones that rarely sit well with other powerful states.

## NOTES

1. White House, "The National Security Strategy of the United States," (Washington, D.C.: September 2002), pp. i, 1. Bush's West Point speech similarly declared: "Moral truth is the same in every culture, in every time, and in every place. . . . We are in a conflict between good and evil." "When it comes to the common rights and needs of men and women, there is no clash of civilizations." "Remarks by the President at 2002 Graduation Exercise of the Unites States Military Academy," White House Press Release, June 1, 2002, p. 3.

2. Thus Samuel Huntington, who agrees that a state's foreign policy is strongly influenced by its domestic regime, argues that conflict can be reduced only by not pushing Western values on other societies: *The Clash of Civilizations and the Remaking of the World Order* (New York: Simon and Schuster, 1996).

3. John Lewis Gaddis, "Bush's Security Strategy," *Foreign Policy*, No. 133, November/December 2002, pp. 50–57.

4. Edward Mansfield and Jack Snyder, *Democratization and War* (Cambridge: MIT Press, forthcoming).

5. Quoted in David Sanger, "U.S. to Withdraw From Arms Accord With North Korea," *New York Times*, October 20, 2002.

6. Quoted in Frank Bruni, "For President, a Mission and a Role in History," ibid, September 22, 2001; "President Thanks World Coalition for Anti-Terrorism Efforts," White House Press Release, March 11, 2002, pp. 3–4; also see "Remarks by the President at 2002 Graduation Exercise," pp. 4–5.

7. "President Bush, Prime Minister Koizumi Hold Press Conference," White House Press Release, February 18, 2002, p. 6.

8. "President, Vice President Discuss the Middle East," White House Press Release, March 21, 2002, p. 2.

9. It is no accident that the leading theorist of this school of thought, Albert Wohlstetter, trained and sponsored many of the driving figures of the Bush administration, such as Paul Wolfowitz and Richard Perle.

10. Letter accompanying "National Security Strategy of the U.S.," p. ii. Calling this aspect of the doctrine and our policy against Iraq "preemptive," as the Bush administration does, is to do violence to the English language. No one thought that Iraq was about to attack anyone; rather the argument was that Iraq and perhaps others are terrible menaces that eventually will do the U.S. great harm and must be dealt with as soon as possible, before the harm has been inflicted and while prophylactic actions can be taken at reasonable cost. For a study of cases, see Robert Litwak, "The New Calculus of Pre-emption," *Survival*, Vol. 44, Winter 2002–03, pp. 53–79.

11. Dale Copeland, *The Origins of Major War* (Ithaca, NY: Cornell University Press, 2000); also see John Mearsheimer, *Tragedy of Great Power Politics* (New York: Norton, 2001). For important conceptual distinctions and propositions, see Jack Levy, "Declining Power and the Preventive Motivation for War," *World Politics*, Vol. 40, October 1987, pp. 82–107 and, for a study that is skeptical of the general prevalence of preventive wars but presents one example, Levy and Joseph Gochal, "Democracy and Preventive War: Israel and the 1956 Sinai Campaign," *Security Studies*, Vol. 11, Winter 2001/2, pp. 1–49. On the U.S. experience, see Art, *Grand Strategy for America*, pp. 181–97. Randall Schweller argues that democratic states fight preventively only under very restrictive circumstances: "Domestic Structure and Preventive War: Are Democracies More Pacific?" *World Politics*, Vol. 44, January 1992, pp. 235–69, and notes the unusual nature of the Israeli cases. For the argument that states are generally well served resisting the temptation to fight preventively, see Richard Betts, "Striking First: A History of Thankfully Lost Opportunities," *Ethics and International Affairs*, Vol. 17, No. 1, 2003, pp. 17–24. For a review of power transition theory, which in one interpretation is driven by preventive motivation, see Jacek Kugler and Douglas Lemke, *Parity and War: Evaluations and Extensions of The War Ledger* (Ann Arbor: University of Michigan Press, 1996).

12. Marc Trachtenberg, *History and Strategy* (Princeton: Princeton University Press, 1991), ch. 3; William Burr and Jeffrey Richelson, "Whether to 'Strangle the Baby in the Cradle': The United States and the Chinese Nuclear Program, 1960–64," *International Security*, Vol. 25, Winter 2000/01, pp. 54–99. Gregory Mitrovich shows how much of

American early Cold War policy was driven by the fear that it could not sustain a prolonged confrontation: *Undermining the Kremlin: America's Strategy to Subvert the Soviet Bloc, 1947–1956* (Ithaca, NY: Cornell University Press, 2000).

13. According to Robert Woodward, George Tenet believed that "Bush had been the least prepared of all of [the administration leaders] for the terrorist attacks": *Bush at War* (New York: Simon and Schuster, 2002), p. 318. Before then his administration had concentrated on Russia and the PRC.

14. *New York Times*, February 1, 2003.

15. Quoted in James Risen, David Sanger, and Thom Shanker, "In Sketchy Data, Trying to Gauge Iraq Threat," ibid., July 20, 2003.

16. Bernard Brodie, "The Development of Nuclear Strategy," *International Security*, Vol. 2, Spring 1978, p. 83.

17. Quoted in Steven Erlanger, "Bush's Move On ABM Pact Gives Pause to Europeans," *New York Times*, December 13, 2001; also see Suzanne Daley, "Many in Europe Voice Worry that U.S. Will Not Consult Them," ibid., January 31, 2002; Erlanger, "Protests, and Friends Too, Await Bush in Europe," ibid., May 22, 2002; Elizabeth Becker, "U.S. Unilateralism Worries Trade Officials," ibid., March 17, 2003.

18. Quoted in Karen DeYoung, "Chirac Moves To Repair U.S. Ties," *Washington Post*, April 16, 2003.

19. Quoted in Bob Woodward interview with Bush in ibid., November 19, 2002 (also see Woodward, *Bush at War* p. 281); quoted in Somini Sengupta, "U.N. Forum Stalls on Sex Education and Abortion Rights," *New York Times*, 10 May 2002.

20. "Remarks by the President at 2002 Graduation Exercise," p. 4. The Wolfowitz draft is summarized in stories in the *New York Times*, March 8 and May 24, 1992. Also see Zalmay Khalilzad, *From Containment to Global Leadership? America and the World After the Cold War* (Santa Monica, CA: RAND, 1995), and Robert Kagan and William Kristol, eds., *Present Dangers: Crisis and Opportunity in American Foreign and Defense Policy* (San Francisco: Encounter Books, 2000). This stance gives others incentives to develop asymmetric responses, of which terrorism is only the most obvious example. For possible PRC options, see Thomas Christensen, "Posing Problems Without Catching Up: China's Rise and Challenges for U.S. Security Policy," *International Security*, Vol. 25, Spring 2001, pp. 5–40.

21. Quoted in James Harding, "Conflicting Views From Two Bush Camps," *Financial Times*, March 20, 2003; for a perceptive analysis, see Bruni, "For President, a Mission and a Role in History." Also see Woodward, *Bush at War*, pp. 102, 205, 281.

22. Richard Betts, "The Soft Underbelly of American Primacy: Tactical Advantages of Terror," *Political Science Quarterly*, Vol. 117, Spring 2002, pp. 19–36.

23. See, for example, Jesse Helms' defense of unilateralism as the only way consistent with American interests and traditions: "American Sovereignty and the UN," *National Interest*, No. 62, Winter 2000/01, pp. 31–34. For a discussion of historical, sociological, and geographical sources of the moralistic outlook in American foreign policy, see Arnold Wolfers, *Discord and Collaboration* (Baltimore: Johns Hopkins University Press, 1962), chapter 15, and Louis Hartz, *The Liberal Tradition in America* (New York: Harcourt, Brace, 1955), chapter 11. For a discussion of current U.S. policy in terms of its self-image as an exceptional state, see Stanley Hoffmann, "The High and the Mighty," *American Prospect*, Vol. 1, January 2003, pp. 28–31.

24. Quoted in Hans Morgenthau, *Politics Among Nations*, 5th ed, revised (New York: Knopf, 1978), pp. 169–70, emphasis in the original.

25. Kenneth Waltz, "America as a Model for the World? A Foreign Policy Perspective," *PS: Political Science and Politics*, Vol. 24, December 1991, p. 69.

26. Alexander Wendt and, more persuasively, Paul Schroeder would disagree or at least modify this generalization, arguing that prevailing ideas can and have led to more moderate and consensual behavior: Wendt, *Social Theory of International Politics* (New York: Cambridge University Press, 1999); Schroeder, *The Transformation of European Politics, 1763–1848* (New York: Oxford University Press, 1994), and "Does the History of International Politics Go Anywhere?" in David Wetzel and Theodore Hamerow, eds., *International Politics and German History* (Westport: Praeger, 1997), pp. 15–36. This is a central question of international politics and history that I cannot fully discuss here, but believe that at least the mild statement that unbalanced power is dangerous can easily be sustained.

27. Wolfers, *Discord and Collaboration,* chapter 5.

28. "President Thanks World Coalition for Anti-Terrorism Efforts"; David Sanger, "In Reichstag, Bush Condemns Terror as New Despotism," *New York Times,* 24 May 2002. Also see "Remarks by President at 2002 Graduation Exercise," p. 3. The question of how broad the target should be was debated within the administration from the start, with Bush initially insisting on a focus on Al Qaeda: Woodward, *Bush at War,* p. 48.

29. *Discord and Collaboration,* chapter 10.

30. Kenneth Waltz, *Theory of International Politics* (Reading, MA.: Addison-Wesley, 1979), p. 200.

31. John S. Galbraith, "The 'Turbulent Frontier' as a Factor in British Expansion," *Comparative Studies in Society and History,* Vol. 2, January 1960, pp. 34–48; *Reluctant Empire: British Policy on the South African Frontier, 1834–1854* (Berkeley: University of California Press, 1963). Also see Ronald Robinson and John Gallager with Alice Denny, *Africa and the Victorians: The Official Mind of Imperialism* (London: Macmillan, 1961). A related imperial dynamic that is likely to recur is that turning a previously recalcitrant state into a client usually weakens it internally and requires further intervention.

32. Robert Jervis, "Was the Cold War a Security Dilemma?" *Journal of Cold War History,* Vol. 3, Winter 2001, pp. 36–60; also see Paul Roe, "Former Yugoslavia: The Security Dilemma That Never Was?" *European Journal of International Relations,* Vol. 6, September 2000, pp. 373–93. The current combination of fear and hope that produces offensive actions for defensive motives resembles the combination that produced the pursuit of preponderance in the aftermath of World War II.

33. Robert Jervis, "Theories of War in an Era of Leading Power Peace," *American Political Science Review,* Vol. 96, March 2003, pp. 1–14.

34. I have discussed how Bush's policy toward Iraq does and does not fit with deterrence thinking in "The Confrontation Between Iraq and the U.S.: Implications for the Theory and Practice of Deterrence," *European Journal of International Relations,* Vol. 9, No. 2, June 2003, pp. 315–37.

35. Quoted in R. W. Seton-Watson, *Disraeli, Gladstone, and the Eastern Question* (New York: Norton, 1972), p. 222.

# Can Democracy Stop Terrorism?

## F. GREGORY GAUSE III

### WHAT FREEDOM BRINGS

The United States is engaged in what President George W. Bush has called a "generational challenge" to instill democracy in the Arab world. The Bush administration and its defenders contend that this push for Arab democracy will not only spread American values but also improve U.S. security. As democracy grows in the Arab world, the thinking goes, the region will stop generating anti-American terrorism. Promoting democracy in the Middle East is therefore not merely consistent with U.S. security goals; it is necessary to achieve them.

But this begs a fundamental question: Is it true that the more democratic a country becomes, the less likely it is to produce terrorists and terrorist groups? In other words, is the security rationale for promoting democracy in the Arab world based on a sound premise? Unfortunately, the answer appears to be no. Although what is known about terrorism is admittedly incomplete, the data available do not show a strong relationship between democracy and an absence of or a reduction in terrorism. Terrorism appears to stem from factors much more specific than regime type. Nor is it likely that democratization would end the current campaign against the United States. Al Qaeda and like-minded groups are not fighting for democracy in the Muslim world; they are fighting to impose their vision of an Islamic state. Nor is there any evidence that democracy in the Arab world would "drain the swamp," eliminating soft support for terrorist organizations among the Arab public and reducing the number of potential recruits for them.

Even if democracy were achieved in the Middle East, what kind of governments would it produce? Would they cooperate with the United States on important policy objectives besides curbing terrorism, such as advancing the Arab-Israeli peace process, maintaining security in the Persian Gulf, and ensuring steady supplies of oil? No one can predict the course a new democracy will take, but based on public opinion surveys and recent elections in the Arab world, the advent of democracy there seems likely to produce new Islamist governments that would be much less willing to cooperate with the United States than are the current authoritarian rulers.

The answers to these questions should give Washington pause. The Bush administration's democracy initiative can be defended as an effort to spread American democratic values at any cost, or as a long-term gamble that even if Islamists do come to power, the realities of governance will moderate them or the public will grow

From F. Gregory Gause III, "Can Democracy Stop Terrorism?" Reprinted by permission of *Foreign Affairs,* Vol. 84, No. 5 (September/October 2005), pp. 62–76. Copyright 2005 by the Council on Foreign Relations, Inc.

disillusioned with them. The emphasis on electoral democracy will not, however, serve immediate U.S. interests either in the war on terrorism or in other important Middle East policies.

It is thus time to rethink the U.S. emphasis on democracy promotion in the Arab world. Rather than push for quick elections, the United States should instead focus its energy on encouraging the development of secular, nationalist, and liberal political organizations that could compete on an equal footing with Islamist parties. Only by doing so can Washington help ensure that when elections finally do occur, the results are more in line with U.S. interests.

## THE MISSING LINK

President Bush has been clear about why he thinks promoting democracy in the Arab world is central to U.S. interests. "Our strategy to keep the peace in the longer term," Bush said in a speech in March 2005,

> is to help change the conditions that give rise to extremism and terror, especially in the broader Middle East. Parts of that region have been caught for generations in a cycle of tyranny and despair and radicalism. When a dictatorship controls the political life of a country, responsible opposition cannot develop, and dissent is driven underground and toward the extreme. And to draw attention away from their social and economic failures, dictators place blame on other countries and other races, and stir the hatred that leads to violence. This status quo of despotism and anger cannot be ignored or appeased, kept in a box or bought off.

Bush's belief in the link between terrorism and a lack of democracy is not limited to his administration. During the 2004 presidential campaign, Senator John Kerry (D-Mass.) emphasized the need for greater political reform in the Middle East as an integral part of the war on terrorism. Martin Indyk, a senior Middle East policymaker in the Clinton administration, has written that it was a mistake for Clinton to focus on Arab-Israeli peace while downplaying Middle East democracy, and he has urged Washington to concentrate on political reform. In a recent book he co-authored, Morton Halperin, the director of policy planning in Clinton's State Department, argues that the roots of al Qaeda lie in the poverty and educational deficiencies of Saudi Arabia, Egypt, and Pakistan, and that these deficiencies were caused by the authoritarian nature of those states and can be combated only through democratization. The *New York Times* columnist Thomas Friedman has done more to sell this logic to the public than anyone else.

Despite the wide acceptance of this connection, the academic literature on the relationship between terrorism and other sociopolitical indicators, such as democracy, is surprisingly scant. There are good case studies and general surveys of terrorists and terrorist organizations, but few that try to determine whether more democracy leads to less terrorism. Part of the problem is the quality of the data available. The Western press tends to report terrorist incidents with a cross-border element more completely than homegrown terrorist attacks. Moreover, most of the statistics identify the location of an incident, but not the identity of the perpetrators—and much less whether they came from nondemocratic countries.

Given such incomplete information, only preliminary conclusions from the academic literature are possible. However, even these seem to discredit the supposedly close link between terrorism and authoritarianism that underlies the Bush administration's logic. In a widely cited study of terrorist events in the 1980s, the political scientists William Eubank and Leonard Weinberg demonstrate that most terrorist incidents occur in democracies and that generally both the victims and the perpetrators are citizens of democracies. Examining incidents from 1975 to 1997, Pennsylvania State University's Quan Li has found that although terrorist attacks are less frequent when democratic political participation is high, the kind of checks that liberal democracy typically places on executive power seems to encourage terrorist actions. In his recent book, *Dying to Win: The Strategic Logic of Suicide Terrorism*, Robert Pape finds that the targets of suicide bombers are almost always democracies, but that the motivation of the groups behind those bombings is to fight against military occupation and for self-determination. Terrorists are not driven by a desire for democracy but by their opposition to what they see as foreign domination.

The numbers published by the U.S. government do not bear out claims of a close link between terrorism and authoritarianism either. Between 2000 and 2003, according to the State Department's annual "Patterns of Global Terrorism" report, 269 major terrorist incidents around the world occurred in countries classified as "free" by Freedom House, 119 occurred in "partly free" countries, and 138 occurred in "not free" countries. (This count excludes both terrorist attacks by Palestinians on Israel, which would increase the number of attacks in democracies even more, and the September 11, 2001, attacks on the United States, which originated in other countries.) This is not to argue that free countries are more likely to produce terrorists than other countries. Rather, these numbers simply indicate that there is no relationship between the incidence of terrorism in a given country and the degree of freedom enjoyed by its citizens. They certainly do not indicate that democracies are substantially less susceptible to terrorism than are other forms of government.

Terrorism, of course, is not distributed randomly. According to official U.S. government data, the vast majority of terrorist incidents occurred in only a few countries. Indeed, half of all the terrorist incidents in "not free" countries in 2003 took place in just two countries: Iraq and Afghanistan. It seems that democratization did little to discourage terrorists from operating there—and may even have encouraged terrorism.

As for the "free" countries, terrorist incidents in India accounted for fully 75 percent of the total. It is fair to assume that groups based in Pakistan carried out a number of those attacks, particularly in Kashmir, but clearly not all the perpetrators were foreigners. A significant number of terrorist events in India took place far from Kashmir, reflecting other local grievances against the central government. And as strong and vibrant as Indian democracy is, both a sitting prime minister and a former prime minister have been assassinated—Indira Gandhi and her son, Rajiv Gandhi, respectively. If democracy reduced the prospects for terrorism, India's numbers would not be so high.

Comparing India, the world's most populous democracy, and China, the world's most populous authoritarian state, highlights the difficulty of assuming that democracy can solve the terrorism problem. For 2000–2003, the "Patterns of Global Terrorism" report indicates 203 international terrorist attacks in India and none in China. A list of terrorist incidents between 1976 and 2004, compiled by the National Memorial Institute for the Prevention of Terrorism, shows more than 400 in India and only 18 in China. Even if China under-reports such incidents by a factor of ten, it still endures substantially fewer terrorist attacks than India. If the relationship between authoritarianism and terrorism were as strong as the Bush administration implies, the discrepancy between the number of terrorist incidents in China and the number in India would run the other way.

More anecdotal evidence also calls into question a necessary relationship between regime type and terrorism. In the 1970s and 1980s, a number of brutal terrorist organizations arose in democratic countries: the Red Brigades in Italy, the Provisional Irish Republican Army in Ireland and the United Kingdom, the Japanese Red Army in Japan, and the Red Army Faction (or Baader-Meinhof Gang) in West Germany. The transition to democracy in Spain did not eliminate Euskadi Ta Askatasuna (ETA) Basque separatist terrorism. Turkish democracy suffered through a decade of mounting political violence that lasted until the late 1970s. The strong and admirable democratic system in Israel has produced its own terrorists, including the assassin of Prime Minister Yitzhak Rabin. It appears that at least three of the suicide bombers in the London attacks of July were born and raised in the democratic United Kingdom. Nearly every day brings a painful reminder that real democratization in Iraq has been accompanied by serious terrorism. And a memorial in Oklahoma City testifies to the fact that even U.S. democracy has not been free of terrorism of domestic origins.

There is, in other words, no solid empirical evidence for a strong link between democracy, or any other regime type, and terrorism, in either a positive or a negative direction. In her highly praised post–September 11 study of religious militants, *Terror in the Name of God*, Jessica Stern argues that "democratization is not necessarily the best way to fight Islamic extremism," because the transition to democracy "has been found to be an especially vulnerable period for states across the board." Terrorism springs from sources other than the form of government of a state. There is no reason to believe that a more democratic Arab world will, simply by virtue of being more democratic, generate fewer terrorists.

## FLAWED

There are also logical problems with the argument supporting the U.S. push for democracy as part of the war on terrorism. Underlying the assertion that democracy will reduce terrorism is the belief that, able to participate openly in competitive politics and have their voices heard in the public square, potential terrorists and terrorist sympathizers would not need to resort to violence to achieve their goals. Even if they lost in one round of elections, the confidence that they could win in the future would inhibit the temptation to resort to extra-democratic means. The habits of democracy would ameliorate extremism and focus the anger of the Arab publics at their own governments, not at the United States.

Well, maybe. But it is just as logical to assume that terrorists, who rarely represent political agendas that could mobilize electoral majorities, would reject the very principles of majority rule and minority rights on which liberal democracy is based. If they could not achieve their goals through democratic politics, why would they privilege the democratic process over those goals? It seems more likely that, having been mobilized to participate in the democratic process by a burning desire to achieve particular goals—a desire so strong that they were willing to commit acts of violence against defenseless civilians to realize it—terrorists and potential terrorists would attack democracy if it did not produce their desired results. Respect for the nascent Iraqi democracy, despite a very successful election in January 2005, has not stopped Iraqi and foreign terrorists from their campaign against the new political order.

Terrorist organizations are not mass-based organizations. They are small and secretive. They are not organized or based on democratic principles. They revolve around strong leaders and a cluster of committed followers who are willing to take actions from which the vast majority of people, even those who might support their political agenda, would rightly shrink. It seems unlikely that simply being out-voted would deflect them from their path.

The United States' major foe in the war on terrorism, al Qaeda, certainly would not close up shop if every Muslim country in the world were to become a democracy. Osama bin Laden has been very clear about democracy: he does not like it. His political model is the early Muslim caliphate. In his view, the Taliban regime in Afghanistan came the closest in modern times to that model. In an October 2003 "message to Iraqis," bin Laden castigated those in the Arab world who are "calling for a peaceful democratic solution in dealing with apostate governments or with Jewish and crusader invaders instead of fighting in the name of God." He referred to democracy as "this deviant and misleading practice" and "the faith of the ignorant." Bin Laden's ally in Iraq, Abu Musab al-Zarqawi, reacted to the January 2005 Iraqi election even more directly: "The legislator who must be obeyed in a democracy is man, and not God. . . . That is the very essence of heresy and polytheism and error, as it contradicts the bases of the faith and monotheism, and because it makes the weak, ignorant man God's partner in His most central divine prerogative—namely, ruling and legislating."

Al Qaeda's leaders distrust democracy, and not just on ideological grounds: they know they could not come to power through free elections. There is no reason to believe that a move toward more democracy in Arab states would deflect them from their course. And there is no reason to believe that they could not recruit followers in more democratic Arab states—especially if those states continued to have good relations with the United States, made peace with Israel, and generally behaved in ways acceptable to Washington. Al Qaeda objects to the U.S. agenda in the Middle East as much as, if not more than, democracy. If, as Washington hopes, a democratic Middle East continued to accept a major U.S. role in the region and cooperate with U.S. goals, it is foolish to think that democracy would end Arab anti-Americanism and dry up passive support, funding sources, and recruiting channels for al Qaeda.

When it works, liberal democracy is the best form of government. But there is no evidence that it reduces or prevents terrorism. The fundamental assumption of the Bush administration's push for democracy in the Arab world is seriously flawed.

## ANGRY VOICES

It is highly unlikely that democratically elected Arab governments would be as co-operative with the United States as the current authoritarian regimes. To the extent that public opinion can be measured in these countries, research shows that Arabs strongly support democracy. When they have a chance to vote in real elections, they generally turn out in percentages far greater than Americans do in their elections. But many Arabs hold negative views of the United States. If Arab governments were democratically elected and more representative of public opinion, they would thus be more anti-American. Further democratization in the Middle East would, for the foreseeable future, most likely generate Islamist governments less inclined to co-operate with the United States on important U.S. policy goals, including military basing rights in the region, peace with Israel, and the war on terrorism. . . .

Although it is not possible to pinpoint from poll data the precise reasons for anti-Americanism in the Arab world, there are indications that it is U.S. policy in the region, not a rejection of American ideals, that drives the sentiment. In the Zogby International–Sadat Chair poll of February–March 2003, respondents in five of six Arab countries said that their attitudes toward the United States were based more on U.S. policy than on U.S. values. Forty-six percent of Egyptians polled identified U.S. policy as the source of their feelings, compared with 43 percent who stressed American values. No fewer than 58 percent of respondents in Jordan, Lebanon, Morocco, and Saudi Arabia also emphasized their opposition to U.S. policy. . . .

Even if democratization could reduce anti-Americanism, there is no guarantee that such a reduction would yield pro-American governments. Anecdotal evidence certainly seems to indicate, for example, that the public in non-Arab Iran has a better impression of the United States than does the Iranian government. The Iranian public's more pro-American stance did not, however, translate into votes for the candidate favoring rapprochement with the United States in the second round of the recent presidential election.

History also indicates that legitimate democratic elections in Arab states would most likely benefit Islamists. In all recent Arab elections, they have emerged as the government's leading political opposition, and in many of them they have done very well. In Morocco, the new Justice and Development Party, an overtly Islamist party, took 42 of the 325 seats in the parliamentary elections of 2002, its first contest. (Only two long-established parties, the Socialist Union of Popular Forces and the Independence Party, won more seats: 50 and 48, respectively.) The same year, in Bahrain, Islamist candidates took between 19 and 21 of the 40 seats in parliament (depending on how observers classified some independent candidates). This success came even though the major Shia political group boycotted the elections, protesting changes in the constitution. . . .

## THE LONG HAUL

The Bush administration's push for democracy in the Arab world is unlikely to have much effect on anti-American terrorism emanating from there; it could in fact help bring to power governments much less cooperative on a whole range of issues— including the war on terrorism—than the current regimes. Unfortunately, there is no good alternative at this point to working with the authoritarian Arab governments that are willing to work with the United States.

If Washington insists on promoting democracy in the Arab world, it should learn from the various electoral experiences in the region. Where there are strongly rooted non-Islamist parties, as in Morocco, the Islamists have a harder time dominating the field. The same is true in non-Arab Turkey, where the Islamist political party has moderated its message over time to contend with the power of the secular army and with well-established, more secular parties. Likewise, the diverse confessional mix of voters in Lebanon will probably prevent Hezbollah and other Islamists from dominating elections there. Conversely, where non-Islamist political forces have been suppressed, as in Saudi Arabia and Bahrain, Islamist parties and candidates can command the political field. Washington should take no comfort from the success of ruling parties in Algeria, Egypt, and Yemen over Islamist challengers: once stripped of their patronage and security apparatus, ruling parties do not fare very well in democratic transitional elections.

The United States must focus on pushing Arab governments to make political space for liberal, secular, leftist, nationalist, and other non-Islamist parties to set down roots and mobilize voters. Washington should support those groups that are more likely to accept U.S. foreign policy and emulate U.S. political values. The most effective way to demonstrate that support is to openly pressure Arab regimes when they obstruct the political activity of more liberal groups—as the administration did with Egypt after the jailing of the liberal reformers Saad Eddin Ibrahim and Ayman Nour, and as it should do with Saudi Arabia regarding the May sentencing of peaceful political activists to long prison terms. But Washington will also need to drop its focus on prompt elections in Arab countries where no strong, organized alternative to Islamist parties exists—even at the risk of disappointing Arab liberals by being more cautious about their electoral prospects than they are.

Administration officials, including President Bush, have often stated that the transition to democracy in the Arab world will be difficult and that Americans should not expect quick results. Yet whenever the Bush administration publicly defends democratization, it cites a familiar litany of Muslim-world elections—those in Afghanistan, Iraq, Lebanon, the Palestinian territories, and Saudi Arabia—as evidence that the policy is working. It will take years, however, for non-Islamist political forces to be ready to compete for power in these elections, and it is doubtful that this or any other U.S. administration will have the patience to see the process through. If it cannot show that patience, Washington must realize that its democratization policy will lead to Islamist domination of Arab politics.

It is not only the focus on elections that is troubling in the administration's democracy initiative in the Arab world. Also problematic is the unjustified confidence that Washington has in its ability to predict, and even direct, the course of politics in other countries. No administration official would sign on, at least not in public, to the naive view that Arab democracy will produce governments that will always cooperate with the United States. Yet Washington's democracy advocates seem to assume that Arab democratic transitions, like the recent democratic transitions in eastern Europe, Latin America, and East Asia, will lead to regimes that support, or at least do not impede, the broad range of U.S. foreign policy interests. They do not appreciate that in those regimes, liberalism prevailed because its great ideological competitor, communism, was thoroughly discredited, whereas the Arab world offers a real ideological alternative to liberal democracy: the movement that claims as its motto "Islam is the solution." Washington's hubris should have been crushed in Iraq, where even the presence of 140,000 American troops has not allowed politics to proceed according to the U.S. plan. Yet the Bush administration displays little of the humility or the patience that such a daunting task demands. If the United States really does see the democracy-promotion initiative in the Arab world as a "generational challenge," the entire nation will have to learn these traits.

# Taming American Power

## STEPHEN M. WALT

### THE GREAT DEBATE

U.S. policymakers have spent the past decade debating how best to wield American power. For the rest of the world, the debate is over how best to deal with it. With so much power in the hands of one country—a country that considers itself destined to lead the world—how should other nations respond? . . .

How do you deal with American power? This question is one for which every world leader must have an answer. And the response of other states to U.S. power is something Americans must care about as well. Basic security is at issue, as the September 11, 2001, terrorist attacks demonstrated. So is the health of the U.S. economy, with the market share of U.S. firms declining in key overseas markets due to anti-American sentiment. The time to worry is now.

To be sure, many governments still value U.S. power and seek to use it to advance their own interests. Yet even Washington's close allies are now looking for ways to tame the United States' might. Many countries fear U.S. influence, and they have devised numerous strategies to manage and limit it. The United States will not and should not exit the world stage anytime soon. But it must make its dominant position acceptable to others—by using military force sparingly, by fostering greater cooperation with key allies, and, most important of all, by rebuilding its crumbling international image.

### OF POWER AND POLICY

Americans tend to see U.S. primacy as beneficial to both their country and the rest of the world. In 2002, the Pew Global Attitudes Project found that 79 percent of U.S. citizens believe it is good that "American ideas and customs are spreading around the world," and more than 70 percent think that U.S. foreign policy takes the interests of other states into account either "a great deal" or "a fair amount." Bill Clinton has described the United States as "a beacon of hope to peoples around the world," and Harvard political scientist Samuel Huntington has declared U.S. predominance to be "central to the future of freedom, democracy, open economies, and international order." In other words, without a benign hegemon maintaining a peaceful global order, many countries would not be able to enjoy the prosperity and security they have come to take for granted.

Unfortunately, this rosy view of U.S. power is not shared overseas, where, according to the 2002 Pew survey, overwhelming majorities say that the United States considers the interests of others "not much" or "not at all." Between 40 percent and 60 percent of foreigners polled think the United States is waging its war on terrorism not solely out of security concerns, but also to "control Mideast oil," "protect Israel," "target Muslim governments," or "dominate the world." A January 2005 BBC survey of 21 countries found only five—India, the Philippines, Poland, South Africa, and South Korea—where a majority of people had "positive" attitudes toward the United States. Although the United States' global standing has rebounded slightly since the invasion of Iraq two years ago, Pew reported in June 2005 that majorities in all 15 countries it surveyed "favor another country challenging America's global military supremacy," and that support for the U.S.-led "war on terror" is declining on every continent. Indeed, citizens in Canada, France, Germany, the Netherlands, Russia, Spain, and the United Kingdom now hold more favorable views of China than of the United States.

The United States' image is especially bleak in the Arab world. Although Arab populations view U.S. popular culture, U.S. science and technology, and the American people somewhat favorably, a 2004 Zogby International poll found that fewer than 10 percent of those surveyed in Egypt, Jordan, Lebanon, Morocco, Saudi Arabia, and the United Arab Emirates approved of U.S. policy on Arabs, Iraq, or the Palestinians. Indeed, when asked to indicate their "first thought" about the United States, the most common response was "unfair foreign policy." The same year, a Pew survey revealed that Osama bin Laden's popularity rating was more than 40 points higher than President Bush's in Jordan, Morocco, and Pakistan. In 2005, Pew reported that majorities in predominantly Muslim countries "express concern that U.S. military power may ultimately be turned against them."

If the United States' primacy is a force for good—as the country's leaders proclaim and its citizens overwhelmingly believe—why do even its allies have concerns about its influence? They have misgivings because they recognize that Washington's power could threaten their own interests. Even those countries that do not fear a U.S. attack are still aware that the United States' position as the world's lone superpower makes it easier for Washington to get its way. And of course, U.S. leaders have sought primacy precisely because they understand that weaker nations have less clout. It should come as no surprise, then, that other states remain wary despite assurances from Washington that U.S. power benefits the entire world. As a Chinese official remarked a few years ago, "How can we base our own national security on your assurances of good-will?" Moreover, even well-intentioned U.S. policies can inadvertently harm other nations, giving them more reason for concern about the long reach of U.S. power. When it supported the Afghan mujahideen in the 1980s, the United States was not trying to create a global terrorist organization. And the United States was not trying to get al Qaeda to bomb the Madrid subway when it courted Spanish support for the war in Iraq. Yet both unfortunate developments were, in part, the unintended consequences of U.S. policy, illustrating why all states must be somewhat concerned about the ways the United States chooses to use its power.

Proponents of a muscular U.S. foreign policy tend to portray anti-Americanism as hostility toward American values or simple resentment of U.S. dominance. President Bush has said that "America was targeted for attack because we're the brightest beacon of freedom . . . in the world." He later explained, "The terrorists who attacked our country on September 11, 2001, were not protesting our policies. They were protesting our existence." And the Pentagon's new National Defense Strategy, issued in March, stated, "Our leading position in the world will continue to breed unease, a degree of resentment, and resistance."

There is a grain of truth in this argument, but foreign opposition to the United States is mostly a reaction to specific U.S. policies. The United States has been the sole great power for nearly 15 years, but its international standing remained fairly high through the late 1990s. Although some foreign leaders expressed concerns about the power imbalance, most nations—their people and their governments— looked favorably on the United States and welcomed Washington's global leadership. Attributing the current unpopularity of the United States solely to its power or values cannot explain the sharp decline in its image that has occurred since 2000, or especially the intense antipathy toward President Bush himself.

Moreover, the United States' main opponents have themselves repeatedly indicated that problematic U.S. policies are their primary concern. For example, bin Laden has made it clear that his hatred is fueled by opposition to what he regards as unjust U.S. actions in the Middle East, not to American values per se. According to the 2002 Pew Global Attitudes survey, "Antipathy toward the United States is shaped more by what it *does* in the international arena than by what it *stands* for politically and economically" (italics in the original). Similarly, a 2004 study by the Pentagon's Defense Science Board concluded that "Muslims do not 'hate our freedom,' but rather they hate our policies." And the State Department's Advisory Group on Public Diplomacy concluded in 2003 that "Arabs and Muslims . . . support our values but believe that our policies do not live up to them."

Disagreement with U.S. foreign policy does not mean the policy is wrong, but it does mean U.S. actions come with a price. When foreign populations disapprove of U.S. policy and are fearful of U.S. dominance, their governments are less likely to endorse Washington's initiatives and more likely to look for ways to hinder them. Rising anti-Americanism also increases the number of extremists who can be recruited into violent movements such as al Qaeda. The United States may still be able to gain others' compliance and overcome overt resistance, but achieving success will be more difficult and more expensive.

Regardless of whether they disagree with U.S. policy or with the simple fact of U.S. power, can other states do anything to tame the American colossus? Historian Niall Ferguson has argued that the central issue is whether Americans have a "will to power" equal to their global responsibilities. President Bush, for his part, has downplayed the risk of going it alone: "At some point we may be the only ones left. . . . That's okay with me. We are America." Such statements imply that the United States can overcome any international resistance to its agenda so long as its resolve is firm.

But this confidence is unwarranted. Although other states cannot diminish U.S. primacy in the near term, there are still many ways they can rein in U.S. power. Some countries seek to manipulate the United States for their own purposes, using accommodation to gain Washington's trust, support, and protection. Others are more confrontational, attempting to oppose and undercut U.S. interests. In either case, the United States' ability to defend or advance its own foreign policy agenda is impaired.

## IF YOU CAN'T BEAT 'EM

Given the reality of U.S. power, some states choose to accommodate it—and in doing so, attempt to ensure that it is used to their benefit. A few countries, wary of coercive measures or even possible military intervention by the United States, may choose to realign their policies to accord with U.S. interests in order to deflect U.S. pressure. More frequently, countries ally themselves with Washington to counter threats posed by their regional adversaries. By developing a close relationship with the United States, as well as with key American constituencies, foreign powers can manipulate U.S. primacy to their own advantage.

Instead of resisting U.S. power, a few states—Libya is the most recent example—"bandwagon" with the United States. To appease Washington, band-wagoners realign their foreign policies according to Washington's dictates. Although the United States has often tried to compel such realignments by pressuring weak and isolated opponents—including Iraq, North Korea, Serbia, and Syria—this strategy rarely works. Even Libya's acquiescence was due as much to prolonged sanctions as to any implied military threat.

More commonly, states choose to ally themselves with the United States out of a desire for U.S. protection from a regional threat. The United States has long been an attractive ally against intimidating neighbors: it is strong enough to shift a regional balance of power, and it generally does so without conquering its allies in the process. Poland, for example, seeks stronger ties with the United States because, as one Polish official explained, Poland "is a country that thinks seriously about security . . . [and] for such a country, it's good to be a close ally of the United States." The specter of China's rising power has created a host of diplomatic opportunities for Washington in Asia: India wants to develop a strategic partnership with the United States, and Malaysia, the Philippines, and Singapore want U.S. forces to remain in the region. Similarly, several smaller Persian Gulf states see the United States as a valuable counterweight to their larger neighbors.

States that do ally themselves with the United States do not do so passively. Indeed, they often go to considerable lengths to ensure that, in return, U.S. power is used in ways that further their own interests. By cultivating personal ties with U.S. officials, especially the president, foreign leaders such as Tony Blair seek to reinforce the United States' commitment to them and to affect how Washington wields its power. . . .

Foreign powers also attempt to take advantage of the unusual openness of the U.S. political system. After the September 11, 2001, attacks, Saudi Arabi launched a multimillion-dollar public relations campaign to counter the perception that the royal family was supporting terrorism. More commonly, foreign governments collaborate with domestic special-interest groups to encourage the U.S. government to support them. The open, decentralized, and divided U.S. political system is extremely vulnerable to this sort of manipulation. And the tradition of free speech and the multitude of media outlets also give organized interest groups considerable latitude. To influence U.S. foreign policy, foreign governments can court American journalists, hire paid lobbyists, cultivate key U.S. legislators and congressional aides, try to co-opt influential members of the executive branch, and mobilize sympathetic Americans to put pressure on their elected officials.

The most significant cases of foreign penetration occur when U.S. ethnic groups lobby on behalf of their traditional homelands. Such lobbying has promoted the causes of Armenia, Greece, Ireland, Israel, and Taiwan, for example. The efforts of these ethnic lobbies rely on familiar tools of political pressure, including campaign contributions, direct congressional lobbying, and extensive letter-writing or media campaigns. Several other ethnic groups are trying to imitate the well-documented success of organizations such as the Armenian Assembly of America, the American Hellenic Educational Progressive Association, and the American Israel Public Affairs Committee. Indian Americans, for example, have formed several political lobbying organizations in recent years. The groups' potential impact has not been lost on the Indian government: in 2004, an official Indian government commission concluded that "the Indian community in the United States constitutes an invaluable asset in strengthening India's relationship with the world's only superpower."

Apart from occasional attempts by some ethnic lobbies to silence U.S. domestic opposition to their agendas (attempts that violate the democratic principle of open debate), these activities are legitimate. But they could also entice the United States into acting against its best interests. Such influence can lead U.S. foreign policy astray precisely because the United States' dominant global position gives U.S. leaders so much latitude in making foreign policy decisions.

## OPPOSING AMERICAN POWER

Although countries use strategies of accommodation to further their own ambitions, the United States usually gets something important out of them: compliance. Many countries, however, are not content to achieve their goals by accommodating or allying themselves with the United States. When foreign powers have aims that are incompatible with U.S. policy, they must develop workable strategies of opposition. Some countries attempt to balance U.S. power by banding together against the United States or by developing specific military options; others try to bind U.S. power within the constraints of international institutions. Some resort to blackmail, attempting to extract concessions from Washington by threatening it with undesirable consequences such as the spread of nuclear weapons; others simply ignore or refuse U.S. demands. And many countries are trying to undermine U.S. power by attacking U.S. legitimacy, a strategy that Washington's recent actions have greatly facilitated. Such efforts to balance the power of the United States have thus far been muted, but they are beginning to hamstring U.S. foreign policy.

Although a number of leaders have openly called for a more multi-polar world, the global response to U.S. primacy does not resemble the coalitions that defeated

Germany in both world wars or the Soviet Union in the Cold War. The reason other nations have not forged a formal anti-U.S. alliance is simple: the United States does not pose the same level of threat. Yet states are beginning to join forces in subtler ways, with the explicit aim of checking U.S. power. Rather than forming an anti-U.S. alliance, countries are "soft balancing": coordinating their diplomatic positions to oppose U.S. policy and obtain more influence together. To name just a few examples: France, Germany, and Russia pursued a unified strategy that helped prevent the United States from obtaining UN Security Council authorization for the invasion of Iraq, and their actions allowed weaker states such as Mexico and Chile to resist U.S. pressure as well. Later, President Bush tried to persuade France, Germany, and the United Kingdom to get tough on Iran's nuclear programs, but he failed to drive a wedge between them and ended up endorsing their diplomatic campaign instead. Beyond Europe, combined opposition from Latin American countries has defeated the Bush administration's efforts to pressure the government of Hugo Chávez in Venezuela, thwarted U.S. attempts to select the new head of the Organization of American States, and blocked a U.S. proposal to create a "democracy review" panel within the OAS.

Some ways of balancing U.S. power are less benign, such as when countries mobilize their military resources and develop defensive strategies that exploit areas in which U.S. strength is not overwhelming. As the Pentagon's 2005 National Defense Strategy notes, "The U.S. military predominates in the world of *traditional* forms of warfare. Potential adversaries accordingly shift away from challenging the United States through *traditional* military actions and adopt asymmetric capabilities and methods" (italics in the original).

Weaker states typically rely on some combination of three broad options. First, they develop conventional military capabilities specifically designed to neutralize U.S. strengths. In the 1999 Kosovo war, Serbia used surface-to-air missiles as well as camouflage and other deceptive tactics to blunt NATO's air offensive. Facing a vastly stronger coalition, the Serbs eventually lost, but they performed far better than NATO expected. Similarly, China is now acquiring military capabilities—including anti-ship cruise missiles, ballistic missiles, and electronic countermeasure technologies—that could hinder U.S. forces if they tried to operate in China's neighborhood.

Second, adversaries sometimes depend on terrorism, the classic "weapon of the weak." Terrorists win by attacking the stronger side's resolve and forcing it to take actions that alienate potential supporters. Al Qaeda and the Iraqi insurgency use terrorism because it allows them to attack vulnerable targets while avoiding direct confrontation with superior U.S. forces. Terrorism can also provoke the United States into overreacting in ways that could increase opposition to the U.S. presence in the Middle East. Sometimes, the strategy works: terrorism helped bin Laden drive much of the U.S. presence out of Saudi Arabia—and it may still defeat the U.S. mission in Iraq.

Third, to balance U.S. primacy, some countries attempt to obtain weapons of mass destruction (WMD), especially nuclear arms. The current nuclear powers developed these weapons to deter their enemies, and that is why Iran and North Korea want them today. As one Iranian reformer stated, "It is basically a matter of equilibrium. If I don't have [nuclear weapons], I don't have security."

Instead of forming such a direct counterpoise to U.S. dominance, many states hope to constrain the United States by binding it within powerful international institutions. Binding works best in areas in which U.S. primacy is not so pronounced, such as international economic affairs. It is not, however, an effective strategy for restraining U.S. action in core areas of national security. The United States failed to obtain Security Council authorization for the wars in Kosovo and Iraq, but that did not stop it from waging them. Nor could Washington keep other states from establishing an International Criminal Court, even though it has refused to acknowledge the court's authority over the United States.

Binding works in economics because the United States is less dominant in that area and because international trade and finance cannot occur without commonly accepted rules. For example, although the rules of the World Trade Organization generally favor U.S. interests, Washington cannot prevent the organization from issuing unfavorable rulings when the United States violates its principles. Nor can Washington ignore these rulings without jeopardizing the trading order on which U.S. prosperity depends. Moreover, the United States cannot simply dictate the terms of multilateral trade agreements—which also helps explain Washington's propensity to negotiate bilateral deals with individual states. The United States can thus be partly bound in this arena, but less easily than other states.

Blackmailing the United States, on the other hand, is an especially effective strategy for states to use—if they can get away with it. Blackmailers must make a credible threat that the United States cannot easily guard against and demands that it can reasonably satisfy. As long as Washington believes that the demands will not be repeated, it may choose to comply. But blackmailing only works in very special circumstances. Threats to use WMD or give them to terrorists are not credible, because blackmailers would thereby trigger their own destruction. Threatening to acquire WMD is, however, another matter. North Korea has been using this threat to great effect, even though the power of the United States dwarfs that of North Korea. Yet Pyongyang was able to extract repeated concessions from Washington and its allies—most obviously in the 1994 Agreed Framework— simply by continuing to develop nuclear weapons. . . .

Even the United States' allies sometimes use blackmail to gain concessions— by threatening their own collapse if they do not receive more U.S. support. Afghan President Hamid Karzai and Pakistan's military leader, Pervez Musharraf, for example, have both won additional benefits by convincing Washington that radicals would seize power if their regimes were to fall.

Another strategy, balking, is a more passive way for states to limit U.S. power: when the United States demands something, they simply refuse. Balking is an especially effective method, too, because even a country as powerful as the United States cannot force every state to do its bidding all of the time. And the more some states balk, the more overextended the United States becomes—making it easier for other states to balk as well. Russia has balked, for example, when asked to end its nuclear collaboration with Iran, just as India and Pakistan balked by resisting U.S. pressure to forgo nuclear testing in 1998.

Balking is sometimes overt—as when Turkey refused to grant the United States use of its territory for the Iraq war—but many countries choose a subtler approach, formally acquiescing to U.S. demands and then doing as little as possible to fulfill them. Thus, Israel has repeatedly pledged to stop building settlements and the Palestinians have promised to crack down on militants, but neither side has actually done much. U.S. leaders are frequently tempted to look the other way when others balk, rather than risk a costly dispute or let others see that they can be openly defied.

Attacking U.S. legitimacy is also a favorite way to erode Washington's international clout. As the world's dominant power, the United States has much to gain from the perception that its power is legitimate. When people around the world believe that U.S. primacy advances broader global interests, Washington finds it easier to rally international support for its policies, leaving its opposition isolated and ineffective. Accordingly, the United States' opponents are currently seeking to convince others that Washington is selfish, hypocritical, immoral, and unsuited for world leadership, and that its dominance harms them. This assault on U.S. legitimacy does not directly challenge U.S. power, but it encourages other people to resent and resist U.S. supremacy.

Unfortunately, the United States has unwittingly given its critics a great deal of ammunition in recent years. Not only did the Bush administration disregard the UN Security Council when it launched its preventive war against Iraq, but its justification for the war turned out to be false, and its bungled occupation has inflicted new suffering on the Iraqi people. . . . The rest of the world sees the invasion as a demonstration of the dangers of unchecked U.S. power.

To make matters worse, U.S. policies since September 11 have reinforced the belief that the United States does not abide by its own ideals. The torture and abuse graphically documented at Abu Ghraib prison, the deaths of Muslim prisoners of war in U.S. custody, the desecration of the Koran by U.S. interrogators, the harsh treatment of and denial of due process to prisoners at Guantánamo Bay, and the conspicuous absence of a single high-level resignation in the wake of these revelations have all made it easy for the United States' critics to portray the country as quick to condemn everyone but itself. . . .

Like President Bush, who said that the Abu Ghraib abuses did not reflect "the America I know," Americans may dismiss these accusations as false, misleading, or exaggerated. But the issue is not what Americans think of their nation's conduct; the issue is how that conduct appears to others. Some of these accusations may be unfounded, but many are seen as valid. And they are rapidly draining the reservoir of international goodwill that makes the United States' status as a superpower acceptable to the world.

The United States is in a global struggle for hearts and minds, and it is losing. If anti-Americanism continues to grow, Washington will face greater resistance and find it harder to attract support. Americans will feel increasingly threatened in such a world, but trying to counter these threats alone will merely exacerbate the fear of U.S. power and isolate the United States even more.

## A NEW APPROACH

Over the last 15 years, the unipolar era has taught an important lesson: Americans may believe that their dominant position is good for the world, but other countries are far more ambivalent about U.S. supremacy and have developed ways to tame U.S. power. Ironically, then, instead of allowing the United States to act with impunity, primacy requires Washington to work harder to convince the other nations of the world that U.S. power is to be welcomed rather than feared.

A retreat to isolationism should be ruled out immediately. True, efforts to restrict U.S. strength would diminish if the United States withdrew from world affairs, but the benefits would not be worth the costs. Despite what critics may believe, the global community does indeed depend on the United States, to maintain the freedom of the seas, wage the war on terrorism, lead the campaign to control WMD, and underwrite the UN, the International Monetary Fund, and the World Bank, among other things. Washington's overarching influence also helps maintain a stable world order by dampening great-power rivalries in several regions. Few states would be safer or more prosperous if the United States withdrew completely.

Instead, the United States should resume its traditional role as an "offshore balancer." This strategy assumes that only a few parts of the world are of strategic importance to the United States, such as Europe, industrialized Asia, and the Persian Gulf. Instead of controlling these areas directly, the United States would rely on local actors to maintain the regional balance of power. The United States would still stand ready to deploy its power against specific threats to its interests, but it would intervene only when absolutely necessary—when the local balance broke down and vital U.S. interests were clearly threatened by hostile forces. In short, while remaining engaged with its allies, the United States should keep its military presence as small as possible. Reducing the size of the U.S. footprint would diminish the likelihood that foreign terrorists—especially suicide bombers—would target the United States, because such responses are most often triggered by perceived foreign occupation.

Being less directly involved on the ground would also bolster the United States' freedom of action. Washington would be able to play hard to get, making its support for others conditional on broad compliance with U.S. goals. Other states would be less likely to take U.S. protection for granted. By diminishing global concerns about U.S. dominance, this approach would also make it easier for Washington to gain global backing on those rare occasions when it needed to use force. Playing hard to get would not win over a recalcitrant regime such as that in Pyongyang, but it would make it easier for the United States to attract broad assistance for its policies in even those hard cases.

Most important, the United States must defend its international legitimacy. Washington must first recognize how it appears to others and then develop a sustained campaign to shape these perceptions. The United States cannot expect to win over the entire world, but it can surely do better than it has of late. . . .

To be effective, a public relations campaign needs a good product. If U.S. foreign policy makes global problems worse while U.S. government and military personnel trample on human rights, then no amount of public diplomacy will rescue the nation's image. To restore the moral stature it possessed before the abuses at Abu Ghraib, at Guantánamo, and in Afghanistan, Washington must sincerely apologize to the victims, and the senior officials responsible should be asked to resign. By failing to hold top officials accountable, the United States demonstrates that it values neither the rights of others nor its own ideals. It is hard to imagine a worse way to rebuild the nation's global image.

U.S. foreign policy must reflect a greater appreciation of what U.S. power can and cannot accomplish. Possessing unmatched strength does not mean the United States can or should impose its values on others, no matter how selfless Americans think their motives are. Instead of telling the world what to do and how to live—a temptation that both neoconservative empire-builders and liberal internationalists find hard to resist—the United States must lead by example. Over time, other nations will see how Americans live and what they stand for, and the rest of the world will want those things too. As Woodrow Wilson once counseled, the United States should "exercise the self-restraint of a really great nation, which realizes its own strength and scorns to misuse it."

. . . The United States' current task is to rebuild the sense of trust, admiration, and legitimacy it once enjoyed, so that the rest of the world can focus not on taming U.S. power but on reaping the benefits that it can bring.

# FAILED STATES, CIVIL WARS, AND NATION-BUILDING

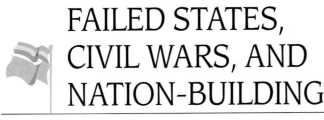

## Failed States, Collapsed States, Weak States: Causes and Indicators

ROBERT I. ROTBERG

This decade's failed states are Afghanistan, Angola, Burundi, the Congo, Liberia, Sierra Leone, and the Sudan. . . . Somalia is a collapsed state. Together they are the contemporary classical failed and collapsed states, but others were once collapsed or failed and many other modern nation-states now approach the brink of failure, some much more ominously than others. Another group of states drifts disastrously downward from weak to failing to failed. What is of particular interest is why and how states slip from weakness toward failure, or not. The list of weak states is long, but only a few of those weak and poorly governed states need necessarily edge into failure. Why? Even the categorization of a state as failing—Colombia and Indonesia, among others—need not doom it irretrievably to full failure. What does it take to drive a failing state over the edge into failure or collapse? . . .

How [could] Somalia, a nation-state of about 9 million people with a strongly cohesive cultural tradition, a common language, a common religion, and a shared history of nationalism . . . fail, and then collapse? Perhaps . . . it never constituted a single coherent territory, having been part of the colonial empires of two suzerains, with other Somalis living outside the boundaries of the two colonies. Then, as was often the experience elsewhere in Africa and Asia, the first elected, proto-democratic, post-independence civilian governments proved to be "experimental, inefficient, corrupt, and incapable of creating any kind of national political culture."[1] General Mohammed

From Robert I. Rotberg, "Failed States, Collapsed States, Weak States: Causes and Consequences," in Robert I. Rotberg, ed., *State Failure and State Weakness in a Time of Terror.* Cambridge, MA and Washington, DC: World Peace Foundation and the Brookings Institution Press, 2003, pp. 1–29.

Siad Barre, commander of the army, decided that the politicians were ruining the country, so he usurped power in 1969, suspending the constitution, banning political parties, and promising an end to corruption. Twenty years and many misadventures later, Siad Barre had succeeded in destroying any semblance of national governmental legitimacy. Backed first by the Soviet Union and then by the United States, Siad Barre destroyed institutions of government and democracy, abused his citizens' human rights, channeled as many of the resources of the state as possible into his own and his subclan's hands, and deprived everyone else at the end of the Cold War of what was left of the spoils of Somali supreme rule. All of the major clans and subclans, other than Siad Barre's own, became alienated. His shock troops perpetrated one outrage after another against fellow Somalis. By the onset of civil war in 1991, the Somali state had long since failed. The civil war destroyed what was left, and Somalia collapsed onto itself. . . .

President Stevens (1968–1985) systematically reduced human security within Sierra Leone so as to maximize his own personal power, and . . . that increase in personal power permitted a quantum leap in his control over the country's rents and riches. Stevens "sold chances to profit from disorder to those who could pay for it through providing services."[2] He created a private military force to terrorize his own people and to aggrandize, especially in the diamond fields. As the official rule of law receded, the law of the jungle, presided over by Stevens, took its place. Institutions of government were broken or corrupted. The state became illegitimate, and a civil war over spoils, encouraged and assisted from outside, turned failure into a collapse. In 2002, after hideous atrocities, a brutal intervention by a West African peace enforcement contingent, much more war, and the arrival of British paratroopers and a large UN peacekeeping force, Sierra Leone recovered sufficiently to be considered failed rather than collapsed. It even held effective elections.

Mobutu used analogous tactics in the patrimony of Zaire. As his people's self-proclaimed *guide*, or as the personalist embodiment of national leadership during the Cold War, he deployed the largesse of his American and other Western patrons to enhance his personal wealth, to heighten his stature over his countrymen, and to weave a tightly manipulated web of loyalties across the army and into all aspects of Zairese society. Every proper political and democratic institution was an obstacle to the edifice that he created. So was civil society, politics itself in the broad sense, and economic development. Letting the country's Belgian-built infrastructure rot, maintaining a colonial type of resource extraction (of copper, other metals, and diamonds), rebuffing the rise of a real bourgeoisie, and feeding his people false glories instead of real substance and per capita growth accentuated his own power, wealth, and importance. As with Stevens and Siad Barre, the modernizing state was the enemy. Mobutu had no sense of noblesse oblige. René Lemarchand says that for Mobutu's state, patronage was the indispensable lubricant. Ultimately, however, "the lubricant ran out and the Mobutist machine was brought to a . . . standstill. . . . The inability of the Mobutist state to generate a volume of rewards consistent with its clientelistic ambitions is the key . . . [to] . . . its rapid loss of legitimacy."[3]

The warring divisions of the failed Sudanese state, north and south, reflect fundamental ethnic, religious, and linguistic differences; Egyptian and British conquest and colonial administrative flaws and patterns; post-independence disparities and discriminations (the north dominating the south); and the discovery of oil in the south. A weak state in the north, providing political goods at minimal levels for its mostly Muslim constituents, became the nucleus of a truly failed state when its long war with the south (from 1955 to 1972 and from 1983 through 2002) entered the equation. The Sudanese war has the dubious distinction of having inflicted the largest number of civilian casualties (over 2 million) in any intrastate war, coupled with the largest internally displaced and refugee population in the world (about 4 million). Slavery (north against south) flourishes, as well. Moreover, in the south, the central government's writ rarely runs. It provides no political goods to its southern citizens, bombs them, raids them, and regards black southerners as enemy. As a result, the Sudan has long been failed. Yet, northerners still regard their state as legitimate, even though the southern insurgents do not and have sought either secession or autonomy for decades. . . . However, so long as oil revenues shore up the north, the Sudan is unlikely to collapse entirely. . . .

The paradigm of failure . . . holds equally well, with similar but differently detailed material, in Afghanistan, Angola, Burundi, and Liberia. . . . Indeed, Angola's killing fields and internally displaced circumstances are almost as intense and certainly as destructive as the Sudan's. The wars in Afghanistan, Angola, Burundi, and Liberia have been equally traumatic for ordinary combatants and hapless civilians unwittingly caught up in a vicious and (until 2002 in Angola) interminable battle for resources and power between determined opponents. Burundi's majority-minority war has produced fewer deaths in recent decades, but it continues an enduring contest for primacy that antedates the modern nation-state itself. From birth economically weak and geographically limited, Burundi's capacity to perform has for a decade been fatally crippled by majority-backed insurgencies against autocratic minority-led governments.

## WEAKNESS AND THE POSSIBILITY OF FAILURE

Collapsed and failed designate the consequences of a process of decay at the nation-state level. The capacity of those nation-states to perform positively for their citizens has atrophied. But . . . that atrophy is neither inevitable nor the result of happenstance. For a state to fail is not that easy. Crossing from weakness into failure takes will as well as neglect. Thus, weak nation-states need not tip into failure. . . .

There are several interesting cases that indeed test the precision of the distinction between weakness and failure:

Sri Lanka has been embroiled in a bitter and destructive civil war for nineteen years. As much as 15 percent of its total land mass has at times in the last decade been controlled by the rebel Liberation Tigers of Tamil Eeelam (LTTE), a Tamil separatist insurgency. Additionally, the LTTE with relative impunity has been able to assassinate prime ministers, bomb presidents, kill off rival Tamils, and in 2001, even destroy the nation's civil air terminal and main air force base. But, as incapable as the Sinhala-dominated governments of the island have been of putting down the LTTE rebellion, so the nation-state has remained merely weak . . . , never close to tipping over into failure. For 80 percent of Sri Lankans, the government performs reasonably well. The roads are maintained and schools and hospitals function, to some limited extent even in the war-torn north and east. Since the early 1990s, too, Sri Lanka has exhibited robust levels of economic growth. The authority of successive governments extends securely to the Sinhala-speaking 80 percent of the country, and into the recaptured Tamil areas. For these reasons, despite a consuming internal conflict founded on intense majority-minority discrimination and deprivation and on pronounced ethnic and religious differences, Sri Lanka projects authority throughout much of the country, has suffered no loss of legitimacy among Sinhala, and has successfully escaped failure.

Indonesia is another case of weakness avoiding failure despite widespread insecurity. As the world's largest Muslim nation, its far-flung archipelago harbors separatist wars in Aceh in the west and in Papua (formerly Irian Jaya) in the east, plus large pockets of Muslim-Christian conflict in Ambon and the Maluku islands, Muslim-Christian hostility in northern Sulawesi, and ethnic xenophobic outbursts in Kalimantan. Given all of these conflictual situations, none of which has become less bitter since the end of the Soeharto dictatorship, it would be easy to conclude that Indonesia was approaching failure. Yet. . . only the insurgents in Aceh and Papua want to secede and are contesting the state. The several other battles take place within the state, not against it. They do not threaten the integrity and resources of the state in the way that the enduring, but low-level, war in Aceh does. In Aceh and Papua, the government retains the upper hand. Overall, most of Indonesia is still secure. In most of the country the government projects power and authority. It manages to provide most other necessary political goods to most of Indonesia despite dangerous economic and other developments in the post-Soeharto era.

What about Colombia? An otherwise well-endowed, prosperous, and ostensibly stable state controls only two-thirds of its territory, a clear hint of failure. Three private armies project their own power across large zones carved out of the very body of the state. The official defense and political establishment has renounced or lost authority in those zones to insurgent groups and drug traffickers. Moreover, Colombia is tense and disturbed. It boasts the second highest annual per capita murder rate in the world. Its politicians and businessmen routinely wear armored vests and travel with well-armed guards, a clear indicator of the state's inability to ensure personal security. Even so . . . the rest of Colombia as a state still delivers schooling and medical care, organizes a physical and communications infrastructure, provides economic opportunity, and remains legitimate. Colombia is weak because of its multiple insurgencies, but is comparatively strong and well-performing in the areas over which it maintains control. When and if the government of Colombia can re-insert itself into the disputed zones and further reduce the power of drug traffickers, the state's reach will expand. Then, a weak, endangered state will be able to move farther away from possible failure toward strength.

Zimbabwe is an example of a once unquestionably strong African state that has fallen rapidly through weakness to the very edge of the abyss of failure. All Zimbabwe lacks in order to join the ranks of failed states is a widespread internal insurgent movement directed against the government. That could come, particularly if the political and economic deterioration of the country continues unchecked. In 2000 and 2001, GDP per capita slid backward by 10 percent a year. Inflation galloped from 30 percent to 116 percent. The local currency fell against the U.S. dollar from 38:1 to 500:1. Foreign and domestic investment ceased. Unemployment rose to 60 percent in a country of 12 million. Health and educational services vanished. HIV infection rates climbed to 30 percent, with about 2000 Zimbabweans dying every week. Respect for the rule of law was badly battered and then subverted. Political institutions ceased to function fully. Agents of the state preyed on its real and its supposed opponents, chilling free expression and shamelessly stealing a presidential election. The government's legitimacy vanished. Corruption, meanwhile, flourished, with the ruling elite pocketing their local and Congolese war gains and letting most Zimbabweans go hungry. Real starvation appeared in mid-2002, despite food aid from abroad. All of this misery, and the tendency to fail, resulted (as it had earlier in the Congo and Sierra Leone) from the ruthless designs and vengeance of an omnipotent ruler. . . .

A number of other nation-states belong in the category of weak states that show a high potential to fail. Nepal has been a clear case since its Maoist insurgency began again roiling the mountains and plains of the monarchist country. Already hindered by geography and poverty, Nepal has never been a robust provider of political goods to its inhabitants. The palace massacre of 2001 undermined the legitimacy of the monarchy, and thus of the ruling government. With the flare-up of a determined rural rebellion in 2002, and Nepal's demonstrated inability to cope effectively, security of persons and of regions became harder and harder to achieve, absent military assistance from India. Under these circumstances, Nepal can hardly project power or credibility. Failure becomes a distinct possibility. . . .

A third variety of weak state includes the enduringly weak. . . . Haiti has always been on the edge of failure, particularly during the nineteenth and twentieth centuries. But its entrenched weaknesses include no ethnic, religious, or other communal cleavages. There are no insurgent movements. Nor has Haiti experienced radical or rapid deflation in standards of living and national expectations, like Argentina in 2002 and Russia in the 1990s. Haiti has always been the poorest polity in the Western hemisphere.

Haiti's national capacity to provide political goods has always been compromised by autocratic and corrupt leadership, weak institutions, an intimidated civil society, high levels of crime, low GDP levels per capita, high rates of infant mortality, suspicion or outright hostility from its neighbors, and many other deficiencies. Narcotics trafficking has been a serious problem since the 1980s. The Haitian government has been unable or unwilling to interdict smugglers in general, and drugs transshippers in particular. Haiti, even under President Jean-Bertrand Aristide (1990–1991, 1994–1995, 2000– ), is gripped in a vise of weakness. Yet, given very limited organized internal dissidence, almost no internal ethnic, religious, or linguistic cleavages within Haitian society except a deep distrust by the majority of the upper classes, and of mulattos because of their historic class affiliations, the ingredients of major civil strife are absent. Failure demands communal differences capable of being transformed into consuming cross-group violence. Haiti seems condemned to remain weak, but without failing.

Nation-states that, given their geographical and physical legacy (and future peril, in several cases, because of global warming and cataclysmic climatic change), can be considered inherently weak include (not a full list) Burkina Faso, Chad, Ghana, Guinea, and Niger, in Africa; Georgia and Moldova in the former Soviet Union, and Cambodia, East Timor, and Laos in Asia. Each has its own distinguishing features, and Georgia and Moldova battle their own so far successful separatist movements. Chad at one time harbored a vicious civil war, and Burkina Faso, Niger, Cambodia, and Laos are all ruled by autocrats unfriendly to civil society and to participatory governance. East Timor is a very new state, having been rescued and resuscitated by the United Nations after two bitter and unrewarding colonial interludes and a brutal final Indonesian spree of destruction and death. East Timor, even with UN help, enters its full majority without a cadre of experienced professionals and bureaucrats and without much in the way of physical resources. The willingness of these weak states to provide political goods in quantity and quality is severely limited at the best of times. Almost any external shock or internal emergency could push them over the brink.

## INDICATORS OF FAILURE

As this chapter has suggested earlier, the road to nation-state failure is littered with serious mistakes of omission and commission. Even in the modern states with inherited weaknesses, failure is not preordained. Poor, arbitrary, absent-minded creations predisposed to failure need not fail. Indeed, Botswana, dirt poor at independence and a forlorn excuse for a state, under determined and visionary leadership created a state strong enough to take full advantage of a subsequent, and much unexpected, resource bonanza. Similarly, a sugar monoculture like Mauritius was transformed by determined visionary leadership into a thriving plural society based on manufacturing for export. In contrast, Malawi and Mali (two examples among many) remain weak and very poor, albeit democratic, having both been unable, in their different circumstances, to overcome the arbitrary configuration of their borders, a common absence of easily exploitable resources, geographical hindrances, and decades of despotism. Climatic change may hit both Malawi and Mali particularly hard, too.

Nation-states are blessed or cursed by the discovery or absence of natural resources, like oil or diamonds, within received borders. But it is not the accidental quality of their borders that is the original flaw; it is what has been made of the challenges and opportunities of a given outline that determines whether a state remains weak, becomes stronger, or slides toward failure and collapse. The colonial errors were many, especially the freeing of Africa south of the Sahara as forty-eight administrative territories instead of six or seven larger ones, and the abysmal failure to transfer the reins of authority much earlier and much more thoroughly to an indigenat. But it is not possible to predict this century's candidates for failure solely or even largely on the basis of colonial mistreatment. . . .

Three kinds of signals of impending failure—economic, political, and deaths in combat—provide clearer, more timely, and more actionable warnings. On the economic front, Indonesia in 1997–1999, Nigeria in 1993–1999, Lebanon in 1972–1979, and Zimbabwe in 2001–2002, each provide instances of how rapid reductions in incomes and living standards indicated the possibility of failure early enough to be noted and for preventive measures to have been attempted. Once the downward spiral starts in earnest, only a concerted, determined effort can slow its momentum; corrupt autocrats and their equally corrupt associates usually have few incentives to arrest their state's slide, since they find clever ways to benefit from impoverishment and misery. As foreign and domestic investment dries up, jobs vanish, and per capita incomes fall, the mass of citizens in an imperiled state see their health, educational, and logistical entitlements melt away. Food and fuel shortages occur. Privation and hunger follow, especially if a climatic catastrophe intervenes. Thanks to foreign exchange scarcities, there is less and less of everything that matters. Meanwhile, in the typical failing state, ruling families and cadres arrogate to themselves increasing portions of the available pie. They systematically skim the state treasury, take advantage of official versus street costs of foreign exchange, partake of smuggling and the rents of smuggling, and gather what little is available into their own sticky palms. If it were possible reliably to calibrate the flow of illicit funds into overseas accounts, nation by nation, robust early warnings would be available. Absent detailed reports of such theft, the descriptors in this paragraph become very suggestive indicators that can be watched, in real time, and can forecast serious trouble, if not an end state of failure.

Politically, the available indicators are equally clear, if somewhat less quantifiably precise. A leader and his associates begin by subverting democratic norms, greatly restricting participatory processes, and coercing a legislature and the bureaucracy into subservience. They end judicial independence, block civil society, and suborn the security forces. Political goods become scarce or are supplied to the leading class only. The rulers demonstrate more and more contempt for their peoples, surround themselves with family, clan, or ethnic allies, and distance themselves from their subjects. The state becomes equated in the eyes of most citizens with the particular drives and desires of a leader and a smallish group. Many of these leaders drive grandly down their boulevards in motorcades, commandeer commercial aircraft for foreign excursions, and put their faces prominently on the local currency, on airports and ships, and on oversize photographs in public places.

The third indicator is the level of violence. If it rises precipitously because of skirmishes, hostilities, or outright civil war, the state can be considered crumbling. As national human security rates fall, the probability of failure rises. Not every civil conflict precipitates failure, but each offers a warning sign. Absolute or relative crime rates and civilian combat death counts above a certain number cannot prescribe failure. But they show that a society is deteriorating and that the glue that binds a new (or an old) state together is becoming fatally thin.

No single indicator provides certain evidence that a strong state is becoming weak or a weak state is heading pell-mell into failure. But a judicious assessment of the several available indicators discussed in this section, taken together, should provide both quantifiable and qualitative warnings. Then avoidance maneuvers can occur and efforts at prevention can be mounted. . . .

## THE HAND OF MAN

State failure is largely man made, not accidental. Institutional fragilities and structural flaws contribute to failure, but those deficiencies usually hark back to decisions or actions of men (rarely women). So it is that leadership errors across history have destroyed states for personal gain; in the contemporary era, leadership mistakes continue to erode fragile polities in Africa, Asia, and Oceania that already operate on the cusp of failure. . . .

Wherever there has been state failure or collapse, human agency has engineered the slide from strength or weakness and willfully presided over profound and destabilizing resource shifts from the state to the ruling few. As those resource transfers accelerated and human rights abuses mounted, countervailing violence signified the extent to which states in question had broken fundamental social contracts and become hollow receptacles of personalist privilege, personalist rule, and national impoverishment. Inhabitants of failed states understand what it means for life to be brutish and short.

In earlier, less interconnected eras, state weakness and failure could be isolated and kept distant from the developed world. Failure once held fewer implications for the surrounding regions and for the peace and security of the globe. Now, however, as much as their citizens suffer, the failings of states also pose enormous dangers beyond their own borders. Preventing nation-states from failing, and resuscitating those that have failed and will fail, have thus become the critical, all-consuming, strategic and moral imperatives of our terrorized time. The chapters in this book demonstrate how and why states have failed and will fail, and how weak states have in several cases been spared the descent into despair and destruction.

## NOTES

1. Walter Clarke and Robert Gosende, "Somalia: Can a Collapsed State Reconstitute Itself," in Robert Rotberg, ed., *State Failure and State Weakness in a Time of Terror* (Washington, D.C.: Brookings Institution, 2003), 129–158.
2. William Reno, "Sierra Leone: Warfare in a Post-State Society," in Rotberg, ed., 75.
3. René Lemarchand, "The Democratic Republic of the Congo: From Failure to Potential Reconstruction," in Rotberg, ed., 37.

# Possible and Impossible Solutions to Ethnic Civil Wars

## CHAIM KAUFMANN

. . . This paper offers a theory of how ethnic wars end, and proposes an intervention strategy based on it.[1] The theory rests on two insights: First, in ethnic wars both hypernationalist mobilization rhetoric and real atrocities harden ethnic identities to the point that cross-ethnic political appeals are unlikely to be made and even less likely to be heard. Second, intermingled population settlement patterns create real security dilemmas that intensify violence, motivate ethnic "cleansing," and prevent de-escalation unless the groups are separated. As a result, restoring civil politics in multi-ethnic states shattered by war is impossible because the war itself destroys the possibilities for ethnic cooperation.

Stable resolutions of ethnic civil wars are possible, but only when the opposing groups are demographically separated into defensible enclaves. Separation reduces both incentives and opportunity for further combat, and largely eliminates both reasons and chances for ethnic cleansing of civilians. While ethnic fighting can be stopped by other means, such as peace enforcement by international forces or by a conquering empire, such peaces last only as long as the enforcers remain.

This means that to save lives threatened by genocide, the international community must abandon attempts to restore war-torn multi-ethnic states. Instead, it must facilitate and protect population movements to create true national homelands. Sovereignty is secondary: Defensible ethnic enclaves reduce violence with or without independent sovereignty, while partition without separation does nothing to stop mass killing. Once massacres have taken place, ethnic cleansing will occur. The alternative is to let the *interahamwe* and the Chetniks "cleanse" their enemies in their own way.

The remainder of this paper has three parts. The next part develops a theory of how ethnic wars end. Then, I present a strategy for international military intervention to stop ethnic wars and dampen future violence and rebut possible objections to this strategy. The conclusion addresses the moral and political stakes in humanitarian intervention in ethnic conflicts.

From Chaim Kaufmann, "Possible and Impossible Solutions to Ethnic Civil Wars," *International Security*, Vol. 20, No. 4 (Spring 1996), pp. 136–175. © 1996 by the President and Fellows of Harvard College and the Massachusetts Institute of Technology. Reprinted by permission of The MIT Press.

## HOW ETHNIC CIVIL WARS END

Civil wars are not all alike. Ethnic conflicts are disputes between communities which see themselves as having distinct heritages over the power relationship between the communities, while ideological civil wars are contests between factions within the same community over how that community should be governed.[2] The key difference is the flexibility of individual loyalties, which are quite fluid in ideological conflicts, but almost completely rigid in ethnic wars.[3]

The possible and impossible solutions to ethnic civil wars follow from this fact. War hardens ethnic identities to the point that cross-ethnic political appeals become futile, which means that victory can be assured only by physical control over the territory in dispute. Ethnic wars also generate intense security dilemmas, both because the escalation of each side's mobilization rhetoric presents a real threat to the other, and even more because intermingled population settlement patterns create defensive vulnerabilities and offensive opportunities.

Once this occurs, the war cannot end until the security dilemma is reduced by physical separation of the rival groups. Solutions that aim at restoring multi-ethnic civil politics and at avoiding population transfers—such as power-sharing, state rebuilding, or identity reconstruction—cannot work because they do nothing to dampen the security dilemma, and because ethnic fears and hatreds hardened by war are extremely resistant to change.

The result is that ethnic wars can end in only three ways: with complete victory of one side; by temporary suppression of the conflict by third party military occupation; or by self-governance of separate communities. The record of the ethnic wars of the last half century bears this out.

### The Dynamics of Ethnic War

It is useful to compare characteristics of ethnic conflicts with those of ideological conflicts. The latter are competitions between the government and the rebels for the loyalties of the people. The critical features of these conflicts are that ideological loyalties are changeable and difficult to assess, and the same population serves as the shared mobilization base for both sides. As a result, winning the "hearts and minds" of the population is both possible and necessary for victory. The most important instruments are political, economic, and social reforms that redress popular grievances such as poverty, inequality, corruption, and physical insecurity. Control of access to population is also important, both to allow recruitment and implementation of reform promises, and to block the enemy from these tasks. Population control, however, cannot be guaranteed solely by physical control over territory, but depends on careful intelligence, persuasion, and coercion. Purely military successes are often indecisive as long as the enemy's base of political support is undamaged.

Ethnic wars, however, have nearly the opposite properties. Individual loyalties are both rigid and transparent, while each side's mobilization base is limited to members of its own group in friendly-controlled territory. The result is that ethnic conflicts are primarily military struggles in which victory depends on physical control over the disputed territory, not on appeals to members of the other group.

### Identity in Ethnic Wars

Competition to sway individual loyalties does not play an important role in ethnic civil wars, because ethnic identities are fixed by birth. While not everyone may be mobilized as an active fighter for his or her own group, hardly anyone ever fights for the opposing ethnic group.

Different identity categories imply their own membership rules. Ideological identity is relatively soft, as it is a matter of individual belief, or sometimes of political behavior. Religious identities are harder, because while they also depend on belief, change generally requires formal acceptance by the new faith, which may be denied. Ethnic identities are hardest, since they depend on language, culture, and religion, which are hard to change, as well as parentage, which no one can change.

Ethnic identities are hardened further by intense conflict, so that leaders cannot broaden their appeals to include members of opposing groups. As ethnic conflicts escalate, populations come increasingly to hold enemy images of the other group, either because of deliberate efforts by elites to create such images or because of increasing real threats. . . .

Once the conflict reaches the level of large-scale violence, tales of atrocities—true or invented—perpetuated or planned against members of the group by the ethnic enemy provide hard-liners with an unanswerable argument. In March 1992 a Serb woman in Foca in Eastern Bosnia was convinced that "there were lists of Serbs who were marked for death. My two sons were down on the list to be slaughtered like pigs. I was listed under rape." The fact that neither she nor other townspeople had seen any such lists did not prevent them from believing such tales without question.[4] The Croatian Ustasha in World War II went further, terrorizing Serbs in order to provoke a backlash that could then be used to mobilize Croats for defense against Serb retaliation.

In this environment, cross-ethnic appeals are not likely to attract members of the other group. The Yugoslav Partisans in World War II are often credited with transcending the ethnic conflict between the Croatian Ustasha and the Serbian Chetniks with an anti-German, pan-Yugoslav program. In fact it did not work. Tito was a Croat, but Partisan officers as well as the rank and file were virtually all Serbs and Montenegrins. Only in 1944, when German withdrawal made Partisan victory certain, did Croats begin to join the Partisans in numbers, not because they preferred a multi-ethnic Yugoslavia to a Greater Croatia, but because they preferred a multi-ethnic Yugoslavia to a Yugoslavia cleansed of Croatians. . . .

Ethnic war also shrinks scope for individual identity choice. Even those who put little value on their ethnic identity are pressed towards ethnic mobilization for two reasons. First, extremists within each community are likely to impose sanctions on those who do not contribute to the cause. In 1992 the leader of the Croatian Democratic Union in Bosnia was dismissed on the ground that he "was too much Bosnian, too little Croat." Conciliation is easy to denounce as dangerous to group security or as actually traitorous. Such arguments drove nationalist extremists to overthrow President Makarios of Cyprus in 1974, to assassinate Mahatma Gandhi in 1948, to massacre nearly the whole government of Rwanda in 1994, and to kill Yitzhak Rabin in 1995.

Second and more important, identity is often imposed by the opposing group, specifically by its most murderous members. Assimilation or political passivity did no good for German Jews, Rwandan Tutsis, or Azerbaijanis in Nagorno-Karabakh. A Bosnian Muslim schoolteacher recently lamented:

> We never, until the war, thought of ourselves as Muslims. We were Yugoslavs. But when we began to be murdered, because we are Muslims, things changed. The definition of who we are today has been determined by our killers.[5]

Choice contracts further the longer the conflict continues. Multi-ethnic towns as yet untouched by war are swamped by radicalized refugees, undermining moderate leaders who preach tolerance. For example, while a portion of the pre-war Serb population remained in Bosnian government-controlled Sarajevo when the fighting started, their numbers have declined as the government has taken on a more narrowly Muslim religious character over years of war, and pressure on Serbs has increased. Where 80,000 remained in July 1993, only 30,000 were left in August 1995. The Tutsi Rwandan Patriotic Front (RPF) showed remarkable restraint during the 1994 civil war, but since then the RPF has imprisoned tens of thousands of genocide suspects in appalling conditions, failed to prevent massacres of thousands of Hutu civilians in several incidents, and allowed Tutsi squatters to seize the property of many absent Hutus.

What can finally eliminate identity choice altogether is fear of genocide. The hypernationalist rhetoric used for group mobilization often includes images of the enemy group as a threat to the physical existence of the nation, in turn justifying unlimited violence against the ethnic enemy; this threatening discourse can usually be observed by members of the target group. Even worse are actual massacres of civilians, especially when condoned by leaders of the perpetrating group, which are virtually certain to convince the members of the targeted group that group defense is their only option. . . .

### Identifying Loyalties

A consequence of the hardness of ethnic identities is that in ethnic wars assessing individual loyalties is much easier than in ideological conflicts. Even if some members of both groups remain unmobilized, as long as virtually none actively support the other group, each side can treat all co-ethnics as friends without risk of coddling an enemy agent and can treat all members of the other group as enemies without risk of losing a recruit.

Although it often requires effort, each side can almost always identify members of its own and the other group in any territory it controls. Ethnicity can be identified by outward appearance, public or private records, and local social knowledge. In societies where ethnicity is important, it is often officially recorded in personal identity documents or in censuses. In 1994 Rwandan death squads used neighborhood target lists prepared in advance, as well as roadblocks that checked identity cards. In 1983 riots in Sri Lanka, Sinhalese mobs went through mixed neighborhoods selecting Tamil dwellings for destruction with the help of Buddhist monks carrying electoral lists. While it might not have been possible to predict the Yugoslav civil war thirty years in advance, one could have identified the members of each of the warring groups from the 1961 census, which identified the nationality of all but 1.8 percent of the population.

Where public records are not adequate, private ones can be used instead. Pre–World War II Yugoslav censuses relied on church records. Absent any records at all, reliable demographic intelligence can often be obtained from local co-ethnics. . . .

Finally, in unprepared encounters ethnicity can often be gauged by outward appearance: Tutsis are generally tall and thin, while Hutus are relatively short and stocky; Russians are generally fairer than Kazakhs. When physiognomy is ambiguous, other signs such as language or accent, surname, dress, posture, ritual mutilation, diet, habits, occupation, region or neighborhood within urban areas, or certain possessions may give clues. Residents of Zagreb, for example, are marked as Serbs by certain names, attendance at an Orthodox church, or possession of books printed in Cyrillic.

Perhaps the strongest evidence of intelligence reliability in ethnic conflicts is that—in dramatic contrast to ideological insurgencies—history records almost no instances of mistaken "cleansing" of co-ethnics.

### The Decisiveness of Territory

Another consequence of the hardness of ethnic identities is that population control depends wholly on territorial control. Since each side can recruit only from its own community and only in friendly-controlled territory, incentives to seize areas populated by co-ethnics are strong, as is the pressure to cleanse friendly-controlled territory of enemy ethnics by relocation to *de facto* concentration camps, expulsion, or massacre.

Because of the decisiveness of territorial control, military strategy in ethnic wars is very different than in ideological conflicts. Unlike ideological insurgents, who often evade rather than risk battle, or a counter-insurgent government, which might forbear to attack rather than risk bombarding civilians, ethnic combatants must fight for every piece of land. By contrast, combatants in ethnic wars are much less free to decline unfavorable battles because they cannot afford to abandon any settlement to an enemy who is likely to "cleanse" it by massacre, expulsion, destruction of homes, and possibly colonization. By the time a town can be retaken, its value will have been lost.

In ethnic civil wars, military operations are decisive. Attrition matters because the side's mobilization pools are separate and can be depleted. Most important, since each side's mobilization base is limited to members of its own community in friendly-controlled territory, conquering the enemy's population centers reduces its mobilization base, while loss of friendly settlements reduces one's own. Military control of the entire territory at issue is tantamount to total victory.

## Security Dilemmas in Ethnic Wars

The second problem that must be overcome by any remedy for severe ethnic conflict is the security dilemma. Regardless of the origins of ethnic strife, once violence (or abuse of state power by one group that controls it) reaches the point that ethnic communities cannot rely on the state to protect them, each community must mobilize to take responsibility for its own security.

Under conditions of anarchy, each group's mobilization constitutes a real threat to the security of others for two reasons. First, the nationalist rhetoric that accompanies mobilization often seems to and often does indicate offensive intent. Under these conditions, group identity itself can be seen by other groups as a threat to their safety.

Second, military capability acquired for defense can usually also be used for offense. Further, offense often has an advantage over defense in inter-community conflict, especially when settlement patterns are inter-mingled, because isolated pockets are harder to hold than to take.

The reality of the mutual security threats means that solutions to ethnic conflicts must do more than undo the causes; until or unless the security dilemma can be reduced or eliminated, neither side can afford to demobilize.

### Demography and Security Dilemmas

The severity of ethnic security dilemmas is greatest when demography is most intermixed, weakest when community settlements are most separate. The more mixed the opposing groups, the stronger the offense in relation to the defense; the more separated they are, the stronger the defense in relation to offense.[6] When settlement patterns are extremely mixed, both sides are vulnerable to attack not only by organized military forces but also by local militias or gangs from adjacent towns or neighborhoods. Since well-defined fronts are impossible, there is no effective means of defense against such raids. Accordingly, each side has a strong incentive—at both national and local levels—to kill or drive out enemy populations before the enemy does the same to it, as well as to create homogeneous enclaves more practical to defend.

Better, but still bad, are well-defined enclaves with islands of one or both sides' populations behind the other's front. Each side then has an incentive to attack to rescue its surrounded co-ethnics before they are destroyed by the enemy, as well as incentives to wipe out enemy islands behind its own lines, both to pre-empt rescue attempts and to eliminate possible bases for fifth columnists or guerrillas.

The safest pattern is a well-defined demographic front that separates nearly homogeneous regions. Such a front can be defended by organized military forces, so populations are not at risk unless defenses are breached. At the same time the strongest motive for attack disappears, since there are few or no endangered co-ethnics behind enemy lines.

Further, offensive and defensive mobilization measures are more distinguishable when populations are separated than when they are mixed. Although hypernationalist political rhetoric, as well as conventional military forces, have both offensive and defensive uses regardless of population settlement patterns, some other forms of ethnic mobilization do not. Local militias and ethnically based local self-governing authorities have both offensive and defensive capabilities when populations are mixed: Ethnic militias can become death squads, while local governments dominated by one group can disenfranchise minorities. When populations are separated, however, such local organizations have defensive value only.

## War and Ethnic Unmixing

Because of the security dilemma, ethnic war causes ethnic unmixing. The war between Greece and Turkey, the partition of India, the 1948–49 Arab-Israeli war, and the recent war between Armenia and Azerbaijan were all followed by emigration or expulsion of most of the minority populations on each side. More than one million Ibo left northern Nigeria during the Nigerian Civil War. Following 1983 pogroms, three-fourths of the Tamil population of Colombo fled to the predominantly Tamil north and east of the island. By the end of 1994, only about 70,000 non-Serbs remained in Serb-controlled areas of Bosnia, with less than 40,000 Serbs still in Muslim- and Croat-controlled regions. Of 600,000 Serbs in pre-war Croatia, probably no more than 100,000 remain outside of Serb-controlled eastern Slavonia.

Collapse of multi-ethnic states often causes some ethnic unmixing even without war. The retreat of the Ottoman Empire from the Balkans sparked movement of Muslims southward and eastward as well as some unmixing of different Christian peoples in the southern Balkans. Twelve million Germans left Eastern Europe after World War II, one and a half million between 1950 and 1987, and another one and a half million since 1989, essentially dissolving the German diaspora. Of 25 million Russians outside Russia in 1989, as many as three to four million had gone to Russia by the end of 1992. From 1990 to 1993, 200,000 Hungarians left Vojvodina, replaced by 400,000 Serb refugees from other parts of ex-Yugoslavia.

## Ethnic Separation and Peace

Once ethnic groups are mobilized for war, the war cannot end until the populations are separated into defensible, mostly homogeneous regions. Even if an international force or an imperial conqueror were to impose peace, the conflict would resume as soon as it left. Even if a national government were somehow re-created despite mutual suspicions, neither group could safely entrust its security to it. Continuing mutual threat also ensures perpetuation of hypernationalist propaganda, both for mobilization and because the plausibility of the threat posed by the enemy gives radical nationalists an unanswerable advantage over moderates in intra-group debates.

Ethnic separation does not guarantee peace, but it allows it. Once populations are separated, both cleansing and rescue imperatives disappear; war is no longer mandatory. At the same time, any attempt to seize more territory requires a major conventional military offensive. Thus the conflict changes from one of mutual pre-emptive ethnic cleansing to something approaching conventional interstate war in which normal deterrence dynamics apply. Mutual deterrence does not guarantee that there will be no further violence, but it reduces the probability of outbreaks, as well as the likely aims and intensity of those that do occur.

There have been no wars among Bulgaria, Greece, and Turkey since their population exchanges of the 1920s. Ethnic violence on Cyprus, which reached crisis on several occasions between 1960 and 1974, has been zero since the partition and population exchange which followed Turkish invasion. The Armenian-Azeri ethnic conflict, sparked by independence demands of the mostly Armenian Nagorno-Karabakh Autonomous Oblast, escalated to full-scale war by 1992. Armenian conquest of all of

Karabakh together with the land which formerly separated it from Armenia proper, along with displacement of nearly all members of each group from enemy-controlled territories, created a defensible separation with no minorities to fight over, leading to a cease-fire in April 1994.

## THEORIES OF ETHNIC PEACE

Those considering humanitarian intervention to end ethnic civil wars should set as their goal lasting safety, rather than perfect peace. Given the persistence of ethnic rivalries, "safety" is best defined as freedom from threats of ethnic murder, expropriation, or expulsion for the overwhelming majority of civilians of all groups. Absence of formal peace, even occasional terrorism or border skirmishes, would not undermine this, provided that the great majority of civilians are not at risk. "Lasting" must mean that the situation remains stable indefinitely after the intervention forces leave. Truces of weeks, months, or even years do not qualify as lasting safety if ethnic cleansing eventually resumes with full force.

### Alternatives to Separation

Besides demographic separation, the literature on possible solutions to ethnic conflicts contains four main alternatives: suppression, reconstruction of ethnic identities, power-sharing, and state-building.

#### Suppression
Many ethnic civil wars lead to the complete victory of one side and the forcible suppression of the other. This may reduce violence in some cases, but will never be an aim of outsiders considering humanitarian intervention. Further, remission of violence may be only temporary, as the defeated group usually rebels again at any opportunity. Even the fact that certain conquerors, such as the English in Scotland or the Dutch in Friesland, eventually permitted genuine political assimilation after decades of suppression, does not recommend this as a remedy for endangered peoples today.

#### Reconstruction of Ethnic Identities
The most ambitious program to end ethnic violence would be to reconstruct ethnic identities according to the "Constructivist Model" of nationalism. Constructivists argue that individual and group identities are fluid, continually being made and re-made in social discourse. Further, these identities are manipulable by political entrepreneurs. Violent ethnic conflicts are the result of pernicious group identities created by hypernationalist myth-making; many inter-group conflicts are quite recent, as are the ethnic identities themselves.

The key is elite rivalries within communities, in which aggressive leaders use hypernationalist propaganda to gain and hold power. History does not matter; whether past inter-community relations have in fact been peaceful or conflictual, leaders can redefine, reinterpret, and invent facts to suit their arguments, including alleged atrocities and exaggerated or imagined threats. This process can feed on itself, as nationalists use the self-fulfilling nature of their arguments both to escalate the conflict and to justify their own power, so that intra-community politics becomes a competition in hypernationalist extremism, and inter-community relations enter a descending spiral of violence.

It follows that ethnic conflicts generated by the promotion of pernicious, exclusive identities should be reversible by encouraging individuals and groups to adopt more benign, inclusive identities. Leaders can choose to mobilize support on the basis of broader identities that transcend the ethnic division, such as ideology, class, or civic loyalty to the nation-state. If members of the opposing groups can be persuaded to adopt a larger identity, ethnic antagonisms should fade away. . . .

However, even if ethnic hostility can be "constructed," there are strong reasons to believe that violent conflicts cannot be "reconstructed" back to ethnic harmony. Identity reconstruction under conditions of intense conflict is probably impossible because once ethnic groups are mobilized for war, they will have already produced, and will continue reproducing, social institutions and discourses that reinforce their group identity and shut out or shout down competing identities.

Replacement of ethnicity by some other basis for political identification requires that political parties have cross-ethnic appeal, but examples of this in the midst of ethnic violence are virtually impossible to find. . . . In fact, even ethnic tension far short of war often undermines not just political appeals across ethnic lines but also appeals within a single group for cooperation with other groups. In Yugoslavia in the 1920s, Malaya in the 1940s, Ceylon in the 1950s, and in Nigeria in the 1950s and 1960, parties that advocated cooperation across ethnic lines proved unable to compete with strictly nationalist parties.

Even if constructivists are right that the ancient past does not matter, recent history does. Intense violence creates personal experiences of fear, misery, and loss which lock people into their group identity and their enemy relationship with the other group. Elite as well as mass opinions are affected; more than 5,000 deaths in the 1946 Calcutta riots convinced many previously optimistic Hindu and Muslim leaders that the groups could not live together. The Tutsi-controlled government of Burundi, which had witnessed the partial genocide against Tutsis in Rwanda in 1962–63 and survived Hutu-led coup attempts in 1965 and 1969, regarded the 1972 rebellion as another attempt at genocide, and responded by murdering between 100,000 and 200,000 Hutus. Fresh rounds of violence in 1988 and 1993–94 have reinforced the apocalyptic fears of both sides.

Finally, literacy preserves atrocity memories and enhances their use for political mobilization.[7] The result is that atrocity histories cannot be reconstructed; victims can sometimes be persuaded to accept exaggerated atrocity tales, but cannot be talked out of real ones. The result is that the bounds of debate are permanently altered; the leaders who used World War II Croatian atrocities to whip up Serbian nationalism in the 1980s were making use of a resource which, since then, remains always available in Serbian political discourse.

If direct action to transform exclusive ethnic identities into inclusive civic ones is infeasible, outside powers or international institutions could enforce peace temporarily in the hope that reduced security threats would permit moderate leaders within each group to promote the reconstruction of more benign identities. While persuading ethnic war survivors to adopt an overarching identity may be impossible, a sufficiently prolonged period of guaranteed safety might allow moderate leaders to temper some of the most extreme hypernationalism back towards more benign, albeit still separate nationalisms. However, this still leaves both sides vulnerable to later revival of hypernationalism by radical political entrepreneurs, especially after the peacekeepers have left and security threats once again appear more realistic.

### Power-Sharing

The best-developed blueprint for civic peace in multi-ethnic states is power-sharing or "consociational democracy," proposed by Arend Lijphart. This approach assumes that ethnicity is somewhat manipulable, but not so freely as constructivists say. Ethnic division, however, need not result in conflict; even if political mobilization is organized on ethnic lines, civil politics can be maintained if ethnic elites adhere to a power-sharing bargain that equitably protects all groups. The key components are: 1) joint exercise of governmental power; 2) proportional distribution of government funds and jobs; 3) autonomy on ethnic issues (which, if groups are concentrated territorially, may be achieved by regional federation); and 4) a minority veto on issues of vital importance to each group. Even if power-sharing can avert potential ethnic conflicts or dampen mild ones, our concern here is whether it can bring peace under the conditions of intense violence and extreme ethnic mobilization that are likely to motivate intervention.

The answer is no. The indispensable component of any power-sharing deal is a plausible minority veto, one which the strongest side will accept and which the weaker side believes that the stronger will respect. Traditions of stronger loyalties to the state than to parochial groups and histories of inter-ethnic compromise could provide reason for confidence, but in a civil war these will have been destroyed, if they were ever present, by the fighting itself and accompanying ethnic mobilization.

Only a balance of power among the competing groups can provide a "hard" veto—one which the majority must respect. Regional concentration of populations could partially substitute for balanced power if the minority group can credibly threaten to secede if its veto is overridden. In any situation where humanitarian intervention might be considered, however, these conditions too are unlikely to be met. Interventions are likely to be aimed at saving a weak group that cannot defend itself; balanced sides do not need defense. Demographic separation is also unlikely, because if the populations were already separated, the ethnic cleansing and related atrocities which are most likely to provoke intervention would not be occurring.

The core reason why power-sharing cannot resolve ethnic civil wars is that it is inherently voluntaristic; it requires conscious decisions by elites to cooperate to avoid ethnic strife. Under conditions of hypernationalist mobilization and real security threats, group leaders are unlikely to be receptive to compromise, and even if they are, they cannot act without being discredited and replaced by harder-line rivals.

Could outside intervention make power-sharing work? One approach would be to adjust the balance of power between the warring sides to a "hurting stalemate" by arming the weaker side, blockading the stronger, or partially disarming the stronger by direct military intervention. When both sides realize that further fighting will bring them costs but no profit, they will negotiate an agreement. This can balance power, although if populations are still intermingled it may actually worsen security dilemmas and increase violence—especially against civilians—as both sides eliminate the threats posed by pockets of the opposing group in their midst.

Further, once there has been heavy fighting, the sides are likely to distrust each other far too much to entrust any authority to a central government that could potentially be used against them. . . .

The final approach is international imposition of power-sharing, which requires occupying the country to coerce both sides into accepting the agreement and to prevent inter-ethnic violence until it can be implemented. The interveners, however, cannot bind the stronger side to uphold the agreement after the intervention forces leave. . . . The British did impose power-sharing as a condition for Cypriot independence, but it broke down almost immediately. The Greek Cypriots, incensed by what they saw as Turkish Cypriot abuse of their minority veto, simply overrode the veto and operated the government in violation of the constitution. Similarly, while at independence in 1948 the Sri Lankan constitution banned religious or communal discrimination, the Sinhalese majority promptly disenfranchised half of the Tamils on the grounds that they were actually Indians, and increasingly discriminated against Tamils in education, government employment, and other areas.

### State-Building

Gerald Helman and Steven Ratner argue that states in which government breakdown, economic failure, and internal violence imperil their own citizens and threaten neighboring states can be rescued by international "conservatorship" to administer critical government functions until the country can govern itself following a free and fair election. Ideally, the failed state would voluntarily delegate specified functions to an international executor, although in extreme cases involving massive violations of human rights or the prospect of large-scale warfare, the international community could act even without an invitation.

As with imposing power-sharing, this requires occupying the country (and may require conquering it), coercing all sides to accept a democratic constitution, enforcing peace until elections can be held, and administering the economy and the elections. Conservatorship thus requires even more finesse than enforced power-sharing, and probably more military risks.

Helman and Ratner cite the UN intervention in Cambodia in 1992–93 to create a safe environment for free elections as conservatorship's best success. However, this was an ideological war over the governance of Cambodia, not an ethnic conflict over disempowering minorities or dismembering the country. By contrast, the growth of the U.S.-UN mission in Somalia from famine relief to state-rebuilding was a failure, and no one has been so bold as to propose conservatorship for Bosnia or Rwanda.

Even if conservatorship could rapidly, effectively, and cheaply stop an ethnic civil war, rebuild institutions, and ensure free elections, nothing would be gained unless the electoral outcome protected all parties' interests and safety; that is, power-sharing would still be necessary. Thus, in serious ethnic conflicts, conservatorship would only be a more expensive way to reach the same impasse.

## Ethnic Separation

Regardless of the causes of a particular conflict, once communities are mobilized for violence, the reality of mutual security threats prevents both demobilization and de-escalation of hypernationalist discourse. Thus, lasting peace requires removal of the security dilemma. The most effective and in many cases the only way to do this is to separate the ethnic groups. The more intense the violence, the more likely it is that separation will be the only option.

The exact threshold remains an open question. The deductive logic of the problem suggests that the critical variable is fear for survival. Once a majority of either group comes to believe that the killing of noncombatants of their own group is not considered a crime by the other, they cannot accept any governing arrangement that could be captured by the enemy group and used against them.

The most persuasive source of such beliefs is the massacre of civilians, but it is not clear that there is a specific number of incidents or total deaths beyond which ethnic reconciliation becomes impossible. More important is the extent to which wide sections of the attacking group seem to condone the killings, and can be observed doing so by members of the target group. In this situation the attacks are likely to be seen as reflecting not just the bloodthirstiness of a particular regime or terrorist faction, but the preference of the opposing group as a whole, which means that no promise of non-repetition can be believed.

Testing this proposition directly requires better data on the attitudes of threatened populations during and after ethnic wars than we now have. Next best is aggregate analysis of the patterns of ends of ethnic wars, supplemented by investigation of individual cases as deeply as the data permits. I make a start at such an analysis below.

## How Ethnic Wars Have Ended

At least 46 significant ethnic civil wars have ended since 1944.[8] Of the total, nineteen were ended by the military victory of one side, sixteen by *de jure* or *de facto* partition, and two have been suppressed by military occupation by a third party. Only nine ethnic civil wars have been ended by a negotiated agreement that did not partition the country. (See Table 1.)

The data support the argument that separation of groups is the key to ending ethnic civil wars. Every case in which the state was preserved by agreement involved a regionally concentrated minority, and in every case but one the solution reinforced the ethnic role in politics by allowing regionally concentrated minorities to control their own destinies through autonomy for the regions where they form a majority of the population. South Africa is a partial exception, since the main element of the agreement was majority rule, although even in this case the powers reserved to the provinces offer some autonomy to whites, coloreds, and Zulus.

TABLE 1 ■ ETHNIC CIVIL WARS RESOLVED 1944–1997

| Combatants | Dates | Deaths (000s) | Outcome |
|---|---|---|---|
| **A. Military victory (19):** | | | |
| Kurds vs. Iran | 45–80s | 40 | Suppressed |
| Karens, others vs. Myanmar | 45– | 400 | Largely suppressed; sporadic violence |
| Chinese vs. Malaya | 48–60 | 15 | Suppressed |
| Tibetans vs. China | 51–89 | 100 | Suppressed |
| Hmong vs. Laos | 59–72 | 50 | Suppressed |
| Katangans vs. Congo | 60–64 | 100 | Suppressed |
| Papuans vs. Indonesia | 64–86 | 19 | Suppressed |
| Blacks vs. Rhodesia | 65–80 | 50 | Rebels victorious |
| Ibos vs. Nigeria | 67–70 | 2000 | Suppressed |
| Hmong vs. Thailand | 67–80 | .30 | Suppressed |
| Palestinians vs. Jordan | 70 | 15 | Suppressed |
| Timorese vs. Indonesia | 74–82 | 200 | Suppressed |
| Aceh vs. Indonesia | 75–80s | 15 | Suppressed |
| Tigreans, others vs. Ethiopia | 75–91 | .600 | Rebels victorious |
| Uighurs etc. vs. China | 80 | 2 | Suppressed |
| Sikhs vs. India | 84 | 25 | Suppressed |
| Bouganvilleans vs. Papua | 88 | 1 | Suppressed |
| Tutsis vs. Rwanda | 90–94 | 750 | Rebels victorious |
| Shiites vs. Iraq | 91 | 35 | Suppressed |
| **B. *De facto* or *de jure* partition (16):** | | | |
| Ukrainians vs. USSR | 44–50s | 150 | Suppressed; later independent 1991 |
| Lithuanians vs. USSR | 45–52 | 40 | Suppressed; later independent 1991 |
| Muslims vs. Sikhs, Hindus (India) | 46–47 | .500 | Partition 1947 |
| Jews vs. Arabs (Palestine) | 47–49 | 20 | Partition 1948 |
| Eritreans vs. Ethiopia | 61–91 | 250 | Independent 1993 |
| Turks vs. Cyprus | 63–74 | .10 | *De facto* partition |
| Bengalis vs. Pakistan | 71 | 1000 | Independent 1971 |
| Armenians vs. Azerbaijan | 88– | 15 | *De facto* partition |
| Somali clans | 88– | 350 | *De facto* partition in N.; ongoing in S. |
| South Ossetians | 90–92 | 1 | *De facto* partition |
| Russians vs. Moldova | 92– | 2 | *De facto* partition |
| Slovenia vs. Yugoslavia | 91 | 1 | Independent 1991 |
| Croatia vs. Yugoslavia | 91–95 | 30 | Independent 1991 |
| Serbs vs. Bosnia | 92–95 | 150 | *De facto* partition |
| Abkhazians vs. Georgia | 92– | 15 | *De facto* partition; sporadic violence |
| Chechnyans vs. Russia | 94–97 | .20 | *De facto* partition |

TABLE 1 ■ (Continued)

| Combatants | Dates | Deaths (000s) | Outcome |
|---|---|---|---|
| **C. Conflict suppressed by ongoing 3rd party military occupation (2):** | | | |
| Kurds vs. Iraq | 60– | 215 | *De facto* partition |
| Lebanese Civil War | 75–90 | 120 | Nominal power sharing; *de facto* partition |
| **D. Regional Autonomy Agreements (8):** | | | |
| Nagas vs. India | 52–75 | 13 | Autonomy 1972 |
| Basques vs. Spain | 59–80s | 1 | Autonomy 1980 |
| Tripuras vs. India | 67–89 | 13 | Autonomy 1972 |
| Moros vs. Philippines | 72–87 | 50 | Limited autonomy 1990 |
| Baluchis vs. Pakistan | 73–77 | .5 | Limited autonomy |
| Chittagong hill peoples vs. Bangladesh | 75–89 | 24 | Limited autonomy 1989 |
| Miskitos vs. Nicaragua | 81–88 | 1 | Autonomy 1990 |
| Mayas vs. Guatemala | 61–97 | 166 | Limited autonomy 1997 |
| **E. Power-sharing Agreements (1):** | | | |
| Blacks vs. South Africa | 60s–93 | 20 | Modified majority rule |

There is not a single case where non-ethnic civil politics were created or restored by reconstruction of ethnic identities, power-sharing coalitions, or state-building.

Further, deaths in these cases average roughly five times lower than in the wars which ended in either suppression or partition: slightly more than 30,000, compared to about 175,000. This lends support to the proposition that the more extreme the violence, the less the chances for any form of reconciliation. Finally, it should be noted that all eight of the cases resolved through autonomy involve groups that were largely demographically separated even at the beginning of the conflict, which may help explain why there were fewer deaths.

## INTERVENTION TO RESOLVE ETHNIC CIVIL WARS

International interventions that seek to ensure lasting safety for populations endangered by ethnic war—whether by the United Nations, by major powers with global reach, or by regional powers—must be guided by two principles. First, settlements must aim at physically separating the warring communities and establishing a balance of relative strength that makes it unprofitable for either side to attempt to revise the territorial settlement. Second, although economic or military assistance may suffice in some cases, direct military intervention will be necessary when aid to the weaker side would create a window of opportunity for the stronger, or when there is an immediate need to stop ongoing genocide.

## Designing Settlements

Unless outsiders are willing to provide permanent security guarantees, stable resolution of an ethnic civil war requires separation of the groups into defensible regions. The critical variable is demography, not sovereignty. Political partition without ethnic separation leaves incentives for ethnic cleansing unchanged; it actually increases them if it creates new minorities. Conversely, demographic separation dampens ethnic conflicts even without separate sovereignty, although the more intense the previous fighting, the smaller the prospects for preserving a single state, even if loosely federated.

Partition without ethnic separation increases conflict because, while boundaries of sovereign successor states may provide defensible fronts that reduce the vulnerability of the majority group in each state, stay-behind minorities are completely exposed. Significant irredenta are both a call to their ethnic homeland and a danger to their hosts. They create incentives to mount rescue or ethnic cleansing operations before the situation solidifies. Greece's 1920 invasion of Turkey was justified in this way, while the 1947 decision to partition Palestine generated a civil war in advance of implementation, and the inclusion of Muslim-majority Kashmir within India has helped cause three wars. International recognition of Croatian and Bosnian independence did more to cause than to stop Serbian invasion. The war between Armenia and Azerbaijan has the same source, as do concerns over the international security risks of the several Russian diasporas.

Inter-ethnic security dilemmas can be nearly or wholly eliminated without partition if three conditions are met: First, there must be enough demographic separation that ethnic regions do not themselves contain militarily significant minorities. Second, there must be enough regional self-defense capability that abrogating the autonomy of any region would be more costly than any possible motive for doing so. Third, local autonomy must be so complete that minority groups can protect their key interests even lacking any influence at the national level. Even after an ethnic war, a single state could offer some advantages, not least of which are the economic benefits of a common market. However, potential interveners should recognize that groups that control distinct territories can insist on the *de facto* partition, and often will.

While peace requires separation of groups into distinct regions, it does not require total ethnic purity. Rather, remaining minorities must be small enough that the host group does not fear them as either a potential military threat or a possible target for irredentist rescue operations. Before the Krajina offensive, for example, President Franjo Tudjman of Croatia is said to have thought that the 12 percent Serb minority in Croatia was too large, but that half as many would be tolerable. The 173,000 Arabs remaining in Israel by 1951 were too few and too disorganized to be seen as a serious threat.

Geographic distribution of minorities is also important; in particular, concentrations near disputed borders or astride strategic communications constitute both a military vulnerability and an irredentist opportunity, and so are likely to spark conflict. It is not surprising that India's portion of Kashmir, with its Muslim majority, has been at the center of three interstate wars and an ongoing insurgency which continues today, while there has been no international conflict over the hundred million Muslims who live dispersed throughout most of the rest of India, and relatively little violence.

Where possible, inter-group boundaries should be drawn along the best defensive terrain, such as rivers and mountain ranges. Lines should also be as short as possible, to allow the heaviest possible manning of defensive fronts. . . . Access to the sea or to a friendly neighbor is also important, both for trade and for possible military assistance. Successor state arsenals should be encouraged, by aid to the weaker or sanctions on the stronger, to focus on defensive armaments such as forward artillery and antiaircraft missiles and rockets, while avoiding instruments that could make blitzkrieg attacks possible, such as tanks, fighter-bombers, and mobile artillery. These conditions would make subsequent offensives exceedingly expensive and likely to fail.

## Intervention Strategy

The level of international action required to resolve an ethnic war will depend on the military situation on the ground. If there is an existing stalemate along defensible lines, the international community should simply recognize and strengthen it, providing transportation, protection, and resettlement assistance for refugees. However, where one side has the capacity to go on the offensive against the other, intervention will be necessary.

Interventions should therefore almost always be on behalf of the weaker side; the stronger needs no defense. Moreover, unless the international community can agree on a clear aggressor and a clear victim, there is no moral or political case for intervention. If both sides have behaved so badly that there is little to choose between them, intervention should not and probably will not be undertaken.[9] Almost no one in the West, for instance, has advocated assisting either side in the Croatian-Serb conflict.[10] While the intervention itself could be carried out by any willing actors, UN sponsorship is highly desirable, most of all to head off possible external aid to the group identified as the aggressor.

The three available tools are sanctions, military aid, and direct military intervention. Economic sanctions have limited leverage against combatants in ethnic wars, who often see their territorial security requirements as absolute. . . .

Whether military aid to the client can achieve an acceptable territorial outcome depends on the population balance between the sides, the local geography, and the organizational cohesion of the client group. . . . The . . . problem with "arm's length" aid is that it cannot prevent ethnic aggressors from killing members of the client group in territories from which they expect to have to retreat. Aid also does not restrain possible atrocities by the client group if their military fortunes improve.

If the client is too weak to achieve a viable separation with material aid alone, or if either or both sides cannot be trusted to abide by promises of non-retribution against enemy civilians, the international community must designate a separation line and deploy an intervention force to take physical control of the territory on the client's side of the line. We might call this approach "conquer and divide."

The separation campaign is waged as a conventional military operation. The larger the forces committed the better, both to minimize intervenors' casualties and to shorten the campaign by threatening the opponent with overwhelming defeat. Although some argue that any intervention force would become mired in a

Vietnam-like quagmire, the fundamentally different nature of ethnic conflict means that the main pitfalls to foreign military interventions in ideological insurgencies are either weaker or absent. Most important, the intervenors' intelligence problems are much simpler, since loyalty intelligence is both less important and easier: Outsiders can safely assume that members of the allied group are friends and those of the other are enemies. Even if outsiders cannot tell the groups apart, locals can, and the loyalty of guides provided by the local ally can be counted on. As a result, the main intelligence task shifts from assessing loyalties to locating enemy forces, a task of which major power militaries are very capable.

On the ground, the intervenors would begin at one end of the target region and gradually advance to capture the entire target territory, maintaining a continuous front the entire time. It is not necessary to conquer the whole country; indeed, friendly ground forces need never cross the designated line. After enemy forces are driven out of each locality, civilians of the enemy ethnic group who remain behind are interned, to be exchanged after the war. This removes the enemy's local support base, preventing counterinsurgency problems from arising. Enemy civilians should be protected by close supervision of client troops in action, as well as by foreign control of internees.

The final concern is possible massacres of civilians of the client group in territory not yet captured or beyond the planned separation line. Some of this must be expected, since ongoing atrocities are the most likely impetus for outside intervention; the question is whether intervention actually increases the risk of attacks on civilians. A major advantage of a powerful ground presence is that opponent behavior can be coerced by threatening to advance the separation line in retaliation for any atrocities.

Once the military campaign is complete and refugees have been resettled, further reconstruction and military aid may be needed to help the client achieve a viable economy and self-defense capability before the intervenors can depart. The ease of exit will depend on the regional geography and balance of power. Bosnia has sufficient population and skills to be made economically and militarily viable, provided that access to the outside world through Croatia is maintained. Although the weakness of the Turkish Republic of Northern Cyprus has required a permanent Turkish garrison, the almost equal weakness of the Greek Cypriots allows the garrison to be small, cheap, and inactive. U.S. Operation Provide Comfort helps secure the Kurdish enclave in northern Iraq by prohibiting Iraqi air operations as well as by threatening air strikes against an Iraqi ground invasion of the region. This intervention has no easy exit, however, since the Iraqi Kurds are landlocked and threatened by Turkey, which is waging a war against its own Kurdish minority. Real security for the Kurds might require partitioning Turkey as well as Iraq, a task no outside actor is willing to contemplate. . . .

## OBJECTIONS TO ETHNIC SEPARATION AND PARTITION

There are five important objections to ethnic separation as policy for resolving ethnic conflicts: that it encourages splintering of states, that population exchanges cause human suffering, that it simply transforms civil wars into international ones, that rump states will not be viable, and that, in the end, it does nothing to resolve ethnic antagonisms.

Among most international organizations, western leaders, and scholars, population exchanges and partition are anathema. They contradict cherished western values of social integration, trample on the international legal norm of state sovereignty, and suggest particular policies that have been condemned by most of the world (e.g., Turkey's unilateral partition of Cyprus). The integrity of states and their borders is usually seen as a paramount principle, while self-determination takes second place. In ethnic wars, however, saving lives may require ignoring state-centered legal norms. The legal costs of ethnic separation must be compared to the human consequences, both immediate and long term, if the warring groups are not separated. To paraphrase Winston Churchill: separation is the worst solution, except for all the others.

## Partition Encourages Splintering of States

If international interventions for ethnic separation encourage secession attempts elsewhere, they could increase rather than decrease global ethnic violence. However, this is unlikely, because government use of force to suppress them makes almost all secession attempts extremely costly; only groups that see no viable alternative try. What intervention can do is reduce loss of life where states are breaking up anyway. An expectation that the international community will never intervene, however, encourages repression of minorities, as in Turkey or the Sudan, and wars of ethnic conquest, as by Serbia.

## Population Transfers Cause Suffering

Separation of intermingled ethnic groups necessarily involves significant refugee flows, usually in both directions. Population transfers during ethnic conflicts have often led to much suffering, so an obvious question is whether foreign intervention to relocate populations would only increase suffering. In fact, however, the biggest cause of suffering in population exchanges is spontaneous refugee movement. Planned population transfers are much safer. When ethnic conflicts turn violent, they generate spontaneous refugee movements as people flee from intense fighting or are kicked out by neighbors, marauding gangs, or a conquering army. Spontaneous refugees frequently suffer direct attack by hostile civilians or armed forces. They often leave precipitately, with inadequate money, transport, or food supplies, and before relief can be organized. They make vulnerable targets for banditry and plunder, and are often so needy as to be likely perpetrators also. Planned population exchanges can address all of these risks by preparing refugee relief and security operations in advance.

In the 1947 India-Pakistan exchange, nearly the entire movement of between 12 and 16 million people took place in a few months. The British were surprised by the speed with which this movement took place, and were not ready to control, support, and protect the refugees. Estimates of deaths go as high as one million. In the first stages of the population exchanges among Greece, Bulgaria, and Turkey in the 1920s, hundreds of thousands of refugees moved spontaneously and many died due to banditry and exposure. When after 1925 the League of Nations deployed capable relief services, the remaining transfers—one million, over 60 percent of the total—were carried out in an organized and planned way, with virtually no losses.

A related criticism is that transfers require the intervenors to operate *de facto* concentration camps for civilians of the opposing ethnic groups until transfers can be carried out. However, this is safer than the alternatives of administration by the local ally or allowing the war to run its course. As with transfers, the risks to the internees depend on planning and resources.

## Separation Merely Substitutes International for Civil Wars

Post-separation wars are possible, motivated either by revanchism or by security fears if one side suspects the other of revisionist plans. The frequency and human cost of such wars, however, must be compared to the likely consequences of not separating. When the alternative is intercommunal slaughter, separation is the only defensible choice.

In fact the record of twentieth-century ethnic partitions is fairly good. The partition of Ireland has produced no interstate violence, although intercommunal violence continues in demographically mixed Northern Ireland. India and Pakistan have fought two wars since partition, one in 1965 over ethnically mixed Kashmir, while the second in 1971 resulted not from Indo-Pakistani state rivalry or Hindu-Muslim religious conflict but from ethnic conflict between (West) Pakistanis and Bengalis. Indian intervention resolved the conflict by enabling the independence of Bangladesh. These wars have been much less dangerous, especially to civilians, than the political and possible physical extinction that Muslims feared if the subcontinent were not divided. The worst post-partition history is probably that of the Arab-Israeli conflict. Even here, civilian deaths would almost certainly have been higher without partition. It is difficult even to imagine any alternative; the British could not and would not stay, and neither side would share power or submit to rule by the other.

## Rump States Will Not Be Viable

Many analysts of ethnic conflict question the economic and military viability of partitioned states. History, however, records no examples of ethnic partitions which failed for economic reasons. In any case, intervenors have substantial influence over economic outcomes: They can determine partition lines, guarantee trade access and, if necessary, provide significant aid in relation to the economic sizes of likely candidates. Peace itself also enhances recovery prospects.

Thus the more important issue is military viability, particularly since interventions will most often be in favor of the weaker side. If the client has economic strength comparable to the opponent, it can provide for its own defense. If it does not, the intervenors will have to provide military aid and possibly a security guarantee.

Ensuring the client's security will be made easier by the opponent's scarcity of options for revision. First, any large-scale conventional attack is likely to fail because the intervenors will have drawn the borders for maximum defensibility and ensured that the client is better armed. If necessary, they can lend further assistance through air strikes. Breaking up conventional offensives is what high-technology air power does best.

Second, infiltration of small guerrilla parties, if successful over a period of time, could cause boundaries to become "fuzzy," and eventually to break down. This has been a major concern of some observers of Bosnia, but it should not be. Infiltration can only work where at least some civilians will support, house, feed, and hide the guerrillas. After ethnic separation, however, any infiltrators would be entering a completely hostile region where no one will help them; instead, all will inform on them and cooperate fully with authorities against them. The worst case is probably Israel, where terrorist infiltration has cost lives, but never comes close to threatening the state's territorial integrity. Retaliatory capabilities could also allow the client to dampen, even stop, such behavior.

## Partition Does Not Resolve Ethnic Hatreds

It is not clear that it is in anyone's power to resolve ethnic hatreds once there has been large-scale violence, especially murders of civilians. In the long run, however, separation may help reduce inter-ethnic antagonism; once real security threats are reduced, the plausibility of hypernationalist appeals may eventually decline. Certainly ethnic hostility cannot be reduced without separation. As long as either side fears, even intermittently, that it will be attacked by the other, past atrocities and old hatreds can easily be aroused. If, however, it becomes and remains implausible that the other group could ever seriously endanger the nation, hypernationalist drum-beating may fall on deafer and deafer ears.

The only stronger measure would be to attempt a thorough re-engineering of the involved groups' political and social systems, comparable to the rehabilitation of Germany after World War II. The costs would be steep, since this would require conquering the country and occupying it for a long time, possibly for decades. The apparent benignification of Germany suggests that, if the international community is prepared to go this far, this approach could succeed.

## CONCLUSION

Humanitarian intervention to establish lasting safety for peoples endangered by ethnic civil wars is feasible, but only if the international community is prepared to recognize that some shattered states cannot be restored, and that population transfers are sometimes necessary. . . .

Ultimately we have a responsibility to be honest with ourselves as well as with the victims of ethnic wars all over the world. The world's major powers must decide whether they will be willing to spend any of their own soldiers' lives to save strangers, or whether they will continue to offer false hopes to endangered peoples.

## NOTES

1. Ethnic wars involve organized large-scale violence, whether by regular forces (Turkish or Iraqi operations against the Kurds) or highly mobilized civilian populations

(the *interahamwe* in Rwanda or the Palestinian *intifada*). A frequent aspect is "ethnic cleansing": efforts by members of one ethnic group to eliminate the population of another from a certain area by means such as discrimination, expropriation, terror, expulsion, and massacre. For proposals on managing ethnic rivalries involving lower levels of ethnic mobilization and violence, see Stephen Van Evera, "Managing the Eastern Crisis: Preventing War in the Former Soviet Empire," *Security Studies* 3 (Spring 1992), 361–382; Ted Hopf, "Managing Soviet Disintegration: A Demand for Behavioral Regimes," *International Security* 17, 1 (Summer 1992), 44–75.

2. An ethnic group (or nation) is commonly defined as a body of individuals who purportedly share cultural or racial characteristics, especially common ancestry or territorial origin, which distinguish them from members of other groups. See Max Weber (Guenther Roth, and Claus Wittich, eds.), *Economy and Society: An Outline of Interpretive Sociology*, Vol. 1 (Berkeley, Calif.: University of California Press, 1968), pp. 389, 395; Anthony D. Smith, *National Identity* (Reno: University of Nevada Press, 1991), pp. 14, 21. Opposing communities in ethnic civil conflicts hold irreconcilable visions of the identity, borders, and citizenship of the state. They do not seek to control a state whose identity all sides accept, but rather to redefine or divide the state itself. By contrast, ideological conflicts may be defined as those in which all sides share a common vision of community membership, a common preference for political organization of the community as a single state, and a common sense of the legitimate boundaries of that state. The opposing sides seek control of the state, not its division or destruction. It follows that some religious conflicts—those between confessions which see themselves as separate communities, as between Catholics and Protestants in Northern Ireland—are best categorized with ethnic conflicts, while others—over interpretation of a shared religion, e.g., disputes over the social roles of Islam in Iran, Algeria, and Egypt—should be considered ideological contests. On religious differences as ethnic divisions, see Arend Lijphart, "The Power-Sharing Approach," in Joseph V. Montville, ed., *Conflict and Peacemaking in Multiethnic Societies* (Lexington, Mass.: Lexington Books, 1990), pp. 491–509, at 491.

3. While the discussion below delineates ideal types, mixed cases occur. The key distinction is the extent to which mobilization appeals are based on race or confession (ethnic) rather than on political, economic, or social ideals (ideological). During the Cold War a number of Third World ethnic conflicts were misidentified by the superpowers as ideological struggles because local groups stressed ideology to gain outside support. In Angola the MPLA drew their support from the coastal Kimbundu tribe, the FNLA from the Bankongo in the north (and across the border in Zaire), and UNITA from Ovimbundu, Chokwe, and Ngangela in the interior of the south. The former were aided by the Soviets and the latter two, at various times, by both the United States and China. . . .

4. Reported by Andrej Gustinčićof *Reuters*, cited in Misha Glenny, *The Fall of Yugoslavia* (New York: Penguin, 1992), p. 166. Another tactic used by extremists to radicalize co-ethnics is to accuse the other side of crimes similar to their own. In July 1992, amidst large-scale rape of Bosnian Muslim women by Serb forces, Bosnian Serbs accused Muslims of impregnating kidnapped Serb women in order to create a new race of Janissary soldiers. Roy Gutman, *A Witness to Genocide* (New York: Macmillan, 1993), p. x.

5. Mikica Babić quoted in Chris Hedges, "War Turns Sarajevo Away from Europe," *New York Times* (July 28, 1995).

6. Increased geographic intermixing of ethnic groups often intensifies conflict, particularly if the state is too weak or too biased to assure the security of all groups. Increasing numbers of Jewish settlers in the West Bank had this effect on Israeli-Palestinian relations. A major reason for the failure of the negotiations that preceded the Nigerian civil war was

the inability of northern leaders to guarantee the safety of Ibo living in the northern region. Harold D. Nelson, ed., *Nigeria: A Country Study* (Washington, D.C.: U.S. GPO, 1982), p. 55.

7. Ethnic combatants have noticed this. In World War II, the Croatian Ustasha refused to accept educated Serbs as converts because they were assumed to have a national consciousness independent of religion, whereas illiterate peasants were expected to forget their Serbian identity once converted. In 1992 Bosnian Serb ethnic cleansers annihilated the most educated Muslims. . . . Tutsi massacres of Hutus in Burundi in 1972 concentrated on educated people who were seen as potential ethnic leaders and afterwards the government restricted admission of Hutus to secondary schools. . . .

8. This total does not include civil wars which stopped temporarily but in which the same combatants later resumed fighting over the same issues (e.g., Burundi or Sudan) or cases in which peace agreements have been signed but not fully implemented as of this writing (e.g., Palestinians vs. Israel, Ovimbundu vs. Angola).

9. This is why the strongest advocates of intervention in Bosnia have emphasized Serb crimes, while those opposed to intervention insist on the moral equivalence of the two sides. Anthony Lewis, "Crimes of War," *New York Times* (April 25, 1994); Charles G. Boyd, "Making Peace with the Guilty," *Foreign Affairs*, 74, 5 (September/October 1995), pp. 22–38.

10. Further, attempts at even-handed intervention rarely achieve their goals, leading either to nearly complete passivity, as in the case of UNPROFOR In Bosnia, or eventually to open combat against one or all sides. At worst, peace-keeping efforts may actually prolong fighting. . . .

# Nation-Building: UN Surpasses U.S. on Learning Curve

## JAMES DOBBINS

Since World War II, the United Nations (UN) and the United States have developed distinctive styles of nation-building derived from their very different natures and capabilities. The United Nations is an international organization entirely dependent on its members for the wherewithal to conduct nation-building. The United States is the world's only superpower, commanding abundant resources of its own and having access to those of many other nations and institutions.

We at the RAND Corporation define nation-building as "the use of armed force in the aftermath of a crisis to promote a transition to democracy." We have examined eight instances in which the United Nations took the lead in such endeavors and eight in which the United States took the lead.

UN operations have almost always been undermanned and under-resourced, because member states are rarely willing to commit the manpower or the money any prudent military commander would desire. As a result, small and weak UN forces are routinely deployed into what they hope, on the basis of best-case assumptions, will prove to be post-conflict situations. Where such assumptions have proven ill founded, UN forces have had to be reinforced, withdrawn, or, in extreme cases, rescued. Nevertheless, UN nation-building missions have often met with success.

Throughout the 1990s, the United States adopted the opposite approach, basing its plans on worst-case assumptions and relying on overwhelming force to quickly establish a stable environment and to deter resistance from forming. By intervening in numbers and with capabilities that discouraged significant resistance, U.S.-led coalitions achieved progressively higher levels of success throughout the 1990s, from Somalia to Haiti to Bosnia to Kosovo.

But in sizing its stabilization operations in Afghanistan and Iraq, the new American leadership abandoned the strategy of overwhelming preponderance, known as the Powell doctrine, in favor of the "small footprint" or "low profile" force posture that had characterized UN operations. In both Afghanistan and Iraq, the original American-led forces proved unable to establish a secure environment.

In both countries, the initial U.S. force levels have had to be significantly increased, but in neither country has this yet sufficed to establish adequate levels of

James Dobbins, "Nation-Building: UN Surpasses U.S. on Learning Curve," *RAND Review*, Vol. 29, No. 1 (Spring 2005), pp. 24–29. Copyright 2005 by RAND Corporation. Reproduced with permission of RAND Corporation in the format Textbook via Copyright Clearance Center.

public security. In Afghanistan, reduced levels of insurgent violence have been replaced by organized crime on a massive level, with some 60 percent of the entire country's gross domestic product now coming from illegal drug production. In Iraq, resistance to a U.S. occupation may be morphing into a sectarian civil conflict.

The low-profile, small-footprint approach to nation-building is much better suited to UN-style peacekeeping than to U.S.-style peace enforcement. The United Nations has an ability to compensate, to some degree at least, for its "hard power" deficit with "soft power" attributes of local impartiality and international legitimacy. The United States does not have such advantages in situations where America itself is a party to the conflict being terminated or where the United States has felt compelled to act without an international mandate.

The United States would be well advised to resume supersizing its nation-building missions and to leave the small-footprint approach to the United Nations. At the same time, the United States would be well advised to emulate the track record of the United Nations in implementing lessons learned from prior operations.

## INPUTS AND OUTPUTS

The UN experience with nation-building began in the newly independent Congo in 1960. Since then, the instances in which UN forces have been used for nation-building have all occurred since the end of the Cold War in 1989, to include Namibia, El Salvador, Cambodia, Mozambique, Eastern Slavonia (in Croatia), Sierra Leone, and East Timor. The U.S. experience began with the occupations of West Germany and Japan in 1945; continued in Somalia, Haiti, Bosnia, and Kosovo after 1989; and expanded to Afghanistan and Iraq in this decade.

Nation-building can be measured in terms of inputs (such as manpower, money, and time) and outputs (such as casualties, peace, economic growth, and democratization). Success depends not just on the inputs, of course, but also on the wisdom with which the resources are employed and on the susceptibility of the society in question to the changes being fostered. Nevertheless, success depends in some measure on the quantity of international military and police personnel, the quantity of external economic assistance, and the time over which they are applied.

In terms of personnel, military force levels for UN missions ranged from nearly 20,000 troops deployed in the Congo and 16,000 in Cambodia to fewer than 5,000 in Namibia and El Salvador. UN missions have normally fielded much smaller contingents than American-led operations. In absolute numbers, the largest UN contingent was smaller than the smallest U.S. contingent. However, the UN missions in Eastern Slavonia and East Timor did deploy sizable military forces relative to the local populations (see Figure 1).

In terms of money, UN-led operations have tended to be less well supported with international economic assistance than U.S. operations, in both absolute and proportional terms. This reflects the greater access of the United States to donor assistance funds, including its own, and to those of the international financial institutions to which it belongs. In effect, the United States can always ensure the level of funding it deems necessary. The United Nations seldom can. Many UN operations are consequently poorly supported with economic assistance.

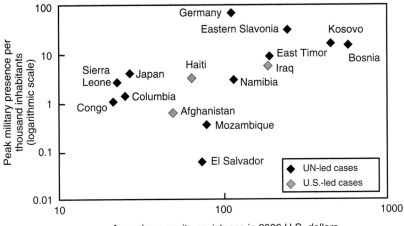

**FIGURE 1** ■ UN Cases of Nation-Building Have Involved Fewer Troops and/or Less Money Per Capita Than U.S. Cases (Except in Some Extremely Small Societies, Like East Timor)

*Source:* Figure 1 is from James Dobbins et al., *The UN's Role in Nation-Building: From The Congo to Iraq,* p. 244. © Copyright 2005 RAND Corporation. Reprinted by permission of RAND Corporation.

In terms of time, UN forces have tended to remain in post-conflict countries for shorter periods than have U.S. forces. In the early 1990s, both UN- and U.S.-led operations tended to be terminated rather quickly, often immediately following the completion of an initial democratic election and the inauguration of a new government. As experience with nation-building grew, both the United Nations and the United States recognized that reconciliation and democratization could require more than a single election. By the end of the decade, both UN- and U.S.-led operations had become more extended.

For each of the eight UN and eight U.S. missions, we measured "outputs," including casualties suffered, peace sustained, economic growth, and democratization. Casualties suffered are a good measure of the difficulties encountered in a nation-building operation. Missions with high casualty levels have been among the least successful.

Among the UN-led cases, the Congo had the highest number of casualties, reflecting the peace enforcement nature of the operation. The Cambodian operation, lightly manned as a proportion of the population, had the second-highest casualty level, followed by Sierra Leone.

Following the loss of 18 U.S. soldiers in Somalia in 1993, the United States took great precautions to avoid casualties through the rest of the decade. But American sensitivity to casualties diminished in the aftermath of the Sept. 11, 2001, terrorist attacks. At the same time, the United States abandoned its strategy of deploying overwhelming force at the outset of nation-building operations. Significantly lower force-to-population ratios in Afghanistan and Iraq than in Bosnia or Kosovo have been accompanied by much higher casualty levels. There have been more casualties among U.S. forces in Afghanistan than in all American nation-building operations studied going back to 1945, and the casualty levels in Iraq are ten times higher than in Afghanistan.

Peace is the most essential product of nation-building. Without peace, neither economic growth nor democratization is possible. With peace, some level of economic growth becomes almost inevitable, and democratization at least possible. Among the 16 societies studied, 11 remain at peace today, and 5 do not (see Table 1). Of the 8 UN-led cases, 7 are at peace. Of the 8 U.S.-led cases, 4 are at peace; 4 are not—or not yet—at peace.

These categorizations are necessarily provisional, particularly for the ongoing operations in Afghanistan and Iraq. Peace in Bosnia, Sierra Leone, East Timor, and Kosovo has been sustained, but so far only with the ongoing presence of international peacekeepers.

The key determinant of economic growth seems to be *not* the level of economic assistance but rather the presence of international peacekeepers and their success in suppressing renewed conflict. As illustrated by. . . . Iraq, security is a prerequisite for growth, and money is no substitute for adequate security forces. Indeed, security without economic assistance is much more likely to spur economic growth than is economic assistance without security.

The final output is democratization. Table 1 characterizes each of the 16 societies as democratic or not based on ratings from Freedom House and the Polity IV Project at the University of Maryland. Among the UN-led cases, all but the Congo

TABLE 1 ■ PEACE AND DEMOCRACY ARE THE MOST IMPORTANT MEASURES OF SUCCESS

| Country or Territory | At Peace | Democratic |
|---|---|---|
| Congo | No | No |
| Namibia | Yes | Yes |
| El Salvador | Yes | Yes |
| Cambodia | Yes | No |
| Mozambique | Yes | Yes |
| Eastern Slavonia | Yes | Yes |
| Sierra Leone* | Yes | Yes |
| East Timor* | Yes | Yes |
| Germany | Yes | Yes |
| Japan | Yes | Yes |
| Somalia | No | No |
| Haiti | No | No |
| Bosnia* | Yes | Yes |
| Kosovo* | No | No |
| Afghanistan* | No | ? |
| Iraq* | No | ? |

* Ongoing operation.
■ UN-led cases ⁻ U.S.-led cases
*Source:* The UN's Role In Nation-Building, 2005.

and Cambodia remain democratic, some of course more than others. Among the U.S.-led cases, Germany and Japan are clearly democratic; Bosnia and Kosovo are democratic but still under varying degrees of international administration; Somalia and Haiti are not democratic; and Afghanistan and Iraq are seeking to build democratic structures in exceptionally difficult circumstances.

## UN 6, UNITED STATES 4

UN-led nation-building missions tend to be smaller than American operations, to take place in less demanding circumstances, to be more frequent and therefore more numerous, to have more circumspectly defined objectives, and—at least among the missions studied—to enjoy a higher success rate than U.S.-led efforts. By contrast, U.S.-led nation-building has taken place in more demanding circumstances, required larger forces and stronger mandates, received more economic support, espoused more ambitious objectives, and—at least among the missions studied—fallen short of the objectives more often than has the United Nations.

There are three explanations for the better UN success rate. The first is that a different selection of cases would produce a different result. The second is that the U.S. cases are intrinsically more difficult. The third is that the United Nations has done a better job of learning from its mistakes than has the United States (see Table 2).

Throughout the 1990s, the United States became steadily better at nation-building. The Haitian operation was better managed than Somalia, Bosnia better than Haiti, and Kosovo better than Bosnia. The U.S. learning curve was not sustained into the current decade. The administration that took office in 2001 initially disdained nation-building as an unsuitable activity for U.S. forces. When compelled to engage in such missions, first in Afghanistan and then in Iraq, the administration sought to break with the strategies and institutional responses that had been honed throughout the 1990s to deal with these challenges.

The United Nations has largely avoided the institutional discontinuities that have marred U.S. performance. Current UN Secretary-General Kofi Annan was Undersecretary-General for Peacekeeping and head of the UN peacekeeping operation in Bosnia throughout the first half of the 1990s, when UN nation-building began to burgeon. The United States and other member governments chose him for his current post largely on the basis of his demonstrated skills in managing the UN peacekeeping portfolio. Some of his closest associates from that period moved up with him to the UN front office while others remain in the UN Department of Peacekeeping Operations. As a result, an increasingly experienced cadre of international civil servants has run UN nation-building missions over the past 15 years. Similarly, many UN peacekeeping operations in the field are headed and staffed by veterans of earlier operations.

Whereas the United Nations has gradually built up a cadre of experienced nation-builders, the United States starts each mission more or less from scratch. The United States tends to staff each new operation as if it were its first and

TABLE 2 ■ THE UN HISTORY OF NATION-BUILDING

| Country or Territory | Years | Peak Troops | Lead Actors | Assessment | Lessons Learned |
|---|---|---|---|---|---|
| Congo | 1960–1964 | 19,828 | UN-led | Partially successful, costly, and controversial. UN ensured decolonization and territorial integrity but not democracy. | Money and manpower demands almost always exceed supply. Controversial missions leave legacies of "risk aversion." |
| Namibia | 1989–1990 | 4,493 | UN-led | Successful. UN helped ensure peace, democratic development, and economic growth. | Compliant neighbors, a competent government, and a clear end state can contribute to successful outcome. |
| El Salvador | 1991–1996 | 4,948 | UN-led | Successful. UN negotiated lasting peace settlement and transition to democracy after 12-year civil war. | UN participation in settlement negotiations can facilitate smooth transition. |
| Cambodia | 1991–1993 | 15,991 | UN-led | Partially successful. UN organized elections, verified withdrawal of foreign troops, and ended large-scale civil war. But democracy did not take hold. | Democratization requires long-term engagement. |
| Mozambique | 1992–1994 | 6,576 | UN-led | Mostly successful. Transition to independence was peaceful and democratic. But negative economic growth. | Cooperation of neighboring states is critical to success. Incorporation of insurgent groups into political process is key to democratic transition. |
| Eastern Slavonia | 1995–1998 | 8,248 | UN-led | Successful. Well-resourced operation and clear end state contributed to peaceful and democratic transition. | UN can successfully conduct small peace enforcement missions with support from major powers. |
| Sierra Leone | 1998-present | 15,255 | UN-led, parallel UK | Initially unsuccessful, then much improved. | Lack of support from major power can undermine UN |

**TABLE 2 ■ (Continued)**

| Country or Territory | Years | Peak Troops | Lead Actors | Assessment | Lessons Learned |
|---|---|---|---|---|---|
| | | | force in support | Parallel British engagement helped stabilize mission. | operations. But even a badly compromised mission can be turned around. |
| East Timor | 1999-present | 8,084 | Australian-led entry followed by UN-led peacekeeping mission | Successful. UN oversaw transition to democracy, peace, and economic growth. | Support of neighboring states is important for security. Local actors should be involved as early as possible in governance. |

*Source: The UN's Role in Nation-Building, 2005.*

destined to be its last. Service in such missions has never been regarded as career enhancing for American military or Foreign Service officers. Recruitment is often a problem, terms tend to be short, and few individuals volunteer for more than one mission.

The UN success rate among the missions studied—seven out of eight societies left peaceful, six out of eight left democratic—substantiates the view that nation-building can be an effective means of terminating conflicts, ensuring against their recurrence, and promoting democracy. The sharp overall decline in deaths from armed conflict around the world over the past decade also points to the efficacy of nation-building. During the 1990s, deaths from armed conflict were averaging over 200,000 per year. Most were in Africa. In 2003, the last year for which figures exist, that number had fallen to 27,000, less than 15 percent of the previous average. Despite the daily dosage of horrific violence displayed in Iraq and Afghanistan, the world has not become a more violent place within the past decade. Rather, the reverse is true. International peacekeeping and nation-building have contributed to this decline in deaths from armed conflicts (see Figure 2).

The cost of UN nation-building tends to look quite modest compared with the cost of larger and more demanding U.S.-led operations. At present, the United States is spending some $4.5 billion per month to support its military operations in Iraq. This is more than the United Nations spends to run all 17 of its current peacekeeping missions for a *year*. This is not to suggest that the United Nations could perform the U.S. mission in Iraq more cheaply, or perform it at all. It is to underline that there are 17 other places where the United States will probably not have to intervene because UN troops are doing so at a tiny fraction of the cost of U.S.-led operations.

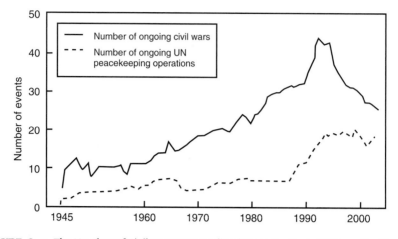

**FIGURE 2** ■ The Number of Civil Wars Has Declined Since the Early 1990s as the Number of UN Operations Has Grown

*Source:* Figure 2 is adapted from James D. Fearon and David D. Laitin, "Neotrusteeship and the Problem of Weak States," *International Security,* Vol. 28, No. 4 (Spring 2004), pp. 5–43, Figure 1. © 2004 by the President and Fellows of Harvard College and the Massachusetts Institute of Technology. Used by permission of The MIT Press.

## HIGHLY INTERDEPENDENT

Despite the United Nations' significant achievements in the field of nation-building, the organization continues to exhibit weaknesses that decades of experience have yet to overcome. Most UN missions are undermanned and underfunded. UN-led military forces are often sized and deployed on the basis of unrealistic best-case assumptions. Troop quality is uneven and has even gotten worse, as many rich Western nations have followed U.S. practice and become less willing to commit their armed forces to UN operations. Police and civil personnel are always of mixed competence. All components of the mission arrive late; police and civil administrators arrive even more slowly than soldiers.

These same weaknesses have been exhibited in the U.S.-led operation in Iraq. There, it was an American-led stabilization force that was deployed on the basis of unrealistic, best-case assumptions and American troops that arrived in inadequate numbers and had to be progressively reinforced as new, unanticipated challenges emerged. There, it was the quality of the U.S.-led coalition's military contingents that proved distinctly variable, as has been their willingness to take orders and risks and to accept casualties. There, it was American civil administrators who were late to arrive, of mixed competence, and not available in adequate numbers. These weaknesses thus appear to be endemic to nation-building rather than unique to the United Nations.

Assuming adequate consensus among Security Council members on the purpose for any intervention, the United Nations provides the most suitable institutional framework for *most* nation-building missions. The UN framework offers a comparatively low cost structure, a comparatively high success rate, and the greatest degree of international legitimacy. Other possible options are likely to be either more expensive (such as coalitions led by the United States, the European Union, or NATO) or less capable (such as coalitions led by the African Union, the Organization of American States, or the Association of Southeast Asian Nations).

The more expensive options are best suited to missions that require forced entry or employ more than 20,000 men, which so far has been the effective upper limit for UN operations. The less capable options are suited to missions where there is a regional but not a global consensus for action or where the United States simply does not care enough to foot 25 percent of the bill.

Although the UN and U.S. styles of nation-building are distinguishable, they are also highly interdependent. It is a rare operation in which both are not involved. Both UN and U.S. nation-building efforts presently stand at near historic highs. The United Nations currently has about 60,000 troops deployed in 17 countries. This is a modest expeditionary commitment in comparison with that of the United States, but it exceeds that of any other nation or combination of nations. Demand for UN-led peacekeeping operations nevertheless far exceeds the available supply, particularly in sub-Saharan Africa. American armed forces, the world's most powerful, also find themselves badly overstretched by the demands of such missions.

A decade ago, in the wake of UN and U.S. setbacks in Somalia and Bosnia, nation-building became a term of opprobrium, leading a significant segment of American opinion to reject the whole concept. Ten years later, nation-building appears ever more clearly as a responsibility that neither the United Nations nor the United States can escape. The United Nations and the United States bring different capabilities to the process. Neither is likely to succeed without the other. Both have much to learn not just from their own experience but also from that of each other.

# Deconstructing Nation Building

## BY JAMES L. PAYNE

When plunging into war, hope generally triumphs over experience. The past—the quiet statistical tabulation of what happened when this was tried before—tends to be ignored in the heat of angry oratory and the thump of military boots. At the outset, it is easy to believe that force will be successful in upholding virtue and that history has no relevance.

Lately, this confidence in the force of arms has centered on nation building, that is, the idea of invading and occupying a land afflicted by dictatorship or civil war and turning it into a democracy. Alas, in their enthusiasm for nation building by force of arms, neither the theorists nor the practitioners have seriously looked at the historical experience with this kind of policy. If, after the troops leave, another dictatorship or another civil war ensues, then one has ploughed the sea. One has suffered the costs of the invasion—Americans killed, local inhabitants killed, destruction of property, tax money squandered, loss of international support, and so on—to no lasting purpose.

To see how nation building in general works out, I have compiled a list of all the cases since 1850 in which the United States and Great Britain employed military forces in a foreign land to cultivate democracy. I included only those cases where ground troops were deployed and clearly intervened in local politics. I have left aside the cases involving lesser types of involvement such as sending aid or military advisors or limited peace-keeping efforts or simply having military bases in the country.

In order to constitute a complete case of attempted nation building, troops have to have left the country (or be uninvolved politically if based in the country) so that we may see whether, in the absence of military support, a stable democracy continued to exist. For this reason we cannot use ongoing involvements such as Bosnia, Kosovo, Afghanistan, and Iraq. The application of this definition identifies 51 instances of attempted nation building by Britain and the United States. The question is, how often did they succeed?

The meaning of success involves more than holding an election and setting up a government. Nation building implies building, that is, constructing a lasting edifice. The nation builders concur in this notion of durability. Their idea isn't just to hold elections, get out, and have the country revert to anarchy or dictatorship. As President Bush has said, the aim in Iraq is to create lasting institutions of freedom. To call a nation building effort a success, therefore, we need to see that the military occupation of the target country was followed by the establishment of an enduring democracy.

James L. Payne, "Deconstructing Nation Building," *The American Conservative*, October 24, 2005, pp. 13–15. Reprinted by permission of the publisher.

To identify results in these terms, I inspected the political history of each country after the troop withdrawal. I looked for events betokening the collapse of democratic rule, including the suppression of opposition leaders or parties, major infringements of freedoms of speech, press, and assembly, violent transfers of power, murder of political leaders by other leaders, and significant civil war. I required large and multiple failures along these lines as evidence of democratic failure. A few arrests of opposition leaders were not enough to disqualify the country as a democracy nor a few assassinations of ambiguous meaning nor a simple military coup nor the resignation of an executive in the face of massive street demonstrations. If numerous free and fair elections were held, this was taken as strong evidence that democracy survived. Elections that were one-sided and to some degree rigged by the incumbents were taken as a negative sign, but they did not, in themselves, disqualify the country as democratic.

The results of applying these principles to the political outcomes in the 51 cases of intervention are shown in the following table. Overall, the results indicate that military intervention succeeded in leaving behind democracies in 14 cases—27 percent of the time. The conclusion, then, is that nation building by force is generally unsuccessful. A president who went around the world invading countries to make them democratic would fail most of the time. One group of countries that seem especially resistant to democracy-building efforts are the Arab lands. There have been nine interventions in Arab countries in the past century. In no case did stable democracy follow the military occupation.

In assessing the effectiveness of nation-building efforts, we should be careful not to confuse conjunction with cause. Just because some military interventions have been followed by democracy, this does not mean that the interventions caused the democracy. There is a worldwide movement against the use of force, and this trend promotes democratic development. Rulers are becoming less disposed to use violence to repress oppositions, and oppositions are less inclined to use force against incumbents. As a result, countries are becoming democracies on their own, without any outside help.

For example, we might be tempted to praise the British occupation of Malaysia as bringing democracy. But in the same period, the neighboring Asian country of Thailand, not occupied, also joined the camp of democratic nations. In fact, in Freedom House's survey of political rights and civil liberties, Thailand ranks ahead of Malaysia. It is quite possible, then, that Malaysia would have become a democracy without British intervention.

South Korea presents an interesting lesson in the effectiveness of nation building. Beginning in 1945, when U.S. troops landed, the United States was heavily involved in guiding political decisions in South Korea. This political involvement essentially ceased after 1961, and the South Koreans were allowed to go their own way politically. This way proved to be a military dictatorship under General Park Chung-Hee, which lasted until his murder in 1979. Thereupon followed two coups, a violent uprising in Kwangju, and many bloody street demonstrations. By 1985, however, the suppression of civil liberties had been greatly relaxed and competitive elections were held. Since that time, South Korea can be called a democracy (albeit a noisy one with plenty of corruption). So here is a case where 16 years of American tutelage brought failure in terms of democratic nation building, while

NATION-BUILDING MILITARY OCCUPATIONS BY THE UNITED STATES AND GREAT BRITAIN, 1850–2000

| U.S. Occupations | | British Occupations | |
| --- | --- | --- | --- |
| Austria 1945–1955 | success | Botswana 1886–1966 | success |
| Cuba 1898–1902 | failure | Brunei 1888–1984 | failure |
| Cuba 1906–1909 | failure | Burma (Myanmar) 1885–1948 | failure |
| Cuba 1917–1922 | failure | Cyprus 1914–1960 | failure |
| Dominican Republic 1911–1924 | failure | Egypt 1882–1922 | failure |
| Dominican Republic 1965–1967 | success | Fiji 1874–1970 | success |
| Grenada 1983–1985 | success | Ghana 1886–1957 | failure |
| Haiti 1915–1934 | failure | Iraq 1917–1932 | failure |
| Haiti 1994–1996 | failure | Iraq 1941–1947 | failure |
| Honduras 1924 | failure | Jordan 1921–1956 | failure |
| Italy 1943–1945 | success | Kenya 1894–1963 | failure |
| Japan 1945–1952 | success | Lesotho 1884–1966 | failure |
| Lebanon 1958 | failure | Malawi (Nyasaland) 1891–1964 | failure |
| Lebanon 1982–1984 | failure | Malaysia 1909–1957 | success |
| Mexico 1914–1917 | failure | Maldives 1887–1976 | success |
| Nicaragua 1909–1910 | failure | Nigeria 1861–1960 | failure |
| Nicaragua 1912–1925 | failure | Palestine 1917–1948 | failure |
| Nicaragua 1926–1933 | failure | Sierra Leone 1885–1961 | failure |
| Panama 1903–1933 | failure | Solomon Islands 1893–1978 | success |
| Panama 1989–1995 | success | South Yemen (Aden) 1934– 1967 | failure |
| Philippines 1898–1946 | success | Sudan 1899–1956 | failure |
| Somalia 1992–1994 | failure | Swaziland 1903–1968 | failure |
| South Korea 1945–1961 | failure | Tanzania 1920– 1963 | failure |
| West Germany 1945–1952 | success | Tonga 1900–1970 | success |
|  |  | Uganda 1894–1962 | failure |
|  |  | Zambia (N. Rhodesia) 1891–1964 | failure |
|  |  | Zimbabwe (S. Rhodesia) 1888–1980 | failure |

the country evolved to democracy on its own 25 years after American involvement in local politics ceased.

Nations around the world are gradually becoming democratic on their own. Therefore, the 14 cases of nation-building "success" cannot be attributed to military intervention. These countries might well have become democracies without it.

The nation-building idea has a critical, generally overlooked, gap: who knows how to do it? Pundits and presidents talk about nation building as if it were a settled technology, like building bridges or removing gall bladders. Huge amounts of government and foundation money have been poured into the topic of democracy building, and academics and bureaucrats have produced reams of verbose commentary. But still there is no concrete, useable body of knowledge.

And, being a non-specialty, there cannot be any experts in it. The people who end up doing the so-called nation building are simply ordinary government employees who happen to wind up at the scene of the military occupation. Many times they are military officers with no background in politics, sociology, or social psychology—not that it would help them. For the most part, these government employees see their mission as getting themselves and the U.S. out of the country without too much egg on their faces. They have no clearer idea of how to "instill democratic culture" than the readers of this page.

A look at some specific examples of nation building illustrates the intellectual vacuum. The 1989 U.S. invasion of Panama is credited in our tabulation as a nation-building success. Was this positive outcome the result of the expert application of political science? One of the nation builders, Lt. Col. John T. Fishel, has written a book on the Panama experience that gives quite a different picture. Fishel was Chief of Policy and Strategy for U.S. forces in Panama, and it was his job to figure out how to implement the mission statement. The orders looked simple on paper: "Conduct nation building operations to ensure democracy." But Fishel quickly discovered that the instruction was meaningless because democracy was an "undefined goal." It seemed to him that it wasn't the job of military officers to figure out how to implement this undefined objective, but, as he observes with a touch of irritation, "there are no U.S. civilian strategists clearly articulating strategies to achieve democracy."

> The fact that there was no clear definition of the conditions that constitute democracy meant that the Military Support Group and the other U.S. government agencies that were attempting to assist the Endara government had only the vaguest concept of what actions and programs would lead the country toward democracy . . .

In practice, what the goal of "ensuring democracy" boiled down to was installing Guillermo Endara, the winner of a previous election, as president, supporting him as he became increasingly highhanded and unpopular, and then stepping away after his opponent was elected in 1994. . . .

Austria presents an instructive example of what nation building has actually amounted to on the ground. In our tabulation, Austria is classified as a case of successful nation building, but a close look reveals that the U.S. role was irrelevant, if not harmful.

After the war, Austria was jointly occupied by Russia as well as the Western powers. The Soviets brought Karl Renner, the elderly and respected Austrian Socialist leader, to Vienna to be the head of a provisional government. Renner's provisional government declared the establishment of the Democratic Austrian Republic on April 27, 1945. For six months, the United States refused to recognize this government (fearing that the Russians were up to no good in supporting it). Finally, when it could not be denied that the provisional government was popular and functioning, the United States recognized it.

Austria thus presents a doubly ironic lesson in how nation building unfolds. The United States—the democratic power—stood in the way of local leaders who were attempting to establish a democratic regime, and the Soviet Union—the world's leading dictatorship—unintentionally acted as midwife for the first democratic administration. Obviously, in Austria, no democracy needed to be "built." The democratic forces in Austria were strong enough to establish a democracy on their own, and they did it in spite of the "nation builders."

The advocates of nation building need to go back and take a close look at what really happened in the postwar political evolution of the defeated powers. In the lore of nation building, it is supposed that American experts applied sophisticated social engineering that forced these countries to become democracies against their will. It wasn't that way at all. These countries became democracies on their own, and the bumptious generals and paper-shuffling bureaucrats of the military occupation were generally more of a hindrance than a help.

The recent intervention in Iraq further illustrates how haphazard and unfocused nation building is in practice. While the military campaign was a success, the occupation and administration has been characterized by naïveté and improvisation. The U.S. had no policy to check looting after victory, nor the forces to do it, and the result was a ravaging of local infrastructure, the rapid formation of gangs of thugs and paramilitary fighters, and a loss of local support for the U.S. effort. The civilian administration was first put in the hands of retired Lt. Gen. Jay Garner, who was two weeks late getting to Baghdad, and who naively expected to find a functioning government in the country. After a month, the hapless Garner was fired, replaced by Paul Bremer as chief administrator. Two months after the invasion, Lt. Gen. William Wallace, the V Corps commander, described the nation-building "technique" U.S. officials were applying in Iraq: "We're making this up here as we go along."

Nation building by military force is not a coherent, defensible policy. It is based on no theory, it has no proven technique or methodology, and there are no experts who know how to do it. The record shows that it usually fails, and even when it appears to succeed, the positive result owes more to historical evolution and local political culture than anything nation builders might have done.

# THE ENVIRONMENT AND CLIMATE CHANGE

## *The Tragedy of the Commons*

### GARRETT HARDIN

We can make little progress in working toward optimum population size until we explicitly exorcize the spirit of Adam Smith in the field of practical demography. In economic affairs, *The Wealth of Nations* (1776) popularized the "invisible hand," the idea that an individual who "intends only his own gain," is, as it were, "led by an invisible hand to promote . . . the public interest."[1] Adam Smith did not assert that this was invariably true, and perhaps neither did any of his followers. But he contributed to a dominant tendency of thought that has ever since interfered with positive action based on rational analysis, namely, the tendency to assume that decisions reached individually will, in fact, be the best decisions for an entire society. If this assumption is correct it justifies the continuance of our present policy of laissez-faire in reproduction. If it is correct we can assume that men will control their individual fecundity so as to produce the optimum population. If the assumption is not correct, we need to reexamine our individual freedoms to see which ones are defensible.

## TRAGEDY OF FREEDOM IN A COMMONS

The rebuttal to the invisible hand in population control is to be found in a scenario first sketched in a little-known pamphlet in 1833 by a mathematical amateur named William Foster Lloyd (1794–1852).[2] We may well call it "the tragedy of the commons," using the word "tragedy" as the philosopher Whitehead used it: "The essence of dramatic tragedy is not unhappiness. It resides in the solemnity of the remorseless working of things."[3] He then goes on to say, "This inevitableness of destiny can only be illustrated in terms of human life by incidents which in fact involve unhappiness. For it is only by them that the futility of escape can be made evident in the drama."

The tragedy of the commons develops in this way. Picture a pasture open to all. It is to be expected that each herdsman will try to keep as many cattle as possible on the commons. Such an arrangement may work reasonably satisfactorily for centuries because tribal wars, poaching, and disease keep the numbers of both man and beast well below the carrying capacity of the land. Finally, however, comes the day of reckoning, that is, the day when the long-desired goal of social stability becomes a reality. At this point, the inherent logic of the commons remorselessly generates tragedy.

As a rational being, each herdsman seeks to maximize his gain. Explicitly or implicitly, more or less consciously, he asks, "What is the utility *to me* of adding one more animal to my herd?" This utility has one negative and one positive component.

The positive component is a function of the increment of one animal. Since the herdsman receives all the proceeds from the sale of the additional animal, the positive utility is nearly $+1$.

The negative component is a function of the additional overgrazing created by one more animal. Since, however, the effects of overgrazing are shared by all the herdsmen, the negative utility for any particular decision-making herdsman is only a fraction of $-1$.

Adding together the component partial utilities, the rational herdsman concludes that the only sensible course for him to pursue is to add another animal to his herd. And another; and another. . . . But this is the conclusion reached by each and every rational herdsman sharing a commons. Therein is the tragedy. Each man is locked into a system that compels him to increase his herd without limit—in a world that is limited. Ruin is the destination toward which all men rush, each pursuing his own best interest in a society that believes in the freedom of the commons. Freedom in a commons brings ruin to all. . . .

In an approximate way, the logic of the commons has been understood for a long time, perhaps since the discovery of agriculture or the invention of private property in real estate. But it is understood mostly only in special cases which are not sufficiently generalized. Even at this late date, cattlemen leasing national land on the western ranges demonstrate no more than an ambivalent understanding, in constantly pressuring federal authorities to increase the head count to the point where overgrazing produces erosion and weed-dominance. Likewise, the oceans of the world continue to suffer from the survival of the philosophy of the commons. Maritime nations will respond automatically to the shibboleth of the "freedom of the seas." Professing to believe in the "inexhaustible resources of the oceans," they bring species after species of fish and whales closer to extinction. . . .

## POLLUTION

In a reverse way, the tragedy of the commons reappears in problems of pollution. Here it is not a question of taking something out of the commons, but of putting something in—sewage, or chemical, radioactive, and heat wastes into water; noxious and dangerous fumes into the air; and distracting and unpleasant advertising signs into the line of sight. The calculations of utility are much the same as before. The rational man finds that his share of the cost of the wastes he discharges into the commons is less than the cost of purifying his wastes before releasing them. Since this is true for everyone, we are locked into a system of "fouling our own nest," so long as we behave only as independent, rational, free-enterprisers.

The tragedy of the commons as a food basket is averted by private property, or something formally like it. But the air and waters surrounding us cannot readily be fenced, and so the tragedy of the commons as a cesspool must be prevented by different means, by coercive laws or taxing devices that make it cheaper for the polluter to treat his pollutant than to discharge them untreated. We have not progressed as far with the solution of this problem as we have with the first. Indeed, our particular concept of private property, which deters us from exhausting the positive resources of the earth, favors pollution. The owner of a factory on the bank of a stream—whose property extends to the middle of the stream—often has difficulty seeing why it is not his natural right to muddy the waters flowing past his door. The law, always behind the times, requires elaborate stitching and fitting to adapt to it this newly perceived aspect of the commons.

The pollution problem is a consequence of populations. It did not much matter how a lonely American frontiersman disposed of his waste. "Flowing water purifies itself every 10 miles," my grandfather used to say, and the myth was near enough to the truth when he was a boy, for there were not too many people. But as population became denser, the natural chemical and biological recycling processes became overloaded, calling for a redefinition of property rights.

## HOW TO LEGISLATE TEMPERANCE?

Analysis of the pollution problem as a function of population density uncovers a not generally recognized principle of morality, namely: *The morality of an act is a function of the state of the system at the time it is performed.*[4] Using the commons as a cesspool does not harm the general public under frontier conditions, because there is no public; the same behavior in a metropolis is unbearable. A hundred and fifty years ago a plainsman could kill an American bison, cut out only the tongue for his dinner, and discard the rest of the animal. He was not in any important sense being wasteful. Today, with only a few thousand bison left, we would be appalled at such behavior. . . .

That morality is system-sensitive escaped the attention of most codifiers of ethics in the past. "Thou shalt not . . . "is the form of traditional ethical directives which make no allowance for particular circumstances. The laws of our society follow the pattern of ancient ethics, and therefore are poorly suited to governing a complex, crowded, changeable world. Our epicyclic solution is to augment statutory law with administrative law. Since it is practically impossible to spell out all the conditions under which it is safe to burn trash in the backyard or to run an automobile without smog-control, by law we delegate the details to bureaus. The result is administrative law, which is rightly feared for an ancient reason—*Quis custodiet ipsos custodes?*—" Who shall watch the watchers themselves?" John Adams said that we must have "a government of laws and not men." Bureau administrators, trying to evaluate the morality of acts in the total system, are singularly liable to corruption, producing a government by men, not laws.

Prohibition is easy to legislate (though not necessarily to enforce); but how do we legislate temperance? Experience indicates that it can be accomplished best through the mediation of administrative law. We limit possibilities unnecessarily if we suppose that the sentiment of *Quis custodiet* denies us the use of administrative law. We should rather retain the phrase as a perpetual reminder of fearful dangers we cannot avoid. The great challenge facing us now is to invent the corrective feedbacks that are needed to keep custodians honest. We must find ways to legitimate the needed authority of both the custodians and the corrective feedbacks.

## FREEDOM TO BREED IS INTOLERABLE

The tragedy of the commons is involved in population problems in another way. In a world governed solely by the principle of "dog eat dog"—if indeed there ever was such a world—how many children a family had would not be a matter of public concern. Parents who bred too exuberantly would leave fewer descendants, not more, because they would be unable to care adequately for their children. . . .

*If* each human family were dependent only on its own resources; *if* the children of improvident parents starved to death; *if,* thus, overbreeding brought its own "punishment" to the germ line—*then* there would be no public interest in controlling the breeding of families. But our society is deeply committed to the welfare state and hence is confronted with another aspect of the tragedy of the commons.

In a welfare state, how shall we deal with the family, the religion, the race, or the class (or indeed any distinguishable and cohesive group) that adopts overbreeding as a policy to secure its own aggrandizement? To couple the concept of freedom to breed with the belief that everyone born has an equal right to the commons is to lock the world into a tragic course of action. . . .

## CONSCIENCE IS SELF-ELIMINATING

It is a mistake to think that we can control the breeding of mankind in the long run by an appeal to conscience. Charles Galton Darwin made this point when he spoke on the centennial of the publication of his grandfather's great book. The argument is straightforward and Darwinian.

People vary. Confronted with appeals to limit breeding, some people will undoubtedly respond to the plea more than others. Those who have more children will produce a larger fraction of the next generation than those with more susceptible consciences. The difference will be accentuated, generation by generation.

In C. G. Darwin's words: "It may well be that it would take hundreds of generations for the progenitive instinct to develop in this way, but if it should do so, nature would have taken her revenge, and the variety *Homo contracipiens* would become extinct and would be replaced by the variety *Homo progenitivus.*"[5]

The argument assumes that conscience or the desire for children (no matter which) is hereditary—but hereditary only in the most general formal sense. The result will be the same whether the attitude is transmitted through germ cells, or exosomatically. . . . The argument has here been stated in the context of the population problem, but it applies equally well to any instance in which society appeals to an individual exploiting a commons to restrain himself for the general good—by means of his conscience. To make such an appeal is to set up a selective system that works toward the elimination of conscience from the race. . . .

## MUTUAL COERCION MUTUALLY AGREED UPON

The social arrangements that produce responsibility are arrangements that create coercion, of some sort. Consider bank-robbing. The man who takes money from a bank acts as if the bank were a commons. How do we prevent such action? Certainly not by trying to control his behavior solely by a verbal appeal to his sense of responsibility. Rather than rely on propaganda we follow Frankel's lead and insist that a bank is not a commons; we seek the definite social arrangements that will keep it from becoming a commons. That we thereby infringe on the freedom of would-be robbers we neither deny nor regret.

The morality of bank-robbing is particularly easy to understand because we accept complete prohibition of this activity. We are willing to say "Thou shalt not rob banks," without providing for exceptions. But temperance also can be created by coercion. Taxing is a good coercive device. To keep downtown shoppers temperate in their use of parking space we introduce parking meters for short periods, and traffic fines for longer ones. We need not actually forbid a citizen to park as long as he wants to; we need merely make it increasingly expensive for him to do so. Not prohibition, but carefully biased options are what we offer him. A Madison Avenue man might call this persuasion; I prefer the greater candor of the word coercion. . . .

To many, the word coercion implies arbitrary decisions of distant and irresponsible bureaucrats; but this is not a necessary part of its meaning. The only kind of coercion I recommend is mutual coercion, mutually agreed upon by the majority of the people affected.

To say that we mutually agree to coercion is not to say that we are required to enjoy it, or even to pretend we enjoy it. Who enjoys taxes? We all grumble about them. But we accept compulsory taxes because we recognize that voluntary taxes would favor the conscienceless. We institute and (grumblingly) support taxes and other coercive devices to escape the horror of the commons. . . .

## RECOGNITION OF NECESSITY

Perhaps the simplest summary of this analysis of man's population problems is this: The commons, if justifiable at all, is justifiable only under conditions of low population density. As the human population has increased, the commons has had to be abandoned in one aspect after another.

First we abandoned the commons in food gathering, enclosing farm land and restricting pastures and hunting and fishing areas. These restrictions are still not complete throughout the world.

Somewhat later we saw that the commons as a place for waste disposal would also have to be abandoned. Restrictions on the disposal of domestic sewage are widely accepted in the Western world; we are still struggling to close the commons to pollution by automobiles, factories, insecticide sprayers, fertilizing operations, and atomic energy installations. . . .

Every new enclosure of the commons involves the infringement of somebody's personal liberty. Infringements made in the distant past are accepted because no contemporary complains of a loss. It is the newly proposed infringements that we vigorously oppose; cries of "rights" and "freedom" fill the air. But what does "freedom" mean? When men mutually agreed to pass laws against robbing, mankind became more free, not less so. Individuals locked into the logic of the commons are free only to bring on universal ruin; once they see the necessity of mutual coercion, they become free to pursue other goals. I believe it was Hegel who said, "Freedom is the recognition of necessity."

The most important aspect of necessity that we must now recognize is the necessity of abandoning the commons in breeding. No technical solution can rescue us from the misery of overpopulation. Freedom to breed will bring ruin to all. At the moment, to avoid hard decisions many of us are tempted to propagandize for conscience and responsible parenthood. The temptation must be resisted, because an appeal to independently acting consciences selects for the disappearance of all conscience in the long run, and an increase in anxiety in the short.

The only way we can preserve and nurture other and more precious freedoms is by relinquishing the freedom to breed, and that very soon. "Freedom is the recognition of necessity"—and it is the role of education to reveal to all the necessity of abandoning the freedom to breed. Only so can we put an end to this aspect of the tragedy of the commons.

## NOTES

1. Adam Smith, *The Wealth of Nations* (New York: Modern Library, 1937), p. 423.
2. William Foster Lloyd, *Two Lectures on the Checks to Population* (Oxford: Oxford University Press, 1853), reprinted in part in *Population, Evolution, and Birth Control*, A. Harding, ed. (San Francisco: Freeman, 1964), p. 37.
3. A. N. Whitehead, *Science and the Modern World* (New York: Mentor, 1948), p. 17.
4. J. Fletcher, *Situation Ethics* (Philadelphia: Westminster, 1966).
5. S. Tax, ed., *Evolution after Darwin*, Vol. 2 (Chicago: University of Chicago Press, 1960), p. 469.

# Environmental Changes as Causes of Acute Conflict

## THOMAS HOMER-DIXON

. . . How might environmental change lead to acute conflict? Some experts propose that environmental change may shift the balance of power between states either regionally or globally, producing instabilities that could lead to war. Or, as global environmental damage increases the disparity between the North and the South, poor nations may militarily confront the rich for a greater share of the world's wealth. Warmer temperatures could lead to contention over new ice-free sea-lanes in the Arctic or more accessible resources in the Antarctic. Bulging populations and land stress may produce waves of environmental refugees that spill across borders with destabilizing effects on the recipient's domestic order and on international stability. Countries may fight over dwindling supplies of water and the effects of upstream pollution. In developing countries, a sharp drop in food crop production could lead to internal strife across urban-rural and nomadic-sedentary cleavages. If environmental degradation makes food supplies increasingly tight, exporters may be tempted to use food as a weapon. Environmental change could ultimately cause the gradual impoverishment of societies in both the North and South, which could aggravate class and ethnic cleavages, undermine liberal regimes, and spawn insurgencies. Finally, many scholars indicate that environmental degradation will "ratchet up" the level of stress within national and international society, thus increasing the likelihood of many different kinds of conflict and impeding the development of cooperative solutions. . . .

## THE RANGE OF ENVIRONMENTAL PROBLEMS

Developing countries are likely to be affected sooner and more severely by environmental change than rich countries. By definition, they do not have the financial, material, or intellectual resources of the developed world; furthermore, their social and political institutions tend to be fragile and riven with discord. It is probable, therefore, that developing societies will be less able to apprehend or respond to environmental disruption.

From Thomas F. Homer-Dixon, "On the Threshold: Environmental Changes as Causes of Acute Conflict," *International Security*, Vol. 16, No. 2 (Fall 1991), pp. 76–116. © 1991 by the President and Fellows of Harvard College and the Massachusetts Institute of Technology. Reprinted by permission of The MIT Press. Portions of the text and some footnotes have been omitted.

Seven major environmental problems . . . might plausibly contribute to conflict within and among developing countries: greenhouse warming, stratospheric ozone depletion, acid deposition, deforestation, degradation of agricultural land, overuse and pollution of water supplies, and depletion of fish stocks. These problems can all be crudely characterized as large-scale human-induced problems, with long-term and often irreversible consequences, which is why they are often grouped together under the rubric "global change." However, they vary greatly in spatial scale: the first two involve genuinely global physical processes, while the last five involve regional physical processes, although they may appear in locales all over the planet. These seven problems also vary in time scale: for example, while a region can be deforested in only a few years, and severe ecological and social effects may be noticeable almost immediately, human-induced greenhouse warming will probably develop over many decades and may not have truly serious implications for humankind for half a century or more after the signal is first detected. In addition, some of these problems (for instance, deforestation and degradation of water supplies) are much more advanced than others (such as greenhouse warming and ozone depletion) and are already producing serious social disruption. This variance in tangible evidence for these problems contributes to great differences in our certainty about their ultimate severity. The uncertainties surrounding greenhouse warming, for example, are thus far greater than those concerning deforestation.

Many of these problems are causally interrelated. For instance, acid deposition damages agricultural land, fisheries, and forests. Greenhouse warming may contribute to deforestation by moving northward the optimal temperature and precipitation zones for many tree species, by increasing the severity of windstorms and wildfires, and by expanding the range of pests and diseases. The release of carbon from these dying forests would reinforce the greenhouse effect. The increased incidence of ultraviolet radiation due to the depletion of the ozone layer will probably damage trees and crops, and it may also damage the phytoplankton at the bottom of the ocean food chain.

Finally, when we consider the social effects of environmental change, especially of climate change, we should be especially aware of changes in the incidence of "extreme" environmental events. Social impacts result "not so much from slow fluctuations in the mean, but from the tails of the distribution, from extreme events." While a two-to-three degree celsius mean global warming might not seem too significant for agricultural production, it may produce a large increase in crop-devastating droughts, floods, heat waves, and storms.

## FOUR PRINCIPAL SOCIAL EFFECTS

Environmental degradation may cause countless often subtle changes in developing societies. These range from increased communal cooking as fuel-wood becomes scarce around African villages, to worsened poverty of Filipino coastal fishermen whose once-abundant grounds have been destroyed by trawlers and industrial pollution. Which of the many types of social effects might be crucial links between environmental change and acute conflict? This is the first part of the "how" question. To address it, we must use both the best knowledge about the social effects of environmental change and the best knowledge about the nature and causes of social conflict.

In thus working from both ends towards the middle of the causal chain, I hypothesize that four principal social effects may, either singly or in combination, substantially increase the probability of acute conflict in developing countries: decreased agricultural production, economic decline, population displacement, and disruption of legitimized and authoritative institutions and social relations. These effects will often be causally interlinked, sometimes with reinforcing relationships. For example, the population displacement resulting from a decrease in agricultural production may further disrupt agricultural production. Or economic decline may lead to the flight of people with wealth and education, which in turn could eviscerate universities, courts, and institutions of economic management, all of which are crucial to a healthy economy.

## Agricultural Production

Decreased agricultural production is often mentioned as potentially the most worrisome consequence of environmental change. . . .

Large tracts are being lost each year to urban encroachment, erosion, nutrient depletion, salinization, waterlogging, acidification, and compacting. The geographer Vaclav Smil, who is generally very conservative in his assessments of environmental damage, estimates that two to three million hectares of cropland are lost annually to erosion; perhaps twice as much land goes to urbanization, and at least one million hectares are abandoned because of excessive salinity. In addition, about one-fifth of the world's cropland is suffering from some degree of desertification. Taken together, he concludes, the planet will lose about 100 million hectares of arable land between 1985 and 2000. . . .[1]

Greenhouse warming and climate change [can affect] . . . agricultural production. Coastal cropland in countries such as Bangladesh and Egypt is extremely vulnerable to storm surges. Such events could become more common and devastating, because global warming will cause sea levels to rise and might intensify storms. The greenhouse effect will also change precipitation patterns and soil moisture; while this may benefit some agricultural regions, others will suffer. . . .

## Economic Decline

If we are interested in environment-conflict linkages, perhaps the most important potential social effect of environmental degradation is the further impoverishment it may produce in developing societies. . . . A great diversity of factors might affect wealth production. For example, increased ultraviolet radiation caused by ozone depletion is likely to raise the rate of disease in humans and livestock which could have serious economic results. Logging for export markets may produce short-term economic gain for the country's elite, but increased runoff can damage roads, bridges, and other valuable infrastructure, while the extra siltation reduces the transport and hydroelectric capacity of rivers. As forests are destroyed, wood becomes scarcer and more expensive, and it absorbs an increasing share of the household budget for the poor families that use it for fuel. . . .

## Population Displacement

Some commentators have suggested that environmental degradation may produce vast numbers of "environmental refugees." Sea-level rise may drive people back from coastal and delta areas in Egypt; spreading desert may empty Sahelian countries as their populations move south; Filipino fishermen may leave their depleted fishing grounds for the cities. The term "environmental refugee" is somewhat misleading, however, because it implies that environmental disruption could be a clear, proximate cause of refugee flows. Usually, though, environmental disruption will be only one of many interacting physical and social variables, including agricultural and economic decline, that ultimately force people from their homelands. For example, over the last three decades, millions of people have migrated from Bangladesh to neighboring West Bengal and Assam in India. While detailed data are scarce (in part because the Bangladeshi government is reluctant to admit there is significant out-migration), many specialists believe this movement is a result, at least in part, of shortages of adequately fertile land due to a rapidly growing population. Flooding, caused by deforestation in watersheds upstream on the Ganges and Brahmaputra rivers, might also be driving people from the area. In the future, this migration could be aggravated by rising sea-levels coupled with extreme weather events (both perhaps resulting from climate change).

## Disrupted Institutions and Social Relations

The fourth social effect especially relevant to the connection between environment change and acute conflict is the disruption of institutions and of legitimized, accepted, and authoritative social relations. In many developing societies, the three social effects described above are likely to tear this fabric of custom and habitual behavior. A drop in agricultural output may weaken rural communities by causing malnutrition and disease, and by encouraging people to leave; economic decline may corrode confidence in the national purpose, weaken the tax base, and undermine financial, legal, and political institutions; and mass migrations of people into a region may disrupt labor markets, shift class relations, and upset the traditional balance of economic and political authority between ethnic groups.

### *The Capacity of Developing Countries to Respond: First-Stage Interventions*

Can developing countries respond to environmental problems effectively enough to avert these negative social effects? The aggregate data on world food production might give us reason for optimism. Between 1965 and 1986, many developing regions suffered serious environmental problems, including erosion, salinization, and loss of land to urbanization. Yet global cereal production increased at 3 percent a year, meat and milk output increased 2 percent annually, while the rate for oil crops, vegetables, and pulses was 2.5 percent. At the regional level, increased food production kept ahead of population growth, except in Africa, and local short-falls were alleviated by exports from developed countries with huge surpluses. We might therefore conclude that developing countries have sufficient capacity, with intermittent assistance from Northern grain exporters, to respond to environmental problems.

But aggregate figures hide significant disparities in food availability among and within developing countries. Moreover, these figures are becoming less promising than they once were: many developing countries have already reaped most of the green revolution's potential benefit, and the rate of increase in global cereal production has declined by over 40 percent since the 1960s. For three successive years—from 1987 through 1989—estimated global cereal consumption exceeded production. Bumper grain crops were again harvested in 1990, but carry-over stocks can be depleted rapidly, and we remain within one or two years of a global food crisis.

Over the long term, the capacity of developing countries to respond effectively to the consequences of environmental change on agriculture will depend on the complex interactions within each society of . . . the society's prevailing land-use practices, land distribution, and market mechanisms within the agricultural sector. Market factors are especially relevant today as numerous developing countries are relinquishing state control over the marketplace, reducing government spending, and removing impediments to foreign investment. Economists often contend that—in a market economy with an efficient price mechanism—environmentally induced scarcity will encourage conservation, technological innovation, and resource substitution. Julian Simon, in particular, displays an unwavering faith in the capacity of human ingenuity to overcome scarcity when spurred by self-interest.[2] Many economists point to the success of the green revolution, which was often driven by market forces; it involved both new technologies and the substitution of petroleum resources (in the form of fertilizer) for inadequate or degraded nutrients in the soil. This argument supports the policies for market liberalization and "structural adjustment" currently promoted by international financial and lending institutions, such as the International Monetary Fund and World Bank. Below, however, I suggest why these policies will not be an effective response to environmental scarcity in the future.

## CORNUCOPIANS AND NEO-MALTHUSIANS

Experts in environmental studies now commonly use the labels "cornucopian" for optimists like Simon and "neo-Malthusian" for pessimists like Paul and Anne Ehrlich.[3] Cornucopians do not worry much about protecting the stock of any single resource, because of their faith that market-driven human ingenuity can always be tapped to allow the substitution of more abundant resources to produce the same end-use service. . . .

Historically, cornucopians have been right to criticize the idea that resource scarcity places fixed limits on human activity. Time and time again, human beings have circumvented scarcities, and neo-Malthusians have often been justly accused of "crying wolf." But in assuming that this experience pertains to the future, cornucopians overlook seven factors.

First, whereas serious scarcities of critical resources in the past usually appeared singly, now we face multiple scarcities that exhibit powerful interactive, feedback, and threshold effects. An agricultural region may, for example, be simultaneously affected by degraded water and soil, greenhouse-induced precipitation changes, and increased ultraviolet radiation. This makes the future highly uncertain for policymakers and economic actors; tomorrow will be full of extreme events and surprises. Furthermore, as numerous resources become scarce simultaneously, it will be harder to identify substitution possibilities that produce the same end-use services at costs that prevailed when scarcity was less severe. Second, in the past the scarcity of a given resource usually increased slowly, allowing time for social, economic, and technological adjustment. But human populations are much larger and activities of individuals are, on a global average, much more resource-intensive than before. This means that debilitating scarcities often develop much more quickly: whole countries may be deforested in a few decades; most of a region's topsoil can disappear in a generation; and critical ozone depletion may occur in as little as twenty years. Third, today's consumption has far greater momentum than in the past, because of the size of the consuming population, the sheer quantity of material consumed by this population, and the density of its interwoven fabric of consumption activities. The countless individual and corporate economic actors making up human society are heavily committed to certain patterns of resource use; and the ability of our markets to adapt may be sharply constrained by these entrenched interests.

These first three factors may soon combine to produce a daunting syndrome of environmentally induced scarcity: humankind will face multiple resource shortages that are interacting and unpredictable, that grow to crisis proportions rapidly, and that will be hard to address because of powerful commitments to certain consumption patterns.

The fourth reason that cornucopian arguments may not apply in the future is that the free-market price mechanism is a bad gauge of scarcity, especially for resources held in common, such as a benign climate and productive seas. In the past, many such resources seemed endlessly abundant; now they are being degraded and depleted, and we are learning that their increased scarcity often has tremendous bearing on a society's well-being. Yet this scarcity is at best reflected only indirectly in market prices. In addition, people often cannot participate in market transactions in which they have an interest, either because they lack the resources or because they are distant from the transaction process in time or space; in these cases the true scarcity of the resource is not reflected by its price.

The fifth reason is an extension of a point made earlier: market-driven adaptation to resource scarcity is most likely to succeed in wealthy societies, where abundant reserves of capital, knowledge, and talent help economic actors invent new technologies, identify conservation possibilities, and make the transition to new production and consumption patterns. Yet many of the societies facing the most serious environmental problems in the coming decades will be poor; even if they have efficient markets, lack of capital and know-how will hinder their response to these problems.

Sixth, cornucopians have an anachronistic faith in humankind's ability to unravel and manage the myriad processes of nature. There is no *a priori* reason to expect that human scientific and technical ingenuity can always surmount all types of scarcity. Human beings may not have the mental capacity to understand adequately the complexities of environmental-social systems. Or it may simply be impossible, given the physical, biological, and social laws governing these systems, to reduce all scarcity or repair all environmental damage. Moreover, the chaotic nature of these systems may keep us from fully anticipating the consequences of various adaptation and intervention strategies. Perhaps most important, scientific and technical knowledge must be built incrementally—layer upon layer—and its diffusion to the broader society often takes decades. Any technical solutions to environmental scarcity may arrive too late to prevent catastrophe.

Seventh and finally, future environmental problems, rather than inspiring the wave of ingenuity predicted by cornucopians, may instead reduce the supply of ingenuity available in a society. The success of market mechanisms depends on an intricate and stable system of institutions, social relations, and shared understandings. . . . Cornucopians often overlook the role of *social* ingenuity in producing the complex legal and economic climate in which *technical* ingenuity can flourish. Policymakers must be clever "social engineers" to design and implement effective market mechanisms. Unfortunately, however, the syndrome of multiple, interacting, unpredictable, and rapidly changing environmental problems will increase the complexity and pressure of the policymaking setting. It will also generate increased "social friction" as elites and interest groups struggle to protect their prerogatives. The ability of policymakers to be good social engineers is likely to go *down*, not up, as these stresses increase.

## NOTES

1. Smil gives a startling account of the situation in China. From 1957 to 1977 the country lost 33.33 million hectares of farmland (30 percent of its 1957 total), while it added 21.2 million hectares of largely marginal land. He notes that "the net loss of 12 million hectares during a single generation when the country's population grew by about 300 million people means that per capita availability of arable land dropped by 40 percent and that China's farmland is now no more abundant than Bangladesh's—a mere one-tenth of a hectare per capita!" See Smil, *Energy, Food, Environment*, pp. 223 and 230.
2. Simon, *The Ultimate Resource*. Population growth, by Simon's analysis, is not necessarily a bad thing; in fact, it may be helpful because it increases the labor force and the pool of potential human ingenuity. See also Ester Boserup, *The Conditions of Agricultural Growth: The Economics of Agrarian Change Under Population Pressure* (Chicago: Aldine, 1965).
3. Ehrlich, Ehrlich, and Holdren, *Ecoscience*; Ehrlich and Ehrlich, *The Population Explosion*.

# Beyond Kyoto

## JOHN BROWNE

### THE CARBON CHALLENGE

In 1997, more than 180 countries gathered in Kyoto, Japan, in search of a coordinated international response to global warming. The provisional agreement they reached appeared to mark a significant step forward. But the Kyoto Protocol is coming unraveled. Despite nearly a decade of effort, it may not even enter into force as a binding instrument. Canada, Japan, and the European Union—the most enthusiastic advocates of the Kyoto process—are not on track to meet their commitments. And the United States has withdrawn from the agreement entirely. Those concerned with the sustainability of the earth's climate could be forgiven for feeling depressed.

Clear-eyed realism is essential. But dismay, however understandable, is a mistaken reaction. There is scope for a different and more positive view of the last seven years and of the future. First, it has become obvious that Kyoto was simply the starting point of a very long endeavor—comparable, perhaps, to the meetings in 1946 at which a group of 23 countries agreed to reduce tariffs. Those meetings set in motion a process that led to the establishment of the General Agreement on Tariffs and Trade in 1948, which, in turn, led to the creation of the World Trade Organization in the mid-1990s. Second, we have improved, if still imperfect, knowledge of the challenges and uncertainties that climate change presents, as well as a better understanding of the time scales involved. Third, many countries and companies have had experience reducing emissions and have proved that such reductions can be achieved without destroying competitiveness or jobs. Fourth, science and technology have advanced on multiple fronts. And finally, public awareness of the issue has grown—not just in the developed world but all around the globe.

Seven years after the Kyoto meeting, it is becoming clear that the reduction of greenhouse gas emissions is a soluble problem, and that the mechanisms for delivering the solutions are within reach. In that spirit of cautious optimism, it is time to move beyond the current Kyoto debate.

### KNOWNS AND UNKNOWNS

Before considering new approaches, it is necessary to distill some basic facts from the voluminous, complex, and incomplete scientific work on global warming.

From John Browne, "Beyond Kyoto." Reprinted by permission of *Foreign Affairs*, Vol. 83, No. 4 (July/August 2004), pp. 20–32. Copyright 2004 by the Council on Foreign Relations, Inc.

Global temperatures have risen by about 0.6 degrees Celsius since the nineteenth century. Other measures of climate bolster the theory that the world is getting warmer: satellite measurements suggest that spring arrives about a week earlier now than in the late 1970s, for example, and records show that migratory birds fly to higher latitudes earlier in the season and stay later. According to the UN's Intergovernmental Panel on Climate Change (IPCC)—by far the most authoritative body of scientists working on this issue—humans are probably not responsible for all the measured warming. But the trend is undoubtedly due in large part to substantial increases in carbon dioxide emissions from human activity. Since the middle of the nineteenth century, the average concentration of carbon dioxide—a so-called greenhouse gas—in the world's atmosphere has risen from some 280 parts per million (ppm) to around 370 ppm. Burning fossil fuels account for about three-quarters of human emissions, with deforestation and changes in land use (mainly in the tropics) accounting for the rest.

There are two main reasons why it has been hard for societies to tackle climate change. First, carbon dioxide has a very long life span: it exists for hundreds of years in the atmosphere, making this a multigenerational issue. Second, reducing carbon dioxide in the atmosphere can be done only on a truly global basis, since emissions mix throughout the atmosphere much quicker than individual processes can limit their impact.

Beyond these known facts, the picture becomes murkier. For instance, nobody knows how rapidly emissions of carbon dioxide and other greenhouse gases will rise in the future. That outcome depends on the pace of global economic growth and on the impact of technology on the ways society generates and deploys useful energy. Equally, it is impossible to determine precisely how the climate will respond as greenhouse gases accumulate to ever-higher concentrations in the atmosphere. The brightness and altitude of clouds, for example, determine whether warming is amplified or diminished, yet it is not known how exactly climate change will affect cloud patterns. Nor is it known how the world's carbon cycle will respond. A warmer climate might make the planet greener—which would mean more carbon dioxide would be sucked from the atmosphere. Alternatively, climate change might impose such severe stress on the biosphere that nature's processes for removing carbon dioxide from the atmosphere would become less efficient than normal.

The most recent IPCC assessment, published in 2001, concludes that if no precautionary action is taken, carbon dioxide concentrations will rise by 2050 to between 450 and 550 ppm and will continue to increase throughout the twenty-first century. The IPCC estimates that temperatures will rise by between 0.5 degrees Celsius and 2.5 degrees Celsius by 2050, with an increase of 1.4 degrees to 5.8 degrees possible by 2100.

One of the most likely effects of global warming is a rise in sea level, as glaciers melt and warmer water expands in the oceans. The best projections suggest seas of between 5 centimeters and 32 centimeters higher by 2050; the outer limit projected for 2100 approaches one meter. These numbers seem small, but coastlines are shallow slopes, not firm walls, so a rise in water levels of just tens of centimeters would erase kilometers of wetlands and beaches.

Industrialized countries will probably be able to handle rising water levels, at least in the next few decades. London and cities in the Netherlands, for example, already have defenses to hold back surging seas. And farmers in wealthy countries can respond to changes in climate by adjusting irrigation and varying the crops they plant, in many cases with government financial support. But the developing world, home to four-fifths of humanity, is likely to fare considerably worse on both fronts. Hundreds of thousands of people have already been displaced by periodic flooding in Bangladesh, and subsistence farmers—who are far less adaptive than their richer counterparts—are already struggling at the climatic margin.

The most dramatic scenarios, although unlikely, would have grave consequences for humanity and ecosystems. Rapid changes in climate could upset the circulation of the North Atlantic, for example—which, ironically, would cause much colder regional temperatures in northern Europe by weakening the heat-rich Gulf Stream. The Amazon rain forest could deplete dramatically due to drying in the atmosphere, in turn releasing huge volumes of carbon that is stored in trees. And an accelerated rise in sea level from melting ice in Antarctica could occur. These uncertain consequences do not lead to crisp timetables for policy. But they mean that precaution and improvements in measurement and learning will be crucial.

A sober strategy would ensure that any increase in the world's temperature is limited to between 2 or 3 degrees Celsius above the current level in the long run. Focused on that goal, a growing number of governments and experts have concluded that policy should aim to stabilize concentrations of carbon dioxide in the atmosphere in the range from 500 to 550 ppm over the next century, which is less than twice the pre-industrial level.

On the basis of known technology, the cost of meeting this goal would be high. But the track record of technological progress in other fields indicates an enormous potential for costs to fall as new ideas are developed and applied. In the energy industry, for example, the costs of deep-water oil and gas development have fallen by a factor of three over the last 15 years, dramatically extending the frontier of commercial activity. There is no reason to think that research and development in the area of benign energy systems would be less successful. Predicting where that success might come will not be easy—but that means progress must be made on multiple fronts.

Many people believe that the 500–550 ppm goal would help avoid the worst calamities. But we must recognize this assessment for what it is: a judgment informed by current knowledge, rather than a confirmed conclusion to the story. . . .

## EFFICIENCY AND TRANSFORMATION

Both the exact level of the peak in global carbon dioxide emissions over time and the subsequent decline are unknown. We can safely assume, however, that emissions from developing countries will keep rising as economic activity and incomes grow. . . . This means that leadership must come from the industrialized world.

In the short term, the developed world can use energy much more efficiently and profitably. With a clear impetus for change, business could put new technologies and services to use: cautiously at first, but more aggressively as the best systems are identified and put into practice with the normal turnover of capital.

Business has already found that it is possible to reduce emissions from its operations. Counterintuitively, BP found that it was able to reach its initial target of reducing emissions by 10 percent below its 1990 levels without cost. Indeed, the company added around $650 million of shareholder value, because the bulk of the reductions came from the elimination of leaks and waste. Other firms—such as electricity generator Entergy, car manufacturer Toyota, and mining giant Rio Tinto—are having similar experiences. The overwhelming message from these experiments is that efficiency can both pay dividends and reduce emissions.

Yet reducing emissions by . . . 25 billion tons per year in 2050 will require more than just efficiency improvements. Given the world's rising demand for energy, we must also transform the energy system itself, making fuller use of low-carbon fuels as well as carbon-free energy systems. Paradigm shifts must occur across the economy: transportation accounts for 20 percent of total emissions, industry contributes another 20 percent, the domestic and commercial sectors emit around 25 percent, and power-generation accounts for another 35 percent. A wide-ranging set of policies is thus called for.

In power generation, options include switching from coal to less-carbon-intensive natural gas. For example, 400 new gas plants, each generating 1,000 megawatts, would reduce emissions by one billion tons per year. Such a reduction would be difficult within the parameters of today's electricity systems—400,000 megawatts is roughly equal to all of China's electric power capacity, or half the installed capacity in the United States. Zero-carbon fuels would also help reduce emissions. If 200,000 megawatts of coal-generated power were to be replaced with nuclear power, carbon dioxide emissions would be reduced by one billion tons per year. Progress on the nuclear front will demand investment in new technologies, as well as a viable plan for locating reactors that ensures that radioactive materials are kept out of the environment and beyond terrorists' reach.

Coal, too, could be made carbon-free, using advanced power plants that gasify the fuel and then generate power while stripping away the carbon for sequestration underground. Coal gasification could become a huge growth industry. China is among the top investors in this technology, not just because these plants are much cleaner, but also because they could be keystones in a program to synthesize clean liquid fuels for transportation needs.

More efficient buildings would also result in large energy savings, since over one-third of today's energy is used indoors. Given that electrification is a central feature of industrial and postindustrial societies, innovators must tap the potential for ultra-efficient electrical appliances. Investment in a digitally controlled power grid could aid this effort by allowing major appliances to "talk" directly with power generators so that the whole system operates closer to its optimum potential. Such a "smart grid" would reduce losses in electricity transmission while also allowing fuller use of waste heat from power generators in factories and homes.

There are efficiency savings to be made in transportation too. Given the massive advantages of gasoline over rival fuels—both in terms of its power density and its ease of storage—transport is unlikely to switch to new fuels in the near future. More promising approaches will focus on making transportation more efficient, while meeting the ever-stricter limits on other emissions that cause air pollution. For example, running 600 million diesel or gasoline cars at 60 miles per gallon (mpg) instead of 30 mpg would result in a billion fewer tons of carbon dioxide per year. Advanced ultra-efficient diesel engines, meanwhile, are so clean that even the strictest regulatory body in the world—the California Air Resources Board—is taking a second look. Advanced techniques for gasoline injection also hold promise, as do hybrid electric-gasoline cars already on the road. Such vehicles have the potential to get more than twice the mileage per gallon of their conventional counterparts. Given the increasing consumer demand for speed and flexibility in air travel, policymakers should also focus on the opportunities for cutting emissions from aircraft.

All of these efforts will require major investments. Some will also require new infrastructures. But we must begin to build and test such systems. Only with evidence from actual experience can we decide how best to direct our efforts.

## DOWN TO BUSINESS

The role of business is to transform possibilities into reality. And that means being practical, undertaking focused research, and testing the different possibilities in real commercial markets. The energy business is now global, which offers a tremendous advantage: international companies access knowledge around the world and apply it quickly throughout their operations.

But the business sector cannot succeed in isolation. Harnessing business potential requires fair and credible incentives to drive the process of innovation and change. In responding to global warming, that role must fall to the government. Neither prescriptive regulations nor fiscal interventions designed to collect revenue rather than to alter behavior provide the answer. Rather, governments must identify meaningful objectives and encourage the business sector to attain them by using its knowledge of technology, markets, and consumer preferences.

Recent experience suggests that emissions trading regimes—whereby government sets a binding cap on total emissions, dividing the total into "emission credits" that are given to those who emit carbon dioxide—are the best policy for encouraging business. Policymakers (notably in the United States) have demonstrated that it is possible to design such systems for other pollutants, such as sulphur dioxide, thereby harnessing the power of innovation and the flexibility of the market to protect the environment, while avoiding crippling costs. The same insights should apply to carbon dioxide. A well-designed trading regime would include a strictly enforced cap, which would make carbon dioxide emission credits scarcer (and thus more valuable) and would thereby increase the incentive for business to control emissions. Such a system would also allow firms and households the flexibility to apply resources where they have the greatest impact, which is essential, because the best measures for controlling carbon dioxide are hard to anticipate with precision and are widely dispersed across the economy. And a credible emission trading system would create incentives to invest in radical new technologies, the kind that will be crucial in building a carbon-free energy system in the future.

Emissions trading systems need not be identical in every country, nor be applied universally from day one. The political reality is that we are unlikely to see the sudden emergence of a single regime; in scope and ambition, that would be comparable to the emergence of a single global currency. Instead, progress is much more likely to come through the gradual process of knitting together diverse national and regional efforts on the basis of their track records of experience and achievement. The key task today is to find practices that will lead to a system that will enable today's diverse and fragmented reduction efforts to be valued on a common basis. The history of trade liberalization over the second half of the twentieth century shows that gradualism can yield impressive results.

At present, the nascent European emission trading system . . . is the most advanced example. Built on sound monitoring and verification policies, the system is the centerpiece of the European effort to implement the commitments adopted at Kyoto. . . . The potential for extending the scope of the trading base is indeed considerable, not least through the incorporation of effective incentives that will reward businesses whose investments reduce emissions outside Europe, such as in Russia and the emerging market economies of Asia—where large and relatively low-cost reductions of emissions are possible.

Markets are emerging in other regions as well. The Chicago Climate Exchange, opened in December 2003, involves 19 North American entities that have agreed to reduce their emissions by one percent per year over four years. Canada may yet create a market for carbon dioxide as it aims to meet the Kyoto targets. And U.S. states have become laboratories for innovation and change. For example, Massachusetts, New York, and New Hampshire are adopting rules that will spur the creation of market-based emission trading systems. Voluntary systems for measuring emissions—such as one being crafted in California—may also provide further foundations for emission trading. There is a strong argument for linking these efforts. U.S. policymakers should also consider establishing a transatlantic partnership to work toward a common market-based trading system.

Offering positive incentives is one key contribution that government can make to stimulate business. Another is organizing research. It is crucial to extend our understanding of the science of climate change: monitoring key variables with sufficient precision to understand both natural variability and the climate's response to human activity. A key target of such work must be to understand the precise connection between the concentration of carbon dioxide in the atmosphere and changes in climate. Such research must also advance our knowledge of available choices: with the clock ticking, we cannot wait for definite answers before we take action.

Government intervention must take other forms too. Transforming the energy system will require new technologies with risks that will be too high (and benefits too remote) for private firms to provide all the needed investment. This is one area in which the United States, with its outstanding technical capacity, should take a leadership role. Innovation will require an across-the-board infusion of resources for basic science and technology, as well as the development of a portfolio of key demonstration projects. The priorities for such work might include photovoltaic cells (which convert sunlight into electricity), fission reactor technology, energy from biomass, and the use of hydrogen.

Given the costs and risks involved in such investment, governments with common interests and common views of the future have every incentive to combine their efforts and resources. Fortunately, there are many precedents of international partnerships in innovation—from high-energy physics to astronomy and nuclear fusion. The global warming challenge is different, in that it involves not only basic science but also the application of novel techniques through products that must withstand the test of competition. But that is why the program of research and development work should involve collaboration not just between different countries but also between governments and business.

There are examples of such collaborative work already underway. In November 2003, a ministerial-level meeting held in Washington, D.C., began the process of building international partnerships for research on the potential of the hydrogen economy. The United States has already pledged $1.7 billion over the next five years for work in this area. A similar collaboration—the International Carbon Sequestration Leadership Forum—is built around the concept of capturing carbon and storing it geologically. Again, this scheme complements programs in the United States, such as FutureGen, a $1 billion public-private partnership to promote emissions-free coal-fired electricity and hydrogen production. These research efforts are a good start, but they must go hand-in-hand with the creation of credible caps on emissions and trading systems, which will create the incentives to transform the energy system.

## DEVELOPING SOLUTIONS

It would be morally wrong and politically futile to expect countries struggling to achieve basic levels of development to abandon their aspirations to grow and to improve their people's living standards. But it would be equally wrong to ignore the fact that by 2025, energy-related carbon dioxide emissions from developing countries are likely to exceed those from the member states of the Organization of Economic Cooperation and Development. Instead of being daunted by the scale of this challenge, policymakers must recognize the scale of the opportunity: developing countries have the potential to leapfrog the developed world's process of industrialization, thereby providing an enormous opportunity to improve energy efficiency and reduce emissions.

So far, most international efforts to engage developing countries have focused on the Kyoto Protocol's Clean Development Mechanism (CDM)—a scheme that would encourage investment by awarding emission credits for the quantity of emission reductions flowing from a particular project. In principle, the CDM was a good idea. In practice, it has become tangled in red tape and has required governments and investors to do the impossible: estimate the level of emissions that would have occurred in the absence of a project and then to calculate the marginal effect of their actions. The only projects that can meet this test are small and discrete: a steel mill that uses sustainably grown wood instead of coal for coke, for example, or a tiny hydroelectric dam that averts the need to build a coal-fired power plant. Such efforts are important, but they are hardly the stuff of radical transformation.

There is no neat, off-the-shelf solution for engaging the developing world. But there are encouraging signs of the process of economic development acting as a force for modernization. In China and India, infrastructure necessary to substitute natural gas for coal is already being put in place. And in many of the oil-producing regions of the world, the spread of international technology is making it possible to capture and reinject the natural gas that is often associated with oil, rather than venting or flaring it into the atmosphere. Efforts to change the incentives that govern land use in the developing world are also encouraging. From the Congo Basin to the Amazon and the forests of Southeast Asia, practical partnerships of governments, nongovernmental organizations, and businesses are showing the way. Small amounts of money and skillfully designed incentives are stemming the tide of deforestation by creating a stake in protecting the forests.

These and other efforts reflect the determination of publics, governments, and business to transcend the harsh and unacceptable trade-off between the desire to improve living standards and allow people the freedom to use energy for heat, light, and mobility on the one hand, and the desire for a clean environment on the other.

## UNFINISHED BUSINESS

The appropriate response to the faltering Kyoto Protocol is neither dismay nor fatalism. A complete international agreement on a subject of such complexity and uncertainty is still a long way off. But as those who championed the cause of liberal trade found after that first meeting in 1946, great causes acquire lives of their own. Consolidated political agreements often follow, rather than lead, the realities on the ground.

Taking small steps never feels entirely satisfactory. Nor does taking action without complete scientific knowledge. But certainty and perfection have never figured prominently in the story of human progress. Business, in particular, is accustomed to making decisions in conditions of considerable uncertainty, applying its experience and skills to areas of activity where much is unknown. That is why it will have a vital role in meeting the challenge of climate change—and why the contribution it is already making is so encouraging.

# NEW ACTORS AND NEW FORCES

# The Rise of China: Getting the Questions Right

## RICHARD K. BETTS AND
## THOMAS J. CHRISTENSEN

. . . It is hardly inevitable that China will be a threat to American interests, but the United States is much more likely to go to war with China than it is with any other major power. . . .

Debate about whether and how China might threaten U.S. security interests has often been simplistically polarized. Views range from alarmist to complacent: from those who see China emerging as a hefty and dangerous superpower, to those who believe the country's prospects are vastly overrated; and from those who see its economic growth as an engine for building threatening military capabilities, to those who see that growth as a welcome force for political liberalization and international cooperation.

Most strategic debate about China still focuses on a few simple questions. With respect to capabilities, these revolve mainly around whether the Chinese armed forces will develop to the point that they rival U.S. military power, and whether the economic surge—with its implications for military transformation—will continue indefinitely or stall. With regard to intentions, China watchers want to know how thoroughly and how soon the country will integrate into a global economy that allegedly constrains conflict; whether Beijing will adopt aggressive aims as its power grows; and whether political liberalization will occur as its wealth

From Richard K. Betts and Thomas J. Christensen, "China: Getting the Questions Right," *The National Interest*, No. 62 (Winter 2000/01), pp. 17–29. This article is reprinted with the permission of *The National Interest*. All rights reserved.

grows. Concern also zeroes in on whether the People's Republic of China (PRC) has the ability to take Taiwan by force.

These are relevant questions at the most basic level, but they are the wrong ones to generate progress in a mature debate. The most worrisome possibilities are those that lie beyond the answers to these questions, and between alarmist and complacent viewpoints. The truth is that China can pose a grave problem even if it does not become a military power on the American model, does not intend to commit aggression, integrates into a global economy, and liberalizes politically. Similarly, the United States could face a dangerous conflict over Taiwan even if it turns out that Beijing lacks the capacity to conquer the island.

## WILL CHINA'S MILITARY POWER RIVAL AMERICA'S?

There is little disagreement that the People's Liberation Army (PLA), a generic designation for all the Chinese armed forces, remains a threadbare force, well below Western standards. Pockets of excellence notwithstanding, most personnel are poorly educated and trained. Weapons systems are old, and even those acquired most recently are inferior to those in Western arsenals. Many units spend a good deal of time in non-military activities; staffs do not practice complex, large-scale operations; exercises and training regimens are limited; and equipment is not well maintained. Even according to the highest estimates, defense spending per soldier is low by First World standards, indicating the dominance of quantity over quality in the Chinese forces.

The main disagreement among Western analysts of China's military is about whether the PLA is poised to move out of its unimpressive condition and into a new era of modernity, efficiency and competitiveness, as anticipated economic reform and growth translate into military improvement. . . .

For China to develop a military on the model of the United States would be a tremendous stretch. The main issue is not whether Beijing will have high defense budgets or access to cutting-edge technology. A rich China might well be able to acquire most types of advanced weaponry. Deeply ingrained habits of threat assessment in the U.S. defense community encourage focusing on these factors. Unfortunately, however, basic "bean counts" of manpower and units and the quality of weapons platforms are poor measures of truly modern military capability. More fundamental to that assessment is whether the PLA establishment is capable of using whatever increase in resources it might receive to build the complex supporting infrastructure necessary to make Chinese forces competitive in combat. . . .

If the PLA remains second-rate, should the world breathe a sigh of relief? Not entirely. First, American military power is not the only relevant standard of comparison. Other armed forces in Asia that the PLA could come up against are much closer to the Chinese standard than to the American. (This is true even of Taiwan's technologically sophisticated military, whose long isolation has eroded its quality.) Second, the United States has global interests and often finds itself distracted or pinned down in other regions. Third, the Chinese do not need to match U.S. capabilities to cope with them. Rather than trying to match an American revolution in military affairs, they might do better to develop a *counter*-revolution by devising asymmetrical strategic options on various parts of the technological spectrum that can circumvent U.S. advantages.

One such example could be "cyberwar" attacks on the complex network of information systems that stitches American military superiority together. Another could be the use of new weapons like land attack cruise missiles or lower tech weapons such as naval mines to impede American access to the region. Still another could be the modification of China's no first-use policy on nuclear weapons, making an exception for repelling an invasion of Chinese territory. Although it is almost unimaginable that China would use nuclear weapons in an effort to gain political concessions from Taiwan, it might threaten their use to deter U.S. military action on behalf of the island. . . .

Taiwan is both the most dangerous and most likely instance of Chinese power projection (more on which below), but it is not the only one. China has conceivable points of conflict in several places that would not require its forces to cross large bodies of water, and where it would not be facing opposition as potent as Taiwan's military. Although less likely than conflict over Taiwan, an imbroglio in Korea would be scarcely less dangerous if the Pyongyang regime were to collapse and South Korean or American forces were to move into the vacuum without Beijing's agreement. Far too little attention has been focused on the odds of miscalculation in a confused situation of this sort. The PLA does not have the American army's logistical capacity, but even a half century ago it managed to project a force of hundreds of thousands of men deep into Korea.

While the Chinese navy is weak, some of its neighbors' navies are weaker still. Two of these neighbors, Vietnam and the Philippines, have outstanding sovereignty disputes with China and have not fared well in naval skirmishes in the past three decades. We also cannot rule out the possibility of a land attack. The PLA did poorly in its invasion of Vietnam over twenty years ago, but the Vietnamese army is now less than half the size it was then, and the Vietnamese economic base is far more inferior to China's than it was in 1978. Logistical limitations would hamper, but not preclude, PRC action in Mongolia, or in the Russian Far East, if that region were to fall out of Moscow's effective control. Granted, conflict over these places is improbable. The problem is that the same could have been said of most wars before they happened.

## WILL CHINA BECOME THE WORLD'S LEADING ECONOMY?

Military potential grows out of economic capacity. China's economy, like its military, is neither to be envied nor denigrated. In recent years it has been the fastest growing major economy in the world. Until strains became evident in the late 1990s, it was common to project high growth rates straight into the future and to see China's GNP surpassing America's early in the twenty-first century. But China's economy faces daunting challenges. And even if it solves many of its problems, the central government may not have sufficient control over the fruits of growth to use them for military coercion.

Even if China achieved the highest GNP in the world, low per capita wealth would persist, limiting disposable income that could be reallocated to the military. . . . Most of the methods available to spur growth involve politically risky measures, such as reform of the financial sector and state-owned enterprises, that threaten to leave tens of millions of additional urban residents jobless. These would join the ranks of the floating population of more than 100 million already in search of work. Similar problems affect the military, as cutbacks in the overall size of the PLA (needed for modernization and professionalization) create yet more disgruntled citizens. To maintain comfortable lifestyles, especially for officers, the military became dependent on business activities and large-scale smuggling of goods otherwise subject to high tariffs. If able officers and soldiers are to stay in uniform, then, the military units need to be subsidized at a high rate in order to implement successfully the plan to get the PLA out of commercial activities and back into the barracks.

All in all, there are no easy ways out for Beijing. Even if all growth-spurring measures work and the Communist Party maintains stability during the transition, the process of doing so will be expensive—especially for a central government that takes in a far smaller percentage of GNP than do Western governments. As China grows through capitalist reforms, Beijing must scramble to find new ways to tax private wealth. However inefficient they may have been, large state-owned enterprises provided a large portion of government revenues. The soft loans that officials forced government-owned banks to give to these enterprises functioned as an indirect tax on families, which, before Chinese membership of the WTO, had no alternatives to the state banks. If the Party is successful in demolishing both the monopoly of state-owned banks and the sturdy safety net for state-owned enterprises, it will need to raise money else-where for the government operating budget. That budget, in turn, will be strained by increases in welfare spending needed to maintain social stability—pensions for the unemployed and retired, and compensations to the military for its lost sources of legal and illegal revenue. . . .

## WILL CHINA BE PACIFIED BY GLOBALIZATION?

To pessimists steeped in realpolitik, a rich China will necessarily be a threat, because economic power can be translated into military power and power generates ambition. To optimists impressed with the revolutionary implications of globalization, however, a more powerful China will not be a threat because it will have too much to lose from disrupting international trade and investment. The latter view is more common in the West than the former, which seems to many to reek of old thinking.

The notion that a web of commercial ties discourages war, however, is itself quite old, if not exactly venerable. It was popularized by Henry Thomas Buckle in the 1850s, by Norman Angell just a year before World War I erupted, and again in the 1970s, when interdependence was said to have reduced the utility of force. . . . Al Gore quoted his father as saying, "When goods do not cross borders, armies will."

The argument this time around is that the proposition is finally true because the nature of interdependence has changed in a crucial way. A century ago it was characterized by vertical trade between imperial centers and colonies, trade in final products between wealthier nations, and portfolio investments. Today there is much more direct investment and transnational production of goods, which fosters "a growing interpenetration of economies, in the sense that one economy owns part of another."[1] With the PRC, Taiwan, Japan, and the United States all owning pieces of each other, how can they fight without destroying their own property? As the Chinese elite make more and more money from bilateral investments with Taiwan, simple greed will prevent huffing and puffing from crossing the line to war. If development thoroughly enmeshes the PRC in the globalized economy, therefore, peace will follow.

There are at least two problems with this latest version of interdependence theory. One is that *both* sides in a political dispute have a stake in not overturning profitable economic integration. The PRC might not want to kill the golden goose, but neither would Taiwan or the United States. Why, then, should Beijing be any more anxious to back down in a crisis than Taipei or Washington? Mutual dependence makes a political conflict a game of chicken, in which each side expects the other to bow to the stakes, and in which collision may result rather than concession.

The second problem is that there is little reason to assume that sober economic interest will necessarily override national honor in a crisis. A tough stand by Beijing may be viewed from the inside as essential for regime survival, even if it is not seen by detached observers as being in China's "national interest." In an imbroglio over Taiwan, which capitals will feel the strongest emotional inhibitions against backing down? Beijing and Taipei both have a greater material, moral and historical stake in the outcome than does the United States.

The global economy does indeed change logical incentives to compromise in political conflict, but not to the degree that it makes Beijing likely to be more "reasonable" than anyone else. Economic globalization does not eliminate the high priority that nations place on their political identity and integrity. Drawing China into the web of global interdependence may do more to encourage peace than war, but it cannot guarantee that the pursuit of heartfelt political interests will be blocked by a fear of economic consequences.

## WILL CHINA BECOME AGGRESSIVE?

Whether China has aggressive motives is what most policymakers want to know about Beijing's strategic intentions. Optimists say the answer is no, because the PRC is ideologically anti-imperialist and seeks only respect as a status quo great power. Pessimists say the answer is yes, because a seething set of Chinese grudges and territorial ambitions are on hold only for a lack of confidence in capability, or simply because all great powers tend to become aggressive when they get the chance.

But such focusing on the unlikely odds of deliberate aggression diverts attention from possibilities that are both much more likely and almost as dangerous. Most countries viewed as aggressors by their adversaries view their own behavior as defensive and legitimate. Whether Beijing is a tiger in waiting, about to set out deliberately on a predatory rampage, is not the most relevant question. No evidence suggests that Chinese leaders have an interest in naked conquest of the sort practiced by Genghis Khan, Napoleon Bonaparte, or Adolf Hitler. The model more often invoked by pessimists is Kaiser Wilhelm's Germany. Like Germany a century ago, China is a late-blooming great power emerging into a world already ordered strategically by earlier arrivals; a continental power surrounded by other powers who are collectively stronger but individually weaker (with the exception of the United States and, perhaps, Japan); a bustling country with great expectations, dissatisfied with its place in the international pecking order, if only with regard to international prestige and respect. The quest for a rightful "place in the sun" will, it is argued, inevitably foster growing friction with Japan, Russia, India or the United States.

Optimists do not have a hard time brushing off this analogy to a state of a different culture on a different continent at a different time, a long-gone era when imperialism was the norm for civilized international behavior. Their benign view, that economic development and trade will inevitably make China fat and happy, uninterested in throwing its weight around, strikes them as common sense. It could turn out to be true. It is more an article of faith, however, than a prediction grounded in historical experience. The United States, for example, is quite interested in gaining the goodies from globalization, yet on the world stage it sometimes throws its weight around with righteous abandon.

Indeed, the most disturbing analogy for China's future behavior may not be Germany but the United States. If China acts with the same degree of caution and responsibility in its region in this century as the United States did in its neighborhood in the past century, Asia is in for big trouble. Washington intervened frequently in Mexico, Central America and the Caribbean for reasons most Americans consider legitimate, defensive, altruistic and humane. The United States and its allies in Asia, however, would see comparable Chinese regional policing as a mortal threat. Even if China does not throw its weight around, the fact that there are others who can respond to the growth of Chinese power sets up the possibility of a classic spiral of tense actions and reactions. China faces alliances involving the United States, Japan, Australia and South Korea, and potential alliances in Southeast Asia.

## WOULD CHINESE LIBERALIZATION GUARANTEE PEACE?

Many assume that as long as democratization accompanies the growth of Chinese power, China will not necessarily pose a security challenge. This would hold true even if China proves able to maintain high levels of economic and technological growth, a healthy degree of government accumulation of the increasing national wealth, and, thereby, military modernization. This theory of the democratic peace—that developed democracies virtually never fight one another—is currently the most influential political science theory among American foreign policy elites.

Even if we accept the democratic peace theory at face value, there are several problems with applying it to China. First, as Fareed Zakaria has noted, the theory really applies only to liberal democracies on the Western model, ones with restraints on government action and guarantees of minority rights. Democratization in China could just as conceivably turn in an illiberal direction, on the model of post-Tito Yugoslavia, Iran or other unpleasant examples of violent activism.

Second, the democratic peace theory does not apply clearly to civil war. Democracies must recognize each other as democracies for the theory to apply.[2] They also have to view each other as legitimate, independent and sovereign states. No matter how many Americans and Taiwanese believe that Taiwan is or should be a sovereign state, this view is widely rejected on the mainland (and is not a premise of past or current U.S. policy).

Third, while liberal democracy is pacific, the process of becoming a democracy can be violent and destabilizing. This is particularly true of democratizing states that lack developed civil societies, independent news media, healthy outlets for popular grievances, and a marketplace for ideas where countervailing views can be debated. This gives elites incentives to manipulate populist or nationalist themes and to adopt tough international policies as an electoral strategy.[3]

The Chinese Communist Party has behaved like many authoritarian regimes, but with much more success. It has systematically prevented the rise of both an independent press and a civil society. Although the foreign press has penetrated China, domestic political publications are still strictly circumscribed by the state. As the . . . crackdown on the Falun Gong demonstrates, the Party is afraid of any group that organizes for any purpose without state sanction, regardless of how apolitical it appears to be.

The Chinese government's concerns about its legitimacy are not mere expressions of paranoia. The intensity of criticism of the leadership that one hears privately in places ranging from taxi cabs to government offices is astonishing. Awareness of its unpopularity gives the government in Beijing incentives to use nationalism as a replacement for the now hollow shell of communist ideology. But the Party is also aware that nationalism is not an inert tool to be pulled out of a kit and manipulated at the whim of the government. It is double-edged. Volatile and potentially uncontrollable, especially on emotional issues such as relations with Japan and Taiwan, nationalism is powerful enough to prop up a communist party in a capitalist society, but it could also severely damage the party if it were turned against the state. Officials in Beijing are aware that nationalism was a major force in the Communist Party's overthrow of the Kuomintang, as it was in the 1911–12 revolution that overthrew the Qing dynasty. . . .

In the early phases of democratization, China should be ripe for jingoism. Hypernationalism could be exploited to mobilize popular support and to deflect criticism of the state, especially given the existence of irredentist claims, and the danger of ethnic and regional "splittism" on the mainland and in Taiwan. If democratization were to occur in the current context of weak institutions, political leaders and opposition parties would have incentives to appeal to nationalism in ways that could destabilize the region. In fact, this is a favorite, though perhaps cynical, argument offered to foreigners by communist opponents of multiparty democracy.

There are, however, plausible scenarios in which Chinese democratization might reduce international conflict. Democratization could make the mainland more imaginative with regard to the frameworks for unification offered to Taiwan, thus making meaningful cross-strait political dialogue more likely. Political liberalization might also make the prospect of eventual accommodation with the mainland more palatable to Taiwan and discourage the island's diplomatic adventurism. But that possibility is not necessarily more likely than its opposite: a renewed belief by Taiwan that the island has its own national identity, that unification with the mainland under any circumstances is unacceptable, and that democratization on the mainland is a threat to Taiwanese goals. Taiwan may see a closing window of opportunity, with the hopes of gaining true independence reduced as the West's sympathy for Taiwan's opposition to unification hardens.

If Americans view mainland democratization as genuine, such fears on Taiwan are well placed. Would the United States risk war to prevent a democratic Taiwan from becoming part of a larger democratic China? The main reasons a president could currently use to mobilize Americans around action in defense of Taiwan's democracy would simply disappear. Many observers view democracy as Taiwan's biggest security asset, because it increases U.S. support. They are right. But it is not just democracy that provides Taiwan's security; it is the current contrast between Taiwan's democracy and the mainland's authoritarianism. . . .

## REASONS FOR PESSIMISM

Optimists on the China challenge are often guilty of contradictory arguments. On the one hand, they argue that China will only become a dangerous enemy if the United States treats it like one. At the same time, they attempt to demonstrate why China will not be able to develop the military capacity to pose any appreciable threat to us for a very long time. How can China be both hopelessly weak and potentially dangerous?

There are ways to square this circle by asking the right questions. China can pose security challenges to the United States even if it is unlikely to narrow the gap in military power. This is true because of geography; because of America's reliance on alliances to project power; and because of China's capacity to harm U.S. forces, U.S. regional allies, and the American homeland, even while losing a war in the technical, military sense.

Optimists are correct to focus on Chinese intentions and the potentially pacifying influences that the United States and other international actors can have on China. But they often assume too much about the positive effects of globalization, interdependence and political liberalization, because they underestimate the role of nationalist emotion and the possibility of misperceptions and inadvertence in war. They also forget that interdependence is a two-way street that restrains not only the Chinese, but China's potential adversaries as well.

In addressing the China challenge, the United States needs to think hard about three related questions: first, how to avoid crises and war through prudent, coercive diplomacy; second, how to manage crises and fight a war if the avoidance effort fails; third, how to end crises and terminate war at costs acceptable to the United States and its allies. . . .

China's growing power causes so many headaches largely because its strategic implications are not fully clear. But before one laments the rise of Chinese power, one should consider an even more uncertain alternative: Chinese weakness and collapse. Nothing ordains that China's march to great power status cannot be derailed. Severe economic dislocation and political fragmentation could throw the country into disorder, and the central government could prove too crippled to use external adventures to rally support and maintain unity. Hard-bitten realists should hesitate before hoping for such developments, however. The last time China was weak and disunified—in the era of warlordism and revolution in the first half of the twentieth century—it was a disaster, not only for China, but also for international peace and stability.

## NOTES

1. Richard Rosecrance, *The Rise of the Trading State* (New York: Basic Books, 1986), pp. 146–7.
2. John M. Owen IV, *Liberal Peace, Liberal War: American Politics and International Security* (Ithaca, NY: Cornell University Press, 1997).
3. Edward D. Mansfield and Jack L. Snyder, "Democratization and the Danger of War," *International Security* (Summer 1995).

# Europe Without Illusions

## ANDREW MORAVCSIK

*It was not the substance of the constitution that attracted opposition but its style and symbolism*

The people of France and the Netherlands have spoken. The constitution is dead, Turkish membership is too, and progress in areas from services deregulation to Balkan enlargement will now be hard. . . .

It is time to view Europe as it really is. Far from demonstrating that the EU is in decline or disarray, the crisis demonstrates its essential stability and legitimacy. The central error of the European constitutional framers was one of style and symbolism rather than substance. The constitution contained a set of modest reforms, very much in line with European popular preferences. Yet European leaders upset the emerging pragmatic settlement by dressing up the reforms as a grand scheme for constitutional revision and popular democratisation of the EU.

Looking back in 50 years, historians will not see the referendums as the end of the EU—not even as the beginning of the end. The union remains the most successful experiment in political institution-building since the second world war. Historians will see instead the last gasp of idealistic European federalism born in the mid-1940s, symbolised by the phrase "ever closer union," and aimed at establishing a United States of Europe. It is time to recognise that the EU can neither aspire to replace nation states nor seek democratic legitimacy in the same way nations do. The current EU constitutional settlement, which has defined a stable balance between Brussels and national capitals and democratic legitimacy through indirect accountability and extensive checks and balances, is here to stay. To see why this is so, we must understand the nature of the current constitutional compromise, the reasons why European leaders called it into question, and the deeper lessons this teaches us about the limits of European integration.

Voting patterns in the recent referendums were a reflection of three related motivations that have dominated every EU election in history. First is ideological extremism. The centre supported Europe, while the extreme right and left, which now account for almost one third of the French and Dutch electorates, voted "no." Second is protest voting against unpopular governments. Third, and most important, is a reaction against the insecurity felt by poorer Europeans. Whereas business, the educated elite and wealthier Europeans favoured the constitution,

Andrew Moravcsik, "Europe Without Illusions," *Prospect*, Issue 112 (July 2005). Reprinted by permission of the author.

those fearful of unemployment, labour market reform, globalisation, privatisation and the consolidation of the welfare state opposed it. Today these concerns dovetail with the perceived economic and cultural threat posed by Muslim immigration.

This type of disaffection is the primary political problem for European governments today, since it is directed both against poor economic performance and against reform measures designed to improve it. As Fareed Zakaria observes, the tragedy is that "Europe needs more of what's producing populist paranoia: economic reform to survive in an era of economic competition, young immigrants to sustain its social market, and a more strategic relationship with the Muslim world, which would be dramatically enhanced by Turkish membership in the EU."

Forgotten in the electoral chaos was the document itself. The constitution is, after all, a conservative text containing incremental improvements which consolidate EU developments of the past 20 years. The "no" campaigns conceded the desirability of the modest reforms from the start—including the foreign minister, stronger anti-crime policy and streamlining of voting procedures. Such changes are popular, not least in France, which proposed most of them. One is forced to conclude that this document became controversial not because its content was objectionable, but because its content was so innocuous that citizens saw a chance to cast an inexpensive protest vote.

What were they protesting against? Here, too, the referendums cannot be viewed as plebiscites directed at the EU's policies. Though the EU is associated . . . with labour market and welfare reform, these matters remain firmly within the competence of the member states. The EU's activities as a whole, while they include oversight of state subsidies and trade policy, may just as reasonably be seen as part of a European effort to manage globalisation rather than promote it. Opponents made occasional mention of EU policies not contained in the constitution, such as the recent enlargement to 25, the introduction of the euro, the deregulation of electricity and Turkish accession. Yet only the last of these seems to have swayed many voters, and they seem to have been unaware that free migration has been ruled even before negotiations begin.

So what lesson should the EU take away? The relative lack of direct criticism of the constitution, the lack of fundamental objections to EU policies and, above all, the stunning lack of positive proposals for reform are striking evidence of the underlying stability of the EU system. The 15 years since the fall of the Berlin wall has been, after all, the most successful period in EU history. The single market, the euro and a nascent European foreign and defense policy came into being. EU enlargement was carried out with surprisingly little disruption in existing member states, and proved the most cost-effective western instrument for advancing global democracy and security. In sum, the EU appears to have quietly reached a stable constitutional settlement.

What is that settlement? The EU is now pre-eminent in trade, agriculture, fishing, eurozone monetary policy and some business regulation, and helps to co-ordinate cooperation in foreign policy. Contrary to statistics one often reads, this amounts to only about 20 per cent of European regulation and legislation. Most areas of greatest public concern—taxes, health, pensions, education, crime, infrastructure, defence, and immigration—remain firmly national. With a tax base a fiftieth the size of the member states, an administration smaller than that of a small city, no police force or army and a narrow legal mandate, the EU will never encompass these fiscally and administratively demanding tasks.

There is no new *grand projet*, akin to the single market of the 1980s or the single currency of the 1990s, to justify change. In 18 months of deliberation, the constitutional convention devoted only two days to the expansion of EU competences. European health, pension, fiscal and education policies have little support, while a US-style military buildup exceeds Europe's means and insults its "civilian power" ideals.

Consider European social policy, of which we heard so much in referendum campaigns. What concrete EU policies should this imply? Blocking sensible efforts to reform the welfare state for long-term sustainability is short-sighted. Many studies show that a division of labour between the new and old members of the EU will generate growth. There is little evidence of a regulatory or fiscal "race to the bottom" driven by the EU, and there remains plenty of room for social policy at national level. The neoliberal "Anglo-Saxon" threat is a myth. Britain is building up its welfare state faster than any of its partners, based partly on a Scandinavian model that tops international competitiveness rankings. Indeed, with continental liberalisation and British social democratisation, Europe's social systems are converging—through the pressure of national politics, not as the result of some EU social policy pipe dream.

A similar constitutional compromise has emerged with regard to institutions. Though Anglo-American Eurosceptics have sought to resurrect the bogeyman of a Brussels superstate headed by the European commission, treaty changes since 1970 have consistently moved Europe in the opposite direction. They have increased the power of the council of ministers (favoured by France and Britain, particularly for matters outside the economic core) and the directly elected European parliament (favoured by Germany) at the expense of the technocratic commission.

The proposed constitution sought to marginally improve the EU's efficiency and transparency, while retaining its basic structure. All of this is the sensible stuff policy wonks love and publics generally support: European parliamentary co-decision was expanded, national parliaments gained an advisory and gatekeeping role, the rotating presidency was abolished, voting weights were adjusted to represent large countries more fairly, foreign policy co-ordination was centralised in a foreign minister and so on. The result was a multinational constitutional compromise that attended to the interests of large and small countries, left and right parties, and Europhile and Eurosceptic tendencies. The reforms enjoyed broad support among member states, and none met a serious challenge in the referendum debates. The biggest change—creation of a European foreign minister empowered to recommend, though not impose, a more co-ordinated foreign policy—enjoys 70 per cent approval across Europe. And recognising the EU as it is, the constitution struck the classic idealist phrase "ever closer union" from the treaty of Rome, and substituted the more balanced "unity in diversity."

So it was not the substance of the emerging constitutional settlement that triggered opposition. The objectionable aspect was its form: an idealistic constitution. Since the 1970s, lawyers have regarded the treaty of Rome as a de facto constitution.

The new document was an unnecessary public relations exercise based on the seemingly intuitive, but in fact peculiar, notion that democratisation and the European ideal could legitimate the EU. In the wake of the Nice and Amsterdam treaties, Euro-enthusiast scholars, politicians and commentators argued that the EU is unpopular primarily because it is secretive, complex, unaccountable and distant from the public—in sum, because it suffers from a "democratic deficit." Joschka Fischer, the [former] German foreign minister, gave the idea of constitutional legitimation a big push with his celebrated lecture on the end point of integration at Humboldt University in 2000. . . .

The idea was to legitimate the EU not through trade, economic growth and useful regulation, as had been the case for 50 years, but by politicising and democratising it. This was to be done via a constitutional convention. Enthused by the prospect of a re-enactment of Philadelphia 1787, millions of web-savvy Europeans were supposed to deliberate the meaning of Europe. More pragmatic voices simply hoped to combat cynicism by simplifying the treaty and delineating EU prerogatives. To justify the need for change, reformers also seized on the perception that the EU would need a radical overhaul to avoid gridlock with 25 rather than 15 members—a fear that now seems unjustified, both because the new states are proving constructive and because the EU is not moving as far or fast as it once did.

Of course, the constitutional deliberation did not mobilise Europeans. Few citizens were aware of the 200 *conventionnels'* deliberations. When testimony from civil society was requested, professors turned up. When a youth conference was called, would-be Eurocrats attended. When those who did attend came to consider democracy, they found that the arrangement Europe currently has is appropriate to a diverse polity in which member states insist on checks and balances at every level. There was little popular or elite support for democratic reform beyond the modest increases in scrutiny by national and European parliaments the constitution contains.

This is as it should be, for there is no "democratic deficit" in the EU—or not much of one. Once we set aside ideal notions of democracy and look to real-world standards, we see that the EU is as transparent, responsive, accountable and honest as its member states. The relative lack of centralised financial or administrative discretion all but eliminates corruption. The EU's areas of autonomous authority— trade policy, constitutional adjudication and central banking—are the same as those in most democracies, where these functions are politically insulated for sound reasons. The notion of imposing democratic control through multiple checks and balances, rather than through elections to a single sovereign parliament, is more American than European—but it is no less legitimate for that. Everyone gets a say in a system in which a European directive needs approval from a technocratic commission, a supermajority of democratic national governments and a directly elected parliament, and must then be implemented by national regulators. Studies show that EU legislation is both consensual and relatively responsive to shifts in partisan and popular opinion.

Enthusiasts for democracy fail to grasp its limits. Engaging European citizens will not necessarily create rational (let alone supportive) debate, because those with intense preferences about the EU tend to be its opponents. Average citizens and political parties keep only a few issues—usually those involving heavy tax and spending—in their mind at any one time, and thus respond only to highly salient ideals and issues. The pull of Europe remains weak, while the bread and butter policies citizens care about most, including the welfare and identity issues that dominated referendum debates, remain almost exclusively in national hands. The failure of European elections to generate high turnouts or focus on EU issues over the years suggests that citizens fail to participate in EU politics not because they are blocked from doing so, but because they have insufficient incentive.

Some democratic enthusiasts propose jump-starting EU democracy by incorporating hot-button issues like social policy and immigration, despite the lack of popular support for doing so. . . . Yet anyone except a philosopher can see that this is the sort of extreme cure that will kill the patient. There is little that could lead the European public to decisively reject an institution as deeply embedded as the EU, but transferring controversial issues like social policy to it without justification might just do it.

More sober voices propose to empower national parliaments, which the constitution sought to do in a modest way. Yet this reveals a final fallacy of the democratisers. For there is little reason to believe that turning policy over to a legislature makes it more legitimate. In western democracies, popularity is inversely correlated with direct electoral accountability. The most popular institutions are courts, police forces and the military. Parliaments are generally disliked. Whatever the source of Europe's declining popularity—a general decline in political trust, unfamiliarity with institutions, xenophobia, discontent with economic performance—it has little to do with its democratic mandate.

Forcing an unstructured debate about an institution that handles matters like telecommunications standardisation, the composition of the Bosnia stabilisation force and the privatisation of electricity production inexorably drove debate to the lowest common denominator. When pro-European political elites found themselves defending a constitution with modest content, they felt they had no alternative but to oversell it using inflated notions of what the EU does and rhetoric drawn from 1950s European idealism. Small wonder they were outgunned by grumpy populists with stronger symbols rooted in class, nation and race (and even more inflated views of what the EU does). Publics became confused and alarmed by the scare tactics of both sides. The referendums came to inhabit a strange twilight zone of symbolic politics, in which claims about the EU bore little relationship to reality, and support and opposition for a status quo constitution became a potent symbol for the myriad hopes and fears of modern electorates.

In the wake of this debacle, European politicians must find a constructive path forward. They should start with a collective mea culpa. The document itself must be renounced. Then over the next few years, the EU should return to its successful tradition of quiet and pragmatic reform. Europeans consistently support incremental advances in the union's foreign, internal security and economic policies along the lines set forth in the constitution. Turkish membership is off the agenda, as it probably would have been even without the referendums. Politicians need to concede this, and concede it loud and clear, in order to preserve continued EU enlargement in the Balkans. Yet a halfway arrangement acceptable to both EU and

Turkish publics remains a realistic goal over the next 20 years and may be better for Turkey than the limited type of EU membership that is currently on offer. No other European policy could contribute as much to global peace and security.

Above all, European politicians need to acknowledge explicitly the existence of a stable European constitutional settlement. The unique genius of the EU is that it locks in policy co-ordination while respecting the powerful rhetoric and symbols that still attach to national identity. Publics will be reassured if it is portrayed as stable and successful. There is no shameful compromise with grand principles here. On the contrary, a constitutional order that preserves national democratic politics for the issues most salient to citizens, but delegates to more indirect democratic forms those issues that are of less concern, or on which there is an administrative, technical or legal consensus, is highly appealing. The EU's distinctive system of multi-level governance is the only new form of state organisation to emerge and prosper since the rise of the welfare state at the turn of the 20th century. Now it is a mature constitutional order, one that no longer needs to move forward to legitimate its past and present successes. Left behind must be the European centralisers and democratisers for whom "ever closer union" remains an end in itself. They will insist that the answer to failed democracy is more democracy and the answer to a failed constitution is another constitution. But Europe has moved beyond them. Disowning this well-meaning, even admirable, band of idealists may seem harsh, but it is both necessary and just. On this basis, Europeans can develop a new discourse of national interest, pragmatic co-operation and constitutional stability—a discourse that sees Europe as it is. The constitution is dead, long live the constitution!

# Transnational Activist Networks

## MARGARET E. KECK AND KATHRYN SIKKINK

Networks are forms of organization characterized by voluntary, reciprocal, and horizontal patterns of communication and exchange. . . . Major actors in advocacy networks may include the following: (1) international and domestic nongovernmental research and advocacy organizations; (2) local social movements; (3) foundations; (4) the media; (5) churches, trade unions, consumer organizations, and intellectuals; (6) parts of regional and international intergovernmental organizations; and (7) parts of the executive and/or parliamentary branches of governments. Not all these will be present in each advocacy network. Initial research suggests, however, that international and domestic NGOs [non-governmental organizations] play a central role in all advocacy networks, usually initiating actions and pressuring more powerful actors to take positions. NGOs introduce new ideas, provide information, and lobby for policy changes.

Groups in a network share values and frequently exchange information and services. The flow of information among actors in the network reveals a dense web of connections among these groups, both formal and informal. The movement of funds and services is especially notable between foundations and NGOs, and some NGOs provide services such as training for other NGOs in the same and sometimes other advocacy networks. Personnel also circulate within and among networks, as relevant players move from one to another in a version of the "revolving door.". . .

Advocacy networks are not new. We can find examples as far back as the nineteenth-century campaign for the abolition of slavery. But their number, size, and professionalism, and the speed, density, and complexity of international linkages among them has grown dramatically in the last three decades. . . .

Transnational advocacy networks appear most likely to emerge around those issues where (1) channels between domestic groups and their governments are blocked or hampered or where such channels are ineffective for resolving a conflict, setting into motion the "boomerang" pattern of influence characteristic of these networks; (2) activists or "political entrepreneurs" believe that networking will further their missions and campaigns, and actively promote networks; and (3) conferences and other forms of international contact create arenas for forming and strengthening networks. Where channels of participation are blocked, the international arena may be the only means that domestic activists have to gain attention to their issues. Boomerang strategies are most common in campaigns where the target is a state's domestic policies or behavior; where a campaign seeks broad procedural change involving dispersed actors, strategies are more diffuse.

It is no accident that so many advocacy networks address claims about rights in their campaigns. Governments are the primary "guarantors" of rights, but also their primary violators. When a government violates or refuses to recognize rights, individuals and domestic groups often have no recourse within domestic political or judicial arenas. They may seek international connections finally to express their concerns and even to protect their lives.

When channels between the state and its domestic actors are blocked, the boomerang pattern of influence characteristic of transnational networks may occur: Domestic NGOs bypass their state and directly search out international allies to try to bring pressure on their states from outside. This is most obviously the case in human rights campaigns. Similarly, indigenous rights campaigns and environmental campaigns that support the demands of local peoples for participation in development projects that would affect them frequently involve this kind of triangulation. Linkages are important for both sides: For the less powerful Third World actors, networks provide access, leverage, and information (and often money) they could not expect to have on their own; for northern groups, they make credible the assertion that they are struggling with, and not only for, their southern partners. Not surprisingly, such relationships can produce considerable tensions. . . .

Just as oppression and injustice do not themselves produce movements or revolutions, claims around issues amenable to international action do not produce transnational networks. Activists—"people who care enough about some issue that they are prepared to incur significant costs and act to achieve their goals"[1]—do. They create them when they believe that transnational networking will further their organizational missions—by sharing information, attaining greater visibility, gaining access to wider publics, multiplying channels of institutional access, and so forth. For example, in the campaign to stop the promotion of infant formula to poor women in developing countries, organizers settled on a boycott of Nestlé, the largest producer, as its main tactic. Because Nestlé was a transnational actor, activists believed a transnational network was necessary to bring pressure on corporations and governments.[2] Over time, in such issue areas, participation in transnational networks has become an essential component of the collective identities of the activists involved, and networking a part of their common repertoire. The political entrepreneurs who become the core networkers for a new campaign have often gained experience in earlier ones.

Opportunities for network activities have increased over the last two decades. In addition to the efforts of pioneers, a proliferation of international organizations and conferences has provided foci for connections. Cheaper air travel and new electronic communication technologies speed information flows and simplify personal contact among activists. Underlying these trends is a broader cultural shift. The new networks have depended on the creation of a new kind of global public (or civil society), which grew as a cultural legacy of the 1960s. . . .

## HOW DO TRANSNATIONAL ADVOCACY NETWORKS WORK?

Transnational advocacy networks seek influence in many of the same ways that other political groups or social movements do. Since they are not powerful in a traditional sense of the word, they must use the power of their information, ideas, and strategies to alter the information and value contexts within which states make policies. The bulk of what networks do might be termed persuasion or socialization, but neither process is devoid of conflict. Persuasion and socialization often involve not just reasoning with opponents, but also bringing pressure, arm-twisting, encouraging sanctions, and shaming. . . .

Our typology of tactics that networks use in their efforts at persuasion, socialization, and pressure includes (1) *information politics*, or the ability to quickly and credibly generate politically usable information and move it to where it will have the most impact; (2) *symbolic politics*, or the ability to call upon symbols, actions, or stories that make sense of a situation for an audience that is frequently far away; (3) *leverage politics*, or the ability to call upon powerful actors to affect a situation where weaker members of a network are unlikely to have influence; and (4) *accountability politics*, or the effort to hold powerful actors to their previously stated policies or principles. . . .

Network members actively seek ways to bring issues to the public agenda by framing them in innovative ways and by seeking hospitable venues. Sometimes they create issues by framing old problems in new ways; occasionally they help transform other actors' understanding of their identities and their interests. Land use rights in the Amazon, for example, took on an entirely different character and gained quite different allies viewed in a deforestation frame than they did in either social justice or regional development frames. In the 1970s and 1980s many states decided for the first time that promotion of human rights in other countries was a legitimate foreign policy goal and an authentic expression of national interest. This decision came in part from interaction with an emerging global human rights network. We argue that this represents not the victory of morality over self-interest, but a transformed understanding of national interest, possible in part because of structured interactions between state components and networks. This changed understanding cannot be derived solely from changing global and economic conditions, although these are relevant. . . .

### Information Politics

Information binds network members together and is essential for network effectiveness. Many information exchanges are informal—telephone calls, e-mail and fax communications, and the circulation of newsletters, pamphlets, and bulletins. They provide information that would not otherwise be available, from sources that might not otherwise be heard, and they must make this information comprehensible and useful to activists and publics who may be geographically and/or socially distant.

Nonstate actors gain influence by serving as alternate sources of information. Information flows in advocacy networks provide not only facts but testimony—stories told by people whose lives have been affected. Moreover, activists interpret facts and testimony, usually framing issues simply, in terms of right and wrong, because their purpose is to persuade people and stimulate them to act. How does this process of persuasion occur? An effective frame must show that a given state of affairs is neither natural nor accidental, identify the responsible party or parties, and propose credible solutions. These aims require clear, powerful messages that appeal to shared principles, which often have more impact on state policy than advice of technical experts. An important part of the political struggle over information is precisely whether an issue is defined primarily as technical—and thus subject to consideration by "qualified" experts—or as something that concerns a broader global constituency. . . .

Networks strive to uncover and investigate problems, and alert the press and policymakers. One activist described this as the "human rights methodology"— "promoting change by reporting facts."[3] To be credible, the information produced by networks must be reliable and well documented. To gain attention, the information must be timely and dramatic. Sometimes these multiple goals of information politics conflict, but both credibility and drama seem to be essential components of a strategy aimed at persuading publics and policymakers to change their minds.

The notion of "reporting facts" does not fully express the way networks strategically use information to frame issues. Networks call attention to issues, or even create issues by using language that dramatizes and draws attention to their concerns. A good example is the recent campaign against the practice of female genital mutilation. Before 1976 the widespread practice of female circumcision in many African and a few Asian and Middle Eastern countries was known outside these regions mainly among medical experts and anthropologists.[4] A controversial campaign, initiated in 1974 by a network of women's and human rights organizations, began to draw wider attention to the issues by renaming the problem. Previously the practice was referred to by technically "neutral" terms such as female circumcision, clitoridectomy, or infibulation. The campaign around female genital "mutilation" raised its salience, literally creating the issue as a matter of public international concern. By renaming the practice the network broke the linkage with male circumcision (seen as a personal medical or cultural decision), implied a linkage with the more feared procedure of castration, and reframed the issue as one of violence against women. It thus resituated the practice as a human rights violation. . . .

Human rights activists, baby food campaigners, and women's groups . . . dramatize the situations of the victims and turn the cold facts into human stories, intended to move people to action. The baby food campaign, for example, relied heavily on public health studies that proved that improper bottle feeding contributed to infant malnutrition and mortality, and that corporate sales promotion was leading to a decline in breast feeding. Network activists repackaged and interpreted this information in dramatic ways designed to promote action: The British development organization War on Want published a pamphlet entitled "The Baby Killers," which the Swiss Third World Action Group translated into German and retitled "Nestlé Kills Babies." Nestlé inadvertently gave activists a prominent public forum when it sued the Third World Action Group for defamation and libel. . . .

A dense web of north-south exchange, aided by computer and fax communication, means that governments can no longer monopolize information flows as they could a mere half-decade ago. These technologies have had an enormous impact on moving information to and from Third World countries, where mail service has often been slow and precarious; they also give special advantages of course, to organizations that have access to them. A good example of the new informational role of networks occurred when U.S. environmentalists pressured President George Bush to raise the issue of gold miners' ongoing invasions of the Yanomami indigenous reserve when Brazilian president Fernando Collor de Mello was in Washington in 1991. Collor believed that he had squelched protest over the Yanomami question by creating major media events out of the dynamiting of airstrips used by gold miners, but network members had current information faxed from Brazil, and they countered his claims with evidence that miners had rebuilt the airstrips and were still invading the Yanomami area. . . .

The media is an essential partner in network information politics. To reach a broader audience, networks strive to attract press attention. Sympathetic journalists may become part of the network, but more often network activists cultivate a reputation for credibility with the press, and package their information in a timely and dramatic way to draw press attention.

## Symbolic Politics

Activists frame issues by identifying and providing convincing explanations for powerful symbolic events, which in turn become catalysts for the growth of networks. Symbolic interpretation is part of the process of persuasion by which networks create awareness and expand their constituencies. Awarding the 1992 Nobel Peace Prize to Maya activist Rigoberta Menchú and the UN's designation of 1993 as the Year of Indigenous Peoples heightened public awareness of the situation of indigenous peoples in the Americas. Indigenous peoples' use of 1992, the 500th anniversary of the voyage of Columbus to the Americas, to raise a host of issues well illustrates the use of symbolic events to reshape understandings. . . .

## Leverage Politics

Activists in advocacy networks are concerned with political effectiveness. Their definition of effectiveness often includes some policy change by "target actors" such as governments, international financial institutions like the World Bank, or private actors like transnational corporations. In order to bring about policy change, networks need to pressure and persuade more powerful actors. To gain influence the networks seek leverage (the word appears often in the discourse of advocacy organizations) over more powerful actors. By leveraging more powerful institutions, weak groups gain influence far beyond their ability to influence state practices directly. The identification of material or moral leverage is a crucial strategic step in network campaigns.

Material leverage usually links the issue to money or goods (but potentially also to votes in international organizations, prestigious offices, or other benefits).

The human rights issue became negotiable because governments or financial institutions connected human rights practices to military and economic aid, or to bilateral diplomatic relations. In the United States, human rights groups got leverage by providing policy-makers with information that convinced them to cut off military and economic aid. To make the issue negotiable, NGOs first had to raise its profile or salience, using information and symbolic politics. Then more powerful members of the network had to link cooperation to something else of value: money, trade, or prestige. Similarly, in the environmentalists' multilateral development bank campaign, linkage of environmental protection with access to loans was very powerful.

Although NGO influence often depends on securing powerful allies, their credibility still depends in part on their ability to mobilize their own members and affect public opinion via the media. In democracies the potential to influence votes gives large membership organizations an advantage over nonmembership organizations in lobbying for policy change; environmental organizations, several of whose memberships number in the millions, are more likely to have this added clout than are human rights organizations.

Moral leverage involves what some commentators have called the *"mobilization of shame,"* where the behavior of target actors is held up to the light of international scrutiny. Network activists exert moral leverage on the assumption that governments value the good opinion of others; insofar as networks can demonstrate that a state is violating international obligations or is not living up to its own claims, they hope to jeopardize its credit enough to motivate a change in policy or behavior. The degree to which states are vulnerable to this kind of pressure varies, and will be discussed further below.

## Accountability Politics

Networks devote considerable energy to convincing governments and other actors to publicly change their positions on issues. This is often dismissed as inconsequential change, since talk is cheap and governments sometimes change discursive positions hoping to divert network and public attention. Network activists, however, try to make such statements into opportunities for accountability politics. Once a government has publicly committed itself to a principle—for example, in favor of human rights or democracy—networks can use those positions, and their command of information, to expose the distance between discourse and practice. This is embarrassing to many governments, which may try to save face by closing that distance.

Perhaps the best example of network accountability politics was the ability of the human rights network to use the human rights provisions of the 1975 Helsinki Accords to pressure the Soviet Union and the governments of Eastern Europe for change. The Helsinki Accords helped revive the human rights movement in the Soviet Union, spawned new organizations like the Moscow Helsinki Group and the Helsinki Watch Committee in the United States, and helped protect activists from repression.[5] The human rights network referred to Moscow's obligations under the Helsinki Final Act and juxtaposed these with examples of abuses. . . .

## NOTES

1. Pamela E. Oliver and Gerald Marwell, "Mobilizing Technologies for Collective Action," in *Frontiers in Social Movement Theory*, ed. Aldon D. Morris and Carol McClurg Mueller (New Haven: Yale University Press, 1992), p. 252.
2. See Kathryn Sikkink, "Codes of Conduct for Transnational Corporations: The Case of the WHO/UNICEF Code," *International Organization* 40 (Autumn 1986): 815–40.
3. Dorothy Q. Thomas, "Holding Governments Accountable by Public Pressure," in *Ours by Right: Women's Rights as Human Rights*, ed. Joanna Kerr (London: Zed Books, 1993), p. 83.
4. Female genital mutilation is most widely practiced in Africa, where it is reported to occur in at least twenty-six countries. Between 85 and 114 million women in the world today are estimated to have experienced genital mutilation. *World Bank Development Report 1993: Investing in Health* (New York: Oxford University Press, 1993), p. 50.
5. Discussion of the Helsinki Accords is based on Daniel Thomas, "Norms and Change in World Politics: Human Rights, the Helsinki Accords, and the Demise of Communism, 1975–1990," Ph.D. diss., Cornell University, 1997.

# NGOs: Fighting Poverty, Hurting the Poor

## SEBASTIAN MALLABY

Last year, I visited Uganda. I wanted to understand how a showcase of African hopelessness turned around, cutting the number of people living below the national poverty line by almost 40 percent during the 1990s. But I wanted to get to the bottom of another issue, too. The World Bank was promoting a dam near the source of the river Nile, at a beautiful spot called Bujagali. Western nongovernmental organizations (NGOs) were in revolt: The International Rivers Network, based in Berkeley, California, maintained that the Ugandan environmental movement was outraged at the likely damage to waterfalls at the site, and that the poor who lived there would be uprooted from their land for the sake of electricity they couldn't afford. It was surely a clash that went to the heart of the globalization struggle. Was the NGO movement acting as a civilized check on industrialization, standing up for millions of poor people whose views the World Bank ignored? Or was it retarding the battle against poverty by withholding electricity that would fuel economic growth, ultimately benefiting poor citizens?

I called the Berkeley activists and asked for some advice. Who ran this Ugandan environmental movement they claimed was so outraged? Where were the villagers who would be cruelly dislocated by the dam project? NGOs such as the International Rivers Network usually love helping Western journalists, and because these journalists are generally far from the scene of the disputed development project, they sometimes simply report what they are told. But now that I was in Uganda, a few hours' drive from the proposed dam, I got a warier response. Lori Pottinger, the International Rivers activist who led the Bujagali campaign, explained that her Ugandan counterparts were preoccupied just then, and that snooping around the villages at the Bujagali site would get me into trouble with the authorities.

Not wanting to give up right away, I tracked down Pottinger's Ugandan counterparts by other means and telephoned their office. A friendly voice invited me to come over straightaway. When I arrived, the group's young director sat me down and plied me with leaflets and reports that gratefully acknowledged the sponsorship of a group called the Swedish Society for Nature Conservation. After half an

Sebastian Mallaby, "NGOs: Fighting Poverty, Hurting the Poor." First published in *Foreign Policy*, September/October 2004. © 2004 by Sebastian Mallaby, by permission of The Wylie Agency hour of conversation, I asked the question that really concerned me: What kind of organization was this?

"This is a membership organization," I was told.

"How many members?" I asked. My host kindly stood up and rummaged about in his desk, returning with a blue notebook.

"Here is the list," he said triumphantly. Uganda's National Association of Professional Environmentalists had all of 25 members—not exactly a broad platform from which to oppose electricity for millions.

My next move was to visit Bujagali. I met up with a Ugandan sociologist who knew the region well and promised to translate for me. She stopped at a cluster of buildings on the edge of the dam site to check in with the local government representative who, far from threatening to call the cops, greeted us cheerfully. For the next three hours, we interviewed villager after villager and found the same story: The "dam people" had come and promised generous financial terms, and the villagers were happy to accept them and relocate. My sociologist companion said we might have sample bias because we were interviewing men, who might value cash more than the land that women tended. So we interviewed some women, who offered the same pro-project line. The only people who objected to the dam were those living just outside its perimeter. They were angry because the project would not affect them, meaning no generous payout.

This story is a tragedy for Uganda. Clinics and factories are being deprived of electricity by Californians whose idea of an electricity crisis is a handful of summer blackouts. But it is also a tragedy for the fight against poverty worldwide, because projects in dozens of countries are similarly held up for fear of activist resistance. Time after time, feisty Internet-enabled groups make scary claims about the iniquities of development projects. Time after time, Western publics raised on stories of World Bank white elephants believe them. Lawmakers in European parliaments and the U.S. Congress accept NGO arguments at face value, and the government officials who sit on the World Bank's board respond by blocking funding for deserving projects.

The consequences can be preposterously ironic. NGOs claim to campaign on behalf of poor people, yet many of their campaigns harm the poor. They claim to protect the environment, but by forcing the World Bank to pull out of sensitive projects, they cause these schemes to go ahead without the environmental safeguards that the bank would have imposed on them. Likewise, NGOs purport to hold the World Bank accountable, yet the bank is answerable to the governments who are its shareholders; it is the NGOs' accountability that is murky. Furthermore, the offensives mounted by activist groups sometimes have no basis in fact whatsoever. If you think this an exaggeration, consider the story of an anti-poverty effort in China's western province of Qinghai.

## OUT, DAM SPOT

There was nothing apparently controversial when, in April 1999, the World Bank concluded negotiations on a project in Qinghai. China was the bank's star client at the time, having lifted around 200 million people out of poverty during the previous decade. The Qinghai project was designed to move 58,000 farmers from a hopelessly parched hillside to another part of the province irrigated by a small dam. Farmers' incomes would rise from around 20 cents a day to a level at which they could actually subsist. China had carried out some 30 such relocation projects in the past. All had reduced poverty.

The day the Qinghai loan negotiations concluded, the bank's project manager, Petros Aklilu, got a call from the Tibet Information Network in London. Qinghai borders on the Chinese administrative division known as the Tibet Autonomous Region. Because the region covers part of historical Tibet and 1 million of Qinghai's 5 million inhabitants are Tibetan, the interest of Tibet-watchers was not surprising. Aklilu explained that the scheme would benefit the 3,500 Tibetans who would move to newly irrigated land, and that Tibetans who stayed behind would benefit from reduced population pressure in their area. In sum, although China's Tibet policy was abominable, the bank's project would actually help Tibetans. Aklilu put down the phone and forgot about the conversation.

He soon had cause to remember it. Within a few days, the Tibet Information Network published a story in its newsletter about a "controversial" World Bank project that would "dramatically affect the demography" of Qinghai by moving ethnic Chinese into a culturally Tibetan area. This was a strange claim. First, no Tibetans lived in the immediate settlement area: The nearest were 276 nomadic herders (the bank had counted them carefully) who wintered 37 miles south of the project. Second, Qinghai had been part of China for as long as the United States had been independent. It was no more Tibetan than Texas is Mexican. But the Tibet Information Network was not deterred. "Population transfer of Chinese into traditional Tibetan areas has become a major concern for Tibetans," the group's newsletter said ominously.

Within a few weeks, the London activists had forged an international coalition. It drew from the various legions of the anti-World Bank army: environmental groups opposed to dams; human rights groups opposed to relocation; other groups opposing cooperation with China. Representatives of 59 organizations—an astonishing worldwide network stretching from Mexico to Thailand—dispatched a long letter to World Bank President Jim Wolfensohn protesting the transfer of "Chinese farmers into a traditionally Tibetan area." Campaigners deluged the bank with e-mails and faxes, anti-bank posters appeared around Washington, and Tibet activists set up camp outside the bank's headquarters. A rap star from the Beastie Boys declared that the bank's loan would lead to the "destruction of the Tibetan peoples."

Despite the inaccuracy of this claim, the activists quickly won allies in Hollywood and the U.S. Congress, most notably the actor Richard Gere, who had recently narrated a documentary film about Tibet, and Democratic Rep. Nancy Pelosi of California. On June 15, 1999, a press release announcing a joint appearance by Pelosi and a pro-Tibet musician stated that the bank planned to move "60,000 ethnic Chinese" into Qinghai, even though Han Chinese constituted only 40 percent of the 58,000 settlers, and even though these Han Chinese were not moving into Qinghai, just relocating within the province. Sixty members of congress fired off a complaint to Wolfensohn, and Sen. Jesse Helms, a far-right Republican politician from North Carolina, leapt at the chance to condemn China and the World Bank in a single breath. When a World Bank delegation went to Capitol Hill to mollify the law-makers, it was confronted with a map that did not even show Qinghai. The entire province had been labeled Tibet, never mind that Tibetans accounted for only one in five people there.

The bank was totally encircled. It was simultaneously up against student protestors and the right wing of the Republican Party, and although the bank's assailants were flat wrong on the facts, nobody was willing to stick up for the insti-tution. In June 1999, the Clinton administration announced that it would vote against the Qinghai project when it came before the World Bank's board. The Lilliputian activists had taken on the bank, and they had won the first round.

## APPEASEMENT DENIED

The most common reaction to this sort of story is that the bank must communicate better with its critics and learn how to compromise with them. Unfortunately, this prescription is naive. It presumes the critics are open to compromise. But cam-paigning NGOs, as distinct from those with real development programs in the field, almost have to be radical. If they stop denouncing big organizations, nobody will send them cash or quote them in the newspapers. Partly for this reason, and partly out of a likeable conviction that the status quo is never good enough, most NGOs do not have an off switch. You can do everything possible to meet them halfway, but they will still demonstrate outside your building. Of course, there will be grown-up groups like Oxfam, World Vision, or the World Wildlife Fund that may accept your olive branch. But they will be the exceptions, and they may coop-erate only cautiously. They don't want to be the next target for the radicals.

The second round of the Qinghai battle illustrated this problem. Confronted with the news that the Clinton administration would block the project, Wolfensohn flew into a rage. He worried about threats by the U.S. Congress to cut contribu-tions to the bank's subsidized lending program if the project went ahead, under-mining the bank's ability to help its poorest clients. He fretted that the adverse publicity might cost him a chance at winning a Nobel Peace Prize and that his Hollywood connections would turn on him. And he feared that one of his central achievements would be jeopardized: Since taking the helm of the bank in 1995, Wolfensohn had done more than any of his predecessors to reach out to NGOs. He welcomed the bank's most ardent critics to private dinners at his home, made a point of meeting with them wherever he traveled, and even created commissions to solicit their advice on World Bank policy.

When the Qinghai battle came to a head, Wolfensohn did everything possible to defuse it. He went out of his way to hear the arguments of the NGOs, treating his own staff with much less deference. He summoned the project team to his office and demanded to know whose arse he should kick first. After much raging and fum-ing, he hit upon a scheme that would meet the NGOs part way. The project would be referred to the bank's Inspection Panel, a tribunal staffed by eminent persons who investigate projects' compliance with the bank's environmental and social safeguards.

The activists alleged several instances of non-compliance. They claimed, for example, that one guideline requiring "special action" to protect ethnic minorities was breached, along with another requiring that resettlement be voluntary. The critics focused particularly on the bank's environmental safeguards. The bank had classified Qinghai as a "Category B" project (posing medium risk to the environment), rather than a high-risk "Category A," and therefore commissioned an arguably skimpy environmental impact study. By referring these claims to the Inspection Panel, Wolfensohn calculated that a political fight over Tibet would now become a technical inquiry into the bank's operational guidelines.

In a sane world, this strategy would have bought some peace with the activists. But the day after the bank decided to convene an Inspection Panel, a pair of students climbed up the face of the bank's headquarters and unfurled a banner proclaiming, "World Bank Approves China's Genocide in Tibet." Privately, other Tibet groups disapproved of these tactics—after all, there was no evidence of genocide— but they were unwilling to speak out publicly against their fellow activists. Meanwhile, members of congress continued to toe the NGO line. Republican Sens. Connie Mack of Florida and Benjamin Gilman of New York accused the bank of "cultural genocide." A House of Representatives subcommittee voted in 1999 to cut contributions to the bank's soft-loan window by $220 million.

When the Inspection Panel inquiry got under way, it only succeeded in bringing the activist attack inside the World Bank's building. The head of the Inspection Panel, Canadian environmentalist Jim MacNeill, clearly favored activists over bank staff, whom he treated with prosecutorial vigor. He seemed more interested in finding technical infringements of the bank's safeguard policies than in asking the big questions: Would the Qinghai project reduce poverty? The answer was yes, but the panel seemed indifferent. Would it cause environmental damage? The bottom line was no, and yet the panel insisted on poking holes in the bank's procedures.

The panel's final report, delivered in April 2000, was a 160-page indictment of the Qinghai project. It insisted that the scheme should have been rated Category A for environmental riskiness, that insufficient attention had been paid to the impact on Mongolian and Tibetan nomads, and that the recruitment of volunteers for resettlement was compromised because interviews were not confidential. The panel's report did not worry too much about whether a Category A environmental assessment would have found reasons to oppose the project or whether nomads might actually benefit from clinics or other facilities created by the project. It did not dwell on the fact that, whatever the circumstances of the interviews, the farmers' desire to relocate was beyond doubt. Indeed, many more people wanted to move than the project could accommodate.

In June 2000, the bank's management made a last-ditch attempt to placate the NGOs by proposing another year's worth of studies and project preparation the bank estimated would cost $2 million. Yet the NGOs continued their calls for canceling the project. In July, the bank board rejected the managers' proposal, and the second round of the Qinghai battle came to a close: China informed the bank that it would withdraw its request for financing.

Not long after the World Bank pulled out of Qinghai, a delegation of Tibet activists went to visit Wolfensohn. They had heard that the Chinese government was pressing ahead with the resettlement project by itself. It later became apparent that China planned to ignore the bank's environmental conditions and move more people to the new area. The NGOs were having a hard time discovering the details of the Chinese plans, so they asked Wolfensohn what was going on.

"How the fuck do I know what they're doing?" Wolfensohn shot back. "You just got us out of there!"

## THE SLEEPING BANK AWAKENS

Versions of this story play out all over the world. The bank designs a reasonable project, which inevitably has flaws. NGOs seize on these flaws and add a large sprinkling of inflammatory rhetoric. The World Bank pulls out, but the project goes ahead anyway, minus the bank's social and environmental safeguards. Because of the fear of NGO assault, the bank is obliged to follow its precautionary guidelines to the letter, adding many months and dollars to project preparation. According to a bank study carried out in 2001, safeguard policies of one kind or another inflate total project preparation costs by somewhere between $200 million and $300 million annually. This money comes out of the hides of the world's poor, and the associated delays mean further months without the electricity or clean water that a bank project might bring—harming the poor a second time over.

The bank's expense and delays do not even benefit the environmental and human rights agendas that NGOs hold so dear. Because of the high cost of doing business with the bank, countries with the option of borrowing on private capital markets increasingly do so. For example, China, which borrowed $1.7 billion from the World Bank in 2000, accepted only half as much in 2001 and 2002—and the infrastructure that China built without the bank's financing was subjected to less scrutiny. Some level of conditionality is essential, but after waves of punishing assault by NGOs, the World Bank has come to reflect the agenda of activists who insist upon perfectionist safeguards. In sum, the world's premier development institution has come perilously close to losing touch with the needs and realities of developing countries.

The good news is that many within the bank have come to understand this dilemma. After experiences like Qinghai and a decade of Wolfensohn's efforts to woo the NGOs, they have rightly realized that you can't win over every critic. For example, the bank invited several NGOs to participate in a commission tasked with setting standards for future dams; the commission responded with a list of standards so onerous as to make most dams unviable. In late 2001, a group within the bank pushed back, persuading the bank's board that the institution should not feel bound by the commission's excessive recommendations. This year, a bank-appointed commission on extractive industries followed the NGOs' lead, calling on the World Bank to pull out of all oil and coal projects because of the pollution they create. But this demand overlooks the developing world's need for energy, which has to be satisfied somehow. And it fails to acknowledge that 2.3 billion people currently depend on wood and other biomass fuels that cause even more deforestation and air pollution. Thankfully, the bank's management rejected the commission's recommendation.

This nascent counterattack must go broader than one institution, however. The lesson of the Qinghai battle is that the bank cannot fight the NGOs alone. Commentators, politicians, and Hollywood celebrities must resist the temptation to side uncritically with feisty activists.

The World Bank's predicament is part of a larger conundrum that bedevils globalization. In many of the world's rich capitals, and especially in Washington, public policy is decided by a bewildering array of interest groups campaigning single-mindedly for narrow goals. A similar army of advocates pounds upon big international institutions like the bank, demanding they bend to particular concerns: no damage to indigenous peoples, no harm to rain forests, nothing that might threaten human rights, or Tibet, or democratic values. However noble many of the activists' motives, and however flawed the big institutions' record, this constant campaigning threatens to disable not just the World Bank but regional development banks and governmental aid organizations such as the U.S. Agency for International Development. If this takes place, the world may lose the potential for good that big organizations offer: to rise above the single-issue advocacy that small groups tend to pursue and to square off against humanity's grandest problems in all their hideous complexity.

# Human Rights in World Politics

## RHODA E. HOWARD AND JACK DONNELLY

The International Human Rights Covenants[1] note that human rights "derive from the inherent dignity of the human person." But while the struggle to assure a life of dignity is probably as old as human society itself, reliance on human rights as a mechanism to realize that dignity is a relatively recent development.

Human rights are, by definition, the rights one has simply because one is a human being. This simple and relatively uncontroversial definition, though, is more complicated than it may appear on the surface. It identifies human rights as *rights*, in the strict and strong sense of that term, and it establishes that they are held simply by virtue of being human. . . .

### WHAT RIGHTS DO WE HAVE?

The definition of human or natural rights as the rights of each person simply as a human being specifies their character; they are rights. The definition also specifies their source: (human) nature. . . .

What is it in human nature that gives rise to human rights? There are two basic answers to this question. On the one hand, many people argue that human rights arise from human needs, from the naturally given requisites for physical and mental health and well-being. On the other hand, many argue that human rights reflect the minimum requirements for human dignity or *moral* personality. These latter arguments derive from essentially philosophical theories of human "nature," dignity, or moral personality.

Needs theories of human rights run into the problem of empirical confirmations; the simple fact is that there is sound scientific evidence only for a very narrow list of human needs. But if we use "needs" in a broader, in part nonscientific, sense, then the two theories overlap. We can thus say that people have human rights to those things "needed" for a life of dignity, for the full development of their moral personality. The "nature" that gives rise to human rights is thus *moral* nature.

This moral nature is, in part, a social creation. Human nature, in the relevant sense, is an amalgam consisting both of psycho-biological facts (constraints and possibilities) and of the social structures and experiences that are no less a part of the essential nature of men and women. Human beings are not isolated individuals, but rather individuals who are essentially social creatures, in part even social creations. Therefore, a theory of human rights must recognize both the essential universality of human nature and the no less essential particularity arising from cultural and socioeconomic traditions and institutions.

Human rights are, by their nature, universal; it is not coincidental that we have a *Universal* Declaration of Human Rights, for human rights are the rights of all men and women. Therefore, in its basic outlines a list of human rights must apply at least more or less "across the board." But the nature of human beings is also shaped by the particular societies in which they live. Thus the universality of human rights must be qualified in at least two important ways.

First, the forms in which universal rights are institutionalized are subject to some legitimate cultural and political variation. For example, what counts as popular participation in government may vary, within a certain range, from society to society. Both multiparty and single-party regimes may reflect legitimate notions of political participation. Although the ruling party cannot be removed from power, in some one-party states individual representatives can be changed and electoral pressure may result in significant policy changes.

Second, and no less important, the universality (in principle) of human rights is qualified by the obvious fact that any particular list, no matter how broad its cross-cultural and international acceptance, reflects the necessarily contingent understandings of a particular era. For example, in the seventeenth and eighteenth centuries, the rights of man were indeed the rights of men, not women, and social and economic rights (other than the right to private property) were unheard of. Thus we must expect a gradual evolution of even a consensual list of human rights, as collective understandings of the essential elements of human dignity, the conditions of moral personality, evolve in response to changing ideas and material circumstances.

In other words, human rights are by their essential nature universal in form. They are, by definition, the rights held by each (and every) person simply as a human being. But any universal list of human rights is subject to a variety of justifiable implementations.

In our time, the Universal Declaration of Human Rights (1948) is a minimum list that is nearly universally accepted, although additional rights have been added (e.g., self-determination) and further new rights (e.g., the right to nondiscrimination on the grounds of sexual orientation or the right to peace) may be added in the future. We are in no position to offer a philosophical defense of the list of rights in the Universal Declaration. To do so would require an account of the source of human rights—human nature—that would certainly exceed the space available to us. Nonetheless, the Universal Declaration is nearly universally accepted by states. For practical political purposes we can treat it as authoritative. . . .

## INTERNATIONAL HUMAN RIGHTS INSTITUTIONS

The international context of national practices deserves some attention. There are, as we have already noted, international human rights standards that are widely accepted—in principle at least—by states. Thus the discussion and evaluation of national practices take place within an overarching set of international standards to which virtually all states have explicitly committed themselves. Whatever the force of claims of national sovereignty, with its attendant legal immunity from international action, the evaluation of national human rights practices from the perspective of the international standards of the Universal Declaration thus is certainly appropriate, even if one is uncomfortable with the moral claim sketched above that such universalistic scrutiny is demanded by the very idea of human rights.

In the literature on international relations it has recently become fashionable to talk of "international regimes," that is, norms and decision-making procedures accepted by states in a given issue area. National human rights practices do take place within the broader context of an international human rights regime centered on the United Nations.

We have already sketched the principal norms of this regime—the list of rights in the Universal Declaration. These norms/rights are further elaborated in two major treaties, the International Covenant on Economic, Social and Cultural Rights and the International Covenant on Civil and Political Rights, which were opened for signature and ratification in 1966 and came into force in 1976. Almost all of the countries studied in this volume have ratified (become a party to) both the Covenant on Civil and Political Rights and the Covenant on Economic, Social and Cultural Rights. . . . Even the countries that are not parties to the Covenants often accept the principles of the Universal Declaration. In addition, there are a variety of single-issue treaties that have been formulated under UN auspices on topics such as racial discrimination, the rights of women, and torture. These later Covenants and Conventions go into much greater detail than the Universal Declaration and include a few important changes. For example, the Covenants prominently include a right to national self-determination, which is absent in the Universal Declaration, but do not include a right to private property. Nevertheless, for the most part they can be seen simply as elaborations on the Universal Declaration, which remains the central normative document in the international human rights regime.

What is the legal and political force of these norms? The Universal Declaration of Human Rights was proclaimed in 1948 by the United Nations General Assembly. As such, it has no force of law. Resolutions of the General Assembly, even solemn declarations, are merely recommendations to states; the General Assembly has no international legislative powers. Over the years, however, the Universal Declaration has come to be something more than a mere recommendation.

There are two principal sources of international law, namely, treaty and custom. Although today we tend to think first of treaty, historically custom is at least as important. A rule or principle attains the force of customary international law when it can meet two tests. First, the principle or rule must reflect the general practice of the overwhelming majority of states. Second, what lawyers call *opinio juris*, the sense of obligation, must be taken into account. Is the customary practice seen by states as an obligation, rather than a mere convenience or courtesy? Today it is a common view of international lawyers that the Universal Declaration has attained something of the status of customary international law, so that the rights it contains are in some important sense binding on states.

Furthermore, the International Human Rights Covenants are treaties and as such do have the force of international law, but only for the parties to the treaties, that is, those states that have (voluntarily) ratified or acceded to the treaties. The same is true of the single-issue treaties that round out the regime's norms. It is perhaps possible that the norms of the Covenants are coming to acquire the force of customary international law even for states that are not parties. But in either case, the fundamental weakness of international law is underscored: Virtually all international legal obligations are voluntarily accepted.

This is obviously the case for treaties: states are free to become parties or not entirely as they choose. It is no less true, though, of custom, where the tests of state practice and *opinio juris* likewise assure that international legal obligation is only voluntarily acquired. In fact, a state that explicitly rejects a practice during the process of custom formation is exempt even from customary international legal obligations. For example, Saudi Arabia's objection to the provisions on the equal rights of women during the drafting of the Universal Declaration might be held to exempt it from such a norm, even if the norm is accepted internationally as customarily binding. Such considerations are particularly important when we ask what force there is to international law and what mechanisms exist to implement and enforce the rights specified in the Universal Declaration and the Covenants.

Acceptance of an obligation by states does not carry with it acceptance of any method of international enforcement. Quite the contrary. Unless there is an explicit enforcement mechanism attached to the obligation, its enforcement rests simply on the good faith of the parties. The Universal Declaration contains no enforcement mechanisms of any sort. Even if we accept it as having the force of international law, its implementation is left entirely in the hands of individual states. The Covenants do have some implementation machinery, but the machinery's practical weakness is perhaps its most striking feature. . . .

The one other major locus of activity in the international human rights regime is the UN Commission on Human Rights. In addition to being the body that played the principal role in the formulation of the Universal Declaration, the Covenants, and most of the major single-issue human rights treaties, it has some weak implementation powers. Its public discussion of human rights situations in various countries can help to mobilize international public opinion, which is not always utterly useless in helping to reform national practice. For example, in the 1970s the Commission played a major role in publicizing the human rights conditions in Chile, Israel, and South Africa. Furthermore, it is empowered by ECOSOC resolution 1503 (1970) to investigate communications (complaints) from individuals and groups that "appear to reveal a consistent pattern of gross and reliably attested violations of human rights."

The 1503 procedure, however, is at least as thoroughly hemmed in by constraints as are the other enforcement mechanisms that we have considered.[2] Although individuals may communicate grievances, the 1503 procedure deals only with "*situations*" of gross and systematic violations, not the particular cases of individuals. Individuals cannot even obtain an international judgment in their particular case, let alone international enforcement of the human rights obligations of their government. Furthermore, the entire procedure remains confidential until a case is concluded, although the Commission does publicly announce a "blacklist" of countries being studied. In only four cases (Equatorial Guinea, Haiti, Malawi, and Uruguay) has the Commission gone public with a 1503 case. Its most forceful conclusion was a 1980 resolution provoked by the plight of Jehovah's Witnesses in Malawi, which merely expressed the hope that all human rights were being respected in Malawi.

In addition to this global human rights regime, there are regional regimes. The 1981 African Charter of Human and Peoples' Rights, drawn up by the Organization of African Unity, provides for a Human Rights Commission, but it is not yet functioning. In Europe and the Americas there are highly developed systems involving both commissions with very strong investigatory powers and regional human rights courts with the authority to make legally binding decisions on complaints by individuals (although only eight states have accepted the jurisdiction of the Inter-American Court of Human Rights).

Even in Europe and the Americas, however, implementation and enforcement remain primarily national. In nearly thirty years the European Commission of Human Rights has considered only about 350 cases, while the European Court of Human Rights has handled only one-fifth that number. Such regional powers certainly should not be ignored or denigrated. They provide authoritative interpretations in cases of genuine disagreements and a powerful check on backsliding and occasional deviations by states. But the real force of even the European regime lies in the voluntary acceptance of human rights by the states in question, which has infinitely more to do with domestic politics than with international procedures.

In sum, at the international level there are comprehensive, authoritative human rights norms that are widely accepted as binding on all states. Implementation and enforcement of these norms, however, both in theory and in practice, are left to states. The international context of national human rights practices certainly cannot be ignored. Furthermore, international norms may have an important socializing effect on national leaders and be useful to national advocates of improved domestic human rights practices. But the real work of implementing and enforcing human rights takes place at the national level. . . . Before the level of the nation-state is discussed, however, one final element of the international context needs to be considered, namely, human rights as an issue in national foreign policies.

## HUMAN RIGHTS AND FOREIGN POLICY

Beyond the human rights related activities of states in international institutions such as those discussed in the preceding section, many states have chosen to make human rights a concern in their bilateral foreign relations.[3] in fact, much of the surge of interest in human rights in the last decade can be traced to the catalyzing effect of President Jimmy Carter's (1977–1981) efforts to make international human rights an objective of U.S. foreign policy.

In a discussion of human rights as an issue in national foreign policy, at least three problems need to be considered. First, a nation must select a particular set of rights to pursue. Second, the legal and moral issues raised by intervention on behalf of human rights abroad need to be explored. Third, human rights concerns must be integrated into the nation's broader foreign policy, since human rights are at best only one of several foreign policy objectives.

The international normative consensus on human rights noted above largely solves the problem of the choice of a set of rights to pursue, for unless a state chooses a list very similar to that of the Universal Declaration, its efforts are almost certain to be dismissed as fatally flawed by partisan or ideological bias. Thus, for example, claims by officials of the Reagan administration that economic and social rights are not really true human rights are almost universally denounced. By the same token, the Carter administration's serious attention to economic and social rights, even if it was ultimately subordinate to a concern for civil and political rights, greatly contributed to the international perception of its policy as genuinely concerned with human rights, not just a new rhetoric for the Cold War or neo-colonialism. Such an international perception is almost a necessary condition—although by no means a sufficient condition—for an effective international human rights policy.

A state is, of course, free to pursue any objectives it wishes in its foreign policy. If it wishes its human rights policy to be taken seriously, however, the policy must at least be enunciated in terms consistent with the international consensus that has been forged around the Universal Declaration. In practice, some rights must be given particular prominence in a nation's foreign policy, given the limited material resources and international political capital of even the most powerful state, but the basic contours of policy must be set by the Universal Declaration.

After the rights to be pursued have been selected, the second problem, that of intervention on behalf of human rights, arises. When state A pursues human rights in its relations with state B, A usually will be seeking to alter the way that B treats its own citizens. This is, by definition, a matter essentially within the domestic jurisdiction of B and thus outside the legitimate jurisdiction of A. A's action, therefore, is vulnerable to the charge of intervention, a charge that carries considerable legal, moral, and political force in a world, such as ours, that is structured at the international level around sovereign nation-states.

The legal problems raised by foreign policy action on behalf of human rights abroad are probably the most troubling. Sovereignty entails the principle of nonintervention; to say that A has sovereign jurisdiction over X is essentially equivalent to saying that no one else may intervene in A with respect to X. Because sovereignty is the foundation of international law, any foreign policy action that amounts to intervention is prohibited by international law. On the face of it at least, this prohibition applies to action on behalf of human rights as much as any other activity.

It might be suggested that we can circumvent the legal proscription of intervention in the case of human rights by reference to particular treaties or even the general international normative consensus discussed above. International norms per se, however, do not authorize even international organizations, let alone individual states acting independently, to enforce those norms. Even if all states are legally bound to implement the rights enumerated in the Universal Declaration, it simply does not follow, in logic or in law, that any particular state or group of states is entitled to enforce that obligation. States are perfectly free to accept international legal obligations that have no enforcement mechanisms attached.

Scrupulously avoiding intervention (coercive interference) thus still leaves considerable room for international action at improving the human rights performance of a foreign country. Quiet diplomacy, public protests or condemnations, downgrading or breaking diplomatic relations, reducing or halting foreign aid, and selective or comprehensive restrictions of trade and other forms of interaction are all actions that fall short of intervention. Thus in most circumstances they will be legally permissible actions on behalf of human rights abroad.

An international legal perspective on humanitarian intervention, however, does not exhaust the subject. Recently, several authors have argued, strongly and we believe convincingly, that moral considerations in at least some circumstances justify humanitarian intervention on behalf of human rights.[4] Michael Walzer, whose book *Just and Unjust Wars* has provoked much of the recent moral discussion of humanitarian intervention, can be taken as illustrative of such arguments.

Walzer presents a strong defense of the morality of the general international principle of nonintervention, arguing that it gives force to the basic right of peoples to self-determination, which in turn rests on the rights of individuals, acting in concert as a community, to choose their own government. Walzer has been criticized for interpreting this principle in a way that is excessively favorable to states by arguing that the presumption of legitimacy (and thus against intervention) should hold in all but the most extreme circumstances. Nonetheless, even Walzer allows that intervention must be permitted "when the violation of human rights is so terrible that it makes talk of community or self-determination . . . seem cynical and irrelevant,"[5] when gross, persistent, and systematic violations of human rights shock the moral conscience of mankind.

The idea underlying such arguments is that human rights are of such paramount moral importance that gross and systematic violations present a moral justification for remedial international action. If the international community as a whole cannot or will not act—and above we have shown that an effective collective international response will usually be impossible—then one or more states may be morally justified in acting ad hoc on behalf of the international community.

International law and morality thus lead to different and conflicting conclusions in at least some cases. One of the functions of international politics is to help to resolve such a conflict; political considerations will play a substantial role in determining how a state will respond in its foreign policy to the competing moral and legal demands placed on it. But the political dimensions of such decisions point to the practical dangers by moral arguments in favor of humanitarian intervention. . . .

Human rights may be moral concerns, but often they are not *merely* moral concerns. Morality and realism are not necessarily incompatible, and to treat them as if they always were can harm not only a state's human rights policy but its broader foreign policy as well.

Sometimes a country can afford to act on its human rights concerns; other times it cannot. Politics involves compromise, as a result of multiple and not always compatible goals that are pursued and the resistance of a world that more often than not is unsupportive of the particular objectives being sought. Human rights, like other goals of foreign policy, must at times be compromised. In some instances there is little that a country can afford to do even in the face of major human rights violations. . . .

If such variations in the treatment of human rights violators are to be part of a consistent policy, human rights concerns need to be explicitly and coherently integrated into the broader framework of foreign policy. A human rights policy must be an integral part of, not just something tacked on to, a country's overall foreign policy.

Difficult decisions have to be made about the relative weights to be given to human rights, as well as other foreign policy goals, and at least rough rules for making trade-offs need to be formulated. Furthermore, such decisions need to be made early in the process of working out a policy, and as a matter of principle. Ad hoc responses to immediate problems and crises, which have been the rule in the human rights policies of countries such as Canada and the United States, are almost sure to lead to inconsistencies and incoherence, both in appearance and in fact. Without such efforts to integrate human rights into the structure of national foreign policy, any trade-offs that are made will remain, literally, unprincipled.

Standards will be undeniably difficult to formulate, and their application will raise no less severe problems. Hard cases and exceptions are unavoidable. So are gray areas and fuzzy boundaries. Unless such efforts are seriously undertaken, however, the resulting policy is likely to appear baseless or inconsistent, and probably will be so in fact as well.

There are many opportunities for foreign policy action on behalf of human rights in foreign countries, but effective action requires the same sort of care and attention required for success in any area of foreign policy. . . .

## CULTURE AND HUMAN RIGHTS

This view of the creation of the individual, with individual needs for human rights, is criticized by many advocates of the "cultural relativist" school of human rights. They present the argument that human rights are a "Western construct with limited [universal] applicability."[6] But cultural relativism, as applied to human rights, fails to grasp the nature of culture. A number of erroneous assumptions underlie this viewpoint.

Criticism of the universality of human rights often stems from erroneous perceptions of the persistence of traditional societies, societies in which principles of social justice are based not on rights but on status and on the intermixture of privilege and responsibility. Often anthropologically anachronistic pictures are presented of premodern societies, taking no account whatsoever of the social changes we have described above. It is assumed that culture is a static entity. But culture—like the individual—is adaptive. One can accept the principle that customs, values, and norms do indeed glue society together, and that they will endure, without assuming cultural stasis. Even though elements of culture have a strong hold on people's individual psyches, cultures can and do change. Individuals are actors who can influence their own fate, even if their range of choice is circumscribed by the prevalent social structure, culture, or ideology.

Cultural relativist arguments also often assume that culture is a unitary and unique whole; that is, that one is born into, and will always be, a part of a distinctive, comprehensive, and integrated set of cultural values and institutions that cannot be changed incrementally or only in part. Since in each culture the social norms and roles vary, so, it is argued, human rights must vary. The norms of each society are held to be both valuable in and of their own right, and so firmly rooted as to be impervious to challenge. Therefore, such arguments are applicable only to certain Western societies; to impose them on other societies from which they did not originally arise would do serious and irreparable damage to those cultures. In fact, though, people are quite adept cultural accommodationists; they are able to choose which aspects of a "new" culture they wish to adopt and which aspects of the "old" they wish to retain. For example, the marabouts (priests), who lead Senegal's traditional Muslim brotherhoods, have become leading political figures and have acquired considerable wealth and power through the peanut trade.

Still another assumption of the cultural relativism school is that culture is unaffected by social structure. But structure does affect culture. To a significant extent cultures and values reflect the basic economic and political organization of a society. For example, a society such as Tokugawa Japan that moves from a feudal structure to an organized bureaucratic state is bound to experience changes in values. Or the amalgamation of many different ethnic groups into one nation-state inevitably changes the way that individuals view themselves: For example, state-sponsored retention of ethnic customs, as under Canada's multicultural policy of preserving ethnic communities, cannot mask the fact that most of those communities are merging into the larger Canadian society.

A final assumption of the cultural relativist view of human rights is that cultural practices are neutral in their impact on different individuals and groups. Yet very few social practices, whether cultural or otherwise, distribute the same benefits to each member of a group. In considering any cultural practice it is useful to ask, who benefits from its retention? Those who speak for the group are usually those most capable of articulating the group's values to the outside world. But such spokesmen are likely to stress, in their articulation of "group" values, those particular values that are most to their own advantage. Both those who choose to adopt "new" ideals, such as political democracy or atheism, and those who choose to retain "old" ideals, such as a God-fearing political consensus, may be doing so in their own interests. Culture is both influenced by, and an instrument of, conflict among individuals or social groups. Just as those who attempt to modify or change customs may have personal interests in so doing, so also do those who attempt to preserve them. Quite often, relativist arguments are adopted principally to protect the interests of those in power.

Thus the notion that human rights cannot be applied across cultures violates both the principle of human rights and its practice. Human rights mean precisely that: rights held by virtue of being human. Human rights do not mean human dignity, nor do they represent the sum of personal resources (material, moral, or spiritual) that an individual might hold. Cultural variances that do not violate basic human rights undoubtedly enrich the world. But to permit the interests of the powerful to masquerade behind spurious defenses of cultural relativity is merely to lessen the chance that the victims of their policies will be able to complain. In the modern world, concepts such as cultural relativity, which deny to individuals the moral right to make comparisons and to insist on universal standards of right and wrong, are happily adopted by those who control the state.

## THIRD WORLD CRITICISMS

In recent years a number of commentators from the Third World have criticized the concept of universal human rights. Frequently, the intention of the criticisms appears to be to exempt some Third World governments from the standard of judgment generated by the concept of universal human rights. Much of the criticism in fact serves to cover abuses of human rights by state corporatist, developmental dictatorship, or allegedly "socialist" regimes.

A common criticism of the concept of universal human rights is that since it is Western in origin, it must be limited in its applicability to the Western world. Both logically and empirically, this criticism is invalid. Knowledge is not limited in its applicability to its place or people of origin—one does not assume, for example, that medicines discovered in the developed Western world will cure only people of European origin. Nor is it reasonable to state that knowledge or thought of a certain kind—about social arrangements instead of about human biology or natural science—is limited to its place of origin. Those same Third World critics who reject universal concepts of human rights often happily accept Marxist socialism, which also originated in the Western world, in the mind of a German Jew.

The fact that human rights is originally a liberal notion, rooted in the rise of a class of bourgeois citizens in Europe who demanded individual rights against the power of kings and nobility, does not make human rights inapplicable to the rest of the world. As we argue above, all over the world there are now formal states, whose citizens are increasingly individualized. All over the world, therefore, there are people who need protections against the depradations of class-ruled governments.

Moreover, whatever the liberal origins of human rights, the list now accepted as universal includes a wide range of economic and social rights that were first advocated by socialist and social-democratic critics of liberalism. Although eighteenth-century liberals stressed the right to private property, the 1966 International Human Rights Covenants do not mention it, substituting instead the right to sovereignty over national resources. . . . To attribute the idea of universal human rights to an outdated liberalism, unaffected by later notions of welfare democracy and uninfluenced by socialist concerns with economic rights, is simply incorrect.

The absence of a right to private property in the Covenants indicates a sensitivity to the legitimate preoccupations of socialist and postcolonial Third World governments. Conservative critics of recent trends in international human rights in fact deplore the right to national sovereignty over resources, as some of them also deplore any attention to the economic rights of the individual. We certainly do not share this view of rights; we believe that the economic rights of the individual are as important as civil and political rights. But it is the individual we are concerned with. We would like to see a world in which *every individual* has enough to eat, not merely a world in which every *state* has the right to economic sovereignty.

We are skeptical, therefore, of the radical Third Worldist assertion that "group" rights ought to be more important than individual rights. Too often, the "group" in question proves to be the state. Why allocate rights to a social institution that is already the chief violator of individuals' rights? Similarly, we fear the expression "peoples' rights." The communal rights of individuals to practice their own religion, speak their own language, and indulge in their own ancestral customs are protected in the Covenant on Civil and Political Rights. Individuals are free to come together in groups to engage in those cultural practices which are meaningful to them. On the other hand, often a "group" right can simply mean that the individual is subordinate to the group—for example, that the individual Christian fundamentalist in the Soviet Union risks arrest because of the desire of the larger "group" to enforce official atheism.

The one compelling use that we can envisage for the term "group rights" is in protection of native peoples, usually hunter-gatherers, pastoralists, or subsistence agriculturalists, whose property rights as collectivities are being violated by the larger state societies that encroach upon them. Such groups are fighting a battle against the forces of modernization and the state's accumulative tendencies. For example, native peoples in Canada began in the 1970s to object to state development projects, such as the James Bay Hydroelectric project in Quebec, which deprived them of their traditional lands. At the moment, there is no international human rights protection for such groups or their "way of life."

One way to protect such group rights would be to incorporate the group as a legal entity in order to preserve their land claims. However, even if the law protects such group rights, individual members of the group may prefer to move into the larger society in response to the processes of modernization discussed above. Both opinions must be protected.

If the purpose of group rights is to protect large, established groups of people who share the same territory, customs, language, religion, and ancestry, then such protection could only occur at the expense of states' rights. These groups, under international human rights law, do not have the right to withdraw from the states that enfold them. Moreover, it is clearly not the intention of Third World defenders of group rights to allow such a right to secession. A first principle of the Organization of African Unity, for example, is to preserve the sovereignty of all its member states not only against outside attack but also against internal attempts at secession. Group rights appear to mean, in practice, states' rights. But the rights of states are the rights of the individuals and classes who control the state.

Many Third World and socialist regimes also argue that rights ought to be tied to duties. A citizen's rights, it is argued, ought to be contingent upon his duties toward the society at large—privilege is contingent on responsibility. Such a view of rights made sense in nonstate societies in which each "person" fulfilled his roles along with others, all of the roles together creating a close-knit, tradition-bound group. But in modern state societies, to tie rights to duties is to risk the former's complete disappearance. All duties will be aimed toward the preservation of the state and of the interests of those who control it.

It is true that no human rights are absolute; even in societies that adhere in principle to the liberal ethos, individuals are frequently deprived of rights, especially in wartime or if they are convicted of criminal acts. However, such deprivations can legitimately be made only after the most scrupulous protection of civil and political rights under the rule of law. The difficulty with tying rights to duties without the intermediate step of scrutiny by a genuinely independent judiciary is the likelihood of wholesale cancellation of rights by the ruling class. But if one has rights merely because one is human, and for no other reason, then it is much more difficult, in principle, for the state to cancel them. It cannot legitimate the denial of rights by saying that only certain types of human beings, exhibiting certain kinds of behavior, are entitled to them.

One final criticism of the view of universal human rights embedded in the International Covenants is that an undue stress is laid on civil and political rights, whereas the overriding rights priority in the Third World is economic rights. In this view, the state as the agent of economic development—and hence, presumably, of eventual distribution of economic goods or "rights" to the masses—should not be bothered with problems of guaranteeing political participation in decision making, or of protecting people's basic civil rights. These rights, it is argued, come "after" development is completed. The empirical basis for this argument is weak. . . . Economic development per se will not guarantee future human rights, whether of an economic or any other kind. Often, development means economic growth, but without equitable distributive measures. Moreover, development strategies often fail because of insufficient attention to citizens' needs and views. Finally, development plans are often a cover for the continued violations of citizens' rights by the ruling class.

Thus we return to where we started: the rights of all men and women against all governments to treatment as free, equal, materially and physically secure persons. This is what human dignity means and requires in our era. And the individual human rights of the Universal Declaration and the Covenants are the means by which individuals today carry out the struggle to achieve their dignity. . . .

## NOTES

1. The International Bill of Human Rights includes the Universal Declaration of Human Rights (1948), the International Covenant on Economic, Social and Cultural Rights (1966), the International Covenant on Civil and Political Rights (1966), and the Optional Protocol to the latter Covenant.
2. Howard Tolley, "The Concealed Crack in the Citadel: The United Nations Commission on Human Rights' Response to Confidential Communications," *Human Rights Quarterly* 6 (November 1984): 420–62.
3. This section draws heavily on Jack Donnelly, "Human Rights and Foreign Policy," *World Politics* 34 (July 1982): 574–95, and "Human Rights, Humanitarian Intervention and American Foreign Policy: Law, Morality and Politics," *Journal of International Affairs* 37 (Winter 1984): 311–28.
4. See, for example, Jerome Slater and Terry Nardin, "Nonintervention and Human Rights," *Journal of Politics* 48 (February 1986): 86–96; Charles R. Beitz, "Nonintervention and Communal Integrity," *Philosophy and Public Affairs* 9 (Summer 1980): 385–91; and Robert Matthews and Cranford Pratt, "Human Rights and Foreign Policy: Principles and Canadian Practice," *Human Rights Quarterly* 7 (May 1985): 159–88.
5. Michael Walzer, *Just and Unjust Wars* (New York: Basic Books, 1977), p. 90. For criticisms of Walzer see Slater and Nardin, "Nonintervention"; Beitz, "Nonintervention"; and David Luban, "The Romance of the Nation State," *Philosophy and Public Affairs* 9 (Summer 1980): 392–97.
6. Adamantia Pollis and Peter Schwab, "Human Rights: A Western Concept with Limited Applicability," in *Human Rights: Cultural and Ideological Perspectives*, Pollis and Schwab, ed. (New York: Praeger, 1979), pp. 1–18.

# The Five Wars of Globalization

## MOISÉS NAÍM

The persistence of al Qaeda underscores how hard it is for governments to stamp out stateless, decentralized networks that move freely, quickly, and stealthily across national borders to engage in terror. The intense media coverage devoted to the war on terrorism, however, obscures five other similar global wars that pit governments against agile, well-financed networks of highly dedicated individuals. These are the fights against the illegal international trade in drugs, arms, intellectual property, people, and money. Religious zeal or political goals drive terrorists, but the promise of enormous financial gain motivates those who battle governments in these five wars. Tragically, profit is no less a motivator for murder, mayhem, and global insecurity than religious fanaticism.

In one form or another, governments have been fighting these five wars for centuries. And losing them. Indeed, thanks to the changes spurred by globalization over the last decade, their losing streak has become even more pronounced. To be sure, nation-states have benefited from the information revolution, stronger political and economic linkages, and the shrinking importance of geographic distance. Unfortunately, criminal networks have benefited even more. Never fettered by the niceties of sovereignty, they are now increasingly free of geographic constraints. Moreover, globalization has not only expanded illegal markets and boosted the size and the resources of criminal networks, it has also imposed more burdens on governments: Tighter public budgets, decentralization, privatization, deregulation, and a more open environment for international trade and investment all make the task of fighting global criminals more difficult. Governments are made up of cumbersome bureaucracies that generally cooperate with difficulty, but drug traffickers, arms dealers, alien smugglers, counterfeiters, and money launderers have refined networking to a high science, entering into complex and improbable strategic alliances that span cultures and continents.

Defeating these foes may prove impossible. But the first steps to reversing their recent dramatic gains must be to recognize the fundamental similarities among the five wars and to treat these conflicts not as law enforcement problems but as a new global trend that shapes the world as much as confrontations between nation-states did in the past. Customs officials, police officers, lawyers, and judges alone will never win these wars. Governments must recruit and deploy more spies,

From Moisés Naím, "Five Wars of Globalization," *Foreign Policy*, No. 134 (January/February 2003), pp. 29–36. © 2002 by the Carnegie Endowment for International Peace. Reprinted with permission.

soldiers, diplomats, and economists who understand how to use incentives and regulations to steer markets away from bad social outcomes. But changing the skill set of government combatants alone will not end these wars. Their doctrines and institutions also need a major overhaul.

## THE FIVE WARS

Pick up any newspaper anywhere in the world, any day, and you will find news about illegal migrants, drug busts, smuggled weapons, laundered money, or counterfeit goods. The global nature of these five wars was unimaginable just a decade ago. The resources—financial, human, institutional, technological—deployed by the combatants have reached unfathomable orders of magnitude. So have the numbers of victims. The tactics and tricks of both sides boggle the mind. Yet if you cut through the fog of daily headlines and orchestrated photo ops, one inescapable truth emerges: The world's governments are fighting a qualitatively new phenomenon with obsolete tools, inadequate laws, inefficient bureaucratic arrangements, and ineffective strategies. Not surprisingly, the evidence shows that governments are losing.

### Drugs

The best known of the five wars is, of course, the war on drugs. In 1999, the United Nations' "Human Development Report" calculated the annual trade in illicit drugs at $400 billion, roughly the size of the Spanish economy and about 8 percent of world trade. Many countries are reporting an increase in drug use. Feeding this habit is a global supply chain that uses everything from passenger jets that can carry shipments of cocaine worth $500 million in a single trip to custom-built submarines that ply the waters between Colombia and Puerto Rico. To foil eavesdroppers, drug smugglers use "cloned" cell phones and broadband radio receivers while also relying on complex financial structures that blend legitimate and illegitimate enterprises with elaborate fronts and structures of cross-ownership.

The United States spends between $35 billion and $40 billion each year on the war on drugs; most of this money is spent on interdiction and intelligence. But the creativity and boldness of drug cartels has routinely outstripped steady increases in government resources. Responding to tighter security at the U.S.-Mexican border, drug smugglers built a tunnel to move tons of drugs and billions of dollars in cash until authorities discovered it in March 2002. Over the last decade, the success of the Bolivian and Peruvian governments in eradicating coca plantations has shifted production to Colombia. Now, the U.S.-supported Plan Colombia is displacing coca production and processing labs back to other Andean countries. Despite the heroic efforts of these Andean countries and the massive financial and technical support of the United States, the total acreage of coca plantations in Peru, Colombia, and Bolivia has increased in the last decade from 206,200 hectares in 1991 to 210,939 in 2001. Between 1990 and 2000, according to economist Jeff DeSimone, the median price of a gram of cocaine in the United States fell from $152 to $112. . . .

## Arms Trafficking

Drugs and arms often go together. In 1999, the Peruvian military parachuted 10,000 AK-47s to the Revolutionary Armed Forces of Colombia, a guerrilla group closely allied to drug growers and traffickers. The group purchased the weapons in Jordan. Most of the roughly 80 million AK-47s in circulation today are in the wrong hands. According to the United Nations, only 18 million (or about 3 percent) of the 550 million small arms and light weapons in circulation today are used by government, military, or police forces. Illicit trade accounts for almost 20 percent of the total small arms trade and generates more than $1 billion a year. Small arms helped fuel 46 of the 49 largest conflicts of the last decade and in 2001 were estimated to be responsible for 1,000 deaths a day; more than 80 percent of those victims were women and children.

Small arms are just a small part of the problem. The illegal market for munitions encompasses top-of-the-line tanks, radar systems that detect Stealth aircraft, and the makings of the deadliest weapons of mass destruction. The International Atomic Energy Agency has confirmed more than a dozen cases of smuggled nuclear-weapons-usable material, and hundreds more cases have been reported and investigated over the last decade. The actual supply of stolen nuclear-, biological-, or chemical-weapons materials and technology may still be small. But the potential demand is strong and growing from both would-be nuclear powers and terrorists. Constrained supply and increasing demand cause prices to rise and create enormous incentives for illegal activities. More than one fifth of the 120,000 workers in Russia's former "nuclear cities"—where more than half of all employees earn less than $50 a month—say they would be willing to work in the military complex of another country.

Governments have been largely ineffective in curbing either supply or demand. . . . Multilateral efforts to curb the manufacture and distribution of weapons are faltering, not least because some powers are unwilling to accept curbs on their own activities. In 2001, for example, the United States blocked a legally binding global treaty to control small arms in part because it worried about restrictions on its own citizens' rights to own guns. In the absence of effective international legislation and enforcement, the laws of economics dictate the sale of more weapons at cheaper prices: In 1986, an AK-47 in Kolowa, Kenya, cost 15 cows. Today, it costs just four.

## Intellectual Property

In 2001, two days after recording the voice track of a movie in Hollywood, actor Dennis Hopper was in Shanghai where a street vendor sold him an excellent pirated copy of the movie with his voice already on it. "I don't know how they got my voice into the country before I got here," he wondered. Hopper's experience is one tiny slice of an illicit trade that cost the United States an estimated $9.4 billion in 2001. The piracy rate of business software in Japan and France is 40 percent, in Greece and South Korea it is about 60 percent, and in Germany and Britain it hovers around 30 percent. Forty percent of Procter & Gamble shampoos and 60 percent of Honda motorbikes sold in China in 2001 were pirated. Up to

50 percent of medical drugs in Nigeria and Thailand are bootleg copies. This problem is not limited to consumer products: Italian makers of industrial valves worry that their $2 billion a year export market is eroded by counterfeit Chinese valves sold in world markets at prices that are 40 percent cheaper.

The drivers of this bootlegging boom are complex. Technology is obviously boosting both the demand and the supply of illegally copied products. Users of Napster, the now defunct Internet company that allowed anyone, anywhere to download and reproduce copyrighted music for free, grew from zero to 20 million in just one year. Some 500,000 film files are traded daily through file-sharing services such as Kazaa and Morpheus; and in late 2002, some 900 million music files could be downloaded for free on the Internet—that is, almost two and a half times more files than those available when Napster reached its peak in February 2001.

Global marketing and branding are also playing a part, as more people are attracted to products bearing a well-known brand like Prada or Cartier. And thanks to the rapid growth and integration into the global economy of countries, such as China, with weak central governments and ineffective laws, producing and exporting near perfect knockoffs are both less expensive and less risky. In the words of the CEO of one of the best known Swiss watchmakers: "We now compete with a product manufactured by Chinese prisoners. The business is run by the Chinese military, their families and friends, using roughly the same machines we have, which they purchased at the same industrial fairs we go to." . . .

Governments have attempted to protect intellectual property rights through various means, most notably the World Trade Organization's Agreement on Trade-Related Aspects of Intellectual Property Rights (TRIPS). Several other organizations such as the World Intellectual Property Organization, the World Customs Union, and Interpol are also involved. Yet the large and growing volume of this trade, or a simple stroll in the streets of Manhattan or Madrid, show that governments are far from winning this fight.

## Alien Smuggling

The man or woman who sells a bogus Hermes scarf or a Rolex watch in the streets of Milan is likely to be an illegal alien. Just as likely, he or she was transported across several continents by a trafficking network allied with another network that specializes in the illegal copying, manufacturing, and distributing of high-end, brand-name products.

Alien smuggling is a $7 billion a year enterprise and according to the United Nations is the fastest growing business of organized crime. Roughly 500,000 people enter the United States illegally each year—about the same number as illegally enter the European Union, and part of the approximately 150 million who live outside their countries of origin. Many of these backdoor travelers are voluntary migrants who pay smugglers up to $35,000, the top-dollar fee for passage from China to New York. Others, instead, are trafficked—that is, bought and sold internationally—as commodities. The U.S. Congressional Research Service reckons that each year between 1 million and 2 million people are trafficked across borders, the majority of whom are women and children. A woman can be "bought" in

Timisoara, Romania, for between $50 and $200 and "resold" in Western Europe for 10 times that price. The United Nations Children's Fund estimates that cross-border smugglers in Central and Western Africa enslave 200,000 children a year. Traffickers initially tempt victims with job offers or, in the case of children, with offers of adoption in wealthier countries, and then keep the victims in subservience through physical violence, debt bondage, passport confiscation, and threats of arrest, deportation, or violence against their families back home.

Governments everywhere are enacting tougher immigration laws and devoting more time, money, and technology to fight the flow of illegal aliens. But the plight of the United Kingdom's government illustrates how tough that fight is. The British government throws money at the problem, plans to use the Royal Navy and Royal Air Force to intercept illegal immigrants, and imposes large fines on truck drivers who (generally unwittingly) transport stowaways. Still, 42,000 of the 50,000 refugees who have passed through the Sangatte camp (a main entry point for illegal immigration to the United Kingdom) over the last three years have made it to Britain. At current rates, it will take 43 years for Britain to clear its asylum backlog. And that country is an island. Continental nations such as Spain, Italy, or the United States face an even greater challenge as immigration pressures overwhelm their ability to control the inflow of illegal aliens.

## Money Laundering

The Cayman Islands has a population of 36,000. It also has more than 2,200 mutual funds, 500 insurance companies, 60,000 businesses, and 600 banks and trust companies with almost $800 billion in assets. Not surprisingly, it figures prominently in any discussion of money laundering. So does the United States, several of whose major banks have been caught up in investigations of money laundering, tax evasion, and fraud. Few, if any, countries can claim to be free of the practice of helping individuals and companies hide funds from governments, creditors, business partners, or even family members, including the proceeds of tax evasion, gambling, and other crimes. Estimates of the volume of global money laundering range between 2 and 5 percent of the world's annual gross national product, or between $800 billion and $2 trillion.

Smuggling money, gold coins, and other valuables is an ancient trade. Yet in the last two decades, new political and economic trends coincided with technological changes to make this ancient trade easier, cheaper, and less risky. Political changes led to the deregulation of financial markets that now facilitate cross-border money transfers, and technological changes made distance less of a factor and money less "physical." Suitcases full of banknotes are still a key tool for money launderers, but computers, the Internet, and complex financial schemes that combine legal and illegal practices and institutions are more common. The sophistication of technology, the complex web of financial institutions that crisscross the globe, and the ease with which "dirty" funds can be electronically morphed into legitimate assets make the regulation of international flows of money a daunting task. In Russia, for example, it is estimated that by the mid-1990s organized crime groups had set up 700 legal and financial institutions to launder their money.

Faced with this growing tide, governments have stepped up their efforts to clamp down on rogue international banking, tax havens, and money laundering. The imminent, large-scale introduction of e-money—cards with microchips that can store large amounts of money and thus can be easily transported outside regular channels or simply exchanged among individuals—will only magnify this challenge.

## WHY GOVERNMENTS CAN'T WIN

The fundamental changes that have given the five wars new intensity over the last decade are likely to persist. Technology will continue to spread widely; criminal networks will be able to exploit these technologies more quickly than governments that must cope with tight budgets, bureaucracies, media scrutiny, and electorates. International trade will continue to grow, providing more cover for the expansion of illicit trade. International migration will likewise grow, with much the same effect, offering ethnically based gangs an ever growing supply of recruits and victims. The spread of democracy may also help criminal cartels, which can manipulate weak public institutions by corrupting police officers or tempting politicians with offers of cash for their increasingly expensive election campaigns. And ironically, even the spread of international law—with its growing web of embargoes, sanctions, and conventions—will offer criminals new opportunities for providing forbidden goods to those on the wrong side of the international community.

These changes may affect each of the five wars in different ways, but these conflicts will continue to share four common characteristics:

***They are not bound by geography.*** Some forms of crime have always had an international component: The Mafia was born in Sicily and exported to the United States, and smuggling has always been by definition international. But the five wars are truly global. Where is the theater or front line of the war on drugs? Is it Colombia or Miami? Myanmar (Burma) or Milan? Where are the battles against money launderers being fought? In Nauru or in London? Is China the main theater in the war against the infringement of intellectual property, or are the trenches of that war on the Internet?

***They defy traditional notions of sovereignty.*** Al Qaeda's members have passports and nationalities—and often more than one—but they are truly stateless. Their allegiance is to their cause, not to any nation. The same is also true of the criminal networks engaged in the five wars. The same, however, is patently *not* true of government employees—police officers, customs agents, and judges—who fight them. This asymmetry is a crippling disadvantage for governments waging these wars. Highly paid, hypermotivated, and resource-rich combatants on one side of the wars (the criminal gangs) can seek refuge in and take advantage of national borders, but combatants of the other side (the governments) have fewer resources and are hampered by traditional notions of sovereignty. A former senior CIA official reported that international criminal gangs are able to move people, money, and weapons globally faster than he can move resources inside his own agency, let alone worldwide.

Coordination and information sharing among government agencies in different countries has certainly improved, especially after September 11. Yet these tactics fall short of what is needed to combat agile organizations that can exploit every nook and cranny of an evolving but imperfect body of international law and multilateral treaties.

*They pit governments against market forces.*   In each of the five wars, one or more government bureaucracies fight to contain the disparate, uncoordinated actions of thousands of independent, stateless organizations. These groups are motivated by large profits obtained by exploiting international price differentials, an unsatisfied demand, or the cost advantages produced by theft. Hourly wages for a Chinese cook are far higher in Manhattan than in Fujian. A gram of cocaine in Kansas City is 17,000 percent more expensive than in Bogotá. Fake Italian valves are 40 percent cheaper because counterfeiters don't have to cover the costs of developing the product. A well-funded guerrilla group will pay anything to get the weapons it needs. In each of these five wars, the incentives to successfully overcome government-imposed limits to trade are simply enormous.

*They pit bureaucracies against networks.*   The same network that smuggles East European women to Berlin may be involved in distributing opium there. The proceeds of the latter fund the purchase of counterfeit Bulgari watches made in China and often sold on the streets of Manhattan by illegal African immigrants. Colombian drug cartels make deals with Ukrainian arms traffickers, while Wall Street brokers controlled by the U.S.-based Mafia have been known to front for Russian money launderers. These highly decentralized groups and individuals are bound by strong ties of loyalty and common purpose and organized around semiautonomous clusters or "nodes" capable of operating swiftly and flexibly. John Arquilla and David Ronfeldt, two of the best known experts on these types of organizations, observe that networks often lack central leadership, command, or headquarters, thus "no precise heart or head that can be targeted. The network as a whole (but not necessarily each node) has little to no hierarchy; there may be multiple leaders. . . . Thus the [organization's] design may sometimes appear acephalous (headless), and at other times polycephalous (Hydra-headed)." Typically, governments respond to these challenges by forming interagency task forces or creating new bureaucracies. Consider the creation of the new Department of Homeland Security in the United States, which encompasses 22 former federal agencies and their 170,000 employees and is responsible for, among other things, fighting the war on drugs.

## RETHINKING THE PROBLEM

Governments may never be able to completely eradicate the kind of international trade involved in the five wars. But they can and should do better. There are at least four areas where efforts can yield better ideas on how to tackle the problems posed by these wars:

*Develop more flexible notions of sovereignty.* Governments need to recognize that restricting the scope of multilateral action for the sake of protecting their sovereignty is often a moot point. Their sovereignty is compromised daily, not by nation-states but by stateless networks that break laws and cross borders in pursuit of trade. In May 1999, for example, the Venezuelan government denied U.S. planes authorization to fly over Venezuelan territory to monitor air routes commonly used by narcotraffickers. Venezuelan authorities placed more importance on the symbolic value of asserting sovereignty over air space than on the fact that drug traffickers' planes regularly violate Venezuelan territory. Without new forms of codifying and "managing" sovereignty, governments will continue to face a large disadvantage while fighting the five wars.

*Strengthen existing multilateral institutions.* The global nature of these wars means no government, regardless of its economic, political, or military power, will make much progress acting alone. If this seems obvious, then why does Interpol, the multilateral agency in charge of fighting international crime, have a staff of 384, only 112 of whom are police officers, and an annual budget of $28 million, less than the price of some boats or planes used by drug traffickers? Similarly, Europol, Europe's Interpol equivalent, has a staff of 240 and a budget of $51 million.

One reason Interpol is poorly funded and staffed is because its 181 member governments don't trust each other. Many assume, and perhaps rightly so, that the criminal networks they are fighting have penetrated the police departments of other countries and that sharing information with such compromised officials would not be prudent. Others fear today's allies will become tomorrow's enemies. Still others face legal impediments to sharing intelligence with fellow nation-states or have intelligence services and law enforcement agencies with organizational cultures that make effective collaboration almost impossible. Progress will only be made if the world's governments unite behind stronger, more effective multilateral organizations.

*Devise new mechanisms and institutions.* These five wars stretch and even render obsolete many of the existing institutions, legal frameworks, military doctrines, weapons systems, and law enforcement techniques on which governments have relied for years. Analysts need to rethink the concept of war "fronts" defined by geography and the definition of "combatants" according to the Geneva Convention. The functions of intelligence agents, soldiers, police officers, customs agents, or immigration officers need rethinking and adaptation to the new realities. Policymakers also need to reconsider the notion that ownership is essentially a physical reality and not a "virtual" one or that only sovereign nations can issue money when thinking about ways to fight the five wars.

*Move from repression to regulation.* Beating market forces is next to impossible. In some cases, this reality may force governments to move from repressing the market to regulating it. In others, creating market incentives may be better than using bureaucracies to curb the excesses of these markets. Technology can often accomplish more than government policies can. For example, powerful encryption techniques can better protect software or CDs from being copied in Ukraine than would making the country enforce patents and copyrights and trademarks.

In all of the five wars, government agencies fight against networks motivated by the enormous profit opportunities created by other government agencies. In all cases, these profits can be traced to some form of government intervention that creates a major imbalance between demand and supply and makes prices and profit margins skyrocket. In some cases, these government interventions are often justified and it would be imprudent to eliminate them—governments can't simply walk away from the fight against trafficking in heroin, human beings, or weapons of mass destruction. But society can better deal with other segments of these kinds of illegal trade through regulation, not prohibition. Policymakers must focus on opportunities where market regulation can ameliorate problems that have defied approaches based on prohibition and armed interdiction of international trade.

Ultimately, governments, politicians, and voters need to realize that the way in which the world is conducting these five wars is doomed to fail—not for lack of effort, resources, or political will but because the collective thinking that guides government strategies in the five wars is rooted in wrong ideas, false assumptions, and obsolete institutions. Recognizing that governments have no chance of winning unless they change the ways they wage these wars is an indispensable first step in the search for solutions.

# The Global Governance of the Internet: Bringing the State Back In

## DANIEL W. DREZNER

. . . Do globalization and the Internet weaken the ability of states to regulate the global economy? This paper argues that . . . states, particularly the great powers, remain the primary actors for handling the social and political externalities created by globalization and the Internet. As the primary actors, the great powers are the most consistently successful in achieving their preferences relative to other actors. Powerful states will use a range of foreign policy substitutes, such as coercion, inducements, delegation, and forum shopping across different international institutions to advance their desired preferences into desired outcomes. Nonstate actors can still influence outcomes on the margins, but their interactions with states are more nuanced than the globalization literature suggests.

The substitutability principle is essential to understanding how globalization affects global governance. States can and will substitute different governance structures, and different policy tools to create those structures, depending on the constellation of state interests. Great-power options include delegating regime management to nonstate actors, creating international regimes with strong enforcement capabilities, generating competing regimes to protect material interests, and tolerating the absence of effective cooperation because of divergent state preferences. Because globalization scholars fail to consider the delegation strategy as a conscious state choice, they have misinterpreted the state's role in global governance.

The international regulation of the Internet provides a fertile testing ground for these arguments. Prior analysis on the Internet has been fuzzy, due in part to the assumption that all Internet-related activity can be defined along a single policy dimension. In fact, the Internet has generated multiple areas of governance, including the development of technical protocols, censorship, e-taxation, intellectual property, and privacy rights. For many of these issue areas, states express divergent interests, halt cross-border Internet transactions that contradict their preferences, and use international governmental organizations (IGOs) and treaties to advance their preferences. Even on issues in which there are large zones of agreement, such as the standardization of technical protocols, the great powers will manipulate private forms of authority to achieve their desired ends.

From Daniel W. Drezner, "The Global Governance of the Internet: Bringing the State Back In." Reprinted by permission from *Political Science Quarterly*, 119 (Fall 2004): 477–498.

The implications for scholars of international relations and globalization are significant. The Internet could be safely described as a tough test for state-centric theories of international relations, and an easy test for global civil society arguments. If states are found to be the key actors for Internet-related issues, the globalization literature will need to reconsider the relationship between states and nonstate actors. The evidence presented here suggests that both IGOs and NGOs have roles to play in global governance. At times they can act as independent agenda setters, but more often they act as the agents of state interests. Only by understanding these actors as governance substitutes in the global Internet regime can one acquire a greater understanding of global governance in an era of economic globalization. . . .

## GLOBALIZATION AND THE INTERNET: THE ACCEPTED WISDOM

Over the past decade, there has been an energetic debate about how globalization alters governance. From this debate, one can distill two clear hypotheses about the effects of globalization on the management of the global political economy. In the first, globalization undercuts state sovereignty, weakening governments' ability to effectively regulate their domestic affairs. Global market forces are both powerful and uncontrollable, stripping governments of their agency. As Thomas Friedman phrases it, globalization forces states into the "Golden Straitjacket," in which they must choose between "free market vanilla and North Korea."[1] A number of international relations scholars have argued that globalization drastically reduces the state's ability to govern.

The second hypothesis is that as state power has waned, globalization has simultaneously enhanced the power of nonstate actors via the reduction of transaction costs across borders. The characterization of these nonstate actors varies from author to author. . . .

. . . The issue area in which the effects of globalization should be at their most concentrated is the regulation of the Internet itself. Internet governance should see states at their most enfeebled and nonstate actors at their most powerful. This is certainly the conclusion of most international relations scholars who study the Internet . . .

## A THEORY OF GLOBAL GOVERNANCE

The theory proposed here assumes that states remain the primary actors in world politics. Their preferences on regulatory issues have their origins in domestic politics. The logic behind this assumption is simple: most social issues originated as domestic problems before globalization made them international issues. Governments will naturally prefer that global regulations mirror their own national standards. This reduces the adjustment costs of any requisite legislative or regulatory changes for governments, as well as the costs for national firms to adhere to a new standard. State power is defined as the size of a state's internal market; the larger the market, the more powerful the state. States with significant internal markets are less dependent on international exchange as a source of goods and capital.

Regulatory coordination can lead to welfare gains for governments, through the reduction of transaction costs for international business and the reduction of social externalities for citizens. At the same time, such coordination can redistribute benefits toward states with domestic standards close to the agreed-upon international standard. If the benefits are significant and the divergence of preferences among the great powers is small, then a sizeable bargaining "core" exists, making successful coordination a likely outcome. If the public benefits of coordination are minor and the divergence of preferences among the great powers is large, then a core will not exist, and the relevant actors will have no incentive to cooperate.

While the perceived size of the public good and the divergence of great-power preferences are the main causal variables, there is one important intervening variable: the preferences of the lesser powers, or peripheral states. These countries' preferences do not affect whether coordination will occur, but they do affect the bargaining process, and therefore, great-power strategies. If peripheral states oppose certain regulatory arrangements, they can effectively block such arrangements in universal membership IGOs that rely on one country, one vote. Therefore, great powers must take the preferences of smaller states into account when they select both the type of bargaining fora and the type of strategies to foster a consensus.

Table 1 displays the typology of governance structures generated from the distribution of state preferences. The key variable determining whether there will be *effective* coordination is the size of the bargaining core among the great powers.

If a large core exists, peripheral state preferences determine the process through which regulatory harmonization takes place. When peripheral states oppose the agreed-upon standard, big states will prefer to employ IGOs with strong sanctioning mechanisms. This makes it easier for the major powers to use joint inducements and sanctions to cajole other actors into compliance. If developing states form blocking coalitions within large IGOs, great powers will rely on club-based IGOs, such as the Organization for Economic Cooperation and Development (OECD) or the G-7, to form "coalitions of the willing" as a coercion mechanism.

When there is minimal divergence of preferences among states, great powers can be more confident in relying on universal-membership IGOs, such as the United Nations, for global governance. Universal IGOs can bring added legitimacy

### TABLE 1 ■ A TYPOLOGY OF INTERNET GOVERNANCE ISSUES

| Great Power Distribution of Preferences | North/South Distribution of Preferences | |
| --- | --- | --- |
| | High Conflict | Low Conflict |
| High Conflict | Sham standards (Censorship) | Rival standards (Consumer privacy) |
| Low Conflict | Club standards (Intellectual property) | Harmonized standards (Technical protocols) |

to an agreement. At the same time, however, great powers prefer to delegate the actual implementation of the regulatory regime to nongovernmental actors rather than IGOs. This is partly for functional reasons; NGOs plugged into public policy networks can have a comparative advantage in gathering information and harnessing the requisite technical expertise. More importantly, the delegation to private actors also provides great powers a less-public and more-effective pathway of ensuring control over the regime's governance structure. Delegation eliminates the transaction costs that are inherent in a universal-membership IGO, particularly one that operates on a one-nation, one-vote principle. Governments can act like a board of directors: states devolve regime management to nonstate actors, while still ensuring that they can influence any renegotiation of the rules of the game.

If the bargaining core between the great powers is small to nonexistent, then global regulatory coordination is far less likely, and the enforcement regime for any proposed global standard will be nonexistent. The preferences of the peripheral states, however, help to determine the tactics of great powers, IGOs, and NGOs. If the peripheral states have moderate preferences, that is, within the zone of great-power preferences, then powerful states have an incentive to attract as many allies as possible as a way to enhance the legitimacy of their own standards. This could be accomplished in a number of ways. One option would be to bring the issue to international bargaining fora in which the membership and the governance structure benefit their position. Another possibility is for great powers to apply their laws extraterritorially, coercing states to adopt their position. Regardless of the chosen strategy, the outcome is one of rival standards. Different fora or alliances will generate alternative sets of regulatory standards, with no clear standard accepted as international law. Nonstate actors may try to advocate for one set of global principles over another, but the divergence of great-power preferences will make such lobbying a largely futile exercise. Any international agreements that do emerge are unstable equilibria. Enforcing such standards on recalcitrant great powers will be next to impossible.

If peripheral states have immoderate preferences, then great powers will lack even the ability to attract natural allies from the periphery, reducing the number of possible bargaining arenas. One possible outcome in this distribution of preferences is the creation of "sham" standards. Governments agree to a notional set of standards with weak or nonexistent monitoring or enforcement schemes. Sham standards permit governments to claim the de jure existence of global regulatory coordination, even in the absence of effective enforcement. Another possible outcome is simple noncooperation, with states enforcing their own national standards. The great powers will try to propagate their preferred set of standards, but their influence will be limited to small, dependent allies.

In the absence of a bargaining core among great powers, NGOs that prefer to see more stringent global regulations can pursue three strategies. First, they can try to enhance the legitimacy of sham standards by engaging in enforcement activities, such as consumer boycotts or "naming and shaming" exercises against actors that violate standards. If this strategy is successful, states and/or firms pay a political price for violating these standards. Second, in the absence of genuine coordination, NGOs can generate their own "voluntary" codes and standards and apply consumer pressure on multinational corporations to adhere to them. If efforts at enforcement fail, they can at least act as monitors of corporate and state behavior. Third, NGOs can act as lobbyists, cajoling core states into narrowing their set of preferences. These efforts can alter the behavior of marginal actors, but are unlikely to be a source of effective governance.

This model suggests that nonstate actors can play important roles in supplying global governance, but only under certain constellations of state interests. The effectiveness of IGOs declines as great power disagreements rise. The role and influence of nonstate actors vary widely from quadrant to quadrant. The salience of great-power preferences remains constant. The presence of a bargaining core among the great powers is a necessary condition for effective global governance. If these states can reach a bargain, the outcome is effective policy coordination, regardless of the preferences or strategies of other actors. If these states have divergent preferences, then global governance is highly unlikely. . . .

## WHEN STATES DISAGREE ABOUT THE INTERNET

The best example of a club standards outcome for Internet issues concerns IPR [Intellectual Property Rights]. Developed and developing countries have divergent preferences on this issue. Because most goods and services produced for the Internet are created in the advanced industrialized states, these countries have an incentive to enforce IPR. Developing countries prefer lax standards as a way of accelerating the transfer of technology and lowering the cost of acquiring new innovations and ideas.

The emerging international regulatory regime on this issue mirrors great-power preferences. In 1996, the World Intellectual Property Organization (WIPO) negotiated two treaties—one on copyrights and one on performances and phonograms—to cover online IPR. Experts agree that these treaties provide "strong" IPR protection.[2] These efforts came in the wake of American and European efforts to apply economic sanctions against countries with lax IPR regimes. Furthermore, the key negotiating parties behind the Uruguay round of the GATT—the "quad" of the United States, Japan, Canada, and the European Union—strengthened the IPR regime by permitting member countries to use the WTO enforcement mechanism to enforce trade-related intellectual property (TRIP). Statistical analyses demonstrate that the threat of WTO sanctions had a significant effect on copyright enforcement. Between 1995 and 2000, software piracy declined by nearly 20 percent in developing countries.[3] The WTO, reflecting great-power preferences, has made it clear that the growth of the Internet will not alter its enforcement of IPR. . . .

The regulation of data privacy is a good example of the rival-standards outcome. As more commerce is transacted over the Internet, there is increased concern about firms or governments taking advantage of the personal information of online consumers. Opinion polls show that privacy is the biggest concern of Internet users. The European Union and the United States adopted different stances on the issue. The U.S. attitude toward privacy rights is based on freedom from state intervention; in Europe, privacy is considered a fundamental right to be protected by the state. As a result, there was no push in the United States for comprehensive regulation of data privacy. . . .

In contrast, in 1995, the EU passed a sweeping Data Protection Directive that set clear guidance and enforcement mechanisms for European firms. The directive was to take effect in late 1998, and to ensure that firms did not evade the law by carrying out operations beyond the EU jurisdiction, the export of EU citizens' personal data to third countries with inadequate protection was banned. This threat proved sufficiently potent for Australia, Canada, and Eastern European countries to revise their own laws in an attempt to comply with EU preferences.

Several nonstate actors tried to mediate a solution on the issue, with no success. Human rights groups lobbied the U.S. government to accept the EU regulatory position because it represented more-stringent protection of consumers.[4] A transnational business group, the GBDe, attempted to develop a common voluntary framework on data privacy. This effort failed miserably, with both U.S. and EU officials criticizing the final product. Instead, the U.S. response was to encourage American multinationals to establish self-regulatory mechanisms that would meet EU standards. Sets of voluntary principles, such as those provided by TRUSTe and BBBOnline, were developed. At the same time, American and European negotiators agreed to a "safe harbor" compromise. The EU would not impose sanctions against U.S. firms that adhered to a voluntary standard consistent with the Data Protection Directive.

The safe harbor compromise went into effect in November 2000, but the EU (state-directed) and U.S. (self-regulation) approaches remain rival standards. Both TRUSTe and BBBOnline have taken steps to become transnational certifiers. At the same time, U.S. compliance with the EU directive remains uncertain. Few companies registered for the safe harbor in the year after the agreement went into effect. Furthermore, Federal Trade Commission studies show that U.S. firms do not enforce their own privacy principles. . . .[5]

The regulation of Internet content—that is, censorship—neatly fits the outcome of sham standards. Governments have wildly divergent preferences regarding the extent to which Internet content should be regulated. Totalitarian governments such as Cuba or Saudi Arabia want absolute control over citizen access to the Internet. Authoritarian governments such as Singapore or China want to exploit the Internet's commercial opportunities while restricting the use of the Internet for political criticism. Liberal democracies also wish to place restrictions on offensive forms of content. These countries' definitions of objectionable content range from child pornography (the United States) to Nazi memorabilia (France). For this issue, there is no bargaining core among nation-states. The predicted outcome would be sham standards and the unilateral use of national regulation to bar undesired content.

Internet enthusiasts have long dismissed the ability of states to take this action. . . . However, the evidence strongly suggests that states can regulate Internet content when they so desire. Such efforts are never 100 percent effective, but that is a goal that few regulatory efforts achieve. As Jack Goldsmith observes: "If governments can raise the cost of Net transactions, they can regulate Net transactions.[6] In particular, governments have discovered that by pressuring Internet service providers, they can exercise significant control over access to content.

The result has been unilateral but successful examples of government regulation of Internet content. For totalitarian states, the modes of regulation have been crude but effective. Cuba simply outlaws the sale of personal computers to individuals; Myanmar outlaws personal ownership of modems. Saudi Arabia censors the Internet by requiring all Web access to be routed through a proxy server that the government edits for content, blocking access to pornographic, religious, and politically sensitive material. . . .

Authoritarian states have succeeded in restricting political content on the Internet without sacrificing its commercial possibilities. Singapore regulates the Internet in the same way that it regulates print or broadcast media, effectively deleting what the government considers to be offensive or subversive material.[7] Singapore's approach has been the model for many East Asian governments, including China. In July 2002, China was able to persuade more than 300 Internet service providers and web portals, including Yahoo!, to sign a voluntary pledge refraining from "producing, posting, or disseminating pernicious information that may jeopardize state security and disrupt social stability."[8]

As for the developed democracies, a French court succeeded in a legal effort to get Yahoo! to drop Nazi paraphernalia from its auction site. Because of the number of "mirror" servers that target Web sites to particular geographic areas, governments have the means to censor the national content of the Web without globally censoring the distribution of information. Unilateral content regulation has succeeded despite the strong normative consensus among Internet enthusiasts against such regulation.[9] The September 11 terrorist attacks and the terrorists' use of the Internet to communicate with each other have only accelerated the pace of content regulation in the developed world. . . .

Human rights NGOs have protested these disparate national efforts to curb Internet content, but this has not led to the creation of any effective system of global governance on the matter. IGOs have been largely hamstrung by the extreme distribution of state preferences over content regulation. This was reflected in the first meeting of the World Summit on the Information Society (WSIS), held in December 2003. One of the key sticking points at this meeting was the language regarding the extent to which any agreement would affect the regulation of speech on the Internet. China, in particular, protested the U.S.-inspired language regarding press freedoms. As a result, although language was inserted into the Declaration of Principles that specifically addressed press freedoms, it was heavily watered down, and language reaffirming state sovereignty was also added. . . .

For each of the issue areas in question, governments have divergent preferences regarding the content of Internet regulation. The resulting global governance structures vary in effectiveness, depending on the distribution of state power. The enforcement of IPR on the Internet has succeeded because the great powers have similar preferences and have been willing to coerce recalcitrant states into compliance. When great powers disagree—over privacy rights—the outcome is the absence of a stable international regime. When all states have divergent preferences, as in the censorship case, the result is effective unilateral steps to regulate access to the Internet. Two facts about these issues are particularly salient. First, nonstate actors have been unable to influence government preferences on these issues. Second, when necessary, governments of every stripe have been willing to disrupt or sever Internet traffic in order to ensure that their ends are achieved.

## GLOBAL GOVERNANCE OF INTERNET TECHNICAL PROTOCOLS

The economics of technical standards on the Internet are a classic example of network externalities at work, in that a standard's utility corresponds directly to the number of consumers using it. For the Internet to be useful for informational and commercial purposes, producers need to agree on the technical protocols that permit users to successfully transmit and access data. Although common protocols create obvious public goods, such standards can also reap disproportionate benefits for actors that either own the standards in a proprietary fashion or have first-mover advantages in exploiting those standards. Because of the huge network externalities that are evident in the Internet, however, we would expect a large bargaining core among states, leading to a harmonized standards outcome.

Popular and scholarly histories of the Internet argue that the technical protocols were created by an epistemic community of computer experts who belonged to the IETF, and that no government could thwart this outcome. A closer look at the origins of these protocols and the regimes for managing them suggests a rather different picture. At two crucial junctures in the growth of the Internet—the acceptance of the Transmission Control Protocol/Internet Protocol (TCP/IP) for exchanging information across disparate computer networks, and the creation of the ICANN regime for governing the Internet Domain Name System (DNS)—governments took active steps to ensure that the outcome serviced their interests and that the management regime remained private but amenable to state interests. In the first episode, governments acted in concert to prevent computer firms from acquiring too much influence over the setting of standards; in the second episode, they acted to prevent particular NGOs and IGOs from acquiring too much influence.

TCP/IP was developed between 1973 and 1978 by members of the Advanced Research Projects Agency Network (ARPANET), the Defense Department's network that connected civilian and military research complexes. The protocols were designed so as to permit interoperability between disparate hardware systems. TCP is responsible for packing and unpacking data such that they can be transferred from one computer to another; IP is responsible for ensuring that data are routed to the appropriate recipients. To use a postal analogy, TCP is the functional equivalent of the envelope, and IP is the functional equivalent of the address/ZIP code on the envelope.

TCP/IP placed minimal code demands on new entrants to the network, which was consistent with the research community's norm of open access.[10] However, this was also consistent with U.S. government preferences as well. . . .

Although Defense Department and ARPANET constituents favored the TCP/IP protocol, other networks did not rely on it. The actors behind these alternative networks had different motivations. Companies with investments in computer networks preferred developing their own proprietary standards, so as to reap the pecuniary rewards of managing their own networks. By the mid-seventies, Xerox was pushing Xerox Network Systems (XNS), Digital was marketing Digital Equipment Corporation's Digital Network Architecture (DEC-NET), and IBM was promoting its System Network Architecture (SNA) to its government buyers. . . . In other words, TCP/IP was far from the de facto standard when the standards debate of the 1970s started, and it faced strong opposition from corporate actors.

The major economic powers feared the prospect of being held hostage to a firm's ownership of the dominant network protocol. This was particularly true for states with government monopolies of the telecommunications sector. This concern was not unfounded. In 1975, IBM refused a Canadian government request to develop a protocol that could interface with non-IBM hardware systems. Instead, the corporation urged Canada to accept IBM's proprietary SNA network protocol. In 1978, the French government issued a report warning other European governments: "If IBM became master of the network market, it would have a share— willingly or unwillingly—of the world power structure."

There were two international responses to this threat. The first was a concerted effort by Canada, Britain, and France to develop a nonproprietary standard, called Recommendation X.25, for the Consultative Committee on International Telegraphy and Telephony (CCITT) of the International Telecommunications Union (ITU), a universal-membership IGO. Created in less than six months, X.25 was designed as a public standard freely available to all private firms. The ITU approved the standard in 1976; the French, Japanese, and British governments immediately adopted X.25 as the standard for their government networks. Because of the significance of these markets for producers, IBM, Digital, and Honeywell reluctantly agreed to offer X.25-compatible software on their computers in addition to their own proprietary standards. . . .

The CCITT initiative was a successful holding action that prevented the emergence of a norm for proprietary standards. The second and more significant initiative was the push by the United States, the UK, France, Canada, and Japan to have the International Organization for Standardization (ISO)—an NGO of technical standard setters—develop compatible network standards for both private and public uses. This push was unusual, in that ordinarily the ISO declared an official standard only after there was a rough consensus among producers. In advocating a role for the ISO at an earlier stage, the major economic powers were clearly trying to accelerate the creation of an international regime consistent with their preferences.

This initiative resulted in the 1978 creation of the Open Systems Interconnection (OSI) model. OSI is not so much a standard as a metastandard, a minimal architecture through which disparate network protocols can communicate with one another. . . .

The creation of OSI had two significant effects on the development of common standards. First, because of the wide ISO membership and the rapid acceptance of its standards, it became prohibitively expensive for any state or firm to create a protocol that was incompatible with OSI. The great powers were particularly enthusiastic about OSI. European governments liked it because it gave their computer producers a chance to compete with IBM, Digital, and other American producers. The U.S. government liked OSI because it was consistent with its preferences for nonproprietary, open source coding.

Second, because OSI stressed openness and accessibility, the TCP/IP code fit more seamlessly with the OSI framework than with other proposed protocols, including X.25. Furthermore, with the ISO as the location for managing network standards, the U.S. government strongly encouraged ARPANET participants to actively participate in ISO committees and meetings, in order to get the TCP/IP protocol accepted as consistent with the OSI framework. By 1984, the ISO had officially recognized TCP/IP as consistent with OSI principles. Because TCP/IP was already widely used in the United States and considered reliable, it became the de facto standard as the Internet grew in size, a classic example of historical "lock-in."[11]

Members of the Internet community often argue that the failure of X.25 or OSI to replace TCP/IP is an example of states being unable to regulate cyberspace. This argument is factually correct but misses the primary motivation of both ventures. The chief concern of both the ITU and ISO initiatives was not to replace TCP/IP but to ward off corporate attempts to lock in a dominant proprietary standard for network protocols. If governments had not intervened, the probable outcome would have been a system of proprietary network protocols. The actual outcome reflected the preferences of governments. Furthermore, consistent with the model presented here, states relied on a universal-membership IGO to boost legitimacy and delegated a nonstate actor to manage the actual standards.

The second government intervention over technical protocols came two decades later. As the commercial possibilities of the Internet and World Wide Web emerged in the early nineties, all of the relevant actors recognized the need to create a more robust regime to manage the DNS for unique Internet addresses. The DNS is responsible for creating unique identifiers for each individual Internet address. This includes, among others, the valued general Top Level Domains (gTLDs), such as .com, .org, or .edu, as well as the country code Top Level Domains (ccTLDs), such as .de or .uk.

There were three reasons for concern about DNS management. First, Internet commentators agreed that the DNS system represented an excellent focal point through which an actor could control access to the Internet. Second, actors with valued trademarks were concerned about the possibility of "cyber-squatters" acquiring valuable addresses, such as www.burgerking.com or www.nike.com. Third, there were significant commercial opportunities in managing the DNS system. Between 1994 and 1998, the U.S. government contracted the DNS registry to Network Solutions Incorporated (NSI). That monopoly was estimated in 1996 to be worth $1 billion to NSI.

The first efforts to develop an international regime to reform the DNS system came from nonstate actors, particularly the ISOC, a network of researchers responsible for developing and managing the original ARPANET. After repeated false starts, ISOC formed the International Ad Hoc Committee (IAHC) to develop a proposal to manage domain names in lieu of NSI. The IAHC was an eminent persons group, with representatives from ISOC, the International Trademark

Association, WIPO, and the ITU. The ITU was particularly eager to be involved, and viewed itself as the natural location for an international regime to manage these issues.

The result of this process was a memorandum of understanding (MOU) among the IAHC parties on gTLDs (gTLD-MOU). The gTLD-MOU proposed assigning governance functions to an entity housed in the ITU, with representation from business interests, IGOs, and ISOC. The ITU arranged a "formal" signing ceremony in Geneva in March 1997 to give the agreement the trappings of an international treaty. This process neatly fits the definition of an epistemic community. Furthermore, the actors involved in the creation of the gTLD-MOU—IGOs, business constituencies, and technical experts—are precisely the actors emphasized in the globalization literature on how the Internet would affect global governance.

The gTLD-MOU immediately ran into opposition from two groups. Governments strongly protested the agreement. The U.S. secretary of state wrote a memo blasting the ITU secretariat. . . . European Union governments opposed the agreement because it was deemed too U.S.-centric. The proposal also ran into opposition from a significant fraction of Internet enthusiasts. They criticized the proposed governance structure as lacking in democratic accountability and as too solicitous of corporate concerns.

The IAHC proposal spurred President Clinton to issue a July 1, 1997 executive order authorizing the commerce secretary to "support efforts to make the governance of the domain name system private and competitive." Presidential advisor Ira Magaziner was put in charge of the initiative, underscoring the high priority the United States gave to settling the issue. U.S. preferences on the issue were clear: to have a nonstate actor—rather than a universal-membership IGO such as the ITU—manage the DNS regime. . . .

Given the ITU's one-nation, one-vote structure, and the secretariat's eagerness to independently manage the issue area, it is not surprising that the United States wanted to switch fora. Historically, the United States has shifted governance of new issue areas away from the ITU in order to lock in its own preferences. . . .

The European Union also wanted three significant changes to the IAHC proposal. The EU commission insisted that the WIPO be involved in any governance structure. This was a hedge against U.S. trademark law being imposed by fiat. The Europeans agreed with the U.S. government that the NSI monopoly of the gTLD registries had to be broken up. The European motivation for this, however, was preventing total U.S. dominance of the Internet. Finally, there was a desire for a formal governmental channel between any private order and governments. This was considered especially relevant to the management of the ccTLDs. The United States was sensitive to these concerns, and promised that there would be a significant number of Europeans on any Internet governance board.

In June 1998, the Commerce Department issued a white paper that officially rejected the gTLD-MOU process and advocated privatization of the DNS system based on four principles: stability, competition, private bottom-up coordination, and representation. There were two reactions to the white paper. Among Internet enthusiasts, a series of self-organized conferences, called the International Forum on the White Paper (IFWP) was held, with the idea of providing citizen feedback to the U.S. proposal. Many people dubbed the IFWP an "Internet constitutional convention." Although U.S. government representatives attended IFWP meetings, there is considerable evidence demonstrating that the IFWP process had no effect on the policy outcome. This was because ISOC, American, and European Union officials were simultaneously negotiating the exact contours of what a private Internet regime would look like.

The result was ICANN. While ICANN was incorporated by key members of ISOC, the resulting governance structure accommodated both U.S. and European concerns. A government advisory committee was created to act as a conduit for government concerns. The NSI monopoly of gTLDs was broken, and the ITU was given only a peripheral role in the new regime. A significant fraction of ICANN's governing board consisted of non-Americans. . . .

While ISOC's wish to manage the DNS system was granted, after a fashion, the negotiating history of ICANN shows that the key actors were states. It was the U.S. government that rejected the IAHC process, shut out the ITU from the process, and ensured the creation of a private order to manage the policy issue. European, Japanese, and Australian governments ensured that the eventual regime would not be dominated by the United States. The key governments vetted the initial roster of ICANN's governing board. In contrast, elements of global civil society were largely shut out of the process. . . .

ICANN's history since its 1998 creation only underscores these conclusions. Nonstate actors out of the ISOC loop have vigorously protested ICANN's governance structure and lack of openness to outside input. In contrast to claims that the Internet would foster greater democratic participation, many individuals have protested at the travel costs of attending ICANN's meetings. Meetings are not widely available on the Web. More generally, its detractors label ICANN as undemocratic and unresponsive, and a threat to the more-decentralized culture of the Internet.

Key governments have been consistent in ensuring their influence and in preferring stability over representation. . . . At the same time, U.S. and European preferences on the matter have been carried out. Since ICANN's creation, competition to provide domain name services has increased, prices have fallen, and trademark disputes have been settled more quickly. ICANN's own governing body has also indicated its eagerness to cater more to government preferences. ICANN currently lists as one of its core values: "Act with sensitivity to the public interest and related governmental concerns, so that *the need for direct governmental action is minimized.* . . . [12]

Had the great powers not intervened, the outcome in this case would have been significantly different from ICANN. The ISOC initially wanted to expand the number of gTLDs to fifty. The management of the DNS system would have been housed in the one-country, one-vote ITU, rather than in a private, non-profit organization. The percentage of Americans running the regime would have been larger. This case demonstrates that nonstate actors have agenda-setting powers. However, once an issue comes to the attention of states, the outcome will reflect great-power preferences.

In both the protocol wars of the 1970s and the creation of ICANN in the 1990s, government preferences were consistent. The great powers repeatedly acted to ensure that the Internet would be governed so as to maximize efficiency without giving monopoly power to any one actor, be it a multinational firm, a nonstate organization, or an IGO secretariat. In the 1970s, governments acted with Internet enthusiasts to ensure that multinational firms would not develop their own proprietary network protocols. In the 1990s, governments acted in concert with multinational firms to prevent NGOs and IGOs from overstepping their policy authority. In both instances, governments delegated regime management to nongovernmental international organizations—ISO and ICANN—to ensure efficient outcomes and to retain their influence over future policy shifts.

## RETHINKING GLOBALIZATION AND GLOBAL GOVERNANCE

The globalization literature argues that the lowering of traditional barriers to exchange, the exponential growth of the Internet, and the rise of networked nonstate actors conspire to weaken the state's role in global governance. The globalization literature is wrong; states are still the primary actors. Furthermore, in focusing on the binary question of state power versus nonstate power, these scholars have glossed over the diversity of relationships that can exist between heterogeneous actors in world politics. A recognition of the substitutability of global governance structures gives us a more powerful lens with which to observe the ramifications of globalization. A review of Internet governance demonstrates that even when states prefer to let private actors take the governance lead, they will intervene to advance their desired ends.

States may be the primary actors, but they are not the only actors. The case studies clearly show that nonstate actors can affect outcomes through their technical expertise and agenda-setting abilities. However, only by giving the great powers pride of place is it possible to set the conditions under which non-state actors will exercise their influence. . . .

By failing to recognize that states can substitute unilateral measures, intergovernmental accords, and delegation to nonstate actors, scholars of global governance have unnecessarily restricted their analyses to simple comparisons of direct state involvement versus the role of nonstate actors. This is particularly true of the delegation option. Unless delegation is recognized as a conscious state choice, researchers inevitably miscode such variables as state power. The value-added of the substitutability concept is that it permits the development of more generalizable theories. . . .

Ironically, globalization scholars have erred not in thinking too grandly about global governance, but in not thinking grandly enough.

## NOTES

1. Thomas Friedman, *The Lexus and the Olive Tree* (New York: Farrar, Strauss, & Giroux, 1999), 86.
2. Catherine Mann, Sue Eckert, and Sarah Cleeland Knight, *Global Electronic Commerce: A Policy Primer* (Washington, DC: Institute for International Economics, 2000), 118.

3. Kenneth Shadlen, Andrew Schrank, and Marcus Kurtz, "The Political Economy of Intellectual Property Protection." Paper presented at the American Political Science Association annual meeting, Boston, MA, August 29–September 1, 2002.

4. Gregory Shaffer, "Globalization and Social Protection: The Impact of EU and International Rules in the Ratcheting Up of U.S. Privacy Standards," *Yale Journal of International Law* 25 (Winter 2000), 1–88.

5. Marcus Franda, *Governing the Internet* (Boulder, CO: Lynne Reinner, 2001), 159.

6. Jack Goldsmith, "Regulation of the Internet: Three Persistent Fallacies," *Chicago-Kent Law Review* 73 (December 1998), 1123.

7. Garry Rodan. "The Internet and Political Control in Singapore," *Political Science Quarterly* 113 (Spring 1998), 63–89.

8. Georgette Wang, "Regulating Network Communication in Asia," *Telecommunications Policy* 23 (April 1999): 277–287; Shanthi Kalathil, "China's Dot-Communism," *Foreign Policy* 122 (January/February 2001), 74–75.

9. Human Rights Watch, "Free Expression on the Internet," accessed at http://www.hrw.org/advocacy/internet/, 25 May 2002.

10. Will Foster, Anthony Rutkowski, and Seymour Goodman, "Who Governs the Internet?" *Communications of the ACM* 40 (August 1997), 17–18.

11. W. Brian Arthur, "Competing Technologies, Increasing Returns, and Lock-In By Historical Events," *Economic Journal* 99 (March 1989), 116–131.

12. Committee on ICANN Evolution and Reform, "ICANN: A Blueprint for Reform," 20 June 2002, accessed at http://www.icann.org/committees/evol-reform/blueprint-20jun02.htm, 10 September 2002

# International Law: The Trials of Global Norms

## STEVEN R. RATNER

The move from describing the world to prescribing for it forms the core of international law. Can those committing human rights atrocities—war criminals from Bosnia or political leaders from Cambodia—be tried in foreign courts or before international tribunals? How can members of the United Nations ensure respect for the decisions of its Security Council? What is the best way to regulate transnational environmental hazards such as greenhouse gas emissions or ocean dumping? Can the United States allow its citizens to sue European companies for their use of land and factories confiscated by the Cuban government from Americans more than a generation ago?

All these questions turn on political decisions by states—but what international lawyers see and seek in such scenarios is a process whose actions are informed and influenced by principles of law, not just raw power. For international lawyers, devising and enforcing universal rules of conduct for states means overcoming two cardinal challenges: how to make such precepts legitimate in a diverse community of nations; and how to make them stick in the absence of any one sovereign authority or supranational enforcement mechanism. . . .

Today, the end of the Cold War has loosened many of the blockages to international lawmaking and implementation. Although legal scholars still ask what states can do on their own—pass extraterritorial laws, use force, or prosecute war criminals—they do so assuming that coordinated action is now more feasible than in the past. Global and regional treaties such as the Chemical Weapons Convention, the Convention on the Prohibition of Anti-Personnel Mines, the Maastricht Treaty, and the North American Free Trade Agreement now serve as the starting point for scrutinizing state behavior according to some objective standard.

The ground seems ready then for an acceleration of this century's great trend in international law: the increasing international regulation of more and more issues once typically seen as part of state domestic jurisdiction. But any attempt to create the lofty, supranational legal edifice idealized by some of the field's practitioners and scholars promises to be problematic at best. Once paralyzed by the deadlock between East and West, and between North and South, the international legal system must now contend not just with the challenge of persuading new states such as Belarus or Croatia to comply with established norms but of coping with Somalia and other failed states, whose circumstances make a mockery of international rules. International law must seek to embrace a growing range of forms, topics, and technologies, as well as a host of new actors. And as it moves further away from strictly "foreign" concerns—the treatment of diplomats or ships on the seas—to traditionally domestic areas—environmental or labor standards—its proponents must increasingly confront new obstacles head-on.

## NEW REALITIES, NEW IDEAS

This new global context surrounding the field has led to at least four fundamental shifts in the kinds of issues that legal scholars now talk about and study.

### New Forms, New Players

Traditionally, most rules of international law could be found in one of two places: treaties—binding, written agreements between states; or customary law—uncodified, but equally binding rules based on longstanding behavior that states accept as compulsory. The strategic arms reduction treaties requiring the United States and Russia to cut their nuclear weapons arsenals offer examples of the former; the rule that governments cannot be sued in the courts of another state for most of their public acts provides an example of the latter. Historically, treaties have gradually displaced much customary law, as international rules have become increasingly codified.

But as new domains from the environment to the Internet come to be seen as appropriate for international regulation, states are sometimes reluctant to embrace any sort of binding rule. In the past, many legal scholars and international courts simply accepted the notion that no law governed a particular subject until a new treaty was concluded or states signaled their consent to a new customary-law rule (witness the reluctance with which human rights norms were considered law prior to the UN's two key treaties in 1966) or, alternatively, struggled to find customary law where none existed. However, today all but the most doctrinaire of scholars see a role for so-called soft law—precepts emanating from international bodies that conform in some sense to expectations of required behavior but that are not binding on states.

For example, in 1992 the World Bank completed a set of Guidelines on the Treatment of Foreign Direct Investment. Though these are not binding on any bank member, states and corporations invoke them as the standard for how developing nations should treat foreign capital to encourage investment. This soft law enables states to adjust to the regulation of many new areas of international concern without fearing a violation (and possible legal countermeasures) if they fail to comply. Normative expectations are built more quickly than they would through the evolution of a customary-law rule, and more gently than if a new treaty rule were foisted on states. Soft law principles also represent a starting point for new hard law, which attaches a penalty to noncompliance. In this case, the bank's guidelines have served as the basis for the negotiation of a new treaty—the

Multilateral Agreement on Investment (MAI)—by the Organization for Economic Cooperation and Development (OECD). The MAI gives foreign investors the right to take any government to international arbitration for compensation when a law or state practice limits their freedom to invest or divest.

Whether in the case of hard or soft law, new participants are making increased demands for representation in international bodies, conferences, and other legal groupings and processes. They include substate entities, both those recognized in some way by the international community (Chechnya, Hong Kong) and those not (Tibet, Kashmir); nongovernmental organizations (NGOs); and corporations. Claiming that the states to which they belong do not always adequately represent their interests, these nonstate actors demand a say in the content of new norms. Some have faced staunch opposition to their participation in decision making: In 1995, China's government relegated NGOs to a distant venue during the UN's Fourth World Conference on Women in Beijing.

But other groups may succeed even as far as effectively taking over an official delegation. For example, U.S. telecommunications companies such as Motorola have seemed almost to dictate U.S. positions in the International Telecommunication Union (ITU), the UN agency responsible for setting global telecommunications standards. At the ITU's 1992 conference on allocating the radio spectrum for new technologies, Motorola's stake in protecting its plans for new satellites became a paramount U.S. interest, resulting in a sizeable Motorola team attending as part of the U.S. delegation. Other corporations have acted outside government channels entirely by promulgating private codes: In response to public pressure, Nike issued a set of self-imposed rules to protect worker rights in the developing world. It is not that states are no longer the primary makers of international law. But . . . these other actors have independent views—and the resources to push them—that do not fit neatly into traditional theories of how law is made and enforced.

## New Enforcement Strategies

Most states comply with much, even most, international law almost continually—whether the law of the sea, diplomatic immunity, or civil aviation rules. But without mechanisms to bring transgressors into line, international law will be "law" in name only. This state of affairs, when it occurs, is ignored by too many lawyers, who delight in large bodies of rules but often discount patterns of noncompliance. For example, Western governments, and many scholars, insisted throughout the 1960s and 1970s that when nationalizing foreign property, developing states were legally bound to compensate former owners for the full economic value, despite those states' repeated refusals to pay such huge sums.

The traditional toolbox to secure compliance with the law of nations consists of negotiations, mediation, countermeasures (reciprocal action against the violator), or, in rare cases, recourse to supranational judicial bodies such as the International Court of Justice. (The last of these was the linchpin of the world of law that Americans such as Andrew Carnegie and Elihu Root sought to bring into being.) For many years, these tools have been supplemented by the work of international institutions, whose reports and resolutions often help "mobilize shame" against violators. But today, states, NGOs, and private entities, aided by their lawyers, have striven for sanctions with more teeth. They have galvanized the UN Security Council to issue economic sanctions against Iraq, Haiti, Libya, Serbia, Sudan, and other nations refusing to comply with UN resolutions.

On the free-trade front, the dispute settlement panels in the World Trade Organization (WTO) now have the legal authority to issue binding rulings that allow the victor in a trade dispute to impose specific tariffs on the loser. . . . And the UN's ad hoc criminal tribunals for the former Yugoslavia and Rwanda show that it is at least possible to devise institutions to punish individuals for human rights atrocities. Nonetheless, as the impunity to date of former Bosnian Serb president Radovan Karadzic and General Ratko Mladic reveals, the success of these enforcement mechanisms depends on the willingness of states to support them: legalism meets realism. . . .

Increasingly, domestic courts provide an additional venue to enforce international law. In Spain, for example, Judge Manuel García Castellóni of the National Court has agreed to hear a controversial human rights case involving charges against Chile's former dictator, General Augusto Pinochet. Meanwhile, Castellóni's colleague, Judge Baltasar Garzón, hears testimony against those responsible for the "Dirty War" of the 1970s in Argentina. (Spain is asserting jurisdiction in both cases because its nationals were among the thousands of victims tortured and killed.) And though Karadzic remains at large, he has been sued in U.S. federal court under the Alien Tort Claims Act, which allows foreign nationals recovery against Karadzic for the rape and torture of civilians during his "ethnic cleansing" campaign in the former Yugoslavia. At a minimum, this provides a symbolic measure of solace for his victims.

## The Legitimacy Problem

Even as scholars seek to devise better enforcement mechanisms, a serious debate is brewing about the legitimacy of such measures. As international organizations are freed up to take more actions by the end of the East-West conflict and the tempering of North-South tensions, the United States and its like-minded allies seem well positioned to impose their agenda on all. Legal scholars question whether Western dominance of the Organization for Security and Cooperation in Europe, UN, WTO, and other international institutions is not merely raw power asserting its muscle again, albeit through multilateral bodies, to the detriment of a genuine rule of law. That this debate is more than academic can be seen vividly in the ongoing discussion about reforming the Security Council. Many Americans may laud the council's new muscle—during the last five years, it has slapped a debilitating embargo and weapons inspection regime on Iraq, prohibited air traffic with Libya due to its sanctuary for those accused of the Pan Am 103 bombing, and approved a U.S.-led occupation of Haiti. But smaller states feel threatened by a Security Council in which the West is often able to convince enough states to approve such council actions, and only a Chinese veto (which was used only once in the last 25 years) seems to protect them. . . .

Focusing on enforcement and legitimacy also provides a useful lens through which to evaluate U.S. reactions to international norms: Even as the United States seeks to strengthen the enforcement of international law for its own ends, it has often recoiled at the prospect that these norms might be enforced against it. In the WTO, the very dispute resolution panels that the United States hopes to use to force open closed markets could order it to choose between environmental protection laws (such as those banning imports of tuna caught in nets that kill dolphins) and the prospects of retaliatory sanctions if those laws have incidental discriminatory effects on trade. In such a scenario, international law, as interpreted by the WTO, becomes the friend of business and bugaboo of environmentalists. But when the UN seeks to promulgate environmental law, as it has with the proposed greenhouse gas convention just concluded at Kyoto, then the tables are turned.

Similarly, the United States wants to use the Security Council to keep in place a comprehensive sanctions regime on Iraq that has the diplomatic appeal of being "international" rather than "U.S.-imposed," all the while holding back on paying its dues because not all UN programs conform to Washington's wishes. As the world's sole superpower, the United States can defy international standards with little fear of immediate sanction; but other states will begin to question its motives in trying to strengthen important legal regimes such as those covering nuclear and chemical nonproliferation.

## New Linkages

The notion of hermetically sealed areas of international law—each a nice chapter in a treatise—is increasingly anachronistic. Environmental and trade law can no longer be discussed separately as the tuna-dolphin example shows; and when private investors have to reckon with serious abuses by local governments, foreign investment law cannot be examined without some consideration of human rights and labor law. The result is a new breed of scholarship linking previously distinct subjects and the realization among some practitioners that overspecialization leads to myopic lawyering.

Moreover, beyond the legal field, international lawyers must address the two-way interaction between international law and broader sociological and cultural trends in society. In one notable example, the debate on a clash of cultures involving so-called Asian values has forced students of human rights to stand back and consider whether rights granted in human rights treaties mean the same thing in all states. Can Singapore suppress free speech for the goal of national unity and development, especially if it claims that its culture sees uninhibited political speech as less than a birthright? Of course, cultural assertions tend to be overly broad, and many human rights activists interpret these claims as excuses for authoritarianism; the arguments, however, can no longer be ignored, and black and white rules of treaty interpretation will not help much.

In the other direction, the proliferation of new norms has direct effects on debates over globalization—the "Jihad versus McWorld" controversy. A global treaty on ozone or greenhouse gases, for instance, will clearly accommodate different perspectives on the priority of environmental protection versus development, but once adopted it cannot tolerate violations in the name of "diversity." Indeed, almost by definition, the decision by states to subject a once strictly domestic concern to international regulation means that cultural, value-based, or "sovereignty" arguments no longer enjoy the upper hand. If a state elects not to sign a major treaty, or ignores one it has assigned—as with the United States and the agreement on the elimination of landmines or Iraq and the one on nuclear nonproliferation—it is more likely to be condemned as a pariah than admired for its rugged individualism.